MODERN COIN MAGIC

MODERN COIN MAGIC

Author, J. B. BOBO

Professional Magician
Specializing in School, College and University Entertainment

Editor, JOHN BRAUN

Editor of The Linking Ring
Past President of The International Brotherhood of Magicians

Illustrator, Nelson C. Hahne

Art Editor of The Linking Ring

A MODERN TREATISE of ways of concealing, producing, altering and multiplying coins from the empty hands, being the first complete explanation of methods for so doing published since Downs' immortal classic of sixty-six years ago. Six hundred sixty-nine illustrations are included for clarity in demonstrating 110 coin sleights and 312 coin tricks.

REVISED EDITION PUBLISHED BY

INC.

5082 North Lincoln Avenue
Chicago, Illinois, 60625
1966

DEDICATION

To JOHN BRAUN,
who has been most helpful
in the gathering, preparing
and writing this material.

PREFACE

IN the summer of 1952 I typed the last page of *Modern COIN Magic,* and in September of that year the late Carl Waring Jones, publisher of *GREATER MAGIC,* added this "treatise on coin magic" to his list of fine "Standard Texts on Specialized Branches of Conjuring." A large first edition was published—large, as editions of conjuring books go when produced exclusively for the fraternity—and after a period of 12 years, the "out-of-print" sign went up.

Carl Jones passed on in January, 1957; his dream of re-establishing coin magic as a popular branch of conjuring had been realized, and what he had been pleased to call "The First COIN Treatise since T. Nelson Downs' *Modern Coin Manipulation* in 1900" had accomplished its mission. Coin magic was back in the repertoires of close-up magicians everywhere; many forgotten sleights and tricks were given a new lease on life, and many clever variations and uses of old plots and principles were finding their way into the magical journals. Yes, coin magic, after lying dormant for years, was "in" again!

Now, in the summer of 1964, I find myself again laboring on an edition of *Modern COIN Magic*—this time a revised edition for The Ireland Magic Company—and a "revised look" at coin magic is in order.

Prior to 1952 little had been written on the subject, and that was scattered throughout dozens of books and magazines. Because of this, it had been difficult for the student to obtain all the information necessary to become a proficient coin worker. The few books devoted partly to coin magic had not filled the need adequately. So—some 15 years ago—I began collecting coin material. I contacted dozens of magicians noted for their ability as close-up workers, and with few exceptions, all complied enthusiastically by contributing their choice material. This process continued, even after thousands of copies of *Modern COIN Magic* had been distributed to magicians all over the world. The result is the book you now hold in your hands.

Of course, not all the material in this book is new. It is not intended to be. My purpose has been to present to the fraternity a complete treatise on sleight-of-hand coin conjuring, and to cover this important segment of the subject in all its *practical* aspects. To do this, it has been necessary to include many of the standard sleights and tricks of the past. Out-of-date or impractical material has been omitted. Only the most useful knowledge has been retained, and only the best sleights needed for the tricks explained have found places in this work. To these tried and tested basic principles have been added many new and revolutionary ideas, all of which should give the student a conception of sleight-of-hand coin magic hitherto unknown.

It will be at once apparent that this book is no encyclopedia of coin magic. In the countless books and magical journals I've sifted through and researched, there are coin puzzles and recreations galore; there are dozens of coin pinches, grips, palms, vanishes, changes, acquitments and even a few wierd finger contortions for which *any* use would be hard to find. There are pieces of apparatus without end, for catching coins, holding coins, vanishing coins, dropping coins, or reproducing vanished coins, most of them of little use today except as "museum" pieces. And there are pieces that were calculated simply to "dazzle" the spectators of a bygone day. On the other hand, there are some ingenious apparatus pieces in the dealer's catalogues, which obviously cannot be explained here; and there are also in current magical literature variations of some of the tricks explained in this book. An insight into this reservoir of coin material can be gained from the Bibliography of other works in which coin material can be found.

Four new chapters have been added to this revised edition, to include the important new material, and here, too, the original purpose of the book has been held to. Only practical, usable, basic tricks could be admitted, but such a plan results in increased value for the coin worker and student. Here is the groundwork—a sound basis upon which to build. There is material here for a lifetime of use, re-use and development!

Now a word or two about coin magic. During the past 12 years this branch of the conjurer's art has become more firmly entrenched than ever, and this is as it should be. Coins are always available. If a magician can do a few coin tricks he is always prepared to entertain. If he does not possess this ability, and has to rely on mechanical gadgets, there will be times when he will have to embarrassingly shun a request for a few tricks by saying, "I don't have anything with me." People will wonder who is the magician—the man, or his bag of tricks. A mastery of coin magic will give anyone an invaluable asset that can be put to practical use every day of the year.

But merely learning the moves of tricks and the sleights is not enough. They should be practiced over and over, dozens of times, so you can do them automatically, without thinking. Only then will you be able to give your attention to presentation, patter, misdirection, and all those things that have so much to do with making a magician a success. The secret workings of a trick are only the means to an end, and that *end* is to entertain your audience.

The best coin tricks require skill, and unfortunately there are few magicians today willing to spend the necessary time and practice to obtain that skill.

The late Jean Hugard summarized the situation well when he said "There is an unfortunate trend among those who dabble in magic, and even those who rate themselves as magicians, to avoid anything that requires a little study and practice and to rely on tricks that work themselves, tricks 'that can be done five minutes after you receive them,' as we see advertised so often."

If you are a beginner, take heart. Not *all* coin magic requires great skill. There are many entertaining tricks in this book that can be mastered easily. Always remember that the tricks you can do "five minutes after you receive them" look like that and nothing more. Magic is a craft you must *master* if you want public admiration. Merely reading this book will not make you an "instant" coin magician. You just *have* to acquire skill! A well-presented trick is like a beautiful piece of music—audiences never tire of it. I have seen Blackstone perform the Dancing Handkerchief dozens of time, but I always enjoyed seeing it again. I'll never forget Thurston's card passes, or LePaul's beautiful card magic. Cardini's magic, and Neil Foster's beautiful magic are rare treats, to be enjoyed time after time. Who could ever tire of watching an artist work? And so it is with all good entertainers—people welcome the opportunity of seeing them again and again. If it be your desire to master this art, you will have to work at it, for "No man is his craft's master the first day!"

J. B. Bobo

Texarkana, Texas
August, 1964

CONTENTS

J. B. BOBO

The Advertisement read:

THE UNBREAKABLE MATCH

A handkerchief is opened flat on a table and an ordinary wooden match is placed in the center and the handkerchief folded up and handed to a spectator who feels the match and breaks it into several pieces. The handkerchief is placed on the table and unfolded, and the match is seen to be fully restored, unbroken. Easy to present anywhere. *Price 10¢.*

THIS was a mystery beyond compare to a boy of thirteen, and the dime that was mailed brought not only the secret of *The Unbreakable Match* but a small, thin paper catalog that illustrated other mysteries that dazzled the imagination and hinted of secret powers that any boy might possess who was able to meet the heavy financial obligations involved. And so the secrets followed as rapidly as capital could be raised by odd-job procurement. It's a familiar story to all magicians. It was either the advertisement or the actual witnessing of a magic show that aroused and crystallized into action that glorious curiosity in the unbelievable, the supernatural and the impossible that enters into the making of a magician. And so *The Unbreakable Match* started young Bobo on a career in magic that has herewith culminated in this book depicting his curiosity in the specialty of coin magic.

Bobo's background is international. His great grandfather, Jean Beaubeaux, immigrated to America after the disastrous Franco-Prussian war, but his new found neighbors never called him by name for the simple reason that they could not pronounce it. So in desperation, Monsieur Beaubeaux changed the spelling of his name to *Bobo*, the way it was pronounced in French. Bobo was born in Texarkana, Texas, in 1910, but the family moved to Ontario, Canada, and ere he was twelve years old, the Johnson Smith mail order catalog arrived, packed in small type with a wonderland of household and shop gadgets and all the gaudy allurements of Fourth of July celebrations, Halloween pranks and carnival entertainment, including that amazing section on Magic that first opened the door to the satisfaction of that *'glorious curiosity in the impossible.'*

Bobo's father operated a restaurant in Windsor, Canada, across the river from Detroit, and Saturday nights found the young Bobo crossing on the ferry to witness the wonderments of Laurant, The Great Leon and Thurston, though he never saw Houdini. The restaurant was a rendezvous too for show people and drummers who displayed the wit and gags of the road, including such 'startlers' as the paper balls under the hat which young Bobo added to his rapidly expanding repertoire.

"My first performance was at an amateur show at the Windsor Theater," writes Bobo, "and if memory hasn't failed me, I got the hook, I was so scared." But persistency prevailed and skills improved thanks to the arrival of *The Tarbell Course* at the age of sixteen. "The *Course* taught me my first real magic, for with the *Course* came a metal box beneath whose padlock were contained the essential gimmicks of a new world of wonders, the thumb tip, the wand shell and the pull, and numerous other shortcuts to the supernatural."

High school days were over, the family had returned to Texas and a career had to be entered, which happened to be as a carpenter at the bench, making kitchen cabinets for a dollar a day. It was a princely income, and it went for magic. After two years Bobo had learned that his eyes were worth more than his hands and he became a free lance window display decorator, splashing merchandise weekly in a hardware store, a department store and nine windows for the J. C. Penney Company. He was also booked as '*The Great Bobo*' at churches, schools and charity dates for his standard minimum fee of three dollars a show. Fancy apparatus was too expensive, and Bobo depended upon sleight of hand with cards, thimbles and coins, and closed with a handcuff escape, the Bean cuffs.

Experience as a window display showman as well as the church and school dates soon led to club dates, and here the price jumped to five dollars per show, "which was a lot of money in those days." The extra income could mean only one thing: '*Illusions*' must be added to the show, and so *Sawing A Woman In Two* was papered all over town. He faithfully pursued *The Tarbell Course* as the lessons came month by month, practicing two hours a day on each lesson for six months to perfect a routine before presenting it.

And then the big break came, his reward for years of patience and persistency, his first contract for a lyceum booking. On the recommendation of Percy Abbott, the magic manufacturer of Colon, Michigan, Bobo was accepted as a substitute for Harold Sterling and went on the road for one hundred and twenty-five dollars a week. He was out for the fall season, September to December, in the Rocky Mountain region for The Grapham Music & Lyceum Bureau, giving school and college shows throughout Colorado, Wyoming, Montana and Idaho. The school houses were so small it was known as the 'Kerosene Lamp' circuit. A charming assistant was now added to the performance who was soon transformed into Mrs. Bobo.

Bobo's schedule now is thirty-five weeks a year. He says his steady booking is a simple system. "If whistle stops want magic, I give it to them at a smaller fee, as the jumps are short and booking is continuous." He has learned in his close-up experience in the smaller school and college auditoriums that this type of audience appreciates a sleight of hand show over an apparatus show because they know that the latter type show means 'trick boxes.' Then, too, there are other advantages in playing the smaller towns. Lyceum and school audiences are of a higher intelligence and appreciate a more cultured show, where success is not dependent upon wisecracks or doubtful humor to get laughs.

Bobo's interest in coin magic began when a medicine-show magician taught him *The Sympathetic Coins,* with pennies. That was long ago—soon after he had acquired proficiency in presenting *The Unbreakable Match.* Sleight of hand always fascinated him—probably because, as he explains, "I am one of those fellows who enjoys working with his hands—learning crafts and skills that require delicacy of touch challenges me. Painting, cabinet making, photography —even just 'making things'—provide my chief sources of enjoyment. Coin magic requires skill, but no magic appears so spontaneous, so "spur-of-the-moment" to an audience. Coin tricks are of a visual nature—they are "sight tricks" and audiences like tricks that require little concentration. Money always fascinates people, and magic with money is doubly fascinating. Even the jingle and clink-ing together of coins is fascinating. Our shows always feature coin tricks. People admire and appreciate skill—coin magic impresses them as magic requiring skill."

"Bobo has extraordinary qualifications for the task of producing a book on coin magic," says John Mulholland, Editor of *The Sphinx.* "He has a canny understanding of the magic the public likes and he selects only such effects for his performances as have genuine appeal. His high reputation as a professional magician has been earned by his delightfully entertaining performances. Both his mastery of magic and his knowledge of audiences he brings into the field of coin magic which long has been his favorite branch of trickery. Mysteries with coins have intrigued him for many years and he has spent a great deal of time and enthusiastic energy collecting, devising, and mastering coin tricks."

This book is the result of Bobo's fascination with the magic of coins. The tricks have been gathered, mastered, tested, catalogued, and filed away like a collection of precious stones, and it has taken many years to get this collection together. Here are superb examples of the art of pure sleight of hand—magic with coins—and magicians the world over will be grateful to Bobo for present-ing to the fraternity his splendid collection of coin tricks.

—JOHN BRAUN

ACKNOWLEDGMENTS

MOST of the material in this book, including my own, is based on accumulated research, ideas, and effects of other magicians. Directly or indirectly, I am therefore indebted to all coin workers.

An honest effort has been made to credit the source of all material as accurately as possible, but slips may have crept in. If I have failed to recognize the originator of any idea, sleight, trick or move in the following pages, I hereby offer my most humble apologies.

I owe thanks to all my contributors, but more especially to Milton Kort, for Milton is one of the most modern-minded and practical of our present day sleight-of-hand artists. He gave unstintingly of his time and help whenever I needed it, and a generous sampling of his genius will be found throughout the book.

I also acknowledge with gratitude the assistance of numerous persons who helped me in gathering and preparing material for this volume. J. G. Thompson, Jr. was responsible for several effects other than his own contributions. Dr. E. M. Robert's revolutionary sleeving technique and tricks therewith should be an inexhaustable source of ideas for years to come. Albert Goshman, C. H. Haden, Stewart Judah, Louis Tannen, John Mulholland, Roland Hamblen, Jimmy Buffaloe, Stewart James and Glenn Harrison did yeoman service in helping me to make this book.

Stanley Collins has rendered the magical fraternity a great service in setting down his recollections of great coin manipulators of the past together with some of their almost-forgotten tricks.

I am deeply grateful for the invaluable assistance given me by my good friend John Braun in editing the material, making suggestions, and for his work on Chapter XIV. Without his help the book could not have been written.

Finally, I want to express the debt of gratitude I owe to my publishers:

The late Carl W. Jones, who first put my book into printed form and added it to his list of outstanding books on magic. As a Publisher of Magic, his record for fine books set a standard for all others to follow.

And to The Ireland Magic Company, whose record as publishers of magic is already an imposing one—so much so that Jay Marshall, the Master Printer of the establishment, now rates the title of "the Ben Franklin of the magical press."

May this edition prove a delight as well as a valuable source of information to all!

J. B. Bobo

PROLOGUE—
OF COINS AND CONJURING

ARCHAEOLOGISTS and numismatists tell us that the first coins were issued in the east and west in the eighth century B.C., and their use soon spread over the civilized world. An ancient tradition has it that coinage was the invention of Pheidon, king of Argos. By the end of the sixth century B.C., the art of coinage had been well established, and Periander had instituted the Corinthian coinage which became one of the great commercial coinages of the world. Electrum (a natural mixture of gold and silver), gold, silver, copper and bronze were the metals coined then, as today, and the oval shaped staters of Lydia, circa 750 B.C., are the earliest examples of the art of coining. By 480 B.C. coins were round, and had become objects of considerable beauty. Many of them were small, but most ranged in size from that of our quarter to our dollar, sizes ideally suited for the purposes of conjuring.

It is at this point that the archaeologists and numismatists fail us completely, for they shed no light upon the earliest use of coins in conjuring. They do tell us the ancient Greeks called the conjurer *psephopaiktes,* from the pebbles which he used, and that the Romans styled him the *calcularius,* or *acetabularius,* from the little stones and cups, respectively. And they have unearthed papyri and inscriptions on tombs depicting the cup and ball conjurers of ancient Egypt. However, we are entirely within the bounds of probability when we assume that these precious and artistically designed bits of metal early fired the imaginations of the cup and ball conjurers, and we can safely place the entrance of the coin into conjuring at full two thousand years before the advent of the Master of the Playing Card and his gift to the magician.

The feats with coins described by Reginald Scot in 1584 in his *Discouverie of Witchcraft* were undoubtedly of ancient vintage in that day, and might well have been devised by the conjurers of the eighth century B.C. Scot defined "legierdemaine" as "the nimble conveiance of the hand, which is especiallie performed three waies. The first and principall consisteth in hiding and conveieng of balles, the second in the alteration of monie, the third in the shuffling of the cards. . . . The conveieng of monie is not much inferior to the ball, but much easier to doo. The principall place to keepe a peece of monie is the palme of your hand, the best peece to keepe is a testor; but with exercise all will be alike, except the mony be verie small, and then it is to be kept betwixt the fingers. . . ." The tricks described by Scot are used to this very day, and the plots are recognizable from his quaintly worded titles:

"To conveie monie out of one of your hands into the other by legierdemaine; To convert or transubstantiate monie into counters, or counters into monie; To put one testor into one hand, and an other into the other hand, and with words to bring them together; To put one testor into a strangers hand, and another into your owne, and to conveie both into the strangers hand with words; To throw a peece of monie awaie, and to find it againe where you list; With words to make a groat or a testor to leape out of a pot, or to run alongst upon a table; To make a groat or a testor to sinke through a table, and to vanish out of a handkercher verie strangelie; A notable tricke to transforme a counter to a groat (the double faced coin consisting of two coins filed thin and joined so the groat showed on one side and the counter on the other); An excellent feat, to make a two penie peece lie plaine in the palme of your hand, and to be passed from thence when you list; To conveie a testor out of ones hand that holdeth it fast; To throw a peece of monie into a deepe pond, and to fetch it againe from whence you list; To conveie one shilling being in one hand into another, holding your arms spread abroad like a rood."

In 1634, *Hocus Pocus Junior* appeared with another trick still used today— "How to make a pile of Counters seem to vanish thorow a Table." This is the Cap and Pence trick, or the Stack of Quarters, or whatever you will, and the making of the shell stack of counters is clearly set forth. The patter, unmistakably Elizabethan, would be frowned upon today. Another trick described is "How to seem suddenly to melt a peice of Coin with words." Required is a small metal box with the bottom in the center and a lid on each end, so that either end can be opened to show a transformation or vanish—even an appearance— the ancestor of the modern coin box. The eighteenth century seems to have advanced coin magic but little. A rhymed account of a visit to Bartholomew Fair in 1717 contains these lines:

> "The large Half-Crown his magick Jaws can blow
> Unseen, unfelt, into the Sleeve of Beau;"

This seems to be the Flying Half-Crown trick with which the French conjurer Ollivier made a reputation almost a century later, and stems undoubtedly from the trick described by Scot "To throw a peece of monie awaie and to find it again where you list."

Jean Nicholas Ponsin's *Nouvelle Magie blanche dévoilée* (1853) contains a more complete section on coin magic than had previously appeared in any book. He lists three different methods for vanishing coins and describes thirty tricks, which include two multiplications of coins or counters in the hands of a spectator; the passage of a coin through a table; the flying coin as performed by the elder Conus and Ollivier; a palm change for changing a coin before the eyes of a spectator; the flying coins in the handkerchief, the first version of the Magical Filtration of Five-Franc Pieces, which L'Homme Masqué used in 1905 as The Expansion of Texture; another flying coin trick in a handkerchief, which is the well known trick of the Coin and Burnt and Restored Handkerchief; and the multiplication of coins in a spectators' hand by means of the money plate or coin tray.

When Robert-Houdin published his *Les Secrets de la Prestidigitation et de la Magie* in 1868, we find, for the first time in any language, the principles of coin conjuring properly explained—the various methods of palming, vanishing and changing the coins, then the tricks. The Melting Coin, The Flying Coins, The Shower of Money (the Miser's Dream, using a top hat!), The Multiplication of Money, The Magical Filtration of Five-Franc Pieces, The Intelligent Coin, The Coins and the Two Hats, and The Golden Coin in a Dinner Roll— all of them magic of the purest kind, just as sound today as they were a hundred years ago. Step by step Houdin instructed in the essentials of the craft—the sleights, preparation, patter and sequence—leaving out none of the subtleties, artifices and manipulations which constitute the art of conjuring. Each trick was a complete lesson, and his book remains one of the best ever written upon the subject. That he did not describe all the coin tricks current in his day he admits, saying "I have selected some of the best, which will serve as specimens whereby lovers of the art may arrange others at their pleasure, making use of the principles laid down at the outset of this chapter."

Modern Magic by Professor Hoffmann in 1876 drew heavily upon Robert-Houdin's treatise, and added to the conjurer's aides such stalwarts as the coin wand, or wand for producing a coin, and the rattle box. In The Shower of Money (Miser's Dream) detailed instructions are given for passing a coin through the side or the crown of the hat, and the use of the coin slide, a form of coin dropper for delivering coins into the hand, is advocated. Also, it is suggested that a few coins be caught on the coin wand.

More Magic (Professor Hoffmann, 1890) acquaints us with the folding coin and the trick of passing a coin into "an ordinary narrow-necked bottle." And in "Multiplying Coins and Tricks Therewith," the multiplying coin is the familiar shell which fits over a coin. Both are popular items today. Professor Hoffmann himself seems to have been the inventor of a "passe passe" effect in which two covers and eight coins, two of which are shell and coin "doubles," are used. This trick has gone through countless variations over the years, and at one time was included in most "boxes of tricks."

The great innovator in coin magic, T. Nelson Downs, presented his famous coin act for the first time in 1895 at the Hopkins Theatre in Chicago. To Downs is credited the invention of the back and front palm with coins, and many other sleights and passes that produced the astonishing effects which made his version of The Miser's Dream the sensation of the vaudeville world, and established him "King of Koins" in spite of a host of imitators. Downs may truly be called the originator of modern coin manipulation; his book, *Modern Coin Manipulation* (1900), established the fashion for coin magicians for the first quarter of this century. It has remained until today the only book in the English language devoted entirely to coins, and in it are disclosed the sleights and passes that enabled the "King of Koins" to reign supreme as a vaudeville favorite both here and abroad.

But even as the "King of Koins" went triumphantly from engagement to engagement, the inventive and restless minds of the world's hanky panky men were evolving new bits of coin chicanery. The best of it was acquired by the "King" and set down for us in *The Art of Magic,* another great book bearing his name as author, and John N. Hilliard's as editor. In this book, which made its appearance in 1909, we find, among other good things, the Downs thumb crotch palm, the coin roll, The Sympathetic Coins (attributed to Yank Hoe), The Expansion of Texture by L'Homme Masqué, and a number of other useful subtleties. The magic of the twentieth century has been greatly influenced by this man from Iowa, whose inventions have stamped him one of the magical giants of his time. Other clever minds have taken up where he left off, and explored the vistas he opened for them, to provide you with the wealth of coin magic you will find collected here.

From the eighth century B.C. to the middle of the twentieth century, a long procession—nay, pageant—of magical craftsmen has contributed to this book of coin magic. As John Northern Hilliard said, "A panorama of civilization. A glorious and sordid pageant, like history itself." May the collected coin magic of these worshippers of the Goddess Maja, to which J. B. Bobo has devoted so much of his magical life, give you pleasure and serve you well!

Monie

Scot's *Discouverie of Witchcraft,* 1584

"He that hath once atteined to the facilitie of reteining one piece of monie in his right hand, may shew a hundreth pleasant conceipts by that meanes, and reserve two or three as well as one. And lo then may you seeme to put one peice into your left hand, and reteining it still in your right hand, and may togither therewith take up another like peice, and so with words seeme to bring both peeces togither. . . . By this devise (I saie) a hundreth conceipts may be shewed."

Chapter I

COIN CONCEALMENTS

The Classic Palm

The coin is held in the center of the palm by a contraction of the muscles at the base of the thumb and little finger, Fig. 1. It is transferred to, and pressed into this grip by the tips of the second and third fingers. Several coins may be held in this manner.

Fig. 1

This is one of the most difficult of all concealments to master but it is one of magic's finest secrets. The layman cannot imagine it possible to conceal a coin in this way.

The beginner may experience difficulty in retaining a coin in this position at the outset, but the ability will come with practice. Once the knack is acquired coins of various sizes can be retained.

A minimum amount of pressure is sufficient to hold the coin in place. Too much grip tends to make the hand appear cramped and tense. A coin is not a heavy object, so hold it lightly and the hand will appear natural. Actually it should be held so loosely that a mere tap with the other hand will dislodge it.

An important point to remember is that no one is misled because the fingers are apart. Only when the hand *looks* natural will it be above suspicion. The ability to palm a coin should be mastered first; naturalness will come later. Make use of the hand that has the coin palmed by picking up something with it, such as another coin, or a small wand or pencil; use it to pull back the sleeve; to snap the fingers or make a gesture. Any of these actions subtly direct attention away from the hand with the concealed coin. Sometimes I grasp a spectator by the arm to draw him closer for a better look, with the very hand that has the coin concealed.

The parlor rug offers an excellent surface for coin work. It is advisable to spread a pocket handkerchief on the rug and place the coins on that, as some rugs have a confusing design, thus making the coins difficult to see. Whether operating from the floor or a table, a natural pose to assume is to rest the fingertips of both hands on the working surface. The hands will then look empty even if something is concealed in one of them, Fig. 2.

In some instances certain tricks must be done while standing and occasionally the spectators will be crowded around you. Just a little thought will solve this problem and

Fig. 2

make you master of the situation. Watch your angles. Form the habit of keeping the palm of the hand in which the coin is palmed, toward the body. Or, if the hand that has the coin concealed is held parallel with the floor there is little chance of detection. The coin can only be seen from a point directly below.

The Edge Palm

The coin is held in the same spot as just explained, by the muscles of the hand which press together from opposite directions against the edge of the coin. It is not held flat as in the classic palm but in a slanting position of about forty-five degrees, Fig. 1.

This palm is more difficult to acquire than the classic palm, but once it has been mastered this one becomes easier. A fairly new coin with a sharp milled edge is easier to

hold than one with a well worn or smooth edge.

To place the coin in this position you must first hold it by its edge between the tips of the forefinger and thumb. Then place the tip of the second finger in front (nail against edge of coin) and third finger behind and grip it with these two fingers as the thumb and forefinger are removed from the coin. Now by bending the two middle fingers inward the coin is carried to the palm, Fig. 2. and retained there while the fingers straighten out again, Fig. 1.

A simple reversal of these moves will return the coin to its starting position.

To palm several coins in this fashion you would proceed exactly as you would with one, but as each coin is palmed it is placed on top of the preceding one with the final coin being closest to the wrist.

Fig. 2

To produce them again bend the second and third fingers inward, place the tip of the third finger on top of the coin nearest the wrist and the tip of the second finger underneath the outer edge of the coin closest to the palm. With the tip of the third finger, slide the top coin forward about a quarter of an inch, then grip it between the tips of the two fingers and bring it into view by straightening these fingers.

Fig. 1

The number of coins that can be palmed and produced in this manner depends entirely on the ability of the performer.

The Thumb Palm

The coin is clipped by its edge in the fork of the thumb by pressure of the latter against the base of the first finger, Fig. 1. The coin should be held rather loosely to permit the

Fig. 1

thumb to assume as natural a position as possible.

To place the coin in this position, begin with it between the tips of the first two fingers, Fig. 2. Curl these two digits inward

Fig. 2

until the top edge of the coin touches the upper palm at the crotch of the thumb, then bring the thumb down and grip it by its edge, Fig. 3, as the fingers straighten out.

To transfer the coin from the thumb palm to the classic palm, bend the second and third fingers inward as you lower the thumb (which action brings the coin closer to the palm), press the tips of these two fingers

Fig. 3

against the flat side of the coin and press it into the palm.

The Downs Palm

The coin is held horizontally in the fork of the thumb by pressure of the latter and the base of the first finger pressing together against opposite edges. Fig. 1 shows this

Fig. 1

position but from a different angle than viewed by the audience.

To bring the coin to this position, hold it vertically between the tips of the first two fingers, Fig. 2. Then curl these two fingers inward, depositing the coin behind the

Fig. 2

Fig. 3

thumb, where it is gripped against the base of the first finger. When the fingers are straightened the hand appears empty, Fig. 3.

This concealment is used mainly as a coin vanish and production. The correct moves for accomplishing this are as follows: Stand with your left side toward the audience and display a half dollar held between the tips of the first two fingers as described. Quickly bring the hand down, then up, in a tossing motion. Under cover of this brief movement, palm the coin. Follow the flight of the non-existent coin upward with your eyes, and if you have executed the moves as described the coin seems to vanish in mid-air. Show the hand empty as in Fig. 3.

To produce the coin, reach out with the hand and seemingly pluck it from the air by a reversal of the above moves.

After you have mastered the moves with a single coin try vanishing several in the same manner. A good number to start with is four. Show them in your left hand and stand with your left side toward the audience. Take the first coin with your right hand and vanish it as described. The remaining three are handled in the same manner but as each coin is placed behind the thumb it goes *underneath* the preceding one. At first this may seem a bit difficult but if you have spent sufficient time in mastering the moves with one coin the extra number should give you little trouble.

The next step is to show the back of the hand empty and produce the coins again.

To do this, turn slightly to the left, and as you swing your arm across your body, curl the fingers inward and touch the tip of the thumb with the tips of the first two digits (which prevents the onlookers from getting a flash of the coins), straighten the fingers and exhibit the back of the hand empty. Reverse these moves, show the palm of the hand empty and proceed to pluck the coins from the air one at a time. As each coin is produced, take it with your left hand, or better still, drop them in a goblet which you hold in your left hand.

A certain amount of care will have to be exercised to prevent the coins from "talking" as they are brought together behind the thumb. The use of old, well-worn coins, such as the Liberty head half dollar, will help greatly in eliminating the noise caused by the coins sliding across each other.

Read Arthur Buckley's description of the Downs palm which he employs in Four Coins to a Glass, (page 160).

A more beautiful coin vanish and reproduction has not been devised.

The Finger Palm

Here is probably the easiest and most natural of all palms. The coin is held at the base of the curled second and third fingers, as in the figure below.

If you will stand in front of a mirror with your arms relaxed at your sides, you will notice that the fingers curl inward naturally. If a coin is placed in the position described above, it can be retained without further movement of the fingers. Apply just enough grip on the coin to hold it in place, for if it is held too tightly the hand will not appear natural. With a coin thus concealed you will find that you can still snap the fingers and use the hand almost as freely as you do normally.

The transfer of the coin from classic or thumb palm to this position can be made during a slight movement of the hand or while the hand hangs naturally at your side.

The Front Finger Hold

The coin is held flat, near the tips of the extended second and third fingers by pressure on its opposite edges with the tips of the first and fourth fingers, The Back Palm, Fig. 2.

The ease in holding a coin in this position depends on the diameter of the coin and the size of the performer's hands. For most hands the half dollar is about right.

The coin can be transferred to this position from the thumb, finger, or classic palm.

The Back Palm

The coin is hidden behind the hand, being held flat against the second and third fingers by the tips of the first and fourth

Fig. I

fingers which press together against opposite edges, Fig. 1.

To get the coin in this position start with

Fig. 2

it in the front finger hold, Fig. 2. Bend the second and third fingers inward, then outward, passing them from one side to the other of the coin, which revolves in this action between the tips of the outer two digits, Fig. 3. When the fingers straighten out the coin will be hidden behind the hand, Fig.

Fig. 3

1, as you show the front of the hand empty, Fig. 4. A slight upward movement of the hand as if tossing the coin into the air will cover the action of back palming.

Fig. 4

To show the back of the hand, reverse the moves as follows: With the palm toward the front, bend the hand downward at the wrist as far as it will go, Fig. 5, and close

Fig. 5

the hand as it continues to turn until it becomes a loose fist, as illustrated in Fig. 6. At this point the two middle fingers bend inward and outward, revolving the coin

Fig. 6

between the first and fourth fingers as the hand completes its turning and the fingers are straightened out. The back of the hand is seen as in Fig. 7. All these moves must blend together in the one action of turning over the hand to show its back.

Fig. 7

An alternate and preferred method of showing the back of the hand is as follows: After the palm is shown, begin turning the hand to show its back just as described above until the position depicted in Fig. 6 is reached. Bend the thumb upward over the lower edge of the coin and release it from the fingers so it can be thumb palmed

as the fingers are extended to show the back of the hand. In other words, the coin is transferred from the back palm to the thumb palm as the hand turns over. This method is not only easier but has several advantages as a trial will show.

To show the front of the hand again, do this: Bend the fingers inward, grip the coin by its edge between the tips of the first two digits and turn it parallel with the floor as the thumb releases its grip and moves out of the way. Now bring the thumb back and press it against the edge of the coin, holding it in the Downs palm position. Still keeping the first finger below and the second finger above the coin, close the hand into a tighter fist and turn it palm toward the audience before straightening the fingers. The position of these two fingers prevents the spectators from getting a flash of silver as the hand is turned palm outward. At the completion of these moves the spectators see the hand as depicted in The Downs Palm, Fig. 3.

To produce the coin simply pluck it from the air as described in The Downs Palm.

All hands are not the same size, consequently all hands cannot handle the same size coin. For most, a half dollar will be just about right, while others will require a larger coin like the silver dollar. The Mexican Peso is slightly larger than the half dollar and the Canadian silver dollar is a trifle smaller than the American coin of the same value. It is advisable to use as large a coin as can be safely handled.

Many interesting foreign coins can be purchased for small sums at coin shops, some almost as cheaply as palming coins. Most coin manipulators prefer real money over the magic shop variety. Palming coins are usually suspected by the layman as being manufactured for magical purposes and for that reason are not recommended for close-up work.

Foreign coins also offer wonderful patter possibilities. Some of the coins available are quite beautiful and interesting in themselves. Use a few foreign coins and weave a story around them—you will find that the spectators will be much more enthusiastic about the trick.

The Back Finger Clip

The coin is clipped behind the hand by its edge, between the first and second fingers, **Fig. 1.**

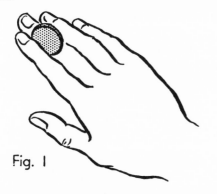

Fig. 1

To get it in this position hold it by its edge between the thumb and the fleshy second phalanx of the middle finger. The forefinger rests on the top edge, **Fig. 2.**

Fig. 2

Bring the forefinger down and place it against the lower edge of the coin as the thumb moves away. Clip the coin between the first two fingers and straighten out the

Fig. 3

hand, which appears empty, as in Fig. 3.

To use this as a vanish, stand with your left side toward the audience and hold the coin as described above. As you pretend to toss it into the air quickly transfer it to the back finger clip. The coin appears to vanish as you apparently toss it into the air. The coin is behind the hand and the hand appears empty.

To show the back of the hand you will have to transfer the coin from one side of the hand to the other. Proceed as follows: Turn the wrist as far as it will go and point the fingers toward the floor. The hand appears the same as shown in The Back Palm, Fig. 5. Now close the hand into a loose fist as you continue turning the hand. The back of the hand is now toward the spectators and it should appear the same as shown in The Back Palm, Fig. 6. With the hand in this position move the thumb around the forefinger and press its tip

Fig. 4

against the underside of the coin. This is done as the forefinger moves away, and the thumb presses the coin tight against the second finger. Thumb slides the coin inward toward the palm where it is clipped by its opposite edge between the first and second fingers. Open the hand and show its back as in Fig. 4.

To bring the coin from front to back of the hand again place the tip of the thumb against the edge of the coin. Push the coin between the fingers to bring it to the back of the hand as the hand turns over. The thumb screens the coin in this action. Finally the palm is shown empty as in Fig. 3.

The Back Thumb Palm

The coin is clipped by its edge with the thumb and is concealed behind the hand, Fig. 1.

Fig. 1

The moves necessary to get the coin into this position are harder to acquire than the Downs palm but this palm has the advantage of being considerably more angle proof. For this reason it is excellent for close work.

There are three ways to get a coin into this position. The first is a method used by T. Nelson Downs, while the other two are my own.

For the Downs method the starting position is the same as The Back Finger Clip, Fig. 1, (page 7). Bend the thumb down and

Fig. 2

clinch the fingers, Fig. 2. As you raise the thumb and return it to its normal position,

Fig. 3

move the coin along with it, Fig. 3, and clip it at the back of the fork of the thumb, Fig. 1. Straighten the fingers, keeping them slightly separated and show your hand

Fig. 4

empty, Fig. 4. Because the coin has a tendency to slant upward the hand must be tilted backward slightly to prevent the spectators getting a flash of silver.

The moves of transferring the coin from the back finger clip to the back thumb palm are made as you make an upward grab at an imaginary coin in the air. Feign disappointment as you open and show your hand empty.

Fix your eyes on another spot in the air even higher than before, then as you make a grab for it raise your thumb and allow the coin to slip into the clinched fist. Triumphantly open your hand and display the coin lying on your palm.

A simpler and easier method with less movement of the hand follows: Stand with your left side toward the spectators and display a half dollar between the tips of the first two fingers of your right hand as in The Thumb Palm, Fig. 2, or The Downs Palm, Fig. 2. Quickly lower, then raise your hand in a tossing motion, pretending to throw the coin upward into the air. Under cover of this movement, bend the first two fingers inward (in practically the same manner as you would for the thumb palm) and clip the coin behind the thumb. The main difference between this move and those used in the thumb palm is that the fingers must clinch tighter and the thumb must go *under* and not above the coin, Fig. 5. When the hand reaches its highest point it should be open and appear empty, Fig. 4.

Produce the coin as already described.

Fig. 5

Another way of getting the coin into the back thumb palm is as follows: Stand with your right side toward the audience and display a half dollar between the tips of your right first two fingers, (The Thumb Palm, Fig. 2). Pretend to place the coin in your left hand but thumb palm it in your right, (the Thumb Palm Vanish, page 25). Close your left hand as if it actually held the coin, then swing to the right and show the right palm empty. It is under cover of this movement that the transfer of the coin from the thumb palm to the back thumb palm must be affected. Here are the moves: Bend the second finger inward, place its tip against the lower edge of the coin, then under cover of the swing to the right, push the coin upward between the thumb and base of the first finger and clip it in the orthodox back thumb palm.

This transfer is made while ostensibly showing the right hand empty, thus proving that the coin is actually in the left hand. Make no verbal comment as you do this— merely show the hand empty and turn your attention back to the left fist. Make crumbling motions with the left fingers, then open the hand and show it empty. Before attention returns to your right hand look up to your right and exclaim, "There it is!" Reach up with your right hand and produce the coin as already described, but do it with only one grab.

Chapter II

BASIC TECHNIQUE

*The Bobo Switch · Utility Switch · One-Hand Switch · Shaw-Judah
Coin Switch · The Click Pass (3 methods) · The Coin Flip · Change-
Over Pass · The Bottom Steal · Producing a Coin from a Spectator's
Clothing · Taking Advantage of a Fumble (3 methods)*

To gain a firm foundation in coin conjuring it is necessary that you learn certain basic principles. Some of these will be described in this chapter. Practice well and master every movement and you will be another step along the road to becoming a proficient coin operator.

The Bobo Switch

One of the most valuable of all coin sleights is a good method for switching one coin for another. Here is one that I have used with success under all conditions for many years. It can be used as an effect in itself or as the means for accomplishing numerous other effects, several of which will be found in the chapters that follow. Learn this sleight and you will have a valuable tool that will serve you well as long as you do close-up magic.

For the sake of clarity suppose you learn this with two coins of contrasting color, such as a silver half dollar and a copper English penny. Have the English penny concealed in finger palm position in your right hand while you show a half dollar in your palm up left hand. Pick up the half dollar with the first two fingers and thumb of the right hand, toss it back into the left hand and close the fingers over it. Do this again. For the third toss, the switch is made and the copper goes into the left hand in-

stead of the silver, yet there is no perceptible change in movement. Regardless of which coin is thrown, the action appears the same.

Instead of tossing the silver coin the third time, the copper one is tossed, as follows: Always hold the visible coin (silver) between the first two fingers and thumb, Fig.

Fig. I

1. When ready to make the switch merely open the second, third, and fourth fingers slightly, releasing the copper coin, but retaining the half dollar with the forefinger and thumb, Fig. 2. It will be noted at this point that the silver coin is completely masked from the spectators' view by the ex-

Fig. 2

tended second, third, and fourth fingers. Only a slight movement is necessary to place the half dollar in finger palm position where it is retained. This should be mastered so that all moves blend into one action of merely tossing a coin into the left hand.

The sleight is not difficult but requires practice to make it indetectable. Performed correctly it is impossible for anyone—layman or magician—to tell that a switch was made.

Remember to close the left hand over the tossed coin each time, and throw the coin in even, consistent speeds—not too fast, yet not too slow, either.

If it is desired to finish with the copper coin in the classic palm position, this can be accomplished as follows: Continue up to the point shown in Fig. 2, but instead of finger palming the half dollar curl the fingers inward pressing the coin into the palm (with the aid of the two middle fingers) and immediately snap the fingers over the closed left hand, which supposedly holds the coin. It is the snapping of the right fingers which covers the move of palming the copper coin.

Master the method first explained, and this one will come easier later. This is the preferred method of the two because it leaves the fingers of the right hand free to pick up other objects or handle them in a natural manner.

The first and most important thing to remember about this exchange is that it must be made under cover of a natural gesture and carefully timed to coincide with an appropriate remark.

Utility Switch

Here is a move that is not only the basis of many coin transposition routines—it aids materially in accomplishing other effects as well. It is a dual purpose move in that it can be utilized to show a number of coins and still keep an extra one hidden.

Suppose you have three half dollars and want the spectators to know of only two. Have these two exposed in your palm up left hand, with one of them lying at the base of the two middle fingers in finger

Fig. 1

palm position. The right hand, with the third coin concealed in finger palm position, points to the left hand, Fig. 1. Call attention to the two coins in your left hand as you show them to the spectators on the left. Swing slightly to the right, retain the forward coin finger palmed in the left hand as you turn that hand inward and over and toss the other one into the right hand, which turns palm upward to receive it, Fig. 2. Show two coins in your right hand to the spectators on the right—one just received from the left hand and one which was already there.

If the moves are made in a natural, unhurried manner, it should appear that you merely showed two coins in your left hand, then tossed them into your right hand to show them to the spectators on the right.

Fig. 1

Fig. 2

This is a convincing method of retaining an extra coin while apparently calling attention to the fairness of the procedure.

For the sake of clarity the moves have been described with three coins, but any small number above this amount will work just as well.

Several tricks and routines in the following pages depend partially or entirely upon this switch for their accomplishment.

One-Hand Switch

Although this one-hand switch is usually made secretly while attention is on the other hand or directed elsewhere, it can be executed openly during some natural gesture or movement of the hand, once it has been completely mastered.

Suppose you have just borrowed a half dollar and wish to exchange it for one of your own which you have finger palmed in your right hand. Proceed as follows: Take the borrowed coin between the tips of your right first two fingers and thumb, Bobo Switch, Fig. 1. Now while you pick up some object with your left hand, or make a gesture with that hand, drop your right hand to your side and switch one coin for the other in the following manner: With the tip of the forefinger, slide the borrowed

coin along the inside of the thumb, Fig. 1, to the thumb crotch, where it is thumb palmed, Fig. 2. Now place the tip of the thumb on top of the finger palmed coin and push it to the tips of the first two fingers. Then allow the thumb palmed coin to drop to finger palm position. At the completion

Fig. 2

of these moves you will have the spectator's coin finger palmed and your own visible at the tips of the first two fingers and thumb in exactly the same position as formerly occupied by the borrowed coin, Bobo Switch, Fig. 1.

The switch, which takes only a moment to make, can be executed while you turn to the right to address the spectators on that side, or during any other natural action.

Shaw-Judah Coin Switch

Quite often the trick at hand requires that a borrowed coin be switched for one of your own, then your own kept in plain

Fig. 1

Fig. 2

view while you do something else with the borrowed one—like secretly loading it into some apparatus or a spectator's pocket (see In a Spectator's Pocket, page 57). This switch of many uses was shown to me by Stewart Judah, who in turn credits it to Allan Shaw.

Besides a coin like the one you intend to borrow, you will require a regular glass goblet. Have the glass on the table and a half dollar classic palmed in your right hand. Ask for the loan of a half dollar and request that it be marked for future identification. While this is being done, pick up the glass by its stem, with the right hand. As you approach the spectator, transfer the goblet to your left hand, then take the marked coin between the tips of the first two fingers and thumb of the right hand and immediately toss it into the glass. This is what you seem to do. Actually you throw your own coin from the palm, Fig. 1, and retain the borrowed one hidden behind the

curled fingers after the fashion of The Bobo Switch. The instant the coin arrives in the glass, rattle it and thumb palm the borrowed coin, Fig. 2.

The exchange is not suspected because every move appears fair and natural. The sound of the coin clinking in the glass adds greatly to the illusion and automatically directs the spectators' attention there. To the spectators it appears that you merely took the borrowed coin with your right hand and tossed it into the glass.

The glass containing the duplicate coin is placed in full view and the borrowed coin is secretly loaded into the piece of apparatus the trick requires. Later in the routine the duplicate coin is taken from the goblet and vanished, and the borrowed coin produced according to the trick at hand.

The spectators believe they see the borrowed half dollar right up to the last minute. Little do they realize that subterfuge entered into this part of the trick!

The Click Pass

Here are two sleights which aid in accomplishing numerous effects. Although both moves appear the same, the results differ slightly. Method (a) is the brainchild of Chester Woodin; the originator of (b) is unknown.

Effect (a): Two half dollars are on the table. The performer picks up one with his right hand, places it in his left hand, and closes his fingers over it. He takes up the second coin with his right hand and drops it into his left hand, where it is heard to strike the first coin. *When the left hand is opened it holds only one coin; the other is shown in the right.*

(b) This action appears the same as described above, but the results differ slightly. *In this case when the left hand is opened it is empty. The right hand opens and displays the two coins.*

Method (a): After showing the two coins on the table, pick up one with the right hand and apparently place it in the left, but really retain it in the right hand in the regular palm position. (See Standard **Vanish, page 22.**) Left hand is closed. The second coin is picked up by the fingers and

thumb of the right hand, which seem to deposit it in the left hand. The left hand opens to receive it, but at the moment of the pretended deposit the coin in the right hand is released, and as it falls into the left hand it strikes the other coin in the process, Fig. 1. The right fingers then press the second coin into the palm, where it is retained.

When the first coin strikes the second coin, as it falls into the left hand, it makes a clink which simulates the sound one coin makes on being dropped onto another. The illusion is so perfect it fools the eye and the ear. Apparently the two coins are in the left hand. Open the left hand showing one coin, then open the right to show the other coin.

(b) The two coins are on the table. Pick up one coin with the right hand, apparently place it in the left, but palm it in the right. Left hand closes as if it held the coin. Take up the second coin with the right hand and

Fig. 2

repeat the previously described maneuver of apparently placing the coin in the left hand, but, at this moment it is palmed in the right hand and strikes the coin already there, Fig. 2, creating the illusion, by sound, of falling on top of the coin supposedly held in the left hand. Close the left hand again, both coins being palmed in the right hand. Wave right hand over left, snap right fingers, close right hand and hold it some distance away from the left. Open the left and show it empty. Open the right hand and show both

Fig. I

coins. The halves have traveled from hand to hand.

The performer apparently places the coins in his left hand, but, with the aid of either of these two passes he can retain one or both coins in his right hand. Although described as tricks, these moves are more effective when used secretly in other routines, several of which are explained in the following pages.

The Click Pass

PAUL MORRIS

Mr. Paul Morris, the famous New York sleight-of-hander, has an entirely different conception of this useful sleight.

In his version the effect is the same as described in method (a) of the foregoing description of The Click Pass. That is, the performer places one coin in his left hand. Then a second coin is ostensibly dropped onto the first, the sound of the two coins coming together offering convincing proof that the left hand actually holds two coins. Nevertheless, only one coin is in the left hand while the other is retained hidden in the right.

Method: Let's say you are using two half dollars. You may start in several ways: (1) While facing front, hold a coin at the fingertips of the two hands about chest high. Place the coin from the left hand between the teeth—most of the coin protruding from the teeth as you smile. The right hand places its coin in the left hand and then takes the coin from the teeth and places it in the left hand with the first one. (2) Place a coin on each of a spectator's hands, then take the coins one at a time and continue from there. (3) Or, have the two coins on the table at the beginning and pick them up one at a time as you commence the trick.

Fig. 1

At any rate, that is how to start. Now let's learn the sleight.

Exhibit coin number one between the tips of the second finger and thumb of the right hand. Hold the left hand palm up and place the coin on it—not on the center

Fig. 2

of the palm, but near the fingertips. Now take coin number two in the right hand, holding it in the same fashion described for number one, and place it on the left hand. It is not placed directly on the center of the left palm but a trifle off-center to the right, as in Fig. 1, the right middle finger and thumb still retaining a grip on the coin. In fact, the right hand never lets go of coin number two. Close the left hand, which action causes the first coin to fall onto the second coin, Fig. 2, and an unmistakable "clink" is heard. Immediately withdraw the right hand from the left, still holding on to the second coin. Fig. 3 shows the beginning of this action. The left fingers hide the movement and what is happening to

Fig. 3

the coins. The closed right fist hides coin number two, which is withdrawn under the right fingers. Just before the hands separate the spectators see the two hands as in Fig. 4. Now, move the right hand away, stealing the second coin with it as in Fig. 5.

Fig. 4

At this point the coin in the right hand is in perfect position for back palming. Simply straighten out the right hand, palm up, and you will find it a simple matter to back palm the coin, Fig. 6. Or, if you prefer, merely push the coin into finger palm position.

Now make a fist of the right hand also, bringing the back palmed coin into the hand as this is done. From here on, the trick is over. The main thing is that the spectators have the impression two coins were placed in the left hand. When you

Fig. 5

open your left hand, however, there is only one coin there. Show the second coin in the right hand, or finish any way you like.

The sleight is very useful in performng numerous 'coin passe' effects, such as Coins into the Glass, Coins Through the Table, etc.

Fig. 6

The Coin Flip

Right hand has a half dollar classic palmed, while the fingers flip another coin into the air a time or two. This is merely a disarming move which tends to show, without saying so, that the right hand holds only one coin. The spectators reason that there is only one because it seems impossible that a second coin could be hidden

Fig. I

in the hand flipping a coin in the air so naturally.

Fig. 1 shows the concealed coin in the palm and the visible coin ready to be flipped into the air. Coin is caught on the extended fingers as shown in Fig. 2. Back of hand is towards spectators.

Fig. 2

A little practice will be necessary to keep the coins from "talking" as the visible one is caught. Once the move is mastered it will be a useful sleight to add to your repertoire of close-up chicanery.

Change-Over Pass

Occasionally the coin operator may wish to vanish a coin and then show both hands empty before reproducing it. This adroit bit of trickery will fulfill that requirement nicely.

Pretend to place a half dollar in your left hand but retain it thumb palmed in the right. (For a method, see Chapter III, Coin Vanishes.) Open the left hand to show that the coin has disappeared. Hands are about waist high and fingers of both

hands point toward the left, Fig. 1. Both hands swing to the right so the right palm may be exhibited empty, and it is in this action that the coin is stolen from the right hand with the left, thusly: About midway in the swing the hands come together and the two middle fingers of the left hand take the coin from the right thumb palm, Fig. 2.

Fig. 2

The left fingers curl inward, hiding the coin as the hands continue without hesitation to the right, where the spectators see the left forefinger pointing to the empty right palm, Fig. 3.

Fig. 3

Left hand can then produce the coin according to the trick at hand.

The same moves can be used to transfer a stack of coins from the edge palm of the right hand to the left hand.

Fig. 1

Fig. 2

Fig. 1

Fig. 3

The Bottom Steal

Paul Morris

Here is a subtle sleight which should find many uses in performing such tricks as Four Coins to a Glass (Chapter VIII), Coins Through the Table, and numerous other effects.

Suppose you have a number of half dollars in your right hand and wish to retain one concealed in that hand as you place the others into the left. The Paul Morris Bottom Steal (with coins!—not cards) accomplishes this in an ingenious manner without any telltale movement whatsoever.

The method: After showing some coins and calling attention to their number, square them into a stack and hold them by their opposite edges between the tips of the right second finger and thumb—the back of the hand toward the spectators and the flat surface of the coins parallel with the floor, Fig. 1. The hands should be held about waist high, the left being palm up a few inches away and in position to receive the coins, Fig. 2. Move the hands toward each other casually. The right hand

is about to place the coins in the palm of the left hand. Take a look at Fig. 3. Fig. 4 shows the performer's view of the action.

As the stack of coins moves toward the left palm the two middle fingers of that hand come in contact with the bottom coin and it remains balanced on their tips hidden from the spectators' view by the right fingers. Fig. 5 shows the spectators' view, while Fig. 6 depicts the action as seen by the performer. As the right hand deposits the stack of coins in the left palm the left middle fingers push upward and press the stolen coin into the right palm, Fig. 7.

The action of sliding off the bottom coin

Fig. 4

Fig. 5

from the stack and pressing it into the right palm is completely hidden by the right fingers which are held close together. Now separate the hands. Allow the spectators to get a brief view of the coins lying in the left hand, then close the fingers over them. In a perfectly natural manner you have

Fig. 6

placed a stack of coins in your left hand but in this action you have stolen a coin, which is now hidden in your right palm. No visible movement of the right hand is necessary to retain the coin as that hand reaches for a glass tumbler and picks it up by its brim. The glass is held between the fingers and thumb of the palm down hand in such a manner that the coin, when released from the palm, will fall into the glass.

Fig. 7

Hold the hands some distance apart, make a tossing motion with the left hand toward the glass and release the coin in the right palm, permitting it to fall into the glass. Open the left hand and show one coin missing. The move can be repeated to cause a second coin to pass into the glass but the third and remaining coins should be caused to pass into the glass by employing different sleights.

This steal is so natural it can be executed in perfect safety at very close range. You may stand face to face with a spectator and execute the sleight without him being aware of anything unusual taking place. After becoming proficient with the sleight you will find that you can even curl back the forefinger to give a view of the coins from above. Even though you may permit the top of the stack to be seen the steal cannot be detected because the chicanery takes place *underneath* the stack while the spectators can only see the *top* of the stack. As far as they are concerned, nothing is hidden—they can see everything as the coins are placed in the left hand. Yet the sleight takes place without their knowing it!

Producing a Coin from a Spectator's Clothing

A prettier and more convincing method of producing a coin from a spectator's clothing has not been devised.

Effect: The wonder worker vanishes a half dollar, then the spectators see both hands empty as he reaches underneath a man's tie and extracts the coin with his fingertips.

Method: Vanish a half dollar, using any method where it is retained in the right hand. Suddenly point to a man's tie with the left hand. The right has dropped to the side and back palms the coin as the left lifts the end of the tie. Right palm is seen

Fig. 1

such difficulties, the more capable we become. Of course, we should be able to perform our tricks so well we do not make mistakes. There is no excuse for a fumble, but mortal man is never perfect. So, why not try to turn a fumble to advantage?

The following are tried and tested ideas that have served many close-up workers well. If you are not familiar with them, here they are for your edification.

For one reason or another you have dropped a coin. Prepare to pick it up by straddling it—that is, the coin is lying on the floor about midway between the feet. Bend down, or rather squat over the coin and pick it up with the right hand.

Now comes a bold move.

Immediately toss the coin backwards between the legs, catching it in the left hand, Fig. 1. The throw should be made just as soon as the right hand removes the coin from the floor, the body and the legs concealing the maneuver from the spectators. Then raise yourself up, pretending to hold the coin in the closed right hand. While

to be empty as the fingers reach underneath. Bring the coin to the front palm and come away with the half dollar lying on the fingers, Fig. 1.

This procedure can be used to produce a coin from other places, such as the bottom edge of a coat, underneath a scarf, or a sweater, or from behind your own knee. When done correctly it appears that you merely reached under the edge of the article and immediately came forth with the vanished money. It looks like real magic!

Taking Advantage of a Fumble

What would you do if you accidentally dropped a coin, or missed one of your vanishes? Would you pick up the coin and apologize for your carelessness, then continue with something else, or would you take advantage of this little mishap and do some unscheduled effect?

The better prepared we are to get out of

Fig. 1

attention is on the right hand the left sleeves the coin. Both hands are shown empty.

If working without a coat the coin can be disposed of in the left hip pocket. However, if you have sleeved it and would like to reproduce it, use one of the methods described in Chapter VII, The Art of Sleeving.

Here is another way of disposing of a coin which has fallen to the floor:

Bend down and pick up the coin with the right hand. Immediately toss it into the left trousers cuff. Do this quickly and without hesitation as you straighten up. You are supposedly holding a coin in the closed right hand. Pretend to place it in the left. Blow on the left hand, then open it to show coin vanished.

Or, you could do this. Bend down and apparently pick up the fallen coin. Actually the coin never leaves the floor. The right hand reaches for it and as the fingers touch the floor in front of the coin they instantly close. This action propels the coin inward along the floor and it slides underneath the right foot which raises slightly, becoming wedged between the toe end of the shoe sole and the floor, Fig. 2. The coin travels inward only three or four inches and is hidden in its flight by the right hand.

This getaway can only be done on a rug-covered floor. On any other surface the sliding of the coin creates a sound, which would be a "give-away."

You straighten up and pretend to vanish

Fig. 2

the coin from the right hand.

Of course, the coin must be recovered—not left there on the floor. To get it, show a second coin and apparently place it in your left hand, retaining it in the right. Slap the left hand on top of your head, remarking that you will cause the coin to penetrate your body, the hard way. Show the left hand empty. Move the right foot to one side exposing the coin on the floor. With your left side toward the spectators bend down to pick up the coin with the left hand. The right hand secretly disposes of its coin in the right trousers cuff on the side away from the audience.

COIN VANISHES

It is impossible to become a good coin conjurer without mastering several methods for vanishing a coin. Here, combined with some of the old standbys, are the best modern methods, contributed by leading coin manipulators.

Standard Vanish

This is given the above title because it holds a high place in my repertoire of coin vanishes. I use this one as much as I do any other because it is so practical and easy to do under almost any conditions.

The coin rests near the ends of the two middle fingers of the right hand, Fig. 1.

Fig. 2

Right hand describes a counter clockwise movement, turning back upward as the fingers curl inward and press the coin into the classic palm position where it is retained. This action takes place under the guise of supposedly placing the coin into the left hand, Fig. 2. The left hand closes as if it holds the coin. Look at and point to the left hand. Then snap the right fingers at the left hand. Open the left hand slowly and mysteriously. The coin is gone.

Reproduce it from behind the knee or keep it concealed, according to the trick at hand.

Fig. 1

Simple Vanish

This is a first-rate coin vanish, and in spite of its simplicity, ranks with the best of them.

Show the coin in the right hand where it rests in the classic palm position. Finger-tips of the left hand gently touch the back of the right hand, Fig. 1. The right hand

Fig. 1

turns inward and over and apparently drops the coin into the waiting left hand, but actually the coin is retained in the right hand, palmed, as the left hand closes, Fig. 2.

Fig. 2

With the right middle finger, tap the closed left hand once. Draw the left hand into a tighter fist by pressing the tips of the fingers into the palm, the thumb angling over the top of the fingers. Placing the fingers in this position makes the next move possible. Open the left hand, slowly and gracefully, a finger at a time, beginning with the little finger. When all the fingers are extended and apart the hand is shown on both sides. It is empty.

Care must be taken to perform this vanish slowly and gracefully. Grace is the important element. Make it look like you really dumped the coin into the left hand. Actually do this a few times before a mirror, then repeat this action but retain the coin palmed in the right hand.

Don't open the left hand too quickly. Take your time and you will have a beautiful and effective coin vanish.

Over the Top

Here is a vanish I have taught in my coin lectures throughout the country. It

Fig. 1

has always been well received. I think you will find it off the beaten path.

The coin rests on the two middle fingers of the right hand, near the tips. The left hand is nearby, held palm up and about the same level. Left hand moves to the right until it crosses over the palm of the right hand. Right fingers toss the coin upward, Fig. 1, into the left hand which immediately turns over, palm downward, the coin falling into the right as the left hand closes,

Fig. I

Fig. 2

Fig. 2. Almost simultaneously the right hand is turned so its back is toward spectators and the second, third, and fourth fingers curl inward slightly on the coin, retaining it where it has fallen. At this juncture the backs of both hands are toward the audience and the right forefinger is pointing to the closed left hand which supposedly holds the coin.

All of these moves must blend into one continuous action. There can be no hesitation. The coin merely makes a hop, skip and jump from the tips of the right fingers onto the left hand and then falls back into the right hand.

After a slight pause the left hand is opened and shown empty.

The only manipulation to this vanish is the knack of tossing the coin from the right middle fingers up into the left hand. The rest of the maneuver follows easily and naturally.

The Tunnel Vanish

Hold the left hand palm downward and

close it into a loose fist so only the thumb and forefinger touch. The right hand holds the coin horizontally between the forefinger and thumb—thumb is on top, Fig. 1.

It will be noted that if the coin is pushed into the left fist and then released it will fall to the floor because of the slightly open left fingers. But if the second, third, and fourth fingers of the right hand are extended when the coin is released it will fall onto these fingers instead. And this is exactly what happens. The coin merely goes over the left thumb and as soon as it is inside the left fist it is turned loose. The extended right second, third, and fourth fingers catch it and curl inward, holding it where it lands, Fig. 2. Without hesitation the right hand moves a few inches to the right with its back toward the onlookers. Left hand closes into a tighter fist and the right forefinger gives a final poke into the left fist.

It appears that the coin was pushed into the left fist and then given a final poke with the right forefinger.

Fig. 2

The left hand is then turned palm up, opened, and shown empty. The coin has faded into nothingness.

Done smartly, this is a coin vanish to fool the closest observer.

Thumb Palm Vanish

This vanish is about as simple and easy as they come, yet it is quite effective.

Display the coin held between the right first and second fingers, Fig. 1. Place the

Fig. I

open left hand in front of the coin, and under this cover bend the first two fingers inward and thumb palm the coin in the right hand, Fig. 2. Quickly straighten the first and second fingers and close the left fingers around them. Move the left fist away to the left, as if removing the coin from the right two fingers, which now separate. To all appearances the coin is now in the left fist—actually it is thumb palmed

Fig. 2

in the right hand. Turn the left fist palm uppermost. Simultaneously transfer the coin in the right hand from the thumb palm position to the classic palm position and snap the fingers over the closed left hand. This is a subtle way of saying that coin is not in the right hand. Open the left hand to show the coin gone.

To transfer the coin from the thumb palm to the classic palm: Bend the two middle fingers inward to the surface of the thumb palmed coin, right thumb bending slightly and pushing the coin lower in the hand. The middle fingers carry the coin from the thumb palm to the classic palm position under cover afforded by snapping the fingers.

This last move should be mastered by all coin workers since many uses will be found for it.

The Drop Vanish

Milton Kort

At the outset the coin rests on its side at the middle joint of the right forefinger, Fig. 1. The hand should be held perfectly relaxed with the fingers curled inward

Fig. I

naturally. Furthermore the hand must be tilted very slightly forward so the lower part of the hand will be closest to the body. The waiting left hand is palm upward and a few inches lower than the left hand. Both hands move toward each other and just as the right hand is over the left it tosses the coin into the air about half an inch—just enough to clear the forefinger— and it is caught in the same hand (right) in finger palm position at the base of the third and fourth fingers, Fig. 2.

Fig. 2

The reason for holding the right hand as just described should now be apparent. With the right hand turned slightly forward the coin merely lands at the base of the third and fourth fingers and stays there without any additional movement of the fingers. In fact, the right fingers must not move at all, but should be sufficiently curled at the beginning so the coin can be retained when it lands. A few trials will be necessary to get the correct tilt of the right hand so the coin will fall from the forefinger, land at the base of the last two fingers and be retained as described. Remember to keep the right hand completely relaxed and you will experience no difficulty in mastering the sleight.

The hands come together just as the coin lands on the lower right fingers. The illusion is that the coin falls down into the left hand. Close the left fingers as the hands are separated. Do not attempt to palm the coin at this stage, but merely hold it where it lands in the right hand by bending the third and fourth fingers a little as the right forefinger points to the closed left hand. After a brief pause the left hand slowly crumbles the coin to nothingness and the hand is shown empty.

A prettier and more convincing method of vanishing a coin has not been devised. At least, I do not know of it.

The sleight can also be used as a switch or as a pass.

As a switch, use it this way: Have one coin concealed in the right hand in finger palm position at the base of the third and fourth fingers. The other coin is lying on the table.

Pick up the coin from the table with the left hand and place it flat on the middle joint of the right forefinger. This should be done under the pretext of showing the left hand empty. Now as you go through The Drop Vanish moves the finger palmed coin is released and falls into the waiting left hand below, while the other coin drops down to finger palm position, occupying the place originally held by the finger palmed coin. At first the sleight will appear a little awkward when used as a switch but with a little practice you will find it quite easy.

The illusion is enhanced if both coins are of the same denomination. The left hand can show its coin momentarily before the fingers close over it.

As a pass, use it this way: Show three coins on the table. Pick up one of them with the right hand and pretend to place it in the left, but retain it classic palmed in the right instead. The left hand is closed. Pick up coin number two with the right hand and apparently place it in the left, but execute The Click Pass (a), (page 14). To the spectators it appears that you are holding two coins in your left hand—the sound created by The Click Pass offering audible proof that this is so. Actually the left hand holds only one coin, while the other is classic palmed in the right. While reaching for the third coin with the right hand, transfer the coin in that hand from classic palm to finger palm position, so it will lie at the base of the third and fourth fingers. Pick up the third coin with the right forefinger and thumb and slide it back to the middle joint of the forefinger in position for the Drop Vanish. Now execute the Drop Vanish moves. As the coin drops from the right forefinger it lands on the finger palmed coin and creates the exact sound it would have if it had fallen into the left hand on top of the coin(s) there. The illusion is perfect. The left hand apparently holds three coins, but actually it holds only one. The other two are finger palmed in the right hand.

Of course, these additional suggestions are not offered as tricks in themselves but as a means for accomplishing other effects.

Many other ideas will suggest themselves by experimenting with the two moves—The Click Pass and The Drop Vanish.

The Bobo Coin Vanish

The main point in favor of this and the three coin vanishes that follow is an illusive element called retention of vision. In other words, not only does the coin actually appear to be placed in the left hand—the spectators think they see it in that hand AFTER the hands separate. The result of the perfect illusion these sleights create is complete deception.

Hold a half dollar by its edge between the tips of the right thumb and middle finger and place it squarely in the palm of the left hand, Fig. 1. Retain this grip on the

Fig. 1

coin as you close your left fingers over it. Open the left first two fingers so the spectators may see that the half dollar is actually in the left hand, Fig. 2.

Although the following moves are carried through as one complete action they will be described separately for better understanding.

Close the first two fingers of the left hand over the coin and hold that hand quite loosely and relaxed. Left little finger rests on outer joint of the right thumb. Study the

Fig. 2

position of the hands in Fig. 2. The left little finger and the outer joint of the right thumb act as a pivot for the two hands as they turn inward together. The left hand turns clockwise as the right hand turns counterclockwise. And both must turn simultaneously, until the backs of both hands are toward the spectators, Fig. 3. The right

Fig. 3

thumb and middle finger still retain their grip on the coin and they bend inward as the two hands turn over. Hands are still together at this point and the half dollar is outside the left fist. (Fig. 4 shows how the hands appear from the rear.)

Although the spectators are never conscious of the hands being in this position

Fig. 4

because there is no hesitation in the action, they are pictured in this position for clarity.

At this juncture the right hand moves inward toward the left shoulder and thence outward again, making a pass over the back of the left fist a couple of times. As the right hand moves back toward the body at the start of this action the coin is thumb palmed.

Going back to Fig. 4 you will observe that the half dollar is held by the thumb and middle finger of the right hand. In order to thumb palm the coin place the forefinger on top of it and remove the thumb, holding the coin between the first two fingers. These two fingers deposit it in thumb palm position as the hand swings inward and outward making the first pass over the left fist. Continue passing the right hand over the left fist a couple more times. Finally, diminish the passes, open the left hand and show that the coin has faded away.

A great many words have been necessary to describe this vanish which only takes a moment to perform and is not difficult once the exact mechanics are thoroughly understood.

The Slide Vanish

JOHN MULHOLLAND

This sleight to cause a coin to disappear was devised by John Mulholland when he was about twelve years old. Because of the reliable peculiarity of the eye called retention of vision, the spectator "sees" the coin go into the hand and is very much surprised when the magician shows it isn't there. The Slide Vanish has the added advantage of being a completely natural move.

This is the effect: The magician holds his right hand out flat to show a half dollar resting on the center of the palm. Tilting his hand he permits the coin to slide from the palm, down his fingers and into the cupped left hand held below to catch it. The left hand is closed about the half dollar and raised to shoulder height. After a rubbing movement of the fingers of the left hand, or with the pronouncement of the magic words, the hand is opened to show that the coin has disappeared.

The sleight depends upon the fact that a half dollar is of such size that it will wedge between the tips of the first and little fingers when those fingers are squeezed tightly against, and just a little above, the two middle fingers. By holding the fingers in this manner, a coin sliding from the palm toward the tips of the fingers will become wedged at the tips of the fingers. As the coin slides down the hand, which should not be tilted so much as to make the movement fast, the left hand is brought underneath and held like a cup. Just at the instant the coin has reached the position on the fingers where it will stay, turn the hand over so that the back is toward the audience. This is done by turning the wrist and in no other way changing the position of the hand. The turn over seems merely to be proof that the coin has left the hand. The instant the right hand is turned it is moved away from the left hand, which then closes "about the coin." The left hand, by the way, should be held so that the palm almost touches the tips of the fingers of the right at the moment the right hand is turned over. The hands being that close together provide complete cover and hide the fact that the coin never goes into the left hand.

Once the left hand is closed the right hand can be dropped to the side. In that position the coin can be brought to the back of the hand so that the palms of both hands may be shown empty after the vanish has occurred. For those who do not back palm, it will be found that the coin is in a position to do the regular palm and, once done, the right hand can aid the disappearance by making passes toward the left hand.

The Illusive Coin Pass

T. J. CRAWFORD in *Greater Magic*

This sleight was given the above title by John Northern Hilliard when he was preparing for T. Nelson Downs that magical classic, *The Art of Magic,* as the coin pass had been submitted to him without a name.

The pass is not one automatically acquired immediately after reading the instructions, but performers who have mastered it have found the effort to perfect it time well spent. It enables the performer to completely vanish a coin from the hand in which it was unmistakably placed. The spectator actually sees the coin lying in the palm of the left hand, yet when the hand is opened, the coin has apparently melted away. Nor is it limited to one coin. Several coins may be vanished singly.

The Method: The coins are picked up from the table, a coin rack, or from the palm of a spectator's extended hand. With the sleeves up and the hands empty, the performer takes one coin between the thumb and index finger of the right hand, holding the coin as near the edge as possible. This scanty grip on the edge is important, as all the surface of the coin possible should be exposed and well polished coins should be used. Much of the effect is psychological and these details are helpful.

What actually happens is this: the coin is really placed in the palm of the left hand and, for a brief interval, the spectators see it lying there, but it is never released from the grip of the thumb and finger on its extreme edge. Strange as it

Fig. 1

may seem, this fact does not dawn on the spectator. To his eye the coin has either melted away or gone into a mysterious pocket in the palm of the left hand.

The timing at this stage is the vital element. The instant the coin is shown openly in the left palm, Fig. 1, the fingers of that hand begin to close over it, and when they have closed to the point of screening the coin from view, the middle, third and little fingers of the right hand are extended full length under the curved fingers of the left,

Fig. 2

Fig. 2. The three right hand fingers form a screen for the coin as the right hand moves away with it. Without this screen, there would be a ruinous flash of the bright coin, which is still held in its original position by the thumb and index finger, Fig. 3.

As the left hand is slowly closed and ex-

tended, and the eyes of the assembly are focussed on that point, the fingers of the right hand are pushing the coin to a center palm. A momentary pause allows the situation to be absorbed, then follows the deliberate process of opening the left hand, showing back and front, with fingers wide apart. The coin is gone. And likewise, several coins are vanished one after the other.

The stack of coins in the left hand can be produced in a fan and showered into a glass after both hands have been shown empty by the change over palm, or transferred to the fork-of-thumb palm (See The Downs Palm, page 3), and after both palms

Fig. 3

have been seen empty, reproduced from the air one at a time.

As a vanish for a single coin, this is one of the best, and is only equalled by a similar vanish by that modern master of subtlety, Dai Vernon, which is simply titled A Coin Vanish.

A Coin Vanish

Reprinted from *Greater Magic*

Hold the coin between the extreme tips of the right thumb and first finger, allowing as much as possible of it to be visible. Place it on the palm of the left hand as

Fig. 1

Fig. 3

shown in Fig. 1. Slowly close the left fingers, keeping them touching one another and extended, the bend being made at the lowest joints, so that they come to touch the back of the middle joints of the right hand, as in Fig. 2.

to the position shown in Fig. 5 and complete the closing of the left fingers on the

Fig. 2

Fig. 4

The instant this position is arrived at, and not till then, extend the right second and third fingers over the coin, the movement being masked by the curved fingers of the left hand, Fig. 3.

With the left finger tips still touching the middle joints of the right fingers, move the right wrist forward, the left finger tips and the middle joints of the right fingers acting as a hinge, Fig. 4. The coin itself should now lie flat on the tips of the right second and third fingers which are curved slightly toward the palm.

Now move the right hand forward a little

palm. From this position relax the right hand and let it drop slowly to the side, but

Fig. 5

on no account make any movement of the right fingers by palming the coin at this moment. In the meantime, move the left hand slowly upwards and make the motions of rubbing the coin away, finally opening it and showing it empty.

While your whole attention is focussed on this action of the left hand, press the coin into the right palm and bring the right hand up, pointing with the forefinger to the empty left hand.

I cannot recommend too strongly that the student follow the instructions given, for there is nothing in the entire realm of coin sleights so deceptive. The whole action is based on the optical illusion known as the persistence of vision.

The Pinch Vanish

Hold a small coin, such as a quarter or a nickel, vertically and by its edges between the thumb and forefinger of the right hand, thumb being on top. Hold the left hand with the fingers pointing downward and palm toward the audience. Place the

Fig. 1

coin directly in front of the left palm, Fig. 1, then slowly close the fingers over it. When the coin is completely covered by the left fingers the forefinger and thumb of the right hand snap together, the edge of the coin against the forefinger sliding off

in this action so coin turns to a horizontal position. The coin is withdrawn from the left fist clipped by its forward edge, Fig. 2, by the pressed-together right thumb and forefinger. To the spectators it appears that the coin remains in the left hand. Try this

Fig. 2

in front of a mirror to get the full effect of this deceptive illusion. Bring the two middle fingers up against the lower side of the coin and quickly press it into the right palm under cover of raising the right hand and immediately snapping the fingers.

Work the left fingers as if crumbling the coin away, then open them slowly to show the coin gone.

Gone

BILL SIMON

Here is a clever coin vanish which has a lot of possibilities. It is one you will enjoy doing, because it depends on misdirection rather than skill for its accomplishment.

Show a half dollar in your open left hand. Close the fingers on it and turn the hand back uppermost. The left fingers then make a rubbing motion as if they were crumbling the coin away. Nothing actually happens, but this is done to lead the spectators to believe that something is taking place. The palm up right hand moves inward and underneath the closed left hand to the sleeve. It grasps the arm just above the wrist and pulls the sleeve back as far as it will go. This is a natural move which is done to convince the spectators that the coin will not vanish up the sleeve. Remark that the coin is still in the left hand and open it, showing the coin again.

Once more close the left fingers over the coin and turn hand over so the fingers will be underneath, but this time they work the coin partially out of the fist until it is held by the tips of the second and third fingers

Fig. 1

and heel of thumb, as in Fig. 1. Watch your angles here. Keep the hand low so no one will get a glimpse of the coin.

It will be found that when the coin is thus held it can be released without any perceptible movement of the fingers.

Now comes a neat move.

The right hand passes underneath the left fist as before. As it moves inward it brushes the coin from the left hand, Fig. 2, and carries it back to the left wrist where it is held in finger palm position and pressed flat against the underside of the left wrist. The action of stealing the coin is one continuous move and is done to illustrate to a spectator how you want him to hold your wrist. It is a clever bit of misdirection and is not suspected.

Do not move the right hand—just turn it inward with its back toward the audience

and retain the half dollar finger palmed as you thrust your closed left hand forward so a nearby spectator can hold your wrist. Apparently the coin is in the left fist, which the helper holds at the wrist, but actually

Fig. 2

it is hidden in the right finger palm. Drop right hand to side.

To the onlookers it seems impossible that a coin could escape under these conditions, and this is what makes the feat so effective. It is this they remember long afterwards. It seems to pack a bigger wallop because they assist in the vanish.

After a proper build-up, slowly open the left hand to show it empty.

This can be made into a complete vanish by merely disposing of the coin in a convenient pocket while attention is on the left hand.

By using a hook coin (see page 256) you can fasten the coin onto a helper's sleeve when you grasp him by the arm to draw him nearer to you, as you offer your wrist to be held. Or, hook it on your own person and retrieve it later.

Or, just use a regular coin and rest the right hand on your helper's shoulder as he holds your wrist, leaving the coin there. The following is a unique way of reproducing it:

Show both hands unmistakably empty,

then reach behind the spectator's ear and produce the coin. As the right hand reaches for the coin, it picks it up from his shoulder, carries it back, and touches it to his ear as it is brought forward into view. The effect on this one person is amazing, because he sees your hand empty as you reach for the coin, and feels it as you apparently produce it from his ear. Try it!

The New Era Coin Go

Jimmy Buffaloe

First, let me describe the effect of this clever vanish so you can better visualize its deceptiveness.

With his sleeves rolled high the wizard places a half dollar in his left hand. He immediately opens his hand to show the coin gone; in fact, both hands are shown with fingers apart, front and back. There is no doubt about it, the coin has completely disappeared. But reaching behind his left leg the performer extracts the missing coin. No trick coins and no gimmicks. Sounds good? It is good!

Here's how: The half dollar is displayed in the right hand between the first two

Fig. 1

fingers and thumb. The left hand is held palm up and the fingers point directly toward the spectators. Right hand places the coin on left palm but right fingers and thumb still retain their grip on the coin. As the left hand closes into a loose fist it is

Fig. 2

raised slightly and the right hand moves inward quickly and deposits the half dollar on the left wrist, Fig. 1.

In this one continuous action the half dollar is screened from view by the closing left fingers and if the left hand is held about chest high the coin will be invisible as it lies flat on the wrist.

Blow into the left hand as it is opened. Both hands are held about chest high and seen to be empty, as in Fig. 2. Be careful not to move the arms too much or the coin may fall off the wrist. Now point fingers of both hands skyward and the audience will observe the backs of the hands as in Fig. 3.

To give the onlookers another view of the empty hands drop them to the sides. The left hand bends inward at the wrist and the coin is held in position by the watch band at one edge and the wrinkles at the heel of the wrist at the opposite edge, Fig. 4.

Fig. 3

As the left hand goes behind left knee the hand straightens, releasing the coin, which is caught in the cupped fingers and brought into view.

The vanish is just as effective without the watch band but a little more skill will be necessary to retain the coin on the left

Fig. 4

wrist. If a wrist watch is not worn the hands can only be shown on both sides at chest height. Either way, this is a beautiful and thoroughly mystifying coin vanish, well worth the time necessary to master it.

Special attention should be given to angles; do not perform this closer than six feet from the spectators.

The Flyaway Coin

FRANK GARCIA

The following feat, although quite easy to do as far as skill is concerned, will test your ability to act and misdirect. The mys-

tery depends almost entirely on subterfuge rather than skill.

Effect: After showing a half dollar the performer places it in his left hand and immediately tosses it into the air where it vanishes. Both hands appear empty as they are seen with the fingers wide apart.

The performer then makes a grab in the air with his left hand, catching the coin. It is tossed toward the right hand where it instantly appears at the extreme fingertips, creating a very pretty effect.

You will not find this an effect with which you can create a reputation for yourself as a sleight of hand artist. But it is a nice bit of chicanery that can be used anytime, since it is entirely impromptu.

Method: Show the half dollar in the right hand. Pretend to place it in the left hand, but retain it classic palmed in the right. Hold both hands shoulder high as you stand facing the spectators. Make crumbling motions with the fingers of both hands simultaneously. Suddenly raise the hands a few inches and open them, pretending to toss the coin into the air. Watch its invisible flight upward. Hold both hands with the fingers wide open and do not try to hold the coin in the palm. Just let it lie flat on the hand. This gives the hands a very natural appearance, and since the palms are above the eye level of the spectators the coin cannot be seen, Fig. 1.

Keep your eyes firmly fixed on the non-existent coin in its upward journey, then pretend to follow its flight downward again to a point directly in front of you. Exclaim, "There it is!" and make a quick grab in the air with the left hand, feigning to catch the coin. Simultaneously with this action the right hand turns palm inward and transfers the coin to the front finger hold (see Fig. 2, The Back Palm, page 5). The left hand, supposedly holding the coin is about 12 inches below the right hand.

Fig. I

"Watch it!"

Make a motion of tossing the coin upward from the left to the right hand. Suddenly expose the half dollar at the extreme fingertips of the right hand, by simply pushing it into view with the thumb. The effect is that you caught the coin with your left hand, then tossed it invisible into your right hand, where it instantly materialized.

The entire effect shouldn't require more than 15 seconds.

Behind the Back

Here is a method which may be used to vanish almost any small object.

Stand with the body turned one quarter to the right and toss a coin into the air a few times with the right hand, but catching it as it descends with *both* hands. Each time the coin is caught, drop both arms to the sides before raising them to toss again. Both arms move up and down in unison as the coin is tossed and caught. After the second or third throw the hands drop to the sides as before and the right hand tosses the coin behind the back into the left hand.

At first this may seem difficult, but after a few trials the knack will come. It will be found that the hands almost come together behind the back as the arms are dropped just prior to the next throw. Actually there is no hesitation when the coin is tossed into the left hand; the toss is accomplished without suspicious movement precisely at the moment the hands drop down. The flight of the coin into the left hand is concealed from view by the body. Just as the coin is caught in the left hand the body turns so left side is toward the spectators. The hands are immediately brought up as before and the right hand tosses the non-existent coin into the air. The left hand has classic palmed the coin in its upward swing and both hands appear to be empty—the spectators viewing the back of the left hand and

Fig. I

the palm of the right—fingers of both hands are wide apart, Fig. 1.

Stand in this position a moment as you watch the upward flight of the invisible coin. It apparently fades into the air.

If the last move appears identical with the preceding ones the illusion will be perfect. The spectators become used to seeing the coin go upward after each toss and their eyes naturally will go upward on the last throw if you have played your part correctly.

The French Drop (Le Tourniquet Vanish)

One of the oldest methods known for vanishing a coin is this one which is known as *Le Tourniquet* or French Drop (literally, the Swivel or Twist). Although it is seldom seen today it is good when properly executed.

With the left hand palm upward, hold a half dollar by its edges between the tips of the left fingers and thumb, tilting the rear of the coin up slightly so its face can be seen by the spectators, Fig. 1.

Fig. I

Bring the palm down right hand over the coin, the thumb going underneath it and between the left thumb and fingers. Lift up and close the right hand, pretending to take the coin away from the left, but allow the coin to make a half turn forward as it slides down to the base of the second and third fingers of the left hand where it is finger palmed, Fig. 2.

Keep the left fingers together during this action or the coin may be glimpsed by the onlookers. Move the closed right hand to the right and downward and turn it fingers

uppermost, keeping your attention fixed on it. Turn the left hand back toward the spectators and point to the closed right hand as it "crumbles" the coin away. Open the right hand and show it empty.

This sleight is especially useful in vanishing a small number of coins, and the action

Fig. 2

is exactly the same as for one, the coins being held in a stack with each flat on top of the other. When the coins fall into the left hand they make a jingle which sounds as if they actually had been taken in the right hand.

Whether you are going to vanish one or several coins you should first actually take the coin(s) in the right hand using the French Drop moves, then place the coin(s) on the table momentarily, pull back the sleeves, pick them up and in apparently repeating the moves, execute the sleight. The action appears the same and the illusion is convincing.

The French Drop can also be employed to exchange one coin for another. To use it for this purpose, have a coin hidden in your right finger palm as you show another in your left hand. Bring the right hand over and pretend to take the coin, but execute the sleight and retain it in the left hand as the right hand closes and moves away with its coin. The moves can be used as a color change (by employing a copper and a silver coin) or simply to secretly exchange a borrowed coin for one of your own.

A group of silver coins can be made to change to copper by employing these moves. The possibilities are numerous.

The Reverse French Drop

Dr. E. M. Roberts

I have given this vanish the above name because the moves resemble the regular French Drop, only they are reversed. Actually this is not so, but I seem to get this impression. Anyway, every trick must have some sort of a name, and this is as good as

Fig. 1

any. It was devised by Dr. E. M. Roberts of Amarillo, Texas.

Balance a half dollar on the balls of the two middle fingers of the right hand as you exhibit it all around. Turn slightly to the left and drop the right thumb on top of the coin, then hold the left hand in a cupped position above the coin, Fig. 1.

Cover the coin with the left hand as in

Fig. 2

Fig. 2, the left fingers grasping the right thumb. Next, lower the two middle fingers of the right hand away from the thumb,

Fig. 3

keeping the coin on the tips of these two fingers, Fig. 3. The closed left hand then moves backward off the extended right

Fig. 4

thumb, supposedly taking the coin. (The coin balanced on the tips of the two middle fingers remains hidden from the spectators' view by the back of the right hand.) Then the two middle fingers press the coin into the right palm, Fig. 4, where it is retained as that hand makes a few passes over the

Fig. 5

closed left hand. (See Figs. 5 and 6, which are the rear and spectators' view, respectively.) Finally the left hand is opened to show the coin gone.

A feint should be made first, by actually taking the coin in the left hand using the moves described above, then in apparently repeating the moves execute the sleight and vanish the coin as described.

Fig. 6

To make this a complete vanish drop the right hand to the side and sleeve the coin using the Dr. Roberts' Method as described in Chapter VII.

The Elusive Silver Dollar

AL SAAL

A silver dollar or a coin of similar size is recommended for this sleight, but some will find that a half dollar will work just as well.

Stand with your right side toward the spectators as you display the coin in the

Fig. 1

right hand. It is lying near the tips of the two middle fingers in position for back palming. Turn the left hand palm down in a cupped position over the tips of the right fingers and, as you pretend to take the coin in the left hand, back palm it in the right. This is accomplished under cover of the left hand, Fig. 1. Move the closed left hand away, and after a brief pause, open it to show it empty, then turn the palm of the left hand toward the spectators. Move the right fingers back of the left hand, and under cover of that hand bring the coin to the front of the two middle fingers as you move the right thumb to the rear of the left hand, then balance the coin on the tip of the right thumb. During this transfer the right hand turns over so its back is toward the audience. The left hand is palm out with its fingers horizontal, while the fingers of the right point upward, but only for a moment, however, because the coin is then clipped between the first and second

Fig. 2

fingers of the left hand, Fig. 2. Now turn the right hand palm toward the audience, keeping the fingers of the two hands in the same relative positions. Then all in one movement reverse the left hand, bend the second, third and fourth fingers of the right hand inward as it turns over, and clip the coin from the left hand to the second finger and thumb of the right hand and immediately transfer it to thumb palm position. Move the left hand away from the right and show it empty once more. Reproduce the coin in your favorite manner.

The effect is not easy to learn quickly. It will be necessary to spend some time on each phase of the trick, paying particular attention to angles and timing. Execute the moves slowly at first, striving for correctness. The fingers must be trained to do their part without fumbling!

The Wrist Watch Vanish

ROYAL H. BRIN, JR.

No, the wrist watch doesn't vanish, but it is used to vanish a coin. Several tricks in print have employed a wrist watch as a hiding-place for a coin but none has seemed quite satisfactory, as the handling has been awkward and unnatural. This hiding-place is too good to be wasted with a half-hearted effort, so here is a practical method of using it, with all moves natural, smooth, and unsuspicious, for the vanish and recovery of a coin.

A coin is apparently placed in the left hand, but really retained in the right; the thumb palm, classic palm, Bobo Vanish, or any equivalent vanish may be used. While gazing at the left fist the right hand drops to the side and the coin is allowed to fall onto the right cupped fingers. The right hand now comes up and grasps the left wrist, thumb above and fingers below, Fig. 1.

Fig. I

With the right thumb, indicate a particular spot on the left wrist, saying that by pressing on that spot the magic is done. At the same time move the hands toward the spectators, and under cover of this larger motion the right fingers slip the coin underneath the wrist watch; it need only go about half way under.

Count to three as you press with the right thumb on the "magic spot," and at "three," the left hand opens to show the coin has vanished. The right hand moves away to the right, palm out, so it also can be seen to be empty. If you are wearing a coat or even a long-sleeved shirt, drop the hands downward to the sides so that the left sleeve will cover the watch, and turn both hands around to show their backs. The effect can even be done with short sleeves, by showing only the palms.

To reproduce the coin, bring the hands together again, left hand closed in a fist, the right hand grasping the left wrist as before. As you count to three, moving the hands forward, the coin is slipped loose by the right fingers and allowed to rest on them. At the count of three, the left hand opens, but is still empty. Look chagrined for a second, and then pretend to remember that to make the coin return, the other wrist must be pressed.

The right hand moves away to the right, carrying the coin and closing into a fist. The left hand now grasps the right wrist, and at the count of three the right hand is opened to show the coin has reappeared.

I have used this quite a bit, and it makes an easy and effective vanish and reproduction.

The Pulse Trick

GLENN HARRISON

Ever since Glenn Harrison showed me this trick in Denver a few years ago, it has been one of my favorite bits of close-up chicanery. The effect is new and different and possesses all the essential elements of smart magic. It is intriguing to the onlookers for the patter fascinates them, and at the same time makes a perfect cover up for the one simple sleight.

Effect: The performer shows a silver dollar as he tells a spectator that he is going to test his nervous system. He asks the spectator to extend his right hand, palm down, then taking the coin in his left hand, performer presses the pulse of the spectator with the other, while the left hand goes underneath the spectator's palm with the coin. The magician explains that by pressing his pulse it sets up a nervous reaction which prevents him from feeling the coin. Opening his hand, the performer runs his fingers over his helper's palm. "Pressing a little harder," continues the performer, "your vision is affected also, and you are not able to see the coin." Accompanying this remark the magician removes his left hand from underneath the helper's and it is seen to be obviously empty.

"But a strange thing happens if I touch a nerve up here at your elbow and release your pulse again. Not only are you able to feel the coin—you can see it as well." With these words the performer brings his left hand into view from underneath the spectator's hand and the missing coin is seen lying on his palm.

Here is one of the best reasons I know of for mastering the back palm. This one secret move is perfectly covered by the subtle misdirection and patter.

Method: Begin the experiment by showing a silver dollar. (If you can back palm a half dollar it will work as well.) Place the coin in your left hand using the same movements as you would to retain it in the right hand, so when you apparently repeat the same action a moment later, nothing will be suspected. (The Slide Vanish is an excellent sleight for accomplishing this effect.)

Approach a spectator as you tell him you are going to test his nervous system. Casually place the coin into your left hand, then toss it back into your right. Gesture with your left hand as you ask the spectator to hold out his right hand. Apparently place the coin back into your left hand but retain it in the right. Then the right hand, which is palm down, makes a movement toward the spectator's outstretched hand as you exclaim, "No, turn your hand palm down." (Spectator usually extends his hand palm up.) Back palm the coin as you take hold of his wrist, your patter running something like this: "Now if I press strongly on your wrist like this, it sets up a strange nervous reaction. Then if I place the coin against the underside of your hand like this . . . (place your closed left hand under his hand, then slowly open it and rub your fingers over his palm) . . . you are not able to feel it. And if I press a little harder on your pulse, your vision is affected also, and you are not able to see it, either." With these remarks slowly open your left hand, rub your fingers across his palm, then bring the hand into view. Slowly show the left hand on both sides with the fingers wide apart. The coin has disappeared.

"But," you state, "a peculiar thing happens if I touch a nerve up here at your elbow . . . (press a spot near his elbow with your left hand) . . . and release your pulse; you are again able to feel the coin, and also you are able to see it." Here your actions must be perfectly timed with your patter. Beginning with "and release your pulse," you do release his pulse with the right hand, and at the same time your left hand, which is palm up, comes straight down underneath his forearm to a position directly under his outstretched hand, which you have cautioned him to keep in this position throughout the experiment. At the exact instant your right hand releases his pulse it also releases the back palmed coin, which falls into the left hand as it passes

underneath on its way down to his palm. There must be no hesitation as the left hand moves down underneath the spectator's forearm. It merely passes underneath the right hand, catches the coin as it falls, and continues on down to the spectator's palm. Then you gently press the coin against his down-turned palm, so that he is able to feel it. Following this you reveal the coin, which ties in with the patter, . . . "and also you are able to see it."

The spectator's right wrist masks the back palmed coin in your right hand, and because all the attention is on the left hand during the action the right is never suspected.

If there is one trick that goes over with the women, this is it. It affords possibility for much comedy and byplay, and is one hundred percent entertainment.

The Cranium Vanish

WALLACE LEE'S VERSION

No, this is not a vanishing head trick but a trick where the top of the head is used as a hiding place for a vanished coin.

Since the coin must be secretly placed on top of the head the trick is only practical to perform before children whose eye level is lower than the top of the head.

Get a group of small-fry in front of you and show them a coin in your right hand. Tell the children that you will place the coin in your outstretched left hand three times, and on the third time you want one child to grab the coin. Keep your eyes on the left hand as you raise the right hand to the top of your head. Next time you raise the hand find the exact spot on top of your head where you can leave the coin. On the third time place the coin on this spot, bring the hand down and pretend to deposit the coin in the left hand. The child grabs, but the coin is gone.

Fig. 1

Fig. 2

To get the coin back, hold your hands at your sides and let the palms extend inward behind your back. With a backward movement of the head the coin will fall into the hands behind the back, and can now be produced from behind a child's ear.

The only difficulty you might experience with this trick is that occasionally you might not catch the coin as it falls from your head. If this happens, feign surprise, look upward and pretend that the coin fell from the ceiling.

As Wallace Lee says: "Aren't we devils?"

Vanish with the Aid of a Handkerchief

Here is an oldie, the method of which can be used to vanish not only a coin but any other small article as well.

Spread a handkerchief over the palm up left hand so one corner will lie on the forearm. Show a half dollar in the right hand, then place it between the thumb and first and second fingers of the left hand, holding it vertically through the cloth, Fig. 1.

With the right thumb and forefinger, pick up the inner corner of the handkerchief and bring it forward over the coin, then turn the left hand palm downward so the handkerchief hangs down over the coin. Make some remark about showing the coin again as you return the hands to their former positions. The coin is again seen as in Fig. 1.

The right hand brings the inner corner over the coin once more and as the left hand turns over it releases the coin which falls onto the cupped right fingers, the handkerchief hiding this action from the audience, Fig. 2. The left hand pretends to hold the coin through the center of the handkerchief. Bring your right hand up with its palm toward the spectators, the forefinger pointing upward and the second, third, and fourth fingers curled slightly to conceal the coin from their view, Fig. 3. (This subtle concealment, when sparingly used, serves as a real convincer and can be used to good effect in many other tricks.) The right hand is brought up in this position as you caution the spectators to "Watch."

Grasp one corner of the handkerchief with the right hand and release your grip on its corner with the other hand. The

Fig. 3

handkerchief floats down and hangs by one corner from the right hand. Done properly, this is a very pretty effect because the spectators expect the coin to fall to the floor. Immediately flick the handkerchief with the right hand and show the left hand empty. Grasp an opposite corner with the left hand, spread it out between the hands and show both sides of the handkerchief. The coin has vanished!

The "Heads and Tails" Vanish

H. Adrian Smith

Effect: After showing several half dollars with the heads all uppermost, the performer places the stack on the fingers of his outstretched hand and closes the hand so that the coins are pressed into the palm. When the hand is opened, the coins are all found to have the tails uppermost. Repeating the process, the performer asks a spectator to guess whether the coins have the heads or

the tails up. When the hand is opened, the coins are found to have disappeared and they are reproduced from behind the performer's knee.

Method: Four or five well worn coins are used. After showing them to be heads up, square them and place the stack near

Fig. 1

the tips of the second and third fingers of the palm up left hand, which is held out flat with the fingers together, Fig. 1. Hold the right hand palm up, fingers together and the thumb parallel to the index finger and about an inch above it. Bring the right hand over to the left at a right angle, the fingers of the right going under those of the left and the right thumb about half an inch above the coins, Fig. 2. With the aid of the right hand, which is brought up rather

Fig. 2

smartly, close the fingers of the left hand, turning the stack over into the left palm. The instant the closing movement begins the right thumb is lowered onto the coins, holding them in place as the left fingers close, thus preventing the coins from making any noise. The right hand turns over in this process as though to press the fingers of the left hand firmly. Withdraw the right hand, then open the left hand, showing the coins in reverse order, tails up.

During the repetition, all moves are identical with the above except that at the exact moment the right hand fingers are under the left to close the left hand, the thumb of the right hand, which is directly above the stack, closes down upon the coins and grasps the whole stack between the first joint and base of the thumb, Fig. 3. The

Fig. 3

whole stack may thus be gripped quietly and with certainty. The closing of the left hand is carried out, this time minus the coins. The right hand moves away casually in a horizontal position, swinging in a short arc as it drops to the side. After the spectator ventures his guess, the left hand is opened and the coins have disappeared. The reproduction from behind the knee presents no problem requiring further explanation.

Vanish for Several Coins

Effect (a): Several coins are shown lying on the performer's right hand. He dumps them into his left hand, the spectators hearing them as they fall. A moment later the left hand opens to show the coins gone.

Effect (b): Similar to the above except that the coins are thrown one at a time from the right hand into the left. The audience sees and hears each coin arrive, but when the left hand is opened it is empty.

Method (a): Place a stack of coins on the right palm. Tilt the fingers downward just

Fig. 1

enough for the coins to slide forward so that they will lie in an overlapping row with the outer edge of the forward coin at the second joint of the two middle fingers, as in Fig. 1.

Turn the right hand inward and downward, apparently dumping the row of coins into the cupped left hand held below. The back of the right is toward the spectators, and the back of the curled fingers of that hand rest momentarily on the upturned left palm, Fig. 2. In sliding into position on the curled right fingers, the coins make a distinct jingle and, since the hands are in close juxtaposition at that moment, the illusion is perfect, both the eye and ear being deceived. Lower the left hand a few inches and close the fingers. Bend the second, third, and fourth fingers of the right hand inward, holding the coins, and point

Fig. 2

to the closed left hand as it then moves away to the left. Keep your attention fixed on the closed left hand for a few moments. Suddenly move the left hand upward, tossing the non-existent coins into the air. Follow their flight upward with the eye and you will be surprised how the spectators will, too. The coins have vanished.

The coins are hidden in the right hand and must be either reproduced or disposed of. The better plan is to quickly reach behind the right knee, jingle the coins, and bring them into view.

Method (b): Stand with your right side toward the audience, holding the coins to be vanished in a stack at the base of the middle finger. With the right thumb, push forward the top coin, then throw it into the left hand. As the right hand throws the coin, the left moves in unison to the right and catches it. The two hands come almost together in this action. Repeat these moves with every coin except the last. Instead of throwing it into the left hand the left hand tosses all its coins back into the right hand. The right hand catches and holds the coins as the left hand closes. There must be no stoppage or slowing down of action as the coins are tossed back. They are tossed back into the right hand without breaking the tempo of movement. Since the right side is toward the audience, the right

hand acts as partial cover for the coins as they are tossed back, it being in the spectator's line of vision.

If the entire action is carried out rather smartly it appears that the last coin is thrown exactly as the rest. The noise of the coins flying back simulates the sound the last coin would have made had it actually been thrown into the left hand. Point to the closed left hand with the right forefinger (second, third, and fourth fingers are curled inward holding the coins) and finish as described in first effect.

A Trio of Vanishes

Ross Bertram

Here are three ways of vanishing a coin, each appearing the same but each entirely different from the other in method. They can be performed in the order given or separately. If performed together each builds on the preceding one, the spectators becoming more puzzled as each vanish is executed.

Number one: Turn your right side toward the spectators and show the coin pinched flat between the tips of the right first and second fingers. Hold the left hand palm down and close it into a loose fist. Fig. 1 shows the two hands with the right hand about to push the coin into the left fist. Move the right hand toward the left and push the coin into the left fist. Once

Fig. 1

the coin is within the fist the two fingers gripping it bend downward, carrying the coin around the left thumb to the right thumb palm. Then extend the fingers before bringing them, empty and separated, out of the left hand, which proceeds to reduce the coin to nothingness in the usual manner.

Number two: Hold the hands in the same position as in the preceding vanish, with the coin between the tips of the first two fingers of the right hand. Apparently repeat the same moves as described in the first vanish except when the coin enters the left fist it is transferred from its position between the first two fingers of the right hand to the ball of the thumb of the same hand. You must be careful not to close the left fingers so tightly as to interfere with this action.

With the back of the right hand toward the spectators slowly withdraw the first two fingers of that hand. Careful attention must be given to angles at this point in order to keep the coin (which is balanced on the tip of the right thumb) hidden from the

Fig. 2

spectators. Fig. 2 shows the performer's view of this action. The back of the right hand acts as a screen and conceals the coin from view. Now bend the right thumb in-

ward and press the coin into finger palm position of the same hand. Curl the second, third, and fourth fingers inward to hide the coin from view and swing your right hand around so its palm is toward the onlookers. The forefinger points upward in a gesturing manner as you caution them to watch what is about to take place. The spectators see the hand as in Fig. 3,

Fig. 3

and since it appears empty it is not suspected, so their attention naturally returns to the closed left hand. Make crumbling motions with the left fingers, and then open the left hand and show both sides to prove that the coin has disappeared.

Number three: The movements in this vanish appear the same as the first two, but with this method the coin vanishes entirely. Both hands are shown unmistakably empty at the finish of the effect.

Take the same positions with the body and the hands as in the first two vanishes. Hold the coin between the first two fingers of the right hand as before and push it into the closed left hand and execute the same movements as described in Number two, up to the point where the first two fingers of the right hand transfer the coin to the tip of the right thumb. Now the similarity ceases.

Immediately after the coin is transferred to the right thumb it swings inward toward

Fig. 4

the left wrist and tosses the coin into the left sleeve. Just prior to this vanish drop your left arm to the side and allow the sleeve to hang down as far as it will go. Without further movement of your left arm bring it up and proceed with the vanish. This slight advance preparation will bring the sleeve well down over the wrist and thus make the action of tossing the coin into the sleeve an easy one. However, you will find in practice that the coin need not be tossed—merely move the right thumb inward toward the left sleeve and allow coin to tumble off into the sleeve, Fig. 4.

This is done while the first two fingers of the right hand are within the left fist. The left fist and the back of the right hand screen this slight action from the spectators.

Withdraw the right first and second fingers from the left fist as in the two previous versions. Make crumbling motions with the left fingers, and then open the left hand and show it empty. Show both hands back and front to prove the coin has completely vanished.

The transfer of the coin from the tips of the first two fingers of the right hand to the ball of the thumb and then into the left sleeve should be made without undue haste, but also without interruption, the hands coming together for only a moment for the depositing of the coin into the left fist. Without presenting too great difficulty, this sleight demands assurance and delicacy in its performance

For additional methods of vanishing a coin see Chapter VI, Cuffing and Chapter VII, Sleeving.

Chapter IV

COMPLETE COIN VANISHES

Here is a collection of time-tested methods for vanishing a coin completely. When I say "completely" I mean they can be performed with the sleeves rolled up and both hands shown unmistakably empty after the coin has vanished. And the coin is not hidden in either hand.

Some of these vanishes now appear in print for the first time. Most, if adroitly executed, are magician foolers. All can be performed with a regular half dollar, and no apparatus is used—just the coin and the two hands. Some of them can even be done without a coat; in fact they are more effective if performed that way.

The Bobo Complete Coin Vanish

This is merely a continuation of The Bobo Coin Vanish, (page 27). At the finish both hands are shown empty. The coin has vanished completely.

Continue The Bobo Coin Vanish up to the point where the right hand thumb palms the coin as it makes its first pass over the closed left hand. It is at the beginning of the second pass that the right hand disposes of the thumb palmed coin. It is dropped in the outer left breast coat pocket as the hand swings inward to begin its second pass, Fig. 1. There must not be the slightest hesitation in getting rid of the

coin; the right hand continues to make a few more passes before the left hand is opened and shown empty.

You will observe that each time the right hand makes a pass over the closed left hand it swings back toward the left breast coat pocket. Therefore it is a simple matter to drop the coin in the pocket on the second pass. The hand must not hesitate when disposing of the coin; make each pass smoothly, blending it into the next without slowing down.

The breast pocket can be held open slightly by stuffing a crumpled handkerchief in it beforehand. The right side is

Right hand drops coin into breast pocket (see arrow)

Fig. 1

toward the audience during the vanish, which shields the getaway and conceals the move of dropping the coin in the breast pocket. And don't forget to keep your eyes firmly fixed on the left fist during the passes with the right hand and the disposing of the coin.

Practice and understand all moves so that you can do them automatically. Blend all moves into one complete action and you will have a baffling coin vanish. This has fooled some of the best posted magicians.

Complete Thumb Palm Vanish

During the years I have been doing close-up magic I have discovered many unique ways of vanishing a coin. Here is one that is both easy and effective.

Proceed with the same moves as described in the Thumb Palm Vanish (page 25), up to the point where the coin has supposedly been placed in the left hand; really it is thumb palmed in the right. Right hand pulls up left sleeve slightly by grasping it midway between the shoulder and the elbow. You will notice that as the sleeve comes up the right hand moves inward towards the left breast pocket. It is in this action that the coin is dropped into the pocket.

This is a casual, offhand move, and appears quite natural. You have apparently pulled up the sleeve to show that the coin cannot go into it, but in this simple move you have disposed of the coin in the breast pocket.

After the proper build-up open the hand to show it empty. Show both hands—the coin has completely disappeared.

Knee-zy Vanish

Effect: A half dollar is held in the right hand. The performer removes it with his left and slaps it against his left knee, immediately reproducing it from behind his right knee with his right hand. This move is repeated, but this time the coin vanishes after being taken from behind the right knee.

Method: Show a coin in your right hand and apparently remove it with the left, actually back palming it in the right hand instead. (Your favorite coin sleight may be substituted.) Slap the non-existent coin against the left side of the left knee and then produce it with the right hand from behind the right knee.

Apparently repeat the same moves, but this time the left hand actually takes the coin and holds it in the closed hand. Slap the left fist against left side of knee as before and then, quickly pivoting on the left foot, swing the body so the right side will be toward the spectators. As you reach behind the right knee to produce the coin, drop it in the left trousers or coat pocket. Pretend to hold a coin in the right hand and go through the motions of placing the coin in the left. Finally reveal the vanish by tossing "it" into the air and showing both hands empty.

Sucker Vanish

Effect: The performer shows a half dollar and apparently places it in his left hand, but the spectators see him remove it and carry it to his pocket. They waste no time in telling him where the coin is, but when he opens his hand the coin is still there. The same moves are repeated. This time the coin actually vanishes.

No better effect than this could be used to close a routine of coin tricks. It is a dandy for the wiseacre and perfect for the kids.

Method: Tell your audience that you will try to do the trick very slowly and that you will give them an opportunity to catch you. Warn them not to say anything, if they should see how it is done, until after it is over. It will be difficult for them to keep from speaking up when they think they know the answer. After that, it's too late!

Show a half dollar and hold it clipped between the first and second fingers as you would to thumb palm it, Fig. 1. Place the

Fig. 1

coin in the left hand and close the fingers over it. Immediately remove it still clipped between the first and second fingers, allowing what you do to be seen, but not being too obvious about it. As soon as the spectators get a flash of the coin, bend the fingers inward as if to conceal it behind the hand. Place the right hand in the trousers pocket, palm the coin and remove the hand. The spectators will think you put the coin in your pocket. Your two hands should be fairly close together at this point; in fact, the extended fingers of the right hand al-

Fig. 2

most touch the closed left hand, Fig. 2. The spectators are sure that you slipped the coin into your pocket—they do not suspect that you removed it again and have it palmed. Say, "I will now strike the back of my left hand three times, like this." At this instant swing both hands to the right so the palm of the right hand is toward the spectators, and drop the coin from the right palm,

Fig. 3

catching it in the left hand. The left fingers open slightly to admit the coin. (Fig. 3 shows the performer's view of this action.) The depositing of the coin in the left hand and the showing of the right hand empty is all done in one move. The coin is actually thrown a distance of three or four inches. It is released from the right hand and caught in the left about midway in the swing from left to right. It cannot be seen if the transfer is made as described. There must be no stoppage or slowing down of action in this maneuver. The hands are brought over to the right in one continuous movement for the ostensible purpose of showing the right hand empty before striking the left hand. Allow the spectators to see the right hand empty then slowly tap the back of the left fist with the right fingers counting, "One, two, three!" Then say, "When I open my left hand the coin will be gone." If someone doesn't speak up at this point and say he saw you put it in your pocket, ask the spectators if they noticed where it went. They will, of course, say it is in your pocket. So you reply, "No, the coin is still here. It hasn't disappeared yet." This is a stunner and prepares you for the payoff!

The next time, you actually vanish it. State, "You know, a great many persons think that when I place a coin in my hand like this . . . (Pretend to place the coin in your left hand, but actually palm it in the right. This time you must fool them. The Bobo Vanish can be used to good advantage) . . . and then place my hand in my pocket, like this, that I put the coin there. (Place the hand in the right trousers pocket and keeping the coin palmed, turn the pocket wrong side out to show that it isn't there. Push the pocket back and leave the palmed coin in the pocket.) However, that is not the case as you can see. All I need do to cause the coin to disappear is to blow on the hand." Open the hand and show it empty. The coin has vanished completely.

At first it may not seem possible to transfer a coin indetectably from one hand to the other as the hands swing from one side of the body to the other, but it can be done. It is primarily a matter of timing and misdirection. Once the secret move is completely mastered it can be done without misdirection because the move is practically indetectable. I have performed it hundreds of times before magicians and not once has the move been detected. So what chance does a layman have?

But with the added advantage of timing and misdirection the effect is sure fire. Be sure to look directly at the spectators as you speak to them and make the secret transfer. Then you will have no trouble.

Timing and misdirection are important in performing any trick, so keep them constantly in mind. The illusion of complete disappearance must be perfect—make it so!

Fig. 1

Pocket Vanish

This naturally follows Through the Pocket (a), (page 65).

Place a half dollar on the right leg outside the trousers pocket, holding it there with the right thumb. The right forefinger pinches the cloth at the bottom of the coin, Fig. 1, and turns it upward, Fig. 2, hiding the coin under the fold of cloth, Fig. 3. It will be observed that the right thumb retains its original position on the

Fig. 2

Fig. 3

coin, only now the coin is on top of the thumb.

Place the left forefinger on top of the fold, retaining it as the right thumb withdraws the coin and presses it into the right finger palm, Fig. 4. The right fingers are extended

Fig. 4

a moment in this action, which conceals the coin from view as it is withdrawn. Coin is in right finger palm as right hand quickly moves down and right thumb and forefinger grasp cloth below the fold. (Fig. 5 depicts position of both hands at this point.) Right hand pulls cloth downward, showing the coin vanished. The left hand slaps the right leg and the right hand reaches into the trousers pocket for the coin. The right hand is partially withdrawn, showing the half dollar lying at the base of the fingers. Coin has apparently penetrated the pocket.

Immediately turn the right hand inward, allowing the coin to fall back into the pocket. The right hand pretends to place the coin into the left hand, which closes. The right hand slaps the back of the left from underneath, as it opens. This action apparently propels the invisible half dollar into the air, for the eyes follow its upward flight. Both hands are then shown empty.

The penetration and apparent removal of the coin from the right trousers pocket blend in one uninterrupted operation.

Fig. 5

Without pausing an instant the right hand seemingly deposits the coin in the left and a moment later it vanishes.

With a Handkerchief

NUMBER ONE

A favorite vanish among coin conjurers is this old standby. It is still a first-rate audience fooler, and best of all, it is not difficult to perform.

Any size coin may be used to good effect.

For better understanding of all moves it is suggested that the feat be rehearsed with the articles in hand.

Stand facing the spectators as you call attention to a half dollar. Hold it vertically, about chest high, between the first two

Fig. 1

the coin, then travels inward until the center of the cloth is over the coin. At this stage the grip on the handkerchief is released, allowing it to drape naturally over the coin held in the left hand. Next, the right hand grasps the coin through the handkerchief from above and turns it over so the fingers of that hand point upward. The coin will now be in view, as shown in Fig. 2. Call attention to the fact that the coin is still there.

Apparently the foregoing moves are repeated, but this time the coin vanishes.

The left hand takes the coin once more as described. The right hand again goes through the motions of covering the coin. This time, however, the right thumb and forefinger snatch the coin from the left hand in the action of draping the handkerchief over hand. The right hand moves back toward the upper breast coat pocket and quickly drops the coin therein. The operation is fully shielded from the spectators' view by the handkerchief, Fig. 3.

During the action of covering the coin the second time, raise the left hand slightly and center your full attention on it. This serves as a bit of misdirection and helps to

fingers and thumb of the left hand. A man's handkerchief is held in the right hand by one edge between the first two fingers, while the third and fourth bend inward pressing a fold against the palm, Fig. 1. It will be found that when the handkerchief is held in this manner, the thumb and forefinger remain free, thus being in the necessary position to pick up the coin, which is what actually takes place later. This grip also spreads the handkerchief considerably, affording more cover for the secret steal.

The right hand, still holding the handkerchief as described above, moves in front of

Fig. 2

Fig. 3

conceal the movement of the right hand as it deposits the coin in the pocket. There should be no noticeable difference in the second covering of the coin over the first, as actually both are almost identical.

As soon as the coin falls into the breast pocket the right hand releases its grip on the handkerchief and pretends to take the non-existing coin through the center of the cloth. Both hands quickly bunch up the handkerchief and toss it into the air. As it falls the hands catch it and spread it out and show it empty. The coin has faded away completely.

Fig. 1

With a Handkerchief

NUMBER TWO

JIMMY BUFFALOE

Effect: The wizard spreads a handkerchief on the table. With his sleeves rolled high, he shows a half dollar and places it underneath the center of the handkerchief where it is heard to strike the table. The handkerchief is immediately jerked away. The coin has vanished! Both hands are positively empty. Nothing is used but a regular coin and a pocket handkerchief.

Method: Prepare for the trick by bunching up a handkerchief and stuffing it in the right coat pocket. This holds the pocket open slightly for what follows.

Stand with the table in front of you and spread a pocket handkerchief on its top. The handkerchief should be of such weight that a coin lying on the table could not be seen through it. Pull back the sleeves and show a half dollar. The left hand lifts the inner edge of the cloth and the right hand goes underneath with the coin. The right fingers snap the coin down on the table at about the center of the handkerchief and immediately pick it up and back palm it. The right hand then moves back to the

right inner corner of the handkerchief and grasps it with the fingers underneath and the thumb on top. The left hand assumes a similar position at the left inner corner, as in Fig. 1.

Suddenly the performer exclaims, "One, two, three—go!" Quickly the handkerchief is jerked from the table, the right hand moving back toward the right coat pocket and

Fig. 2

dropping the back palmed coin therein, Fig. 2. Without hesitation pop the handkerchief between the two hands and toss it into the air. As it descends it is caught, opened and shown empty. The coin has disappeared.

It should appear to the observers that you merely jerked the handkerchief from the table and threw it into the air. This is all you apparently do.

At the beginning the spectators hear the coin strike the table underneath the handkerchief, and are expecting to see it lying on the table when the handkerchief is removed. They are so bewildered by the unexpected vanish of the coin that the action of the right hand goes unnoticed. The whole action should be done in a smooth continuous manner, without hesitation or fumbling.

With a Handkerchief

NUMBER THREE

MILTON KORT

Begin the trick by showing a half dollar in the right hand and a handkerchief in the left hand. Hold the right hand palm up with the coin clipped between the tips of the first and second fingers. The left hand drapes the handkerchief over the coin, making sure coin will be at its center, then the left hand grasps the coin through the cloth from above, with the fingers at the front and the thumb at the rear. That is what apparently happens, but actually the left hand grasps only the center of the cloth as the right hand moves downward and inward toward the left and tosses the coin into the left coat pocket. Without hesitation the right hand continues in an arc as it is brought up about chin height, the right forefinger gesturing toward the spectators, as you caution them to "watch!"

After the left hand grasps the handkerchief by its center the right hand is immediately brought downward in a counterclockwise movement before it swings up to assume the position described. As it swings around in this circular movement it passes very close to the left coat pocket. As it passes it tosses the coin into that pocket, Fig. 1. To facilitate the coin going into the

Fig. 1

pocket, a handkerchief can be wadded up and placed in beforehand. The pocket then remains open and makes an easier target.

The coin should not be aimed at the pocket itself but at a spot two or three inches above its opening, and should be in a vertical position as it strikes the coat at this point. It then falls easily into the pocket. The pocket opening presents a difficult target to hit but if the coin strikes the coat flatly somewhere not too far above the pocket it will find its mark automatically.

The act of bringing the right hand up to a point in front of you as you direct the spectators to "watch" is a perfectly natural one. Even though you should actually take the coin in the left hand the right hand would still follow the same movement as described to dispose of the coin. Try it before a mirror, going through the action slowly until you are thoroughly familiar with the course the right hand must follow. Once you are familiar with it you will be able to remove the right hand from underneath the handkerchief, toss the coin into the coat pocket, and bring hand up for the gesture without hesitation. It should be all one motion and should appear that you merely grasped the coin through the handkerchief with the left hand and then gestured with the right forefinger as you commanded "watch."

When the right hand with the coin leaves the handkerchief, the left is holding the handkerchief not directly in front of the body but a bit to the left. Handkerchief must be held about eight inches in front of the left breast coat pocket to mask the flight of the coin. Although coin actually travels only two or three inches before it enters the pocket it is completely hidden in its flight by the handkerchief.

After cautioning the spectators to "watch," the right hand grasps one corner of the handkerchief and flicks it into the air. It is caught with both hands, opened and shown on both sides. The coin has vanished without a trace.

The effect is worth the necessary time to master it.

In a Spectator's Pocket

Who would suspect the magician of disposing of a vanished coin in a spectator's pocket? Yet, this is exactly what is done. In each instance the coin is secretly deposited in a helper's breast coat pocket. Here are three methods.

(a) Display a coin lying in the right hand on the two middle fingers in position for back palming. The left hand turns palm down over the end of the right fingers and pretends to take the coin, but it is back palmed with the right hand. (See The Back Palm, page 5.) The left hand is closed while the palm of the right hand appears empty. This should be done right under the nose of the observer for the action that follows. "Would you mind standing back a little," remarks the wizard, gesticulating with the right hand. In this movement the performer's hand nears the spectator's breast pocket, and the coin is tossed therein, from the back of the right hand, Fig. 1.

Fig. 1

Coin is tossed from back of right hand into pocket (see arrow)

The distance the coin is thrown depends on the skill of the operator. Even if the spectator's coat is touched in this tossing motion he does not notice it, or pays little attention to it. The coin is disposed of in a natural movement, gesturing for the spectator to move back.

Instead of actually tossing the coin into the spectator's pocket you can deliberately drop it in from the back of the hand as you give him a gentle push backward. If the spectators should notice the move they would not see anything wrong because they would see an empty palm as the secret deposit was made.

This may seem dangerously daring at first, but experience will bring confidence. Soon the subtlety can be executed with nonchalance. The move will pass unnoticed if done smoothly, without haste, but without delay.

Finally, the left hand is opened and shown empty.

The vanished coin should not be immediately reproduced from the spectator's pocket, but recovered later, in a more subtle manner, after a few other effects have been performed. In due course you direct the spectator to hold his hands together in a cupped fashion over his heart while you display another coin. Explain that you will cause the coin to travel from your own hands to those of your helper so fast the eye will be unable to follow it. Vanish the coin in your best magical manner, but when the assistant opens his hands they are empty. Apparently you have failed, but then you remember, "Maybe the coin went so fast it missed your hands altogether. Perhaps it is in your breast coat pocket; would you please see." The spectator extracts the coin from his pocket.

The entire effect is greatly enhanced if the original coin is a borrowed half dollar. It is marked for future identification and vanished as explained. A duplicate coin is magically reproduced instead of the marked coin, and it in turn is vanished. It is this coin that you attempt to pass into the spectator's hands, and fail. Then when the spectator extracts the missing half dollar from his pocket and identifies it, you have a superb magical problem indeed.

(b) In this method the prestidigitator drops the coin into the assistant's breast coat pocket from the right thumb palm.

The coin is vanished in any manner that leaves it retained in the right thumb palm. It is from this concealment that it is dropped into a spectator's pocket. The performer requests the spectator to move back a little so the others may get a better view. He gently pushes back the nearest observer under this pretext, and disposes of the thumb palmed coin in his pocket in the action.

It will be found that a coin in the right thumb palm protrudes from the hand at the perfect angle for dropping it into an onlooker's pocket. In this instance the coin is not tossed, but merely allowed to fall into the spectator's pocket, as he is given a gentle nudge backward.

The coin is later recovered using the ruse explained in method (a).

(c) **Wallace Lee Method.**

After you have performed several sleights with a half dollar, and the spectators are convinced you are using only one coin, steal another from a clip underneath the coat, or from a pocket, and keep it concealed in the right hand. Face a spectator. Ask him to come a little closer, and as if to encourage him, hook your right fingers over the top of his outer breast coat pocket and gently pull him toward you. The coin should be near the ends of the fingers and held in this position by the tips of the first and fourth pressing together against its edge, Fig. 2. As you pull the spectator toward you, drop the half dollar into his pocket, at the same time taking his hand and placing it over his pocket, instructing him to keep it there so nothing can get in.

During this action let the other coin be plainly seen in the left hand. Since the spectator still sees the original coin he is aware of no other, and he never dreams that a coin has been loaded secretly into his breast pocket.

Announce that you will cause the coin

Fig. 2

Coin is dropped into pocket as spectator is pulled toward performer

to fly into his pocket and caution him to hold his hand tightly over the pocket opening lest you slip it in when he isn't looking. Vanish the half dollar and pretend to cause it to penetrate the bottom of his pocket. Tell him to see if the coin has arrived, and while he is fumbling to get it out, either sleeve or pocket the other one.

The trick takes boldness and plenty of it, but what a surprise it creates!

Bluff Vanish

All that is needed to perform this little feat is a handful of change and a lot of nerve.

Effect: The wonder-worker takes a handful of change from his pocket and removes one coin. The remaining coins are returned to the pocket. The single coin is then caused to vanish in a mysterious manner.

The secret of this effect depends entirely on your ability as a magician to bluff your way through.

Let us suppose you have thoroughly baffled your audience with some clever close-up chicanery. You have convinced them that miracles *can* happen and they are ready to believe *anything. Now* is the time to spring this vanish.

Method: If you carry your loose change in your left trousers pocket you will always be ready to work this little effect; otherwise prepare for it beforehand by placing a few small coins in that pocket.

Remove these coins with the left hand and show them. Move the coins about with the right fingers as if searching for a particular one. Say something about needing a coin for your next trick. Suddenly remark, "Oh, this penny (or dime, or nickel) will be all right." Pretend to remove one of the coins with the first and second fingers and thumb of the right hand. Hold the first two finger tips and thumb together as if they actually held a coin. The left hand drops the rest of the coins back into the left trousers pocket. Go through the motions of placing the non-existent coin in the left hand. Show the right hand empty. After a bit of by-play open the left hand and show it empty.

Performed at the right moment this vanish is just as startling as the more complicated ones. I have used it for years and can vouch for its effectiveness.

Sucker Bluff Vanish

Milton Kort

Using the foregoing method, a sucker vanish can be worked that is a real fooler to magician and layman alike. I'll wager it will become one of your favorites.

Opening for coin
to slide out

Coin is allowed
to slide out of open-
ing into palm

Besides having a handful of coins, you must be wearing a wrist watch with an expansion band.

Proceed as in the above vanish up to the point where the non-existent coin is placed in the left hand. From here on the effect differs greatly.

As you pretend to place a coin in the left hand, that hand closes over the first two fingers and thumb of the right hand. Then the right two fingers are quickly removed and placed in back of the left hand. The right thumb is still within the left fist

as the first two fingers slowly move inward toward the wrist. Place these two fingers between the hand and the wrist and stretch the band a couple of times. This action causes the band to visibly move on the top side of the wrist, creating the impression that the coin is being inserted under the band. Remove the right thumb from the left fist, then show the right hand empty with a flourish. With considerable ceremony open the left hand and show it empty.

Naturally everyone will suspect that the coin is hidden underneath the watch band

and it won't be long until someone lets his suspicions be known. After some reluctance remove the wrist watch and show it. If someone doesn't want to examine the watch and take it apart I miss my guess.

The Coin Fold

Here is a useful method of vanishing a coin by wrapping it in a piece of paper. Although the vanish is described using a half dollar, any size coin may be used.

Method: From fairly heavy paper cut a piece approximately five inches square. In an emergency almost any paper can be used, even newspaper.

Hold the piece of paper in your left hand, about chest high, the fingers on the front side of the paper and the thumb at the rear. Show a half dollar in the right hand, then place it under the left thumb slightly above center, Fig. 1.

Turn the left hand around and show the coin at this position to the audience. Turn the paper back and, with the aid of the right hand, fold up the bottom edge to within half an inch of the top edge, Fig. 2.

Crease the right side of the paper about a quarter of an inch from the edge of the coin and fold it forward, Fig. 3.

Now fold the left side of the paper toward the front in the same manner, Fig. 4.

Fold the top half inch edge down in front. To all appearances the coin is securely wrapped in the paper, but actually there is an opening at the top where it can escape at the proper time, Fig. 5.

Turn the paper over so the opening will be downward and hold it in the right hand between the fingertips and thumb, Fig. 6.

To prove the coin is still within the paper you can allow someone near you to feel it or you can tap the parcel on the table or a glass.

When ready for the vanish loosen your grip on the paper and the coin will slide from the opening into your hand where it is finger palmed. Take the paper in the left hand and go to your right pocket for a match. Leave the coin in the pocket and bring out the match. Light it and set fire to the paper. Before it burns up entirely place it on an ash tray.

Or, if you desire, you can tear up the paper with the coin still finger palmed, then produce it according to the trick at hand.

This vanish is especially startling and pretty when flash paper is used. In this case, when the paper is ignited, both the coin and paper seem to vanish in a burst of flame.

The Envelope Vanish

A fairly heavy Manila paper envelope is prepared beforehand by cutting a slot at the bottom right corner. With a pair of scissors trim a small sliver of paper from the bottom of the envelope. When the envelope is prepared this way the opening will offer no resistance to the coin and it will fall freely into your hand.

From a piece of paper the same color as the envelope, cut a round piece the same size as the coin you intend to vanish and paste it inside the envelope at the bottom center, Fig. 1.

To perform: Show the envelope empty, then very slowly and openly place the coin into it. Coin falls to the bottom of the envelope where it is held with the fingers

Fig. 1

Disc of paper   Slit

Coin drops
thru slit
into hand

Fig. 2

of the left hand. Seal the flap and hold it by the ends with both hands. Raise the left end of the envelope slightly so the coin will roll down to the right corner. Hold it there with the right fingers and thumb.

While talking to the spectators allow the coin to slip through the slot into the right hand, Fig. 2. Hold the envelope in the left hand as you reach into your right pocket for a match or cigarette lighter. Light the match and hold it behind the envelope a moment as you call attention to the coin (circle of paper) in the envelope. The small piece of paper shows up as a shadow, creating the impression that the coin is still within the envelope. Light the envelope and as it burns the coin seems to melt away to nothing. You have apparently burned the coin.

When searching for a method to vanish a coin do not overlook cuffing and sleeving, Chapters VI and VII, respectively. Then there are the hook and magnet coins, pages 256, 258. And the method used in Coin To Key (page 78), is an old standby.

QUICK TRICKS

The most practical and usable tricks are the kind that can be performed on the spur of the moment with little or no apparatus. Here are 27 of the most effective mysteries of this variety that I have been able to gather together.

Through the Leg

Effect: A coin placed in the fold of the pants leg, vanishes. It is reproduced from behind the same leg, having apparently penetrated it. Here are two methods.

(a) Show a half dollar and place it flat on the left trousers leg, about six inches above the knee. Hold it in place with the tip of the right second finger while the thumb of the same hand pinches a small fold of cloth at the top edge of the coin and turns the coin over, downward. The coin is now hidden in the fold of cloth with the tip of the right third finger underneath it. Insert the tips of the left second and third fingers underneath the fold of cloth just to the left of the coin, in such a manner that the tips of the two thumbs will be brought together outside the fold and directly above the coin. Now move the hands

apart with the thumbs pressing against the edge of the crease in the cloth, and under cover of an adjusting process, slide the coin out of the fold and press it into the right palm with the aid of the right two middle fingers. If the moves are made as described the removal of the coin will be completely hidden by the back of the right hand. Bring the thumbs together and again run them along the edge of the fold. Finally allow the fold to fall away. The coin has vanished. Produce it from behind the right knee.

(b) Although this method makes use of the same moves described in Pocket Vanish (page 52), the effect is entirely different.

Show a half dollar, place it flat on the left leg about six inches above the knee and hold it in place with the tip of the right thumb. The right forefinger pinches the cloth at the bottom of the coin and turns it upward, hiding the coin under the fold of cloth. At this juncture the right thumb is underneath the coin. (Refer to Figs. 1, 2, and 3, Pocket Vanish, page 52, for comparable positions.)

Place the left forefinger on top of the fold, retaining it. As this is done the right fingers straighten and the right thumb withdraws the coin from the fold and presses it into right finger palm. The right hand immediately moves down and grasps the cloth below the fold, between the thumb and forefinger, then pulls it downward, showing the coin gone. Slap the left leg with the left hand. Reach behind the left leg with the right hand and produce the coin.

For best effect this must be performed briskly, with no hesitation between moves. It appears to the spectators that you have slapped a coin through the leg.

Follow this with Rubbed Through the Leg.

Rubbed Through the Leg

Here is a companion effect to the one described above. Although both produce the same effect, they are accomplished by different means. They are alike, however, in that both are direct and convincing.

Fig. I

Effect: The *right* hand rubs a coin on the left leg and it disappears. The same coin is produced from behind the same leg with the *left* hand. Only one coin is used.

Method: The right hand flips a half dollar in the air a few times. Bend over and apparently place the coin on the left leg, but actually toss it into the left hand, Fig. 1. The right hand makes a rubbing motion on the leg and the left hand produces the coin from *behind* the leg. Basically that is what happens.

You may wonder how it is possible for a coin to be tossed from the right hand into the left without anyone seeing it. Well, it can be done, and it isn't as difficult as would be imagined. I will try to break down every move so there will be a thorough understanding.

First of all—the flipping business. This is most important; in fact, the trick practically depends on it. What it does is to focus attention on the coin so that when you suddenly bend over to rub coin on the leg, the eye has to refocus for this different position. It is at this instant that the coin is tossed into the left hand. The coin travels only a few inches, but it is not seen because of the rapidity of its flight, and because the eye has not had time to focus on this action.

The human eye is like a camera lens in that it has to focus at a specific range for an object at that distance to appear in sharp definition. For instance, if the camera lens is focused at ten feet anything at twenty-five feet will be blurred. This would hold true if the distances and settings were reversed.

To fully understand how the eye compares to the camera lens in this matter, try looking at something nearby, then suddenly shift your eyes and gaze at an object farther away. Notice how it takes the eye a fraction of a second to refocus on this new distance. It is on this brief time-lapse that the secret of this effect is partly based. This phenomenon is used to advantage by quite a few top-flight magicians.

Now let's go back to the beginning. Show a half dollar and flip it into the air a few times with the right hand. Suddenly bend over and pretend to place the coin on the left leg a few inches above the knee, but really toss it into the left hand. The hands are in front of the left leg as this happens, and the coin travels only a few inches. It is thrown from the tips of the right fingers and when it strikes the open left hand that hand is quickly placed against the left side of the leg. The right hand makes a rubbing motion on the left leg, and simultaneously the left hand moves up the left side of the left leg, coming to rest in a natural position just below the left trousers pocket. As the right fingers continue to rub the left leg the fingers are slowly spread apart. Then the fingers flick an imaginary speck off the leg and the right hand is seen to be empty. Slide the left hand down the back of the leg and bring the coin into view.

A lot of words have been necessary to explain this feat, but the mechanics are simple. Mostly it is a matter of timing. Once this is understood the reader should have no difficulty in mastering it. This trick has an astonishing effect when smoothly performed.

Through the Pocket

This bit of close-up coin chicanery has been a favorite with magicians for many years. It is one trick that can be performed anytime with excellent results, as it is strictly impromptu. Here are three methods.

Effect: A half dollar placed in the right trousers pocket is caused to penetrate the cloth in a mysterious fashion.

(a) Call attention to a half dollar clipped flat between the tips of the right first and second fingers, in position for finger palming. Holding the coin thus, the right hand enters the right trousers pocket. Immediately thumb palm the coin while the left forefinger presses against the outside of the pocket as if holding the coin. This action with the left forefinger is a natural one and serves as a bit of misdirection for the moves that follow. Withdraw the right hand with the coin hidden in the thumb palm. Next, release the coin from the thumb palm allowing it to fall onto the cupped right fingers. It is then pressed flat against the right leg as the left forefinger is taken away. At this moment the right hand lies flat against the right leg, fingers pointing downward. The coin is hidden underneath the fingers which press it to the leg.

The right thumb pinches a small fold of cloth behind the upper portion of the coin. The right hand turns the coin over, downward, forming the fold over the coin. Maintain this fold with the left forefinger as the right hand moves away. Snap the right fingers. Then grasp the cloth below the fold and pull downward slowly, allowing the hidden coin to come into view. When the coin is about two-thirds the way out of the fold, slide the left forefinger downward on top of it to prevent it from falling to the floor.

(b) In this version the coin is visibly dropped into the pocket, without the hand leaving sight of the audience.

Two identical coins are required. Have one finger palmed in your right hand as you display the other between the tips of your left forefinger and thumb. Reach across your body with your right hand, hook the fingers in the left pocket opening and hold it wide open while you slowly and deliberately drop the coin from your left hand into that pocket. Be sure to make these moves in such a manner that there will be no doubt in the spectators' minds that the coin did actually enter the pocket. Allow the finger palmed coin to drop on the cupped right fingers, then press it flat against the left leg and finish as described in the first version.

Because the coin is actually seen to drop into the pocket this makes an excellent version to have on tap in case you have to repeat the trick before the same group of spectators.

(c) Dave Coleman Method.

Show the coin in the left hand. Execute The French Drop (page 37), as you pretend to take it with the right hand. Place the right hand (apparently holding the coin) in the right trousers pocket. The palm-inward left hand is brought over and placed flat against the right hand, which is still within the pocket. As this is done the coin is secretly deposited on the leg where it is held hidden underneath the left fingers. Actually the coin should be between the tips of the fingers of the two hands. Turn both hands over together, forming a *vertical* (and not a horizontal) fold in the cloth. Remove the left fingers from the fold, leaving the coin hidden underneath the cloth. The right fingers facilitate this action by holding the coin through the pocket until the left fingers are withdrawn. Retain this fold with the tip of the left thumb as you remove the right hand from the pocket.

With the right thumb above and forefinger below, grip the coin by its edges through the cloth so its form can be seen. Apparently the coin is in the pocket. Now, press the right thumb and forefinger together which causes the coin to emerge, apparently through the fabric, in an uncanny manner. Catch the coin in the left hand as it falls from the fold. Shake the trousers leg with the right hand and give the last fading fold a flick with the forefinger.

The Pocket Vanish (page 52) makes a

fine follow-up trick. The two effects complement each other and blend perfectly into a nice routine.

First, perform Through the Pocket (a) or (c). Then explain that if a coin will come through the pocket it should penetrate *back* through the cloth, into the pocket again. This you proceed to demonstrate by performing the Pocket Vanish.

Through the Hand

There are many occasions when the magician needs a little trick to perform on the spur of the moment—an incidental effect that can be done quickly without special props. This is just such an effect. I will describe three methods.

(a) Clyde Cairy Method.

A half dollar is shown in the left hand. The hand is then closed on the coin and turned over so the back of the hand is uppermost. The fingers work the coin partially out of the fist until it is barely held by the tips of the second and third fingers and the heel of the hand, Fig. 1. Care must be taken

Fig. 1

here lest the spectators glimpse the coin. Hold the left hand rather low, and watch your angles.

Show the right hand empty and begin massaging the back of the left hand with the fingertips. The right thumb is underneath the left hand during this motion and prepares to steal the coin from the left hand. The right hand slows down its rubbing almost to a standstill. Then the left fingers release the coin so that it lies balanced horizontally on the top of the right thumb, Fig. 2. Suddenly lift up the right

Fig. 2

hand, then quickly bring it down, slapping the fingers on the back of the left fist.

Centrifugal force causes the coin to leave the thumb as the right hand is brought down on the left, the coin being transferred from the thumb to the inside of the fingers, and is slapped down on the back of the left hand. The right hand is then taken away revealing the half dollar lying on the back of the left hand. The right hand removes the coin and the left hand is opened and shown empty. Apparently the coin has penetrated up through the back of the left hand.

One of the first rules we learn in magic is never repeat the same trick before the same audience. But there are exceptions to all rules, and this one can be broken providing a different method is used to obtain the end result. The feat may be repeated in a slightly different manner by using the

following version. The two versions blend perfectly.

(b) Show the left hand empty, close it into a loose fist, and turn it over so the fingers will be underneath. Hold the half dollar near its edge between the tips of the right fingers and thumb. Press its milled edge against the back of the left hand, Fig. 3.

Suddenly push the fingers of the right hand down over the coin. The illusion is that the coin is pushed through the back of the left hand. At this moment the coin

Fig. 3

is concealed behind the right fingers, which rest momentarily on the back of the left hand. Without changing the position of the right fingers and thumb, quickly move the hand about six or eight inches to the right, turning the left hand over and opening it at the same time. As the spectators see the empty left hand, say "Nothing in the hand." Immediately swing the right hand back to the left, tossing the coin into the left hand as it closes and turns over. The right fingers assume the original position on the back of the left hand, as you add, "One more little rub and the coin goes right through."

Diminish the rubbing motion, finishing by
separating the fingers and giving the last
rub with the tip of the middle finger. This
convincing move tends to show without saying so that the coin has left the right hand.
Move the right hand aside as you open the
left hand to display the coin.

In the first version the coin penetrates
the left hand from the inside out, while in
the second version it penetrates from the
outside in.

(c) Ross Bertram Method.

Face the spectators as you show a half
dollar lying at the base of the first finger

Fig. 4

on your open left hand, Fig. 4. Place the
left thumb on top of the coin and turn the
hand over and close the fingers. As the hand
turns over the thumb moves inward toward
the body, carrying the coin with it. Coin
will now be outside the fist, clipped by its
edge by the thumb and base of the first
finger, Fig. 5.

Let's go over that again. Actually the
hand turns over *before* the fingers are

Fig. 5

closed. Begin by placing your thumb on top
of the coin as described above and turn the
hand over. The coin will then be lying
horizontally on the side of the thumb,
which now moves inward, carrying coin
with it as the fingers close. These are the
actual mechanics of the sleight, but to the
spectators it must appear that you merely
closed your hand and turned it over. The
coin is now outside the fist and completely
hidden from the spectators' view by that
hand.

Raise the right hand and hold it palm
down over the left fist. Call attention to the
ring you wear on your left third finger.
Comment on its mystical powers and tell
the spectators that by rubbing it you can
cause unexplainable things to happen. Rub
the ring with the tip of the third finger of
the right hand and while doing so edge
palm the coin in your right palm. In making this steal, pay special attention to hold
the hands at such an angle that the coin
cannot be seen at any time by the audience.

Lower the hands a few inches and place
the right finger tips on the back of the left
fist, then make a massaging movement. In
this action release the coin from the right
palm and allow it to slide down the right
fingers onto the back of the left hand. Keep
the right fingers together lest the spectators
see the coin. Finally spread the right fingers slightly and show the coin on the back
of the left hand, it having apparently penetrated the back of the hand.

Through a Handkerchief

There are methods in great variety for
performing this trick. Perhaps because the
effect is simple and direct—and because no
special props are used. Since no special
preparation *is* required, the trick is a perfect one for close-up impromptu work. Here

Fig. 1

left thumb pinches over a small fold at the base of the coin. This fold is to the rear and is not seen by the spectators, Fig. 1.

Say, "Let me show you that the half dollar is still underneath the handkerchief." With the right hand, seize the front edge of the handkerchief and lift it up, thus giving a brief view of the coin, Fig. 2. The right hand then returns the handkerchief to its original position, as the left simultaneously tosses forward the back half of the handkerchief. This subtle action causes *all the folds* of the handkerchief to fall down-

Fig. 3

are two methods—both appear entirely different in effect.

Effect: A coin is caused to penetrate the fabric of a pocket handkerchief in a baffling manner.

(a) Display a half dollar in your left hand, holding it upright between the finger tips and thumb. With your right hand, spread a borrowed handkerchief and drape it over the left so its center covers the coin. Allow a spectator to feel the coin through the cloth and verify the fact that it is still there. With the aid of the right hand, the

ward *in front of the coin*, Fig. 3. At this point the coin is *outside* the handkerchief, and is held in a horizontal position between the middle finger underneath and the thumb on top, Fig. 4.

With the right hand, grasp the handkerchief a few inches below the coin and pull downward as you twist it counterclockwise, Fig. 5. Next, grip the handkerchief with the right second, third, and fourth fingers while the forefinger and thumb press against opposite edges of the coin. Finally, squeeze the coin into view, and show the handkerchief undamaged.

Fig. 2

Fig. 4

Several astounding tricks utilizing this
principle will be explained in later chapters.

(b) Few close-up stunts have more eye-
appeal than this version. It is startling and
different in effect.

Fig. 6

dle finger and thumb. With the coin thus
held, it is placed over the center of the left
palm on top of the handkerchief, Fig. 6.
The right middle finger and thumb retain
their grip on the coin as the left hand

Fig. 5

Fig. 7

Show the left hand empty, then hold it
palm up as the right hand spreads a white
pocket handkerchief over it. The center of
the handkerchief should be over the palm
and one corner on the forearm.

Display a half dollar in the right hand,
gripping it near its edge between the mid-

slowly closes over it. The left hand opens again to give one more view of the coin, then it closes. Immediately move the right hand inward and grasp the inner corner of the handkerchief lying on the forearm. In this movement the right hand thumb palms the half dollar. The handkerchief affords cover for the coin as it is withdrawn from the left hand and the back part of the right shields it from view as that hand reaches back to grasp the inner corner of the handkerchief.

The first and second fingers of the right hand pull the handkerchief forward exposing the empty left palm, Fig. 7. Say, "Nothing in the hand." The coin is dropped into the left hand as right returns the handkerchief to its original position on the arm, Fig. 8. It should appear that you merely

Fig. 8

uncovered the left palm and then pulled the handkerchief back over it. As the left palm is exposed, be careful that the right hand does not pull the handkerchief away entirely. A little pressure with the left thumb on a fold of the fabric will prevent this happening.

Open the left hand to show the handkerchief empty as you continue, "Nothing, that is, except the half dollar." Grasp the corner of the handkerchief toward the audience and slowly pull it away, showing the coin lying on the left palm.

It looks like real magic!

For a third method, see Perfected Coin Through Handkerchief, page 270.

Double Penetration

JIMMY BUFFALOE

Effect: A handkerchief is spread over the left hand by the performer. Two half dollars are placed on the handkerchief and hand is closed. Then the left hand is shaken and the clinking of the two coins is clearly heard. The closed hand is turned over so the corners of the handkerchief hang down, thus forming a bag with the coins inside. A spectator verifies that the two coins are still within the handkerchief by feeling them through the cloth. Grasping the coins through the cloth the performer suddenly yanks them through the handkerchief. The handkerchief is shown unharmed.

Method: Although the spectators know of only two coins, actually four are used. Two are in the left trousers pocket along with a pocket handkerchief, while the other two are in the right trousers pocket.

Begin the effect by removing the two coins from the right trousers pocket and placing them on the table. With the left hand, reach into your left trousers pocket, classic palm the two coins and bring out the handkerchief. It is shown casually and then thrown over the palm up left hand, but take care not to expose the two palmed coins.

Pick up the two coins from the table with the right hand and hold them together as one between the first and second fingers.

Pretend to place these two coins on the handkerchief but thumb palm them instead. Immediately close the left hand and rattle the two coins which lie on the palm underneath the cloth. This creates a perfect illusion that the two coins were actually placed in the left hand on the handkerchief.

An alternate and preferred method of apparently placing the two coins in the left hand would be to perform The Click Pass (b), (page 14). This gives a more perfect illusion because the second coin can be heard to fall onto the first.

Now turn the left hand over so the folds of the handkerchief hang down. Place the left thumb above the two coins and open the left hand. The coins make a complete revolution in this action and they are now underneath the center folds of the cloth being held horizontally between the thumb underneath and the fingers above. Next, remove the second, third, and fourth fingers from the cloth and exhibit the handkerchief and coins between the left thumb and forefinger only, Fig. 1.

The right hand, with the coins still palmed, grips the handkerchief about half way down toward the four corners and pulls

downward with considerable force, forming a pocket around the coins. Maintain this grip on the coins and the handkerchief as you lower the left hand and raise the right. The right hand now holds the handkerchief near its corners from above, while the left, which grips the coins and the handkerchief, pulls down from below. Release your grip on the two coins and the center of the handkerchief with your left hand, and if the above moves were made correctly the coins will be held in the folds of the handkerchief without danger of their fall-

Fig. 2

2 coins lying horizontally in folds of handkerchief

ing out, Fig. 2. Remove the right hand from the handkerchief and grasp it at the same point with the left hand. This leaves the right hand free to reach into the right trousers pocket for a small wand or pencil. The two coins are left in the pocket and the wand is removed. Tap the two coins from underneath with the wand a couple of times, causing them to jingle together slightly, then place the wand aside.

If you like you can allow a spectator to feel the coins in the handkerchief at this point. To do this, place the right thumb on top of the two coins and the forefinger underneath the cloth, and move the right hand forward. Pull back on the handker-

Fig. 1

chief with the left hand as you do this and the coins will be completely covered on top and bottom with the folds of the cloth and you can offer them to be felt with safety.

Bring the handkerchief back to its original position. With the aid of the right thumb and fingers, turn the coins into an upright position behind the handkerchief. Then with two or three quick downward jerks, pull the two coins from the cloth, the effect being that they are pulled through the handkerchief. Show the coins in the right hand and toss them onto the table. Exhibit the handkerchief unharmed.

Pants Leg Miracle

JIMMY BUFFALOE

Effect: Showing a half dollar, the performer places it in the folds of his left pants leg. When the fold is pulled away a moment later, a dime emerges. The half dollar has vanished.

Method: When you remove the half dollar from your right trousers pocket have a dime concealed behind it. Call attention to the half dollar and place it (with the dime concealed behind it) on the left leg about six inches above the knee. Hold it in position with the tip of the right third finger, then using the moves described in method (a), Through the Leg (page 63), form a fold over the two coins. At the completion of this move the dime will be the outer coin. Place the tip of the left forefinger on the dime through the cloth, then as you move the right hand away, the half dollar is withdrawn, under cover of the back of the right hand, and pressed into the right palm. Snap the right fingers a couple of times to emphasize the emptiness of that hand, then grasp the cloth below the fold and pull downward slowly causing the dime to gradually come into view.

Half Dollar to Quarter

MILTON KORT

Effect: The conjurer displays a half dollar in his right hand while showing his left hand unmistakably empty. He takes the half dollar with his left hand and shows his right hand equally empty. The coin is then returned to his palm up right hand and the hand is seen to be holding only the single coin.

A spectator is requested to hold out his hand. The performer turns his hand over and drops the coin into the spectator's hand, but when it lands in the spectator's hand it is seen to have changed to a quarter. The performer then shows both of his hands positively empty. Apparently a half has changed into a quarter!

Method: Have a half dollar and a quarter in the right trousers pocket. Place the right hand in the pocket, clip the quarter by its edge between the first and second fingers so it will be hidden underneath the hand (see The Back Finger Clip, page 7), and bring the hand out showing the half dollar lying on the outer joints of the first and second fingers, directly above the hidden quarter, Fig. 1. Or, if you prefer, you may secretly get the quarter into the back finger clip position while asking for the loan of a half dollar. At any rate, display the fifty cent piece as described, with the

Fig. 1

hand held about waist high and the fingers pointing forward and slightly downward.

Give the half dollar a couple of little tosses into the air, causing it to turn over each time. This natural gesture tends to give convincing proof that the hand is otherwise empty. Keep the hand low as you make this and the following moves.

Show the left hand to be empty by spreading the fingers wide apart and slowly turning the hand over a time or two. Drop the arm to your side and shake it vigorously to show that you have nothing concealed in your sleeve. Make no comment on this fact as you do this, however.

Now comes the part that fools them all. Still keeping the right hand low, point the fingers to the left as you bring the left hand over and grip the half dollar in the following manner: Press the left thumb against the edge nearest to your body while the forefinger presses against the edge farthest from it. As you grip the half dollar in this manner extend the left second, third and fourth fingers underneath the right fingers and clip the quarter between the tips of the second and third fingers. Slide the half dollar off the right fingers to the left, taking the quarter along underneath it. The quarter protrudes upward from between the tips of the left second and third fingers, but by lowering the half slightly it covers the quarter completely. The left hand seems to be holding only a half dollar. If you will stand in front of a mirror while making these moves you will quickly discover the proper position the hand and coins must be held to prevent the spectators seeing the quarter. Fig. 2 shows the position of the half dollar in the left hand as seen by the spectators. Because of the special angles necessary to perform the trick it should not be done when the spectators' line of vision is low. It is best when performed at close range with only a few spec-

Fig. 2

As audience views it. Half dollar conceals quarter, which is clipped between tips of second and third fingers.

tators viewing the trick from a standing position.

Now slowly and deliberately show the right hand empty and shake the arm as you did the left. Reverse the above moves to replace the half dollar in its original position on the right fingers. As this is done the quarter goes back to its previous back finger clip position underneath the right hand. Except for the half dollar, you have apparently shown both hands empty.

With the right hand, again toss the fifty cent piece into the air a few times and contrive to have it fall in position for palming. When you have it in the center of the palm, turn the hand counterclockwise and close it. Hold the half dollar in the palm and keep the fingers pointing slightly downward as you do this so as not to expose the quarter. While making the final closing movement with the right hand, bring the quarter inside the fist with the aid of the thumb. These moves should be blended into one continuous movement—that of closing the hand.

Ask a spectator to hold out his hand. Reach out and drop the twenty-five cent piece into his hand, then as you bring your hand back, sleeve the half dollar. The sleeving move must be made immediately after dropping the quarter into the spectator's hand. All eyes will be on the quarter for a brief moment, then they will return to your hands. By this time the deed is done—the half dollar is up the sleeve and there is no clue to the mystery of how the half dollar changed into a quarter.

The Charmed Coin

Here is a quick trick that is a real eye popper.

Effect: A half dollar is shown and tossed into the left hand a few times. Suddenly the coin changes to a candy charm, which is eaten by the performer.

Method: Begin with a candy charm (sold in the dime stores and candy shops) up the right coat sleeve.

Show a half dollar and toss it back and forth from hand to hand. This action convincingly demonstrates without saying so that the hands are otherwise empty.

Next display the coin in the left hand. While attention is on the coin the right hand drops to the side allowing the charm to fall from the sleeve. It is caught on the curled right fingers and immediately finger palmed.

Take the half dollar from the left hand with the right, holding it between the first two fingers and thumb. Toss it into the left hand and close the fingers over it. Repeat this action a couple of times. Pretend to toss the coin again, but throw the charm instead. (See The Bobo Switch, page 10.) The coin is retained in the right palm. Wave right hand mysteriously over the closed left hand. Open the left hand and display the candy charm. As this is done the right hand sleeves the coin. Slowly remove the foil from the charm, letting it be seen that the hands are otherwise empty. Eat the candy.

After eating the candy, drop the right hand to the side and retrieve the coin from the sleeve. Drop it in the pocket as you remove your pocket handkerchief to wipe your hands.

The effect will be greatly enhanced if a coin the same color and approximately the same size as the charm is used. If the charm has a silver foil wrapper use a silver coin. If the charm has a gold foil wrapper use a brass or bright copper coin. Under these conditions the switch can be made more slowly without fear of detection.

Instead of a charm a small cookie can be used.

The Coin of Metamorphosis

Dr. E. M. Roberts

Numerous methods have been devised for causing one coin to apparently change to another. Here is one which just about tops them all for sheer effectiveness. Although it requires only about a minute to perform, it packs such a terrific wallop it will be remembered long after other tricks are forgotten.

Effect: A borrowed penny instantly and visibly changes to a half dollar while held in the performer's right hand. Then the coin is tossed into the left hand, and after a couple of mysterious passes are made over it, changes back to a penny. The penny is returned to its owner and the performer shows his hands positively empty.

Method: Begin with a half dollar hidden in your right hand as it hangs by the side. Ask for the loan of a penny and while it is forthcoming get the half dollar into the Downs palm position. Receive the penny with the left hand, then take it with the right between the first two fingers and thumb, Fig. 1.

Swing the right hand upward to the right and exhibit the penny as in Fig. 2, the half dollar being hidden behind the

Fig. I

Fig. 2

Fig. 4

half dollar from the Downs palm, Fig. 5. Straighten the fingers, withdrawing the half from behind the thumb, Fig. 6, and exhibit the half clipped between the first and sec-

thumb. The existence of another coin is not suspected since the right hand appears empty.

Bring the forefinger down in front of the penny then back to its original position, which action clips the coin between the first two fingers as in Fig. 3. The moves

Fig. 3

Fig. 5

Fig. 6

which follow happen in quick succession. The right hand is brought up to the mouth and the coin is blown upon, then returned to its original position to show the penny has changed to a half dollar. As the right hand comes up to the mouth and back again the penny is exchanged for the half as follows:

With the aid of the right thumb move the penny down and deposit it on the tip of the third finger, Fig. 4. Then bend the fingers inward, pressing the penny into classic palm position with the tip of the third finger as the first two fingers clip the

ond finger tips, Fig. 7. The hand is held with the palm turned partly downward, in which position the penny cannot be seen.

Figures 4 through 7 depict the moves which are performed with the two coins in the moment it takes to raise the hand,

Fig. 7

blow on the coin, and return the hand to its original position. The action of removing the half dollar from the Downs palm and pressing the penny into the palm is performed as the hand is brought up and returned to its former position. Figures 4 and 5 show the moves that must be executed as the hand is brought up to the mouth, while Figures 6 and 7 show the moves that are performed as the hand swings back to its original place. When the hand has returned to its original position it should be holding the half dollar between the tips of the first two fingers as in Fig. 7. Then the first two fingers revolve the half dollar round and round a few times, indicating without comment that the hand is otherwise empty. Actually, the right hand should be held about waist height as the half dollar is shown. The penny cannot be seen. With care you will be able to turn your right palm partially toward the audience and keep the penny hidden. The thumb bends down, holding the half dollar, and partly covers the penny in the palm. Watch your angles. Try this before a mirror and you will quickly realize the position the right hand must assume. Of course, the safe position is as in Fig. 7 but when you are performing this at close range for only two or three people more of the palm can be shown with safety.

Revolve the half dollar between the fingers and thumb as described above, then apparently toss it into your left hand but throw the penny instead. This is executed as follows: Turn the body to the left and thumb palm the half dollar by bending in the first two fingers with the coin and straightening them. As the right hand approaches the left it releases the penny from its palm (Fig. 8 shows the performer's view of the right hand as it approaches the left hand) and it falls into the left hand as it closes. The right hand continues in its swing

Fig. 8

inward, passing over the left hand and back to the upper left breast pocket where the half dollar is released and allowed to fall into the pocket (See The Bobo Complete Coin Vanish, page 49, for a detailed description of a vanish using this principle.) Quickly move the right hand outward again and brush it briskly over the left fist a couple of times. The moves of tossing the penny into the left hand in lieu of the half dollar, depositing the half dollar in the breast pocket and brushing the right hand briskly over the left fist must all be blended in one continuous movement, without hesitation, yet without haste. Finally open the left hand to show the penny. As you return it to its owner let both hands be seen unmistakably empty.

Suggested Patter: "The penny, as you know, is made from copper which is a soft metal, very susceptible to quick changes in temperature. For instance, if I should blow on it like this, it changes to a silver coin. However, if I should squeeze it like this, it quickly changes back to its original form and substance. But I'll let you in on a secret—actually nothing happened. It was just an illusion."

The trick is particularly startling if performed with the sleeves rolled up. And, of course, it can be done without a coat providing you stuff a small piece of facial tissue, Kleenex, in the shirt pocket beforehand to keep it open slightly. But with or without a coat it is a real puzzler, even to magicians.

Coin to Key

Courtesy J. G. THOMPSON'S *My Best*

Effect: The performer shows a half dollar which he holds by its edge between the thumb and forefinger of his right hand, and the hand is seen to be otherwise empty. After showing his left hand empty he places the coin on the left palm and closes his fingers over it. To satisfy the spectators that the coin is still in the left hand he opens it slightly to give them another view. Then he makes mystic passes over the left hand and opens it to show a key. The coin has completely vanished.

Method: The trick makes use of a clever concealment and an old sleight combined with The Bobo Complete Coin Vanish (page 49). It is especially puzzling because the key is actually much larger than the coin, thus proving it could not have been concealed behind it. Nevertheless the key is partly hidden behind the coin at the beginning. The key must be of the padlock or automobile lock variety. The head, or larger end of the key, is covered with the half dollar, while the smaller end (the end which goes into the lock) is covered with

Fig. 1

the right thumb. The coin is held by its extreme edge between the right thumb and forefinger as in Fig. 1, the forefinger holding the key in place behind the coin and thumb.

Stand with your right side toward the spectators as you call attention to the half dollar, holding it as explained. Hold your left hand about shoulder high, with its palm outward, and slowly and deliberately

Fig. 2

place the coin on its palm, Fig. 2. Close the left fingers over the coin and key, being careful that the smaller end of the key is not seen as this is done. If you retain your grip on the coin and key until the left fingers close over them you will be safe. Tell the spectators that at this point most people think the coin has already vanished but you would like to show that this is not so. Open the first and second fingers of the left hand, giving the spectators a partial view of the coin. The third and fourth fingers remain closed to cover part of the coin and the key, Fig. 3. Close the two fingers again and turn the hand over so its back will be toward the audience. With

Fig. 3

Fig. 5

the aid of the left fingertips work the coin partially out of the hand until it is held at its extreme edge by the fingertips and the heel of the thumb, Fig. 4.

"I will perform the feat in slow motion," you announce. "Watch! Not a finger moves." Hold the left hand about shoulder high and rest the tip of the right forefinger

Fig. 4

closed left fingers. The right hand does not move as the left hand turns over, and just as it completes its turn the coin comes between the tips of the right thumb and forefinger. The right hand then moves downward carrying the coin with it as the forefinger is brought across the left fingers as explained above. Perform this steal in front of your mirror to appreciate its clever-

Fig. 6

on its back, Fig. 5. As you say "not a finger moves," slowly turn the left hand over, which brings the coin to the front, hidden from the spectator's view by the right hand. As the left hand turns over take the coin by its edge between the right thumb and forefinger, Fig. 6, then slide the tip of the right forefinger downward slowly across the

ness. Actually it can be done quite slowly, and if properly executed there will be no visible movement of either hand. It is clean and indetectable. Ostensibly you are demonstrating the fairness of your movements but while so doing you have gotten possession of the coin in your right hand.

"Now by making a few mysterious passes over my left hand I will cause a peculiar transformation to take place. Watch!" Move the right hand inward and outward, making a few passes over the left fist, and under cover of this action thumb palm the coin, then drop it into the upper left breast pocket on the second or third swing inward. (See The Bobo Complete Coin Vanish, page 49, for a detailed description of this principle.) Finally stop the passes altogether, then open the left hand and show the key. The half dollar has apparently changed into a key!

Change for a Half

Effect: The performer shows a half dollar which he slowly places in his left hand. He closes the left fingers over the coin, makes a few passes over the left hand, then opens it. Instead of a half dollar he has change for a half—a quarter, a nickel and two dimes. Nothing used but ordinary coins.

Method: No doubt you have guessed the secret. It depends on the same concealment and moves described in the foregoing effect. Instead of a key—a quarter, a nickel and two dimes are hidden behind the half dollar at the beginning of the trick. Care must be taken to prevent the coins from "talking." Steal the half dollar out of the left hand as described, dispose of it in the upper left breast pocket, then open the left hand to show change for a half.

The same moves can be used to vanish a single coin, or to cause a larger coin to change to a smaller one, or to a foreign coin. As a transition effect you can cause a coin to change to a thimble, a ring, a button, a coil of ribbon, etc. Such "incidental" effects often create more astonishment than carefully planned program items. Change for a Half will serve you well—**learn it.**

Much from Little

John Braun's Version

Effect: The trickster shows a nickel in his right hand between the tips of the forefinger and thumb, and the hand appears otherwise empty. After showing his left hand empty he brings it over to his right hand for a moment. When the two hands separate he is holding an English penny in his right hand and a half dollar in his left. The nickel has vanished.

Method: This clever mystery depends on an old method of concealment which should be known to all coin workers.

Stick a bit of wax about the size of a small pea on the upper side of an English penny or similar copper coin, and flatten it out somewhat. Place a half dollar below this coin and hold the two together horizontally between the right thumb and forefinger. The extreme tips of the thumb and forefinger curl around the two coins and press against opposite edges of a nickel.

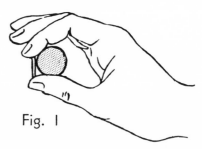

Fig. I

The nickel is in a vertical position and conceals the two larger coins from view of the spectators. Fig. 1 shows how this looks from above, while Fig. 2 shows how it should appear to the spectators.

Hold the right hand about shoulder height with fingers wide apart as you point the face of the nickel directly toward the onlookers. The hand appears to be holding only the five cent piece. (Using this method

Fig. 2

of concealment even such a large coin as a silver dollar can be concealed behind a dime.) Angles are very important, so be sure to keep the larger coins parallel with the floor at all times, otherwise the spectators may get a flash of them.

Casually show your left hand empty without mentioning this fact, then bring it up to the right hand so the left thumb tip touches the flat side of the nickel and the tips of the second and third fingers rest on the underside of the half dollar.

Fig. 3

(See Fig. 3 for performer's view of this action.) With the aid of the left thumb, slide the nickel back onto the English penny and press it down onto the wax. At this point all three coins are horizontal. Quickly separate the two hands, taking the English penny and nickel between the tips of the first two fingers and thumb of the right hand, holding them vertically with

the thumb pressing against the nickel at the rear. The left hand grips the half dollar in like manner. Hold the two coins in front of your chest with the hands about a foot apart. The nickel is hidden behind the English penny and is held in place by the wax.

Bring the left hand down, even with the waist, and hold it palm up with the half dollar resting on the fingers. Toss the English penny onto the left palm so the nickel is on the underside; the coin lies perfectly flat because the nickel fits into the hollow of the palm. Immediately pick up the half dollar with the right hand and toss it down again on top of, and overlapping, the English penny. The sound of the coins clinking together offers perfect proof that they are genuine, and they are. But don't omit this one little point. It is important. The effect is so startling and puzzling that the spectators need final proof that everything is legitimate. The two coins clinking together puts the final touch on this bit of close-up chicanery.

Pocket the English penny and use the half dollar for your next experiment.

The Topsy Turvy Coins

KARREL FOX AND ROY KISSEL

Effect: Five borrowed half dollars are placed in an overlapping row on the performer's left hand so they alternate heads up, tails up, etc. The wonder-worker pushes the coins together and holds them in a stack between the fingers and thumb of his right hand. He then releases them one at a time, allowing them to fall onto the left hand. As the coins fall they are seen to be all one way, i.e., all heads up. Somehow they have mysteriously rearranged themselves.

Method: Borrow five half dollars and

Fig. 1

Fig. 2

Fig. 3

the fifth and last coin, allowing it to fall without turning over, and it lands head up also, Fig. 2, for this action, which is the same move as used with the Okito Coin Box to cause its bottom to turn over as it falls onto the left hand. The move is a standard one and is known to all magicians who use the Okito Coin Box. (For further details, see The Okito Coin Box, page 217.)

Done at a quick pace the spectators will believe that the coins rearranged themselves so they all faced one way.

Although the effect is not particularly astounding, it makes a nice interlude between deeper mysteries.

The Impromptu Mint

JIMMY BUFFALOE

Effect: The performer goes to his pocket and brings forth a nickel which he exhibits on his outstretched right hand. With his left hand he shows a playing card on both sides and the hand is otherwise empty. He brings the card over the nickel hiding it from view. He immediately removes it. The nickel has changed to a half dollar!

The magician quickly covers the half dollar for a moment. When the card is removed the spectators see the nickel again. The nickel is tossed onto the card and both can be examined. No clue to the mystery will be found.

This makes a perfect transition effect. After doing a few card tricks make a few remarks regarding the relation of money to cards. Reach into your pocket for a nickel and proceed with the effect.

Method: Have a half dollar and a nickel in the right trousers pocket and you are ready to begin.

Remove any card from the deck and show it on both sides, snapping it with the

place them on the left hand as described above. Call attention to the way the coins alternate—every other coin being reversed. Push the coins together slowly with the right fingers then hold them between the thumb and fingers of the same hand. The right fingers point downward and the coins are held in a stack by pressure on their edges with the fingers and thumb, Fig. 1. Hold the left hand palm up a few inches below the coins as the right hand drops them onto it one at a time. Allow the bottom coin to fall naturally, releasing it with the fingertips and the thumb. It lands on the left hand heads up. The second coin is released with the thumb only. This causes the coin to make a half turn as it falls onto the first, heads up. Release the third coin as you did the first so it does not turn over and it falls onto the other two naturally—heads up. Control the fourth coin so it will land heads up. Finally, drop right fingers. Then hold it in the left hand. With the right hand, reach into the right trousers pocket, quickly back palm the half dollar and bring out the nickel lying on the two middle fingers between the two outer joints. The spectators see the nickel lying on the right hand and the hand appears otherwise empty.

The left hand now brings the card over the nickel, hiding it from view. Under cover of the card bend the middle fingers inward, then outward again, pivoting the half dollar between the first and fourth fingers. (This is merely a reversal of the regular back hand palm move. See Chapter I for a detailed description of the moves.) At the completion of the move the half dollar will have been brought from the back of the hand (back palm) to the front of the hand (front palm), and covering the nickel. Much care and precision will have to be exercised here lest the coins "talk." Remove the card to reveal the half dollar.

The above action takes but a moment, and it should appear to the spectators that you merely passed the card over the coin slowly.

The pasteboard is brought back over the right hand, covering the half dollar. Under cover of the card the following action takes place: The half dollar is not rotated this time but held firmly by its edges between the first and little fingers while the second and third fingers (with the nickel resting on them) arch back, and as they straighten out again they slide over the half dollar, which ends up in back palm position. The card is taken away to show nickel again.

Hold the card tray fashion in the left hand. Turn the right hand counterclockwise and close the hand into a loose fist, which position puts the half dollar in easy thumb palming position. Quickly thumb palm the half and toss the nickel onto the tray as the right hand swings to the left.

Display the nickel on the card for a second. While attention is on the nickel sleeve the half dollar. Show the nickel and card, then as you drop the nickel back into your right trousers pocket let the larger coin drop out onto the cupped fingers and place it into the pocket with the nickel.

An alternate finish: Instead of sleeving the coin take the nickel with the right hand and place it and the half dollar into the pocket. In this case the card would not be shown on both sides until *after* the nickel and the "evidence" had been put in the pocket. You would hold the card rather suspiciously to draw attention to it, then slyly turn it over and snap it with the right fingers. Let them examine it if they wish. There is nothing to find.

The reason for throwing the nickel onto the card is so that you may silently show both sides of your right hand. This is very necessary because the entire action takes place in such a small area the spectators think the half dollar is near by. But throwing the nickel onto the card at the finish, and thumb palming the half dollar, eliminates all suspicion from their minds.

The effect is both startling and pretty.

Smart Coin Trick

FRANK M. CHAPMAN, *courtesy The Bat*

Try to figure this out before you read the explanation. It's a beauty!

A borrowed half dollar is balanced on the tip of the right forefinger. The left hand forms a fist around it. The right hand is withdrawn and shown empty back and front, fingers wide apart. Right hand removes a handkerchief from the breast pocket, and holds it by one corner. Left hand is slowly opened, palm toward spectators, fingers wide apart. The coin has faded away!

The handkerchief is taken by the left thumb and forefinger. The right hand is again shown empty. The right hand then catches opposite corner of the handkerchief and stretches it out taut. The left hand lets go of its corner and is again shown empty, back and front. The handkerchief is merely drawn across the empty left palm in one continuous motion, and

Fig. 3

Fig. 1

Fig. 4

the half dollar instantly appears on the palm.

It is a perfect piece of modern, impromptu magic. You'll like this one a lot.

Method: First, balance the half dollar on your right forefinger as in Fig. 1. Now bring the left hand over it, and close the left fingers loosely around the coin and the right fingers. Under cover of the half-closed left fist, bend the right forefinger inward, carrying the coin with it, Fig. 2. The coin goes around the base of the left thumb and the right thumb slides it into position on the back of the left wrist, Figs.

Fig. 2

3 and 4. The coin remains balanced on the back of the wrist. If you are inclined toward nervousness, better push the coin slightly under the edge of the coat cuff for security.

The right forefinger is then drawn from the left fist and the right hand shown empty. Show the back and front with the fingers wide open. Make every move deliberately. The slower, the more effective it will be. Take the handkerchief from the breast pocket, and hold it by one corner between the thumb and forefinger. The left hand is slowly opened, palm toward spectators, and the coin remains hidden on the back of the hand, Fig. 5. Swing the right hand over to the left and place the corner of the handkerchief held by the right hand between the left forefinger and thumb. Hold the left hand steady. (Let the right hand place the handkerchief in position.) The right hand is shown to be empty once more, and now grasps an opposite corner

Fig. 5

and stretches the handkerchief out taut. As this is done the left hand turns slightly, allowing the coin to fall off, and it is caught with the right, the action being concealed from spectators' view by the handkerchief, Fig. 6. Immediately release the corner from the right hand and shake the handkerchief a few times. Show the left hand empty, back and front, then hold it out flat with the palm up. Draw the handkerchief across the left hand and drop the coin in the same action. As the handkerchief is drawn over the left hand the coin mysteriously reappears.

Fig. 6

Tuck the handkerchief back into your breast pocket and return the coin.

IMPROMPTU VERSION

J. G. THOMPSON, JR.

Smart Coin Trick is a very effective stunt, its one weak spot being that there is no logical reason for using the silk. Eliminate it, and you obtain an additional feature— that of making the feat strictly impromptu.

To accomplish this, bring the coin to the back of the left hand and give it an extra shove with the right thumb so that about half of it slips under the edge of the coat sleeve.

In disclosing the vanish of the coin from the left hand, raise the latter almost to a vertical position. Then move it slightly to the left, turning the palm up and opening the fingers at the same time.

If the combined moves just described are properly executed, the coin will slide up your sleeve and permit the showing of both front and back of the left hand.

At this point, suspicion will be centered on the right hand. As you demonstrate its innocence, drop the left hand to your side, whereupon the coin will drop onto your curled fingers.

Pretend to catch something from the air with your right fingers and drop it into the left fist. When the left fingers are opened, there is the coin.

The Switchover

JIMMY BUFFALOE

Here is a clever method for magically producing a coin from an ordinary pocket handkerchief.

Effect: A handkerchief is shown on both sides and the performer's hands are obviously empty. Taking the handkerchief by its center he shakes it gently and out drops a half dollar into the waiting hand below.

Method: Begin by reaching into your pocket with your left hand for your pocket handkerchief. While the hand is in the pocket get a half dollar into classic palm position, then bring out the handkerchief and hold it by one corner between the thumb and forefinger. Call attention to the emptiness of the handkerchief as you pull it through your right hand a few times, letting it be seen at the same time that the hand is empty. Grasp the opposite corner from the one held by the left hand between the right forefinger and thumb, and stretch it out to show its front side to the audience. To show the back of the handkerchief without letting go of the corners the arms must cross each other and this is where a transfer of the coin takes place.

As the right hand moves to the left it passes directly underneath the left which releases the coin and drops it onto the cupped right fingers, Fig. 1. The right hand continues without pause to the left, and the back of the handkerchief is then seen by the audience. At this point the arms have changed positions and the coin is concealed

Fig. 2

Fig. 1

in the right hand. This is a perfectly natural move which is necessary to show a handkerchief back and front, and is not suspected. After showing the back of the handkerchief the arms are uncrossed and brought back to their original positions as the front is shown again. Release the corner of the handkerchief held by the right hand. Left hand then throws the handkerchief over the right. Keep the right palm away from the audience (so the coin will not be seen) until it is completely covered with the cloth, then turn it palm up.

Reach over with your left hand and grasp the coin through the center of the handkerchief, being careful that the form of the coin is not seen through the cloth. Hold the handkerchief, tent fashion, a few inches above your upturned right hand and gently shake out the coin, Fig. 2. Catch it in your right hand and show it to the spectators.

Although the explanation of the moves takes a lot of space, the production actually requires about 10 seconds to perform. The dropping of the coin from the left hand into the right during the cross over of the arms is never suspected because all you seem to be doing is showing the two sides of the handkerchief.

The Appearing Half

JIMMY BUFFALOE

This effect employs The Switchover and produces the coin in an entirely different manner. Although the sleeve could be used to conceal the coin, The Switchover enables you to produce the coin with the sleeves rolled up.

Effect: The performer's hands are seen to be empty as he shows a handkerchief on both sides. He spreads the handkerchief over his palm up left hand, and then closes the hand into a fist, folding the cloth over with the fingers as they close. The outer corner is given to a spectator to hold. As the spectator holds the outer corner, the performer pulls on his end and a coin emerges from the fist in a mysterious fashion.

Method: Show the handkerchief empty by means of The Switchover and transfer the coin to the right hand where it is concealed in classic palm position. Release the

left corner of the handkerchief, show it empty, then spread the handkerchief over it with the right hand, making sure its center is over the palm. Spread the handkerchief over the left hand so a corner will be lying on the forearm. The right hand retains its grip on this corner as handkerchief is adjusted into position. Slowly close your left fingers over the handkerchief. Ask a spectator to hold the outer corner of the cloth, and to illustrate what you want done, release the inner corner with the right hand and take hold of the outer diagonally opposite corner, and hand it to the spectator. As the right hand moves forward to pick up the outer corner it passes

Fig. 1

directly over the left fist. The instant the right hand is over the left fist it releases the half dollar which falls into the left hand, the fingers opening slightly to receive it, Fig. 1. Without hesitating the right hand continues to the front corner of the handkerchief as you pick it up and offer it to the spectator.

The movement of the left fingers opening slightly is not noticed since the eyes are following the right hand.

After the coin has been deposited in the left fist, and the assistant is holding the outer corner of the handkerchief, the right hand again takes hold of the corner lying on the left forearm. Gently pull inward on this corner, and as you do so the coin will slowly emerge from the left fist. The effect is both startling and pretty.

Coin Production from Two Cards

If my memory serves me correctly, this little gem appeared in *The Sphinx* some years back. I have never met anyone who has seen it. It is so good I would like to record it here for the benefit of all. It is a nice thing to know when you have to produce one coin, either at the beginning of a trick or at the climax, after a duplicate coin has been vanished.

Effect: The prestidigitator shows two playing cards several times, front and back, in the fairest possible manner. Placing the two cards together he tips them downward and a coin slips from between them.

Method: Begin with a half dollar classic palmed in the right hand, and a deck of cards face down in dealing position in the left hand. With the aid of the right hand,

Fig. 2

deal two cards face up onto the table, and lay the deck aside.

As you pick up the two cards with the left hand allow the palmed coin in the right to drop onto the curled fingers. Transfer the two cards to the right hand, which turns palm up and takes them by their inner ends between the thumb (on top) and fingers (below) in such a manner the coin will be covered by the cards, Fig. 1.

With the left hand, remove the top card from the right, holding it by one end. Show the faces of both cards as you hold them about waist high. Now raise them to chest level and show their backs. As you do this slide the coin inward toward the palm (almost off the card) and display the two cards held by their extreme ends, Fig. 2.

Now lower the cards to waist level and show their faces again. As you lower the cards slide the coin back underneath the right hand card so it will be completely hidden. Without hesitating a moment, place the right hand card diagonally across the top of the left in such a manner the half dollar will slide underneath the left hand card, where it is held by the tip of

Fig. 1

Fig. 3

Fig. 5

the left second finger, Fig. 3. With the right hand (which has never released its grip on its card), slide the top card forward (paint brush fashion) off the lower card, Fig. 4, show its back, then turn it face up again and replace it in its crossed position above the left hand card, Fig. 3. Retain

Fig. 4

the coin in position with the tip of the right second finger while the left hand removes its card (duplicating the above action as much as possible, Fig. 5), shows its back, and returns it underneath the right hand card *AND* coin. The coin is now between

the two cards. And if you have blended the moves together perfectly, no one—not even a magician—will know of its presence.

The next step is to produce the coin. This you do by holding the crossed cards between the fingers and thumb of the right hand (with pressure on the coin to hold it in place between the two cards), then tipping them downward allowing the coin to come into view from between the two cards, Fig. 6. Rest the edge of the lower card on the upturned left hand, which stops the coin before it is entirely out from between the two cards. This shows that the coin actually comes from between the cards.

Another way of using this is to show the two cards front and back as described,

Fig. 6

without producing the coin. The cards are merely placed on the table in the crossed position with the half dollar between the two. A second coin is vanished and the top card is blown away, exposing the supposedly vanished coin lying on the lower card.

A lengthy description has been necessary to give you these moves. The actual performance of the effect takes only a few seconds. All moves smoothly combine into a progressive sequence. The appearance of the coin is both baffling and pretty.

The Touch of Midas

CARDINI

Effect: The conjuror shows his left hand empty and closes it. A spectator touches his left wrist. When the hand is opened it contains a coin! The coin is removed. This procedure is continued until four or five coins are produced.

Method: At the outset four half dollars are classic palmed in the right hand. Call attention to your left hand as you show it with fingers wide apart. Snap the fingers of the right hand over the left as it closes. The snapping of the right fingers shows without saying so that the hand is empty.

Fig. 1

Laymen do not suspect that anything can be concealed in the hand when the fingers are snapped. This disarming move can be used many times when a coin is classic palmed.

While attention is on the closed left hand, drop the right to the side and release one of the palmed coins, allowing it to fall onto the cupped fingers. At first this may seem difficult, but the following move facilitates the action. Bend the third finger in and press it against the top coin in the palm, sliding it downward from the rest about a quarter of an inch, Fig. 1. Relax the muscles in the palm slightly and this coin will fall onto the cupped fingers as described above, Fig. 2.

Fig. 2

With the coin resting on the fingers, bring the right hand up and point to the left. Open left hand and show it empty. Quickly drop the coin from the right fingers into the left hand and close it. Immediately swing the right arm to the right and pretend to catch something from the air with that hand. The right fingers are closed and the three coins in the palm are hidden. The sudden action at the beginning of this maneuver is sufficient misdirection to cover the coin as it is caught in the left hand. Pretend to toss something toward the left hand, then extend it slightly, asking a nearby spectator to touch the wrist with his forefinger.

Illustrate by touching the left wrist with the right forefinger. Say, "I have discovered a magic way of making money. Watch!" Open the left hand showing a half dollar. During this brief action the right hand has dropped to the side and a second coin has been released from the palm and now rests on the curled fingers.

As the right forefinger and thumb remove the first coin from the left hand the second coin is dropped therein. The left fingers are partially closed which shields

Fig. 3

this action, Fig. 3. The left hand quickly closes on the second coin, as the right fingers flip the first one into the air. (See The Coin Flip, page 16.) The right hand catches it and slaps it down on the back of the closed left hand. Move the left hand toward your helper as you ask him to take the coin from its back. While he is thus occupied the right hand drops to the side again and the third coin is dropped from the palm onto the fingers as before.

Have the spectator touch the left wrist as before. Then open the hand showing the second coin. The right hand removes it

and secretly loads in the third one, as described previously. The left hand quickly closes over the third coin as the right fingers flip the second into the air. Right hand catches it and slaps it onto the back of the closed left hand. While the spectator removes this coin from the back of the left hand the right prepares the last coin for loading. The spectator again touches the left wrist and the hand is opened to disclose the third coin. The right hand removes it and loads coin number four into the left hand.

It is produced in the same manner as the first three were.

The entire series of actions should not require more than forty-five seconds, and should run something like this: Left hand shown empty and first coin loaded therein. Spectator touches left wrist. Left hand opens to show coin. Right hand removes it and loads second coin in the left as it closes. Right hand flips the coin into the air and then slaps it down on the back of the left hand. While spectator removes it and touches left wrist, right hand drops to the side and gets next coin ready for loading. This is continued until four coins are produced.

Except for the first coin there is no necessity for hurried or quick movements. Rather a rhythmic and synchronous blending of all moves should be practiced. Therein, alone, lies the success or failure of this effect.

The element of surprise in the appearance of each coin serves as sufficient misdirection, and acts as cover for the secret movements of the right hand.

The effect is worth the time necessary to master it.

Suggested Patter: Relate briefly the story of King Midas, and how everything he touched turned to gold. But don't make a lengthy harangue or give a lecture.

One to Four

CAL EMMETT

Effect: The performer removes a half dollar from his left trousers pocket and takes it in his right hand. Then making a tossing motion in the air he causes the coin to vanish. After showing the hand empty on both sides he reaches into the air and produces the half. He holds his left hand in a fist and places this coin between the middle joints of the third and fourth fingers. Reaching into the air again with his right hand he produces a second coin, then places it in a similar position between the middle joints of the left second and third fingers. This is continued until four coins are produced and displayed in the same fashion in his left hand. Each time he produces a coin with his right hand that hand is seen to be otherwise empty.

Method: Have four worn half dollars in the left trousers pocket. Reach in with the left hand, finger palm three of them, and bring the fourth out held visibly between the tips of the forefinger and thumb.

Turn your left side toward the spectators and take the coin in the right hand. Flip it into the air a couple of times in such a manner it will be obvious that you have only the one coin. Now, as you pretend to toss the coin into the air again, back palm it. Show the hand empty on both sides, then reach out and produce it again. (If the distance and angles permit, the Downs palm could be employed instead of the back palm.) After the coin is produced, display it vertically between the tips of the right first two fingers.

Turn to the left and place the coin between the middle joints of third and fourth fingers of the closed left hand (the thumb end being lower than the little finger end), which is held back up and about chest

Fig. 1

high. As this is done the left thumb slides one coin to the right from the finger palmed stack in the left hand, into the right finger palm. (See Figs. 1 and 2, which are front and rear views, respectively.) Keep the

Fig. 2

right fingers together to cover the movement made by the left thumb as it pushes a coin out of the thumb end of the fist into the right finger palm. Be sure that you make no movement with the left thumb until it is completely hidden behind the right hand. As you separate the two hands, point to the coin between the left fingers with the right forefinger.

Under cover of turning to the right again, drop the right hand to the side and back palm the coin in that hand. Show the hand empty, then reach out and seemingly produce the coin from the air. Display it as you did the first coin. Turn to the left and as you deposit this coin between the middle joints of the left second and third fingers, repeat the previously described moves to steal a third coin with the right hand.

Instead of back palming this third coin and producing it as you did the first two, vary the procedure by simply producing it without first showing the hand empty. Or, if you wish, you can reach down behind the right knee and extract it from there. Show this coin by flipping it into the air a time or two, letting it be seen at the same time that the hand is otherwise empty. Deposit it between the middle joints of the first and second fingers of the left hand but *do not* steal the fourth coin from the left hand. Retain it finger palmed for the time being.

While showing the right hand empty, release the last coin from the left finger palm, allowing it to lie flat on the two middle fingers near their tips. Turn to the left, close the left hand into a tighter fist and as you raise it to a position about shoulder high, maneuver the coin to a place

Fig. 3

outside the fist where it is held by an extreme edge against the heel of the hand by the tips of the two middle fingers. (Fig. 3 shows the hand from the rear.) Close the right hand into a fist but keep the forefinger extended. Bring it up, back outward, to the left hand and touch the edges of the three coins with the tip of the forefinger, counting, "One, two, three." Turn the left fist over, counterclockwise, which movement brings the coin to the front, but hid-

den by the right hand. As the left hand turns over, take the coin between the tips of the right second finger and thumb (after the fashion described in Coin to Key, page 78), then open the left hand and point to its palm, saying, "Nothing here." Turn the left hand back toward the spectators again, showing the three coins, adding, "Just three coins." Still retaining your grip on the three coins, close the hand into a fist and hold it as before. Under the guise of showing the left hand on both sides you have stolen the fourth coin with the right hand. Turn to the right and back palm

Fig. 4

the coin. Show the hand empty, then produce it from the air and deposit it in the left hand between the middle joint of the first finger and tip of the thumb, Fig. 4.

If you are not proficient with the back palm you need not show the right hand empty at all. And as a variation the coins could be produced from different parts of the body instead of from the air as described.

One to Six

JACK CHANIN

Effect: The magician removes a half dollar from his pocket and displays it in his left hand, and the hand is seen to be otherwise empty. He takes the coin with his right hand and produces a second coin from the air with his left. Now he has two coins —one in each hand. He places the right hand coin between his lips and transfers the coin in his left hand to his right. A third coin is immediately produced from the air with his left hand and he again displays a coin in each hand. Each time he produces a coin with his left hand, that hand is seen to be unmistakably empty, except for the one coin. As he produces the coins with his left hand he takes them with his right and places them between his lips until six coins are produced.

Method: All six coins are in the right trousers pocket at the beginning. When you are ready to present the mystery, reach into your pocket, classic palm five coins (Jack employs his own Chanin Single Coin Production Palm, but I have found the classic palm to be simpler and easier for most magicians) and bring out the sixth, visible between the fingers and thumb.

Take the coin in the left hand, and as you show it all around, allow the spectators to see that you have nothing else in the hand. Make no verbal comment on this fact—just show the hand and coin in such a manner that everyone will have no doubt that you are holding but one coin. While you are doing this, casually drop the right hand to the side, release one coin from the palm, and hold it on the cupped fingers as illustrated and described in The Touch of Midas, (page 90). Turn your body slightly to the left as you show the visible coin for the last time. Bring the right hand up to the left, then as you swing to the right, take the coin from the left hand between the tips of the right forefinger and thumb and drop the coin from the curled right fingers into the left hand, Fig. 1. Make sure the fingers of both hands are held together so the spectators cannot get a flash of the secret transfer.

Pretend to see something in the air to

Fig. 1

your left. Reach out suddenly with the left hand and produce the coin that was hidden in that hand at the tips of the forefinger and thumb. Face the spectators, hold the hands about chest high and palm inward, and show a coin at the tips of the fingers and thumb of each hand. Place the right hand coin between your lips, then while showing the coin in the left hand again, drop the right hand to the side, release another coin from the palm and catch it on the curled fingers. Bring the right hand up to the left hand and as you take the just-produced coin in the right, secretly drop the coin from the right curled fingers into the left hand exactly as you did before, Fig. 1.

After taking the visible coin in the right hand, reach out with the left hand and produce another coin from the air. Again show a coin in each hand. Place the right hand coin between your lips with the coin already there, and repeat the moves until you have produced all six coins. Drop the coins into a glass and continue with the next trick at hand.

After mastering the production of the six coins you might try this finish by way of variation: Instead of placing the last produced coin between your lips with the others, hold it a moment in the left hand, while you drop the five coins from your lips into the palm up right hand. Now place the coin from the left hand between your lips and hold the other five coins in a stack by their edges between the tips of the fingers and thumb of the palm up right hand. Execute The French Drop (page 37) or the Vanish for Several Coins (a), (page 45) as you pretend to take the five coins in the left hand. Keep your eyes on the closed left hand as you remove the coin from between your lips with the right hand. Fan the closed left hand with the visible coin in the right hand, then open the left and show it empty. The five coins have vanished.

To bring them back, do this: Remove the visible coin from the right hand with the left and show it. Then take the coin again in the right hand, and as you do so steal the five coins between the tips of the left second and third fingers as shown in Fig. 2.

Fig. 2

Swing to the right as you do this and curl the left fingers inward, hiding the five coins. Show the single coin in the right hand. Close the left hand into a fist and place this one coin in it. Unknown to the spectators, the left hand now contains all six coins. Pick up a glass with the right hand and dribble the coins from the left hand into it one at a time to mark the climax of the trick.

For another method of producing several coins, see The Modern Miser, (page 285).

Chapter VI

CUFFING

Dr. E. M. Roberts' Method · Louis Tannen's Method

Have you ever accidentally dropped a coin, had it accidentally land in your trousers cuff, and then speculated on the miracles you might create if you could do this every time?

To throw or toss a coin into the cuff with any degree of certainty is next to impossible. Unfailing accuracy is not easily attained. However, there is a simple, practical method of accomplishing this feat which can be mastered by anyone in a short time. Here are two methods.

Dr. E. M. Roberts' Method: Stand fairly close to your audience as you show them a half dollar. Turn slightly to your left and place the left foot forward so its heel is about even with, and about eight inches to the left of, the right toe. Pretend to place the coin in your left hand but retain it palmed in the right hand. The left hand is closed, pretending to hold the half dollar. With the right hand palm down and about waist high, reach out toward the nearest spectator in a gesturing manner as you caution him to "watch." Immediately drop the right arm down, pendulum fashion, and swing it to the left, tossing the coin into the left cuff in the action. Without hesitation bring the right hand up and make a few passes over the closed left hand. Finally open it to show the coin vanished.

The foregoing action is made easier with the thorough understanding of the following preparation. Be sure the trousers legs hang straight down. If there is the slightest

break in them there will be danger of the coin glancing off and falling to the floor. Sometime before attempting the feat glance down and check the trousers legs. If they are not hanging correctly seize an opportune moment and pull the trousers up at the waist.

The coin is not tossed from the right palm. Instead, it is dropped onto the cupped right fingers as the arm moves downward, and is thrown from there. Do not aim at the cuff itself, but toss the coin

Coin strikes trouser at "X"

Fig. 1

so that it will strike flatly against the loose part of the inside of the left trousers leg. This area is indicated in Fig. 1, and it lies between the front crease and the inside center seam, not higher than about 10 inches above the cuff. If the coin strikes anywhere in this area, the fabric will give so that there will be no rebound and the coin will slide smoothly down into the cuff.

The tossing of the coin into the cuff must be done exactly at the right moment. Timing is very important. Combine the pretended placing of the coin into the left hand with the gesture cautioning the spectators to watch the left hand. The right arm then swings down naturally, tossing the coin into the cuff. Without pause it is brought up to the left hand where it makes a few passes, or the fingers are snapped a couple of times.

To perform this method of cuffing without fear of detection the spectators must be standing fairly close to you. (Not over four or five feet away.) They can even be all around you and they will not see the coin go into the cuff if you "cuff" it properly. At such close range the human eye covers only a small area and this area is above your waist. When the coin leaves the hand it is below the waist and out of their line of vision, and therefore cannot be seen. For this reason this method of cuffing cannot be performed with assurance before a seated audience, or an audience at a distance.

The best coin to use for cuffing is a dark, dull-metaled coin—a copper coin such as the English penny is excellent. It does not reflect light as readily as a silver coin and is therefore less likely to be observed as it travels into the cuff.

Not only can this method of cuffing be used as a vanish; it may also be used for exchanging one coin for another. Here are two methods:

Have a half dollar up your right sleeve, keeping the elbow bent so it will not fall out. Call attention to an English penny which you toss from hand to hand. This shows without saying so that your hands are otherwise empty. Hold it in your left hand momentarily and as you make some remark about it, drop the right arm to the side and allow the silver coin to slip out into the cupped right fingers. Quickly press the coin into the right palm then reach over and take the copper coin from the left hand. Grasp it between the fingers and thumb, keeping the hand palm down so the other coin concealed in the palm cannot be seen. Raise the left hand and pretend to blow a few particles of dust from it. This serves as misdirection for the following action: Drop the right arm and toss the copper coin into the left cuff. Without pause, bring the right hand up and deposit the half dollar in the left, which quickly closes over it. Without calling attention to the fact, let it be seen that the right hand is empty. Pronounce the magic words, then open the left hand to show the transformation.

When working at a table there is practically no chance of detection even if the spectators are seated and at a distance. Here is the procedure:

Start with the silver coin already in your right palm. The copper coin is lying on the table in front of you, a few inches from the rear edge. With the right hand palm down, reach out and slide the coin off the table toward you. Just as the coin leaves the table it is tossed into the trouser cuff, its flight being hidden by the table. The right hand then continues on its swing upward to the left and places the silver coin in the left hand. After a bit of byplay open your left hand to show the change.

A variation to the above method: Start the effect with the copper coin on the table and the silver coin in finger palm position of the right hand. Pick up the copper coin and pretend to toss it into the left hand, but throw the silver coin instead. (See The Bobo Switch, page 10.) Then extend your right arm toward the spectators and caution them to "watch" as you did in the basic vanish method. Drop the right arm and toss the copper coin into the trouser cuff, then swing it up and make a pass or two over the closed left hand. Open your left hand to show that the copper coin has changed to silver.

The foregoing method is clean and offers wonderful possibilities for other effects.

Fig. 2

Louis Tannen's Method: In this version the coin is tossed into the right trousers cuff in a manner similar to a method you might employ to vanish a hook coin.

Stand with your left side toward the spectators and toss a coin into the air a couple of times with your right hand, each time watching its flight upward. As the hand reaches its lowest point prior to the third tossing movement it drops the coin into the right trousers cuff, Fig. 1. Immediately bring the right hand up and pretend to toss the invisible coin into the air. Watch its flight upward with amazement and the spectators will follow your gaze. The coin has vanished into the air.

The advantage of this method is that the left side is toward the spectators and the body hides the coin as it is tossed into the cuff.

After vanishing a coin by cuffing it you can either leave it there or openly reproduce it from the cuff at any time. No one will know how it got there.

Many combinations are possible by combining cuffing with a complete coin vanish from Chapter IV. For instance, a coin could be vanished by cuffing, then later reproduced after a similar coin has been vanished. You vanish the second coin completely, then after showing the hands positively empty, reach down and apparently produce the same coin from the cuff. If the first coin was a borrowed, marked half dollar, this becomes quite a baffler when the identical coin is reproduced.

Other effects should suggest themselves.

Chapter VII

THE ART OF SLEEVING

Before attempting sleeving in any form it is important that the student understand that this type of chicanery cannot be successfully performed while wearing just any kind of coat. To sleeve with absolute certainty the sleeves must be of the proper length and size. Of course, after you become proficient in the art of sleeving you will find that it can be done fairly well while wearing any coat. But to be sure of yourself it is advisable not to attempt sleeving unless you are wearing a coat with sleeves suited for the purpose. An old or ill-fitting coat is not good. Chances are you have outgrown it and, no doubt, the sleeves are too small and too short. It is not necessary that you have your coat tailored for the purpose, although some magicians do keep this in mind when they have their suits made. But any coat that fits you correctly (remember, I said correctly) has sleeves the proper length and size. The sleeves do not have to be extra long or extra large, merely the correct length and of average fullness at the wrist.

And remember, it is harder to sleeve while wearing a coat which has the sleeves pressed with a crease in them, than in one which has "rolled" sleeves. Pressing the sleeves with a crease tends to flatten them out, thus creating a smaller opening for an object to enter. Most of the better suits of today come with the coat sleeves "rolled." A "rolled" sleeve is the ideal type for sleeving.

There are certain types of sleeving that are difficult to perform with the shirt sleeves down, and it is difficult and risky to attempt sleeving while wearing a shirt with "French" cuffs. Wear a shirt with regular cuffs, and if you intend performing any effect utilizing the Dr. Roberts' Method it is absolutely necessary that the right shirt sleeve be turned back to above the elbow. This leaves plenty of room in the coat sleeve for free passage of a coin, which is necessary in performing his method of sleeving.

The majority of effects using sleeving can be performed with the shirt sleeves down, but make certain that the coin goes up the coat sleeve—not the shirt sleeve, for it may become entangled in the folds of the shirt and be more difficult to retrieve when that time comes. Try pulling the shirt sleeves up a little by grasping them at the top, inside of the coat at the armpit. This will make the cuff fit snugly around the forearm and permit cleaner passage for the coin.

A very convincing move to use immediately after a sleeving operation and the subsequent showing of both hands, involves the pulling up of the coat sleeve until it fits tightly around the forearm. Then the shirt sleeve can be unbuttoned and turned back, which permits the arms to be lowered and shaken without fear of the coin making a premature appearance. Do this without comment and the effect is convincing. The spectators cannot imagine that you would do anything so audacious as this if the coin had gone up the sleeve.

This is not recommended for use every time a coin is sleeved—just once in a while to allay any suspicion which may arise.

Methods

Probably the most widely used sleeving method is embodied in what might as well be termed

DELAYED ACTION SLEEVING

Apparently place a coin in your left hand, actually retaining it in the right. You can open the left hand and show it empty, but you cannot display the other hand unless you do a change over. Wouldn't it be cleaner to be completely rid of the coin, yet be able to produce it at will?

Sleeving is the answer. After the apparent placing of the coin in the left hand, hold it in the right. Then allow the coin to rest on the fingers near the tips, the hand, back up, being held in a loose fist, Fig. 1. The coin is only about an inch from the coat sleeve and a slight forward jerk will send

Fig. 1

it up the sleeve. This movement should be executed in connection with some natural gesture. You can drop the coin into the sleeve as you point or raise your arm to run your fingers through your hair, to take a cigarette from your lips, or to tap the person near you on the arm or chest, or to start a count of One, Two, Three, gesturing as you do so, and so on. In this way your action will appear natural and reasonable. With the coin safely up the sleeve, you can open the left hand and show it empty. When the attention turns to the right hand, you are in a position to show that hand also.

To retrieve the coin, simply lower the right arm and hold your hand in a cupped position. The coin will fall directly into it.

This method requires practice, but it is well worth the effort, as anyone who has seen Jarrow vanish a handful of salt or loose tobacco will attest.

IMPROVED METHOD

After you become thoroughly acquainted with this method of sleeving you will find that you can get a coin into the sleeve without any forward movement of the right arm whatsoever.

The right forearm is held in a horizontal position with the coin lying on the fingers near the tips as in Fig. 2. The fingers then bend inward and enter the coat sleeve opening as the arm is raised for some gesture as suggested above. The coin merely tumbles off the fingertips into the sleeve

Fig. 2

and there is absolutely no movement of any kind to give you away.

It is this "delayed" variety of sleeving most magicians have in mind when they think of sleeving. However, there are other types not so commonly associated with this phase of chicanery. One, which will be dealt with at length, because of its effectiveness, is called, for want of a better name,

THE "PUMPKIN SEED" VANISH

This very descriptive title is slightly ambiguous. Actually it refers to the method— not the article to be vanished.

The action is instantaneous and consists of holding a coin in one hand and "squirting" it up the sleeve under cover of taking it in the other hand.

The actual mechanics are these: Hold a coin by the edges, between the thumb and first finger of the right hand, and cover it with the left hand as if about to take it in that hand, Fig. 1. Squeeze the thumb and forefinger together and the coin will "squirt" from between the fingers and fly up the left coat sleeve, the entire action being covered by the left hand. Immediately close the left fingers around the right finger and thumb, then remove the right

hand slowly from the left with the finger and thumb empty and separated, letting it be seen that the right hand is empty. Snap the right fingers and open the left hand, showing the coin has vanished.

Reach over with the right hand and pluck a non-existent coin from a spectator's lapel, at the same time lowering the left arm to your side and catching the coin in the left hand as it drops out of that sleeve. Slap the invisible coin into the left hand and show the genuine coin.

This apparent plucking of the coin from the spectator's clothing is perfect misdirection for retrieving the coin. The movement of both hands must be synchronized, however.

One of the easiest items to sleeve in this manner is a coin. It is best to start with a small one, either a penny or a nickel, for the unmilled edge slips from between the fingers easily. After mastering these, try a quarter next and finally a half dollar.

The coin should be propelled up the

Fig. 1

sleeve with such speed and force, due to the "squirt" and a half-throw, that it will not stop until it reaches the elbow. This takes some practice to master. However, when the coin is up this far (you can usually feel it stop at the elbow), there is less danger of it falling out. You will soon learn to hold the arm that secretes the coin with the forearm parallel with the floor.

REVERSE "PUMPKIN SEED" VANISH

Ross Bertram

In the regular "Pumpkin Seed" Vanish as described above, the coin is "squirted" from the right hand into the left sleeve, while in this method the coin goes into the right sleeve.

With the right hand palm up, display a half dollar, holding it by its edges between

Fig. I

the second finger and thumb, Fig. 1. Turn the right hand over, palm down, and pretend to place the coin in the left hand which is held palm up, with the fingers in a cupr_d position, to receive it.

A_tually as the right hand turns over the second finger and thumb quickly press together, "squirting" the coin inward to the right and up the right sleeve, Fig. 2. This is done immediately after turning the right hand over. The right hand, without pausing, moves to the left and pretends to deposit the coin in the cupped left hand,

Fig. 2

which closes. Make crumbling motions with the left fingers, then open the hand to show the coin has vanished.

THE CATAPULT

A coin is resting on the left fingers and the right hand is about six inches away, back up. Both hands move toward each other rather rapidly and the flat surfaces meet with a jar, which sends the coin shooting up the right sleeve, Fig. 1. The left

Fig. I

hand must be tilted downward slightly in order to permit easy passage of the coin.

As soon as the right hand stops, resting on the left, it begins a circular rubbing motion, which ends with the disclosure that the coin has disappeared, the entire action appearing as if the right fingers rubbed the coin out of existence.

Variation—Show the coin lying on the palm up left hand. Bring the right hand over the coin, palm down, and place the four fingers, held close together, in front of and against the edge of the coin, hiding it from the spectators' view. As you pretend to remove the coin from the left hand, quickly close the right fingers, which action sends the coin into the right sleeve. Now move the right hand away as if it really held the coin, and conclude by opening the right hand a moment later to show the coin vanished.

Instead of the coin lying on the left hand as explained above, it can be lying on the table near the edge closest to you, then when the right hand pretends to remove it the coin is propelled up the right sleeve as described and the vanish concluded according to the trick at hand.

JUDAH METHOD

STEWART JUDAH

Standing full face to the audience, hold both hands open (palm up, with the tips of the fingers stretched out to the front), and about two inches apart. Show a coin in the right hand, and then toss it back and forth from one hand to the other a

Fig. 1

few times. When the coin arrives back in the right hand after a few tosses, place the right thumb on top of the coin and pretend to toss it back into the left hand. Actually the right thumb retains the coin as the left hand closes, Fig. 1. Immediately move the right hand forward with its back toward the spectators, passing it first over the knuckles of the left fist, then inward, underneath the fist to the wrist which is grasped with the right thumb and fingers, thumb on top and fingers underneath. Under

cover of this movement, which is done to illustrate to a spectator how you want him to hold your wrist, the coin is tossed into the left sleeve, Fig. 2.

Fig. 2

If this action is executed in a casual, natural manner the spectators will be unaware that anything unusual had happened.

Extend your closed fist toward a spectator with a request that he hold your wrist as you have just illustrated. Explain to the audience how difficult it would be for you to remove the coin from the left fist without being detected. Then slowly work the fingers together pretending to crumble the coin to nothingness, and finally open the hand to show the coin vanished.

A vanish of a coin performed under these conditions is quite intriguing to the spectators and they are at a loss to explain its disappearance.

A UNIQUE SLEEVING MOVE

ROSS BERTRAM

Stand facing the spectators as you show a half dollar held flat and parallel with

Fig. 1

the floor between the left forefinger and thumb, Fig. 1. Close the right, back up, hand into a loose fist (actually the first and second fingers are less curved than the other two) and hold it about six inches to the right of the left hand. Move the left hand toward the right and push the coin into the right fist so it will lie flat on the cupped third and fourth fingers near their tips, Fig. 2. As you remove the right thumb and

Fig. 2

forefinger from the left fist, allow the coin to tumble off the right fingers into the sleeve, similar to the improved method described in Delayed Action Sleeving. It will require a little practice to get the knack of this, but once acquired it can be done with assurance every time. The right hand immediately turns over and both hands are shown empty.

While the left hand is exhibiting the coin prior to its deposit in the right fist, drop the right arm to the side, which action allows the sleeve to hang all the way down

over the wrist. This slight preparation eliminates any awkward movement later.

The vanish requires only a few seconds, and it appears that you merely pushed a coin into the right fist then immediately showed both hands empty.

The vanish is quick, startling and pretty.

THE THROW

J. A. BOWLING

When the trick at hand requires several coins to be vanished one at a time, the following method by Jim Bowling of Houston, Texas serves the purpose admirably. It is especially effective when used in conjunction with Bob Kline's Copenetro (the effect where several coins appear visibly in a tumbler-covered whiskey glass).

In the right trousers pocket is one coin. Yes, only one. That is all that is needed. It is this one coin which is vanished over and over, the number of times depending on the trick you are performing. It can be used in many other effects, but let's suppose you wish to perform the above named trick. Hold the apparatus in your left hand. Reach into your right trousers pocket and bring out the coin. Display it lying on the two middle fingers. Bring the right arm up and make a throwing motion toward Copenetro. As the arm is brought up the hand closes into a loose fist and the coin slides off the fingers into the sleeve. The action goes like this: After showing the coin in the right hand turn that hand counterclockwise as you close it into a loose fist. At the same time raise the arm for the throwing motion. Just as the arm is brought up, the wrist bends inward a bit and the tips of the curled fingers enter the sleeve opening, Fig. 1. The coin automatically slides from the fingers into the sleeve. Admittedly this is a bold procedure, but a logical one. As you go through the throwing motion

Fig. 1

with the right arm another coin appears visibly in Copenetro.

Drop the right hand to the side, retrieving the coin from the sleeve, and reach into the right trousers pocket for another coin. Bring the same one out and vanish it all over again in the same manner. Continue ad infinitum.

A few minute's practice before a mirror will convince you how natural the moves are. The sleeving action must take place as the arm is brought up for the throw, not after it has been raised. Do not hesitate as you sleeve the coin. Merely raise your arm, allow the coin to fall into the sleeve, and throw. Performed at a rather brisk pace the move is indetectable.

KORT METHOD

Milton Kort

Turn the right side toward the spectators and show the coin pinched flat between the tips of the right forefinger and thumb. Hold the left hand about shoulder high with its palm toward the spectators. Place the coin in the center of the left palm, Fig. 1, and slowly close the fingers over it. It is now that the invisible removal of the coin should be effected; and you must be careful not to close the left fingers so tightly as to interfere with this withdrawal.

As you turn the right hand toward the body (counterclockwise) nip the lower edge of the coin between the tips of the second and third fingers and bend them inward, withdrawing the coin from the left hand. The coin is concealed from the spectators by the back of the right hand and the

Fig. 1

action of that hand turning over. At this moment the end of the right forefinger should still be within the left fist. (Fig. 2 shows a rear view of the hands in this position.)

Fig. 2

If the movement of the right hand is well executed, in the manner just described, it will be impossible for the spectators to see the coin at any moment during its withdrawal.

With the hands in this position extend the two middle fingers of the right hand enough to deposit the coin in the left

Fig. 3

sleeve, Fig. 3. Very little movement of these two fingers will be required to do this, as a trial will show. The movement is indetectable because it is perfectly hidden by the back of the right hand. Slowly withdraw the right forefinger from the left hand, which then proceeds to reduce the coin to nothingness in the usual manner.

KIRK STILES METHOD

This method accomplishes the same thing as the preceding one, only in a slightly different manner.

Stand with your right side to the spectators and show a coin held pinched flat by its outward edge between the tips of the right forefinger and thumb. The open left hand should be held about chest high waiting to receive the coin. As you transport the coin toward the left hand, place the tip of the little finger against the under

Fig. 1

surface of the coin, Fig. 1, and retain it balanced there while the thumb and forefinger let go of it. As the right hand approaches the left, the coin becomes hidden behind the fingers, therefore the movement of the little finger cannot be seen. The little finger, with the coin balanced on its tip, bends inward toward the palm while the forefinger and thumb pretend to deposit the coin in the left hand. As the left fingers close on the right forefinger and thumb, the right little finger drops its load into the right sleeve, Fig. 2, the entire action being covered by the back of the right hand and

Fig. 2

the movement of making the pretended deposit in the left hand. The moment the left fingers close over the tips of the right forefinger and thumb the two hands are raised slightly, which causes the hidden coin to tumble off the right little finger into the left sleeve. Practically no movement on the part of the right little finger is necessary to cause the coin to leave it and fall into the left sleeve. Actually the little finger practically enters the left sleeve to drop its load.

Slowly withdraw the right forefinger and thumb from the left fist and show the right hand empty. Make crumbling motions with the left fingers, then open the hand and show it empty also.

A METHOD OF SLEEVING ONE OF SEVERAL COINS

Milton Kort

The following method of sleeving one coin from a handful should find many uses. Two effects using this method will be described in the section, Tricks Using Sleeving.

For the sake of clarity the method will be described using four coins. However, any small number of coins either mixed or all one size may be used.

Place a stack of four half dollars on the right palm at a position just inward from the base of the first and second fingers, Fig. 1.

With a slight movement of the hand allow the coins to fall from their stacked position and lay in an overlapping row, the original topmost coin near the heel of the hand, at the left side of the palm, Fig. 2.

Close your fingers over the coins and you will find that the innermost coin will be only partially covered by the third and fourth fingers, Fig. 3. The spectators must not be aware of this fact. As you close your hand, turn it over.

Now, by relaxing pressure on the innermost coin with the third and fourth fingers and quickly moving the hand forward slightly, this one coin will shoot up the sleeve. The movement is made as you extend your hand and offer the coins to a person near you to hold. Or, the coin may be sleeved during the brief interval while attention is directed to an object in the

Fig. 1

Fig. 2

Fig. 3

left hand. The actions of closing the hand, turning it over, and sleeving the coin are all combined into one continuous movement. Actually it is the Delayed Action Sleeving method applied while holding several coins. If you have mastered the Delayed Action Sleeving method you should have no trouble with this.

DR. E. M. ROBERTS' METHOD

Here is a method of sleeving that is so good, so practical and flexible I feel that it will become one of the most popular methods. It is a feat of pure skill which, on the face of it, seems absolutely impossible. Properly used it will puzzle the initiated as completely as the veriest layman.

The method of sleeving about to be described is a radical departure from the general conception of this neglected phase of sleight of hand. There are no extraneous moves to telegraph your actions, such as the obvious finger snapping a coin up the sleeve from an outstretched hand and arm. Nor is there a tell-tale movement of the arm when the coin is sleeved. The act of sleeving is made under perfectly natural movements and when properly done it is

Fig. 1

impossible to detect. To date, this is the finest method extant.

It is advisable to first master the mechanics of the sleeving act itself, which will be described in detail, then proceed to the methods of concealing the act by timing and misdirection. The related factors, such as the position of the hand, timing, gestures, etc., are very important and are to be considered as the synchronizing element whereby all efforts are blended into one indetectable move.

Fig. 2

Now for the mechanics of the sleeving act itself. The right hand will be used in the illustrations.

1. Place the coin on the inside of the tip of the third finger as in Fig. 1.

2. Lower the thumb and place it on top of the coin as in Fig. 2.

3. Bring the second finger down and place it against the forward edge of the coin as in Fig. 3.

Fig. 3

4. Now remove the coin leaving the fingers in exactly the same position as though the coin was still there, Fig. 4.

5. Press the thumb against the second finger and push upward toward the first finger, causing the thumb to slide off and above the second finger with a snap-like

Fig. 4

action. (This should not be confused with the common method of audibly snapping a coin up the sleeve.) This method is entirely noiseless, because the coin is not snapped but given a tremendous push with the second finger. Fig. 5 shows the fingers after the snap action. It will be noted that the second finger moves only a fraction of an inch but with terrific force. It is this force that propels the coin up the sleeve.

6. Now place the coin back in the fingers

Fig. 5

as shown in Fig. 3 and repeat the above action. You will discover that the coin can be propelled many feet through the air. The third finger acts as a rest for the coin and is the guiding influence for controlled direction on the flight of the coin up the sleeve. The second finger pushes—the thumb generates the force. If any other effort is brought into play, all is lost. Use only the two fingers and thumb as designated. Under no circumstances should there be any wrist movement, or throwing or tossing motion to get the coin into the sleeve. Only the push of the second finger is used to shoot the coin up the sleeve.

The coin is not sleeved while the arm is in a horizontal position as in most common methods, but while the arm hangs naturally at the side.

Now let's consider the position of the hand as it hangs at the side. The hand is perfectly relaxed and must be held so that the wrist does not bend either inward or outward, but is along the direct axis of the arm.

Before attempting this method of sleeving take off your coat and roll back the right sleeve as far as it will go. It must be turned back to a position well above the elbow, otherwise the coin will become entangled in its folds and be difficult to extricate. Put your coat on again and you are ready to begin.

Hold the coin as described above and allow your arm to hang loosely at your side. Fig. 6 shows the position of the hand and arm at the side as seen from the rear.

With the arm in this position propel the coin up the sleeve but make no attempt to keep it there. You will find that the coin flies up the sleeve with such force it goes way above the elbow, and it is not propelled with sufficient and proper force unless it does go above the elbow. After you have mastered the action completely you will be able to shoot it as far as the sleeve of the coat will allow. As it falls from the sleeve catch it on the curled fingers and repeat the action again and again until you are thoroughly familiar with it.

At first you may experience difficulty in hitting the opening of the sleeve with the coin, but with a little experimenting—turn-

Fig. 6

ing the wrist slightly right and left—you will find the correct position to insure the coin going into the sleeve every time.

Make no attempt to mask the action at this point. The masking is accomplished by the aid of timing and will be explained later.

Watch your actions as you stand before a mirror. Practice sleeving the coin until there is no noticeable give away move evident. It will take an hour or so for several days to become thoroughly familiar with the action before you can do it naturally and casually. Practice the mechanics over and over until they become second nature. Not until you feel that you have complete mastery over the move should you attempt to proceed further.

Timing: Timing in magic has been defined as the proper instant to execute a sleight, and in the matter of sleeving it is most important. Once the mechanics have been mastered you are ready to learn how to employ the timing to mask the act itself.

Place the coin in proper position for sleeving. Now synchronize the sleeving move with the action of raising your arm. Actually the coin is sleeved while the hand hangs at your side, not while the arm is being raised. Then before it can fall out, the hand is raised so the forearm is parallel with the floor. There is no need to raise it any higher, as the coin cannot fall out with the arm in this position. After a momentary pause any gesture may be used to show the hand empty. Almost any ruse will suffice as misdirection if cleverly used. You can raise your hand to take a cigarette from your mouth, to point, to rub the hands together, to begin a count of One, Two, Three, etc.

One important advantage this method of sleeving has over other methods is this: Anytime you wish, you may shoot the coin up your sleeve as you raise your arm for any reason. But you need not hold your arm in this horizontal position as in former methods. You can drop your arm to your side at any time and regain possession of the coin. This has never been possible before. In former methods the performer had to hold his arm horizontally at all times, otherwise the coin would fall out. This is particularly annoying when one accidentally drops a coin. The performer cannot pick it up with the hand that has the coin concealed in that sleeve because that coin would fall to the floor also. The performer could never lower his hand below his elbow for any reason. He could not remove a coin from the floor or the table unless he did it with the other hand. When the arm is held in a horizontal position

for any length of time it becomes suspicious looking, and consequently such a position should be avoided. This method eliminates such problems, because much more freedom of action is possible. A coin on the table or floor can be picked up with the same hand that has the coin in its sleeve! Merely let the coin fall onto the cupped fingers and immediately palm it. Then reach down and pick up the coin.

This method is especially useful when working standing at a table. You can use one hand just as freely as the other. Anytime you wish to show the hands empty merely sleeve the coin again as you raise your arm, then allow it to fall into your hand when you wish.

A subtle use of this handling is as follows: Suppose you want to do a switch or color change. Have an English penny and a half dollar in the right trouser pocket. Reach in with the right hand and palm the English penny. (You can tell the difference by the unmilled edge of the copper coin.) Bring out the half dollar and toss it onto the table. Immediately drop the right arm to the side and sleeve the English penny. Bring your hands up and rub them together. Do this without comment, letting the hands be seen empty. This natural gesture is used by a great many close-up workers to call attention to the hands without verbal comment. Drop the right arm to the side and gain possession of the English penny. Hold it finger palmed as you reach for the half dollar. Pick it up with the thumb and fingers and pretend to toss it into the left hand, but throw the English penny instead. (See The Bobo Switch, page 10.) Close the left hand over the copper coin then bring the hand up and blow gently on it. Simultaneously with this action drop the right arm to the side and sleeve the half dollar. Bring the right arm up and open the hand in front of you.

Open the left hand to show the transformation and toss coin into the right hand. Toss coin back and forth a few times letting it be seen that the hands are otherwise empty. Adroitly executed, there is no prettier coin switch than this.

Not only can the method be used to vanish a coin; it can also be used at any time as a clean-up move. If an effect requires one coin hidden in the hand at the beginning of a certain trick it would be best to sleeve the coin so the hands could be shown unmistakably empty. A coin can be sleeved from the hand that has a coin in its palm just as easy as without the hidden coin. At the finish of a trick if there is a coin that must be palmed or hidden in the hand in some manner it would, in most cases, be best to sleeve the extra coin, thus bringing the effect to a clean finish.

A careful study of the various methods described is recommended to all lovers of close-up magic. The time devoted to this and the mastery of the different sleeving moves will pay off in big dividends of mystery.

Loading

No tricks are suggested in the following methods of loading a coin into a sleeve. The methods are suggested as a means of beginning or ending a given effect cleanly, and are invaluable in the performance of many effects described in other parts of this book. Other uses should suggest themselves.

Beginning a trick with the hands unmistakably empty oftimes adds tremendously to the effect about to be presented. If the trick at hand requires an extra coin for its execution, this coin might as well be hidden in one of the sleeves, then secretly obtained at the proper time.

1. A Simple Method of Loading a coin into either sleeve is as follows: Have the extra coin in either upper vest pocket or held outside the pocket by means of a pencil or fountain pen clip. By reaching under the coat to pull up the shirt sleeves, or to obtain an article from the pocket, the coin can be secured and dropped into the inside opening of the coat sleeve. Just as the sleeve is pulled, the arm should be crooked and the coin dropped.

2. A Method of Sleeving One of Several Coins, previously described, can be used as a means of secretly loading a coin into the sleeve. Suppose you intend performing a trick with several coins and for the sake of explanation let's say the trick requires five coins, yet you want the spectators to be aware of only four. Proceed as follows: Reach into your right trousers pocket for the five coins. Bring them out and hold them in the outstretched right hand. Do not call attention to the number, but as you hold them manage to get one near the heel of the hand, which is proper position for this method of sleeving. Ask a spectator near you to hold out his hand. As he complies with your request close the hand and turn it over. Then as you extend your arm to drop the coins into his hand, sleeve one coin. Casually show both hands empty and have him count the coins into your right hand. Toss the coins into your left hand. Show the coins to the spectators on the left and while attention is thus momentarily diverted, drop the right arm to the side and gain possession of the coin from the right sleeve.

You have shown without a doubt that you have only four coins, yet in this action you have secretly obtained the extra coin necessary for the performance of the trick in a clean, indetectable manner.

3. The Dr. Roberts' Method of Sleeving can be put to good use to sleeve one of several coins. The following procedure has proven practical: Reach into the right trousers pocket for the coins, getting one into classic palm position. Bring them out and immediately drop all but the palmed coin into the left hand. As you call attention to the coins, drop the right hand to the side and sleeve the coin in that hand using the Dr. Roberts' Method. Immediately bring the right hand up alongside the left and count the coins into it from the left hand.

The hands have been shown and the coins counted. Everything seems fair and above board. The extra coin can now be easily obtained any time you wish.

4. The Delayed Action Vanish offers a variation to the one just described. To load a coin secretly in the sleeve proceed as follows: Reach into the right trousers pocket for the coins, getting one into classic palm position. Bring them out and drop all but the palmed coin into the left hand. As you gesture for a spectator to step closer to assist in the effect or count the coins, sleeve the coin.

Switching

An excellent method for switching one coin for another by sleeving has already been described, using the Dr. Roberts' System. To this and the ones to be detailed later, I would like to add the following:

Suppose you wish to exchange a half dollar for an English penny or a similar sized coin. Have the copper coin finger palmed in the right hand and a half dollar lying on the table. Show a handkerchief on both sides then throw it over the right hand. Pick up the half dollar with the left hand and carry it underneath the handkerchief. Under cover of the handkerchief drop the silver coin into your right sleeve while the left fingers push up the copper coin. Bring the left hand from underneath the handkerchief and grasp the copper coin through the cloth, from above, with that hand. The change can be shown immediately or later, depending on the effect you wish to produce. If you wish to affect an immediate transformation merely turn the left hand over to bring the copper coin into view. Both hands and the handkerchief are then shown empty. As the right hand drops to the side to return the handkerchief to the hip pocket the coin is caught in that hand as it falls from the sleeve and placed in the pocket with the handkerchief.

If the trick being performed requires a delayed transformation, grasp the copper coin through the cloth with the left hand and show the right hand empty. Wad up the handkerchief and lay it aside. When the proper time comes, unfold the cloth to show the English penny.

Sleeving can be used as a means for exchanging a borrowed coin for one of your own. To make such a switch proceed as follows: Sometime before you intend asking for the loan of a coin get the duplicate into right finger palm position. You can do this by casually placing your right hand in the right trousers pocket at a time when the action would receive no attention. However, this is a minor problem. Ask for the loan of a coin and receive it with the right hand between the first two fingers and thumb. Execute The Bobo Switch, (page 10) as you pretend to toss the borrowed money into the left hand. As you fix your attention on the duplicate coin in the left hand, sleeve the other in the right sleeve using either the Delayed Action or Dr. Roberts' Method. Then proceed with the trick at hand.

The Sleeve Pocket

A practical means for keeping a coin readily available for any length of time is the sleeve pocket. This is simply a small

Fig. 1

Pocket open at this end— stitched on other sides

pocket sewed inside the lower part of the sleeve. It should be stitched on three sides, the one nearest the elbow being the "mouth," Fig. 1.

A coin (or other small object) placed therein cannot fall out while the hand is being used normally. But, if the arm is raised, say, to scratch your head, the coin will emerge into the sleeve proper. When the arm is dropped, it will fall into your hand.

Tricks Using Sleeving

Sleeving is no panacea, but when judiciously used it offers a powerful means of increasing the effect of many tricks. As a rule it is not wise to use sleeving in your opening feat. The sleeves are more likely to be suspected then. Use it later when everyone is satisfied that the sleeves are playing no part in your mysteries. And don't overdo it. Include only one or two such effects in an entire routine.

PENETRATION

Effect: The performer is seated on one side of a table, with a spectator either to his right or at the opposite side. He shows a coin and taps it on the table. The spectator places his hand on top of the performer's and presses downward. This apparently forces the coin through the table, for the hand is shown empty and the coin

is produced from beneath the table with the other hand.

Method: Sit at a table with the left forearm resting on the edge. Show a small coin and hold it flat between the right forefinger and thumb, Fig. 1. Extend the other fingers and the coin will be hidden from the spectator as you tap it on the table.

Fig. 1

Show it again and tap it once more. Then ask the spectator to place his hand on top of yours. Regardless of how he does this, jerk your hand from beneath his and say, "No, not that way. Turn your hand the other way." Move your hand inward in this gesture and toss the coin into the left sleeve, Fig. 2. A little experimenting will help you decide on the correct position to take at the table for accomplishing this move. The right hand moves inward only a

Fig. 2

few inches, tosses the coin in the left sleeve and returns to its original position on the table. It is held exactly as if it still held the coin. (A clever ruse, suggested by Frank Garcia, can be used here. Immediately remove your left arm from the table and drop it to the side, gaining possession of the coin. Carry it underneath the table to the exact spot occupied by the right hand above the table. Pretend to tap the non-existent coin on the table with the right hand while the left hand does the actual tapping underneath. Properly synchronized the illusion is perfect. Apparently the right hand still holds the coin!) Have the spectator place his hand on top of your hand again and press downward. Just as your hand is pressed flat, snap the coin against the underside of the table with the left hand. Have spectator lift his hand from yours, then show yours empty. Produce the coin from beneath the table.

If a borrowed, marked coin is used the effect will be much greater.

MIGRATION

Effect: The performer places a borrowed, marked half dollar in his left hand. Showing his right hand unmistakably empty he closes it into a fist. Two spectators hold his wrists to prevent the use of the sleeves. Despite these precautions the coin is caused to travel from the left hand to the right. Only one coin is used.

Method: Here again the sleeves play a vital part in the mystery. Borrow a half dollar and have it marked for future identification. Receive it in your right hand. Pretend to place it in the left but retain it palmed in the right. Ask a spectator near you to step forward and assist in the effect. When you single out a particular person all eyes will be upon him, and it is during this momentary diversion that you sleeve the coin in the right sleeve. As the spectator comes forward have him stand on your left and hold your left wrist. The reason for this, you explain to the spectators, is that so many people accuse you of using your sleeves and that you would like to eliminate this possibility from their minds. During this explanation let it be clearly seen by all that the right hand is empty. Say nothing about the emptiness of the hand, just use it in gesturing in such a way that there will be no doubt as to its innocence. Ask a second spectator to step up, and as you point to the spot where you want him to stand, allow the coin to fall from the right sleeve and catch it on the curled fingers. Then extend your right arm and have him to hold your wrist in the same manner as the other spectator.

The feat is accomplished as far as the sleight of hand goes. All that remains is to announce that you intend causing the borrowed coin to fly from the left hand to the right hand with such tremendous speed it will be impossible to follow. Call attention to the seemingly impossible conditions under which you have subjected yourself. Caution each man to hold tightly onto your wrists, then go through the necessary hocus pocus as you pretend to make the coin pass. Slowly open your left hand and show it empty. Allow a moment for the spectators to speculate as to whether the coin will be in the right hand or not. Then open it as dramatically as possible to show the coin in that hand.

Dismiss your helpers and return the coin. Have it identified by the owner as being the same coin originally loaned you.

Second method: The effect of this version is identical with the previous one except a duplicate coin is used.

Commence the trick with one half dollar already up the right sleeve. Show a second half dollar and toss it from hand to hand. Ask a spectator to step forward and stand at your left. While the coin is in the right hand place the thumb on top of it and pretend to toss it back into the left hand. Close the left hand, and as you illustrate how you want your helper to hold your wrist, toss the coin into the left sleeve. (For a full description of this sleight see the Judah Method, page 103.) Show the right hand empty. Then ask a second spectator to step up, and as you direct him where to stand allow the coin to fall from the right sleeve and catch it in the right hand. Keep the coin in classic palm and hold hand palm down. Extend your arm for him to hold your wrist. Just before he takes hold, close your right hand into a fist.

Finish as in the preceding effect.

TRANSPOSITION

DR. E. M. ROBERTS

The following is just about the cleanest method of causing two coins to change places that I have yet run across. The handling is so fair and above board that the ultimate effect is unfathomable.

Effect: The wizard spreads a colored handkerchief on the table and places a copper coin on its center. About a foot away to the right he spreads a white handkerchief and places a silver coin on its center. He then shows both hands empty and begins the experiment. The copper coin is wrapped in the dark handkerchief and given to a spectator to hold. The silver coin is wrapped in the white handkerchief and given to a second spectator to hold. At command the coins are caused to change places. The spectators unwrap their respective coins themselves to disclose the transposition.

All moves are clean, fair and natural. And no trick coins are used.

Requirements: Two pocket handkerchiefs, one white and one colored. Two half dollars and an English penny.

Working: Despite the apparent impossibility of the sleeves playing a part in this feat, they are responsible for much of the trickery. The Dr. Roberts' Method of Sleeving is the first means used to accomplish the mystery. The duplicate half dollar is the second aid to deception.

Have the three coins in the right trousers pocket and the handkerchiefs lying on the table. Begin the trick by unfolding the colored handkerchief and spreading it on the table in front of you. Show the white handkerchief and spread it on the table a little to the right of the other one. Reach into the right trousers pocket and palm one of the half dollars. (You will be able to detect a half dollar by its milled edge.) Bring the other two coins out, holding them at the fingertips of the palm down hand. Take the copper coin with the left hand and hold it in the same manner as you place the two coins on the center of their respective handkerchiefs. (The copper coin goes on the colored handkerchief while the silver coin is placed on the white.)

As you do this, say, "Two handkerchiefs and two coins. On the center of the colored one I'll place this colored coin, while on the center of the white handkerchief I'll place this white coin. The reason for this is so that it will be an easy matter for you to keep track of the two coins. You can associate the copper coin with the colored handkerchief and the silver coin with the white handkerchief." While saying this, casually turn the two coins over, showing their reverse sides. Turn the copper coin over with the left hand and the silver coin over with the right hand. You still have the extra half dollar palmed in the right hand.

The action of turning over the two coins proves without comment that they are ordinary, and at the same time gives the hands something to do.

Take a step backward so all may see the position of the coins and the handkerchiefs. As you step away from the table get the palmed half dollar in the Dr. Roberts sleeving position and sleeve the coin. Immediately raise the hands and rub them together in a warming up action. Then gesture with the left hand toward the copper coin saying, "Remember the position of the two coins. The copper coin is on the colored handkerchief." Gesture with the right hand as you say, "And the silver coin is on the white handkerchief." This action demonstrates the fairness of the situation, implanting the position of the two coins in the minds of the spectators before you begin, and at the same time shows that both hands are empty.

As you step back to the table, drop the right hand and catch the coin on the cupped fingers as it falls from the sleeve, then classic palm it. Reach over and pick up the English penny between the fingers and thumb of the right hand. Say, "Here's the copper coin." Pick up the handkerchief by its left border with the left hand. At the same time drop the right hand and sleeve the copper coin. As you raise your arm to prevent the coin from falling out of the sleeve swing the left hand over to the right and throw the handkerchief over the right hand. The sleeving action must be synchronized with the action of the left hand picking up the handkerchief. Without hesitation the left hand moves to the right, and as the right hand comes up the handkerchief is thrown over it. Just as the handkerchief covers the right hand, that hand quickly pushes up the silver coin so its form is seen by the spectators. This is the only crucial move in the trick so practice it until you can do it naturally and without hesitation or haste. Blend the movements of the

two hands together in one smooth continuous action. Done as described, it appears that you merely picked up the copper coin with the right hand and threw the handkerchief over it with the left.

Allow the form of the coin to show through the handkerchief a moment, then grasp coin through the cloth, from above, with the left forefinger and thumb. Remove the right hand from underneath the handkerchief with its palm toward the spectators, fingers wide apart. Make no comment as you do this. The spectators see both hands empty at the same time and assume the form they see in the handkerchief to be that of the copper coin. (Actually it is the silver coin. The copper coin is in the right sleeve.) Daintily, and with the aid of the fingers of both hands, fold the coin over a few times, covering it with several folds of cloth. This is done as a precaution against a spectator discovering the fact that an exchange has been made. Finally hand the bundle to a spectator on your left to hold.

Ask him if he can feel the coin. Caution him to hold it tightly. If you have performed the exchange smoothly, no one will suspect that it is a silver coin and not a copper coin which is wrapped in the colored handkerchief.

As you step back to the table, drop the right hand and retrieve the copper coin from the right sleeve, immediately classic palming it. "And here," you say, "is the silver coin." Pick it up with the right hand. At the same time the left hand removes the white handkerchief from the table. The same moves are used for this switch as were used for the first one. Drop the right arm, sleeve the coin, and as you bring up the hand throw the handkerchief over it. By the time the hand is completely covered the copper coin should be at the fingertips. It is taken to be the silver coin by the spectators. Grasp it through the fabric from above with the left hand and remove the right from beneath the handkerchief and show it empty. Fold this coin into the handkerchief slowly and neatly, just as you did the previous one. Hold the bundle in the left hand. As you reach across the body to hand it to a spectator on the right to hold, drop the right arm, retrieve the silver coin from the sleeve and drop it in the right coat pocket. The action is completely hidden by the body.

The spectators think the copper coin is wrapped in the colored handkerchief and the silver coin in the white. Actually the opposite is true. All moves have been so clean and fair that nothing unusual is suspected.

The trick is now over as far as you are concerned. Recapitulate what has been done. Caution each spectator to hold his coin tightly and explain that you intend causing the coins to change places. In your best magical manner command the two coins to change places. Clap your hands together, wave the magic wand, snap your fingers, or pronounce some gibberish. At any rate, announce that the change has taken place. Have both parties remove the coins from the handkerchiefs to verify this statement.

From the spectators' viewpoint you have caused the transposition of the two coins under impossible conditions. They will have no solution to the mystery.

DEVALUATION

Effect: The performer shows his hands empty except for a half dollar. The left hand is turned palm down and the half placed on its back. Then he passes his right hand over the coin and it instantly changes to a quarter. The hands are shown unmistakably empty except for the quarter.

As with many effects in this book, this is not new. However, it is not generally known. It was shown to me by Harold Agnew of Oakland, California. He credits it to Tenkai. Regardless of who it belongs to it is a beautiful effect that, when performed correctly, looks like genuine magic.

Method: At the start of the experiment have the quarter already up the right sleeve. Keep the arm crooked so the coin won't fall out as you show a half dollar in the right hand. Hold the half at the fingertips and turn the hand around so the spectators can see that there is nothing but the half in the hand. Slowly show the left hand empty in like manner, then hold it palm downward, about chest high, with the fingers pointing forward. Flip the half dollar into the air with the right hand and place it on the back of the left. Show the right hand empty once more.

Turn your attention to the half dollar on the back of the left hand as you say, "Watch the half dollar." With the pronouncing of these words drop the right hand to the side, retrieve the quarter from the right sleeve, and hold it classic palmed. This takes but an instant and is done as you direct attention to the half dollar. Bring the right hand up, holding it palm down with the fingers pointing to the left as you move it toward the left hand. Move the hands toward each other rather rapidly

Fig. I

until the palm of the right hand is directly above the back of the left hand. Stop the hands with a jerk. This sends the half dollar into the right sleeve, Fig. 1. The right hand immediately drops the palmed quarter to the back of the left hand, then moves away to the right to reveal the quarter lying on the exact spot previously occupied by the larger coin. Turn the right hand over and show it empty, then take the quarter with the right hand and show the left empty also. There is no clue to the change. It happens quick as lightning.

To facilitate the coin going into the right sleeve you might try raising the hands slightly as they are brought together, and lowering the thumb side of the left hand a trifle. The half dollar can't miss. It just slides off the back of the left hand into the right sleeve. This raising and tilting movement will be unnecessary once the moves are thoroughly mastered. You will find that with a little practice you will be able to send the half dollar into the right sleeve simply by stopping the movement of the two hands suddenly. The move is so beautiful it is surprising even to you!

Be sure your right side is toward the spectators as you perform the actual sleeving move. If this precaution is taken the flight of the half dollar into the right sleeve will be amply covered by the right hand and arm.

INFLATION

FOLLOW-UP TO DEVALUATION

An old rule says, *Never repeat a trick.* But there are exceptions to all rules, and this rule is no exception.

The end result of this feat is identical with Devaluation—the preceding trick—but since the moves are slightly different the two make excellent companion effects.

Suppose you have just performed the pre-

vious change and the half dollar is still up your right sleeve. To change the quarter back to the half dollar do this: Show the quarter and the hands freely, then let the quarter lie on the left palm. As you show the quarter once more, drop the right hand, catch the half dollar as it falls from the sleeve, and palm it.

Here the similarity in moves ends.

Quickly move the hands toward each other, stopping them suddenly just as the right palm arrives over the left palm. This sends the quarter flying into the right sleeve. Immediately place the two palms together and turn the hands over so the left hand will be on top. To do this the hands will have to be revolved, the palms acting as a pivot. The right hand is now palm up below the left hand, and the left hand is palm down above the right. Keeping the left side of the left hand pressed against the right, raise the thumb side of the hand, book-fashion, revealing the half dollar lying on the right palm.

The main difference in this change over the preceding one is the twisting action of the hands immediately following the sleeving action. Do not hesitate after bringing the hands together. Continue the action by promptly revolving them to bring the palm of the right hand uppermost. Reveal the half dollar on the right palm as described.

TRANSFORMATION

Effect: "A nickel is made from a rather soft metal," remarks the performer. "In fact, it is so soft that if I take it in my left hand and blow on it, it immediately becomes so malleable that I can, by slapping it onto my right hand, flatten it out like a pancake." While pronouncing these words the magician shows his hands empty except for a nickel. This he places in his left hand and then shows his right hand empty. After blowing on the coin he slaps it down onto his right hand. When he raises his left hand the nickel has apparently flattened out as he said, for there on his right hand is a half dollar. The nickel has vanished.

Method: The "Pumpkin Seed" Vanish is responsible for most of the trickery in this change. There are two ways of beginning the effect. Either have the half dollar up the right sleeve when you display the nickel in the right hand, or get it there as you remove the nickel from the pocket by using the Delayed Action Method. (A full description of this technique has already been given under Loading.) At any rate, you have a half dollar in your right sleeve as you toss a nickel back and forth between the two hands, showing without comment that the hands are otherwise empty.

Take the nickel in the right hand, holding it by its edges between the index finger and thumb. Bring the cupped left hand palm down over the nickel and pretend to take it in that hand. At the instant the nickel is covered press the right index finger and thumb together, "squirting" the nickel into the left sleeve ("Pumpkin Seed" Vanish). Close the left hand as if it held the coin and show the right hand empty. Explain that by blowing on the coin you can soften it up to a malleable state. Bring the left hand up and blow into the fist from the thumb side. While attention is thus diverted, drop the right hand to the side and catch the half dollar as it falls from the sleeve. Move both hands toward each other simultaneously and bring the palms of the hands sharply together. This action, you explain, "flattens out the coin like a pancake." Lift the left hand to show the half dollar lying on the right. Apparently the nickel has "flattened" out to a larger coin.

You can quit here or change the fifty-cent piece back into the nickel as you prefer.

If you wish to change it back to the five-cent piece do this: Allow a moment for the spectators to realize what has happened and that you have nothing else in your hands. Drop the left hand, retrieving the nickel from the left sleeve, and hold it finger palmed. Show the half dollar in the right hand, holding it parallel with the floor between the tips of the index finger and thumb—the thumb on top. Bring the left hand up to waist level, hold it palm down, and close it into a loose fist. Push the half dollar into the left fist but steal it out again as you execute The Tunnel Vanish (page 24). The finger palmed nickel will not interfere with this move. Blow into the left fist again, then open it to show the transformation. At the exact instant that you open the left hand, sleeve the half dollar in the right sleeve using the Delayed Action Method.

Sometimes I make a third change by doing Devaluation (page 117). I'll guarantee that the three changes performed in a sequence will leave the most blasé audience goggle-eyed!

VARIATION

The "Pumpkin Seed" Vanish serves as a clever device in many transition effects. Using the method described above you can change a coin to a ring, a ball, a thimble, a pipe, a pack of cigarettes, or any other small object. Merely have the article up your right sleeve at the beginning. Show a coin in the right hand. Do The "Pumpkin Seed" Vanish as you get rid of the coin in the left sleeve. Drop the right arm, catch the article as it falls from the sleeve in the hand, then bring the two hands together suddenly as if slapping the coin onto the right hand. Remove the left hand to show the article lying on the right hand.

Many unusual and startling changes can be accomplished in this manner. Try it.

DIME AND PENNY FOR THE WISEACRE

AL SAAL AND MILTON KORT

Most magicians are interested only in entertaining the general public with their magic. But there are others whose specialty is performing tricks designed especially for the bewilderment of their brother wizards. Among these are such men as John Ramsay of Scotland, and the late Dr. Samuel Cox Hooker. Quite a number of our contemporary close-up workers are also experts in this field.

Nowadays, with so many secrets of magic available from magic and novelty shops throughout the country, more and more people are becoming more and more familiar with the workings of our once-guarded art. That clever contrivance, The Dime and Penny, is now almost public property. The following version is purposely contrived to baffle those who know the workings of the mechanical set. This version makes use of a genuine dime and penny, plus a clever sleeving move.

With the two coins in your right trousers pocket you are ready to begin. Let's suppose you are working the trick for a few magical friends. Tell them that you have just purchased a dime and penny outfit and that you would like to demonstrate it. Reach into the pocket, getting the two coins between the tips of the right index finger and thumb. Bring them out together, with the dime concealed behind the penny. Begin tapping the edge of the penny on the table as you ask your audience if they have seen the new version of the effect. They will, of course, say that they haven't. Finally release the dime allowing it to fall to the table. Properly handled, it will look as though you had a nested set and that you jarred the dime loose. This action of dislodging the dime is familiar to all magicians who own the outfit, and it builds

them up for what is about to come.

Explain that the only trouble with the original effect was that the larger coin had to be placed over the smaller one and that a tell-tale sliding move was necessary so the two coins would nest. In the new version, you tell them, the dime goes ON TOP of the penny and no sliding movement is necessary. This throws the wise guy completely off the track. Place the penny in the palm of the right hand, then take the dime from the table and place it ON TOP OF and overlapping the inner edge of the penny. Close your hand so the tip of the third finger presses against the surface of the two coins and turn the hand over. Turn the hand back and open it to show the two coins once more. The small coin is still on top of the larger one. Place the tip of the third finger back on top of the two coins as you again close the hand and turn it over.

Now comes the part that fools them all.

While the hand is back up, press against the dime with the tip of the third finger, sliding it toward the wrist and away from the penny. The penny then falls inside the cupped fingers. Explain to the spectators that in the new version someone can even hold your hand and the trick will still work. In a logical way, extend your hand toward a nearby spectator for him to hold. As you do this relax the pressure on the dime with the third finger and it will fly into the sleeve. (See A Method of Sleeving One of Several Coins, page 107.) Work the fingers a little as if nesting the coins, then turn the fist over for the spectator to hold. After a brief moment have him release his hold on your fist. Then open it to show the penny. The dime has vanished but everyone will think it is in the penny. As you hand them the penny to look over tell them to notice the precision workmanship. It won't take long for someone to discover that the penny is genuine and that they have been hoodwinked. Then it's too late.

If, however, you are working the trick for the layman, say nothing about using trick coins. Just work it as described, then give the penny to someone as a souvenir.

A NOVEL VANISH AND REPRODUCTION

Here is an ingenious method of vanishing and reproducing a coin which was shown to me by the late Paul Rosini. Although it makes use of the sleeves it does so in such a subtle manner they are never suspected.

The only advance preparation necessary is to have a small wand or pencil in the upper left vest or shirt pocket. And you must be wearing a coat.

Stand facing the spectators as you show them a half dollar in your right hand. Pretend to place it in your left hand but retain it palmed in your right. Keep the left hand closed as you say, "In my pocket I have a magic pencil." (This remark is necessary before making the following action—otherwise the spectators' suspicions would be aroused.) Reach under the coat with the right hand and quickly drop the palmed coin into the top opening of the coat sleeve. Keep the left arm bent at the elbow and the coin will fall only that far. Bring out the pencil and show it. Say, "If I tap my left hand with the magic pencil the coin will vanish." Suit the action to the words as you touch the left fist a couple of times with the pencil. Slowly open the left hand to show the coin vanished. Let it be seen that BOTH hands are unmistakably empty except for the pencil, before proceeding.

Raise the pencil up high as you suddenly exclaim, "Look! Here it is on the pencil." During this brief bit of action drop the left arm and catch the coin in the hand as it falls from the sleeve. Bring the left hand up closed. Tap it with the pencil as you say, "I'll put it back in the hand so you can see it." As dramatically as possible open the left hand to show the missing coin. "There it is!"

George Kaplan makes excellent use of this principle in an effect called "The Kaplan Coin Transposition," which is described on page 447 of *Hugard's Magic Monthly*. I urge you to investigate it.

THE VAGABOND COINS

MILTON KORT

The Kort Method of Sleeving One of Several Coins, previously described, is employed in this trick to cause four half dollars to pass from one hand to the other.

Method: Prepare for the trick beforehand by placing five half dollars in the right trousers pocket.

Reach into the pocket for the five coins. Palm one as you bring them out. Toss four into the left hand and immediately sleeve the fifth in the right sleeve, using the Delayed Action Method. Hand the four coins to a spectator and show both hands empty. Have him count the coins into your right hand. Show the left hand once more and slowly count the coins into it yourself. Extend the left arm slightly to show the four coins to the spectators on the left. At the same time drop the right arm and gain possession of the sleeved coin. Move the left hand toward the right and apparently toss the four coins into the right hand. Actually you execute the Utility Switch, (page 11) as you retain one coin and throw the other three. Immediately show four coins in the right hand, three just received from the left hand, and the other which was already there. At this point you have four coins lying on the open right hand and one hidden in the left hand. Show the four coins to the spectators on your right. Showing the coins first to one group of spectators, then another group, creates a logical excuse for tossing the coins from one hand to the other.

Close the left hand and hold it in front of you as you maneuver one of the four coins in the right hand into sleeving position. (The coins should lie in an overlapping row with the innermost coin at the heel of the hand.) As you close your hand and turn it over, the inner coin is held only slightly by the tips of the third and fourth fingers. Ask a spectator to hold out his hand. Thrust your right arm forward and relax pressure on the innermost coin. This will cause it to fly into the right sleeve. Count the coins one at a time into his waiting hand. There are only three. Direct your attention to your left hand and open it to show that one coin has arrived there. While attention is on the left hand, drop the right hand and catch the coin as it falls from the right sleeve. Reach over and pretend to take the coin from the left hand with the right. Show the coin at the right fingertips while the left hand retains its coin finger palmed. Point to the coin at the right fingertips with the left hand as you say, "One coin has passed." Place the right hand's coin in the left hand, being careful that the two coins do not touch. Otherwise they would "talk" and give away the presence of the extra coin. Apparently the left hand holds just one coin. Actually it contains two.

Take the three coins from the spectator in your right hand, and get one in sleeving position as you close the hand and turn it over. Say, "In my right hand I have three half dollars." Look over to the left hand and add, "While in my left I have only one." Before attention can return to the right hand thrust it forward and say to your helper, "Count these." As you extend

your arm, sleeve the inner coin. Drop two into his hand and show your hand empty. "Where did the coin go? Why over to my left hand, of course." Open the left hand and show two coins. While showing the two coins in the left hand, drop the right and regain the sleeved coin. Toss one of the two into the right hand as you again execute the Utility Switch. Show two coins in the right hand, one just received from the left hand, and one which was already there. Place these two coins in the left hand. The left now contains three coins while the audience thinks it holds only two.

Have the spectator return the two coins to your right hand. Show them again and close the hand, getting one coin into sleeving position. Repeat the preceding moves to cause the third coin to pass. Open the right hand and show one coin. Drop it into the spectator's hand. Open the left and show three coins. Say, "Three coins have passed." As you show the three coins in the left, drop the right hand to the side and retrieve the sleeved coin as before. Bring the right hand up and toss into it two of the three from the left hand, again executing the Utility Switch. Show three coins in the right hand, one which was already there, and two which arrived from the left hand. Repeat, "Three coins." Place them in the left hand along with the one already there. Four coins are now in the left hand, but the audience know of only three.

Take the single coin from your helper and vanish it in the same manner as you did the others. A better plan would be to vanish it in a different way, so execute The Throw vanish (page 104), to sleeve the last coin. Open the left hand and show that the coin has arrived. A nice touch is to allow the coins in the left hand to jingle together just as the right vanishes the last coin.

To get rid of the sleeved coin, get possession of it by dropping the right hand. Hold it classic palmed as you remove the four coins from the left hand. Drop all five into the right pocket.

SPLITTING THE ATOM

Dr. E. M. Roberts

Effect: A borrowed half dollar instantly and visibly changes to two quarters.

Method: Before asking for the loan of a half dollar, have two quarters classic palmed in the right hand.

When someone offers a half dollar, take it in the palm down right hand between the fingers and thumb. Display it for a moment, then, as you bring the left hand up in front of you as if you intended tossing the half into it, drop the right hand to the side and sleeve the coin (Dr. Roberts' Method). Raise the right hand and quickly transfer the two quarters to the fingertips, displaying them fanned. After receiving the half dollar in the right hand it is a natural move to drop the arm in preparation for an intended toss. The left hand should be brought up and held in front of you at the same instant the right hand is lowered. Center your attention momentarily on the left hand then on the right hand as the two quarters are brought into view.

When you take the borrowed half in the right hand, quickly get it into the Dr. Roberts' sleeving position. Then the instant the hand reaches its lowest level the coin is propelled up the sleeve. (The two palmed quarters in no way interfere with this move.) Of course, the forearm will have to be raised to prevent the half dollar falling from the sleeve. Once the half dollar leaves the hand the fingers are free to bring the two palmed quarters to their tips. This they do as the hand is brought up. By the time the right hand is even with the left,

it should have the two quarters displayed in a fan. The intended throw is interrupted and the two coins are seen in the right hand. Drop them singly into the left hand and show the right hand empty.

When performed at an even, unhesitating tempo the effect is beautiful to behold. It appears that you visibly split the larger coin into two smaller ones.

If you care to change the two quarters back to the half dollar, the method about to be described will do the trick. Otherwise, you can get rid of the sleeved half dollar by using this stratagem: While showing the two quarters in the left hand, drop the right and gain possession of the sleeved half. Hold it thumb palmed, then raise the hand and take one of the quarters between the tips of the thumb and first and second fingers. In the action of pulling back the left sleeve slightly, drop the thumb palmed half dollar into the outer left breast pocket. The left hand repeats the same action with the right sleeve, for effect. This move of disposing of the half dollar in the breast pocket is similar to the one used in the Complete Thumb Palm Vanish, (page 50).

To change the two quarters back to a half dollar do this: Have a small blob of magician's wax on the lower button of the coat or vest. While showing the two quarters in the left hand get the sleeved half into the right hand by dropping that hand. Then hold it classic palmed. Secure the blob of wax on the tip of the right second finger. Then take one of the quarters from the left hand and as you display it momentarily, press the wax to its back. You are now showing a coin in each hand. Place the left hand's quarter in the right hand, BEHIND the other quarter, and press the two together.

The exchange of the two quarters for the half dollar is made during the following brief action: Raise the left hand and blow a few imaginary dust particles from it. At the same time drop the right hand and sleeve the two quarters. The wax holds them together as one coin, thus preventing their rattling. Immediately raise the right hand and drop the half dollar into the left hand. Show the right hand empty.

Return the borrowed half dollar with the left hand. As you do this drop the right, catch the sleeved coins as they fall from the sleeve and dispose of them in the right coat pocket.

Dr. Roberts tells me that he is often approached by someone who has witnessed the first part of the experiment—the splitting process—with two quarters, wanting him to put them together. For this reason he always carries a blob of wax on a button, and a half dollar handy. He is then ready to perform the restoration process at any time.

When a trick is performed under these conditions it packs a greater wallop than if it had been performed in a planned routine.

CHANGE FOR A DOLLAR

Dr. E. M. Roberts

Even more startling and puzzling than the foregoing splitting effect is this one in which two half dollars change to a dollar bill.

The handling is identical with the restoration part just described (changing the two quarters to the half dollar), except a bill is used instead of the half dollar.

Prepare for the trick by folding a dollar bill and concealing it in the right palm. The bill and halves could all be together in the right trousers pocket and the bill palmed as the halves were brought forth. In this case a small blob of wax would already be on one of the halves. At any

rate, show a coin in each hand, holding each at the fingertips with the backs of the hands toward the spectators. Transfer the coin from the left hand to the rear of the coin in the right and press the two together. Raise the left hand to blow on it as in the preceding effect. During this brief bit of business, which serves as misdirection, drop the right hand and sleeve the two halves (Dr. Roberts' Method). Then as you raise the right hand bring the bill to the fingertips and begin unfolding it. When you return your attention to the right hand the bill is practically unfolded. Finish unfolding it with the aid of the left hand. Exhibit the dollar bill and show the hands otherwise empty.

The change is a pretty one.

THE STRATOSPHERE QUARTERS

Dr. E. M. Roberts

Effect: The performer shows four quarters which he places in a row on the table. Nothing is concealed in either hand. Picking up one of the quarters with the right hand he tosses it into the air where it vanishes. The remaining three coins are caused to disappear in a like manner. After tossing the last coin into the air he shows his right hand empty. Making a grab in the air with his left hand he produces the missing money.

Method: Once again the Dr. Roberts' Method of Sleeving plays a big part in the mystery. Besides the ability to perform this method of sleeving you will need four duplicate quarters. Actually, however, you will need only seven quarters in all; the eighth is borrowed from a spectator. The reason for this will soon be apparent.

Prepare for the trick in advance by sticking a small blob of wax on one side of three of the seven quarters. Cut a piece of waxed paper about an inch wide and four inches long. On it place the three waxed coins. Fold the paper accordion-fashion, and place it in the right trousers pocket. Wedge the other four quarters between the prongs of a safety pin and fasten it underneath the left side of the coat, in a position for the left hand to steal later.

Seize a favorable moment, separate the three quarters from the paper and bring them from the pocket. Place them waxed side down in a row on a table. As you remove these three quarters from the pocket remark that you need four for the trick about to be performed, and ask for the loan of a quarter from a spectator. Place it at the right end of the row of three quarters already on the table. This subtly throws anyone off the scent of the correct solution. Borrowing a quarter emphasizes the "impromptu" nature of the effect, and this is the impression you wish to create.

Stand with your right side toward the spectators as you pick up with your right hand coin number one from the left end of the row. Pretend to toss this coin into the air, and as you go through a throwing motion with the hand, classic palm the coin with the waxed side away from the palm. Repeat this operation with coins number two and three. Each time a coin is apparently thrown into the air the eyes follow its invisible flight. Each time a coin is vanished it is pressed into the palm to become fastened to the others by means of the wax. The left hand is seen empty as it moves more or less in unison with the throwing motions on the right hand. The three quarters are now stuck together in the right palm.

As you reach for the last (unprepared) coin with the right hand, steal the four quarters from underneath the coat with the left hand. This is accomplished by placing the fingers underneath the coat and forcing the stack from the pin by pressing against

their edges with the thumb from outside the cloth. The coins fall onto the cupped fingers. Go through the motions of tossing the last coin into the air with the right hand and press it into the palm onto the waxed side of the third coin. As you watch the invisible flight of the last coin upward, drop the right hand to the side and sleeve the stack of four coins using the Dr. Roberts' Sleeving Method. All four coins are propelled up the sleeve as one. Raise the right hand so the coins will not fall from the sleeve. Then turn it palm toward the audience as you say, "Oh, no! (If there are any magicians in your audience they will be thoroughly mystified at this point, because they will think you are concealing the coins in the palm.) Not here, but here." As you pronounce these last words suddenly make a grab in the air with the left hand. Then show the quarters in that hand. Pour the coins into the right hand and let it be clearly seen that these are the only coins you have.

Keep the right arm bent so the sleeved stack will not fall out. Toss the coins back into the left hand. With your left side toward the spectators count the coins one at a time onto the table. While this is being done drop the right hand, retrieve the waxed stack from the sleeve, and drop it into the right coat pocket.

Pick up one of the four quarters from the table and return it to the spectator from whom it was borrowed at the beginning of the trick.

THE WORLD'S FASTEST COIN VANISH AND REPRODUCTION

Dr. E. M. Roberts

One of the fastest and most baffling coin vanish and reproduction tricks in existence is this one by Dr. Roberts.

Turn your right side to the spectators,

Fig. 1

To bring it back proceed as follows: Drop the right hand to the side, catch the sleeved coin on the cupped fingers, and say, "To bring the coin back, all we have to do is close the hand, tap it on the back, rub the heel of the hand again, and the coin returns." Slowly close the left hand and turn it back toward the spectators. Bring the right hand up and tap the back of the left fist with the right fingers. As this is done the coin is loaded into the left fist. These are the actual mechanics: With the coin lying on the cupped fingers, bring the right hand up rather fast to tap the left fist. As the right hand nears the left

show a half dollar held vertically by its edge between the tips of the right second finger and thumb, and place it flat against the palm of the left hand, which is stretched out, palm toward the audience, Fig. 1. Now execute The Bobo Coin Vanish as you pretend to retain the coin in the left hand. At the completion of this sleight the left hand will be closed (apparently holding the coin) and the coin hidden in the right hand. While looking directly at the left hand, drop the right hand to the side and sleeve the coin in the right sleeve, utilizing the Dr. Roberts' Method. Without any undue delay, raise the right hand and place the tip of its forefinger against the heel of the left hand at a position just inward from the tip of the closed left little finger, and with a circular motion, massage the heel of the hand. As you do this say, "By rubbing the heel of the hand in this fashion the coin disappears." Beginning with the little finger, slowly open the left hand a finger at a time and show it empty. Show both hands empty at the same time by holding the fingers wide apart and turning the hands over slowly a time or two. The coin is gone.

Fig. 2

fist the (right) fingers open and the coin is tossed upward, and it is caught in the left hand which opens slightly to receive it, Fig. 2. The right fingers immediately tap the back of the left fist once. The left hand is turned over and the right forefinger repeats the rubbing movement on the heel of the left hand; then the left hand is slowly opened, a finger at a time, showing the coin lying in the palm. Tilt the left hand slightly, causing the coin to slide off into the waiting right hand below.

DIE TO DIME

KIRK STILES

Here is a one-hand change of a die to a dime, ring, or any other object small enough to be concealed under the curled third and fourth fingers.

Have the die and dime in the right trousers pocket. Reach in, finger palm the dime at the base of the third and fourth fingers and bring out the die, visible at the fingertips, and toss it onto the table. Pick it up with the aid of the first two fingers and spin it on the table a couple of times, which action shows without saying that it is ordinary, and at the same time gives the right hand a natural, empty appearance.

Fig. 1

Take up the die between the tips of the right first two fingers and thumb as in Fig. 1, and hold the hand palm up in a position some six or eight inches below your chin and a similar distance from your chest. Blow on the die, then under cover of a flourish, the die is sleeved and the coin shown. To accomplish this change, begin by holding the hand as just described. Turn the hand palm inward and lower it, then as you bring it up and swing it to the right, sleeve the die. The forefinger snaps between the thumb and second finger, which acts as a channel and directs the die up the

sleeve. (This move is quite similar to the Dr. Roberts' Method described elsewhere in this chapter. If you are familiar with it this sleeving move with the die will be simple.) Before the die has a chance to fall out of the sleeve the arm is raised and the hand (still closed) turned palm upward. Every move except the forefinger snap should be done slowly and deliberately. As soon as the die is gone the fingers begin a snapping movement and the hand is returned to its original position near the chin. Blow on the hand, then open it to reveal the dime.

ALMOST A TRANSPOSITION

STEWART JAMES AND MILTON KORT

Effect: The performer displays a penny in his left hand and a dime in his right. As he closes his hands on the two coins and holds them some distance apart, he announces that he will cause the coins to transpose themselves. Opening his hands a moment later he shows the transposition—the penny is now in his right hand, but in his left hand he holds not the dime that was expected, but two nickels!

Method: At the outset, have a dime and a penny in the left trousers pocket and two nickels and a penny in the right trousers pocket. Announce a trick with a dime and penny. Thrust both hands into the pockets, and while pretending to search for the necessary money, finger palm the two nickels in the right hand at the base of the third finger, and hold the penny between the outer two joints of the second finger. Remove both hands from the pockets and show the dime and penny in the left hand, but keep the three coins in the right hand concealed. (The right hand does not appear suspicious when the coins are gripped as just described.)

Hand the dime and penny from the left

hand to a spectator to look over. Don't tell him to examine them. Just say, "Look these over, please," or some such thing. While he looks over the coins, drop the penny from the right hand into the left coat sleeve. (Just do it casually and it won't be noticed.) Show the left hand empty back and front, then have the spectator place the dime and penny in your hand. Ask him if he noticed the dates on the coins. When he replies that he didn't, dump them back in his hand. While he is checking the dates drop the left hand to the side, let the sleeved penny drop into the hand and finger palm it at the base of the third finger.

Now take the two coins from the spectator—the dime with the right hand and the penny with the left, holding them between the tips of the forefingers and thumbs of the two hands which are about chest high and palm uppermost (the fingers curl inward naturally hiding the finger palmed coins). Explain that you are going to cause the two coins to change places. Very slowly bring the hands together and slide the two coins across each other, ending with the dime between the tip of the left forefinger and thumb, and the penny in the same position in the right hand. Smile and say that there was no trick to that because they were able to see you do it. (Or, you could use the old wheeze as you ask the spectators if they wish the coins to transfer visibly or invisibly. When they say "visibly," make the exchange as described.) "Now," you say, "I will do it by magic. I will cause the one cent to change places with the ten cents." (Do not use the words "dime" and "penny." This is important, as you will see in a moment.) As you close your hands and turn them back uppermost, bring the two coins inside the fists and balance them on the pads at the ends of the middle fingers, in position for executing A Method of Sleeving One of Several Coins, (page 107).

Ask the spectator who looked over the coins to hold out his hands. As he does so thrust your two hands forward, sleeving the dime in the left sleeve and the penny in the right sleeve, and drop the finger palmed penny from your left hand into his right hand and say, "Here is the *one cent*." Then as you drop the two finger palmed nickels from your right hand into his left, add, "And here is the *ten cents*." Turn both hands over and show them empty.

Retrieve the sleeved coins and dispose of them in the pockets while the spectators are examining the penny and nickels.

SECOND VERSION

In this verson the climax is slightly different.

In your left pocket you have a dime and a penny, but in your right pocket you have ten pennies. All ten are brought out concealed in the right hand as you show the dime and penny in the left. Proceed as in the first version by secretly loading one of the ten pennies into the left sleeve while the dime and penny are in the spectator's hands. You sleeve the dime in the left sleeve as in the first method, but you do not sleeve the penny in the right sleeve. It is merely added to the nine already in that hand. At the finish you dump the "one cent" (penny) from the left hand and the "ten cents" (ten pennies) from the right into the spectator's hands.

THIRD VERSION

MILTON KORT AND ROBERT UNGEWITTER

In this version you hold a duplicate dime in the right hand, instead of the two nickels. At the climax you show an actual transposition by dropping a penny from the left hand and a dime from the right hand.

For a fourth version, using mechanical coins, see page 238.

Chapter VIII

COINS ACROSS

*Copper and Silver Transposition (4 methods) · Guess Which Hand ·
Quarter and Half Dollar Transposition · The Curious Nickel · Two
Pennies on the Leg · The Inseparable Pair · Coins in the Teeth · The
Drop Pass · The Hippity Hop Half · Rapid Transit · Winged Silver
(3 versions) · The Flying Eagles · Variation · Three and Three ·
Chinese Money Mystery · Drobina's Coin Routine · Four Coins to a Glass
(2 versions) · The Traveling Centavos · Miracle Coins to the Pocket*

Without a doubt some of the most puzzling effects possible with coins are those of the transposition and "passe-passe" variety. Tricks of this nature seem to hold a special fascination for most spectators. How a magician can cause coins to travel from one place to another is completely beyond their comprehension.

In this chapter you will find many unique and different effects of this nature, all worthy of your consideration. All are time-tested and, with the exception of one, they are strictly impromptu.

The effect of the first four tricks is the same—the transposition of a copper and a silver coin—but each method is entirely different.

Copper and Silver Transposition

MILTON KORT

Effect: The performer shows two coins —a half dollar and an English penny. He puts the copper in his left hand, holds the silver in his right hand, then commands them to change places. The copper coin is slapped onto the table with the right hand. Then after making a mysterious pass over

his left hand, he opens it, showing the silver coin. The coins have changed places!

Method: The effect depends on standard sleights plus an ingenious loading move for its accomplishment.

Show the two coins and place them on the table—the English penny on the left and the half dollar on the right. Pick up the copper coin with the right hand and pretend to place it in the left hand but retain it palmed in the right. Say, "Copper coin in the left hand." Close the left hand as if it held the coin and turn it over, palm down. Take the silver coin from the table with the fingers and thumb of the palm down right hand. Thumb palm the coin as the hand closes. (The copper coin is in the classic palm and the silver coin is in the thumb palm.) As the right hand closes over the half dollar state, "And the silver coin in the right hand." Hold the fists back uppermost and about a foot apart.

To the spectators it appears that you are holding a copper coin in your left hand and a silver coin in your right. Actually both are in the right hand.

As you command the coins to change places rap the knuckles of both hands on the table. Release the copper coin from

Fig. 1

the right palm, allowing it to rest on the closed fingers, then open that hand and slap the copper coin onto the table. As you do this say, "The copper coin has jumped over here to my right hand."

To show the silver coin in the left hand do the following: With the right hand palm down and the fingers pointing to the left, bring it over and touch its fingertips to the back of the left fist, Fig. 1. Turn the left hand over, counterclockwise, and as you do so open the left fingers slightly and drop the coin from the right thumb palm into the left hand, Fig. 2. Without hesitating, the left hand continues turning until it is palm up. The right hand, with its fingertips still pressed lightly against the back of the left fist, moves forward to facilitate this action. At the completion of this move the right hand is palm up with its finger-

Fig. 2

tips pressed upward against the underside of the left fist, Fig. 3. Slap the back of the left fist once with the right fingers and immediately open the left hand, showing the silver coin. Toss it onto the table. "And here is the silver coin."

If the loading move is made in an even, unhurried manner it appears perfectly natural. Make the move as you look directly into the eyes of the spectators and say the last words, "And here is the silver coin." Ostensibly you have merely made a mystic pass around the left fist but in this

Fig. 3

action you have imperceptibly dropped the coin into the left hand.

Master this move and you will have a clever subterfuge which can be used effectively with other small articles as well. I have seen Milton Kort use this move to load dice and small balls into his left hand, with great effect.

Actually, it is a utility move with many uses.

Second Method

STEWART JUDAH

With the exception of the final move, the handling in this version is identical with the one just described. Instead of employing a sleight to load the half dollar into his left hand, Stewart Judah utilizes a move that is not only completely deceptive but entirely natural as well.

Proceed as in the first version up to the point where you have apparently placed the English penny in your left hand—actually you have it concealed in the right hand, classic palmed. And you have just taken up the half dollar with the same hand, the half being held in thumb palm position. The fists are backs up and about a foot apart. Emphasize the position of the coins: "Copper in the left hand—silver in the right."

Go through whatever business that appeals to you as you pretend to make the coins change places. Keeping the right hand back up, open it and drop the copper coin onto the table. Now as the left hand moves over to the right, that hand turns palm up, the left hand opens and the palms are slapped together. Quickly turn the left hand back to the left and palm up, exposing the half dollar briefly on the right palm. Instantly slap the coin onto the left hand, which in turn tosses it onto the table. The effect is that you opened your left hand, slapped the coin onto the right, then back onto the left. The action is perfectly natural as a trial will show.

Third Method

ARTHUR PUNNAR, *by permission of Hugard's Monthly*

The effect of this version is the same as the first two but the method is entirely different.

Method: Show an English penny and a half dollar on the table. Pick up the penny with the right hand and pretend to place it in the left, but retain it classic palmed instead. Close the left hand and turn it back

uppermost. Take up the silver coin with the palm down right hand and as you apparently close the fingers over it, back palm it and hold it outside the fist where it cannot be seen when the back of the hand is uppermost. Now release the penny from the palm, allowing it to rest on the two middle fingers inside the fist.

Ask the spectators, "Which hand holds the penny; which holds the half dollar?"

After the spectators reply correctly open the hands and announce, "The half dollar is now in the left hand and the penny is in the right." Move the hands toward each other. Then as you open them and turn them palm upward, bring the back of the right hand over the palm of the left as in Fig. 1. At this point the penny is visible in the right hand (which is still holding the half dollar back palmed) and completely

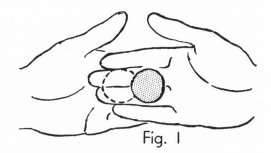

Fig. I

shielding the left palm. Release the back palmed half so it will drop onto the left palm and separate the hands. The coins have changed places since the copper is now seen resting in the right hand while the silver is lying in the left hand.

In performance, the action of the hands coming together, turning, opening and separating coalesces into one graceful and natural gesture.

Alternate procedure: Have a duplicate penny palmed in the right hand. Pick up the penny from the table and deliberately place it in the left hand. In the action of closing that hand and turning it over, sleeve the penny. Take up the half dollar with the right hand and proceed as described.

Fourth Method

Ross Bertram

Ross Bertram, who is one of the finest coin manipulators I know, has some excellent ideas on how to transpose an English penny and a half dollar. Here is one of his pet routines which combines the transposition of the two coins with a couple of surprises. It is a routine for the connoisseur!

The performer shows an English penny and a half dollar and apparently repeats the same moves three times in succession. The first time, the coins transpose themselves. The second time, one travels from one hand to join the coin held in the other hand. And the last time, when the hands are opened they are empty. Both coins have vanished!

Working: Show an English penny and a half dollar and place them on the table about a foot apart, the penny on the left and the fifty cent piece on the right. Pick up the copper coin with the right hand and place it on the palm of the left hand. Then take the silver coin in the right hand and hold it in the same manner. Call attention to the position of the two coins as you slowly close your hands and turn them over.

Ask a spectator, "Which is which?" or, "Where is the penny?" If he names their correct positions say, "That's right." If he calls the position of the coins wrong say, "You were not watching." In either event, open your hands and show the coins again, this time lying on the fingers. The penny rests on the left second and third fingers with its left edge protruding slightly toward

the index finger, so that it can be nipped between the index and second fingers a moment later when the hands close. The half dollar is displayed in the right hand resting on the index and second finger with its edge extending slightly toward the third finger, so it can be nipped between the second and third fingers. Fig. 1 shows the correct position of the coins on the hands.

Close the hands and turn them over. As this is done the fingers make the following movements: The left index finger presses down on the edge of the English

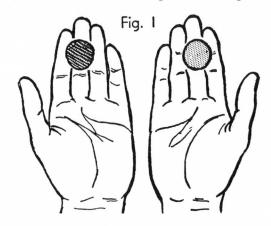

Fig. 1

penny, levering it up. It is then clipped by its lower edge between the index and second fingers. A similar action takes place with the right hand as it closes. The third finger presses down on the edge of the half dollar so it can be nipped between the second and third fingers. In the action of closing the hands and turning them over, the coins are nipped as mentioned. By pressing the fingertips to the palms the coins will be forced through the fingers to the outside of the fists. They will still be held by the same fingers but will be gripped by their opposite edges. The move is accomplished simultaneously with both hands, and must be made in the action of closing them. If executed as described the move cannot be detected. Now, unknown to the spectators, the coins are *outside* the fists. (Fig. 2 shows a view of the hands as seen from below.) Hold the hands about a foot apart and keep the middle joints of the fingers pointing down or resting on the

Fig. 2

table. This will conceal the protruding coins from view of the spectators.

As a gesturing movement, swing both hands upward together, bringing the under-side of the fists just close enough together for the coins to be transferred—the penny from the first and second fingers of the left hand to the first and second fingers of the right hand—the half dollar from the second and third fingers of the right hand to the second and third fingers of the left hand. And the hands return to the table. (The performer's view of the transfer is shown in Fig. 3.) This action takes but a fraction of a second and is made during a gesture as you direct a spectator near you to "watch."

At first this move will seem awkward,

Fig. 3

mainly because it is so foreign to the average coin move. However, with a little practice the knack of transferring the two coins indetectably will come. The transfer must be made quickly and timed exactly with your words to the spectator. There is a certain tempo and grace of movement that serves as misdirection for the maneuver. Master the transfer first, then practice the timing.

As you return the fists to the table, draw the coins into their respective hands, then turn the hands over. Open the left hand and say, "Here is the half dollar." Open the right hand as you say, "And here is the English penny." Turn both hands over and slap the coins onto the table.

Offer to repeat the experiment.

Put the half dollar on the palm of the left hand and the English penny on the palm of the right hand. Close the hands and turn them over as before. Pretend to hear someone say that the coins have already changed places. Open the two hands and show the coins again, resting on the fingers in preparation for the transfer move. Remind the spectators that the left hand contains the half dollar, and the right, the English penny. As you close the hands nip the coins as before, and as the hands turn over, the coins are transferred to the outside of the fists. (They are now held outside the fists in exactly the same manner as in the first effect.) Bring the hands together as in the first experiment, but instead of exchanging the coins only the English penny moves. It is taken with the left hand by its edge between the second and third fingers. Both hands return to the table. Both coins are now held by the fingers of the left hand—the half dollar between the first and second fingers, and the English penny between the second and third fingers.

Draw the penny into the hand and press it into the palm. Draw the half dollar into the hand and allow it to rest on the closed fingers. Hold the hands about a foot apart and about six inches from the table. Gesture with the left hand as you say, "Remember, the silver coin is here." Keeping the left hand palm down, open it and snap the half dollar onto the table. Since the spectators see only the half dollar and the hand appears otherwise empty, they naturally assume that the English penny is still in the right hand. Slowly pick up the half dollar with the same hand and as you close it into a loose fist allow the half dollar to rest on the fingers.

Gesture with the right hand and say, "And here is the copper coin." (Actually the right hand is empty.) Make a tossing motion with the right hand toward the left hand. Release the English penny from the left palm so it will fall onto the half dollar with a decided CLINK. Open the right hand and show it empty. Then open the left, revealing the two coins, and allow them to fall to the table.

Now comes an apparent repeat of the same moves but this time the spectators get a surprise, for the coins mysteriously vanish.

Here's how: Put a coin on the palm of each hand as before. (It makes no difference which hand holds what coin.) Caution the spectators to again remember the positions of the coins. Close the hands and turn them over. Hold them in a loose fist, the coins resting on the cupped fingers. Ask a spectator near you to hold out both hands. As he does so extend your arms and sleeve both coins simultaneously, one coin going in the left sleeve and one going in the right sleeve. (See Kort Method of Sleeving One of Several Coins, page 107.) Make motions with the fingers of both hands as if crumbling the coins to dust. Turn the hands over as you make the final crumbling

motions with the second fingers and thumbs. Open the hands widely and show them empty. Both coins have vanished. This comes as a genuine surprise, since the spectators were expecting another transposition.

The sleeved coins can be retrieved by dropping the arms to the sides at an opportune time and catching the coins on the cupped fingers as they fall from the sleeves. Thrust both hands into the pockets in search for another article for the next trick and leave the coins.

Guess Which Hand

C. James McLemore

I think the average magician would welcome the opportunity of obtaining the secret of a trick that had been a pet of another magician for over three decades. Here is just such a trick. It has been performed by "Jim" McLemore literally thousands of times, under every conceivable condition, until it has reached a state of perfection seldom found in tricks. This is the first time it has been explained to anyone.

Here is the effect: The performer reaches into his pocket with his right hand, takes out a handful of coins, selects one and returns the rest to his pocket. He seats himself directly in front of a seated spectator, with any number of persons gathered around, looking on at all angles, and asks the seated spectator to watch his hands and try to guess which hand holds the coin.

The performer takes the coin in his right hand, closes both hands into a fist, holds them about a foot apart and asks the spectator to touch the hand he thinks is holding the coin. The spectator is never right, or always right—at the discretion of the performer. The routine is continued for six or eight guesses, then the spectator is permitted two guesses. Still he fails to find the coin unless the magician desires. When a final choice is allowed the spectator fails to find the coin in either hand because it has vanished.

The routine may be varied for comedy and effect according to the skill of the performer and the existing circumstances.

Required: A handful of coins (including two matching pennies) in the right trousers pocket. Although any size coins up to a quarter can be used, the trick will be described using pennies.

PHASE ONE

Working: Since the over-all effect is best with the assistance of a woman, choose one who you think might be receptive to the trick and seat her directly in front of you. Remain standing for the time being as you speak to her. "I want to prove to you that most people need glasses." If she is wearing glasses say, "Oh, I see you wear glasses. Well, you should have them changed. They seem to be a little weak for you. Now I want you to be very frank with me—just like a child would be—and if you see me do anything tricky or wrong and are able to catch me, please say so immediately." Turn to the surrounding spectators and say to them, "Now don't any of you people help her a bit—I'm only fooling her—you'll see what I'm doing easily.

"This is a trick I learned a few days ago and I'm not very good at it yet. First, let me get a coin." Remove the coins from your right trousers pocket, and as you go over them with your left fingers move one penny into right finger palm position, remove the other with your left hand and as you return the remaining coins to your pocket retain the duplicate penny finger palmed in your right hand. "See this penny?

(Show coin in left hand.) I'm going to take it in one hand, close my hands, and I want you to touch the hand you think holds the coin. Are you ready? Let's go."

Hold the visible penny in the left hand in position for executing The French Drop (page 37). Bring the right hand over and pretend to take it in that hand. Execute The French Drop (the finger palmed coin in the right hand in no way prevents this action), close the hands and hold them backs uppermost and about a foot apart. (A penny is in each hand.) Have her touch one hand. Regardless of which one she touches say, "No, you are wrong, it's in this hand." (Optional: "I told you you needed glasses.") Keep the hand she chose closed and open the other hand and show the coin.

If she touches the right hand, keep it closed and show the penny in the left hand. If she chooses the left hand keep it closed as you open your right and show a coin in it. In either case you can, by employing this stratagem, prove her wrong by showing the coin in the other hand.

Now if she touches your right hand and you show the coin in your left you are in position to repeat the trick immediately. But if she chooses your left hand and you show the coin in your right you have to vary the procedure slightly by pretending to return that coin to your left hand before repeating the trick. To do this, show the coin in your right hand and reach over and pretend to take it with your left. As you do so retain the right coin finger palmed in that hand and display the one in the left hand that was already there. This is not difficult as a trial will show.

Repeat the trick two more times showing her wrong each time as described. The surrounding spectators will be enjoying the proceedings, and that's what you want.

PHASE TWO

"Well, I see you missed every time. I forgot to tell you that I am a mindreader as well as a crook—I mean, magician—so by reading your mind I can foretell the future and, believe it or not, even if you *try* to miss you are going to win the next three times. That is the law of averages for a blind person. Because, as I explained, you are fundamentally blind, and so if you touch my hand often enough, and since the coin is bound to be in one of them, you ought to win half the time. Now on account of my being a great mathematician it stands to reason that since you have missed three times you ought to win three times. See if you can keep from winning."

Repeat the previous moves three more times, allowing her to win each time by opening and showing a coin in whichever hand she chooses. By this time she will be getting more and more exasperated with herself and the situation will become funnier each time she guesses.

PHASE THREE

"Let's try it again." Slowly repeat the same moves until she discovers that you are using two coins. If she doesn't catch on after three or four more trials, hold your fists close together and open first one then the other until it dawns on her that there must be two coins. Sometimes they become so befuddled you almost have to deliberately expose the two.

After she discovers that you have an extra coin say, "Oh, I see you have discovered that I have two coins. Well, I told you I was just learning the trick and I find it easier to fool you by having a coin in each hand. In that way I can make you think you won or lost as I please. If I want you to win I simply open the hand you touch and show that coin. But if I want you to lose, I merely open the hand you

did not touch and show you a coin in it. You have such little confidence in yourself since you know you are blind—at least subconsciously you know you are blind—that you forgot to make me open the hand that you touched. Then I simply reached over with my right hand and touched the fingers of my left hand and started the trick over again. That just shows you how weak-minded or weak-eyed we can be."

PHASE FOUR

"To convince you of your eye trouble, I am going to repeat the trick for you, but this time with one coin. (Lay one coin aside, but make sure it stays in plain view.) Honest now, only one coin." Show both hands with fingers wide apart, then take the single coin in your left hand as you continue. "Now, I'll take the coin again but no matter which hand you touch you will miss."

This stage of the routine requires that the coin be back thumb palmed in your right hand, which is accomplished as follows: The palm up left hand is holding the penny between the tips of the first

Fig. 1

two fingers and thumb, Fig. 1. Note that in this position the coin is hidden from the spectator by the cupped right fingers. As you pretend to grab the coin with the right hand, raise both hands slightly, move the left hand to the right and deposit the

Fig. 2

coin in the crotch of the right thumb, Fig. 2; then without hesitation close both hands into fists and hold them palms uppermost and about a foot apart. Normally the fingers stop when they reach the coin, so it is a very sensible thing to do when making the back thumb palm to start curling the right fingers down against the left forefinger, thus creating the illusion that the right hand travelled the same distance that it normally had before when you simply reached and pretended to take the coin.

Let's go over that again. Bring both hands together as in Fig. 1. Now as you deposit the coin in the back thumb palm of the right hand, raise both hands slightly (to cover this move), close them into fists and separate them as described. At first reading, this move may sound a little difficult, but it isn't. If the move is made fairly quickly it will appear that you took the coin in your right hand. But even if the spectator thinks you left the coin in your left hand the effect is not changed, because she is still trying to guess which hand holds the coin.

Back thumb palm the coin as described and have her touch either hand. If she touches your left open it and show it empty. The instant you do this, bring the back thumb palmed penny into the right fist. A quick snap of the wrist will accomplish

this as you open the fingers slightly to admit the coin, then close them. After showing your left hand empty open your right hand and show the penny in it.

If she touches your right hand, open it and show it empty, then give her a second choice. As she turns her attention to your left hand and touches it quickly bring the back thumb palmed penny into the right fist as described, then after showing the left hand empty, open the right hand and show the coin in it. Actually you can give her two chances to win and she will lose. No matter which hand she chooses she loses—entirely under your control.

Repeat this three or four times, then let her discover that you are hiding the coin behind your right hand. Just keep doing it over slowly until she catches on.

PHASE FIVE

"Oh, well, you caught me again, but I must explain to you how I should have done the trick." Take the coin from the left hand with your right, visibly making the back thumb palm and continue with the patter. "Now you know where the coin is so I'll let you guess. If you touch my right hand I open and close it quickly (do so) and you don't see the coin because it is hidden behind my hand. Then when I give you a second choice and you look over to my left hand—boy, oh, boy,—I'm sure watching your eyes—I make this move with my right hand." Look over to your right hand and crudely demonstrate how you throw the penny into that hand. "Then after I show that the coin isn't in my left hand, I open the right hand and show it there. Confusing, isn't it?"

After the exposé you apparently continue in the same manner but still you fool her. "I'll do it again and I want you to watch closely so you will see how I do it. You see, I take the coin in my right hand . . . (execute The French Drop as you pretend to take the coin in your right hand, but retain it in your left) . . . and hide it on the back of that hand (make a movement with the right fingers as if you were back palming a coin). But if I want to—instead of throwing the penny into my right hand—I can throw it all the way across into my left hand, like this." Make a motion of tossing a coin from the right to the left hand, open the right hand and show it empty on both sides, then open the left and show the coin in it. Properly done, it appears that you did actually throw a coin from one hand to the other.

"Well, I see you didn't see the coin go across, so I'll do it again." Execute The French Drop again, leaving the coin in your left hand. Next time go through the same moves but actually take it in your right hand. Alternate taking it with your right hand and leaving it in the left three or four times. After this she will be completely bewildered.

PHASE SIX

"Well, I'm going to give you one last chance, after which I'll stop, but to make things easier for you I'll let you make two guesses." Hold the coin in your left hand as before. Take it with your right and immediately snap it up the right sleeve as you close and separate the hands. Whichever hand she touches, open it and show it empty, then give her a second choice. When she touches the other hand open it also and show it empty. The coin is gone and the trick is over.

SUMMARY

When taking the coin in Phase One of the trick, you will, of course, execute The French Drop. When you are making the spectator miss, you simply open the hand she *did not* touch, which proves to her that she missed. Then, regardless whether she chooses the right or left hand, bring the hands together with a natural sweeping motion and replace the left hand coin back at the fingertips of that hand, retaining the right hand coin finger palmed, and start over again. Do this three times.

In Phase Two you repeat the same moves as used in Phase One, but allow her to win each time by opening and showing a coin in whichever hand she touches. Do this three or four times.

In Phase Three the same moves as used in Phases One and Two are repeated over and over, slower and more obvious each time until she discovers that you have two coins. After this place one coin aside and offer to repeat the trick with the single coin.

In Phase Four you can, by virtue of the back thumb palm, show either hand empty and actually allow a second choice if you wish. While showing the left hand empty the back thumb palmed coin is tossed into the right palm and finally shown in it. Do this three or four times, then let her discover that you are hiding the penny behind your right hand.

In Phase Five you continue with The French Drop; alternate leaving the coin in the left hand and actually taking it in the right hand until she is completely befuddled. And she will be if you do your sleight of hand well.

In Phase Six duplicate the preceding moves as much as possible as you take the coin in your right hand and sleeve it as described.

The moves to accomplish the different phases of the trick are, in the order used: The French Drop (first three phases), the back thumb palm (Phase Four), The French Drop again (Phase Five), and finally the sleeving move (Phase Six) to vanish the coin.

The trick has some elements of exposure in it because you do expose the duplicate coin, but that is so unimportant it is hardly an exposure at all. Then you increase the excitement by letting the spectator discover how you are hiding the coin behind your hand. Of course this is a sleight of hand principle, but the back thumb palm is used so infrequently in magic that it is the basis of no actual trick that I know of. If it should be used in other manipulations it would not be suspected after this exposure. The French Drop and the sleeving are not exposed, and if you would rather not expose the back thumb palm just carry on two or three times as described *without* exposing it, then proceed with the next phase of the routine.

The sleeving move can either be made as described or The "Pumpkin Seed" Vanish (page 101) can be used. To do this you would have to show the coin in your right hand, then "squirt" it up the left sleeve as you pretended to deposit it in the left hand.

If you wish, you can do what I have seen the originator do many times—cuff the coin, then remove your coat and permit yourself to be searched.

The only difficult move in the entire routine is the back thumb palm, and that can be quickly mastered. Actually the move is made under a grabbing movement of the hands and is quite easy to cover. Showmanship and window-dressing amount to 99 percent of the effect.

Quarter and Half Dollar Transposition

After a version which appeared in *Ireland Writes a Book*

This trick, the brainchild of Laurie Ireland, is one of the most novel effects of its kind I have ever run across. Glenn Harrison showed me a version of it, to which I have added a few ideas of my own. The composite version follows.

General effect: A quarter and a half dollar change places a couple of times in a unique manner. Finally the half dollar changes to two quarters.

Requisites and Preparation: You will require three quarters and a coin clip to hold one coin. The clip can be either of the magic shop variety or simply a paper clip. Fasten the clip to the lining of the coat just underneath the lower right side, in such a position that the right hand can easily steal a coin from it while the arm hangs naturally at the side. Place one quarter in the clip, one in the right trousers pocket, and one with some change (but no half dollars) in the left trousers pocket.

Working: Thrust both hands into the pockets, classic palm the quarter in the right pocket in the right hand, and bring out the loose change in the outstretched left hand. Do this as you remark that you need a quarter and a half dollar for your next experiment. With the fingers of the right hand (which is held back toward the audience) search through the coins in the left for the necessary coins. Finding only a quarter, remove it with the right first two fingers and thumb and return the remaining coins to the left pocket. Ask for the loan of a half dollar. When it is proffered take it with the left hand, then place the two coins on the table with the half dollar a few inches to the left of the quarter. Drop the right hand to the side and transfer the palmed quarter to finger palm position.

Pick up the half dollar and toss it into the left hand. This is what you pretend to do. In reality, you execute The Bobo Switch (page 10) and throw the finger palmed quarter instead. At the completion of this sleight you will have a quarter in the left fist and a half dollar finger palmed in the right. To the spectators it should appear that you merely picked up the half dollar with the right hand and placed it in the left. Without pausing a moment, take up the quarter with the right hand and hold it vertically between the first two fingers with the thumb resting at the lower inside edge of the coin, Fig. 1. This is exactly the same position you would put the coin in if you were about to execute the back finger

Fig. 1

clip. Show first the quarter in the right hand, then the left fist and say, "Here is the quarter, and here is the half dollar. Right?" Before the spectators can answer and turn their attention back to the right hand, lower that hand, back palm the quarter and push the half dollar forward from its finger palm position to a new position at the outer joints of the first two fingers. The change is instantaneous. The quarter appears to transform itself visibly to a half dollar. The hand is held about waist level, with the fingers pointing slightly downward so as to conceal the fact that a quarter is clipped between the first two fingers and underneath the hand. With the half dollar lying on the fingers as just described there is no danger of the spectators getting a flash of the edge of the quarter, Fig. 2. Simultaneously with this action open the left hand and show a quarter there. The quarter and half have changed places.

Many words have been necessary to de-

Fig. 2

scribe this first transposition adequately, but in actual practice the series of moves blend into one and happen so fast it is impossible for the spectators to follow.

Offer to repeat the trick.

Place the quarter from the left hand on top of the half dollar in the right hand, holding them in place with the tip of the right thumb. Then show the left hand empty. Remember to keep the right fingers pointing slightly downward to conceal the hidden quarter. Now bring the left hand over to the right and grasp the fifty cent piece in the following manner: Hold the left hand palm up, and as you grip the for-

Fig. 3

ward edge of the large coin between the tips of the thumb on top and forefinger below, extend the left fingers underneath the right fingers and clip the hidden quarter between the tips of the left second and third fingers, Fig. 3. Now swing the left hand upward and to the left, curling the last three fingers inward hiding the quarter from view, and display the half dollar and quarter in the two hands as shown in Fig. 4.

Fig. 4

Lower the left hand, press the quarter into the palm and rest the half dollar on the curled fingers. Bring the right hand over to the left and pretend to rub the twenty-five cent piece into the left arm. Palm the quarter as you swing the right arm over to the left and rub the tips of the fingers on the coat sleeve near the elbow. As you do this say, "The quarter goes down the sleeve into the left hand." Release the quarter from the left palm, allowing it to fall onto the half dollar lying on the fingers, and immediately rattle the two coins. Show the quarter and half in the left hand and place them on the table—this time with the quarter on the left. At this juncture the extra quarter is palmed in the right hand.

Say, "I will do the trick once more, *especially for you.*" Turn your body slightly to the right and as you speak these last three words to the spectators on your right, drop the right hand and quickly steal the quarter from the clip underneath the edge of the coat, and hold it finger palmed. Two quarters are now hidden in the right hand —one in the palm and one in the finger palm. Turn to the front again, pick up the quarter from the table with the right hand and toss it into the left hand. Permit the spectators to get a flash of this coin before you close the hand. Take up the half dollar with the right hand and as you go through the motions of tossing it into the left execute The Bobo Switch and throw the finger palmed quarter instead. The sound of the

thrown quarter striking the one in the left hand enhances the illusion that the half dollar was thrown. The deception is further heightened by immediately rattling the two coins. Apparently the left hand holds a quarter and a half dollar. Actually it contains two quarters. While rattling the two coins in the left hand the positions of half and quarter in the right hand must be reversed. To do this, drop the right hand to the side and as you close the hand, get the half dollar into the position shown in Fig. 5. The half dollar is raised up on the

Fig. 5

middle fingers against the heel of the hand and the quarter drops onto the base of the fingers, then the half dollar slides down and is pressed into the palm. The jingling of the coins in the left hand will cover any noise made by this move. Now ask the spectators if they all remember that a half dollar and a quarter are in the left hand. Then as you say, "We will now make the quarter fly up the sleeve," reach over with the right hand and produce the quarter from the left elbow. "Now what do we have in the hand?" If they say, "The half dollar," you say, "The fifty cents?" "That's right." Open the left hand, show the two quarters and give them to the spectator from whom you borrowed the half dollar in the first place. Dispose of the half dollar as you place your quarter in your pocket.

The repetitions are cumulative in effect, making the trick more puzzling each time. Using borrowed coins also adds to its effectiveness.

The Curious Nickel

THOMAS H. BEARDEN

The performer extends both hands toward a spectator, showing a nickel lying on the right palm and the left hand empty. He closes his right hand on the nickel and allows the spectator to hold both wrists. In spite of this precaution against trickery, the right hand is opened a moment later and shown empty, and the left is opened to show the coin has passed to that hand.

The effect is repeated under the same conditions and the nickel peregrinates to the right hand.

Placing the nickel in his left hand the performer takes a rabbit's foot from his pocket and touches his left with it. When he opens that hand the coin has vanished. Both hands are shown absolutely empty except for the rabbit's foot. He closes his left hand and again touches it with the rabbit's foot. As he opens it the nickel is seen to have mysteriously returned.

Requirements: Two nickels exactly alike, a rabbit's foot or some similar token (in an emergency almost any small article will serve the purpose), and the ability to sleeve a coin.

Working: Begin the effect with the rabbit's foot in the right trousers pocket and one of the nickels in the left sleeve. Keep the left forearm parallel with the floor as you toss the other nickel from hand to hand. Finally, extend both hands toward a spectator with the five-cent piece lying on the right palm. Have him take it and look it over. As he does this drop the left arm to the side and catch the other nickel on the cupped fingers as it falls from the sleeve. Then bring the closed left hand up to the same height as the right. Take the coin back in the right hand. Close the hand, turn it over and hold it in a loose fist with the nickel resting on the fingers. As you ask the spectator to hold both wrists, thrust both hands forward and sleeve the coin in the right sleeve.

Make a motion with the right hand as if tossing the nickel toward the left hand. While your wrists are still being held, slowly open the right hand and show it empty. Now slowly open the left to show that the nickel has passed to it.

Since the trick is apparently finished the spectator will be less watchful. Take advantage of this by dropping the right hand to the side and regaining the sleeved nickel.

Offer to repeat the trick.

Show the nickel in the left hand, pointing to it with the right forefinger. Slowly close the left hand and turn it over. Do the same with the right hand. As you again extend your arms for the spectator to hold your wrists, sleeve the coin in the left hand in the left sleeve. Make a throwing motion with the left hand toward the right as before, then open the left and show it empty. Slowly open the right hand and display the nickel back in that hand. Let it be clearly seen that both hands are empty except for the nickel. (The other one is up the left sleeve.)

Take the visible nickel in the right hand, holding it in position for The French Drop (page 37). Pretend to take the nickel in the left hand but retain it in the right. The left hand is closed. Say, "In my pocket I have a magic rabbit's foot." Reach into the right trousers pocket for the rabbit's foot. Leave the nickel and bring out the rabbit's foot and show it. Comment briefly on its mystical powers, then tell the spectators that by merely touching the left hand with it the nickel will disappear. Stroke the left hand with the rabbit's foot, then open it and show it empty. Without comment show the right hand empty with the exception of the rabbit's foot.

"It's all in the rabbit's foot," you say, as you thrust it up close to a spectator's face. As you do this drop the left arm to the side and quickly retrieve the sleeved nickel in the left hand. Raise the closed left hand and say, "Once again I touch my hand with the rabbit's foot and the nickel returns." Dramatically open the left hand to show the nickel has returned.

Two Pennies on the Leg

J. G. THOMPSON, JR.

Here is a close-up quickie that should find favor with a great many magicians. It is easy, effective, and requires no advance preparation. Because of a clever bit of misdirection it can be repeated with safety—even for magicians.

Effect: While seated, the performer shows two pennies and puts them on his left leg about six inches apart. The outer one is taken in the left hand and the inner one in his right. At command, the coin in the left hand is caused to pass over to the right. The left hand is opened and shown empty. Both coins are shown in the right hand.

Method: The trick is equally effective performed seated or standing. If no chair is available, merely stand on the right foot while you raise your left leg and place the pennies on it. It should not be difficult to balance yourself for the short period necessary to perform the trick. If you are near a wall or table you can lean on it slightly while you stand on one foot.

Show two pennies and put them on the left leg about six inches apart. Cover the inner one with the back of the left hand. Pick up the outer one between the fingertips and thumb of the right hand, holding it flat near its edge so most of the coin will be visible. Pretend to place it in the left hand but retain it in the right as fol-

lows: Press the edge of the penny against the left palm and as that hand closes, slide the right fingers down over the coin so it will be hidden behind the ends of the fingers. Do not attempt to palm the coin but merely hold it in this fashion as the right hand moves away and the left hand closes. Properly done, the coin appears to be in the left hand. Immediately draw the penny inward so it lies on the curled fingers. This leaves the forefinger and thumb free to pick up the second coin.

When the left hand closes the inner coin will be exposed. Without hesitation the following actions take place simultaneously: Raise the left fist and blow into it at the thumb end while the right forefinger and thumb pick up the inner penny. *It is important* that these two actions be carried out together, not separately. Draw the penny into the right fist and hold the fists about a foot apart. Gesture with the right hand, then with the left as you say, "A penny here and a penny here. Right?" Before a spectator can answer, say, "No, nothing here." Open the left hand and show it empty, then say: "Both are here." Slowly open the right hand and show both coins in that hand.

The blowing into the left fist as the right hand picks up the second coin serves as a distracting element. It is impossible for the spectators to concentrate on both actions at once. The blowing business is the key to the trick. Without it the trick would fool no one. But performed as described it is guaranteed to baffle layman and magician alike. You must remember not to perform the trick too fast or too slow, but in a smooth, even tempo. Learn to blend all moves together in one harmonious whole and you will have a trick that will be a delight to perform. It is so easy, yet so baffling.

Once you have the trick thoroughly

mastered you may feel safe in repeating it several times without fear of detection.

The Inseparable Pair

Although the end result of this effect is the same as the one that follows the handling is entirely different. Since both versions require two coins, they can be worked together or as companion effects.

Effect: Showing two coins on the table, the performer picks up one in each hand, then closes the fingers over them. He crosses his arms at the wrists and opens his hands to show a coin in each, then closes them again and turns them over. To further convince the spectators, he releases the coin from his left hand and allows it to fall on the table. Picking it up again with the same hand, he releases the coin from his right hand and allows it to fall, picking it up immediately with the same hand. The hands are held far apart while the left hand makes a tossing motion toward the right. A coin is heard to arrive in the right hand. Left hand is opened and shown empty, then the right is opened to show both coins.

Method: Show two half dollars and place them on the table about six inches apart. Pick up a coin with each hand and display them for a moment lying on the palms. Then close the hands, turn them over and cross the arms at the wrists. With the arms

still crossed at the wrists, turn them palm up and open both hands, showing a coin in each, Fig. 1. Close the hands and turn them over again, still keeping them crossed. As this is done, the fingers of the right hand should press its coin firmly into the palm and hold it there. This is just a "get ready" move in preparation for what is to follow. Both hands are closed and appear the same, but the coin in the left hand is held loosely, while the coin in the right is held securely in the palm.

Fig. 2

To show that each hand still contains a coin, swing both to the left, opening the left hand as you do so. This allows that coin to fall to the table, Fig. 2. Pick up the coin with the left hand, but, instead of closing the fingers over it, hold it clipped

Fig. 3

Fig. I

between the finger tips and the base of the hand. (Fig. 3 shows how the coin is held as viewed from underneath the hand.) At this point the hands should be quite close to the table, so that the coin is not visible to the spectators. Just be sure this is viewed from above and not from a low vantage point. Arms remain crossed at the wrists.

Open the right hand as the arms are swung to the right, but, instead of dropping the coin from that hand, hold it palmed and release pressure on the other coin, which falls to the table. There is no visible movement as the left hand releases its coin, because it is synchronized with the

Fig. 4

opening of the right hand. It appears as though you dropped the coin from the right, Fig. 4. Apparently you have dropped first one coin, then the other. Actually the same coin was dropped both times. Properly executed, this subterfuge is a perfect illusion. Left hand is still closed, but empty. The right hand has the coin palmed.

Uncross arms and pick up the coin from the table with your right fingers and thumb. Close the hand into a loose fist, allowing the coin to rest on the fingers directly underneath the other palmed one. Hold the hands some distance apart, then move the left fist quickly to the right a few inches in a tossing motion. An instant later release the coin from the right palm, permitting it to clink down on the one lying on the fingers. Open the left hand and show it empty, then show both coins in the right.

Apparently you have tossed the coin from the left hand invisibly through space into the right.

Do not underestimate the effect of this last movement. Fix your attention firmly on the left fist as you go through the tossing motion with it. Turn your eyes quickly to the right hand as that hand allows its two coins to come audibly together.

The effect is a good one.

As a variation, the same moves can be utilized to obtain a penetration effect. To accomplish this, proceed as described up to the point where the right hand has just picked up the coin which was secretly dropped by the left. Carry the right hand underneath the table to a point directly below the left hand, which is held a few inches above the table top. Announce your intentions, then suddenly open the left hand and bring it down noiselessly, flat on the table. A fraction of a second later release the coin in the right palm permitting it to fall noisily onto the one lying on the fingers. Turn the left hand over and show it empty. Rattle the two coins in the right hand as you bring it up and toss the coins onto the table.

Royal Brin performs this trick with a copper and a silver coin. How? Simple! He uses that double faced coin which shows a silver coin on one side and a copper coin on the other. (See Copper and Silver Transposition, page 243, for a description of this coin.) He holds the gimmicked coin copper side up in his left hand. Using the same moves just described he drops the same coin twice—once as a copper coin, once as a silver coin.

The illusion of apparently showing the two coins is much more convincing when this subterfuge is employed. The only precaution necessary is to be sure the surface on which you drop the coins is a soft one, otherwise the fake coin will sound very unnatural. Special care will also have to be exercised in controlling the fake coin so it will land proper side up each time. However, that is a simple matter.

Coins in the Teeth

Equally as mystifying as the preceding trick, but much more showy, is this trick with two coins.

Effect: The performer shows a coin in each hand. The left hand's coin is placed between the teeth. The right hand's coin is tossed into the left, then the coin between the teeth is dropped into the right hand.

This is repeated.

For the third time he shows a coin in each hand and places the coin held by the left hand between his teeth. The right hand's coin is placed in the left hand which closes over it. Taking the coin from between his teeth he places it in the left hand also, it being heard to fall onto the other one already there, audible proof that both coins are actually in the left hand. Yet a moment later the magician opens his left hand and shows it empty. The missing coins are produced by the right hand from behind the knee.

Method: This depends mainly on the Click Pass (b), page 14. The rest is window dressing.

Stand facing the spectators as you show a half dollar in each hand, holding each upright at the tips of the fingers. Place the left hand's coin between the teeth, then deposit the right hand's coin in the left. Now, drop the coin from between the teeth and catch it in the right hand.

Repeat the entire procedure.

Apparently repeat for the third time by placing the left hand's coin between the teeth. Turn slightly to the left and go through the motions of putting the right hand's coin in the left, but retain it classic palmed instead. Close your left hand as if it actually held a coin. Keep the back of the right hand toward the spectators as you remove the coin from between the teeth with the fingers. Execute The Click Pass as you pretend to place this second coin in the left hand. Because of the sound created by The Click Pass the spectators believe both coins to be in the left hand when actually both are classic palmed in the right.

After pausing a moment for effect, open the left hand and show it empty. Reach behind the right knee for the two coins. Rattle them as you bring them into view and toss them onto the table.

The Drop Pass

JIMMY BUFFALOE

Effect: The magician shows two coins and places them on the table about a foot apart. He takes the right hand coin in his left hand in such a manner there is no doubt that the coin is actually in that hand. The remaining coin is taken in his right hand. Holding the hands some distance apart, he opens his left, showing it empty. At this instant the missing coin is heard to join the other in the right hand, which is then opened to show the two coins.

Method: A clever new sleight is responsible for the trickery in this two coin puzzler. Begin by showing a half dollar in each hand. Slap them onto the table so they will lie about a foot apart, then rest the fingertips of both hands on the table behind the coins. Keeping the left hand palm down, reach across and pick up the coin on the right as follows: Holding the hand in a loose fist, place the base of the thumb on top of the inner edge of the coin and press this edge to the table as the outer edge is lifted by inserting the nail of the second finger underneath it. Push the tips of the two middle fingers under the outer edge so the coin will stand upright on its edge. Grip the top edge of the coin between the tips of the two middle fingers and heel of hand. (Fig. 3, The Inseparable Pair.) The hand is closed and from the spectators' viewpoint appears perfectly natural. Apparently the coin is within the hand. Actually it is outside the fist and can be instantly released by slightly relaxing the two middle fingers.

Immediately after the left hand has picked up the coin on the right as described, and before it returns to its former position, the right hand prepares to reach for the coin on the left. In its journey to the coin on the left, it passes underneath

Fig. 1

the left hand (as it is being withdrawn to its original position), which drops its coin, and it is caught on the cupped right fingers, Fig. 1. Both hands are moving together—the left hand inward to the left, and the right hand outward to the left. Pick up the coin on the left with the right hand, and as the hand is brought back to its original position, transfer the coin lying on the cupped fingers to the palm, then allow the one just picked up to rest on the

cupped fingers. Close the right hand into a loose fist and hold the hands far apart. The instant the left hand is opened and shown empty, release the coin in the right palm permitting it to fall onto the other one with a "clink." Open the right hand showing two coins.

Follow this with The Hippity Hop Half.

The Hippity Hop Half

JIMMY BUFFALOE

Two coins are on the table. The performer puts one in his left hand, then takes the other in his right. (And the right hand is seen to be holding only *one* coin.) Both hands are turned over and slapped on the table. Apparently there is a coin underneath each palm, but when the hands are lifted none is under the left—both are under the right.

Method: Call attention to the two coins on the table—they are about a foot apart. Pick up the left coin with the right hand and pretend to put it in the left hand, but retain it palmed in the right. Close the left as if it held the coin, then rest the knuckles on the table. Take the remaining coin with the palm down right hand, and under cover of the action of moving it a few inches to the right to do so this is what takes place: The instant the right hand picks up the coin from the table, back palm it (a simple matter, since the hand is in a loose fist and the action is covered by the back of the hand), then drop the palmed coin onto the cupped fingers. Turn the hand clockwise as you open it out flat, showing a coin lying on the two middle fingers (this is taken to be the coin just removed from the table). It should appear that you merely picked up the second coin with the right hand, which you then turned palm up to show the coin. Keep the right hand very close to the table, then release the back palmed coin allowing it to rest on the table underneath the fingers, Fig. 1. (Obviously, the trick must be performed on a cloth covered table or on a rug.) Move the hand forward slightly so the coin on the table will be covered by that portion of the

Fig. 1

Coin backpalmed

Fig. 2

Coin under knuckles on table

fingers between the knuckles and middle joints. Because the right hand appears very natural and to all appearances holds only one coin, the belief is further strengthened that the other coin must be in the left hand.

Close the right fingers over the visible coin, being careful not to expose the one underneath the hand. The position of the right hand at this juncture is shown in Fig. 2. Quickly turn over both hands simultaneously and slap them palm down on the table. As this is done the coin held by the right hand is brought down with an audible clink onto the one resting on the table. Lift

both hands simultaneously, showing that the left half has apparently hopped over to join the one on the right.

Rapid Transit

ROYAL H. BRIN, JR.

Effect: Showing two coins, the performer places one in his left hand, closes it and turns it over. The second coin is put on the back of the left hand. The right hand is then closed into a fist and held some distance from the left. A spectator moves the outside, visible coin from the back of the left fist to the back of the right fist. As this is done, performer explains that when this coin is moved the other follows it. To prove this, he opens his left hand. It is empty. The missing coin is found in the right hand.

Method: Call attention to two coins on the table, and for the sake of explanation let's call one A and the other B. Pick up A and place it on the palm of the left hand. The right hand now takes the second coin (B), and puts it on the back of the left, which closes and turns over for the purpose. However, it is in this action that coin A is sleeved in the right sleeve. This is accomplished in a manner similar to the one described in Inflation, (page 118). The exact mechanics are: After taking coin B in the right hand, turn slightly to the left and move both hands toward each other. Bring them to a halt suddenly. This causes the coin A lying on the left palm to shoot into the right sleeve. (This specific action is concealed from view by the back of the right hand.) Immediately close the left hand and turn it over so coin B may be deposited on its back. As you separate the hands let it be clearly seen that the right hand is empty.

Face the spectators, and as you remind

them that one coin is inside the fist and the other on top, drop the right hand to the side, retrieving coin A as it falls from the sleeve. Keep your eyes on the left hand so the spectators' attention will also be focussed there. Now bring up the right hand, close it into a fist and hold it back up about a foot from the left fist. Ask a spectator near you to move the visible coin B from the back of the left hand to the back of the right.

When this is done, announce that the concealed coin passes invisibly from one hand to the other when the visible coin is moved. Open the left hand and show it empty. Then to show that coin A has arrived in the right hand, the following little flourish is effective: Toss B upward from the back of the right hand, then turn hand over and open it, allowing coin B to strike A when it is caught. Leave the right hand extended for a few seconds so it can be seen that both coins are there. Pausing thus adds to the effect of the unusual climax.

Of course, it is obvious that a somewhat similar effect can be obtained without sleeving, by merely retaining A in the right hand when apparently placing it in the left, by use of the many sleights for the purpose. However, the method just described has these two advantages: (1) the spectators actually see coin A resting on the palm of the left hand and thus know that it was really put there; (2) the right hand is seen to be empty after both coins have been deposited, which gives further proof of fairness of procedure. The sleeving move is easy to do and is justified by those strong points.

The trick works equally as well with almost any size coins, but the effect is enhanced if coins of contrasting color are used, such as a half dollar and an English penny, or a half dollar and a Chinese coin. Or, instead of B being a coin, it could be a small magnet or rabbit's foot. If a rabbit's foot were used you could explain that the transportation was due to the potency of the rabbit's foot. It's funny, but people like to believe such things.

Winged Silver

(A basic method using an extra coin.)

NELSON C. HAHNE

The principle used in this coin migration effect is almost as old as magic itself. It has been used in various forms by magicians for so long it is considered basic and standard.

The trick will first be described in its original form, then in its improved version. Although any small number of coins may be used, four seems to be ideal.

Effect: Four coins pass one at a time invisibly from one hand to the other.

Method: You will require five half dollars for the feat, although the spectators are aware of only four. Either borrow the four coins from the spectators or provide them yourself. In each case you must secretly obtain a fifth coin and conceal it in the right palm. There are numerous ways of doing this. A simple plan would be to palm the extra coin as the others are brought from the pocket. If you intend borrowing the four coins, casually place the right hand in the trousers pocket and palm the fifth coin while you ask for the loan of the others and wait until they are forthcoming.

Having obtained the four coins one way or another, display them in the palm up left hand with the forward coin lying at the base of the two middle fingers in readiness for finger palming. With the aid of the right fingers, move the coins about slightly, calling attention to the number—four. Go through the motions of tossing the coins into the right hand, but toss only three of them, the forward coin being finger palmed. Turn the left hand inward and over as you do this so as not to expose the coin held in the left finger palm. Show four coins in the right hand, three just received from the left and one which was already there. (See the Utility Switch, page 11.) The coins are transferred from the left hand to the right under the pretext of showing them to the spectators on the right. In fact, every time this move is made it must be done apparently as an excuse for giving the spectators on the right a better look at the coins. Display them in the right hand for a moment, then toss them onto the table (or give them to a person near you to hold).

The Utility Switch accomplishes two things—it enables you to show both hands in a fair manner, and to emphasize the fact (?) that you have only four coins. Correctly executed, the spectators will be unaware of the extra coin finger palmed in your left hand.

Pick up one of the four coins from the table with the right hand, and as you show it, raise the left to about waist level, keeping its back toward the spectators. Turn slightly to the left and go through the motions of throwing the coin from the right hand toward the left, but retain it classic palmed in the right. The actual mechanics used to accomplish this are as follows: Display the coin in the right hand, holding it between the tips of the index finger and thumb, then in the action of raising the hand for the pretended throw, place the tips of the two middle fingers against the coin and press it into the palm. Make the throw with the right hand, then make a grab in the air with the left hand, pretending to catch the coin. Immediately open the left hand and show the coin.

Now you must simulate taking the coin from the left hand with the right. This is done as follows: When you open your left hand the coin will be lying at the base of the two middle fingers. Hold the left hand in front of you with the fingers pointing to the right. Place the right fingers (which are held close together) against the front edge of the coin and the thumb against the inner edge, hiding coin from view. Pretend to carry away the coin between the right fingertips and thumb, simultaneously turning the back of the left hand toward the audience. Retain the coin finger palmed and point to the right hand as it moves away. Turn the right hand palm up, close it into a loose fist, then open it, showing the half dollar lying on the palm (which is the one that had been there all the time).

Immediately transfer the coin from the palm to the fingers and flip it into the air, catching it in its descent. This serves as misdirection, enabling the left hand to shift its coin from the finger palm to the classic palm. It is then held in a loose fist with the fingers downward. Push the right hand coin into the left fist from the thumb end, allowing it to rest on the fingers. To the spectators it appears that you merely took the coin in the right hand, flipped it into the air, then replaced it in the left hand. Unknown to the spectators, there are now two coins in the left hand (one in the palm and one lying on the fingers)—they believe it contains only one.

Pick up coin number two from the table with the right hand and hold the hands far apart. Go through the motions of throwing this coin toward the left hand as you did the first, but palm it instead. Left hand immediately releases the coin in its palm, permitting it to fall with a "clink" onto the one lying on the fingers. The move produces a perfect illusion of the coin actually being thrown into the hand. Turn the left hand palm up and open it, showing the two coins. (One is still palmed in the right.)

Execute the Utility Switch as you apparently toss these two coins into the right hand. In reality you retain one finger palmed in the left hand as you throw the other. Immediately show two coins in the right hand, one just received and the other which was already there. While the right hand displays the two coins to the spectators on the right, transfer the coin in the left hand from finger palm to classic palm, keeping the back of the hand toward the audience. Hold the left hand in a loose fist as before and replace the two coins from right hand, being sure they go on the curled fingers, directly below the palmed coin.

Take the third coin from the table with the right hand and as you repeat the moves of apparently throwing it toward the left hand, release the coin in the left palm permitting it to clatter down on the two resting on the curled fingers. Turn the left hand palm up and open it, showing three coins.

Again execute the Utility Switch as you apparently toss these three coins into the right hand. Actually, you retain one finger palmed in the left hand as you throw two. Show three coins in the right hand, two just received from the left and one which was already there. Again shift the finger palmed coin in the left hand to classic palm position as you exhibit the three coins in the right. Place them back in the left hand as you did the others, the coins going on the curled fingers.

Three coins have now passed magically into the left hand. One remains on the table. To conclude the trick properly you must dispose of this last coin as you pretend to pass it into your left hand, so that at the finish you can show that you have only four coins. To do this, proceed as follows: Pick up this last coin from the table with the right hand and turn slightly to the left. Hold it between the tips of the first two fingers and as you go through the motions of tossing it straight up into the air, thumb palm it. As you follow its invisible flight upward, lower your right hand to the breast coat pocket and drop the coin in it. Keep your eyes firmly fixed on the non-existent coin, following its descent. Just as it apparently nears the left hand, release the palmed coin so it will fall on top of the other three resting on the fingers. Rattle the coins in the left hand, then show the right hand empty. Open the left hand and show the four coins. The hands are otherwise empty and there is no clue to the mystery.

Although it has taken a great many words to describe this trick in detail, actually it is quite simple. The transmission of each coin from the right hand to the left is accomplished through the repetition of the same moves over and over.

If, for some reason, you prefer not to get rid of the last coin in your pocket as explained, you may palm it in the right hand as you did the others, then, as a clean-up move, execute the Utility Switch by tossing three of the four coins into the right hand. The spectators see four coins in the right hand and naturally assume that there are no more. Finally toss the four back into the left hand and place all five into the pocket.

IMPROVED VERSION

The moves in this version are identical with the ones just described, except an additional smaller coin is used. This can be almost any coin, such as a quarter, a Chinese coin, a gold coin, or an unusual pocket piece. It is not concealed from the spectators but used openly along with the others and, because of it, a more puzzling effect is created. For the sake of explanation, let's say the extra coin is a Chinese coin. You will still need five half dollars, one of which must be kept concealed from the audience as in the original method.

Begin the feat by showing four half dollars and the Chinese coin in the left hand, one of the halves being in position for finger palming. The fifth half dollar is concealed in the right palm. Perform the Utility Switch as you toss three of the half dollars and the Chinese coin into the right hand (retain the fourth in the left finger palm). Show four halves (one of which was already there) and the Chinese coin in the right hand, then toss them onto the table.

Explain that the Chinese coin will be used as a magnet to draw the others to it. Pick up the Chinese coin and push it into the left fist so it lies on the curled fingers as in the above method.

The trick continues from here exactly as in the first version; that is, you take the first half dollar from the table and as you pretend to toss it into the left hand, palm it. As this is done, release the half dollar in the left palm, letting it fall audibly onto the Chinese coin. Open the left hand and show that the half has arrived. Go through the motions of tossing both coins into the right hand, but do the Utility Switch, and throw only the Chinese coin. Immediately show a half dollar (which was already there) and the Chinese coin in the right hand. Place both back in the left hand and continue these moves until all four halves have passed into the left hand.

Adding the Chinese coin to this ancient trick not only enhances the mystery but usually confuses those who are acquainted with the secret of the old method.

The Flying Eagles

Effect: Three coins leave the right hand to join three in the left hand, one by one, in a convincing manner.

Method: Borrow six half dollars, or, to save time you may have six of your own ready. Better, have four of your own and borrow two, giving the impression you have no more of your own. A seventh coin is concealed in the right palm. Take the six coins in the left hand and move them about with the right fingers while you call attention to the number. This natural action draws all the attention to the six coins.

Pick up three coins between the fingertips and thumb of the right hand and place them in a row on the table to your right, then take the remaining three in the same manner and put them in a row on your left. With the palm down right hand, take up one of the coins from the row on the left and drop it into the left hand, counting, "One." As you reach for the next coin allow the palmed coin to fall onto the cupped fingers. Pick up the second coin and drop it AND the hidden coin in the left hand, counting, "Two." Turn the right hand palm up and gesture toward the third coin, then pick it up as you say, "And one more makes three." Drop it into the left hand on top of the others.

The right hand group of three coins is taken in the right hand in the following manner: Pick up the first one and press it into the palm, counting, "One." Take up the second and third, counting, "Two, three," and hold them on the cupped fingers. You now have four coins in the left hand and three in the right. Hold the hands some distance apart and command one coin to pass from the right hand to the left. Make a slight throwing motion with the right hand toward the left, then keeping the right hand palm down, open it, allowing two coins to tumble to the table, counting, "One, two." (One is still palmed in the hand.) Open the left hand to show four coins, then count them onto the table to your left.

Go through the same set of movements to cause the next coin to pass. Add the concealed coin as you count the five coins back into the left hand. Show the last coin openly in the right hand, then as you go through the motions of throwing it toward the left, sleeve it, using The Throw method (page 104). Display an empty right hand, then open the left, showing all six coins. You can get rid of the sleeved coin later at an opportune moment by dropping it into your pocket, or immediately as you count the six coins from your left hand onto the table.

Variation

One of the easiest and most effective coin transposition effects I know is this one which was shown to me by Señor Mardo during the S. A. M. Convention at Denver in 1949.

It is similar in effect to the preceding version but eight coins are used—four copper and four silver.

Working: Arrange four copper coins in a vertical row on the table. Parallel with this row, and about five or six inches to the right, place four half dollars. With the right hand, pick up one copper coin and as you pretend to place it in your left hand, palm it in the right. Close the left hand into a fist and turn it thumb side up. Keeping the right hand palm down, gather up the remaining copper coins and insert them part way in the top of the left fist, then allow them to sink into the fist. Apparently the left hand holds four copper coins. Actually it contains only three, the fourth being concealed in the right palm.

Now as you pick up one of the silver coins with the right hand and place it on top of the left fist, say, "Every time I remove a silver coin from this row and add it to the copper coins (allow silver coin to sink into

left fist, then take up the remaining three with the right hand) a copper coin travels over to take its place." Open the right hand and spread four coins on the table, three silver and the copper which you had palmed previously. Open the left hand, and as you spread the three copper and one silver on the table, call attention to the fact that one copper and one silver have changed places.

Go through the same motions three more times until all the copper coins are lined up on the right and all the silver coins are lined up on the left.

One of the nicest things about this routine is the method. Only one sleight is necessary to perform it—that is the one that retains the copper coin in the right hand.

Even though the mystery makes use of only one sleight it is best to vary your methods. Instead of beginning as described, do this: With the left hand, pick up the four copper coins and arrange them in a row in the palm up right hand. Show them, then as you turn the right hand over retain one coin classic palmed and dump the other three into the left hand, which immediately closes and rattle them. Proceed as described.

For retaining a copper coin in the right hand the next three times execute the following three vanishes: Simple Vanish, Drop Vanish, and The Tunnel Vanish, or any three different vanishes from Chapter III.

Three and Three

Because of its simplicity, this has become one of my favorite "coin pass" effects. I hope it will become one of yours, too.

Effect: Three coins pass one at a time from the left hand to join three others held in the right hand.

Method: Show six half dollars, then place them on the table, in two parallel rows, three on the left and three on the right. With the left hand, pick up a coin from the left row and put it squarely in the palm of the palm up right hand; then take the remaining two and place them slightly forward of the first one. Show the three coins, then toss the forward two into the left hand, retaining the inner one classic palmed. Immediately rattle the two in the closed left hand and say, "Three half dollars."

Keeping the right hand palm down so as not to expose the coin in its palm, gather the right hand row of three coins and allow them to rest on the cupped fingers. Say, "And three half dollars here." With the backs of both hands toward the audience and both held far apart, make a tossing motion with the left hand toward the right and release the coin from the right palm allowing it to fall onto the three on the fingers with a "clink." Open the left hand, show the two coins, and put them on the table to the left. Open the right hand showing that the coin has arrived, then place the four coins on the table to the right.

With the right hand, pick up one of the two coins from the left row and pretend to place it in the left hand, but retain it palmed instead. Take the second coin and go through the motions of placing it in the left hand also, but execute The Click Pass (a), (page 14) instead. Because of the sound created by The Click Pass the spectators believe the left hand to contain two coins. Actually it holds only one, the other being palmed in the right. Gather the four remaining coins from the table with the right hand, and hold them on the cupped fingers as before, as you say, "Four coins here," then gesturing with the left hand, add, "and two coins here." Keep the hands some distance apart as you repeat the tossing motion with the left hand, and as you do so allow the coin in the right palm to

drop audibly onto the other four resting on the cupped fingers. Open the left hand and show one coin. Put it on the table to the left. Open the right hand and show five coins. Place them on the table to the right.

Pick up the single coin from the left and apparently place it in the left hand, but retain it in the right palm. With the right hand, gather the five coins from the table and hold them on the cupped fingers as before. The spectators think you have one coin in your left hand and five in your right. Actually, however, all are in the right, while the left is empty. Tell the spectators to watch the last coin as it travels across to the right hand. Repeat the tossing motion with the left hand, then open it and show it empty. Open the right hand, show the six coins and dump them onto the table.

Practice releasing the palmed coin in the right hand to coincide with the throwing motion of the left. Herein lies the effect of the trick.

The real beauty of this little mystery is that a different move is used to cause each coin to leave the left hand and pass into the right. For this reason it is practically impossible to follow.

Chinese Money Mystery

Effect: The performer places eight pennies on a table, four in each of two vertical rows. Beginning at one end of the two rows and using both hands, he picks up a coin from each row simultaneously. To show that everything is fair, he tosses the two coins back on the table and again picks them up, one in each hand. He gathers the next two in exactly the same manner, throws them to the table, takes one in each hand as before and continues in this manner until none remain. Although he should have four pennies in each hand, when he opens his hands, he holds all of the coins in the left and none in the right. Just eight coins are used.

Method: The trick is performed more easily on a soft surface, such as a rug or sofa. A towel or a piece of heavy cloth can be spread on any hard surface for performing the effect. If the trick is performed on a hard surface, the coins bounce too much when thrown from the hands.

Lay two rows of four coins on the table, or floor, parallel with each other and vertical, the rows being about four inches apart. Any even number of coins can be used in the trick, but eight seems to be just right.

Call attention to the fact that you have two rows of four coins. Show your hands

Fig. 1

empty, close them into a loose fist and then turn them backs up. Start at the inner end of the two rows and work outward. Use the thumb and second joint of the first finger of each hand to pick up the first two coins, Fig. 1, which you grasp simultaneously and then throw quickly to the table, saying, "Two by two." Pick them up again, a coin in each hand. Keep the coins from view, holding them between the thumb and fore-finger at the middle joint, Fig. 2.

Fig. 2

Say, "Two by two," as you pick up the next two in the same manner and apparently throw them to the table. However, both coins are thrown from the right hand and none from the left. The hands swing downward in an arc with the thumbs pointing inward toward each other. As the fists are raised in preparation for the throw they are held the same distance apart as are the two rows of coins. Then as they move quickly downward they swing toward each other in the arc and both coins are released from the right hand the exact instant the hands are closest to each other. They continue on downward without hesitation, finally coming to rest on the table, a fist at the inner end of each row of coins. The illusion is that a coin came from each hand. Properly executed, the deception is so perfect it is impossible for the closest observer to detect that this was a fake throw and that both coins came from the same hand. When the throw is made correctly the coins will land a few inches apart, one on the right and one on the left.

Pick up the two coins just tossed to the table, one in each hand, which places three in the left hand and only one in the right. At this point the spectators think that you hold two coins in each hand. Four coins remain on the table.

Continue picking up pairs and throwing only the ones in the right hand until all have been so handled. At the finish of these actions you will have seven coins in the left hand and one in the right. Each time you pick up a pair of coins and throw them to the table say, "Two by two."

Hold the hands far apart, then gesture with the left hand as you ask, "How many coins do I have here?" The answer will, of course, be "Four." "And how many here?" (indicating the right hand). The answer will again be "Four." "Apparently this is so," you say, "but actually they are all here." As you say this, open the left hand showing the seven coins. Simultaneously turn the right hand palm down, open it and rest the finger tips on the table, the single coin being classic palmed. Before the spectators are able to count the coins in the left hand, quickly turn the right hand palm up and toss the coins into it. Immediately throw them back into the left hand, which then tosses them onto the table.

An alternate finish is this: Hold the fists far apart as you pretend to toss the four (?) coins from the right hand invisibly into the left. Follow the flight of each coin with your eyes until only one remains in the right hand. As you pretend to toss the last coin, accidentally (?) drop this one to the table. Apologize for fumbling on the last coin, pick it up with the LEFT hand, then open it to show all eight coins. Open the right hand and show it empty.

The trick works best with small coins, such as pennies. It is most effective if done with the small Chinese coins with the square holes, but be sure they match.

If you can procure some old Chinese coins at a coin dealer's, you will have the added advantages of glamor and antiquity to work into your patter for the trick.

If you work the trick on the floor, spread a white pocket handkerchief on the rug first. This not only dresses the trick but makes the coins easier to see because of the contrast.

Frank Drobina's Coin Routine

FRANK DROBINA

Several years ago, while attending the Texas Association of Magicians Convention in San Antonio, Texas, I saw this effect for the first time. Although the routine makes use of simple, actually elementary sleights, it is a real baffler, and is calculated to puzzle the keenest observer, whether layman or magician.

To make this book complete I felt that I must have Frank's routine, but when I wrote him he replied that he couldn't do the trick justice without demonstrating it in person. He said he would be glad to teach it to me on our first meeting. Time went by, and to make a long story short I had to make a special trip into Flint, Michigan to get the full working details.

So, it is with great pleasure that I now present Frank Drobina's Coin Routine.

Effect: Five coins pass through the air from one hand to the other, invisibly.

Time: Five to seven minutes.

Requirements: Six small coins, dimes preferred.

Preparation: Place the six coins in the right trouser pocket sometime before you intend doing the trick.

Sleights: A thumb palm that is a little different from the one explained in Chapter I. With this one the coin lies at a right angle to the hand and thumb, and is pressed into the fleshy part of the hand at the base

Fig. I

of the thumb, being held in this position by its edges, Fig. 1.

With the coin thus concealed, there is more freedom of movement than with the regular thumb palm. The hand appears very natural and the thumb does not lie flat against the hand in a tell-tale fashion.

Whenever the thumb palm is mentioned in this routine it refers to the one just described.

PHASE ONE

Reach in the pocket, thumb palm one of the coins, and remove the other five. Toss the five dimes into the left hand and jingle them, then toss them back and forth a few times, letting it be seen that the hands are otherwise empty. Keeping the back of the right hand toward the spectators, place the five coins onto the table. Move them about with the right fingertips as you call attention to the number.

With the right fingers, slide two of the coins to the left a few inches. Now there are two coins on the left and three on the right.

The following business is designed to confuse the spectators. Look first at the left hand then at the right hand as you say, "This is my left hand and this is my right." Keep the backs of both hands toward the spectators and move them back and forth as you call attention to each hand. "I'm going to place two coins in my left hand." Pick up the two coins from the left side of the table and drop them into the left hand, closing it immediately. Pick up the remaining three coins with the right hand and close the fingers over them. "Remember, this is my right hand and this is my left hand." Slap all of the coins (except the palmed coin) onto the table and draw the hands away. Five coins are seen. Again call attention to the two hands as you repeat, "Don't forget, this is my right hand and

this is my left. If I turn around, *this* will be my left hand and *this* will be my right hand. Right?" They will agree. You say, "No, no, *this* will always be my left hand and *this* will always be my right hand." So

Fig. 2

you point to each hand again to get them straight.

Pick up the two dimes with the right fingers and thumb and drop them into the cupped left hand. Place the two coins over on the left side of the hand at the base of the first finger, and simultaneously, drop the palmed dime so it will land on the opposite side of the hand at the base of the third and fourth fingers, Fig. 2. The coins are placed in this position in preparation for the next move. If the left hand is held as described there will be no need to hurry in closing it. The cupped fingers prevent

Fig. 3

the extra coin from being seen. Close the left hand slowly and let your eyes travel to the other three coins on the table. Pick them up and hold them in a row on the right fingers, the outer one lying on the tip of the forefinger in readiness for the thumb palm, Fig. 3. As you close the right hand press the dime into the thumb palm with the right forefinger. "Remember, this is my right hand and this is my left. Let's assume I placed three coins in my left hand and two coins in my right hand, but *actually* how many do I have (look back and forth from hand to hand, finally stopping on the right hand) . . . in this hand?" They will answer "Two." You say, "No, I mean *actually* in this hand." (Shake the right hand again.) The spectator, thinking he was mistaken, will correct himself and say, "Three." You say, "No, no." Drop the three coins from the left hand onto the table and slap down two with the right hand, keeping the extra dime hidden in the thumb palm. "Don't try to guess."

Pick up the two coins with the right fingers and thumb and drop them into the left hand, but do not load in the extra coin. Remove the remaining three from the table with the right hand and close the fingers over them. Repeat your question, "How many coins do I have in my right hand?" He will answer, "Three." You say, "*Actually!*" He will change his mind and reply, "Two." Slap the five coins onto the table to show two in the left hand and three in the right hand, as you say, "No. Stop guessing!" By now he is thoroughly muddled.

Regardless of his reply set the stage for the next phase and give him another chance.

"Look, it seems like I'm confusing you in some way. Let's do this *one at a time* so you won't get mixed up." With the right forefinger, slide one of the two dimes over with the three, making four on the right and one on the left.

PHASE TWO

Pick up the single coin with the right fingers and thumb and throw it into the left hand, immediately closing the fingers over it. "Did you see it?" Open the left hand and show the dime. Remove it with the right hand and toss it back as you repeat the question. "Did you see it?"

Open the left hand and as you remove the dime with the right fingers and thumb drop the palmed coin at the same time so it will fall at the base of the third and fourth fingers. Clip it between those two fingers and turn the hand back toward the spectators, holding it about shoulder high. (In case the coin does not land in the correct position merely bend the fingers inward slightly and retain it where it does land.) Show the dime lying on the end of the right forefinger.

Draw the right hand back, press the dime into thumb palm, and make a throwing motion toward the left hand. The palming of the coin in the right hand takes place as the hand is drawn back for the throw. As the right hand pretends to throw the coin, the left hand closes. Then open the left hand to show that the dime has arrived. Remove it with the right hand as you say, "It goes right through and doesn't hurt a bit." (The reason you remove this coin from the left hand is to give you a chance to add the palmed coin when you replace it a moment later.) The right hand drops the dime back into the left hand and adds the palmed coin at the same time. As the right fingers and thumb place the dime in position on the left side of the hand the palmed one is dropped so it will land at the base of the third and fourth fingers. This not only prevents the two coins from clinking together—it puts them into position for the next move. Close the left hand over the coins keeping them in their original positions and turn the back of the hand toward the audience. Hold the left hand about shoulder height as before as you reach for another coin with the right.

Repeat the throwing motions with the right hand and thumb palm the dime. Follow the flight of the invisible coin over to the left hand with your eyes. Relax the left hand slightly, allowing the upper coin to fall onto the lower one with a decided "clink," as you exclaim, "Did you hear it?"

Acting very surprised, open your left hand to show the two coins. Remove them with the right fingers and thumb and show the left hand empty. As you place the two coins back into the left hand drop the palmed coin also. Drop the two on the left side of the hand and the single coin about an inch away on the right side of the hand in preparation for the next move.

Take another coin from the table and pretend to pass it into the left fist, but thumb palm it as before. Follow its flight to the left hand and allow the upper single coin to fall down onto the other two making a "clinking" sound.

"Did you hear it? You can always hear it, but never see it. You see, I throw curves and as they go by I grab them very quickly."

"Anybody can throw them like this." Pick up another coin and actually throw it into the open left hand so everyone can see it. Reach over with the right hand and remove the coin, simultaneously dropping the palmed coin so it will land at the base of the left third and fourth fingers. Close the left hand and hold it with its back toward the audience, about shoulder height. "Look," (put the coin in the right hand on the table and point to the back of the left fist)—"see the scars! That's where they go through." Pick up the coin again with the right hand, keeping the palm turned down. (Of course, there is no coin in the thumb palm now.) As you tell them to watch the fourth coin turn the right hand

over so they can see clearly that you have only the single coin. (It lies on the tip of the forefinger.) Pretend to toss this coin into the left hand but thumb palm it as before. Open the left hand to show the coin has arrived. Each time a coin is caught in the left hand allow the coins to "clink" together. This helps create the illusion you are striving for. Dump the four coins into the right hand and rattle them, then place them on the table. (One dime is concealed in the right thumb palm.)

An easy, careless handling of the right hand at all times will convince the most skeptical spectator that the hand is empty.

PHASE THREE

Allow a moment for the spectators to grasp what has happened, then pick out a person near you and tell him you will throw the last coin into his hand. As you reach for the four coins on the table allow the thumb palmed coin to drop onto the cupped fingers. Pick up the coins and give them to him to hold. Keep talking to him as you drop the coins into his hand. Ask him if he is right or left handed, or move him from one side to another. The spectator believes he has four coins, but actually he has five. Caution him to hold the coins tightly as you pick up the last dime from the table with the right hand. Tell him it won't hurt a bit. Pretend to throw the dime, but thumb palm it instead. Quickly ask him if he felt it go in. If he says, "No," say, "Oh, so you're not feeling so well." If he says, "Yes," say, "Oh, so you're feeling pretty good." At any rate, have him open his hand. He will have five coins. Point to the coin farthest away from the others as you exclaim, "There it is!"

PHASE FOUR

Take the five coins from your helper and thank him for his assistance. Place the five coins onto the table. (A sixth is thumb palmed in the right hand.)

Pick out another spectator (one wearing a coat), and as you move him back load the thumb palmed coin into his outer left breast pocket. (See In a Spectator's Pocket (b), page 58.) Tell him you intend passing a coin by magic into his closed left hand, but he will have to imagine the coin flying through space—you usually throw it so fast no one can see it.

Pick up one of the coins from the table and as you go through the motions for throwing it toward him, thumb palm it as you did the previous coins. Follow its invisible flight with your eyes, and as it nears his hand have him make a quick grab for the coin. Suddenly shout, "Now!" Regardless of how he grabs tell him he did it wrong. He grabbed either too high, too low, too fast, or too slow.

"You didn't do it right. You missed the coin and it fell into your pocket."

Ask him to reach in his pocket and remove it. Take it and place it on the table with the rest. (One coin is thumb palmed in the right hand.)

PHASE FIVE

Tell the spectators that some of them may doubt that the coin that went into your helper's pocket was the same one you started with. So to convince them, you will have a coin marked. Allow someone to select and mark one of the dimes. As this is being done drop the right hand to the side and let the thumb palmed coin drop onto the curled fingers. When the coin has been marked receive it in the right hand and hold it between the forefinger and thumb. Now, direct everyone's attention to your left trouser pocket as you turn it inside out with the left hand. While you are doing this, the right hand thumb palms the marked dime and drops the other one onto

the table. (The Bobo Switch, page 10, can be substituted for this move.) This is done apparently to give you an extra hand to help show the pocket. Handle pocket with both hands as you call attention to its emptiness, no holes, etc. Turn the pocket back, then take the supposedly marked coin from the table and slowly and deliberately drop it into the pocket. Have someone verify that the coin is actually in the pocket by allowing them to feel it through the fabric. After everyone is satisfied, back up a little so they may have a better view. Allow the thumb palmed coin to fall onto the curled right fingers and place it flat against the leg outside of the pocket. With the right thumb pinch a fold of cloth above the coin and turn it downward over the coin concealing it from view. (For a more detailed description of this move see Through the Pocket (b), page 65.) Go through a rubbing motion as you bring the dime into view. Show that the coin did not make a hole in your trousers, then have it identified. It is the same coin!

The moves in this routine are so worked out that you will always be a step ahead of the spectators. Throughout the routine there are certain points that are designed to upset any solution which may begin to form in the minds of the spectators.

In Frank Drobina's hands the routine never fails to make a vivid impression on all who see it.

Four Coins to a Glass

Described by ARTHUR BUCKLEY

I rate this as one of my best coin illusions. Ever since I first read the "Coins to Glass" in Tommy Downs' book way back in 1908, I have been fascinated with the possibilities this feat offers. Other ways of performing the trick have appeared in *The*

Fig. 1

Sphinx and some in *The Linking Ring* under my name, but I consider this method my best.

The illusion: Proceed to gather four silver dollars, one by one, from the air, dropping them into an empty drinking glass held by the left hand. Pour the four coins

Fig. 2

from the glass onto the open right palm, and then set the empty glass aside. The four coins are tossed from the right palm into the open left palm and spread out by the fingertips of the right hand for all to see plainly that there are just four coins. The left hand is closed on the four coins. The fingers of the right hand pick up the glass by its rim. Gaze at the closed left hand, give it a little shake, and then look toward the glass. A coin is seen and heard to fall into the glass. Place the glass on the table in plain view. Toss the coins from the left hand into the open palm of the right. Spread them so that it can be seen there

are but three. Toss the coins from the right hand to the left hand and again spread them to assure there are three. The left hand is closed on the three, and the glass is picked up by the fingertips and thumb of the right hand. The drama is re-enacted and another coin is seen and heard to fall into the glass. These moves are repeated for each of the remaining two coins, and they pass the same way as the first two coins, falling visibly into the glass held by the right hand. After the fourth coin has fallen into the glass, the left hand is slowly opened, and it is unmistakably empty.

These are the sleights required to perform this beautiful coin illusion:

Fig. 3

The production of four or five coins at the fingertips, one at a time, from the Downs palm position, as in Figs. 1, 2, 3, and 4.

Palming a coin and holding a glass by its rim with your fingertips and thumb, and releasing the coin at the desired instant so that it falls into the glass, as in Fig. 8.

Fig. 4

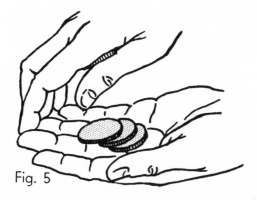

Fig. 5

The thumb palm, either hand, Figs. 5 and 6.

Tossing a coin or coins from the right hand into the left and retaining one coin, and repeating these moves from left hand to right hand, as in Figs, 5, 6 and 7. (In-

Fig. 6

stead of retaining a coin each time in the thumb palm, it can be retained in the finger palm as described in the Utility Switch, page 11.)

Holding a coin in the left hand and releasing it so that it will fall from your left palm into your handkerchief pocket, the fall of the coin completely concealed by your left arm.

Reviewing these sleights in the order given: The production with the five coins held in the crotch of the thumb as shown in Fig. 1. (This is the Downs palm.) The fingers close, the ball of the second finger

pressing lightly against the top four coins, and not against the bottom coin, the third finger passing beneath the bottom coin,

Fig. 7

Fig. 2, and doing so in a manner that permits it to be concealed by the thumb until the moment arrives for its appearance at the fingertips. When the coin has been carried past the tip of the thumb, the second finger releases it, and the thumb instantly presses it near the rim against the third fingertip, giving a startling reality to its

Fig. 8

sudden appearance at the fingertips. I have not hitherto revealed this very important detail of this sleight for producing coins at the fingertips, from the Downs palm, and I trust you may profit by its explanation. The figures are viewed from a side angle for explanatory reasons.

As each of the four coins is produced, it is allowed to fall into the glass held in the left hand. No one has the slightest reason to suspect that another coin remains hidden.

The four coins are spilled from the glass into the right hand to join the fifth. The glass is placed aside. The right thumb secretly retains one coin as the right hand turns the four coins back into the left palm; the coin retained in the right hand being thumb palmed, Fig. 5. This is best accomplished by bending the first finger around and over the edge of the coin, whereupon it is pressed against the fork of the thumb which easily presses down upon it to hold it securely but lightly in place. (Figs. 5 and 7 are the same as seen from the side and front.) The fingertips can easily spread the four coins in the left palm without danger of exposing the thumb palmed coin in the right hand, or imparting any suspicion of same to the onlookers. The right hand takes up the glass, and in doing so shifts the retained coin to the classic palm, Fig. 8. The left hand closes on the four coins, and the right hand releases the palmed coin, and it falls into the glass. The right hand places the glass on the table.

The left hand turns over to spill out the coins as the right turns palm up to receive them; and the left thumb retains the coin resting against the left palm, and only three coins are spilled on the right palm. The fingers of the left hand spread the three coins on the right hand. The right hand turns two of the three coins back into the left hand, and thus produces a perfect illusion of showing only three coins in the

hands. The right hand with the thumb palmed coin reaches for the glass, and in doing so the coin is dropped momentarily onto the fingertips, then pressed into the palm. The little drama of pretending to pass the coin from the left hand to the glass is enacted, and the coin is allowed to fall from the right palm into the glass. The moves as described are repeated for the third coin. When only two coins are left, one in the left hand known to the audience, and one in the right hand unknown to them, the left hand is brought up, with the arm bent at the elbow. The hand is about eight inches above the handkerchief pocket. As a trial will reveal, the coin may be released and will fall unseen by the audience into the pocket. The left hand is not immediately opened, the arm being first extended away from the body, and the fourth coin falls into the glass. The left hand opens, thus completing a beautiful illusion.

Second Version

Although the effect of this routine is similar to the one just described, the moves are entirely different. In fact, the sleights necessary for its performance have already been described in preceding pages.

Method: Begin the experiment with a drinking glass on the table and four half dollars concealed in the right palm. Execute The Touch of Midas (page 90) as you produce these one at a time, and drop them into the glass. If you prefer, you may have the coins already in the glass and start from there.

Take up the glass from the table with the right hand and empty the four coins into the palm up left hand, then set the glass on the table. Call attention to the number of coins, then square them up in a stack. Pick up the stack of coins by their edges between the right second finger and thumb. Show the left hand empty on both sides, and as you replace the stack of coins in the left hand execute The Bottom Steal (page 18), which action secretly puts one coin in the right palm. Immediately close the left hand on the three coins as you reach for the glass with the right hand. Pick it up by the rim between the fingertips and thumb (see Fig. 8, preceding version) and hold it some distance from the left hand. Make a slight throwing motion with the left hand toward the right and instantly release the coin in the right palm, allowing it to fall into the glass. Place the glass on the table, then open the left hand showing three coins.

Count them into the right hand. Pretend to toss all three back into the left hand but retain one palmed in the right. As the two coins arrive in the left hand they clink together and it is impossible to detect the fact that only two coins were thrown. Take the glass in the right hand as before and repeat the throwing motion with the left hand to effect the passage of the second coin into the glass. Put the glass on the table, and open the left hand to show two coins which are then placed on the table.

Silently show both hands empty front and back. Do The Click Pass (a), (page 14), as you apparently return both coins to the left hand. At the completion of this sleight there will be one coin in the closed left hand and one concealed in the right. The sound of the two coins striking each other as this move is executed offers convincing proof that the left hand does actually contain two coins. Pick up the glass with the right hand and again go through the motions of passing a coin into it. Allow the palmed half to clatter down into the glass, then set it on the table. Open the left hand showing one coin.

Take the coin in the right hand, holding it by its extreme edge between the tips of the forefinger and thumb. Hold it high so all may see, and while pretending to replace it in the left hand, perform The Tunnel Vanish (page 24), which sleight retains coin in the right hand. Keep the left hand closed as if it actually held the coin. While reaching for the glass with the right hand, get the coin into the palm, then take up the glass and hold it as described. Hold the hands far apart and repeat the same set of movements to effect passage of the last coin. Finally open the left hand and show it empty, then pour the coins from the glass into the left hand, letting it be plainly seen that there are only four.

The Traveling Centavos

Reprinted through the courtesy of *The Sphinx Publishing Corporation*

After returning to the States from a trip below the border I found I had a pocket full of Mexican coins, among them several 20 Centavo Pieces. A handmade, leather dice cup was also brought back. Playing around with the 20 Centavo Pieces and the dice cup, the following routine was born. A 20 Centavo Piece is a copper coin about midway between the size of a quarter and a half dollar, but I see no reason why quarters or half dollars cannot be used. In an emergency an opaque plastic or metal tumbler, as used in bathrooms, will serve instead of the leather cup.

Effect: On the table in front of the performer is a dice cup. Showing his hands empty, the performer picks up the cup and dumps a few coins onto his right hand. The coins are placed on the table—there are four.

The dice cup is shown empty and the right hand picks up a coin and makes a tossing motion toward the cup. The coin is heard to arrive in the cup. This is continued until all four coins pass one at a time into the cup. The passage of each coin is accomplished by a different move.

Method: Although the spectators know of only four coins, actually five are used. These are in the leather dice cup on the table at your left. If the cup is unlined and has a wider mouth than bottom, it will not only be easier to handle but the sound of the coins as they arrive in the cup will be more distinct.

Show the hands empty without calling attention to the fact. Take up the dice cup with the left hand and empty the five coins into the palm up right hand. Replace the cup on the table *upside down*. The right hand places the four coins in a row on the table to the right of the cup. The fifth coin is retained hidden in the palm. The right hand removes one coin from the table and places it on the open left hand at finger palm position. (This is at the base of the two middle fingers where it can be retained later.) The remaining three coins are arranged in an overlapping row, extending inward toward the palm. Right hand with its concealed coin in the palm points to the coins on the left hand as you call attention to the number—"Four."

These are apparently tossed into the right hand, but the forward coin is retained in finger palm position. The exposed right hand shows four coins, one which was hid-

Fig. 1

den in the palm and the other three just received from the left hand (the Utility Switch, page 11).

The left hand picks up cup as the right hand places its four coins in a row on the table. The back of the left should be toward the audience as it grasps the cup near the bottom. The cup is picked up in this position and turned mouth toward spectators allowing them to view the inside. Because of this position the cup can be shown all around—to the spectators on the left and to the ones on the right. The coin remains concealed by the curled fingers and is not seen from any angle except from the rear, Fig. 1.

As the right hand picks up the first coin from the row on the table the cup is turned

Fig. 2

mouth upwards and allowed to slide down between the fingers and thumb of the left hand, then the hand turns clockwise with the cup revolving between the thumb and forefinger, remaining upright and assuming the position shown in Fig. 2. Back of the left hand is toward the audience.

The right hand makes a tossing motion toward the cup and palms the coin. The left immediately releases its coin from finger palm position, and it falls audibly into the cup. Shake the cup vigorously so all can hear that the coin has arrived. Turn the cup counterclockwise and dump the coin onto the fingers of the right hand. The cup is tipped inward for this action and you are turned slightly toward the left. The extra coin palmed in the right hand will not be seen. The right hand flips the coin just received into the air a couple of times, catching it on the fingers each time, but be careful that the two coins do not clink together in this action. (See The Coin Flip, page 16.) This subtle move shows without saying that the right hand is otherwise empty.

Holding the visible coin between the first finger and thumb of the right hand, lower

Fig. 4

Fig. 3

the hand slightly so that the coin in the palm will slide down to finger palm position. (Fig. 3 shows how the two coins are held at this point.)

Bring the left hand up, holding the cup tilted slightly to the right to facilitate the following move: Toss *both* coins together from the right hand toward the cup. The visible coin is aimed at the mouth of the cup and goes into it as the other lands on the cupped fingers of the left hand. Be sure to release both coins simultaneously and you will have no difficulty. Fig. 3 shows the position of the two coins in the right hand immediately before the throw, while Fig. 4 shows the left hand after the throw,

with one coin lying on the cupped fingers and the other entering the cup.

Turn the left hand clockwise and let it assume the position shown in Fig. 2. Rattle the coin in the cup so it can be heard.

Pick up a second coin from the table with the right hand and make a tossing motion toward the cup. Palm the coin as before as the left hand releases its coin, which falls into the cup onto the other coin, and both are then rattled.

Apparently dump both coins from the cup into the right hand but retain one in left finger palm as the two slide across the cupped fingers. As the two coins slide across the fingers of the left hand one is retained and the other one falls into the waiting right hand, Fig. 5. Rattle the two coins in the right hand as the left hand again allows the cup to assume an upright position. The right hand openly drops its two coins into the cup, which is then shaken vigorously. One coin is in finger palm position, Fig. 2, and the right hand is empty.

The right hand picks up the third coin and seems to toss it invisibly into the cup. Actually, the coin is palmed as before while the left hand releases its coin so that it falls into the cup. The three are rattled in the cup to convey the idea that one actually did pass.

Fig. 5

The left hand turns the cup mouth toward the onlookers and empties the three coins onto the table. Cup is then placed *upside down* to the left of the coins. The right hand picks up the three coins and places them onto the open left hand, one going in finger palm position. Call attention to the three coins and toss two of them into the right hand, retaining one in finger palm. The right hand shows three coins, two just received from the left hand and the third which was hidden in the palm (the Utility Switch). As the coins are shown in the right hand, the left picks up the cup from the table and shows it empty as in Fig. 1. Cup is again allowed to assume position as shown in Fig. 2. The right hand daintily drops its three coins into the cup, one at a time. The cup is shaken, rattling the three coins therein. A fourth coin is concealed in the finger palm.

The right hand takes up the last coin from the table and repeats the same set of movements as it pretends to toss the coin into the cup. The coin is palmed and the left hand permits the finger palmed coin to fall onto the three in the cup. As the left hand rattles the coins in the cup, drop the

right hand and shift the coin in that hand to finger palm position. As the right hand takes the cup from the left hand it presses its coin against the outside of the cup near the bottom and dumps the four coins from the cup onto the table. The right hand appears quite empty in this action.

Set the cup on the table *mouth up,* and return the fifth coin from the fingers to the palm while reaching for one of the coins on the table. Place this coin in finger palm position on the open left hand and the other three overlapping it inward toward the palm. Toss the three innermost coins into the right hand, retaining the forward one in finger palm position. Show four coins in the right hand, three just received and one which was already there (the Utility Switch). Place these four coins on the table in a row as the left hand picks up the cup and shows it empty as in Fig. 1. (One coin is finger palmed.) Cup assumes position as in Fig. 2 as the right hand picks up the first coin from the table. Apparently toss it into the cup as described, but palm it and release the coin from the left hand so that it falls into the cup. The right hand picks up the second coin and visibly drops it into the cup. The third coin is removed from the table, it and the one concealed in the right hand are dropped together into the cup as one. Just toss them together, that's all. Finally, the right hand takes the last coin and flips it into the air. The left hand catches it in the cup and the cup is placed on the table.

The last part of tossing the coins back into the cup is just a "clean-up" move. It gets rid of the extra coin nicely and puts a finish on the effect at the same time.

Master this trick and you will have one of the prettiest and most baffling of all coin transposition effects. There is a certain rhythm or poetry of motion to the moves which you will enjoy—even for yourself!

Miracle Coins to the Pocket

GLENN HARRISON

This ingenious feat of magic won its inventor, Glenn Harrison, a prominent coin manipulator of Denver, first prize in the sleight of hand contest at the Society of American Magicians' Convention in 1949.

The method used to accomplish the effect is not one which will be quickly adopted by many magicians, and for this reason it will be more of an exclusive item for those who do go to the trouble to prepare for the trick. Those who do use it will find that they have one of the most baffling feats possible with coins, one that will create a veritable sensation whenever shown.

Effect: The magician shows three silver dollars and a glass. The coins are marked for identification while the glass is placed in the empty right coat pocket. Taking one of the dollars, magician places it in his left hand and announces his intention of causing the coin to pass up the left sleeve, across the body, then into the glass in the coat pocket. No sooner does he make this declaration than the coin is heard to arrive in the glass. The second, and finally the third are treated in like manner, each apparently going up the sleeve, across the body, then down into the glass where they are heard to arrive. A spectator is permitted to remove the glass from the performer's pocket and examine the coins. They are the marked coins!

The effect appears exactly as described. Only three coins are used. They are the ones which were marked at the beginning, and they are the ones which finally appear

in the glass. The sound of the coins arriving in the glass one at a time is actually created by the coins themselves.

Sounds impossible? It looks just as impossible as it sounds. Presented as described, the feat is calculated to baffle all who see it, magicians and laymen alike.

Method: Besides the three silver dollars you will need a glass as used to serve Old-Fashions, and a coat prepared as follows: Take your coat to a tailor and have him make a flat tube of cloth long enough to reach from the breast pocket to the right

Fig. 1

pocket. The material for this tube should be of a soft variety, such as a rayon the same as, or similar to, that used in the lining of dress coats. After making this tube and pressing it flat it should be a little wider than the diameter of a silver dollar. The breast pocket will have to be altered, making it "funnel" shaped. One end of the tube is fastened to the bottom of the breast pocket, then it follows the inside of the coat around the back and down to the right coat pocket where it enters near its top. About an inch of the tube should protrude inside the pocket from the body side. It is this tab that is placed over the rim of the glass when it is put in the pocket. The tube is fastened to the coat by its top edge as it goes around the back of the coat. (See Figs. 1, 2 and 3

Breast Pocket

Fig. 2

for detailed construction of pockets and tube.) When constructed as described, the tube serves as a slide or passage-way for the coins as they travel from the breast pocket to the side pocket. Almost any single-breasted coat can be altered for the trick. A double-breasted coat sometimes fits too tight and because of this the coin may hang up in the tube enroute to the side pocket. If this should happen you can loosen the coin and speed it on its way by merely shrugging the shoulders.

Warning: Do not attempt this trick with

Coat Pocket

Fig. 3

half dollars. They are not heavy enough. After a coat is thus prepared, experiment with it to determine to your utter satisfaction that it will not fail when put to actual use. The tube may require an additional adjusting after it is installed in the coat, to give it the right slant.

Working: Show the three silver dollars and the glass. If you live where silver dollars are readily procurable you might begin the trick by borrowing the coins. In any event, have them marked for identification by three different spectators. Show the glass empty and as you place it in the right side pocket adjust the end of the tube over the rim so it will hang on the inside.

Take one of the silver dollars from a spectator and apparently place it in your left hand, but retain it thumb palmed in the right hand instead. Say, "I will cause the silver dollar to pass up my left sleeve, across my body, then down into the glass in my right pocket." Suiting the actions to the words, pass your right forefinger along your coat sleeve, across the chest, then gesture toward the right pocket, being careful not to let the hand get too close to the pocket lest someone suspects you of dropping the coin in the pocket. As the hand passes across the breast pocket the coin is dropped in it, then without hesitating it continues on its way as you indicate the route the dollar will take in its journey to the glass. Pay no attention to your actions as you do this, but look directly at the spectators. Timed right, the dollar will arrive in the glass about the time you have completed your movements of showing how it will travel, Fig. 4. Open your left hand and show it empty.

Take the second coin from the spectator and repeat the above described movements of causing it to pass into the glass in the pocket. For the third coin, instead of dropping it in the breast pocket, leave it thumb

Clink

Fig. 4

ently extract the coin from the body. Say, "Occasionally the coin strikes a rib, which makes the trick much more difficult and much more painful." This usually gets a laugh.

Pretend to replace the dollar in the left hand but thumb palm it in the right instead. Then, as you repeat the moves of indicating the path the coin will travel, drop it in the breast pocket. After the coin is heard to arrive in the glass, show the left hand empty, then the right. Have a spectator reach into your pocket and remove the glass. The markings on the coins are verified, proving that they are the same ones.

The only crucial move in the entire routine is the act of disposing of the thumb palmed coin in the breast pocket as the hand passes it. It is vitally important that this be thoroughly and completely mastered. The trick is too good to expose through carelessness and insufficient practice. Strive for a perfect illusion!

palmed while you go through the motions used for causing the first two to pass into the glass. Wait for the sound of the coin arriving in the glass, but it doesn't come. After a moment of suspense, accompanied by the proper facial expressions, reach under the left side of the coat and appar-

COIN CLASSICS

Gathered together in this chapter are the coin classics—tricks that have stood the test of time. Even though some of them are centuries old they are still being performed today. Together with these mysteries you will discover many new effects by contemporary magicians which, in my opinion, are also classics.

Coin Through a Ring

Almost every close-up worker is familiar with that oldie, the Coin Through a Ring, which requires a gimmicked coin for its accomplishment. Now comes a new method which depends on a trick fold in the handkerchief instead of a trick coin. Both methods will be described.

First, the original method: A coin is placed in the center of a handkerchief, then the four corners are gathered together and pushed through a man's finger ring. The ring is pushed up snugly against the coin and a spectator holds the bunched together corners of the handkerchief. Under these conditions it does not seem possible that the ring could be removed from the handkerchief since it would be virtually impossible to slip the ring over the coin. Nevertheless this is exactly what the performer does do.

This seemingly impossible feat is accomplished through the use of a folding coin (see page 286). Begin the experiment with the fake coin concealed in your right hand. Borrow a pocket handkerchief, a man's ring, and a half dollar. Spread the handkerchief on the table and lay the ring nearby. Take the borrowed coin in your right hand and switch it for the folding coin (see The Bobo Switch, page 10) as you pretend to toss it onto the center of the handkerchief. (Be sure the table is cloth covered, otherwise the dull thud of the fake coin striking the table will give you away.)

Gather up the four corners of the handkerchief and pass them through the ring, watching your angles so that the concealed coin will not be discovered. Slide the ring down to the coin and have a spectator hold the four corners of the cloth bunched together in his hand, Fig. 1. Call attention to the fact that the half dollar is much larger than the ring, and for this reason it cannot slip through the ring. Announce that while the four corners of the handkerchief are being held you will attempt

Fig. 1

to remove the ring. Take the ring and coin in your hands, and under cover of them fold the coin, slide the ring off, and allow the coin to return to its original shape. Place the ring on the table, then take the handkerchief and unfold it and remove the fake coin. (Care should be taken to keep the flat surface of the fake coin toward the spectators, to better conceal the grooved edge.) Apparently by mistake, place the coin in your pocket. Leave it there and remove the other one as you notice your error. Return it and the other two articles to their owners.

If you would rather not keep the borrowed coin concealed in your hand all during the trick you might favor this handling. Have the fake coin concealed in your right hand while you borrow the three articles necessary for the trick. Have someone near you hold the ring for a moment while you do the following: Throw the handkerchief over your right hand, take the borrowed half from the

spectator with your left hand and carry it underneath the handkerchief. Under cover of the cloth, drop the borrowed coin in your right sleeve while the fingers push up the fake coin. Bring the left hand from underneath the handkerchief and grasp the fake coin through the fabric from the outside with that hand, then remove the right hand. Do not make a display of showing either hand empty; just let this fact be seen as you proceed as described.

After removing the ring from the handkerchief and returning it, drop the right hand to the side and retrieve the sleeved coin. Remove the coin from the handkerchief and return the latter. Switch the fake coin for the genuine coin, then give it back to its owner.

Now, the new method: After borrowing a ring, a handkerchief, and a half dollar, give the ring to a spectator to hold while you proceed to place the coin in the handkerchief in the following manner: Hold the coin upright between the tips of the left forefinger and thumb. Throw the handkerchief over the coin with the right

Fig. 2

hand. Then, with the aid of the right thumb, obtain a tiny pinch of cloth with the left thumb at the base of the coin at the rear, Fig. 2. Now grasp the top edge of the coin at X through the cloth between the tips of the first finger and thumb of the right hand and turn the coin back on top of the left thumb, the thumb nail acting as a hinge. The small fold of cloth must be retained as the coin assumes a horizontal position. This will be facilitated if you will press the coin inward against the tip of the left thumb as you turn it back. While the right forefinger and thumb hold the coin in place, slide the left thumb inward and secure a new hold on the inner edge of the coin (at X) between the thumb on top and the forefinger underneath, Fig. 3.

With the right hand, raise the front edge of the handkerchief, briefly exposing the coin. Now as the right hand returns the front edge of the handkerchief to its original position the left hand is lowered and the portion from the left forearm falls forward also. This simultaneous action should appear to the spectators as though you merely raised the front portion of the handkerchief to give them another view of the coin. In spite of the fairness of the procedure the coin is now outside

Fig. 3

the handkerchief, being covered by a fold of cloth at the rear, Fig. 4.

Twist the handkerchief a few times, then request the spectator who is holding the

ring to take the coin while you relieve him of the ring. Say, "I'll take the ring while you hold the coin." Do not fear detection here. I have performed this trick hundreds of times and no one has ever suspected a thing unusual or tried to

Fig. 4

examine the fold. (The action of folding the coin in the handkerchief takes but a moment, and it is done in a casual manner while you are looking and speaking to the spectators.) Caution the spectator to hold tightly to the coin. While the coin is thus being held you have your hands free to push the four corners through the ring. Slide the ring down to the coin, then take all from him. Grasp the handkerchief just below the ring and show it all around. If you have made the fold with care and twisted the handkerchief properly, the cloth-covered coin will appear exactly the same on both sides.

Have the spectator take the four corners and hold them together in one hand while you take the cloth-covered coin in your hands. Point out the fact that the coin is larger than the ring and that it would be impossible to remove the ring from that end of the handkerchief. Cover the coin and ring completely with your hands and quickly work the coin from the fold of the cloth, explaining that the only way to remove the ring would be to first remove the coin. Bring the coin into view and hold it in one hand as you slide the ring off the handkerchief with the other. Return these two articles to their owners. Then take the handkerchief, unfold it, show it undamaged and return it.

The handling just described is especially suited for performing the trick for only

gimmicked coin only the ring is removed from the handkerchief; the new method not only accomplishes the same effect but has the additional feature of being a penetration as well. Actually two mysteries in one!

With both methods in your repertoire you will be well equipped to present the mystery on any occasion, whether you have the folding coin with you or not. If you have to repeat the trick before the same

Fig. 5

Fig. 6

one person, but when there are more than two persons the following presentation is far superior:

Proceed up to the point where the ring is placed over the handkerchief and pushed down against the coin. Take the handkerchief from your helper and have two others assist you by holding a corner in each hand with the handkerchief spread out between them, the ring being on top, Fig. 5.

Under cover of the hands work the coin from the folds of the cloth, thus freeing the ring. The moment it is free take the hands away, exposing the coin and ring lying on the handkerchief as in Fig. 6. The effect is very startling and puzzling.

Although the two methods of performing the trick do not appear exactly the same, they are for all practical purposes the same. In the original version using the

group of people you can use the real money method. A good magician should not have to make excuses for not being able to perform any one of his mysteries.

In this book you will find a variety of methods for the tricks described.

Silver or Copper Extraction

Effect: Showing a copper and silver coin in his right hand, the magician wraps them in a borrowed handkerchief. A spectator verifies that the coins are actually in the handkerchief by feeling them through the cloth. A second spectator is given absolutely free choice in choosing one of the coins. Whichever one he names is actually removed, leaving the other still wrapped in the handkerchief. Here are three methods.

Fig. 1

Fig. 3

(a) Stewart Judah Method.

Borrow a handkerchief and hold it in your left hand while you show an English penny and a half dollar in your right hand. Hold the coins between the fingertips and thumb of the palm up hand. The silver coin is underneath and protrudes from the rear of the upper coin a quarter inch, Fig 1. It is necessary to hold the coins

Fig. 2

exactly in this manner to facilitate the next move.

Now as you throw the handkerchief over the coins, raise the right hand about chest high, the fingers pointing upward. With the left hand, grip the top edge of the copper coin (through the handkerchief) between the tip of the forefinger in front and the thumb at the rear, Fig. 2, and lift the

handkerchief up and away from the right hand. Fig. 3 shows the performer's view of the two hands and handkerchief at this point. (Notice that the right thumb holds the silver coin against the fingers.) Lower both hands together, the right hand going behind the handkerchief to assume the position shown in Fig. 4, then the copper coin is placed flat on top of the silver coin lying on the right fingers, Fig. 5.

Transfer the coins and handkerchief to the left hand, holding them so that the thumb will be on top and the forefinger underneath. Now grasp the cloth a few inches below the coins with the right hand and pull inward, stretching the handkerchief taut between the two hands, Fig. 6.

Fig. 4

Have a spectator feel the two coins through the fabric. Owing to the position of the handkerchief the outside silver coin is covered by a fold of cloth from underneath

Fig. 5

and feels like it is on the inside. Next relax your grip on the handkerchief with your right hand, allowing the handkerchief to hang down from your left.

Ask a spectator to choose a coin and tell him whichever one he names you will extract from the handkerchief. Let's suppose he names silver. (I have found from experience that most people will choose the half dollar.) Again grip the handkerchief with the right hand a few inches below

Fig. 6

the coins, then with a series of little jerks with the left hand, bring the silver coin into view, apparently through the cloth.

Grip the copper coin through the fabric with the left fingers and thumb and turn the hand palm up so the handkerchief will drop down around the hand, bringing the copper coin into view.

As mentioned above most people will choose the half dollar, but in case this doesn't happen you will have to proceed differently. If the copper coin is named you will have to continue from Fig. 5 as

Fig. 7

follows: With the left hand, grip both coins by their inner edges between the forefinger on top and thumb below, lift them up and away from the right hand, turning them upright and holding them about chest high, Fig. 7. Move the right hand underneath the handkerchief and grip both coins together at their lower edges between the forefinger and thumb of the palm up hand, Fig. 8. With the left hand, grasp the lower front edge of the handkerchief and lift it up and back over the right forearm, showing the copper coin, Fig. 9. The spectators are given only a brief look at the coin and the absence of the silver coin is never noticed since it is supposedly behind the copper one. Both hands move together simultaneously as you quickly release the edge of the handkerchief with your left hand and immediately lower your right hand, permitting all the folds of the handkerchief to hang down in front of the coins. The position at this point is the same as

Fig. 8

shown in Fig. 5, except the silver coin is now within the handkerchief and the copper coin lies on the fingers underneath. Adroitly executed, this subtle switch is indetectable. To all appearances the two coins are still inside the handkerchief. Actually the copper coin is now outside, covered by the cloth.

Fig. 9

Transfer the coins to the left hand and grip the handkerchief with your right a few inches below the coins. Gradually work the

copper coin into view as previously described. Finally show the silver coin in the handkerchief and the latter free from damage.

(b) Orville Meyer Method.

Proceed as in the Judah method up to the point where the coins are covered with the handkerchief. Then as you take the copper coin through the cloth between the tips of your left forefinger and thumb, thumb palm the silver coin in your right

Fig. 10

hand. Lift the copper coin up and away from the right hand. Fig. 10 shows the performer's view of the two hands and handkerchief at this point. In the action of stroking the handkerchief a couple of times with the right hand, leave the half dollar behind the folds of the cloth, gripping it by the tip of the left thumb, Fig. 11. Now lower the hands to the position shown in Fig. 5 and proceed as described.

(c) A third method popular with coin workers for stealing the silver coin and placing it outside the cloth is to back palm it as follows: Hold the coins as in Fig. 1. Spread the handkerchief with the left hand and throw it over the right so its center covers the two coins. Grasp the forward edge of the copper coin through the hand-

Fig. 11

kerchief, between the left forefinger underneath and the thumb on top. Immediately
back palm the silver coin with the right
hand. With the left hand, lift the copper
coin and handkerchief away from the
right, giving the spectators a brief view of
the empty palm, Fig. 12, then move the
right hand behind the folds of the handkerchief. The moment the right fingers are
hidden behind the handkerchief the back
palmed half dollar is brought to its original
position on the front of the fingers, Fig. 4,
and the handkerchief-wrapped copper coin
is laid flat on top of the half as in Fig. 5.
The effect is then continued as described
in the first method explained.

Fig. 12

Regardless of the method you choose (I
alternate between the three) for stealing
the silver coin from the handkerchief and
getting it underneath the copper coin, the
balance of the moves are the same.

Sometimes, however, I resort to an equivoque and simply remove the silver coin,
which I always get outside the handkerchief by one of the methods just described.
I ask the spectator which he prefers—the
silver or the copper. If he names the silver
coin I remove it by extracting it as described. But if he names the copper coin I
tell him to hold the handkerchief, then I
remove the silver, and he has the coin he
asked for. He still thinks he had a free
choice, for I have not told him I would
remove the coin he named.

The equivoque enables you to eliminate
one move that might, under certain circumstances, prove objectionable. Magicians, working for each other, like to stress
the "absolute free choice" angle in various
tricks. But to the layman, the broad effect
is all that counts, and for him it is just as
good the simple way.

Copper Penetration

This makes an excellent "follow-up"
trick for Silver or Copper Extraction. In
fact, the two go so well together I seldom
perform them separately. They are top-
notch foolers.

Effect: Two coins are shown, one copper
and one silver. The copper is given to a
spectator to hold while the performer
wraps the silver coin in a borrowed handkerchief. A spectator then holds the silver
coin through the cloth in one hand and
the bunched together corners in his other
hand, the handkerchief being stretched out
horizontally between them. Taking the
copper coin, the performer causes it to
vanish. The exact instant the coin vanishes

it is heard to strike the silver coin as it arrives in the handkerchief.

Method: To perform this startling feat you will require two English pennies (or two other copper coins of the same size) and one half dollar. One of the copper coins must be in your left coat pocket.

Suppose you have just performed the effect of removing either of two coins from a borrowed handkerchief. Hand the handkerchief to a spectator to remove the remaining coin. Apparently this is done so he may see for himself that there is only one coin remaining in the handkerchief. Actually it is done so you may steal the copper coin from your coat pocket with your left hand. Since all attention will be on the spectator's actions as he removes the coin, casually place your left hand in your

Fig. I

pocket, finger palm the copper coin, then remove the hand.

Have someone hold the copper coin used in the previous trick while you take the silver coin and hold it vertically between the tips of the forefinger and thumb of your left hand. Keep the second, third and fourth fingers curled inward, covering the finger palmed copper coin. Spread the handkerchief with your right hand and throw it over your left hand so its center covers the half dollar.

Now you need someone to hold the coin through the handkerchief. If possible, choose a lady because her reaction adds considerably to the over-all effect. As you offer her the coin and handkerchief to hold, transfer them to your right hand as follows: With the right forefinger and thumb grip the right edge of the silver coin through the cloth, Fig. 1, then curl the second, third and fourth fingers around

Fig. 2

the handkerchief just below the coin. Release your hold on the silver coin with your left hand and press the copper coin into the right finger palm (a fold of cloth will be between the coin and the right curled fingers, Fig. 2, then remove the left hand from underneath the handkerchief. Have her take the silver coin through the fabric by its edge between her thumb (on top) and forefinger. Caution her to hold it tightly, then release your grip from the copper coin, but keep your fingers curled around the handkerchief and slide your hand to the right. Do not lower your right hand as you do this but keep it on the same level as her right hand. The moment the right hand moves away from the copper coin, grip the handkerchief with the left hand at the exact spot just vacated by the right.

Fig. 3

Say, "Will you also hold this end with your left hand?" Since you are holding the bunched together corners with your right hand and gripping the portion just below the silver coin with your left, she can only take the handkerchief at the spot between your two hands, Fig. 3. Before taking your hands away say, "Hold the handkerchief and coin tightly. Don't let go with either hand until I tell you. When I say 'Go!' release the coin with your right hand." Then as a safety measure repeat your instructions something like this: "Don't forget, hold both ends tightly. When I say 'Go!' let go with this hand." (Touch her right hand.) "But hold tightly with this hand." (Touch her left hand.) Most people

Fig. 4

are willing and anxious to cooperate, but if your instructions are not thoroughly understood, assistants from the audience can certainly ruin a trick. In this case if she should let go of the wrong end the copper coin would fall to the floor and spoil your trick. So be sure there is no misunderstanding of your instructions. The lady should be holding the handkerchief between her two hands as shown in Fig. 4.

With your right hand, take the copper coin from the spectator who has been holding it for you and say, "Here is the copper coin." Then to the lady, "You are holding the silver coin inside the handkerchief. Do

clink!

Fig. 5

you feel it?" She will reply that she does. Then say, "Watch the copper coin!" Pretend to place it in your left hand but retain it palmed in your right. Go through the motions of tossing the coin toward the handkerchief with your left hand as you exclaim, "Go!" The moment she releases her grip on the silver coin with her right hand the weight of the coin will cause that end of the handkerchief to drop and the copper coin to clink down on top of it, creating a very startling effect, Fig. 5. Take advantage of this surprise by disposing of the palmed coin in the right pocket.

I cannot recommend this and the preceding trick too highly.

The Expansion of Texture— Expanded!

Robert-Houdin called the great-grandfather of this pretty feat "The Magical Filtration of Five-Franc Pieces." A still later version of the trick, "The Expansion of Texture," was said to be the masterpiece of the celebrated L'Homme Masqué, and is described on page 240 of Downs' *The Art of Magic*. The routine described here is a combination of the two preceding tricks, Silver or Copper Extraction, and Copper Penetration, and follows closely the version taught by that arch-hierophant of sleight of hand, Dai Vernon, in his lectures a few years ago.

Requisites and Preparation: Two matching copper coins, a half dollar, and a pocket handkerchief.

Have one of the copper coins finger palmed in your left hand, the other copper coin and the half dollar in your right trousers pocket, and the handkerchief in your breast coat pocket.

Working: With the right hand, remove the half dollar and the duplicate copper coin from the pocket. Show them, then as you pretend to toss them into the left hand execute the Utility Switch (page 11), retain the copper coin finger palmed and throw only the half dollar. Left hand immediately shows two coins, the half dollar that just arrived from the right hand and the copper coin which was already there. Toss the coins onto the table as the right hand removes the handkerchief from the pocket.

Pick up the silver coin with the left hand and hold it vertically between the fingers and thumb as the right hand covers it with the handkerchief. Grasp the right edge of the coin through the cloth with the right forefinger and thumb and give it a half turn inward, then secure a new grip on the inner edge of the coin with the left forefinger and thumb. With the right hand, lift the front portion of the handkerchief, giving the spectators a brief view of the coin inside. Left hand now gives a slight shake and the handkerchief falls around the coin, but the coin is now in an outside fold. (This is the same move as used in the new method of the Coin Through a Ring, this chapter.)

Pick up the copper coin from the table with your right hand and slowly place it inside the handkerchief alongside the silver coin. However, a thickness of cloth separates the two coins (one inside, one outside).

Have a spectator hold the bunched together corners of the handkerchief while you retain your grip on the two coins and the center of the cloth. Ask, "Which coin shall I remove—copper or silver?" Regardless of which coin is named you remove it as follows: (Remember, the silver coin is in an outside fold, the copper coin is inside the handkerchief, and the duplicate copper coin is finger palmed in your right hand.) If the silver coin is named, remove it. But if the copper coin is chosen, which seldom happens, pretend to extract it, and show the copper coin which you had concealed in your right hand. Pretend to work it back into the handkerchief, then extract the silver one (which was in an outside fold), explaining that one is as easy to remove as the other. Have the spectator remove the copper coin from the handkerchief.

Offer to repeat the trick.

Hold the half dollar vertically between the forefinger and thumb of your right hand (duplicate copper coin concealed in finger palm position) as the left hand covers the coin with the handkerchief. Now as you grip the half dollar through the fabric with the left hand, secretly hold the copper coin directly below it with the same hand. As a spectator is directed to hold the silver coin by its edge, the right hand gathers in the four corners and the copper coin is released and falls to the bottom of the little bag thus formed.

When the spectator has taken hold of the silver coin with his right hand, with your left hand grasp the handkerchief where the copper coin rests, as the right hand gives the four gathered corners of the handkerchief to the spectator to hold in his left hand. Handkerchief is held horizontally between the spectator's hands, the copper coin resting in the folds between his hands. Instruct the spectator to hold the handkerchief corners tightly in his left hand—and touch his left hand so he understands. Pick up the copper coin with your right hand. Pretend to transfer it to the left hand (Standard Vanish, page 22), then bring the left hand down smartly onto the handkerchief held by the spectator, opening hand as it touches handkerchief, and knocking coin end of handkerchief from spectator's right fingers, causing the two coins inside the handkerchief to clink together with startling effect. Apparently the copper coin has passed back into the handkerchief to rejoin the silver.

If the spectator has been instructed to hang on tightly to the corners of the handkerchief in his left hand he will be astonished to find two coins in the handkerchief. As you bring up the right hand to gesture toward the handkerchief in telling spectator to unwrap it and take out the coins, sleeve the extra coin palmed in the right hand.

The Gadabout Coins

In January 1950 *The Linking Ring* carried an effect called The Alleurian Coins, by George F. Wright. It appealed to me, so I experimented with it—making a change here and there, and came up with the routine which follows. The easy sleights are described in the foregoing chapters. The effect is simple and direct, and the routine is so designed that the performer will always be one jump ahead of the spectators.

Effect: In this bit of hocus pocus the wonder-worker calls attention to three half dollars on the table. He places two of these in his left hand, and the third goes in his pocket. Opening his left hand he shows three coins, one having apparently traveled from the pocket into the hand. This is repeated three times. Finally the coins vanish altogether leaving both hands entirely empty.

Method: Four half dollars are required. All four coins are in the right trousers pocket at the beginning. Place the right hand in the pocket and finger palm one coin as the other three are brought forth and placed on the table in a row. Say something about these coins having been so closely associated for so long a time they have great affinity for each other. The right fingers and thumb pick up the first coin and toss it into the left hand, which closes on it. The left hand opens again as you say, "One half dollar."

The right fingers and thumb remove the second coin from the table and toss it into the left hand with the first, as you add, "Two half dollars." Slowly close the left fingers over the two coins. Open the hand again to show the two coins. The right hand removes the two coins from the open left hand and fans them, being careful that the finger palmed third coin is not seen. Place them back in the left hand, adding the finger palmed coin. There is nothing fancy here, just drop all three together and close the hand around them. Reiterate, "Two half dollars."

"The third coin I shall place in my

pocket." The right hand picks up the last coin from the table and apparently places it in the right trousers pocket. It is not left there, however, but is brought out again, finger palmed. Gesture with your closed left hand, as you exclaim, "Watch!" Drop the coins from the left hand onto the table one at a time, counting, "One, two, three." Apparently the third coin has passed from the pocket into the left hand.

"I will do it again," you say. The right hand again places two of the three coins into the left hand, one at a time. Close the left hand slowly over the two coins. Open it again, as you remark, "Just two coins." These are apparently tossed into the right hand, but one is retained in left finger palm position. The exposed right hand shows the two coins, one of which was hidden in finger palm position, and the other just received from the left hand. (See Utility Switch, page 11.) "Two half dollars," you repeat.

One coin remains concealed in the left hand as it closes into a fist. The right hand places its two coins on top of the left fist, and slowly allows them to sink down in the hand. The right hand is shown empty. The audience knows of only two coins in the left fist, but actually there are three. Right hand picks up the third and last coin from the table and places it in the pocket, as you say, "Once again I will place the third half dollar in my pocket." Remove the right hand from the pocket with the coin hidden in the finger palm. "But, do you think it will stay there? No!" you state, as you look at the closed left hand. "It has returned to the fold." Slowly and deliberately the left hand releases its three coins, one at a time, allowing them to clatter onto the table, as you count, "One, two, three! Puzzling, isn't it?" The left hand is empty.

The right hand places the three coins onto the open left hand, one going in

Fig. 1

finger palm position. Execute the Utility Switch as you toss two of them into the right hand, retaining one finger palmed in the left. The right hand displays three coins, two just received from the left hand, and one which was concealed in finger palm. "Very remarkable coins," you say. Toss them onto the table. (One coin is still finger palmed in the left hand.) "The most remarkable coin of the three is this one." Pick up one of the coins from the table with the fingers and thumb of the right hand, and press its edge against the back of the left hand, Fig. 1. "Watch it!" Apparently push the coin through the back of the left hand. This is done by holding it loosely, and merely pushing the fingers down over the coin. Gradually the coin dis-

Fig. 2

appears from view, and, at the same time, the fingers of the left hand close slowly. The coin is now hidden behind the fingers and thumb of the right hand, Fig. 2. Open the left hand, letting the duplicate coin be seen. "It has mystical powers." Right hand finger palms its coin.

Close the right hand into a fist over the coin there. Left hand then places its coin on top of the right fist. The second coin is picked from the table and deposited along side the first. Both are allowed to sink down into the right fist.

"Once more," you say, as you pick up the last coin from the table with the *left hand,* and place it in the *left pocket* leaving it there. "Again the coin returns to the fold," you remark, as you show the right hand containing the three coins. Count them onto the table, and show the hands empty, without calling attention to them verbally.

Three times you have placed a half dollar in your pocket. Three times the coin returns to join the other two. Now comes the startling surprise.

After showing the three coins on the table, pick up one with the right hand and apparently place it in the left, but, in reality, retain it in the right hand classic palmed. Close the left hand as if it really held the coin. Pick up the second half with the right hand, and repeat the previously described maneuver of apparently placing the coin in the left hand, but execute The Click Pass (b), (page 14), retaining it palmed in the right with the first. Close the left hand which apparently holds the two coins—actually it is empty. Both coins are in the right hand. The right hand then removes the last coin from the table, executing The Coin Flip (page 16) for effect. Right hand then carries this coin to the pocket, leaving it, AND the two which were palmed. Wave right hand over left,

and snap fingers. Open left hand and show it empty. The halves have vanished.

For a different climax see Routine No. 14, page 347.

The Three Coin Trick

MILTON KORT

Effect: Three coins are shown and vanished one at a time. Two are reproduced in the performer's hands, while the third is found in a spectator's pocket.

Working: Show three half dollars and give them to a spectator to hold. Take one of them from him with your left hand, then as you pretend to take it with your right, toss the coin into the right sleeve. (See The Catapult, page 102.) Make crumbling motions with your right hand, then open the hand and show it empty.

Take a second coin from your helper with your right hand. Execute The "Pumpkin Seed" Vanish (page 101) as you pretend to place it in your left hand. Go through the motions of crumbling this coin away with your left hand, then open it and show it empty. Now you have a coin up each sleeve.

Take the third coin from your assistant with your right hand. Perform The French Drop (page 37) as you apparently take it in your left hand. Keep the left hand closed as if it actually held the coin and turn the right hand palm toward the spectators with the second, third, and fourth fingers curled over the coin and the forefinger pointing upward. This is done as you simply gesture and caution the spectators to "Watch." (See Vanish with the Aid of a Handkerchief, page 43, for a full description of this subtle concealment.) Make crumbling motions with the left hand, then open it and show it empty. As things now stand, you have vanished three coins—one is hidden in the right sleeve, one in the left sleeve and one is finger palmed in the right hand.

Explain to the spectators that you will now attempt to bring the three coins back. Show the left hand empty on both sides, then slowly close it and turn it back uppermost. Bring the right hand palm down over the back of the left fist, and under cover of tapping the back of the left hand and turning it over, load the coin from the right hand into the left using the method described in the first version of Copper and Silver Transposition, (page 129.) Open the left hand to show that one coin has returned. Take it in your right hand and as you do so, let your left drop to your side and catch the coin that was in the left sleeve, and hold it finger palmed. Now bring the palm down left hand up to about waist level and form it into a very loose fist. Bring the right hand with its coin (which is held between the tips of the fingers and thumb) over the left fist and rest the lower edge of the coin on its back. Pretend to push the visible coin through the back of the left hand by suddenly sliding the right fingers down over the coin. (This is the same move described in method (b), Through the Hand, page 67, except a coin is already in the left hand.) The instant the right fingers are brought down over the coin, close the left fingers, then turn the hand over and open it to show the coin that was already there. The illusion is that you pushed a coin through the back of your left hand. (This method for apparently causing a coin to penetrate the hand belongs to John Ramsay of Ayr, Scotland.) At the completion of this move a coin will be hidden in your right hand and an exposed coin in your open left hand.

Tap the spectator on the chest and say, "I'll bet you thought the coin wouldn't penetrate my hand," or words to that effect. As you do this, drop the coin from the right hand into his upper breast coat pocket. (More nerve than skill is required to perform this loading operation, but once the knack is acquired it is easy.) Take the coin from the left hand with the right hand, show it, and as you pretend to return it to the left hand, sleeve it in the left sleeve by executing The "Pumpkin Seed" Vanish. The left hand is closed, apparently holding the coin. Show the right hand empty, which convinces the spectators that the coin must actually be in the left. After a brief pause, open the left hand and show it empty. As you do so, drop the right hand and retrieve the coin from the right sleeve, then reach up and apparently pluck coin from the spectator's left ear. The effect is that you placed a coin in your left hand, caused it to vanish, then immediately reproduced it from your assistant's ear.

While producing this coin with your right hand, drop your left hand to your side and catch the coin from that sleeve. A moment later produce it with your left hand from his right ear. Have him remove the third coin from his pocket which climaxes the routine to excellent effect.

Second Method

The effect is practically the same as the one just described except one of the coins is a hook coin. Show the three coins and give them to a spectator to hold. If you will let him hold the stack of three coins between the tips of his fingers and thumb, with the hook coin on the bottom, there will be no danger of him discovering the gimmicked coin. Take the top two coins one at a time and vanish them as explained. Then take the hook coin in your right hand and perform The French Drop, retaining coin finger palmed in that hand as the closed left hand moves away. Place your right hand on his back, and as you draw him a little closer for a better look, hook the coin on his coat. Now open your left hand and show it empty, letting it be seen that your right hand is also empty.

The trick now proceeds exactly as the first version, but instead of having him remove the third coin from his pocket, you show your right hand unmistakably empty, then produce the coin from behind his back.

Third Method

This version requires an additional two coins. As you begin the trick have one finger palmed in each hand, the other three coins in a convenient pocket.

Have a spectator step forward to assist you, and while moving him about directing him where to stand, load a coin in each of his two side coat pockets. Remove the three coins from your pocket and hand them to him to hold.

Take the coins from him one at a time and go through the same routine described in the first version, up to the point where you have just performed the penetration of the coin through the left hand. At this point you will have an exposed coin in your left hand and a coin hidden in your right. Tap him on the chest with your right hand and drop the coin from that hand into his breast pocket. Now take the visible coin and vanish it completely, using The Bobo Complete Coin Vanish (page 49). Show both hands unmistakably empty then have the spectator take the coins from his pockets. Each coin will come from a different pocket, thus creating a very strong effect.

At the completion of this routine you will have a coin in your own breast pocket (which you leave there) and one up each sleeve. These last two can be retrieved easily and disposed of in the pockets while

the spectator is removing the three coins from his pockets.

Still other variations are possible by combining the moves in different combinations.

The Bent Penny

It is an accepted fact that audience participation tricks are always sure-fire. This one is no exception. Because of the unusual climax the trick is much more effective when performed with the assistance of a lady.

Effect. The magician borrows a penny and gives it to a lady to hold tightly in her hand. After a bit of byplay he announces that the penny has vanished. The lady opens her hand. The penny is still there, but apparently she held it too tight because it is now badly bent.

Method: Quite a bit of fun can be had in the performance of this little trick, especially if you borrow the penny from a man and give it to his wife to hold.

Prepare for the trick beforehand by bending a penny. This can be done by placing it about half way in a vise and with the aid of a pair of pliers bending the protruding half slightly. Have the bent penny finger palmed in your right hand as you ask for the loan of a penny. Receive the penny in your left hand. Then pick it up with your right fingers and thumb and toss it back a couple of times while talking. Ask a lady to hold out her right hand, then place the penny in it with your left hand. Tell her to close her hand and as she does so assist her with your hands. Suddenly notice that she is holding it wrong. Have her open her hand. Take the penny with your right fingers and thumb and execute The Bobo Switch (page 10) as you pretend to toss it into your left hand. Throw the bent penny instead and hold it between the tips of the fingers and thumb (a small portion of the bent penny will be visible but not enough to tell that it is bent), while you hold the borrowed penny in finger palm position in your right hand. Close the right fingers as tightly as possible over the coin and direct her attention to that hand as you illustrate how you want her to hold the coin. As you take the

Fig. 1

penny from her and show her how to hold her hand say, "No, you're not holding it right. Let me show you. Hold your hand tightly like this." Although the right hand actually contains the borrowed penny, it appears to be empty as a trial will show, Fig. 1. No one suspects that you would be so bold as to try to conceal a coin in your right hand while showing it so freely as you illustrate how you want her to hold hers.

Have her hold out her right hand again and deliberately place the bent penny in it. Keep it covered with your fingers as you assist her in closing her hand. Caution her to hold the penny tightly so it would be impossible for you to remove it. Ask her if she can still feel it. When she replies that she can, tell her to squeeze it a little more. Finally snap your fingers and announce that the coin has vanished from her hand. She will, of course, deny this because she can still feel the penny. She doesn't know it is bent because it is impossible to tell the difference while holding it tightly. Pre-

tend that something has gone wrong. Have her open her hand to see what is the matter. When she discovers the bent penny she will be quite surprised. Say, "No wonder I couldn't make the penny disappear. You held it too tightly. Look, you have bent it." During this momentary surprise drop the borrowed penny in your pocket. Let her keep the bent penny as a souvenir.

Silver Extraction

Dr. Boris Zola

Effect: After showing a silver coin, the magician gives it to a spectator to hold tightly in his hand. He then lights a match and moves it in a wide circle around the spectator's hand, claiming that the heat from the match will soften the silver enough to enable him to remove it. The match is discarded, then the performer extracts a small nugget of silver apparently through the back of the spectator's hand. The spectator opens his hand. What he now holds appears to be a coin but it is entirely transparent. Apparently the magician did exactly what he said he would do—remove the silver from the coin.

Requirements: A silver coin, a plastic coin to match, a wad of tin foil about the size of a pea, and a packet of matches.

Working: Have all together in your right pocket and you are ready to begin. Reach into the pocket, finger palm the plastic coin, and bring out the silver coin between the tips of the fingers and thumb. Comment on the peculiar quality of the silver in the coin as you toss it into your left hand a few times. Ask a spectator to hold out his right hand. Pretend to toss the silver coin back into your left hand as you make this request but execute The Bobo Switch (page 10), throwing the plastic coin instead. The instant you receive the plastic coin in your left hand close the fingers over it and turn the hand over, then immediately open it again, keeping the coin pressed to the underside of the fingers with the thumb. (The coin should be as near the tips of the fingers as possible without actually showing.) Put the plastic coin in the spectator's right palm, keeping it covered with the fingers, then ask him to close his hand. Assist in closing his hand with the fingers of your two hands, then hold his fist a few moments as you caution him to hold tightly. If you make the switch in a casual, natural manner while talking to him, he will not suspect anything unusual. It's the boldness of the procedure that is so disarming.

Say, "In my pocket I have a match." Reach into the right pocket after the matches. Quickly press the ball of foil into the crotch of the two middle fingers, grasp the packet of matches and remove the hand from the pocket. Hold the hand so there is no danger of the foil being seen. Open the packet, remove a match and strike it. Say, "I do not intend burning you. I just want to pass the match around your hand in this manner to warm up the silver content of the coin." Begin passing the lighted match around his hand in a wide circle so as not to burn him, then say, "When the silver gets soft enough I can remove it." Blow out the match and toss it in an ash tray. As you move your right hand back to a position just above his, place the thumb tip on the ball of foil and roll it out to the tips of the fingers, keeping it hidden for the time being. "I believe I can remove the silver now." Place your right fingertips on the back of his fist and execute a circular rubbing motion with them. Suddenly bring the foil into view as you exclaim, "Here it is!" Hold the ball of foil in your right palm and have him open his hand. He will be holding the plastic coin, much to his surprise.

Occasionally someone may want you to put the silver back into the coin. If you should have such a request merely use a Wallace Lee gag as you explain that to do this you would have to go into a dark room. This seems to amuse the spectators and gives you an excuse for not complying with the request.

The Ghost of a Coin

This unusual audience participation trick is always well received. Two versions are given, both time-tested.

Effect: While being tightly held in a spectator's hand, a half dollar changes to a glass disc.

Requirements: A half dollar and a glass disc the same diameter and thickness. Go to a glazier and have him cut several glass discs each the size of a half dollar. The glass should be as nearly the thickness of a half dollar as possible. The kind of glass that is used in small picture frames is usually about right. And the discs should not be polished—just have the sharp edge taken off. When prepared in this manner the rough edge makes the disc feel more like a real coin. Since you may break or lose one occasionally it would be wise to have a supply on hand.

Working: At the outset both the glass disc and the half dollar are in the right coat pocket. The metal coin is in the main part of the pocket while the glass disc is in the little match compartment. Reach into the pocket, finger palm the glass disc and bring out the silver coin visible at the fingertips. Approach a spectator and ask him to assist you with your next experiment. Say, "How good are you at holding on to money?" Regardless of his answer, state, "Here is a half dollar." Toss it into your left hand a few times. "Would you mind holding out your hand?" With this request, execute The Bobo Switch (page 10) throwing the glass disc instead of the coin. The instant the disc strikes the left hand, close it. Then without hesitating turn the hand over, open the fingers, and hold the disc pressed against the underside with the thumb. (A good switch in coin magic can be compared to a good top change in card magic. It isn't the move that is so important, it's the misdirection which hides the move.) Learn to make the switch in a casual, natural manner, and *don't* look at your hands when the critical move is made. Look directly at the spectator as you ask him a question. A split second later make the switch. But you are not through yet. You must hold his attention for a few seconds until you get the disc in his hand and his fingers closed over it.

As you place the disc in his hand keep talking to him but say nothing about the half dollar. If you mention the half dollar he may immediately question whether the article he feels is a half dollar or not. Say, "Do you feel it? Do you think I can remove it while you are holding it?" To these questions he will naturally reply, "No." After placing the glass disc in his hand hold your left hand so it can be seen to be empty. The half dollar is actually palmed in your right hand but if that hand is held naturally and is used to assist in closing his hand, it will not be suspected. He will have only one logical conclusion: he is holding the half dollar.

Say, "I'll cause the half dollar to disappear from your hand." Keep your right hand palm down as you snap the fingers over his fist and exclaim, "It's gone!" He will deny that the coin has vanished from his hand. Say, "Don't tell me you still have it." He will let you know that he still feels it. Ask, "What are you holding?" He will reply, "A half dollar." Pretend that something must have gone wrong. Ask him to

open his hand. The moment he does, sleeve the half dollar in the right sleeve. When he sees the glass disc lying in his hand he will be surprised. A moment later he will look at your hands. He will see nothing because they are empty, and he has no clue to the mystery.

There are few close up coin mysteries more puzzling than this. It is always an unfathomable mystery to the layman how something he is holding in his own hand can be made to disappear or change.

Second Method

WALLACE LEE

To present this version, hold the glass disc concealed in the left palm and the metal coin plainly visible in the right hand

Fig. I

in correct position for back palming. Ask a spectator to open his hand widely. Apparently take the coin from your right hand into your left and place it on the spectator's palm. Actually a switch is made as follows: Cover the coin on the right fingers with the palm down left hand, Fig. 1, and under cover of the left fingers, back palm the coin with the right hand. Close the left hand on the glass disc and as it moves away, turn the right palm down and bring the coin to the palm. Place the glass disc in the specta- tor's hand and finish as in the first method.

Coins Through the Table

One of the finest tricks of close-up coin conjuring is this classic attributed to Han Ping Chien. It ranks with such old-timers as The Miser's Dream, The Cap and Pence, and The Sympathetic Coins. Until recently not too much has been generally known about the trick, since its secret has been closely guarded by a few top-notch perform- ers.

Effect: The magician shows eight half dollars and one quarter. He arranges these in two parallel rows on the table so that there are four halves in the left row and four halves and the quarter in the right row. He picks up the row of four coins with his left hand and the row of five with his right. He shows the coins again, then places his right hand underneath the table. Open- ing his left hand suddenly, he brings it palm down on the table and the four coins are heard to arrive in his right hand under- neath the table. He raises his left hand—the four coins *have* vanished. Bringing his right hand from underneath the table he pours from it all nine coins. Four coins have ap- parently penetrated the table top!

No duplicate coins are used and the trick can be done while surrounded.

Method: The success of the trick hinges on one ingenious move, and the important element in its execution is timing rather than skill.

Seat yourself at a table and show the nine coins, then place four halves in a vertical row on the table. Parallel with this row and about three or four inches to the right place the remaining coins, the quarter oc- cupying a position at the inner end, Fig. 1. Explain that the reason you add a quarter to the right row is to differentiate between the two groups of coins. Stress the fact that there are four half dollars in the left row and four half dollars *AND* a quarter in the right row, making five altogether in that particular row.

Starting at the outer end of the left row pick up the four coins one at a time with

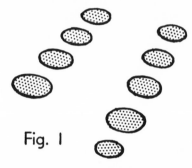

Fig. 1

your palm down left hand, then turn the closed hand so the back of the fist rests on the table. Do the same thing with your right hand. Turn the left hand palm down and slap its four coins on the table, saying, "Four." Quickly arrange these in a row again, then pick them up one at a time as before and rest the back of the fist on the table. Slap the five coins from the right hand on the table in exactly the same man- ner as you say, "Five." Arrange them in a row so there is no doubt about the number, then pick them up again one at a time. As each half dollar is taken up it is pressed into the palm and held there. The quarter is taken up last. The reason for this will soon be apparent.

Both groups of coins are shown again in the following manner: Slap the four coins from the left hand onto the table as you did the first time and say, "Remember, there are four coins in my left hand." Begin at the inner end this time; pick up the four coins and hold them together outside the

Fig. 2

fist between the tips of the fingers and the heel of the hand. (Fig. 2 shows the correct grip on the coins as seen from below.) To facilitate getting the coins into this position pick them up as follows: Keep the left hand palm down as you pretend to pick up the first coin. The coin is not actually removed from the table but its forward edge is lifted by inserting the tips of the curled fingers underneath it. Slide this coin forward onto the second coin. Lift these together in the same fashion and push them forward onto the third coin. The same moves are repeated to pick it up, then the three are pushed forward onto the last coin. All four are levered up to a vertical position with their edges resting on the table. With the coins in this position it is a simple matter to grip them as shown in Fig. 2. Keep the hand close to the table to conceal the coins protruding from the underside of the fist.

Now comes the crucial move. Turn your right hand palm downward and drop its five coins onto the table. At least, that is what you appear to do. Actually you retain the four half dollars palmed and drop the quarter only which falls onto the four coins which are released from the left hand as it turns fingers upward and swings to the left. The right hand is brought palm down on the exact spot occupied by the left hand, and to the spectators it appears that you

merely moved your left hand away as you slapped the right hand down on the table, Fig. 3. This is the only difficult move in the entire trick and it must be executed with the utmost precision. Lift the right hand exposing the five coins and say, "And don't forget, there are five coins here."

Place your right hand underneath the table and deposit the four half dollars on your right knee as you adjust yourself a little closer to the table. This is a bold move but it is never suspected. Bring the right hand back to the top of the table and gather up the five coins. Display them in the palm up hand as you state your intention of passing the coins through the table. Slowly close the fingers on the coins and carry the hand under the table and pick up the four coins from the right knee. Turn

Fig. 3

your attention now to your left fist, which supposedly contains four coins, and bring it to the center of the table. Open it suddenly exclaiming, "Watch!" and bring it palm down onto the table. At the same instant the right hand, which is underneath the table, allows the four coins to drop audibly onto the others in the palm, the sound enhancing the illusion of the coins having actually passed through the table.

Lift the left hand and turn it palm up to show that the coins have vanished, then bring the right to the top of the table and dump out the nine coins.

Second Version

The effect of this version is exactly the same as the one just described except the four coins from the right hand are not secretly placed on the knee. They are merely retained palmed in the right hand as the crucial move is made where the four coins are secretly dropped from the left hand, then all nine coins are carried underneath the table and the trick is concluded as in the first version.

Of course, this method is not quite as clean as the first since the right hand cannot be shown empty before taking up the last four coins from the table, but it is offered here as a variation.

Third Version

In this version you use eight quarters and one half dollar. These are placed on the table in two rows as in the first version, with the half dollar occupying a position at the inner end of the right hand row.

Proceed as in the first version by picking up the left row with the left hand. Take up the right row with the right hand, beginning with the half dollar. Press it into the palm, then hold the four quarters in the loose fist. Bring the left hand to the center of the table and open it, displaying the four quarters. Then as you explain that you intend to pass these four coins through the table, carry the right hand underneath the table and place the four quarters from it on the knee (retain the half dollar palmed). While you are talking bring your right hand back to the top of the table. Say, "Remember, there are four coins here." Turn the left hand over and slap its coins on the table. Pick them up as in the first version, holding them outside the fist as in Fig. 2. Turn your attention to your right hand and as you say, "and there are five coins here," drop the four coins from your left hand and swing it away, and slap the right hand

down on top of them. Lift the right hand showing four quarters and a half dollar. Apparently they all came from the right hand. After letting it be seen that the right hand is empty, pick up the five coins and carry them underneath the table. Pick up the four quarters from the knee and hold them above the others in the palm of the hand. Conclude as in the first version.

Fourth Version

Stewart Judah

Here is probably one of the best versions of all. It is by that master of subtlety, Stewart Judah, and has several superior points in its favor.

The effect is the same in this version, except six pennies and one nickel are used.

Method: Place the six pennies in two parallel rows about four inches apart, then add the nickel to the outer end of the right hand row. Explain that the reason you use seven coins is because seven is a lucky number. There are seven days in the week, and seven has been a mystical number since time immemorial.

Working inward, the right fingers and thumb pick up the nickel and place it on top of the outer penny. These two coins are placed on top of the second penny, and finally the three are placed on top of the inner penny. Simultaneously the left fingers and thumb pick up the left row, working from the outer coin inward. At the completion of this action there will be three pennies in your closed left hand, while the other three pennies and nickel are held vertically between the thumb and first two fingers of the right hand, the nickel being next to the fingers. (This is important.) No pretense is made of concealing the four coins in the right hand from the spectators. The left hand is vertical as it rests on the table, thumb upward. A few inches to the right is the right hand, back up, pressing the edges of the four coins to the table top.

Tap the edges of the four coins in your right hand on the table a few times as you say, "I think you will agree that the table top is quite solid, and it is just as solid from underneath." Move the right hand underneath the table and leave the three pennies on the leg. (To facilitate this, place the stack of four coins on the leg, then lift off the top coin, the nickel.) Without too much hesitation move the right hand on to the center of the table and tap two or three times with the edge of the nickel. To the spectators it appears that you first tapped the top of the table with the four coins, then tapped the underside of the table with the same coins.

Bring the closed right hand to the top of the table. The spectators are unaware that it contains only the five cent piece. Place the right hand about six inches to the right of the left fist. Both fists are thumb up. Pound the right fist on the table as you emphasize, "Yes, the table is quite solid." Hold the nickel rather loosely in the right fist so that it will slip down to the lower part of the fist underneath the little finger. The pounding aids in getting the coin into this position.

"Remember, I have three pennies in this hand." So saying, move the left hand slightly to the right and slap down its three coins. Turn the left hand palm up so the spectators can see that it is empty but make no comment on this fact. Gather up these three coins but do not remove them from the table. Immediately the right hand moves to the left and slaps its nickel to the table. The left hand releases its three pennies as it quickly turns fingers upward and moves to the left to make way for the right hand. The left hand closes and the right palm comes down on top of the three pennies.

Properly executed, it appears that you slapped down three pennies from your left hand, then repeated the same action with your right. The right hand now turns palm up and the spectators assume the three pennies and nickel they now see are the ones that were originally held in that hand. The left hand is closed and empty.

An important point to remember is to slap down the coins from both hands at the same spot on the table. The hands are close together and the left hand merely moves away from the right as it comes down on the table with the four coins it supposedly holds. Practice the move until even you cannot detect the fact that the three pennies did not come from the right hand, and you will have nothing to fear. When smoothly done the illusion is perfect.

Pick up the three pennies and nickel with your right hand and as you place it underneath the table take the three pennies from the leg. All the coins are now in the right hand. Bring the left hand, apparently containing three pennies, to the center of the table. Open it and slap it palm down on the table. Immediately rattle the coins in the right hand underneath the table. Lift your left hand from the table to show that the three pennies have vanished. Bring up the right hand and pour from it all seven coins.

Regardless of the version you choose, practice it well and you will have one of the finest table tricks in existence.

For still another version, see Coins Through the Table, page 276.

The Magical Filtration of Four Half Dollars

Al Baker

This trick, by Al Baker, is considered by most magicians a close-up classic. A book of this kind would not be complete without it.

The plot is of the simplest nature—four half dollars are passed one by one through the table top from the left hand to the right. No duplicate coins are used.

The trick must be done while you are seated at a table and, before making any mention of doing a trick, a little preparation has to be made. With your right hand grip the cloth of the left leg of your trousers at the seam midway down the inside of your thigh and pull the loose part over onto your right thigh, at the same time pressing your knees together. This can be done easily under cover of adjusting your chair. The cloth will thus form a flat surface onto which you can safely drop a coin and from which you can just as easily take it again, with no one being any the wiser.

This done, you are ready either to borrow four half dollars or to produce four of your own, which you drop onto the table in front of you. Casually rub your hands together so that all can see you have no other coin, but for goodness sake don't say anything about your hands being empty or about what you propose to do.

PASSAGE OF THE FIRST COIN

Hold your right hand out flat and palm upwards. Pick up one coin with the left hand and drop it onto your right palm, counting one. This coin must lie in the exact position for the classic palm so that by merely contracting the hand the coin will be retained there.

Pick up the other three coins one by one and drop them successively into the right hand, letting the second fall a little in front of the first and the remaining two in line toward the tips of the fingers, in an overlapping row, as in Fig. 1. Hold the left hand palm upwards with the fingers curled and turn the right hand over just above it,

Fig. 1

apparently dropping all four coins into it, but really retaining the one in the right palm as explained above. Let the right hand rest momentarily on the edge of the table, drop the palmed coin onto your improvised servante and immediately make an outward brushing movement with the backs of the fingers on the table top as if removing some particle of dust.

Now for the first time announce what you will try to do, that is, to pass the coins through the table top. Make some remark about the texture of the wood, that you are not sure the experiment will succeed, and again brush off the surface. Show your right hand empty, holding it flat, palm upwards, and fingers pointing straight to the front. Thrust it straight under the table up to the bend of the arm, lean forward, bend the hand inwards from the wrist and pick up the coin you dropped onto your lap.

Close your left hand, turn it over and open it, letting the three coins fall on the table underneath it. Press downwards, pretending great exertion, then say, "One coin has passed." Lift the left hand and show three coins only; bring the right hand from under the table, flat and palm upwards, and show the coin lying on it.

PASSAGE OF THE SECOND COIN

Drop the coin from the right hand about four inches from the edge of the table and in line with your trousers servante, rub your hands together and make some remark such as, "Well, one went through, let's try another." Pick up one of the three with the right hand at the tips of the thumb and fingers counting, "One," the second coin under the first, counting, "Two," and the third under these two counting, "Three," Fig. 2. Hold the left fingers curled and ap-

Fig. 2

parently drop the three coins into that hand; really push off the upper two coins only, retaining the third with the tip of the thumb against the first joints of the fingers, as in Fig. 3. Without pausing, move the right hand back towards the fourth coin and, apparently, pick it up by sweeping it to the edge of the table, really letting it fall onto your little servante under cover of the fingers and, turning the hand upwards, show the coin you retained at the tips of the thumb and fingers.

Properly timed, this move makes a perfect illusion. Above all, do not hurry, just act naturally and the spectators seeing only one coin in your right hand will be con-

Fig. 3

vinced that there are three in your left. Let the coin lie on the palm of your outstretched right hand and thrust that hand straight forward under the table just as you did the first time. Lean forward, pick up the dropped coin, turn the left hand, dropping its coins on the table underneath it and, at the same moment, let the two coins in the right hand clink together. Lift the left hand, showing two coins only, and bring the right hand up with two coins lying on it.

PASSAGE OF THE THIRD COIN

Lay the four coins on the table thus:

A   D
B   C

the two rear coins, B C being about six inches from the edge of the table. With the right hand pick up D C, one at a time, clicking them together, then with the left hand pick up A and, in apparently picking up B, sweep it off the edge of the table onto your trousers servante and hold the left hand with the fingers curled as before.

Show the two coins lying on your outstretched right hand and thrust it straight under the table as before. Lean forward and secure the coin from your trousers servante. Turn the left hand, letting its one coin fall on the table beneath it. Rub this hand on the table as if forcing a coin through and let one coin in the right hand clink against the other. Lift the left hand showing one coin only and bring the right hand up flat with three coins lying on it. Throw the coins on the table.

PASSAGE OF THE FOURTH COIN

Pick up one coin with the left hand and drop it into the right. Then turn the right hand over the cupped left hand and apparently drop the coin, really retaining it in the right palm. With the right hand slide one coin to the edge of the table and pick it up. Place this coin on another, draw them both to the edge of the table and pick them up but this time drop the palmed coin onto your trousers servante. Put the two coins on the third and pick up all three, drawing them back to the edge of the table as before. Turn the hand and show the three coins lying on it, silent but convincing proof that the fourth coin is in the left· hand.

Place the right hand under the table in the same manner as before and, leaning forward, pick up the coin from your lap. Hold this coin edgewise between the right thumb and fingers. With the left hand pretend to place the coin it is supposed to hold edge downwards on the table and then press it flat with a sharp click, and really do this with the coin in the right hand under the table. If the movements are properly timed the illusion is so perfect that the spectators are forced to believe the coin is really under the left hand.

Rub the table with the left hand, then raise it showing the table top bare. Bring the right hand up with the four coins lying on it and toss them onto the table.

It should be carefully noted how subtly the coin which is to pass is secured at a different point in the routine each time; if the moves are done neatly and naturally, without hurry, they are indetectable. Mastery of this trick will go a long way towards convincing the student of the vast importance of timing and misdirection in conjuring.

An alternate method for passing the fourth coin through the table is offered by Frank Garcia. It is as simple as it is ingenious.

By the time you have passed three coins through the table the spectators will usually be watching you like hawks. Therefore the move for causing the fourth coin to penetrate the table needs to be a very clever one.

Here is Frank's method:

Pick up one of the four coins from the table with your right hand and slowly and deliberately place it in your left palm. Slowly close the left fingers over the coin, then turn the hand fingers downward. Take the remaining three coins in your right hand, and as you place the hand underneath the table, deposit one coin on your right knee.

Move the left toward the center of the table and raise it a few inches. Just as you are about to bring it down on the table, stop suddenly and look at the spectators. Smile slyly and say, "You probably doubt that I still have a coin in my left hand." With these words open the left hand and slap its coin onto the table. Pick it up again and hold it outside the fist by its edge between the tips of the fingers and the heel of the hand in the same manner as shown in Fig. 2, page 191. The left hand is back up and held close to the table and the coin cannot be seen. Now slap the two coins from your right hand onto the table as your left hand drops its coin and moves away. (See Coins Through the Table, page 191, for a detailed description of this move.) Apparently you slapped first one coin, then three onto the table. Move your left fist away to the left as you pick up the three coins from the table and display them in your palm up right hand. Close the fingers slowly over the coins, then carry them underneath the table. As you do so, quietly pick up the coin from your right knee.

Move the left hand to the center of the table, open it and slap it palm down onto the table. At the same instant click the coins together in your hand which is underneath the table. Turn the left hand palm up and show it empty. Bring up the right hand and pour the four coins from it onto the table.

The method for passing the last coin through will baffle the closest observer.

The Sympathetic Coins

Here is one of the oldest and best close-up coin tricks of all time. Almost every magician who does intimate magic has one or more versions in his repertoire. Several versions will be described on the following pages, but to better acquaint the reader with it in its pure and simple form I would like to give the original Yank Hoe method which was first described in T. Nelson Downs' *The Art of Magic*.

Effect: The performer borrows a handkerchief and four half dollars. He spreads the handkerchief on the table and places a coin on each of its corners. The coins are covered alternately with two squares of paper, then they are placed over the two coins at the outer corners. The two visible coins are caused to pass one at a time to one of the papers. Finally the last coin vanishes from underneath its paper, to join the others underneath the other paper.

Requirements: A pocket handkerchief (preferably one of a dark color so the coins will show up by contrast), four half dollars (which you borrow and have marked), and two pieces of stiff paper (the quality used for magazine covers is about right) about four inches square.

Working: Stand behind a table, spread out the handkerchief and place a half dollar on each corner. Show the two pieces of paper freely and hold one in each hand between the thumb on top and the fingers below. Explain that the experiment you are about to present is more of an optical illusion than it is a feat of magic. This explanation is necessary to account for the moves you are about to make with the squares of paper.

Cover the two front coins with the squares of paper and call attention to the fact that the two back coins are visible.

Shift the papers to the two rear coins, leaving the two forward coins in sight.

Move the papers to cover the coins at the front left corner and right rear corner, showing the other two in position.

Now cover the right front and left rear coins, reminding the spectators that each time you cover two coins, two others remain visible.

While talking and looking directly at the spectators, pick up the right front coin and hold it underneath the paper with the fingers. To facilitate this move press down on the left edge of the coin through the paper with the right thumb. This causes the right side of the coin to lever up slightly, permitting the tip of the third finger to be inserted beneath it. The coin is then held against the underside of the paper.

Now comes the crucial move. Retaining your right hand in the same position, move the left paper up and hold it directly above the square held by your right hand. Immediately move your right hand away, with its piece of paper and coin, a few inches to the right, and drop the paper from your left hand directly on the spot where the outer right coin is supposed to lie. Then move the right hand over to the left and place its paper over the coin at the front left corner, releasing the coin at the same time. Be careful that the two coins do not clink together and give you away as you do this.

The most difficult part of the trick is now over but the spectators think the trick hasn't begun. Pick up the coin from the left inner corner of the handkerchief with your right hand, then lift that corner with your left hand, the *fingers well underneath and the thumb above*. Show the coin plainly, then place it underneath the handkerchief and push it forward toward the front left corner. This is what you seem to do. In reality, you place the coin between the tips of your left first and second fingers (back finger clip) the moment the right hand is out of sight, then without hesitation move the hand forward to the left outer corner. Now, with a slight upward movement of the fingers one coin will be thrown upon the other, causing an audible "clink." Apparently you have pushed the coin through the fabric.

Remove your right hand from beneath the handkerchief, show it empty, then lift the outer left paper, showing the two coins. Without pausing, bring the paper back to the left rear corner, release that corner and take the paper from your right hand with your left hand. Properly done it is impossible to get even the smallest flash of the coin between the fingers because the paper is placed under the left thumb *before* the fingers are removed from underneath the corner of the handkerchief. The two coins are uncovered and the paper placed in the left hand all in one continuous move.

The instant the left hand takes the paper from the right hand, that hand moves up, picks up one of the coins and drops it onto the other. (This makes room for the third coin which will be added momentarily.) Now replace the paper—this time with a coin underneath—over the two coins, making three coins under that paper.

Repeat the above movements with the coin from the inner right corner, then raise the paper and show the three coins. As the paper is returned the fourth coin is added.

At this point the spectators are convinced that there are three coins under the left paper and one under the right. Actually all four are under the left paper and none is under the other. In order to pass the last coin you vary the procedure. Bend over and pretend to blow the last coin across, then lift the right paper to show the coin vanished. Raise the left paper to show all four coins there.

Various ruses have been devised for passing the last coin, but the above method is time tested.

Second Version

Besides the four borrowed half dollars you will require an additional one of your own. Have this one concealed in your left palm while you spread the handkerchief on the table and place the four coins on its corners. Cover the coins in the same way as before but do not remove the outer right coin. Leave it under the paper. Add the palmed coin to the outer left one as you cover it for the last time before actually commencing the trick.

Proceed from here as in the first version up to the point where you have brought three coins under the left paper and secretly added the fourth. Lift the paper from the outer right corner, then vanish it using a method from Chapter IV.

Because of the secret use of an extra coin in this version it is safe to repeat the trick before the same audience, especially if you employ

The Al Saal Stratagem

Instead of repeating the move of placing the coin between the left first and second fingers as it is carried under the corner of the handkerchief, you might try this move of Al Saal's which appeared in *The Sphinx* for November, 1937:

As you place the coin beneath the cloth back palm it with your right hand, then as you remove that hand from beneath the cloth place the left paper over the right hand. This move does not have to be hurried because the hand appears quite empty. Now as you turn the right paper over to show its other side, transfer the coin to the front finger hold where it will be concealed between the fingers and the paper. You are now in position to continue the effect.

The move just described is one of continued motion and is perfectly covered in the action of turning the paper over to show its other side.

Third Version

One of the most popular versions of to-day employs pennies and playing cards. Perhaps the reason for this is that the trick is a little easier to perform with pennies. They are not as difficult to conceal in the hands or under the cards and there is less danger of an accidental give-away clink as a coin is secretly added to the one at the outer left corner. And as a rule a white handkerchief is more readily available than a colored one. If playing cards are not handy, business cards can be used.

Pennies and cards can be used in either of the first two versions, the only difference being that when the right hand steals the penny from the outer right corner it is clipped by its edge (back finger clip) between the first and second or second and third fingers (whichever is the most convenient), then the trick proceeds exactly as was described using half dollars.

Suggestion: If you will work the trick on a soft surface you will find it easier to lever up the penny at the right corner in preparation for stealing it.

Some performers get down on their knees and perform the trick on the rug. It appears much more impromptu this way.

Fourth Version

THE CHANGING CHANGE

STEWART JAMES

Effect: Same as the first version except four coins of different values are used.

Requisites and Preparation: A half dollar, two quarters, a nickel, and a dime in your right trousers pocket.

A folded opaque handkerchief in your right coat pocket, and a dime.

A billfold containing two bills in your left hip pocket.

Presentation: Stand behind a cloth cov-ered table, place your hand in your right coat pocket, finger palm the dime and remove the handkerchief.

Reach over with your left hand and take the handkerchief by one extreme corner between the tips of the forefinger and thumb, allow it to unfold and display it palm toward the audience.

While showing the left hand and handkerchief freely, place the right thumb on top of the dime and slide it down near the tip of the fingers. Hold the handkerchief in front of your chest, then with your right hand, grasp the cloth near the corner held by your left hand and as you do so leave the dime. Hold it hidden behind the handkerchief with your left thumb, then slide your right hand along the edge of the cloth to the opposite corner, stretching it out between the two hands. Make the secret deposit of the dime behind the corner and the stretching out of the handkerchif one continuous move. The handkerchief is now held by its extreme corners between the tips of the forefingers and thumbs, the dime being hidden behind the left thumb, Fig. 1.

Give the handkerchief a flick, extend your arms, then draw it back toward you with your hands barely clearing the table top. As you do this, deposit the dime on the table so it will be covered and will lie about midway between the inner and outer left corners. Release your grip on the handkerchief and smooth it out.

Fig. 1

Take out your billfold, extract the two bills from it and drop them on the center of the handkerchief. Do not return the billfold to your pocket but place it on the table some distance to your left. This is merely to eliminate the couple of times the hand would approach the pocket—once to replace the billfold and once to take it out again to return the bills. Neither action is essential and might be considered suspicious, and might thus make the routine less clean cut.

Thrust your hand in your right trousers pocket, palm one of the quarters (it is easy to locate one of the quarters because of the difference in the size of the coins), bring out the others at the finger-tips and toss them into your outstretched left hand. Spread them about with the tips of your right fingers, calling attention to their values. As you show the coins and move them about, get the quarter into position for finger palming. Execute the Utility Switch (page 11) as you retain the quarter finger palmed and toss the nickel, dime, and half dollar into your right hand. Apparently show the same four coins in your right hand. Actually the quarter was already there. All seems fair.

Immediately pick up the bills with your left hand so they will lie across the fingers, hiding the finger palmed quarter. Holding the bills in this position permits the hand to assume a natural position and the reason for doing so is immediately apparent. With your right hand, place the four coins at the center of the handkerchief in this order:

50¢   5¢

25¢   10¢

Draw off the top bill with your right hand, then hold a bill in each hand between the fingers underneath and the thumbs on top. (A quarter is concealed underneath the left bill.) Cover the half dollar with the left

bill and the nickel with the right bill, lift the two coins underneath the bills and move them out about half way toward the two outer corners of the handkerchief.

Cover the quarter and dime in the same manner and move them to the corners nearest you.

Cover the half dollar and nickel again and move them to the outer corners and leave the bills on top of them. This is what you apparently do. In reality, you steal the nickel with your right hand while your left leaves its quarter with the half dollar. Be careful that the two coins do not clink together as you do this.

From this point on, the effect is the same as the original version except for the different size coins used, and because of this fact the trick is very puzzling, especially to the informed.

The state of things at this juncture is this: Underneath the bill lying at the outer left corner of the handkerchief are two coins—a half dollar and a quarter. The nickel that the right bill is supposed to cover is now finger palmed in your right hand. Pick up the quarter from the left inner corner of the handkerchief with your right hand, then lift that corner of the cloth with your left hand. Place your right hand underneath the handkerchief (with its visible quarter and finger palmed nickel) and move it up the left side of the cloth to where the dime lies. As you explain that you will cause the quarter to penetrate the fabric and join the half dollar, leave the quarter and nickel on the table and pick up the dime (which has been lying on the table from the time the handkerchief was spread on the table), then move the hand on up to the outer left corner and give that corner a little upward kick with the fingers, causing the two coins under the bill to clink together. Draw your right hand back to the left inner corner of the handkerchief, and place the dime between the left first and second fingers (back finger clip), then remove the right hand. Pick up the bill from the outer left corner of the handkerchief to show the half dollar and quarter.

Bring the bill back to the left inner corner of the handkerchief and take it with your left hand, fingers underneath and thumb on top. Return the bill to its former position, leaving the dime underneath it.

Take up the visible dime from the right inner corner with your right hand and carry it underneath the handkerchief. Leave it on the table and finger palm the nickel, then move the hand on up and click the coins together as before. Place the nickel between the left first and second fingers, then remove the right hand and lift the right bill showing a half dollar, a quarter, and a dime.

Bring the bill back to your left hand which replaces it (with the nickel underneath) back over the three coins. Now all four coins are under this bill, but the spectators believe the nickel to be under the right bill. Explain that you will pass the five cent piece the hard way. You will pull it down through the cloth, move it across, and shove it up through the cloth again to join the other three coins. Put your right hand under the left side of the handkerchief, finger palm the dime, then move the hand underneath the right bill. As you move the hand back to the left bill, finger palm the quarter. This makes for better timing and you can be sure that the coins will not "talk" as they might if you tried to secure them both at once.

Pick up the left bill with your left hand, revealing the four coins together. Simultaneously remove your right hand from beneath the handkerchief and bring your left hand back and place the bill in your right hand, covering the finger palmed coins.

Pick up the right bill with your left hand

to show that the coin is actually gone from beneath it, then place the bill in your right hand *underneath* the coins and bill in that hand. Take up the billfold and return the two bills to it with the coins in between. This is natural and leaves your hands empty with nothing on the table but the four coins and the handkerchief.

Suggestion: Have two quarters and a dime in your right trousers pocket and another dime finger palmed in your right hand. Show the handkerchief and as you spread it on the table leave the dime as explained. Reach into your pocket, finger palm one quarter and bring out the other quarter and dime and toss them into your left hand. Tell the spectators that you need two more coins. It doesn't make any difference what you get (even foreign coins or tokens) as they require no duplicates.

All four coins may be borrowed if you are sure of getting a quarter and dime that will look like yours.

For a fifth version see page 282.

The Coin Roll

This age-old flourish was a favorite with coin men long before the days of Downs.

With the right hand closed and back uppermost, show a large coin pinched flat between the tips of the thumb and outer side of the knuckle of the forefinger, and protruding as much as possible, Fig. 1.

Fig. I

Fig. 2

Push the coin up slightly and release it with the thumb, permitting the coin to be balanced on the back of the forefinger between the knuckles and the middle joint as in Fig. 2. Raise the second finger and bring it down on the right edge of the coin causing it to assume a temporary position pinched flat between the first and second

Fig. 3

fingers, Fig. 3. Without hesitating, the coin is allowed to fall onto the back of the second finger and the same action is continued until the coin is pinched in a vertical position between the last two fingers.

At this stage of the flourish you may reverse the process, thus bringing the coin back to its starting position, or better still, allow the coin to slip between the last two fingers onto the tip of the thumb which is brought underneath the hand to receive it. It is then carried balanced flat on the ball of the thumb back to its starting place and the same set of moves repeated as many times as you wish.

Several variations are possible with this beautiful flourish. Some performers can keep two or more coins going at the same time with both hands simultaneously.

The Downs Coin Star

This is more a feat of digital dexterity than a trick of magic. It is generally credited to T. Nelson Downs who used it primarily in his close-up work.

Because the coins are balanced on the tips of the fingers and thumb it is important that large, heavy coins be employed. The feat is made easier and more sure-fire through the use of a little wax on the coin that is balanced on the thumb. (See Note at end.)

Hold the right hand palm upward with the fingers extended and well apart. Show five coins in your left hand, then balance them on the ball parts of the thumb and four fingers as shown in Fig. 1. Turn to the left and pretend to dump the five coins into your left hand, but retain them in your right. To accomplish this, turn the right palm toward the body, bend the fingers inward and snap the coin on the tip of the thumb down onto the one on the tip of the forefinger. As the fingers thus curl inward one or two coins will usually clink together; this combined with the noise of the two balanced on the forefinger and thumb snap-

Fig. 1

Fig. 2

ping together creates the illusion, by sound, of the coins actually falling into the left hand, Fig. 2.

Close the left hand as if it actually held the coins, then turn back facing the spectators and drop the right hand to the side at a position just out of sight behind the right hip. Center your complete attention on your closed left hand, then open it suddenly and bring it palm against the chest as if throwing the coin through the body. Turn the left hand palm toward the spectators, showing it empty. While this is be-done, the right hand, which is holding the coins flatwise between the fingers, moves further behind the body as if catching the coins as they penetrate the body, and opens as shown in Fig. 1. The most difficult part of this move is getting the original coin back on the tip of the thumb. This can be facilitated by pointing the thumb and fore-finger upward and separating them first, then the others are extended and the hand brought into view with the five coins balanced on the tips of the fingers and thumb in the form of the original star.

Note: It is generally known that some of our top magicians do not always employ standard procedure in the presentation of certain effects. They have their own pet methods—methods known only to themselves. This is one reason why one magician is often mystified by another.

T. Nelson Downs guarded well his pet method for performing The Coin Star because it has never before appeared in print.

Although it is possible to perform the trick with ordinary coins after a considerable amount of practice, there is always a chance of failure. A good magician—a magician with a reputation to uphold—does not wish to take chances. He cannot afford to miss! The trick must work everytime!

The fact that Mr. Downs employed an aid other than skill in the performance of this trick was suspicioned by many but actually known to few. In September, 1951 I had the privilege of examining some of Mr. Downs' effects, which are now in the hands of C. R. (Bud) Tracy. Among the gadgets and gimmicks I noticed a clip holding six dollar-size palming coins. Two of these were well-worn and smooth. One of

Fig. 3

these two was specially prepared by having a shallow cavity, the size of a dime, on one side, Fig. 3. In this hollowed out place was a bit of wax, now green with age. Discovering this I realized, here were the very coins that Downs used for performing the Coin Star! And this prepared coin was the one he placed on his thumb! Because of the wax the coin would safely adhere to the thumb and not fall off during the critical move of the trick. But you may wonder, why the indentation. Why wouldn't any coin do, providing it had a bit of wax on it? The reason for the cavity is twofold. First, the wax could be spread around the cavity, thus affording better adhesion to the ball of the thumb than a single ball of wax. Second, a coin thus prepared could be handled quite freely, manipulated, or stacked with the other coins without fear of sticking to them.

I am told that Mr. Downs would sometime flip the coins into the air after performing the feat to show the absence of trickery. The prepared coin always landed wax-side down, therefore appearing quite ordinary.

As mentioned earlier, this prepared coin stood out slightly from the rest because it was smoother in appearence. The spectators were unaware of a sixth coin which matched the prepared coin in appearance. On certain occasions after executing the Coin Star, Mr. Downs would switch the prepared coin for the extra, unprepared one, then the coins were shown freely without any preparation whatsoever. A clever bit of subtlety!

A trapeze artist can do his act without tape on his wrists or rosin on his hands, but *WHY TAKE CHANCES!* Use a little wax and play safe.

Roll Down Flourish with Four Coins

Hold a stack of four coins in your right hand between the tips of the first and third fingers, with the tip of the second finger resting against the outer edges and the tip of the thumb against the opposite inner edges, Fig. 1. Lower the thumb until it touches the inside of the outer joint of the third finger, then with a slight pressure on the two inner coins with the thumb, sep-

arate them a bit from the other two coins. Hold them in this position momentarily with the thumb and first and second fingers, while the third finger adjusts itself up against the tip of the thumb. Now by raising thumb and lowering the third finger the four coins will separate, a pair rolling out between the thumb and forefinger, and

Fig. 2

a pair rolling out between the second and third fingers, Fig. 2.

Next, the little finger is brought up so its tip will be touching the side of the second finger and its back pressed against the edge of the outer coin. Simultaneously the thumb is lowered and its tip placed against the inside of the outer joint of the third finger which then presses against the edge of the rear coin, Fig. 3. The fingers are then separated, causing the coins to roll out and assume the position depicted in Fig. 4.

Besides pratice, a considerable amount

Fig. 1

Fig. 3

Fig. 4

of feel and balance is required to execute this flourish with precision.

Downs Eureka Pass

This beautiful vanish and reproduction of several coins was devised by that master coin manipulator, T. Nelson Downs.

Effect: The magician shows four coins. Taking them one at a time in his right hand, he causes them to disappear by apparently tossing them into the air. After showing his hand empty back and front he proceeds to reproduce them one at time.

Procedure: Show four coins (of a size you can easily back palm) and place them on a nearby table. Standing with your left side toward the audience, pick up one of the coins with your left hand and place it between the tips of the right forefinger and thumb. Keep the palm of the right hand toward the spectators, and as you go through the motions of tossing the coin upward into the air, back palm it. As soon as the coin is out of sight behind the right hand, remove the little finger from the lower edge, then hold it clipped in an oblique position between the first and second fingers. (See The Back Finger Clip, page 7.)

Take up a second coin between the forefinger and thumb of the left hand (which is held back toward the spectators) and place it between the same fingers of the right hand. As this coin is placed in position, it

is natural for the left second, third, and fourth fingers to go behind the right fingers. Under cover of the right fingers, and the action of placing the second coin between the right forefinger and thumb, seize the coin from behind the right fingers between the tips of the left second and third fingers as in Figs. 1 and 2, which are front and

Fig. 1

Fig. 2

rear views, respectively, then separate the hands with the first coin concealed in the left hand. Actually the right hand is raised slightly to give the audience a better view of the coin it holds while the left hand moves inward toward the body and points at the right hand.

Under cover of pretending to toss the second coin into the air with the right hand, back palm it, then hold it in the back finger clip as you did the first. While reaching for the third coin with the left hand, edge palm the first coin. (See The Edge Palm, page 2.) Then as you place this coin in the right hand, steal the second one from behind the right fingers in the same manner as you did the first. Continue these moves until three coins are edge palmed in the left hand and one is back palmed in the right hand.

The second part of the routine consists of showing the right hand empty on both sides, then reproducing the coins one at a time with that hand. To accomplish this, a reversal of the foregoing moves must be executed. After vanishing the last coin with the right hand, show it empty on both sides by performing the front and back palm. Finally, reach up into the air and produce the coin between the forefinger and thumb. While doing this with your right hand you must ready a second coin with your left hand by removing it from the edge palm and holding it clipped between the tips of the second and third fingers. Bring your left hand up to your right to remove the just produced coin, and as you do so, deposit the coin from the left fingers between the first and second fingers of the right hand in the regular back finger clip. The left hand moves away visibly bearing the just produced coin, and drops it onto the table.

Repeat the same set of moves to reproduce the remaining three coins.

If you wish you may vary slightly the method of reproducing the last coin. After you have produced the third coin and deposited the fourth coin to the back of the right hand, instead of showing that hand empty in the orthodox fashion of the front and back palm, do this: Turn the right hand over to show its back, and as you do so transfer the coin to the Downs Palm (behind the thumb), then turn the hand over showing the palm and produce coin in the fashion described on page 3.

Downs considered the "Eureka" Pass one of his prettiest and most puzzling feats—an opinion shared by most coin manipulators.

"Eureka" Routine

Arthur Punnar

The following routine employs Downs' Eureka Pass and Roll Down Production of Four Coins in a novel combination of effects.

Procedure: Stand with your left side toward the audience and show four coins (dollars or halves) held in a fan between the left forefinger and thumb. Take one of the coins with your right hand, flip it into the air and catch it. Extend your right arm, close the fingers over the coin, then as you slowly turn your hand over, back palm the coin so it will be outside the first. The movement required to revolve the coin into position is hardly suspicious and should simulate a pulverizing action.

Keeping the fingers together, turn the right hand around and open it. The empty palm now faces the audience with the coin in the familiar rear pinch between the first and second fingers. Both sides of the hand have been shown empty without the usual tricky manipulations.

Let's go over that again. The coin, you recall, is outside the fist, the back of the hand toward the audience. Before the hand is opened the tips of the thumb and first finger meet and when the hand is opened the thumb makes a circular rubbing motion against the finger to "annihilate" the last particle before the hand is shown empty.

The effect is truly magical.

Bring the left hand over to the right, and while placing a second coin between the tips of the right forefinger and thumb, the last three fingers of the left hand pass to the back of the right hand and seize the coin held there between the second and third fingers, after the fashion of the standard Eureka Pass. As the hands separate, after placing the second coin in position for its vanish, you transfer the first coin to the edge palm. Follow the same procedure to vanish the second and third coins.

The fourth coin, after being maneuvered into the finger hold outside the fist as previously described, is then "worked" into a rear thumb palm. The foregoing position is probably the most convenient one to accomplish the back thumb palm, then the action of vanishing all four coins will appear practically identical. Separate the fingers, thus indicating that at no time were the closed fingers used to conceal the coin. (With practice, the thumb can be almost fully extended, resulting in a convincing acquitment.)

The first part of the routine is now finished. At this point you have three coins edge palmed in your left hand, and one coin hidden behind your right hand in the back thumb palm.

The next phase of the experiment consists of reproducing the four vanished coins, which is done in an entirely different manner from the Downs Eureka Pass, previously described. After a suitable pause, make a short upward thrust with your right hand, at the same time relaxing your grip on the coin and closing the hand into a fist. This causes the coin to fall into the hand which is then opened and the coin shown. Display the coin between the tips of the forefinger and thumb, then bring the left hand up to take it. In the action of doing this the right second and third fingers clip the edge palmed coins and carry them away as you quickly swing your body to the left. As you finish the turning movement of your body the back of your right hand should be toward the audience (with the three coins held between the tips of the curled middle fingers) and pointing to the coin held in the left hand. Do not attempt to palm the coins; if the second and third fingers are sufficiently curled the coins will be well concealed. Center your complete attention on the visible coin in your left hand as you maneuver the three coins in the right hand so they will be gripped by their edges between the tips of the first three fingers and thumb. As you swing back to the right, quickly execute the Roll Down move (page 204) with the three coins so that only the space between the forefinger and thumb is vacant. Place the coin held by the left hand between the forefinger and thumb of the right, thus signifying the completion of the effect.

Rattle Box Routine

STEWART JUDAH

An effective routine for small intimate groups is this easy-to-do mystery by magicdom's master of sublety, Stewart Judah.

Effect: The mystery is in two parts. From a small wooden box, the performer removes a Chinese coin, which he shows and places in full view on the table. He then asks for the loan of a coin from a spectator, who marks it for future identification and drops it into the box. The performer never touches this coin. The box is shaken, proving the spectator's coin still inside, then it is placed on the table. Picking up the Chinese coin, performer drops it into an opaque tumbler, which he holds in one hand a few inches above the table as he places his other hand underneath the table. He commands the coin to penetrate the table and pass into his hand as the glass is brought suddenly down onto the table. He brings up his other hand, shows the Chinese coin and tosses it onto the table.

In the second phase of the mystery the spectator's coin is caused to travel invisibly from the box to the glass. Taking up the box in one hand and the tumbler in the other he holds them some distance apart. He shakes the box again to prove that the coin is still there, then commands it to pass into the glass, where it is heard to arrive. The box is opened and shown empty and the coin dumped from the tumbler into the spectator's hand, who identifies it as his own.

As the ads would say—no duplicate coins and no difficult moves!

Requisites and Preparation: A rattle box, a Chinese coin (or any unusual coin), and an opaque tumbler such as the plastic variety used in the bathroom.

The rattle box containing the Chinese coin is on the table and the tumbler nearby.

Working: With the right hand, pick up the rattle box and shake it, causing the coin inside to rattle. Open the box and dump the coin into your left hand. Show it to a few nearby spectators, then place it on the table in full view. Ask for the loan of some small coin such as a nickel or a quarter and have it marked for future identification, then permit the spectator to drop the coin into the box. As you return to the table tilt the box slightly so the coin will slide out into your right hand, close the box, shake it (causing the rattle in the double bottom to sound), then place it in full view on the table. Apparently the coin is still in the box. Actually it is finger palmed in your right hand.

Pick up the Chinese coin with your right hand and the tumbler with your left hand. Show the tumbler empty, then toss the Chinese coin into it. This is what you pretend to do. In reality you execute The Bobo Switch (page 10) as you retain the Chinese coin finger palmed and toss the spectator's coin into the glass instead. Don't try to be fancy here. Make the switch as simple and natural as possible and no one will suspect an exchange. After rattling the coin in the glass, place it on the table. If the switch has been made properly the spectators will be convinced that the Chinese coin is in the tumbler. Actually it is hidden in your right hand and the spectator's coin is in the tumbler.

State, "I will now cause the Chinese coin to penetrate the bottom of the glass and pass through the table into my hand." Suiting the action to the words, move your right hand underneath while the left hand raises the glass a few inches above the table. "Listen!" As the left hand brings the tumbler down onto the table the right hand snaps the coin against the underside of the table. "Did you hear it?" Bring the right hand up, show the coin and toss it onto the table, saying, "Here it is." Although you have not shown the tumbler empty (it still contains the spectator's coin) it will not be suspected.

Pick up the glass with your left hand and the box with the right hand as you announce your next feat. "I will now cause the coin to leave the box (shake box, rattling it), describe an arc in the air and land in the glass." As you speak these words indicate the passage the coin will take with your eyes. Shake box again and exclaim, "Here it goes! Watch it!" Pretend to follow the flight of the non-existent coin as it leaves the box, flies upward through the air, then downward into the glass. The instant your eyes reach the glass lower it suddenly, causing the coin inside it to jingle, thus creating the illusion that the coin was actually caught in the glass. Open the box, show it empty and place it aside. Rattle the coin in the glass as you walk over to the spectator and dump it into his hand. He identifies it as his own.

Thieves and Sheep

MILTON KORT AND STEWART JAMES

Here is a new version of an ancient trick. Originally it was worked with paper wads. A method using wooden blocks appeared on the magic market a few years ago, also a new version by Stewart Judah, called "The Alibi Twins," which makes use of two little figures and five imitation cookies.

Effect: Relating a story about two thieves and some sheep, the performer shows two nickels and five pennies, which he places on the table in a row. His hands represent the two barns, the two nickels represent the thieves, and the five pennies represent the sheep. He takes up a nickel in each hand, then alternating with each hand, he picks up the five pennies so that after all have been removed from the table he has one nickel and two pennies in his left hand and one nickel and three pennies in his right. The coins are returned to the table, then picked up again according to the story. But when he opens his hands he shows the two nickels together in his left hand and the five pennies in his right.

Working: Sit at the table and secretly place two pennies on your right leg, which should be underneath the table. Borrow five pennies and two nickels. Arrange the pennies in a horizontal row in front of you near the edge of the table, with a nickel at each end. Begin the trick by saying, "A little mystery with five pennies and two nickels. The story concerns two notorious thieves—represented by the nickels, who are out to steal the five sheep—represented by the pennies. My hands will be the two barns into which the thieves sneak in an effort to steal the sheep."

Holding the hands palm downward, take up a nickel in each hand and say, "While the sheep herder is away the thieves creep into the barns. Then each thief takes a sheep." Pick up a penny with your right hand, then take the next one with your left hand. Alternate hands in picking up the pennies until there are none left on the table. You will have one nickel and two

pennies in your left hand and one nickel and three pennies in your right. "The thieves are about to make their get-away when they hear the sheep herder returning. Quickly, they put the sheep back." Starting with your right hand, replace a penny on the table, then put back one from your left hand, and so on alternating hands, until all five pennies are back on the table in a row. Finally place the two nickels back in their original positions at the ends of the row.

Lower your hands to the chair and hitch yourself a little closer to the table. While doing this, steal the two pennies from your right leg with your right hand, and hold them finger palmed at the base of the third and fourth fingers. Bring your hands to the top of the table and continue your story. "After the sheep herder leaves, the thieves again sneak into the two barns to steal the sheep." Pick up a nickel in each hand as before and hold the one in the right hand outside the fist between the tips of the fingers and the heel of the hand as described in Coin to Key, Fig. 4 (page 78). As you say, "Remember, there is a robber in each barn," bring your fists up together in a gesture and pass the nickel from the right fist to the left fist after the fashion described in the Fourth Method, Copper and Silver Transposition (page 132). Now you have both nickels in your left hand, two pennies in your right. Both hands are back up, and as you begin picking up the five pennies in the same order as before, state, "Each thief steals a sheep." Place the tips of the right first two fingers over the penny at the right end of the row and slide it off the edge of the table toward yourself and take it in your hand. Apparently do the same thing with your left hand, but slide the penny at the left end of the row off the table into your lap instead. Repeat the same moves as you take the next coin legitimately with your right hand, then slide the next one off into your lap with your left hand as you pretend to take it in that hand. Take the remaining penny honestly in your right hand. The spectators now think you have a nickel and two pennies in your left hand and one nickel and three pennies in your right. Actually the left hand holds only the two nickels (as already explained), while the right holds the five pennies (two others are in your lap). "The sheep herder, sensing something wrong, returns again. But when he looks in the first barn he finds all the sheep." Open your right hand, showing the five pennies. "And when he looks in the second barn he finds the two thieves all by themselves." Open your left hand, showing the two nickels. At an opportune moment pick up the two pennies in your lap and pocket them with the coins on the table.

A slightly different version using a trick coin can be found under the same title on page 249.

Just Pretend

STUART CRAMER

A trick that requires simple sleights is usually favored by most magicians because such a trick allows the performer to concentrate on presentation and showmanship. The following trick, although not very difficult, requires careful timing and misdirection to put over successfully. Properly done it is a classic.

As the spectators see it: With his sleeves rolled up, the magician shows a fifty-cent piece, places it in his left hand, then gestures with his right, showing unmistakably that the coin is actually in the closed left hand. He then makes a magic pass around his left hand, explaining that he is drawing the coin out of the hand. Pretending to hold the invisible coin in his right hand, he throws it away and his right hand is seen

to be empty. The left hand is opened and it is seen to be empty also.

Saying that the trick would not be complete unless he could bring the coin back, the magician pretends to pluck the coin from the air with his right hand, then pretends to put it back in his left. Another magic pass is made around his left hand and when it is opened a moment later the coin is seen to have returned.

Required sleights: Three sleights are used, and all three are blended together into one continuous movement. The first involves the secret removal of the coin from the left fist; the second, getting the coin into the Downs palm and holding it there while you make a gesture of throwing it away and showing the right hand empty; and third, secretly putting the coin back into the left hand after it has been shown empty. These moves will be explained in detail.

Working: Turn back your sleeves and stand with your body turned slightly to the left as you display a half dollar between the tips of the right fingers and thumb. Hold your left hand chest high, palm toward the audience, and say, "I will tell you exactly how this trick is done, but I assure you, you won't believe me. First, we will

Fig. I

place the coin in the left hand." Bring the right hand over to place the coin in the left hand but push it between the left thumb and the base of the forefinger as in Fig. 1. The back of the right hand conceals

Fig. 2

this action from the spectators, and to them it appears that you merely placed the coin in the palm of the left hand. Fig. 2 shows the left fist with the coin hidden in a back thumb clip.

Move the right hand back to the right so it will be palm outward as you gesture, Fig. 3, and say, "And now we start to pretend.

Fig. 3

Fig. 4

But first, we must make a magic circle around the hand, like this." With a circular motion, pass the right hand around the left fist, Fig. 4, and as you do so, steal the coin. **The actual mechanics are these:** Move the right hand, palm down, over the top of the left fist and scoop the coin from the back of the left thumb with the right fingers as it makes a circular pass around the left hand, Fig. 5.

Fig. 5

Immediately after making the mystical pass and stealing the coin, say, "And now we pretend to draw the coin out of the fist." You are still turned slightly to the left and your left fist is held stationary at all times. An actual drawing, or pulling, motion is made, as though the fingertips, which never go near the left hand, were really trying to magically draw the coin out of the left hand. Under cover of this motion, which is a combination of an arm and finger movement, the coin is worked into the Downs palm. (See The Downs Palm, page 3.)

This is the most difficult part of the manipulation, but it has the advantage of being covered by the motion of the right hand feigning to draw the coin out of the left fist. Just keep on pretending to pull it out of the left hand (and this is exactly what you tell the audience you are doing!) until you get the coin into the Downs palm position. The best way to do this is to use the thumb to push the coin between

Fig. 6

Fig. 7

the first and second fingers, Figs. 6 and 7, then bend them inward and place the coin behind the thumb so it will be horizontal with the floor, Fig. 8.

After the coin is Downs palmed make one more drawing motion, only slower, and

Fig. 8

say, "After we pretend to draw the coin out of the hand, we pretend to throw it away." Accompany these words by turning the body to the right and making a throwing motion with the right hand with a wrist action. (To prevent the spectators getting a flash of the coin as you swing right, place the tip of the thumb and forefinger together momentarily.) Follow the flight of the non-existent coin as you pretend to toss the coin to your right, Fig. 9.

Special attention should be given to the footwork to make the turn a graceful one. As you turn your body to the right, take a short step to the right with the right foot, while the other goes up on its toes.

After pretending to toss the coin away with your right hand, reverse the foot and body movements and assume your original position, that is, your body turned slightly to the left. Your left hand is closed and the back of the right is toward the audience.

Say, "Now if we have pretended well enough and used our imagination to the fullest extent, we will find that the coin has really flown away." After all movement

Fig. 9

has ceased, turn your gaze toward your left hand and slowly open it. Turn the hand over several times, showing it back and front with the fingers wide apart.

Pause a split second after showing the left hand empty, then before the spectators' attention returns to the right hand, raise it, back outward and forefinger pointing partly upward in a gesture, and say, "The trick would not be very good if we were not able to get the coin back, so. . . ." And with these words, turn again to the right (using the same body and foot movements as before), extend your right hand palm toward the audience (with the coin hidden in the Downs palm) and pretend to pluck an imaginary coin from the air, saying, ". . . we simply pretend to pluck the coin out of the air, like this. . . ." (Do not produce the coin; do exactly what you tell the spectators you are doing—*pretend* to pluck a coin from the air.) ". . . and pretend to put it back into the hand. . . ."

As these words are spoken, turn back to the left and go through the motions of placing an imaginary coin in your left hand,

Fig. 10

Fig. 10. Left hand is open and obviously empty as the right draws away. Continuing, say, ". . . like that." On the words, "like that," repeat the motion of pretending to put a coin in the left hand, but this time you really DO drop the coin from the thumb palm into the left hand, Fig. 11, which immediately closes over it.

Fig. 11

"Then we make another magic pass around the hand." Move your right hand around your left but keep it clearly away from that hand. Turn to the audience and

say, "And since we have been pretending all along, naturally the coin is right there in the fist where it has been all the time." With these last words, slowly open your left hand to disclose the coin lying on the palm.

For best results perform the trick with a borrowed, marked coin.

In essence the trick is a coin vanish and reproduction, but with the proper presentation and showmanship it becomes a beautiful little drama that is guaranteed to make a profound impression on magician and layman alike.

The Free and Unlimited Coinage of Silver

This is the nonpareil of after-dinner tricks and smartly worked has a bewildering effect. Mr. Downs saw it performed by an itinerant conjurer in a Viennese café, and was so charmed that he purchased the secret and included it in his book *The Art of Magic*.

Effect: A half dollar is exhibited in the performer's hand. A spectator is asked to select one of the objects on a dinner table. The coin disappears and is found under the object selected. A number of objects on the table are lifted in turn, and under each one a coin is found.

Requisites and Preparation: Four half dollars, three of which are palmed in the right hand at the beginning of the experiment.

Working: The conjurer calls attention to three objects on the table, say a napkin, a salt cellar and a cruet. In handling the objects he slips a coin under each, a la the cups and balls. One of the three objects is selected, and the performer, holding a half dollar in the right hand, apparently takes it in the left hand, and, holding this hand above the article, commands the coin to pass under it. The left hand is shown empty, and the performer lifts up the article with the right hand, revealing the coin. He takes this coin in the left hand and in replacing the article the coin in the right hand is introduced underneath. In the same manner coins are found under the other two articles, and there is always one coin palmed in the right hand. The performer, by the mere act of lifting up any article on the table, for the ostensible purpose of showing that there is nothing under it, can introduce a coin under it by the mere act of replacing the article. The production of coins under six or seven articles will be sufficient.

Coins and Cards

GLENN HARRISON, *courtesy The Sphinx Publishing Corporation*

This is a pet trick of that well-known manipulator Glenn Harrison, from Denver, Colorado. Although the general effect is not new to magicians, the misdirection and complete surprise make it unique. The surprise comes when the spectators, believing they are witnessing a card trick, are suddenly aware of coins, coins, coins.

Requisites and Preparation: Six well-worn half dollars (the old Liberty head halves are ideal for this particular trick because they are usually very smooth) and a deck of cards.

Have three coins in your right coat or trousers pocket, the other three finger palmed in your left hand and hidden by the deck of cards, which is held in dealing position, Fig. 1.

Working: Using both hands, spread the cards in a fan and have three spectators each select a card with special attention to free choice. After they have remembered their cards gather them together with your right hand, toss the deck onto the table with your left hand and immediately transfer

Fig. 1

the three chosen cards to your left hand, where they are held in the position shown in Fig. 1. Both hands now take hold of the cards by the fingertips underneath and thumbs on top, taking care to hold the coins snugly underneath and out of sight.

State that you will show the three cards one at a time so all will know what they are. As you say this begin fanning the cards face down by pulling the bottom card to the left with the left fingers and the top card to the right with the right fingers. The coins automatically fan with the cards, left fingers holding onto the two top coins and right fingers drawing bottom coin to the right in a fan, Fig. 2.

Fig. 2

Now for the showing of the cards, which is bold but very clean cut. Draw off the coin to the right as you draw off the card to the right. Do not draw if off with pressure or the coin will "talk," but rather let the coin drop onto the right fingers. When it is free of the other coins simply hold the card (with the coin underneath) between the tips of the right fingers and thumb, then bring it to a vertical position, showing its face. As you do this the right fingers pull the coin to the extreme right edge of the card, thus showing the card's full face, Fig. 3. When it is turned face down again

Fig. 3

the fingers slide the coin back under the card and it is placed, coin underneath, on the table or floor. This move of showing the card is so innocent no one ever dreams you are hiding a coin. To prevent the coins "talking" perform the trick on a cloth covered table, or better still, on the rug. The other two cards are shown in exactly the same way, always letting the coin drop onto the fingers before pulling the card away.

You now have three cards in a row with the coins underneath. The spectators still think you are doing a card trick.

Remove the three coins from the right pocket and place them on the table. Now you go through a routine of vanishing the three coins one at a time and causing them to appear underneath the cards. The moves for accomplishing this are as follows: Pick up one coin with your palm down right hand and as you pretend to deposit it in the left retain it palmed in the right. Make a throwing motion with the left hand toward the card on the left end of the row as you

open and show the hand empty. With the palm down left hand, grip the outer left corner of the card between the tips of the fingers underneath and thumb on top, and lift it up, exposing the coin. The instant the left hand lifts the card the right hand releases its palmed coin, permitting it to drop onto the cupped fingers. Without hesitating, the left hand turns the card face up, brings it back to the right hand, which turns slightly clockwise and takes it between the fingers underneath and thumb on top in such a manner that the coin will be hidden underneath the card. Fig. 4 shows

Fig. 4

how the card is lifted to expose the coin, while Fig. 5 shows card being taken in the right hand. As the right hand moves toward the table with the card and hidden coin, the left hand draws the visible coin inward a few inches, then the right hand deposits the card and coin over the exact

Fig. 5

spot originally occupied by that card. The moves of vanishing the coin, picking up the card, drawing the coin inward with the left hand and returning the card to the table with the right must be executed as one continuous, unhesitating action—not too fast, and certainly not too slow either. If the moves are made as described it should appear that you picked up a coin with your right hand, placed it in your left, tossed it toward the end card, lifted the card to expose the coin, then returned the card to the table.

Treat the second and third visible coins in the same manner to cause them to apparently vanish and appear under the next two cards. At the finish of this action there will be three face up cards, with a coin under each one, and three visible coins,

Fig. 6

Fig. 6. No one will be aware of the presence of the three hidden coins under the cards, so the next phase of the trick comes as a genuine surprise.

State that you will now do the trick the hard way. Pick up the three visible coins and display them in an overlapping row in your palm up right hand. Execute the Vanish for Several Coins (a), (page 45) as you turn your hand inward and over, pretending to dump the coins into your waiting left hand below, but retaining them in the right hand. The sound created by this pass convinces the spectators that the coins actually arrived in the left hand. Make a throwing motion with your left hand toward the three cards, then, with the left hand, turn them over one at a time with a snapping action, exposing the three coins.

Instead of using the above named vanish you can employ The French Drop (page 37) or The Click Pass (b), (page 14). Coins are picked up quickly with the fingers of the right hand where they mingle with the palmed coins and are placed back in the right pocket.

The routine requires more confidence than skill. When you come to the coin vanishes breeze right through them. Don't worry about making an expert coin pass. Just toss the coin back and forth from hand to hand, then retain it in the right hand as you pretend to toss it back in the left and immediately throw it toward one of the cards. Each move blends smoothly into the next one and they all happen so fast it is impossible for the spectators to follow them.

Chapter X

COIN BOXES

The Okito Coin Box

If it hadn't been for a chronic case of indigestion the Okito coin box probably would not have been invented. Back in 1911, Theodore Bamberg (Okito) operated a magic shop at 1193 Broadway, New York City, and had as his partner a man named Joe Klein, who suffered constantly from indigestion. Joe kept a drawer full of pills for his ailment. One day, while waiting for a customer to drop in the shop, Okito was idly toying with one of Joe's pill boxes when he suddenly discovered that the lid would fit on the bottom as well as on the top of the box. This gave him an idea. He turned the box upside down in his hand and placed the lid on the bottom. Shaking the box, the pills would rattle inside, but when he lifted the box from his hand the pills would stay in his hand. He immediately tried the mystery on his partner by causing the pills to vanish from the box, then reproducing them elsewhere. Joe was completely fooled.

Okito then conceived the idea of making the box of a size to take a fifty-cent coin so it could be used for a magic trick. Thus the Okito coin box was born. The boxes were manufactured in large quantities and sold to magicians all over the country by Roterberg, Yost and Company, Sam Bailey, W. D. LeRoy, and Martinka and Company. The box sold for fifty-cents in those days and couldn't be produced fast enough to meet the demand. It became so popular that today there are few magicians who do not own an Okito coin box in one form or another.

In recent years the box has been modernized and specifically weighted, which makes it easier to handle. Fig 1 shows the original

Fig. 1

Fig. 2

Okito coin box while Fig. 2 shows it modern counterpart. Although either box can be used in most of the routines, many magicians still prefer the old style box.

Upon examining the box you will note that the lid can be placed on either the top or the bottom and the box will look the same either way. This is the simple prin-

Fig. 3

ciple on which all tricks with the box depend.

Handling: Place a coin in the box and allow it to rest on the left fingers as in Fig. 3. The lid is in the right hand between the forefinger and thumb. Tilt the box so the spectators can see the coin, then bring the lid over and place it on the box—not on the top, but the bottom. This is done as follows: As the right hand approaches the

Fig. 4

left hand it screens the box from view while the left fingers bend inward, turning the lower part of the box upside down, Fig. 4. Straighten the left fingers and put the lid on the bottom of the box, Fig. 5.

Fig. 5

If these moves are properly executed it appears to the spectators that you merely placed the lid on the box.

As the right hand moves away the spectators see the box lying on the left fingers as in Fig. 6. Place the left thumb on top of

Fig. 6

the lid and shake the box to show that it still contains the coin.

You can now remove the box from your left hand with your right and the coin will remain on the left fingers in finger palm position. But you will have to watch your angles as you do this. Otherwise the spectators may get a flash of the coin. If you are performing standing, with the spectators seated, you will have nothing to worry about, but if this is not the case you will have to curl your left fingers slightly as you remove the box with your right hand, Fig. 7. This action conceals the coin until it can be finger palmed and the hand turned back toward the spectators.

Fig. 7

Another way of secretly turning over the box is as follows: Hold the lower section of the box between the tips of the first three fingers and thumb. The palm up right hand is nearby, holding the lid between the tips of the forefinger and thumb, Fig. 8.

Fig. 8

Show the coin in the box, then bring the right hand over to place the lid on. As this is done the extended second, third and fourth fingers of the right hand shield the

box from view as the left fingers turn it over, Fig. 9. The lid is then placed on the bottom of the box and the right hand moves away, revealing the covered box lying on the fingers in exactly the same position it would had the bottom not been reversed. The box is immediately shaken to show that

Fig. 9

the coin is still inside. Although this move is slightly more difficult than the first it is much more convincing and for this reason it should be preferred.

One Hand Method: With this method you may allow a spectator to place the coin in the box and put on the lid.

After this has been done, take the box in your right hand, allowing it to rest on the outer joints of the two middle fingers. Under cover of rattling the coin in the box you make a secret turn-over move with the bottom section as follows: Grasp the lid between the forefinger and thumb and lift it up so the second, third and fourth fingers can bend inward, causing the bottom of the box to turn over on the palm, Fig. 10. At

Fig. 10

the same time, bend the forefinger inward and slide the lid back into the crotch of the thumb, Fig. 11. Hold the lid in this position while the thumb goes to the top of the

Fig. 11

lid and presses it down onto the bottom of the box in the palm, Fig. 12. Practice the moves so you can blend them together smoothly as you shake the box.

Fig. 12

When the hand comes to a halt, after shaking the box, the bottom will be upside down on the hand, covering the coin underneath. Everything seems fair.

Hand to Hand Throw: After making one of the above secret turn-over moves you can toss the box and its contents from hand to hand without losing or exposing the coin. Even though the bottom is inverted the coin will not fall out if the toss is made with care. Allow the box to rest on the fingers, then simply toss it into the other hand. Hold the receiving hand a little lower than the other and move the hand downward a trifle the instant the box lands on the fingers. This helps to prevent the box from turning over or the lid sliding off. The moment the box lands in the receiving hand, place the thumb on the lid and shake

the box. Continue the rattling for a moment, then toss it back into the other hand. Actually no great skill is required to execute this move properly. It is more a knack than a feat of skill. If the move is made in a casual, offhand manner it appears very convincing.

All the foregoing moves can be performed with any number of coins up to four. (The modern Okito coin box holds four half dollars.)

After performing a trick with the box it will be necessary to show the box empty. To do this, hold the box in the right hand between the tips of the first two fingers and thumb, keeping the open bottom of the box away from the audience. Hold the palm up left hand about eight or ten inches below and directly underneath the right hand. Press the tip of the second finger against the front rim of the bottom section of the box as the thumb releases it from the inner side. This causes the bottom to begin turning over the instant it leaves the lid. Since the bottom part of the box is its heaviest part, it will turn over in mid-air, Fig. 13, and land right side up in the palm of the left hand below. Lower the right hand slightly, and drop the lid opening upward beside the bottom section in the left hand.

Fig. 13

Coins Through Box and the Hand

Effect: The magician shows a half dollar and an Okito coin box. The coin is placed in the box and the lid put on. He shakes the box to prove that the coin is still there, then places it on the back of his palm down hand, which he holds a few inches above the table top. Giving the box a tap with a pencil, the coin is caused to penetrate the box and fall to the table. The box is then opened and shown empty.

Working: Show the box and the half dollar. Have the box examined if you wish, then place the coin in the box. As you put on the lid, execute the secret turn-over move, then shake the box with the left hand as you show the right empty. Toss the box and the half dollar into the right hand and shake it again while you show the left hand empty.

With the left hand, grasp the box and lift it off the right hand, leaving the coin finger palmed as the hand turns over and the box is placed on the back of the right hand. Give the box a tap with a pencil or small wand and release the finger palmed coin, which falls to the table. Show the box empty using the moves for the purpose.

An excellent "coins through the table" effect can be performed using practically the same moves.

Seat yourself at the table and show the box. Borrow four half dollars and have them marked for future identification. Have a spectator place the coins in the box and put on the lid. Take the box, execute the one hand secret turn-over move and toss the box into the left hand, then back into the right. Steal the coins in your right hand as you take the box and place it on the table with your left hand. Move the right hand underneath the table and quietly place the stack of coins on the right leg. Do this while talking to the spectators and telling them

what you intend to do. By this time the right hand is again on top of the table.

Move the box to the center of the table, show your right hand empty and place it underneath the table. Lift the box a few inches from the table and bring it sharply down on the table as you say, "Pass!" Immediately rattle the coins underneath the table with your right hand, then bring them up and pour them onto the table. Show the box empty. Return the coins and have their owners identify their marks.

Okito Box, Coin and Handkerchief

Effect: A borrowed, marked coin is caused to pass from an Okito coin box into the knot of a spectator's handkerchief which he tied himself.

Method: Have an Okito box and a half dollar in the right trousers pocket, and a pencil in a coat pocket. Reach into the trousers pocket, finger palm the half dollar, remove the box and pass it for examination. While the box is being examined, remove the pencil from your coat pocket and place it on the table. Take the box back and place it on the table with the pencil, then request the loan of a half dollar and a handkerchief. When the coin is produced ask that it be marked for future identification, and while this is being done take the handkerchief and throw it over your left forearm. Take the marked coin and as you pretend to toss it onto the table beside the box, execute The Bobo Switch (page 10) instead. Or, if you prefer, you may have a goblet on the table and execute the Shaw-Judah Coin Switch (page 12) as you pretend to toss the coin into it.

Drop your right hand to your side, let the spectator's coin slide down to the fingers and hold it by its edges between the tips of the first and little fingers. (This is the same grip you would use if you were about to back palm it.) Take a corner of the handkerchief in such a manner that the coin will go underneath it and be covered by the fingers. Grasp the diagonally opposite corner of the handkerchief with your left hand and stretch it out taut between your two hands. The coin is now between the folds of the right corner of the handkerchief, held in place with the fingers in front and the thumb at the rear, Fig. 1. Twirl

Fig. I

the handkerchief rope-fashion, tossing the lower corners over toward the front, thus forming the handkerchief in a kind of a tube.

Ask the spectator from whom you borrowed the handkerchief to take it by the corners and tie it into a knot, As he reaches for it, bring the hands together slightly so the handkerchief will sag in the middle, and release the coin, which slides down inside the tube to the center, Fig. 2, then place the corners in his hands. As you give him

Fig. 2

the two ends of the handkerchief do so with a little flourish to cover the movement of the coin sliding to the center. Instruct him to tie a knot in the center of the handkerchief and to release either end. The borrowed coin is now safely within the knot of the handkerchief but the spectators think it is still on the table.

Go to the table, pick up the supposedly marked half dollar and place it in the Okito box. As you put on the lid, execute the secret turn-over move. Rattle the coin and toss the box from hand to hand a time or two, finishing with it in the right hand. Take the box with your left hand and retain the coin finger palmed in your right.

Pick up the pencil with your right hand, being careful not to expose the palmed coin. Touch the tip of the pencil to the box saying that you will remove the coin from the box on the point of the pencil. Pretend to carry the coin away on the tip of the pencil and say, "Here it is. No, it isn't in the box." Shake the box. It doesn't rattle because there is nothing in it. "You see, the coin is actually on the tip of the pencil." Walk over and touch the knot of the handkerchief with the pencil and say, "It is now in the knot. Will you feel it, sir. Is it there?" He will admit that it is. Have him untie the knot and remove the coin, and while all eyes are on him, place the pencil in your pocket and leave the duplicate coin. After he removes the coin have it identified and return it to its owner. The only thing left to do is to show the Okito box empty, which you do, using the move for the purpose.

The trick can also be performed without the use of a duplicate coin. In this case, allow the spectator to place the coin in the box himself. Take the box from him and steal out the coin using the one hand method, then place the box aside for a moment. Load the coin in a second spectator's handkerchief and have him tie a knot in it as in the first version. Pick up the box and tell the spectators that you will cause the coin to fly from it into the knot of the handkerchief held by the spectator. Make a mystical pass, then show the box empty. Conclude as already described.

Routine with an Okito Coin Box and a Silk

Jack Chanin

Fig. 1

Effect: Four half dollars are placed in the bottom section of the Okito box and covered with a silk handkerchief before placing on the lid. In this condition the box and coins are placed on the back of a spectator's hand. The performer gives the spectator a small wand with which to tap the box three times. After tapping the box the silk is pulled from between the two sections of the box, then the box is shown empty. The coins have vanished without a trace.

Requisites and Preparation: A dark colored silk handkerchief about 15 inches square, four half dollars (old, worn ones are best), a small wand about the size of a toothpick (these can be purchased cheaply from your magic dealer in lots of 100), and an Okito box.

Have the coins in the box in the right trousers pocket, the silk in the right coat pocket and the small wand in the left coat pocket.

Working: Remove the silk from your pocket, show it, then drape it over your left forearm. Take out the Okito box next and dump out the four coins onto the table. After showing the box, place the lid on the table and hold the bottom part at the base of the two middle fingers of your palm up left hand.

Pick up the coins and drop them into the box. With your right hand, remove the silk

from your left forearm and drape it over the coin filled box. Pick up the lid and place it on top, so the silk will be between the lid and the box, Fig. 1.

Place the left thumb on the lid and shake the box so everyone can hear that the coins are still inside. With your right hand, pick up one corner of the silk and make a few passes over the box. Snap your right fingers and announce that the coins have disappeared. Remove the lid with your right hand and pull the silk back over your left forearm exposing the coins still in the box. Act surprised that the coins are not gone.

Grasp the silk with your right hand and again spread it over the box and coins. Under cover of doing this, and while making some remark about not saying the proper magic words, quietly turn over the box with your left fingers. Take the lid from the table and place it on the box as before, only this time, unknown to the spectators, the bottom section of the box is upside down. Place your left thumb on the lid and rattle the coins to prove they are still there.

Ask a spectator to hold out his left hand, back up. Grip both sections of the box through the handkerchief with your right forefinger and thumb, and lift it up and away from the coins which are retained finger palmed in your left hand. The silk acts as a screen and conceals the coins momentarily as the box is lifted away. As the right hand moves away with the box and silk, turn the left hand palm inward and point to the box and silk in the right hand. Place the box with the silk on the back of the spectator's hand and tell him you will let him be the magician. As you caution him to hold his hand still, place your left hand in your coat pocket, leave the coins, and bring out the wand. Hand him the wand with the request that he tap the box with it three times, then allow him to keep the wand as a souvenir.

Place the fingers and thumb of your palm down right hand over the box and hold it lightly while your left hand grasps a corner of the silk and pulls it free. As the silk comes away the lid remains on the box. Shake the silk to show it empty and throw it over your right forearm. Take the box from him and show it empty using the moves described earlier. The coins are gone and there is no clue to the mystery.

All moves are standard, but the clever addition of the silk and the small wand create an entirely different and baffling effect.

Silver to Copper with the Okito Coin Box

Dr. Carl L. Moore

Effect: A spectator drops a silver coin in the Okito box. The lid is placed on and the box shaken to prove that the coin is still there. The box is then given to a spectator to hold. He shakes the box and the coin is again heard to rattle, but when he opens the box the silver coin is seen to have changed to a copper one. The performer's hands are empty.

Method: No new moves are necessary to perform this startling change. As you begin the trick have an English penny (or some foreign coin) up your right sleeve. Hand the fifty-cent piece to a spectator to look over, then have him drop it in the box. As you put on the lid execute the secret turnover move so the lid goes on the bottom. While rattling the coin in the box with your left hand, drop your right to your side, catch the copper coin as it falls from the sleeve and hold it finger palmed. The box lies at the base of the two middle fingers of the palm up left hand. Grip the box between the thumb on the inner side and the forefinger on the outer side, lift it up and away from the coin, and place it in the right hand directly over the finger palmed copper coin and immediately rattle the box. Watch your angles as you do this. Turn your left hand inward slightly and curl the second, third and fourth fingers inward on the coin as you swing slightly to the right to place the box in the right hand. The box is transferred from the left hand to the right under the pretext of showing it to the spectators on the right. Now the copper coin is in the box and the silver coin is finger palmed in your left hand.

Now you must make the one hand turnover move before handing the box to a spectator. This you do as you rattle the coin in the box. When you turn to the left to hand the box to a spectator, the left hand, hidden by the body, disposes of its coin in the left coat pocket. After a bit of byplay have the spectator open the box to discover the copper coin. Everything may now be examined.

The Half Dollars and the Okito Box

J. Elder Blackledge

Effect: The magician empties five half dollars from an Okito coin box, places the coins on the table and covers them with the bottom section of the box. One coin leaves the box and travels to his left hand. Then the remaining four are held in his right hand, but again a coin passes to his left hand. Now he places two coins on the back of his left hand, covers them with the box and holds his right hand below. One coin penetrates his left hand and appears on the back of his right. Finally, he places four coins on the table, covers them with the box and holds the fifth one in his left hand. This coin leaves the hand and joins the others underneath the box.

Requisites and Preparation: An Okito coin box, four half dollars and one cut down half and shell.* Because this old style shell coin looks exactly like any other half dollar in size and thickness it will stack perfectly with the other coins and fit into the box. The coins are placed heads up in the box as follows: First, the three half dollars, then the shell covered coin, then the other half dollar on top. Put the lid on the box and you are ready to begin.

Working: Hold the box containing the coins with your left hand. Lift off the lid and place it aside—it plays no further part in the trick. Dump the coins out of the box onto the fingers of your right hand, tails up, show the box empty and place it upside down on the table.

Transfer the stack of coins to your left hand so they will still be tails up, spread them out in an overlapping row with the right fingers, showing and counting five coins. The shell covered coin (opening of shell up) lies second from the inner end of the row, Fig. 1. With the right fingers and thumb, push the coins together and slide them forward onto the left fingers. Take the top three coins with the right fingers

Fig. 1

(underneath) and thumb (on top) and spread them out in a fan. Fan the two remaining coins with the left hand; call attention to the number you have as you show the two fans on both sides. Place the fan of three *underneath* the two coins in your left hand, square them together and place the stack, tails up, on the palm of your left hand. The shell covered coin (opening of shell up) is on top.

Grip the stack of coins by its edges between the tips of the thumb and middle finger of the palm down right hand, with the tip of the forefinger resting on top, Fig. 2. Lift off the four top coins, retaining the bottom one palmed in the left hand, and *turn both hands over simultaneously.* At the completion of this maneuver you will be holding the stack of four coins, heads up, between the tips of the thumb and middle finger of your palm up right hand,

Fig. 2

* A description of The Cut Down Half and Shell will be found on page 265.

Fig. 3

Fig. 5

with the tip of the forefinger pressing upward against the nested coin from below. Fig. 3 shows the correct position of the coins in the right hand, and the left hand (with the fifth coin hidden in its palm) about to retake the stack in preparation for the next move which follows immediately.

Take the coins between the thumb and middle finger of the palm down left hand and spread them on the table from right to left so that each coin overlaps about half the other, Fig. 4. The cut-down coin is allowed to drop from the shell first, then the shell, then the other three coins. Let it be clearly seen that there are five coins on the table. In reality there are only three half dollars. The shell and its coin make the other two. And there is one real half palmed in the left hand.

Pick up the upside down box between the fingers and thumb of the palm down left hand, then with the aid of the inside

rim of the box (which is tilted slightly) and the right forefinger, Fig. 5, slowly push the coins together and cover them with the box. As this is done the shell slips over its coin.

Close the left hand into a fist and hold it some distance away from the box. Pretend to extract a coin from the box with the right hand and toss it toward the left. Open the left hand, show its coin and drop it on the table to the left. Lift the box with the right hand, then using the tips of the right and left first fingers, spread out the coins so they do not overlap, showing four coins.

Now slide the three real half dollars off the table one at a time and place them, tails up, in an overlapping row in the left hand. Take the shell covered coin last and add it to the forward end of the row (opening of shell up). Show and count them as four coins. With the right fingers and thumb, push the coins together.

Repeat the first moves as you retain one palmed in your left hand and spread the others in an overlapping row on the palm up right hand, Fig. 6.

While showing the coins, drop the left hand to your side and shift the coin in that hand to finger palm position. While you slowly close your right hand over the coins (which action causes the shell and its coin to nest), bring up your left hand, palm toward the spectators, with the second, third and fourth fingers curled over the coin and the forefinger pointing upward as you

Fig. 4

Fig. 6

gesture and caution the spectators to "Watch." (For a full description of this subtle concealment, see page 43.) Close the left hand into a fist and hold both hands far apart. Make a throwing motion with the right hand toward the left, then open the left hand showing the half dollar, and place it on the table with the first one. Open the right hand, show three coins (two real coins and the shell covered coin on the bottom) and spread them out on the palm with the left fingers. All are heads up.

Remove one of the genuine coins with the left hand and place it on the table with the other two. Two remain in the right hand—one is the real half dollar, the other is the shell covered coin. Take the real coin with the left fingers and thumb and display it on both sides as you show one in the right hand in the same manner. Shift the real coin in the left hand so it rests, heads up, at the base of the two middle fingers (finger palm position), then place the shell covered

coin (opening of shell down) on top of and slightly overlapping the real coin to the right, Fig 7. Show the two coins in the left hand—the right hand is empty.

Holding the right hand vertically (palm inward and fingers pointing to the left), grip the shell by its opposite edges between the tip of the thumb and forefinger with the tip of the second finger underneath, Fig. 8. Now the following moves must be

Fig. 8

executed simultaneously: Lift the shell covered coin away from the left hand as that hand retains the real half dollar finger palmed and turns back uppermost. At the same time the right thumb and forefinger raise the shell up off the cut-down coin and the second finger (with the cut-down coin balanced on its tip) moves inward, separating the two parts and making them appear as two coins, Fig. 9. The lifting away and

Fig. 7

Fig. 9

separating the shell from its coin is all one movement and must be done as the left hand turns back uppermost. Practice this move in front of a mirror and realize its complete deceptiveness. Properly done it appears that you merely lifted the two coins from the left hand and turned that hand over.

Place the shell on the back of the left hand, show the cut-down coin on both sides, then slip its edge under one edge of the shell, Fig. 10. In finger palm position in the same hand is the real half dollar.

Fig. 10

Pick up the box with the right hand and slip it over the coin and shell on the back of the left, which action causes them to nest as one coin. Show the right hand empty and as you do this release the finger palmed coin in the left hand allowing it to drop onto the curled fingers, then move the fingers of the palm up right hand between the ends of the left curled fingers and the

Fig. 11

left palm, Fig. 11. Grip the coin lying on the left fingers in back palm position of the right hand, turn the right hand back uppermost and straighten the left fingers, all in one move. At this point both hands are palm down and the real half dollar is lying on the back of the right fingers directly underneath the box, which you remember is on the back of the left hand, Fig. 12.

Fig. 12

Ask a nearby spectator to press lightly on the top of the box with his forefinger. Raise the left hand and move it to the left, exposing the half dollar lying on the right fingers, then let it slide off beside the three on the table. Lift the box with the right hand from the back of the left hand, show the box empty and place it on the table. Pick up the shell covered coin and show it as one coin. Apparently the other coin passed through the back of the left hand onto the right fingers.

Now take up the four real coins from the table, square them in a heads up stack, add the shell covered coin (good side of shell up) to the top and hold them by their edges between the first two fingers and thumb of the palm up left hand, Fig. 13. With the right forefinger and thumb, lift off the shell (only) and immediately turn the left hand back uppermost and deposit the stack, tails up, on the table behind the box. The box

Fig. 13

partially conceals the coins and prevents the sharp eye of a spectator from discovering that there are five and not four as you pretend. Lift the box with the left hand and place it over the stack. To the spectators it should appear that you merely lifted off the top coin, put the remaining four on the table and covered them with the box. Actually there are five coins underneath the box, four of which are genuine, while the bottom one is the cut-down coin. The shell is exhibited in the right hand as a coin.

Deposit the shell (good side up, of course) on the fingers of the palm up left hand, then apparently turn it over as follows: Grip the shell by its forward edge between the tips of the right forefinger (below) and thumb (on top) and place the second finger in position as shown in Fig. 14. With a counterclockwise movement of the right

Fig. 14

hand, pretend to turn the shell over but revolve it between the tips of the first and second fingers (which action is hidden by the back of the right hand) and deposit it heads up on the left fingers in the same position it originally occupied. The move should be made immediately after placing the shell on the left fingers, and *before* the spectators have had a chance to notice which side of the coin was up. It should appear to the spectators that you simply turned the coin over.

Pick up the shell with the right hand, show the left hand empty front and back, close it into a fist and hold it back uppermost and about waist high. Holding the shell vertically between the tips of the fingers and thumb of the palm down right hand, bring it over and rest its lower edge on the back of the left fist. Perform Through the Hand (b), (page 67) as you apparently push the shell through the back of the left hand. At the completion of this move show the shell lying on the fingers of the palm up left hand.

The final phase of the routine is to vanish the shell and lift the box and show five coins. This is accomplished as follows:

Grip the shell (which is still lying on the fingers of the left hand) by its inner edge between the first two fingers (on top) and thumb (underneath) of the right hand and drag it back onto the left palm, at the same time closing the left fingers over it. Release your grip on the shell with the right hand and point to the box. Open the left hand, show the shell still there, then move it back onto the fingers. Take the shell as before and again drag it back onto the left palm. Under cover of this and the action of closing the left fingers, clip the shell by its right edge between the tips of the right second and third fingers, then curl those fingers inward, extracting the shell from the left hand. The forefinger alone remains in the left fist as the right second and third fingers straighten and carry the shell underneath the left hand, where it is held (good side up) against the back of the left hand by the tip of the right second finger, Fig. 15.

Fig. 15

Withdraw the right forefinger from the left fist and move the hand back and grip the left wrist. As this is done the right second finger slides the shell along underneath the left hand to the wrist where it is finger palmed in the right hand as you illustrate to a spectator how you want him to hold your wrist, Fig. 16.

Fig. 16

Let go of your wrist (retaining the shell finger palmed) and have the spectator hold it. Point to the box with the right hand as you suddenly exclaim "Go!" Ask the spectator if he felt anything. Regardless of what he says, slowly open your left hand and show it empty. Lift the box from the stack of coins with the right hand, then

with the tips of the first fingers of each hand, spread out the coins, showing five. Apparently the coin (shell) passed from your left hand to join the other four underneath the box.

Pick up the cut down coin with the left hand and take it in your palm down right hand. While reaching for a second coin with the left hand, add the shell to its coin in the right hand. Place the four real coins with the shell covered half in the right hand and show them as five coins. Return them to the box, place on the lid and put the box in your pocket.

The George Boston Combination Coin Box

The newest version of the Okito coin box has a recessed bottom just deep enough to take a half dollar or an English penny. Otherwise, the box appears the same as the one shown in Fig. 2, page 217. With a coin hidden in the recessed bottom, the box may be balanced on one finger and coin will not fall out.

The box takes four half dollars, and with an extra one hidden in the recessed bottom it will still appear full of coins after the secret turn-over has been made and the four coins stolen.

Practically all routines using the standard Okito box can be worked with this one.

Here is a version of the Coins Through Box and the Hand by George Boston, which will give you a general idea on the overall handling. After learning this routine you will find that others can be readily adapted to the box also.

Effect: Some half dollars are placed into the box, which is set on the palm of the hand and shown to still contain the halves. The lid is put on the box. The hand is turned over and the box placed on the back of the hand. Again the lid is raised to show the coins. The lid is then replaced and the coins are commanded to leave the box one at a time and pass through the hand onto the table. The box is then opened and shown empty.

Method: Take five half dollars in the right hand but *DO NOT* call attention at any time to the number of coins used. Show the box and place it on top of the coins in the hand. On removing the box from the stack, the rim will pick up one coin from the top of the stack. Hold this hidden coin in place as you put the box on the palm of the right hand. Take off the lid and drop the four coins within. Put the lid back on. Now pick up the box from the palm of the hand and while shaking it to show that the coins are still there, execute the one hand turn-over move, putting the lid on the bottom, then hold box in the palm of the right hand. Lift the lid to show coins still in the box. In reality, the spectators see only the coin in the recessed bottom, but believe they are seeing the stack of coins.

Lift the box quickly from the palm, turn over the hand and place box on the back of the same hand. As this is done the four coins are retained in the palm. Lift the lid again to show the coin(s). Replace lid and command the coins to pass through the hand. Allow one coin at a time to drop onto the table from the right fist. After all of the coins have apparently passed, raise the box and allow the bottom to fall, turn over and drop right side up on top of the coins. This will add the coin from the recessed bottom to the rest, where it will be unnoticed due to the fact that at no time did you call attention to the number of coins used.

And here is an entirely new effect with the box not possible with the regular Okito box.

Copper and Silver Transposition with the Combination Coin Box

A half dollar is dropped in the box and the lid put on. An English penny is placed on the palm of the right hand and the box set on top of it. The idea is to cause the two coins to change places—the half dollar to come out of the box and the penny to enter the box.

Here is where the new feature comes in—simple, but effective. When the box is set over the penny, move it so the penny will slide into the recessed bottom. This will keep it from moving as the box is handled. Now reverse the box, using the secret turn-over move. Due to the fact that the penny is in the recessed bottom of the box it will follow through as the turn-over is made and apparently be INSIDE the box, while the half dollar will be OUTSIDE the box on the palm of the hand. Lift the box and show the half dollar on the hand, then shake the box so the audience can hear the penny rattling inside.

Sounds impossible, but try it yourself. You will be amazed at the simplicity of its working.

State that you will repeat the effect. This time put the half dollar on the palm and the box containing the penny on top of it. Repeat the former move and the half dollar will be back in the box and the penny will be outside on your hand. Everything may now be examined.

The German Coin Box

This box, which supposedly originated in Germany, is actually the forerunner of all modern coin boxes. The box is straight sided, has no lid, but does have a recessed bottom to take one coin. Fig. 1 shows the box upside down.

Fig. 1

Although the box I own takes seven half dollars—six in the box and one in the recessed bottom—one could be made to take any small number of coins.

Since the box has no lid it has to be secretly reversed while closing the fingers over it, or in placing it underneath a handkerchief, etc.

Here is a simple, but effective "passe" effect using this box:

Show the box and the seven coins, but *DO NOT* call attention to the number. Hold the coins on the left fingers and place the box on top of them so it will cover one coin. With the right hand slide the box away from the coins onto the palm, with a coin in its recessed bottom. Now take the box (and the coin) and display it neatly balanced on the tip of your right second finger.

Move the box back onto the right fingers, then drop the coins from the left hand into it. Show the coins in the box to the spectators on the right; then, as you place the box in your left hand to show the coins to the spectators on the left, turn it over. The spectators see the single coin in the recessed bottom and suspect nothing.

An alternate method of reversing the box is as follows: Take the box legitimately in the left hand near the tips of the fingers. Close your fingers and turn the hand over. Now if you turn your hand back (palm up) and open it, you will find the box upside down.

After secretly turning the box over, take it again in your right hand, but leave the stack of six coins finger palmed in your left hand as you do so. Face the spectators as you make this move, and curl your left fingers upward to conceal the coins as you take the box in the other hand. Curl the fingers over the coins as you point to the box in the right hand. After displaying the box and coin(s) in the right hand close the fingers over the box, causing it to turn over in the action. Close the left hand and hold it some distance from the right.

Command the coins to pass from your right hand into your left. Open your right hand and show the empty box. Rattle the coins in your left hand, then open it to show the coins there. Display the empty box in the right hand and the coins in the left just long enough for the spectators to realize what has happened, then toss box onto the coins in the left hand, adding the coin from the recessed bottom to those in the hand. The extra coin will go unnoticed due to the fact that you didn't call attention to the number of coins used.

The late Bert Kalmar used this box in a slightly different manner. He had a hole cut in the bottom large enough to insert the tip of his forefinger. He could then convincingly show the box free from preparation by looking through the hole or inserting his finger in it.

To work the preceding effect with a box thus prepared you will also require a gimmicked coin. This coin has been ground smooth on one side, then this side painted flesh color.

Have the gimmicked coin finger palmed in the right hand, painted side away from the fingers. Show the box, then take it in the right hand so it covers the coin. By sliding the box back onto the palm the spectators can apparently look right through it, the flesh colored side of the coin appearing as the hand. Place the coins in the box and continue as in the first version. At the finish the spectators see the coins in the left hand and an empty box in the right. The illusion is perfect.

Palm off the gimmicked coin and add it right side up to the others. Put them all together in the pocket.

The Paul Fox Coin Boxes

Still another variation are these unique boxes by Paul Fox. In this case there are two boxes which match in every way, except that one has a recessed bottom. Although both boxes are the same height, it takes seven quarters to fill each one. A thicker bottom in the ungimmicked box accounts for this.

Here are three excellent effects using these boxes:

NUMBER ONE

Fasten an extra quarter in the recessed bottom of the gimmicked box with a bit of wax and place both boxes in the right coat pocket. In the right trousers pocket have seven quarters.

Reach into the coat pocket, finger palm the gimmicked box and bring out the other one, visible at the fingertips. Pass the box for examination. (And if there are magicians present watch them scrutinize the bottom.) Take the box back in the right hand and toss it into your left hand. That is what you pretend to do. Actually you execute The Bobo Switch (page 10) and throw the gimmicked box instead.

Place your right hand in your trousers pocket, leave the ungimmicked box and bring out the seven quarters and place them in the box. Now you cause the coins to pass from one hand to the other using the method already described under The George Boston Combination Coin Box.

NUMBER TWO

Have an extra quarter stuck in the recessed bottom of the gimmicked box. This box and the ungimmicked one are in your right coat pocket, and the seven quarters are in your right trousers pocket.

Reach into the right coat pocket, finger palm the gimmicked box and bring the other one out at the fingertips. Pass it for examination. Take it back with your right hand, and as you pretend to toss it into your left, make the switch as before. Remarking that you have a second box in your pocket, reach in to get it. Bring the same box back out; have it examined. Apparently the spectators have examined two different boxes. In reality they have examined the same box twice. Because the boxes look exactly alike this clever ruse is never suspected.

After the box has been examined, take it back and place it in your left hand alongside the gimmicked one already there. Bring the seven quarters from your right trousers pocket and place them in the ungimmicked box. Both boxes are side by side in the palm up left hand with the gimmicked box to the left of the ungimmicked one.

Close your fingers over the boxes and turn the hand over. With your right hand, reach into the thumb side of your left fist and remove the gimmicked box upside down. The single coin in the recessed bottom gives the illusion that the box is full of coins. Display the box lying on your right fingers apparently full of coins. Actually the seven coins are in the box in the left fist.

As you close your right hand, the gimmicked box turns over. Hold the hands some distance apart and shake them. "This," you say, "causes the coins to travel from one hand to the other." Open your right hand, showing the box in that hand empty. Open your left hand, show the box in that hand full of coins, then dump them into your right hand and place the two boxes and coins back into the pocket.

NUMBER THREE

Requisites and Preparation: Seven quarters with different dates and an eighth with a date to match one of the other seven. This extra coin, of a known date, is fastened with wax to the bottom of the gimmicked box, "head" side showing. Have the two boxes together in your right coat pocket and the quarters in your right trousers pocket. In your right hip pocket have a clean, folded handkerchief, and on the table have two pieces of paper about three inches a square, and a pencil.

Working: Inform the spectators that before you begin the experiment you will make two predictions. Write the date of the coin in the recessed bottom on the first piece of paper, then fold it and number it "one." Put it on the table and take up the second paper. Pretend to write a prediction on it but leave it blank. Fold the paper, number it "two," and place it on the table beside the first paper.

Reach into your coat pocket, finger palm the gimmicked box and bring the other one out at the fingertips. Have it examined, then take it back with the right hand and switch it for the gimmicked box as you pretend to toss it into the left hand.

Place the right hand in the trousers pocket, leave the ungimmicked box and bring out the seven quarters. Pass the coins to a spectator near you to verify that each has a different date. After he has done so, give him the box and tell him that he is to hold it with the coins behind his back, and then put the coins in the box in any order he pleases. When he has finished this task have him hand the box to you behind your back, so no one will see the box or the coins. The moment you receive the box, turn it over and bring it forward in your closed right hand. Now ask him to pick up paper number one, unfold it and read your prediction. While he is unfolding the paper and reading the date, pick up the box from

your right hand with your left (leaving the seven coins finger palmed in your right hand) and place the box on the table without turning it over. Reach into your hip pocket, leave the coins, bring out the handkerchief and throw it over your left forearm. When he has read the date on the paper ask him to read the date of the top coin in the box. They are the same!

Now comes the surprising climax. Take the handkerchief from your arm, show it and spread it on the table. Pick up the box and place it underneath the center of the handkerchief. As you do this turn the box right side up. Have a second spectator open the second piece of paper. When he gets it open say, "What do you see written on the paper?" He will reply, "Nothing," because the paper is actually blank. Pull the handkerchief from the box and say, "What do you see in the box?" Again his answer will be, "Nothing." Show the empty box to the other spectators, then drop it in your right trousers pocket. Pick up the handkerchief, show it and put it in your pocket. The coins have vanished and there is no clue to their disappearance.

Although the box was apparently examined before the trick began, occasionally there may be some inquisitive soul who might wish to see it again. If this happens, remove the ordinary box from the right trousers pocket and let him examine it to his heart's content. Of course, there is nothing to find.

If you handle these boxes well you will be surprised at the number of magicians you will fool. The average magician is acquainted with the recessed bottom box, so when you apparently use an ordinary box to accomplish an effect he thinks only possible with a gimmicked one, he is puzzled. And a layman has no chance at all!

Chapter XI

TRICK COIN TRICKERY

How long trick coins have been employed by magicians will probably never be known. Almost every close-up performer owns one or more of them. Who has not heard of the Dime and Penny Trick or the Half Dollar in the Bottle? This latter trick has been a reputation maker for more than one magician.

Gimmicked coins make possible many unique and mystifying effects which would be impossible with ordinary coins under similar circumstances. But it must be remembered that while they will pass for real coins in looks, they will not sound like real coins. For this reason a certain amount of care must be exercised in handling them. If a tricked piece of money is accidently dropped or tossed onto another coin or on the hard surface of a table, its unnatural sound will immediately attract attention. So if the trick requires the use of a table, be sure it has a cloth on it; otherwise get down on your knees and perform the trick on the rug.

Never polish a trick coin. The more it looks like ordinary "filthy lucre" the better. If a gimmicked coin needs cleaning wash it with soap and water or clean it with a soft rubber eraser.

Guard the secret of your trick coins. The layman should never know such a thing as a trick coin exists. Life would be easier for every magician if no one knew we employed anything but the real article.

In this chapter will be found a choice collection of gimmicked coin bafflers—old friends as well as new, each one a veritable miracle when properly presented.

Squeeze Play

STEWART JAMES

Effect: The performer shows a silk handkerchief and spreads it on the table. A nickel is placed on the center of the silk and covered with a poker chip which has a quarter inch hole through its center. Thus the coin remains visible through this hole up to the last minute. The four corners of the handkerchief are gathered together and passed through a harness ring. Two spectators hold the handkerchief spread out between them, with the opening formed by the coin and ring toward the floor. The performer reaches underneath the handkerchief and removes the nickel although it is too large to pass through either the ring or the hole in the poker chip.

Requisites and Preparation: A Nickel and Penny set (made same as the Dime and Penny), a harness ring with an inside measurement of approximately three-quarters of an inch, a silk handkerchief, and a poker chip with a hole about the size of a pencil through its center.

Have the ring, poker chip and silk in your left coat pocket and the two parts of the Nickel and Penny set in your right coat pocket. (To keep them from nesting have one in the small match pocket.)

Working: Remove the handkerchief, ring and poker chip. Pass the ring and chip for examination and spread the handkerchief on the table. After the two articles have been examined take them back and put them on the table beside the silk. Reach into your right coat pocket, finger palm the shell and remove the double faced part, nickel side showing. It is this coin you place on the center of the handkerchief as a nickel. Of course, it is a little smaller than a regular five cent piece, but before this is noticed by the spectators you cover it with the poker chip. Allow someone to look through the hole and verify that the coin is still there, then gather the four corners of the silk together and push them through the harness ring. Turn the handkerchief over so the opening into the little bag in the center will be from the bottom, then have two spectators hold the handkerchief stretched out between them.

Place your right hand underneath the handkerchief, then with the aid of your left hand which grasps the center of the silk

from above, work the coin around the poker chip and through the ring. The moment it is in the right hand, press it into the shell which you are holding in that hand and bring it out as a nickel. Allow the spectators to remove the harness ring and the poker chip from the silk. All can now be examined. Since the nickel is now bigger, thanks to the shell now covering it, it cannot be forced through the ring.

Of course, a folding coin could be used in place of this nickel and penny set but it would not stand examination of any sort.

Jimmy Valentine Picks a Lock

Stewart James

Effect: The performer shows a small padlock, a silk handkerchief and two coins. The handkerchief is spread on the table. The two coins are placed on the center of the silk, then its four corners are gathered together and pushed through the bow of the lock. Two spectators hold the handkerchief with the lock in view, the opening into the bag formed by the two coins being underneath. A spectator names either one of the two coins in the handkerchief and the performer removes it. All is then examined.

Requisites and Preparation: A Nickel and Penny set, a genuine penny, a small padlock such as is used on dog collars (this must have a bow too small for either a penny or a nickel to pass through), and a silk handkerchief.

Have the silk and padlock in your left coat pocket and the two parts of the Nickel and Penny set in your right coat pocket, separated as in the first trick. The regular penny is finger palmed in your right hand.

Working: Remove the handkerchief and padlock from your left pocket. Pass the padlock for examination and spread the handkerchief on the table. Remove the gimmicked nickel and penny from your right pocket and place them on the center of the handkerchief with the shell part overlapping the other section slightly. After the lock has been examined take it back, then gather the four corners of the silk together and push them through the bow of the lock. Have two spectators hold the four corners with the handkerchief stretched out between them. The lock is above and the opening into the bag is underneath.

Ask a spectator to name either the nickel or the penny. If he names the penny place your right hand underneath the handkerchief while you grasp the center from above with your left hand. Under cover of the left hand, slide the two coins together so they will nest, then bring your right hand up and show the penny which you had concealed in your hand all the time. If, however, the nickel is named, say that you will leave the nickel locked in the handkerchief and remove the penny. Regardless of which coin is named you bring out the penny. Have the two spectators remove the lock from the silk and show that only the nickel remains.

Attention should be directed to the lock and not the coins.

When working this trick for magicians use the unfaked duplicate from a Brema Nut set and let them worry about when you switched nuts.

Money Paper

STEWART JAMES

Effect: The performer shows four pennies, a nickel and a business card. One penny is selected by a spectator and the date of that penny is written on a paper disc. The business card is placed on the table and the four pennies are stacked on top of it. The paper disc is put on the top penny, then covered with the nickel. The performer says he will cause the paper disc to travel down through the stack of pennies and the card and appear under the card on the table. The nickel is lifted and the disc is gone. Pennies are tilted from the card and the card lifted, but there is no paper disc on the table. Performer says that he may not have waited long enough for the disc to penetrate the card. He tears the card in two and out drops the missing disc from between the layers of cardboard! Apparently the paper disc penetrated only half way through the card.

Requisites and Preparation: A Nickel and Penny set, four ordinary pennies (one of which must bear the same date as the penny of the faked set), an ordinary nickel, several paper discs slightly smaller than a penny, and a fake business card prepared as follows: Take one of the paper discs and write on it the date of the fake penny. Glue two business cards together around their edges with the disc bearing the printed date between them.

Have the ordinary nickel and one penny of an indifferent date in the left trousers pocket. The right trousers pocket contains the remaining three pennies, shell nickel, and some change of other denominations. Have the fake business card wherever you usually carry your regular business cards, and the paper discs in a small envelope or in the stamp compartment of your wallet.

Procedure: Take out your wallet, remove a paper disc and place it on the table. Next, remove the prepared business card. Finally, take the change from the right trousers pocket and remove the four pennies and nickel (actually three genuine pennies and the penny-nickel fake).

Arrange the four pennies in a row on the table with their dates up. The fake penny and penny bearing the same date are side by side at one end of the row. Have a spectator name a number not over four. No matter what number is called you can force either of the two pennies with the identical dates by simply counting from the left or right as the case may require. If the ordinary coin bearing the force date is arrived at, you may permit the spectator to pick it up and note the date. If the fake coin is the one selected by number, it must be left on the table for obvious reasons. In either case there must be no doubt as to the actual date. Should the fake coin be arrived at, tell the spectator he must not touch the coin lest he be accused of being your confederate. When the coin has been counted to, give the spectator a magnifying glass to check the date.

The date on the selected coin is printed on the paper disc. Stack the pennies with the fake coin occupying the top position on the gimmicked business card. Place the paper disc on top of the fake penny and cover it with the shell nickel. Press the shell down so it will trap and conceal the paper disc as the fake penny nests. As you return the magnifying glass to your left trousers pocket, finger palm the nickel and penny.

State that the disc will penetrate the stack of pennies and the card. Lift the nickel from the stack of pennies between your right forefinger and thumb. Turn it over and show the paper disc gone, then place it on the card to the right of the stack of pennies. With the right thumb on top and fingers underneath, pick up the card and look underneath (card may be near table edge to facilitate this action). Appear surprised that the paper disc is not on the table. Apparently tip all the coins into the left hand as you turn the card over to examine the other side. In reality the right thumb retains the fake nickel as the three pennies are dumped into the left hand. Almost immediately the left hand allows the four pennies and the nickel that it holds

(the nickel and one penny were already there) to slide onto the table. The left hand, now obviously empty, grasps the left end of the business card and assists the right in tearing it in half. The paper disc falls to the table and its date is then checked. It is the same as that on the selected penny. Apparently the paper disc penetrated the stack of pennies but only passed half way through the business card.

When gluing the cards together, the pocket can be in one end of the card so the disc will be in the half in the left hand. The half in which the disc rests is easily recognizable by the printing on the card. By pressing on the sides of the half card, the disc can be seen inside and handed to a spectator to remove. While he is doing that, it is a simple matter to dispose of the fake nickel and toss the remainder of the card on the table.

Everything on the table may now be examined as there are just four ordinary pennies—*all dates different,* and an ordinary nickel. The paper disc bears the freely (?) selected date and any peculiarity of the card explains little.

Instead of a business card, use a playing card split as explained in card books, then glued back together with the paper disc in between. Use a card with one or more reversible pips so that you will know where the disc is before the tear.

The trick can also be performed with a stack of dimes and a penny by employing the Dime and Penny set.

Almost a Transposition

Stewart James

The effect of this mystery is identical with the one of the same name described on page 127, except in this case mechanical coins are responsible for the trickery.

This is the effect: The performer shows a penny in his left hand and a dime in his right, and announces that he will cause them to change places. He closes his hands on the coins and holds them some distance apart. Opening them a moment later he shows the transposition—the penny is now in his right hand, but in his left hand he holds, not the dime that was expected, but two nickels!

Requirements: A Dime and Penny set, a Nickel and Penny set, and a genuine nickel.

Working: Have the shell penny (of the Dime and Penny set) finger palmed in the right hand at the base of the third finger, opening away from the finger. Concealed in the same position in the left hand is the regular nickel with the shell nickel (of the Nickel and Penny set) on top of it, opening away from the hand.

Hold the hands chest high, backs toward the spectators and fingers curled in naturally. Between the tips of the right forefinger and thumb hold the double faced section of the Dime and Penny set, dime side toward the spectators. The double faced section of the Nickel and Penny set is displayed, penny side outward, in the same manner in the left hand. To the audience you are merely holding a dime in your right hand and a penny in your left hand.

Call attention to the two coins by saying, "Watch the two coins! I will cause the one cent to change places with the ten cents." (Do not use the words "dime" and "penny." This is important as you will see later.) With the aid of the thumbs, slide the two visible coins down behind the fingers and press them into their respective shells as you close and lower the hands. Go through whatever business that appeals to you for causing the transposition. Open your right hand first, show the penny and say, "Here is the *one cent.*" Now open your left hand, show the two nickels and say, "And here is the *ten cents.*"

Considering the fact that these two gimmicked sets were designed for the specific purpose of vanishing a coin, this routine is unique indeed.

The Homing Coins

AL CAROSELLI

Effect: After showing his handkerchief unprepared, the magician spreads it on the table, folds it in half, then places two nickels, a dime, and a penny in a row upon it. He folds the handkerchief over the coins "tent fashion" and removes them one at a time and places them in his left fist. One of the coins is removed from his fist and placed on the table. The remaining three are caused to travel back to their original positions under the "tent."

Requisites and Preparation: A 21¢ Trick (which consists of two nickels, a dime, and a penny so prepared they will nest together and appear as a regular five cent piece), two genuine nickels, a dime, and a penny.

Have one of the regular nickels in the right trousers pocket. The 21¢ Trick and the three remaining coins are in left trousers pocket. The handkerchief is on the table or in one of the pockets.

Working: Show the handkerchief freely, spread it on the table, then fold it in half by bringing the forward edge over the rear edge. Remove the 21¢ Trick (as a nickel) and the three real coins from the left trousers pocket and place them on the handkerchief, near its inner edge, as follows: The 21¢ Trick (opening of outer shell down), the nickel, the dime, the penny, Fig. 1.

Fig. 1

Count and name the four coins. From the outer edge, fold the already-folded handkerchief toward yourself forming a double thickness of cloth over the coins. Pull up the center of the handkerchief, covering the coins by forming a "tent" over them so that you alone can see them, Fig. 2.

Fig. 2

Reach into the "tent" with the right hand, lift off the outer shell of the 21¢ Trick and set it slightly to one side, but still under the "tent." Turn over the balance of the nested set, lift off the outer shell (nickel), show it and place it on the fingers of the palm up left hand, saying "A nickel." Close the fingers, which action causes the shell to turn over (opening up) onto the palm, and hold the hand in a loose fist. Go into the tent with the right hand again, lift off the shell penny and as you show it say, "A penny." Put it in the left hand, nesting it in the nickel. Remove the fake dime from the "tent" next, name it, and nest it in the other two nested shells in the left fist. Finally remove the remaining section of the 21¢ Trick, which is the outer shell. Show it as a nickel and place it in the left fist, nesting all four parts together as you do so. The four coins have been removed from the handkerchief singly, and slowly deposited in the left fist. Apparently you hold 21¢ in your left hand—two nickels, a dime, and a penny. Actually the three genuine coins remain in the "tent" unknown to the spectators. They are: a dime, a penny, a nickel.

Say, "Two nickels, a dime, and a penny in my left hand. I'll remove one nickel and put it in my pocket." Suiting the action to

the words, with the right forefinger and thumb reach into the left fist, daintily remove the nested coins and show them as a nickel. Let it be clearly seen that you have nothing else concealed in your hand, then place it in your right trousers pocket. Pretend to change your mind as you add, "No, I believe I'll leave it right here on the table in plain view." Leave the gimmicked set in the pocket and bring out the real nickel and place it on the table close to the handkerchief.

The trick is now over as far as you are concerned. The fake coins are safely hidden in your pocket and your left hand apparently still contains 16¢—a nickel, a dime, and a penny.

Now go through the motions of removing the coins from the left hand with the right and tossing them one at a time toward the handkerchief. Open the left hand, show it and the right hand empty, dusting off the hands to emphasize the disappearance, then throw back the top fold of the handkerchief exposing the three missing coins. All four coins are in plain view and are available for examination. Say nothing about this—just leave them there on the table.

The Circus Trick

Effect: While relating a story about visiting a circus as a boy, the performer shows two nickels, a dime, and a penny which he places in the center of his handkerchief. Removing a nickel, he places it in his pocket. Apparently three coins should remain. But when he shakes out the handkerchief the coins have vanished.

Requirements: A 21¢ Trick and a pocket handkerchief.

Working: Place the four gimmicked coins on the table (being careful that they do not "talk") and call attention to their total— 21¢. Begin the trick as you say, "I remember when I was a boy this much money was quite a lot. At least, it was for me. One time when I heard that the circus was coming to town I began saving my money so I could see it. Although I was quite young at the time, I had heard of pickpockets. I didn't want to lose all my money so I put my savings in my handkerchief and hurried off to the circus." As you say this, show your handkerchief, throw it over your left fist, make a little well in the handkerchief and place the four coins therein one at a time, nesting them as you do so.

"When I arrived at the circus I noticed that the admission to the "big top" was only 15¢ for children, plus a penny tax. This left me a nickel for pink lemonade." Take out the nested coins as a nickel, show this on both sides, and place it in your pocket. "After drinking the lemonade I pushed my way through the crowd to see the outdoor demonstration at the sideshow. When it was over I went to the ticket window to buy my ticket. I opened my handkerchief to take out my 16¢, but it was empty. It was then I realized that my handkerchief had been picked." Show both hands and the handkerchief empty. Without wasting too much time, begin another trick so no one will ask to examine the nickel.

The 16¢ Vanish

Effect: The performer shows two nickels, a dime, and a penny which he places in his left fist. Whatever three coins the spectators name the performer removes invisibly and tosses away. He then opens his hand and shows a single coin. The chosen three have vanished!

Requirements: A 21¢ Trick.

Working: Place the four gimmicked coins of this set on the table, naming each coin as you do so. Show your left hand empty and close it into a loose fist. Place the four

coins into the fist one at a time in the proper order, nesting them.

Tell the spectators that you have four coins in your hand—two nickels, a dime, and a penny—three different kinds of coins—nickel, penny, dime. Have someone name one of these three. Suppose the dime is named. Go through the motions of removing an invisible coin from your left fist with your right forefinger and thumb. Pretend to hold a coin, but let it be clearly seen that you hold nothing. Toss the non-existent coin into the air. Repeat this same business with the next two coins. After you have apparently tossed away a nickel, a penny, and a dime, say, "What does that leave?" The reply will be, "A nickel." "That's right," you say, as you open your hand showing the nickel.

Actually the choice of coins given the spectators is a bluff, but no one ever seems to notice it.

85¢ Through the Table
(The $1.35 Trick)
ROLLAND HAMBLEN

Effect: The performer spreads his handkerchief on the table and shows four coins—a dime, a quarter, and two half dollars—which he places on the four corners of the handkerchief. Taking up the coins one at a time, he places them in his left fist. Then he removes the coins, shows them again, and returns them to his left fist. Showing his right hand empty, he places it underneath the table while he moves his left fist to the center of the handkerchief. Suddenly he brings his fist down on the table and then opens it. It contains only a half dollar. The right hand is brought up showing the missing coins. Apparently they passed through the handkerchief and table.

Requirements: A $1.35 Trick. (This consists of two half dollars, a quarter, and a dime. When nested, the set appears to be a regular half dollar.) A real half dollar, a real quarter, a real dime, and a pocket handkerchief.

Working: After seating yourself at the table, spread the handkerchief in front of you, then distribute the coins on the corners as follows: Put the dime on the outer right corner and the quarter on the outer left corner. The regular half dollar goes on the inner right corner, while the fake half dollar ($1.35 Trick) goes on the inner left corner, opening down.

Make no comment on the four coins as you pick them up one at a time with your right hand and place them in the left fist. The dime is taken up first. It is put squarely in the left hand. While reaching for the quarter with the right hand, close the left hand into a loose fist, then place the quarter in on top of the dime. Follow these two with the regular half dollar and finally the fake half.

Remarking that perhaps everyone did not remember the exact denominations of the coins, you apparently remove them. Actually you remove the four gimmicked coins of the $1.35 Trick and place them on the corners of the handkerchief. This is done as follows: Open your left hand slightly and as you do so, lever up the outer shell of the half at its inner edge with the tip of the third finger. With the right forefinger and thumb, grasp the shell and flick it over onto the nested coins. After this operation the shell will be upside down resting on the nest of three coins. Now, the right forefinger and thumb approach the fake coins and shell, and at the same time the left hand turns palm down; but on the way down the right fingers firmly press the real coins into the left palm, and immediately remove the nested coins and shell right side up. Hold the gimmicked coins between the right fingers and thumb while you momentarily rest the fingertips of the palm down left

hand on the table. Apparently the right hand is holding all the coins and the left hand is empty.

The fake coins are now resting on the right fingers in the following order: On the bottom is the "top" or outer shell of the set, right side up. Then, on top of this rests the "bottom" or inside section of the half dollar (the section that holds the nested quarter and dime). These are all right side up.

With the tips of the fingers and thumb of the palm down left hand, remove the "bottom" section of the half dollar (the section that holds the nested quarter and dime), and place it on the inner left corner of the handkerchief. This leaves exposed the quarter (with its nested dime) and the "top" section of the half dollar. Remove the quarter and place it on the outer left corner of the handkerchief. Next, put the dime on the outer right corner, and finally, the "top" section of the half dollar on the inner right corner. To the spectators it appears that you merely placed the four coins in your left hand, then returned them to their original positions on the handkerchief. The regular dime, quarter and half dollar are still palmed in your left hand.

While calling attention to the values of the four coins on the corners of the handkerchief, move the left hand underneath the table and quietly place its palmed coins on the right leg. Bring up the left hand and hold it, palm up, above the table. Pick up the dime from the outer right corner of the handkerchief and place it in the palm of the left hand and close the fingers over it. Take up the quarter next and place it in the left fist over the dime. Deposit the half dollar from the left inner corner of the handkerchief in the left hand over the first two coins and turn all three over together. The "top" section is put in last, covering all.

Show the right hand empty and as you

move it underneath the table, pick up the three genuine coins from the leg. Carry your left fist to the center of the handkerchief and as you bring it down on the table, rattle the coins in the right hand underneath the table. Turn the left hand over and open it. It contains only one coin—the half dollar ($1.35 set). Immediately bring the right hand to the top of the table and pour its three genuine coins onto the table.

Copper and Silver Transposition

(Using the Double Faced Coin)

Transpositions utilizing a half dollar and an English penny have appeared in magical literature for years. A variety of methods have been explained. The following four are presented as a contribution to the ever-growing collection. Among them will be found, at least, one presentation which should appeal to every type of performer, for there are methods with and without sleight of hand.

In each instance a fake coin is used. It is double faced, showing a copper coin on one side and a silver coin on the other. Originally such coins were made by splitting copper and silver coins in half and soldering a silver half to a copper half. Since such coins would not stand the close scrutiny of an intimate performance because of the obvious center joining, they have been improved upon. The best ones are made by filing down one surface of a silver coin until it is perfectly smooth, and then soldering to it the thinnest possible section of a copper coin. A coin prepared in this manner does not show a tell-tale middle joint and is to be preferred for this reason over the old "half and half" variety.

For the four routines following, the fake coin used shows a half dollar on one side and an English penny on the other.

NUMBER ONE

Effect: An English penny and a fifty-cent piece are used. The spectator closes his hand over the copper coin, seeing it up to the last moment. The performer holds the half dollar in his fist. When each opens his hand, the coins have changed places; that is, the spectator holds the half, while the performer has the penny. Both are tossed into the spectator's hand for examination. They are genuine coins!

Method: Despite the fact that the spectator is given the coins for examination after the climax of the trick, the extra, fake coin is used.

Begin by showing the prepared coin and the genuine half dollar in the palm of the left hand, copper side of the fake uppermost, the English penny being finger palmed in the right hand. Ask the spectator to hold out both hands, palm up. Pick up the half dollar, with the right hand, from the left and place it in the spectator's left hand. Then put the prepared coin, copper side uppermost, on the right fingers of the spectator.

Call attention to the fact that the spectator holds a silver coin in his left hand and a copper coin (the fake) in his right. Ask him to close his left fingers over the silver coin. At the same time, assist him in doing this with pressure from your two hands. Then ask him to close his right hand over the copper coin. Assist him again with your left fingers. Since the coin rests on his fingers, it will be turned over when he closes his hand, bringing the silver side up. The right hand aids slightly in this action, acting also as a cover, which prevents the spectator from seeing the coin.

Request him to hold both coins tightly. Point to his left hand, saying, "Open this hand." As soon as he does, pick up the half dollar with the right thumb and first and second fingers. Caution him again to hold the coin in his right hand tightly, for it is important that he does not ruin the climax.

Say, "I have the silver coin, while you have the copper. Is that correct?" He will, of course, reply, "Yes." While talking to him, toss the half dollar into your left hand a few times, finally making the switch as described in The Bobo Switch, (page 10).

At this point, your left hand holds the genuine English penny, while the half dollar is palmed in your right hand. The spectator holds what he thinks is a copper coin, but is, in reality, the fake coin, silver side up.

Tell him that when you snap your fingers, he is to open his hand. Snap the fingers of the right hand and, as soon as he lifts his fingers, pick up the coin from his hand with your right hand, silver side up, saying, "No, you have the silver coin while I have the copper." Open your left hand, revealing the genuine English penny and apparently toss the fake coin on top of it, but actually switch it for the genuine half dollar in the process. Then throw both coins into his right hand. You will be left holding the fake coin in the right hand and he will have the unprepared coins in his hands. Say nothing about examining them, as he will do so without the suggestion.

When the spectator opens his right hand and sees he is holding a silver coin instead of the copper one, he will be quite surprised. A moment later he will turn the coin over, so you must be a little faster than he is. As soon as it is apparent that he is holding a silver coin, pick it up with the right fingers. Immediately open your left hand revealing the copper coin, which draws his attention and, before his mind can return to the coin he was holding, apparently toss it into your left hand, switching it for the genuine coin. Then immediately toss both coins into his still outstretched hand.

All the dirty work is covered by a series of misdirectional surprises. However, timing and boldness are important, and you must not hesitate in your movements.

It is all very natural and convincing, and a trick that will be talked about. Spectators are always impressed by tricks that seem to take place in their own hands.

NUMBER TWO

If you wish to have the coins examined beforehand, finger palm the fake coin in the right hand, copper side against the fingers; hold the genuine copper coin in view between the thumb and forefinger of the same hand, and the half dollar in the same position in the left hand, the backs of both being up.

Have the spectator extend both hands, palm up. On his right palm, place the half dollar and, on his left, place the English penny. After he has looked at them, exclaim, "Oh, the coins should be reversed. The copper goes over here, while the silver should be in this hand." As you say this, pick up the copper coin from his left hand, with your right fingers, the silver coin from his right hand, with your left fingers, and apparently transfer the two, but actually place the silver one in his left hand and the fake coin in his right, executing The Bobo Switch in order to accomplish this. At the finish of this seemingly innocent maneuver, the fake coin will be in his right hand, copper side up, the genuine half will be in his left hand and you will have the *bona fide* penny finger palmed.

From this point, the trick proceeds as already described in method Number One.

NUMBER THREE

This is a non-sleight version that is both effective and easy to perform.

Have the genuine penny in the right trousers pocket. Exhibit the genuine half and the fake, copper side uppermost, on the left palm. (The half dollar should overlap the copper coin a trifle.)

Call attention to the two coins, saying, "A copper coin and a silver coin." Close your left hand and turn it back up, allowing the half to slide over the fake as you do this. With your right forefinger and thumb, reach into the closed left hand and remove the upper coin (the fake, silver side up). Show the silver side, saying, "I will place the half dollar in my pocket." Thrust your right hand in the pocket and exchange the fake for the genuine penny. Leave your hand in the pocket for a moment.

Say, "I placed a silver coin in my pocket. Therefore, I still have in my hand, what?" Spectator will say, "Copper coin." Reply, "No, my left hand holds the silver coin, while here I have the copper coin." Remove your right hand from the pocket at this point and show the genuine penny. Remark, "You see they have changed places." Both coins can be examined.

If you should be asked to show the pocket empty, this can be accomplished easily by utilizing the top-of-pocket concealment, known to all magicians.

NUMBER FOUR

J. G. THOMPSON, JR.

Have the prepared coin in your right trousers pocket. Hand the unprepared half and penny to a spectator, asking him to examine them and drop them into his coat pocket.

Reach into your trousers pocket, finger palm the coin, pull out the pocket to show it empty, push it back and leave the coin there.

Instruct the spectator to remove one of the coins from his pocket and hand it to you. Which ever it is, place it in your trousers pocket, making sure the two coins don't "talk." Then ask him if he can name the coin he still has. When he does, have him lay it on the palm of your left hand. Tell him that, naturally, leaves you with the other. Reach into your pocket and remove the prepared coin, laying it also on your left palm, the correct side showing.

Suggest trying it again, enter his pocket, drop the genuine coin and bring out the prepared one, with the side showing that matches the coin in his pocket. Apparently place it in your pocket, actually finger palming it.

Then ask, "Which one do I have?" When he answers, say, "No, you're wrong. See for yourself." Turn your right side toward the spectator and raise your right arm, laying it across your chest in order to afford him easy access to your pocket. In this position, the hand will be above the opening of your breast coat pocket into which the prepared coin is dropped.

When he finds he has named your coin incorrectly, he will immediately look into the situation in his own pocket and be left holding two unprepared coins.

Presto Chango

THOMAS H. BEARDEN

Here is a top notch trick that packs a real surprise. Few close-up stunts are as unique as this spectator fooler. Sandwiched in with the more complicated mysteries it adds zest to the performance.

Effect: Performer shows two silver coins in his open left hand. He quickly closes, then opens the hand. The coins have instantly changed to copper. Again he closes his hand and opens it. This time the coins have turned back to silver. The action is repeated for the third time, but this time only one coin changes to copper. The two coins are tossed onto the table for examination.

Requisites and Preparation: An English

penny, a half dollar and a fake coin which shows copper on one side and silver on the other. (See the preceding trick for a complete description of this coin.)

Place the copper side of the fake coin against the silver coin and put them together in the little match or change pocket inside the right coat pocket. The regular copper coin is in the pocket proper.

Working: Thrust the right hand into the coat pocket, finger palm the copper coin, and bring out the fake coin and the silver coin together between the fingers and thumb. Take them with the left hand, between the thumb and fingers, holding them together in alignment and casually showing both sides. The right hand then takes them and places them on the palm of the open left hand. With the right forefinger slide the top coin forward until it lies on the two middle fingers near their tips. The left hand appears to be holding two silver coins. The regular copper coin is still concealed in the right finger palm.

With the right forefinger and thumb turn over the coin on the left palm as you state, "Two silver coins. Watch them." The right hand picks up the silver coin from the left palm and apparently tosses it back, but it is switched for the copper coin from the right hand. (See The Bobo Switch, page 10.) The left hand closes immediately, causing the fake coin to turn over. The fake coin is brought back on the copper as the hand closes. Open the left hand and tilt it downward slightly, which allows the top coin (fake) to slide forward onto the fingers.

At this juncture the coin on the left palm is the regular copper, while the one lying on the fingers is the fake coin, copper side uppermost. The regular silver coin is in the right finger palm.

Apparently the coins have changed to copper.

With the right thumb and finger turn over the regular copper coin lying on the left palm, showing its other side as you exclaim, "Copper coins!"

The right hand removes the copper coin from the left and pretends to toss it back, but The Bobo Switch is executed instead. The silver coin goes in the left hand as it closes and the forward (fake) coin turns over on top of the just arrived silver coin. Open the left hand and show two silver coins, the regular silver coin lying on the palm, and the fake coin (silver side uppermost) lying on the fingers.

Apparently the two coins have changed back to silver.

Close the left hand again, allowing the fake coin to turn over, then open it. This time the spectators see one silver and one copper coin. The silver coin lies on the palm and the fake coin (copper side uppermost) at the base of the two middle fingers.

Coins from the left hand are apparently tossed into the right hand, but the forward (fake) coin is retained finger palmed. The right hand then shows two coins—the one which was hidden in the finger palm, and the one just received from the left hand. (For a more complete description of this move see the Utility Switch, page 11.) The right hand then tosses the copper and silver coins onto the table. They are regular coins.

Left hand can get rid of the fake coin by reaching into the pocket for a handkerchief to perform an effect with one or both of the coins.

The Inferior Coin

Milton Kort

Effect: After showing two silver coins and a copper coin, the performer places them on a spectator's outstretched hand. He shows them again, then places them in his left hand, but when that hand is opened the copper coin has vanished. Showing his right hand empty, he reaches behind his right knee and produces the missing coin. This is repeated twice more. Next, he deposits one of the silver coins in his pocket and closes his hand over the other silver coin and copper coin. When the hand is opened it is holding two silver coins. The wayward coin is extracted from the pocket. He places the copper back in his pocket and shows two silver coins in his hand. Suddenly they both change to copper and a silver coin is taken from the pocket.

Requisites and Preparation: Two half dollars, an English penny, and a gimmicked coin which shows copper on one side and silver on the other. (See page 243 for a description of this coin.)

In the beginning the two silver coins and the copper coin are together in the right coat pocket. In the small match compartment of the same pocket is the gimmicked coin, copper side away from the body.

Working: Remove the three regular coins and show them. Request a nearby spectator to assist you by holding out one hand, then place the three coins in his hand. Show both hands empty, then with the right hand turn over the three coins one at a time, showing their other sides and counting them. Say nothing about the coins being ordinary—just show them as you count and name them.

Fig. 1

Pick up the copper coin from the spectator's hand and place it on the palm of your right hand, then take up the two silver coins and drop them on the fingers of the hand, Fig. 1. Say, "Two silver and one copper." Turn the right hand inward and over, toss the two halves into the left hand (which immediately closes and rattles them) and retain the copper coin hidden in the right palm, Fig. 2. Move the left fist away from the body and at the same time sleeve the copper coin from the right hand in the

Fig. 2

right sleeve. Apparently the left hand holds all three coins. Actually it holds only the two silver coins. The copper is up the right sleeve.

Say, "As you know, we are using three coins— two silver and one copper. Copper, compared to silver, is an inferior metal. As a result a coin made from copper would be inferior to one made from silver." While pronouncing these words, show the right hand empty, and continue, "Because the copper coin feels inferior to the silver coins it runs away and hides. We find it hanging around one of the joints." Lower your right hand, catch the coin as it falls from the sleeve on the cupped fingers, then produce it from behind the right knee. Open the left hand, show the two silver coins and toss the copper coin on top of them.

Replace the three coins in the spectator's hand, and offer to repeat the trick. The effect this time is the same but the moves are slightly different. Here they are: Pick up a silver coin from the spectator's hand and pretend to place it in your left hand, but retain it classic palmed instead. The left hand is closed. Take up the copper coin next. Execute The Click Pass (a), (page 14) as you palm it and drop the silver coin instead. The sound created by this sleight gives the illusion that the second coin was dropped into the left hand also. Remove the remaining silver coin from the spectator's hand and toss it into your left hand. Apparently the left hand holds all three coins. Actually it holds only the two silver coins. The copper is palmed in the right hand. Rattle the coins in the right hand and as you move it away from the body, sleeve the copper coin in the right sleeve.

Show your right hand empty and repeat the same patter as before (which gets funnier each time), then produce the sleeved coin from behind the right knee in the same manner as you did the first time. Open the left hand, show the two silver coins and toss the copper coin on top of them.

Offer to do the trick once more. Toss the three coins from your left hand into your right, then display them again. If the copper coin does not land near the heel of the right hand, move it there with the left, so that when you close the hand and turn it over, the copper coin will be held partly outside the fist in preparation for executing the Kort Method of Sleeving One of Several Coins. (See page 107.) Sleeve the copper coin as you toss the two silver coins into the left hand, which immediately closes and rattles them. Show the right hand empty as you again recite the same patter, then produce the copper coin from behind the right knee.

Open the left hand, show the two silver coins and toss the copper coin on top of them.

Pick up the copper coin from the left hand with the right, commenting on its waywardness. "Because it feels inferior to the silver coins it would much rather be off by itself—in such a place as my pocket." As you say these last words place the real copper coin in the coat pocket, leave it and remove the gimmicked coin, copper side out. Explain that you would like to show them what happens if one of the silver coins is placed in the pocket. Drop the gimmicked coin (copper side up) on the left fingers, remove one of the half dollars and place it in the match compartment of the right coat pocket. (It is placed in this compartment to prevent the coins clicking together.) Let your right hand be seen empty as you remove it from your pocket. Close your left hand, which action causes the gimmicked coin to turn silver side up, then snap the right fingers over the left. Open the left hand and show two silver coins. (Actually one is the real half dollar and the other is the gimmicked coin, silver side up.) Reach into your right coat pocket, remove and show the regular copper coin. The copper coin has apparently changed places with the silver coin.

Pretend to drop the copper coin back in the pocket, but retain it finger palmed. With the right forefinger, push the gimmicked coin forward from the left palm onto the left fingers and show the two coins, both apparently halves. Pick up the gimmicked coin between the tips of the first two fingers and thumb of the palm down right hand. State, "Here we have a silver coin." Toss it back onto the left fingers, then pick up the real half from the palm in the same manner, adding "And here is another silver coin." Pretend to toss the real half dollar back, but execute The Bobo

Switch (page 10), and throw the English penny instead. The instant the copper coin lands in the left hand it closes. In the action of closing the hand the gimmicked coin turns over, copper side up onto the real copper coin which was just thrown onto the palm. (This part of the routine will be familiar to you if you have mastered Presto Chango, page 245, as they are the same.) The real half dollar is now palmed in the right hand.

"By the way, do you remember what coins we are using?" The reply should be, "Two silver coins and a copper coin." "No," you say. "It's two copper coins . . ." Open your left hand, showing the copper coins (actually one is the gimmicked coin, copper side up), then reach into your coat pocket with your right hand and bring out the half dollar that was palmed. Show it as you add ". . . and one silver coin." Toss the half dollar into the right hand, show all three coins, then drop them in the left coat pocket.

Thieves and Sheep

LILLIAN BOBO

This is the same effect as the one described on page 208, except half dollars and English pennies are used.

For this version you will require, besides six English pennies and two half dollars, a double faced coin (English penny–half dollar).

Arrange five of the copper coins in a horizontal row on the table in front of you. Place a half dollar at the left end of the row and the double faced coin, silver side up, at the right end. To all appearances you have five copper and two silver coins. Beforehand, as you sat down, you placed a half dollar on your left leg and a regular English penny on your right leg.

Pick up the seven coins from the table and lay them down again as in the first part of the experiment on page 208. Then as you adjust your chair closer to the table, palm the half dollar from the left leg in the left hand, and the English penny from the right leg in the right hand. Bring your hands up and pick up the two end coins from the table but do not make the secret transfer as in the first method. Take up the five copper coins in the same order as you did the pennies in the first version, dropping the same two with the left hand in the lap as you slide them off the table. Now when you open your right hand, show the copper side of the double faced coin and you will appear to be holding five copper coins (sheep). Open your left hand and show the two regular halves (thieves). There will also be two copper coins in your lap which you can secretly pick up and add to the others as you put them all in your pocket.

In and Out

"HEN" FETSCH

Tricks utilizing the double faced coin which shows copper on one side and silver on the other have gained considerably in popularity among close up workers in recent years. Practically every coin worker has his own pet effect with this gimmicked coin. Following are three such tricks from the fertile brain of "Hen" Fetsch.

Effect: Two coins—an English penny and a half dollar—are covered with a borrowed handkerchief. The half dollar is removed and held outside the handkerchief and directly over the covered penny, while a spectator holds the bunched together four corners of the handkerchief. The magician covers the center of the cloth and the two coins with his hand and causes a transposition. When he opens his hand he is holding the English penny, while the spectator unfolds the handkerchief to find the half dollar.

Because there are some people who have never seen an English penny and may want to examine the coin, it is best to precede this trick with one utilizing a regular English penny. After becoming familiar with the coin in another trick they will naturally take this one for granted.

Fig. 1

Method: Show a half dollar and a double faced coin in your palm up right hand as a copper and silver coin. Borrow a handkerchief and spread it over your hand and the coins, Fig. 1. With the left hand, pick up the half dollar through the cloth and lift it up and away from your right hand as you say, "Here is the copper coin." At the same time turn over the gimmicked coin and bring it

Fig. 2

out silver side up adding, "And here is the silver coin." Display the handkerchief and visible coin as in Fig. 2.

Place the double faced coin, silver side up, directly over the covered half dollar and have a spectator hold the bunched together corners of the handkerchief in one hand as you retain your grip on its center and the two coins, Fig. 3.

"The copper coin is inside the handkerchief and the silver coin is outside. Watch!" Close your left hand over the coins and

Fig. 3

the center of the handkerchief and as you do so secretly reverse the outside coin, which will now be copper side up. Instruct your helper to hold tightly onto the corners, then with a couple of little jerks, pull your hand free of the handkerchief and open it, showing a copper coin. "Here is the copper coin, while you have the silver coin." Have him unfold the handkerchief to find the regular half dollar.

Follow this with Up Their Sleeve.

Up Their Sleeve

"Hen" Fetsch

This is an effective and practical follow-up trick to the one just described, as it sells the transposition and serves to exchange the gimmicked coin for a genuine one.

Effect: The spectator who assisted you in the previous trick is requested to hold up his arm as for drinking a tall cool one. The magician shows a half dollar and an English penny, drops the English penny into his assistant's sleeve and the half dollar into his own. He commands the coins to transpose themselves. The assistant and the performer lower their arms over a table which permits the half dollar to drop from the assistant's sleeve and the English penny to drop from the performer's sleeve. The coins have changed places and both may now be examined.

Requisites: A regular half dollar, a regular English penny, and a double faced coin.

Preparation: Have the regular English penny under your watch band as in Fig 1.

Working: Immediately after performing In and Out, show the half dollar and gimmicked coin as a copper and silver coin

Fig. 1

and say, "I'll do it again, but I'll need your assistance." Request the spectator who assisted you in the previous trick to stand on your left and hold up his right arm as if he was holding a drink. Holding the two coins together, place them in his sleeve opening, release the half dollar, and turn over the double faced coin as you bring it out and show it as a half dollar. Since he sees you holding what he thinks to be the half dollar

he reasons that you must have dropped the English penny into his sleeve. Actually the half dollar is in his sleeve and you are holding the gimmicked coin, silver side up.

After dropping the coin into his sleeve state, "In your sleeve is the copper coin and here is the silver coin, which I will drop into my sleeve." With this remark, raise your left arm and pretend to drop the silver coin (gimmicked coin) down your sleeve. What actually happens is this: As the right hand enters the sleeve it finger palms the gimmicked coin and pushes the English penny from underneath the watch band, which drops to your elbow. The action of apparently dropping the coin into your sleeve, finger palming it, and dislodging the other one should be all one move. Don't try to be clever—just do it. Lay thinking just doesn't suspect an exchange. At this point, pick up his handkerchief from the table (which you had placed there after performing the preceding trick) and place it part way in your right coat pocket, disposing of the finger palmed gimmicked coin at the same time. You do this apparently to clear the table for what is about to happen.

The usual magic mumbo-jumbo is executed, then you lower your arm, permitting the copper coin to fall out of your sleeve onto the table. The spectator repeats your actions and the half dollar drops from his sleeve. Again the coins have changed places! The handkerchief is returned to its owner and the coins may now be examined. But please don't say, "Here, examine the coins." It is better to make some casual remark such as, "Have you noticed that both coins are about the same size? Of course today's values make them just about even." This amusing side remark allows you to turn the coins over and offer them for comparison.

The third version of Copper and Silver Transposition (page 244) can be used instead of the above to follow In and Out, if you so desire. Both tricks get rid of the gimmicked coin in the course of the routine.

Buddha's Coin

"HEN" FETSCH

This routine features the English penny-half dollar coin and what appears to be the Buddha Money Papers, which is just about the oldest trick ever palmed off on the public by the circus, side-show, and street pitchman. Many a pleasurable moment has been derived by watching the knowing smile at the beginning and the puzzled look at the finish when they remove the coin from the papers.

Effect: A set of Buddha papers is shown and unfolded, disclosing a copper and silver coin within the smallest paper. The silver coin is removed, the papers refolded over the copper coin and the packet placed on a spectator's outstretched right hand. The performer shows two copper coins, then after sandwiching the silver coin between them, places all three coins in the spectator's left hand and commands a transposition. The three coins are shown to be all copper—the silver has vanished. The spectator unfolds the papers and finds the missing silver coin.

Requisites and Preparation: Two English pennies, a double faced coin, and a set of ungimmicked Buddha papers. The outfit consists of a set of folded papers (plain or each a different color), usually four, that nest within each other. The gimmicked papers consist of two such sets with the outer papers of each set glued back to back so that either set of papers could be opened and a production, vanish, or change shown. Almost every school boy is familiar with this novelty store item so a further explanation is unnecessary here. The papers should be handled exactly the same as if you were using the gimmicked set. That

is, the turn over move should be made with each paper after it is folded.

Have the half dollar and the gimmicked coin (copper side up) within the smallest paper and the two regular copper coins in your right trousers pocket.

Working: Show the nested papers saying, "Here is an unusual trick I saw performed the other day by a street pitchman." This remark serves to jog the memory of your viewers so that they will recall the secret of the papers. Unfold the papers one by one until the two coins are revealed. "A half dollar and an English penny," you state. As you cover the coins with one fold of paper with your left hand, the right hand turns over the gimmicked coin and brings it into view, silver side uppermost. "He left the penny in the paper and placed the half dollar in full view on his stand." With this remark, deposit the gimmicked coin, silver side up, on the table and complete the fold of the paper around the penny (half dollar). After the folding is completed turn the paper over and place it on the next paper, which is folded, turned over and placed on the next paper. This is repeated until all the papers are folded and the last one turned over. The packet of papers is then placed on a spectator's extended right palm. Remove the two pennies from your pocket, show them, sandwich the silver coin (gimmicked coin) between them and deposit the stack on top of the folded papers, Fig. 1.

The papers and stack of coins are picked up as a unit, turned over and placed on the spectator's left palm. Clap your hands to-

Fig. 1

gether, say the magic words, then transfer the nested papers back to his right hand. "These moves," you explain, "are the ones the pitchman made in presenting the trick to his sidewalk audience." Really it's all done to turn over the gimmicked coin.

Pick up the top penny with your right hand and toss it into your left. The next coin, which should be a half dollar but is a penny, is tossed into the same hand. This is repeated with the last penny. The spectator unfolds the papers one by one and in the last paper he finds the missing half dollar. If he suspects the papers and examines them he will find nothing.

"At this point the pitchman asked me if this was the same half dollar I gave him just a minute ago. To which I replied, "Yes." He then pocketed the coin and said, 'You gave it to me? Thank you sir!' I didn't mind as the trick was worth a half dollar."

If you borrow the half dollar in the beginning, finish the above patter by saying, "You must agree that the trick *is* worth a half dollar. Right?" and pocket his coin. Of course you return his coin immediately following the chuckle.

The Stack of Quarters

NATE LEIPZIG

One of the real classics of coin magic is "The Cap and Pence" or "The Stack of Quarters." It has been a pet effect in the repertoires of many great magicians of the past and present. The effect of the trick is unique and startling.

The most difficult part of the trick is the switch of the real coins for the gimmicked stack. This is accomplished in two different ways in the following two routines. The first is by that master of dexterity, Nate Leipzig, and was shown to me by a contemporary master, Rolland Hamblen.

Effect: The magician borrows six quar-

ters and shows a conical wooden form which is covered with a thin leather cone. He stacks the quarters and places them on the back of his left hand. A spectator is requested to remove the leather cone from the wooden form and place it over the stack of coins. At the count of three the spectator is invited to lift the leather cone, which he does. "No," corrects the performer. "Not that way, this way!" And suiting the action to the words, the performer lifts the leather cone, which in turn leaps from his fingers toward the spectators. In place of the quarters is a pile of pennies, while the quarters drop from the performer's left hand.

Requirements: A fake stack of quarters, hollowed out to hold six pennies.

Six pennies.

Six quarters, which you may borrow or provide yourself.

A thin leather cone (approximately 1¼ x 2¼ inches), to fit loosely over the stack of coins.

A conical wooden form, over which the leather cone must fit. This form serves a dual purpose. It keeps the leather cone in proper shape, and furnishes excellent misdirection for the switch of the six single coins for the fake stack. Cone and form are shown in Fig. 1.

Preparation: Have the fake stack loaded with the six pennies, opening up, in the left trousers pocket, the cone covered wooden form in the right coat pocket, and the six quarters in the right trousers pocket.

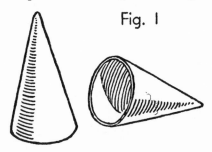

Fig. 1

Working: Announce a trick with six quarters. Thrust both hands into your pockets, finger palm the fake stack (opening away from fingers) in your left hand and remove it as you bring out the six quarters with your right hand. If you wish to borrow some of the coins follow the same procedure, but in this case you provide three or four and borrow the rest.

At any rate, toss the six quarters onto the table, then remove the cone and its form and place it beside the quarters. Pick up the quarters one at a time with the right hand and place them in a stack at the base of the curled forefinger and crotch of thumb of the left hand, which is held back toward spectators, Fig. 2.

Request a spectator to remove the wooden form from the leather cone. All eyes will be momentarily diverted from the stack of quarters on your fist to the spectator's action of removing the wooden form from the leather cone. During this short

Fig. 3

Fig. 2

cone, Fig. 4. State that on the count of three he is to lift the leather cone from the coins. Count, "One, two, three!" No matter how he lifts the cone, say, "No, not that way." Have him replace it over the

Fig. 4

interval, the loose quarters are allowed to slip into the left fist and, as though retrieving them, the right fingers extract from the finger palm of the left hand, the fake stack. The real coins are retained finger palmed as the right hand places the fake stack (slightly fanned) on the back of the left fist, which turns back uppermost for the purpose, Fig. 3.

Make a pretense of evening up the stack of coins on the back of your hand, then have a spectator cover it with the leather

stack, then lift it yourself and exclaim, "This way!" You now proceed to illustrate the proper way of removing the cone, which is as follows:

With the right forefinger and thumb, grip the leather cone at the base, lift it AND the fake stack from the back of the left hand, just high enough to clear and expose the stack of pennies. Then the first finger rolls the cone inward toward the base of the thumb permitting the fake stack to drop into the right fist and, as soon as the stack is free of the cone, the first finger (which is now curled in toward the base of the thumb) straightens out in a flicking motion, and propels the cone straight at the spectators, Fig. 5. Taking advantage of the slight turmoil caused by the flying cone, the right hand moves down to the side and

Fig. 5

quickly drops the fake stack in the coat pocket.

The left fist, still possessing the six loose quarters, releases them into the spectator's hand.

Admittedly, this last move is a bold one, but it is indetectable if done smoothly. The surprise created by the appearance of the six pennies and the falling quarters furnishes ample misdirection for the secret disposal of the gimmick.

The cone and the coins can now be inspected as there is nothing to find.

SECOND METHOD

Effect: A stack of six quarters is placed on the back of a spectator's hand and covered with a tube which was formed from a dollar bill. When the tube is lifted the quarters have vanished—in their place is a stack of pennies. The performer removes the quarters from his purse.

Requisites and Preparation: Needed, besides the prepared stack of coins, are six pennies to fill the shell, fourteen extra quarters, a coin purse and a dollar bill. Put the six quarters in the coin purse

and place it in the right trousers pocket, together with seven loose quarters. Fill the stack with the pennies and set the quarter on top. Fan it slightly and deposit it in the left trousers pocket with the opening upward, so the pennies will not spill out. Fold a dollar bill lengthwise and roll it into a tube a trifle larger than the circumference of a quarter. Tuck in one end of the bill to keep it from unrolling, Fig. 1, and put it in the left coat pocket. This idea of using a bill instead of a cone belongs to Bert Allerton.

Fig. 1

Working: Thrust both hands into the trousers pockets. Finger palm and stack with the loose quarter on top, holding it so that the opening is against the fingers and, with the right hand, remove the seven genuine quarters. Show the quarters, letting it be seen that they are ordinary.

Pretend to dump the loose quarters into your left hand, but retain them in your right hand by executing the move as explained in method (a), Vanish for Several Coins (page 45). Immediately turn the left hand palm upward and show the fake stack with the loose quarter on top. The switch is indetectable, when properly done. Ask a spectator to hold out his right hand, back up. Take the fake stack between the thumb and first finger of the now palm down right hand and place it on the back of his, the left hand steadying his hand in the action, Fig. 2. Then drop your right hand, which contains the seven loose quarters, to your side.

Fig. 2

Square up the stack of quarters with your left fingers, then reach into your left coat pocket and remove the rolled up dollar bill. Show it empty and place it on his right thumb, Fig. 3.

Make some remark about there being six quarters and then count them. Finding

Fig. 3

seven, say, "As this trick requires just six quarters, I'll remove one." Take the loose coin from the top of the stack with your right hand and place it in your **right coat** pocket, together with the seven palmed quarters. This accomplishes two things:

First, it conveys the impression that all the quarters on the back of the spectator's hand are loose and, second, it provides an opportunity for disposing of the extra quarters, leaving both of your hands empty.

With your right hand, remove the dollar bill from the spectator's thumb, show it empty again and place it over the stack of quarters. Be sure he holds his hand high enough so that he can't look down into the tube. Remove the dollar bill and place it in the palm of your left hand, using your right hand to elevate or adjust his hand a little. Again replace the dollar bill over the quarters and clap your hands together once. Quickly take away the dollar bill AND the stack, leaving the pile of pennies on the back of his hand. Place the bill, with the hidden stack, again in your left hand and retain it by curling the fingers over it. Toss the empty bill on the table, reach into your left trousers pocket, leave the stack in the pocket and remove the coin purse. Open it and dump the six quarters on the table.

Apparently the quarters have found their way into your purse.

The Hook Coin

One of the most common, yet one of the most neglected gimmicked coins is the hook coin. This is simply a coin with a hook (usually made from a steel pin) fastened to its edge in such a manner it can be hooked onto the clothing, Fig. 1.

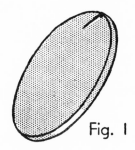

Fig. 1

The original, and probably the simplest method for vanishing the coin is as follows: Stand with your left side toward the spectators as you show the coin, keeping the hook covered with the thumb. Toss it into the air about a foot with your right hand and catch it in the same hand. Lower your hand and throw the coin upward again, this time higher than before. Catch it in your right hand, and as you lower your hand to your side for a more forceful throw, hook the coin onto the right trousers leg, then swing the hand up as before and toss the coin still higher into the air. As you follow the non-existent coin upward with your eyes, it seems to fade away in mid-air. Show both hands empty.

Few magicians vanish the coin as just described. Most of them are content to show the coin, then crudely hook it on the trousers leg as they make a motion of tossing it into the air.

The coin should be tossed into the air two or three times before hooking it onto the trousers leg. And it is important that the eyes follow the coin each time in its upward journey. After two or three throws the spectators become accustomed to seeing the coin go upward, so when you pretend to throw it the last time it becomes perfectly natural for them to look upward again. In fact, some people even imagine they see it. Furthermore, there must be no hesitation as the coin is hooked onto the trousers. Each throw should be in perfect tempo with the preceding one. And when you pretend to toss the non-existent coin into the air the last time follow its flight upward a bit longer than before, then turn your attention to your right hand. Turn it over a time or two as if looking for the coin. Pretend to be puzzled yourself as to where the coin might be. Upon not finding the coin in your right hand it is only natural for you to look next at your left

hand. Not seeing it there either give a little shrug of the shoulders and look at the audience to convey the idea that the coin has completely disappeared.

Do not try to get rid of the coin immediately. Seize an opportunity later, unhook it and drop it in the right coat or trousers pocket.

As a variation to the foregoing, try this: Pretend to place the coin in the left hand but retain it hidden in the right. Extend the closed left hand toward a person on your left, requesting him to hold the coin. Before he can take it change your mind and offer it to a person on your right. As you turn to the right, secretly hook the coin onto the right trousers leg, Fig. 2. This action serves as ample misdirection for the

Fig. 2

secret maneuver. When the spectator holds out his hand for the coin the left hand crumbles it to an invisible dust and sprinkles it on the spectator's palm. Both hands are then shown empty.

The coin can be detached and pocketed later.

Sometimes I use the hook coin this way: I vanish it as mentioned above. Then I show both hands with fingers wide apart and roll up the sleeves. This convinces the onlookers that the coin is not concealed about the hands. Suddenly I exclaim, "Oh, there it is!" as I reach out with the left hand and apparently pluck the vanished coin from a spectator's ear, or some part of his clothing. All eyes are on the left hand. I close the left hand as if it actually held a coin. During this brief action the right hand drops down to the side and quickly unfastens the hook coin from the trousers leg. I then pretend to slap the vanished coin onto the right hand, where it is displayed. Try it.

Instead of employing a clip to hold an extra coin under the edge of the coat you can use a hook coin. Merely hook it on the lining just under the right lower edge of the coat where it can easily be stolen with the right hand.

Perhaps the most ingenious method for disposing of a hook coin is to boldly fasten it on a spectator's arm or back while gently drawing him closer for a better look. This is easy and extremely effective. Merely show the coin in your right hand and pretend to place it in your left hand, but retain it hidden in your right. As you request a nearby spectator to step a little closer, grasp him by the left arm and hook the coin on his sleeve. After the proper build up, open your left hand and show it and your right hand empty.

To reproduce the coin, close your left hand into a loose fist and hold it about waist high and back uppermost. Tell the spectator that if he will make a mystic pass around your left hand the coin will return. Take hold of his left arm again, getting possession of the coin, and draw him along side of you. Then as you demonstrate how you want him to pass his hand around your left fist, perform the secret loading move

of Milton Kort's which is described on page 129. After he passes his hand around your left fist, open it and show that the coin has returned. This is a real baffler when performed with the sleeves rolled up. He is at a loss to explain where the coin went or how it returned.

Milton Kort tells me of an interesting experience he had with a hook coin and another magician. He pretended to place the coin in his left hand, but retained it in his right. Then as he gently pushed his friend back so the others could see, he hooked the coin on his sleeve. Having a little knowledge of trick coins, the magician smiled knowingly and felt his shoulder and found the coin. Right then, there was born an idea for fooling magicians—especially those who may know about the hook coin.

This is it: Hold an ungimmicked half dollar in your right hand in position for sleeving. Push the magician back a little and as your hand almost touches his shoulder, snap the coin up the sleeve. Pretend to place the coin in your left hand and vanish it. Watch him smile knowingly and notice his expression when he feels for the hook coin that is not there. The cover for the sleeving move is perfect.

This trick is not intended for the layman, but the magician, whom we all like to fool once in awhile.

The Magnet

The lastest wrinkle on the hook coin is no hook at all. The coin appears perfectly ordinary and can even be handled by the spectators without them suspecting anything unusual.

Secret: The coin is either a steel coin, or a silver one which has been faked by adding a piece of steel. (The wartime American pennies are ideally suited for this purpose, also.) A magnet is either in the right hip pocket or fastened inside the right trousers leg about midway between the knee and the hip. One of the best magnets for this purpose can be obtained at a beauty parlor supply house. These are attached to a bracelet, or leather strap, so they can be worn on the wrist, wrist watch fashion. Beauty operators use them to hold bobby pins while working on a customer's hair. The cheapest ones have a leather strap, which is easier to remove than the plastic bracelet that most of them have. Remove the leather strap and attach in its place a length of tape to the magnet. To the opposite end of the tape fasten a small metal hook so that it can be hooked over the waistband of the trousers, Fig. 3. The magnet then hangs down inside the right trousers leg at a position about even

MAGNET

TAPE

Fig. 3

HOOK

with the right hand as it hangs naturally at the side.

Now by using a steel coin, or one that has been gimmicked as described, you can utilize the same moves as you would to vanish a hook coin. The coin merely becomes attracted by the magnet and stays in position on the leg until it is removed. The real advantage to this method is that since there is no hook on the coin it can be handled and shown quite freely.

Although a hook coin can be used in this clever vanish by Milton Kort, it is especially clean cut and baffling when the gimmicked coin and magnet are employed.

The moves appear so fair and natural they can be executed with perfect safety even at extremely close range.

Roll back your sleeves, turn slightly to the right—just enough so the coin may be fastened to the right trousers leg without the action being detected by the spectators—and display the coin lying on the fingers of the palm up right hand. Hold both hands fairly low (slightly below waist level), lower the right hand to the side, bring it up and toss the coin into the left hand, which immediately closes over it. Repeat the process. As the right hand drops to the side in preparation for the third toss the coin is placed flat against the right leg where it is held by the attraction of the magnet. Without hesitating an instant, the right hand comes up and duplicates the preceding action of tossing the coin into the left hand. The left hand closes as before, pretending to hold the coin. Allow the right hand to be seen empty, then after a suitable pause, open the left hand and show the coin vanished.

The success of the vanish depends entirely on attention to the following details. The distance the coin travels in its journey from the right to the left hand is actually not more than three inches. As the right hand comes up from the side it comes to a sudden halt just as the tips of the fingers touch the

Fig. 4

right side of the palm up left hand, Fig. 4. As the hand comes to a halt the coin leaves the fingers of the right hand, forms a small arc in the air and lands in the left palm. The left fingers immediately close over the coin.

It is important that the tempo of each action be identical. Do not move the left hand but keep your attention firmly fixed on it at all times. In the first two tosses the spectators become accustomed to seeing the coin land in the palm of the left hand. When the same moves are duplicated on the third toss they imagine they see the coin leave the right hand again and land in the left. When the hand is opened and shown empty a moment later they will be completely baffled.

Dispose of the coin in the pocket at an opportune moment later on, or reproduce it the same way as you would the hook coin.

Another use for the gimmicked coin and magnet is as a holdout. The coin is secretly attached to the right trousers leg prior to beginning a trick. After showing the hands unmistakably empty the coin is secretly obtained and concealed in the hand according to the trick at hand. This method of stealing a coin is easier, quicker, and offers less chance of detection that if it were stolen from the pocket of a clip underneath the coat.

A gimmicked coin of this variety can be used in other routines and not saved for just one effect. It all adds up to cleaner presentation. The coin is especially fine for intimate conjuring, not to mention that it also throws the wise guy, or magician, off the track.

Sundry Gimmicked Coins and Tricks Therewith

This chapter does not describe all the trick coins, nor does it give every trick

that is possible with them. Here then, are a few more of a lesser known variety to add to the collection.

Nickel to Half Dollar

This is a folding half dollar with a hollowed out place on one side to take a nickel. The nickel is soldered to the center section of the folding coin so it fits in this cavity when the half is in its normal position. With the two outside sections folded back the coin can be exhibited as a nickel

Fig. 1

by holding it as shown in Fig. 1. The protruding parts of the half are hidden with the thumb and first and second fingers.

The nickel is allowed to change visibly to a half dollar under cover of a slight up and down movement of the hand.

The effect is startling and mysterious.

Liberty Head Half and U. S. Penny

This coin, like the Dime and Penny, is in two parts. The half is a shell and the penny, which is about the size of a quarter, shows the reverse side of the silver coin on one side. When the two pieces are nested together they appear as a regular Liberty head half dollar and can be casually examined.

The usual working is as follows: With a regular quarter concealed inside the shell, display the half and old penny, sliding them over and under each other. The last time the penny goes under, slip it between the quarter and shell and press it into position. (See How to Make Money, page 266, for a more detailed description of this move.) Ask a spectator to extend his left hand, place the coins therein, close his hand around them and tell him to hold both hands behind his back, transfer one of the coins to the other hand and then extend both fists, back up, in front of him.

Now you make a guess as to which hand contains the silver coin. In making your choice, select the one in which you originally put the coins; this advice stems from the fact, that, for some strange reason, such has always been the case in all times I have performed the feat.

Whether right or wrong, have him open only the hand containing the half. With your right fingers, turn it over as you pick it up, so that he will remember that he saw both sides, then have him open his left hand. When he does so, he will find he is holding, not the penny as he expected, but a regular twenty-five cent piece, which he may then examine.

The only weakness I have found in the trick is that the penny cannot be examined at the beginning. Because this coin can only be found in numismatic shops, most people are unfamiliar with it and want to examine it. Of course, this cannot be permitted. I have solved the problem with an extra genuine penny which I obtained from a coin dealer. Here is how you would do it using the real penny:

Have the shell half, with the regular quarter concealed in it, in your right trousers pocket. In finger palm position of your right hand is the prepared penny, copper side against the fingers, and at the fingertips of the same hand is the genuine penny. Hand the real penny to a spectator to look over and pass around first, then take it back with your right hand and pretend to toss it in your left hand, but execute The Bobo Switch (page 10), and throw the gimmicked penny instead. Show it lying in your left hand, copper side up, as you remark that you need another coin for the experiment you are about to perform. Reach in your right trousers pocket, leave the genuine penny and bring out the shell half with the concealed quarter. The half dollar attracts no particular attention so you can proceed now as described, without any inhibitions.

The Ring Coin

This coin, said to have been used by T. Nelson Downs in his close-up work, is simply a half dollar with a broken ring soldered to it as shown in Fig. 1.

Fig. 1

Here is how Frank Garcia employs it: With the ring over the tip of the right middle finger exhibit the coin apparently balanced on that finger. Place the tip of the right forefinger on top of the coin and slowly deposit it in the palm of your left hand as shown in Fig. 2.

Fig. 2

As you close your left hand, turn your right hand over and withdraw the right middle finger, carrying the coin with it into the right palm. Slowly pull your right forefinger from the left fist, then after a brief pause open your left hand and show it empty. Produce the coin from behind your right knee, neatly balanced on the tip of the right middle finger.

Variation: Show the Ring Coin and a regular half dollar clipped between the tips of your right first and second fingers as in Fig. 2. Close your left hand and withdraw the Ring Coin as described. Apparently your left hand contains both coins. Say the magic words, then open the two hands displaying a coin balanced on the tips of the two second fingers.

Very pretty.

Short Changed

GENE GORDON

Effect: While relating a story on how he was short changed at a circus, the magician shows a handful of change consisting of seven coins. He tosses the money into his left hand where it is heard to arrive, but when he opens that hand a moment later all but two of the coins have vanished. He shows his hands otherwise empty and allows the coins to be examined, as they are genuine.

Requirements: The trick depends on a special gimmick which is simply a group of five coins (two pennies, two nickels, and a quarter) soldered together with a hook on one of the coins, Fig. 1. This idea of fastening a group of coins together was first used by George Starke and described in *Hugard's Monthly.*

Besides this you will require a duplicate group of the same coins which are not fastened together. These are in your left

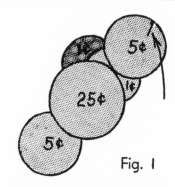

Fig. 1

trousers pocket and the gimmick is in your right trousers pocket.

Working: Thrust both hands into your pockets, finger palm the gimmick in the right hand with the hook side away from the fingers and the hook at the little finger side of the hand. Bring out both hands. In the left hand show a loose quarter, two nickels, and two pennies, with the two nickels lying on the base of the forefinger in preparation for a later move.

As you show the loose change say, "The reason I took up magic was because I learned a lesson while a boy that I never forgot—a lesson that made me decide I should smarten up a bit or be fooled again. A ticket-seller in a side show was the villain. He showed me my change and dropped it in my hand and told me to hold it tight until I got home so I wouldn't lose it. I'll show you just what happened. Here's some loose change—twenty-five, thirty-five, thirty-seven cents—I"ll need a couple more nickels to really show you." Reach into the left trousers pocket, retain the two nickels with the thumb, drop the other three coins and bring out the hand back outward. "Here, I'll arrange them just as they looked to me." Bring the left hand over the right and pretend to place a handful of coins in that hand. Place the two nickels in the right hand so one will cover the hook on the gimmick, the other lying nearby, Fig. 2.

Fig. 2

(By raising the little finger slightly there will be no danger of the hook being seen.)

Show the gimmick and the two coins in your right hand as you continue. "Twenty-five, thirty-five, forty-five, forty-seven cents. He tossed all the coins into my hand. . . ." Turn your right hand inward and over, retain the gimmick with the thumb and toss the two nickels into the left hand, Fig. 3. The clinking together of the two nickels arriving in the left hand creates an illusion, by sound, that all the coins were thrown.

Fig. 3

Close the left hand as the right drops to the side and hooks the gimmick on the trousers leg. Bring up the hand and gesture. . . . "And do you know, when I got home, all I had left was just enough to buy a small package of aspirin for the headache I had."

Open the left hand, show the two nickels and toss them onto the table. While the coins are being examined, unhook the gimmick from the trousers and drop it in your pocket.

With a little practice the trick can be done entirely surrounded. To perform it under these conditions you would hook the gimmick a little higher on the trousers—underneath the edge of the coat.

Instead of hooking the gimmick to the trousers as described it could be sleeved immediately after tossing the two nickels into the left hand. And if the gimmick enters the sleeve hook down, it will in all probability fasten itself to the inside of the sleeve where it is safe from view. However, if you intend to dispose of the gimmick by sleeving it would be best not to have a hook on it at all. Merely dispose of it in the pocket in the usual fashion later.

The Marksman

JIMMY BUFFALOE

Effect: The performer shows a half dollar and holds it in his left fist. He removes a small pistol from his pocket and extols his marksmanship. He aims the pistol at his left fist and pulls the trigger. Instead of a shot being heard a flame shoots up. The pistol turns out to be a cigarette lighter which the performer uses to light a cigarette that he previously placed between his lips. After blowing a puff of smoke toward his left hand, he opens it. Sure enough, there is the half dollar, but it has a real bullet hole through it!

Method: The working should be obvious from the above description, but here are the details. You will require one of those cigarette lighters that resembles a small pistol, a pack of cigarettes, and two half dollars. One half dollar has a hole in it.

The hole can be one that has been drilled, or, better still, one that has been made with a real bullet. Have the two coins in your right trousers pocket and the pistol-lighter in your right coat pocket.

Working: Begin the trick by casually placing a cigarette between your lips. Put your right hand in your right trousers pocket, finger palm the coin with the hole and bring out the other one, visible at the fingertips of the palm down hand. Show the good coin and casually toss it into your left hand a few times as you explain what a good shot you are. Pretend to toss the half back into your left hand but execute The Bobo Switch (page 10) and throw the one with the hole instead. The move need not be fast because the effect is better if the spectators get a flash of the coin as it is thrown into the left hand. Then close your fingers over it before they detect the hole.

Reach into your right coat pocket, leave the good coin and bring out the pistol-lighter. Hold out your left fist and take aim at it with the pistol. Caution the spectators to hold their ears because of the terrific noise the gun will make. When you pull the trigger a flame shoots up. Everyone sees that it is a lighter and laughs. Look surprised, shrug your shoulders and light your cigarette. Take a puff and blow some smoke toward your left hand. Open the hand. There is the coin, but it has a hole through it, which proves that you may not be a good marksman but you are a good magician!

The Squirting Nickel

Most magicians are familiar with the squirting nickel. It looks like a genuine coin, but is actually hollow and may be filled with water, which will squirt from a small hole near the edge, when the nickel is pressed. It will send out a fine stream for a distance of approximately six feet. Often it will hold enough for five or six squirts.

Perhaps you have one and have wondered how to use it. Following are a few suggestions.

When filling the coin, submerge it completely with the hole up. Press on it until no more air bubbles appear, whereupon you will know that it is full. It can be carried in the little match compartment within the right coat pocket without danger of leaking.

After a little experimenting, you will find you can control the stream of water so it will hit your victim in the eye, which makes a perfect weapon for use when you encounter a persistent heckler or a "wise guy" who thinks he knows all the answers and insists upon displaying his knowledge to the rest of your audience.

Indiscriminate use of the nickel is not recommended. Your friends will accept it as a funny bit of business if you present it correctly, which is *not* in a "smart-alecky" manner. But don't inflict it on strangers.

Following is an effective patter presentation: "Being a magician, my work carries me from coast to coast. Once, while playing out West, I visited a buffalo ranch and I learned something I never knew before. Most persons think the buffalo on the nickel is a regular American buffalo, but it isn't. It's a water buffalo." Then you let him have it!

Chapter XII

SHELL AND FOLDING HALF

The Shell Half

There are two types of shell half dollars. The old-style shell will only fit over a special cut down half—one that had been reduced in size and its edge remilled. The two parts are an integral part of each other and must be used together.

The expanded shell is a shell that has been stretched to fit over *any* regular half dollar. The best expanded shells are hollowed out from the head side of the coin. Since the tail side is not as deeply embossed as the head side a deeper cut can be made from that side, thus creating a shell that will cover a regular coin more completely.

Although the old style shell and cut down half are still being used, the expanded shell is by far the most popular. The reason for this is that practically every trick that can be done with the old style set can be performed with the modern expanded shell. By employing the expanded shell the magician can borrow the needed coins and secretly add the shell to one of them. At the end of the routine the shell is secretly removed and the money returned without anyone being the wiser.

The expanded shell is an ingenious device that has made possible many clever and

baffling mysteries heretofore impossible. On the following pages you will find some of best ones. All except one can be performed with the expanded shell.

The first, a simple effect, has to do mainly with the correct handling of a coin and shell and is called

Mystery with a Half Shell

Magicians who own either the expanded shell or the old style set have found it difficult to separate the two noiselessly and invisibly. Here is a simple and natural method of accomplishing this, together with an easy routine.

Display the nested shell and half on the ends of the two middle fingers of the palm up right hand, opening of the shell being up. Turn the hand inward, so its back will be toward the audience, toss the real coin into the left hand and retain the shell in the right by pressure on its edges with the first and fourth fingers, Fig. 1. Transfer the shell to the regular palm while bouncing the coin up and down in the left hand.

Pick up the half with the right hand and flip it into the air, catching it in the same hand (see The Coin Flip, page 16), then toss it into the left hand. Reach out with the right hand and produce the shell from the

Fig. 1

right hand, reach behind your left elbow and produce the shell and half as one coin.

Let it be seen clearly that you have just this one coin. Hold the coin and shell together in the right hand, as previously explained, and toss the former into the left hand. Reach behind the right knee and produce the shell and lay it beside the genuine half in the left hand as before. Explain that you need only one coin, place the shell in your pocket and continue with a trick using the single coin.

How to Make Money

Effect: The performer shows a half dollar in his right hand and tosses it into his left. He reaches underneath his left hand and produces a second half dollar. He shows these, one in each hand, and his hands are seen otherwise empty. Now, as he slides the coins across each other a few times, one half suddenly transforms itself into a quarter.

Method: Have a half dollar, with a shell covering it, and a quarter, in the right trousers pocket. Reach into the pocket with the right hand, classic palm the quarter and bring out the half dollar and shell as one coin. Keep the back of your right hand toward the spectators while revolving the half and shell between the first two fingers and thumb. As you do this, show your left hand empty on both sides.

air, keeping the faked side toward yourself. Toss it into the left hand along side the real half. Move both coins so they will rest on the first and second fingers, thumb on top, with the shell overlapping the real coin at its outer edge, Fig. 2. Pretend to remove one coin, but, as the coins are covered momentarily by the right hand, slide the shell over the half with the left thumb as the right moves away. Blow on your right hand and then open it to show the coin has vanished.

Take the shell and half as one coin in the right hand while you show your left empty on both sides. Pretend to place the nested half and shell back in the left hand but retain it palmed in the right hand. Make a tossing motion with the left hand and show the "coin" has vanished. Then, with the

Toss the half dollar into the left hand, retaining the shell in the right. (See preceding effect for method.) As soon as the half lands in the left hand, reach underneath that hand and produce the shell between the tips of the right first and second fingers. Hold the regular half in the left hand near the tips of the fingers and lay the shell on top of it so it overlaps the forward edge slightly. As these two coins are exhibited, drop the right hand to the side and allow the palmed quarter to fall onto the

Fig. 2

cupped fingers. Pick up the shell from the left hand with the right, adding the quarter underneath, Fig. 1, then display the shell balanced on the tip of the right second finger as you show the real half in the same

Fig. 1

manner in the left hand, Fig. 2. The hands are otherwise empty.

Bring the hands together, holding them about waist high, and pass the two coins over one another a few times, always moving the real half across the top of the shell from right to left, then underneath it from

Fig. 2

left to right. The real half will not nest within the shell because it contains the quarter. Show the two halves in this manner three or four times. When the shell (and quarter) are in the right hand, pass the genuine half underneath from left to right, lifting up the left side of the shell slightly so the real half will slide between it and the quarter. This action causes the shell and half to nest while the quarter slides to the right and is immediately shown in the right hand. If the right fingertips, which are underneath the shell at the time of the

above action, will slide the quarter to the right as far as it will go, it becomes a simple matter to lift the left edge of the shell for the real half to slide between it and the quarter, Figs. 3 and 4, and become nested as the right hand brings the quarter into view from underneath the right side of the half. It is important that the passing of the

Fig. 3

two coins across one another from hand to hand be done in an even tempo—not too fast, yet not too slow either. The effect is that one half dollar suddenly changes into

Fig. 4

a quarter. At the finish of this move you will be holding a quarter in your right hand and the half and shell, as one coin, in your left hand.

Place the quarter and nested half and shell on the palm of the right hand (opening of the shell up), with the quarter on top of and overlapping the half. Turn the right hand over, and as you toss the coins into the left hand, retain the shell classic palmed in the right. Show the real half and quarter in the left hand. Remove the quarter from the left hand with the right fingers and thumb and place it (and the palmed shell) in the right trousers pocket, explaining that you require only the half dollar for the next experiment.

Three Questions

DAVE COLEMAN

Effect: The magician shows a half dollar of his own and borrows another to go with it. So that there will be no doubt as to which coin is which a large X is made on the borrowed coin with a marking pencil. Then as the performer begins passing the coins across each other from hand to hand he explains that in order to get all his money back the spectator must give the same answer to three questions. Spectator is correct with his first two answers, but no matter how he answers the third question he loses. As the spectator answers the third question, his half dollar instantly transforms itself into a quarter with the original X still on it.

Requisites and Preparation: An expanded shell, a quarter, and a black china marking pencil, or crayon. Put a large X on the tail side of the quarter, nest it in the shell half and place them in the small compartment of the right coat pocket. Have the pencil in any other pocket.

Working: Borrow a half dollar, then mark a large X on its tail side with the marking pencil. Hold the coin, X side up, between the fingers and thumb of your palm up left hand as the right hand removes the shell and nested quarter from your coat pocket. Hold the shell (with the quarter hidden underneath) exactly as you hold the real half and state, "Two half dollars. The reason I marked yours is so that we will know which coin is yours and which coin is mine. We are going to play a little game. I am going to ask you three questions and no matter how ridiculous they sound you must answer, 'No, twenty-five cents.' Do you understand?" If he fails to understand thoroughly, explain further, then continue. "Remember, all you have to do to get your money back is answer, 'No,

twenty-five cents,' to each question I will ask you."

Begin passing the real half and the shell (containing the quarter) across each other from hand to hand as explained in the previous trick, as you ask, "When the collection plate is passed to you in church you always drop in a five dollar bill, don't you?" He will reply, "No, twenty-five cents." Continue the action with the coins and ask him the second question. "When you buy a present for your wife (or sweetheart) you always spend at least twenty-five dollars, don't you?" He will reply, "No, twenty-five cents." "You are doing fine. Now for the last question. When you loaned me this half dollar a few moments ago you expected to get it back, didn't you?" (Regardless of his answer, he loses.) As he sputters his answer, "No, twenty-five cents," allow his half dollar to slip into the shell (as explained in the previous trick) and bring the quarter into view, X side up. The effect is that his coin suddenly reduced itself in size with the X still on it.

Hand him the quarter saying, "Well, you didn't win, but you didn't lose either—at least not all of your money."

You won't want to use this as a method of subtly cheating your victim out of twenty-five cents, so have a second quarter with an X on it in your pocket, which you remove and hand to him a few seconds after giving him the first one. State, "That was a double cross, wasn't it? Here is another one with a cross on it."

Coin Through a Glass

Effect: The performer shows two drinking glasses and two half dollars. Holding one of the glasses horizontally in his right hand, he places the two coins just inside of the glass so that they overlap each other slightly. Then he picks up the second glass and holds it opening upward directly underneath the bottom of the upper glass. As he turns the upper glass upright the two coins slide to the bottom of the glass where one is seen to penetrate the bottom and fall into the lower glass. The coins are poured out onto the table and the glasses and coins can be examined.

Requisites and Presentation: Besides two clear, straight sided drinking glasses, you will require two half dollars and an expanded shell. At the outset the coins and shell are in the right trousers pocket and the two drinking glasses are on a cloth covered table.

Begin the mystery by placing the right hand in the pocket. Classic palm one of the halves and bring out the other half and shell as two coins at the fingertips of the palm down hand. Place the half and shell on the table a few inches apart. (Warning: Be sure that you perform this feat on a cloth covered table or a rug covered floor. Otherwise the unnatural sound of the shell will give you away.)

Pick up one of the glasses with the left hand, turn it horizontally and take it in the palm down right hand, holding it near its bottom, and with its mouth pointing to the left. Take up the real half with the left hand and place it inside the glass about an inch from the rim. Next, pick up the shell and put it inside the glass partly overlapping the real half, Fig. 1.

the half and shell to slide to the bottom. As they strike the bottom of the glass the shell slides over the half and they nest. At this instant the right hand releases its palmed half allowing it to fall into the lower glass, Fig. 2. The effect is that one half dollar penetrated the bottom of the upper glass and fell into the lower one.

Do not turn the upper glass entirely upright during the above action or the shell and half may accidently come apart.

Fig. 2

Merely tip it just enough to cause the coin and shell to slide to the bottom, then turn it back on its side. The final step is to pour the coins out onto the table. This you do by bringing the glasses down and resting their rims on the table. Tilt both slightly and the coins will slide out onto the table, Fig. 3. A certain amount of delicate han-

Fig. 1

Take the second glass from the table with the left hand and hold it upright directly below the bottom of the upper glass. Now tilt the upper glass just enough to cause

Fig. 3

dling is necessary at this point to prevent the shell from bouncing off its half dollar as they slide out of the glass onto the table.

And that is another reason the table must be cloth covered.

Place the two glasses bottom upward on the table a few inches in front of the two coins. With the right hand, pick up the nested half and shell and place them on top of the real half, then lift them from the table together and display them momentarily overlapping each other on the two

Fig. 4

middle fingers of the palm up right hand, Fig. 4. Toss the two genuine coins into the left hand and retain the shell in the right as previously described. While showing the two coins in the left hand, shift the shell in the right to classic palm position. Then take one of the halves from the left hand with the palm down right, and, as the right hand places its coin on the bottom of the glass on the right, the left hand places its coin on the bottom of the glass on the left. Coins and glasses can now be examined.

Perfected Coin Through Handkerchief

Jimmy Buffaloe

Here is a method for performing the Coin Through Handkerchief that is not only different and convincing, but so designed that it will mystify even magicians. There are no secret folds or pinches as in some versions, and the coin is clearly shown to

be in the handkerchief right up to the last moment.

Requisites and Preparation: A regular half dollar and an expanded shell (or the old style half and shell) and an opaque pocket handkerchief. The shell covered half is in one of the right pockets and the handkerchief is in any other pocket.

Working: While standing facing the spectators, remove the handkerchief, show it on both sides, then hold it by one edge with your left hand while you remove the nested half and shell (as one coin) from the pocket with the right hand. After casually showing the shell covered coin, balance it (opening of shell down) on the tip of the right second finger. Let it be clearly seen that you only have the one coin, then cover it with the handkerchief, Fig. 1.

With the left second finger and thumb, grasp the shell by its edges through the

Fig. 1

cloth and lift it up off the real coin, which remains balanced on the tip of the right second finger, Fig. 2. Under cover of the handkerchief, thumb palm the real half in the right hand and turn it palm inward as the left hand removes the handkerchief completely. Turn slightly to the left, show the handkerchief on all sides and point to it with the right hand, Fig. 3. Now change your grip on the shell so it will be upright

Fig. 2

Fig. 4

and you will be holding it by its upper edge between the tip of the forefinger (on the front) and thumb (at the rear).

Now in the action of stroking the handkerchief a couple of times, as if straightening out the wrinkles, the right hand leaves its coin behind the cloth and against the hollow side of the shell, Fig. 4. The moves for accomplishing this are as follows: Bring the right hand over and grasp the handkerchief directly below the left hand, and as you do this, the left thumb grips the real coin and retains it behind the cloth (and shell), then the right hand moves down, stroking the handkerchief.

Face the spectators again, turn the coins to a horizontal position and lay them on the ends of the two right middle fingers (with the real half against the fingers), then remove the left hand. The way the coins rest on the right fingers is important. The two coins are gripped as one, exactly the same way as you would hold a coin if you were about to back palm it. With the left hand, grasp the front corner of the handkerchief and lift it up and back on the right forearm, exposing the shell, which is right side up, Fig. 5. Be sure to keep the front edge of the shell down so the hollow underside cannot be seen. This is the convincing

Fig. 3

Fig. 5

part of the effect: The spectators actually see the coin in the center of the handkerchief. The real coin is directly underneath the cloth and shell and cannot be seen.

While exhibiting the shell in this manner obtain a little extra slack in the handkerchief at the rear of the shell. The reason for this will be obvious in just a moment. The left hand, still gripping the corner of the handkerchief, returns it to its original position, but as it passes downward in front of the shell, the right thumb kicks it off and it is caught in the curled left fingers, Fig. 6, the action being hidden by the folds of the handkerchief. The left hand im-

Fig. 6

mediately grasps the handkerchief near the corners and pulls downward. The form of the real coin under the center folds of the cloth, is presumed by the spectators to be the same one they saw only a brief moment before.

Now as the left hand pulls gently downward on the handkerchief, the real coin comes into view, having apparently penetrated the cloth. The shell, which has been in finger palm position in the left hand, is shifted to classic palm position as the right hand tosses the real coin onto the table. The handkerchief is then taken by a corner in each hand and spread out to show it undamaged. Return handkerchief and palmed shell to pocket.

25¢ and 50¢ Transposition

DR. CARL L. MOORE

Effect: After showing a half dollar and a quarter, the performer holds the large coin in his left hand and the small coin in his right. He slowly closes his hands on the two coins and holds them some distance apart. A spectator is asked to guess which hand holds the quarter. No matter which hand he guesses, the performer shows that hand to contain the half dollar. Now the performer pretends to transpose the coins several times, each time showing that the half dollar has changed places with the quarter. Finally he opens both hands, showing a half dollar in each hand. The quarter has vanished.

To climax the mystery he causes one of the half dollars to change back to a quarter.

Requisites and Preparation: A regular half dollar and an expanded shell (or the old style shell and cut down half), and a quarter. Have the shell covered half and the quarter in the right trousers pocket.

Working: Remove the coins from the pocket with the right hand and display them lying near the ends of the two middle fingers. The shell covering the half is opening up and the quarter is overlapping it, Fig. 1.

Turn the right hand inward and over, toss the real coins into the palm up left

Fig. 1

hand and retain the shell in front finger hold as previously described. Call attention to the two coins in the left hand and name them. With the palm down right hand, pick up the quarter between the tips of the fingers and thumb, then move the half dollar to the tips of the left fingers and display them as in Fig. 2. Note that the quarter

Fig. 2

slightly overlaps the top edge of the shell in the right hand.

Remind the spectators that the half dollar is in the left hand and the quarter is in the right hand as you slowly pull the coins down behind the fingers and close the hands. As the right thumb pulls the quarter down behind the right fingers it goes into the shell, then the fingers close onto the palm and the shell turns right side up, covering the quarter. Lower the fists to about waist level and hold them fingers uppermost and about a foot apart.

Ask a spectator to guess in which hand you hold the quarter. If he guesses the right hand, say that he is wrong as you open it and show a half (shell covering the quarter). If he names the left hand, call him wrong by opening the left hand and showing the real half dollar there.

Tell the spectators that you can cause the half and quarter to transpose at will. Shake your two fists, open the right and show a half (shell) there. Close the hand,

shake the fists again, then open the left one and show a half (real) there. Continue this a time or two, then state that the reason you can show a half dollar in either hand is that you have two half dollars. Open both hands and show the real half in the left hand and the shell half (covering the quarter) in the right hand.

Now to bring the trick to a logical climax you change one of the halves back to a quarter using the moves described in How to Make Money (page 266).

The Peregrinating Halves

Reprinted through the courtesy of
The Bat

Effect: Four borrowed half dollars are made to travel one at a time from the left hand to the right in the fairest possible manner.

Method: Again that clever magical accessory, the expanded shell, is responsible for most of the trickery. Although you may provide the necessary coins yourself, the effect of the mystery will be increased considerably if you use borrowed money. Have the shell in the right trousers pocket and some loose change (but no halves) in the left trousers pocket. Begin the trick by thrusting both hands into the trousers pockets and remarking that you need four half dollars for your next experiment. Palm the shell (hollow side against the palm) in the right hand as it is removed and bring the loose change from the left pocket with the left hand.

Exhibit the odd coins in the left hand, going over them with the fingers of the right as if looking for some half dollars. This natural gesture happens almost every time you remove some change from your pocket. Upon not finding any half dollars, return the loose change to the left pocket and ask for the loan of four half dollars.

When these are received, place them in the left hand, then with the right fingers, spread them out in an overlapping row, saying, "Four half dollars."

Tilt the left hand downward, which causes the coins to slide forward into a stack, but make sure that the topmost coin is tails up. (Assuming the shell has a tail-side, otherwise the topmost coin should be heads up.) As this is done, drop the right hand to the side, release the shell from the palm, catch it on the curled fingers and

Fig. 1

grip it (opening away from the fingers) by its edges between the tips of the first and fourth fingers (Front Finger Hold).

Pick up the stack of coins from the left hand with the right, adding the shell to the top coin in the process, Fig. 1. Turn the right hand palm up and spread out the coins in a fan, Fig. 2. The half with the

Fig. 2

shell becomes the bottom one in this action.

Show the left hand empty back and front, then count the coins back into that hand one at a time, the one with the shell going in last and becoming the topmost coin. Show the right hand empty on both sides, then count the coins back into that hand. At the completion of this count the shell covered coin will be on the bottom. Show the left hand empty once more, then proceed to count the coins back into that hand in the following manner: With the right thumb, push the top half forward from the stack and place it in the left hand, counting "One." Count "Two" and "Three" as you place the second and third coin in the left hand in the same manner. Finally, show the last coin lying on the fingers of the right hand and apparently place it into the left hand also as you count, "Four." Actually the shell is placed in the left hand and the coin is retained finger palmed in the right hand.

Here is the basic move on which the trick depends. It is used three times and is the most important sleight in the entire

Fig. 3

routine. The shell covered coin lies on the second and third fingers between the first and second joints. The right thumb lies along the inner edge of the shell and coin, Fig. 3. The thumb and forefinger press together and lift the shell up away from the coin, Fig. 4, as the other fingers curl inward carrying the coin to finger palm posi-

Fig. 4

Fig. 5

the right. Open the left hand to show three coins (shell covers top coin), and toss the coin from the right hand onto the table.

Count the three coins from the left hand into the right as first described, then count them back, retaining the genuine half in the right hand as the shell is placed in the left. (Basic move.)

Pick up the coin from the table with the right hand, calling attention to the one

Fig. 6

tion. The right hand turns slightly inward during this action, to cover the coin while the thumb lifts the inner edge of the shell so that only its top side is seen by the spectators. Fig. 5 shows the right hand holding the shell, as viewed by the spectators. Figs.

3, 4 and 5 depict the moves made by the right hand with the shell in the action of moving to the left and depositing the shell with the three genuine coins in the left hand. It is important that the coins be counted with the same tempo each time, then the last count will appear perfectly legitimate.

Place the shell in the left hand so it will overlap the forward coin, Fig. 6. As the coins are thus exhibited transfer the coin in the right hand from finger palm to classic palm position. Close the left hand, allowing the shell to slide over the topmost coin. Close the right hand and hold it a foot or so from the left, then make a small tossing motion with the left hand toward

coin, there, being careful that the one in the palm is not seen. Show the three coins on the open left hand (actually two coins and the shell), then close the hand so that the shell will slide over the coin underneath it. Go through the motions of causing the next coin to pass. Jingle the two coins in the right hand and toss them onto the table as the left hand opens to show only two coins remaining. (The shell covers the top one.) Make as much noise as possible with the coins in the right hand each time they are tossed onto the table. This gets attention away from the coins in the left hand and shows without saying that the coins are genuine. They are, aren't they? You borrowed them!

Count the two coins from the left hand into the right, then show the left hand empty. Right hand counts them back, retaining the real half dollar and placing the shell into the left hand in its place. (Basic move.) Pick up the two coins from the table with the right hand and exhibit the two in the left as you say, "Two and two." Close the left hand, allowing the shell to slide over the one half dollar. Close the right hand over its two coins so they will lie on the cupped fingers directly below the third one in the palm. Make a tossing motion with the left hand toward the right. An instant later release the coin in the right palm, permitting it to drop audibly onto the other two, then toss all three onto the table. Open the left hand showing a single coin which has the shell over it. Place the shell covered coin in the right hand and show the left hand empty.

Apparently place the last coin, which is covered by the shell, back into the left hand, actually palm it in the right with the opening of the shell *away* from the palm. (Simple Vanish, page 23, is a good method.) The reason for this will be evident later.

Take up the three coins from the table with the right hand and hold them on the cupped fingers. Repeat the tossing motion with the left fist toward the right and release the coin from the shell in the right palm so it will clatter down onto the three resting on the cupped fingers. At first it will seem difficult to release the coin and retain the shell from the right palm, but the knack can be acquired easily with a little practice. The muscles of the palm simply relax just enough for the coin, which is heavier than the shell, to be released and drop down onto the other three coins. Keeping the right hand palm down, toss all four coins onto the table, then slowly open the left and show it empty.

Pick up the four coins and start to put them into your pocket, disposing of the shell in the pocket, then suddenly remember that the coins are not yours. Return them to their owners.

If you wish, you may simply gather up

the coins from the table and return them while concealing the shell in the right palm. There is no reason for anyone to suspect that you used anything but the four coins. The shell can be dropped into the pocket a few moments later.

And you need not use borrowed coins. If you use your own you can have the shell already on one of the coins, or add it later in the fashion as first described with borrowed coins.

If there is a cleaner, or more baffling method for causing a number of coins to pass from one hand to the other I have not seen it.

Coins Through the Table

Milton Kort

Effect: The performer borrows four coins, places them on the table and covers them with a whiskey glass. He shows his left hand empty and holds it underneath the table. One coin is then caused to penetrate the table and pass into his left hand. Two more coins pass through the table into the performer's hand in the same manner. The last one is made to penetrate the table and pass into a spectator's hand.

Requisites and Preparation: A small, transparent whiskey glass, four half dollars (which may be your own or borrowed) and an expanded shell.

Working: Seat yourself at the table and secretly adjust your pants leg as described in The Magical Filtration of Four Half Dollars (page 193), in preparation for dropping coins into the lap.

If you use your own coins have the shell already on the top one of the stack. If you wish to use the spectators' coins you can secretly add the shell as described in the preceding trick. In either event, show the four halves in the right hand (shell covering the top one), then count them one at a time onto the left fingers, reversing their order so the shell covered half becomes the bottom one. With the left fingers underneath, and thumb on top, spread out the coins in a fan, Fig. 1 and show the two hands otherwise empty.

Fig. 1

With the right forefinger and thumb, remove the shell covered coin and place it on the table before you, not more than three inches from the edge of the table. Take the remaining three coins one at a time and place them on the table in a vertical row so each will overlap the other, Fig. 2.

Fig. 2

Now square up the coins in the following manner: Hold both hands palm down, place the tips of the thumbs against opposite edges of the inner shell covered coin and the tips of the middle fingers against opposite edges of the outer coin. Bring the thumb and fingers together, squaring the coins into a stack, then show both hands empty.

With the palm down right hand, grasp

Fig. 3

the stack of coins by its edges between the thumb at the inner edges, and the fingers at the outer edges, slide it off the table toward yourself and place it in the palm up left hand. As the stack of coins slides off the table the bottom coin drops out of the shell, Fig. 3, into the lap. After placing the three coins and shell in the left hand, tilt that hand downward just enough for the coins to slide forward, and they are exhibited in an overlapping row as four coins, Fig. 4.

Fig. 4

Remove the three coins with the right hand one at a time and place them back on the table overlapping each other as before. Then take the shell from the left hand and place it on the table slightly overlapping the forward coin. Show your left hand empty, and as you move it underneath the table, pick up the coin from your lap. Before completing this action pick up the

Fig. 5

glass with the right hand. Show it freely, inside and out. Then with the aid of the glass, which is held upside down, slide the shell and coins toward yourself, Fig. 5, into a stack, then cover the stack with the glass, Fig. 6. This action causes the shell to cover the top coin. Immediately bring up the left hand and toss its coin onto the table. Lift the glass and spread out the coins, showing

Fig. 6

three (shell covers one). One coin has apparently penetrated the table and passed into the left hand.

Slide the shell covered coin off the table with the right hand and place it on the fingers of the left hand. Slide off the other two and place them in the left hand on top of the shell covered coin. Spread the coins in a fan and show the hands otherwise empty, as before.

Take the shell covered coin and place it on the table before you, then put the other two on top so they overlap forward. Square

the coins in the same manner as you did before, then grasp the stack with the right fingers and thumb (as previously described) and repeat the preceding moves of drawing it off the table and placing it back into the left hand. As this is done the bottom coin drops out of the shell into the lap. Show the two coins and the shell as three coins in the left hand. Return them to the table so the shell will go down last and occupy the outer position of the row. With the left hand, pick up the coin that apparently penetrated the table and as you carry it underneath the table, pick up the other coin from the lap. Take up the glass with the right hand, scoop the two coins and shell into a stack and cover them as before. Once again the shell slides over and hides the top coin. Let the two coins in the left hand clink together, then bring them up and toss them onto the table to the left. Lift the glass, spread and show two coins (one covered by shell).

Repeat the above moves for passing the third coin through the table into the left hand. At the completion of this action you will have one shell covered coin before you on the table and the other three (which passed through the table) will be lying a few inches to the left.

Ask a spectator, who is sitting across the table from you, to hold out his right hand. When he has complied, pick up the three regular coins and place them in a stack on the palm of his hand, counting them as you do so. Ask him if he would like to see the fourth coin pass visibly into his hand. After he replies that he would, take up the shell covered coin and add it to the stack of three already in his hand. Remark that since that was a poor trick you will do it again, only next time you will do it by magic.

With your right fingers and thumb, lift off the shell, and as you do so have him close his hand over the coins. Assist him with the closing of his hand with your left hand. He thinks he is holding only three coins. Actually he is still holding four. Have him place his hand beneath the center of the table. Show the shell and lay it on the table in front of you. Pretend to draw it off with the right hand, but let it fall in your lap. Move your closed right hand to the center of the table, holding it back uppermost. Open it suddenly, bring it down flat on the table, then turn it over and show it empty. Have the spectator bring up his hand and open it. Lo and behold, he is holding four coins! Apparently the last coin passed through the table into his hand!

Instead of sliding the shell off the table into the lap you can show it in your right hand, pretend to place it in the left, but retain it palmed in the right. Then the left fist is brought to the center of the table and the trick finished as described.

The Protean Coin

MILTON KORT

Effect: A silver coin changes to copper, then back to silver. After repeating this several times, the performer shows the coin to be an ordinary one and his hands empty.

Requisites and Preparation: An expanded shell, a gimmicked coin which shows silver on one side and copper on the other, and a regular half dollar. The genuine coin is in the small match compartment of the right coat pocket and the shell covers the copper side of the gimmicked coin so it resembles a regular half dollar.

Working: Hold the shell covered gimmicked coin (shell side up) between the tips of the right forefinger and thumb and casually show it on both sides without comment. Rest the coin (shell side up) on the right two middle fingers, between the outer first and second joints. Turn slightly to the

Fig. 1

left, then, using the moves described in The Peregrinating Halves (page 273), retain the coin in the right hand and deposit the shell (good side out) between the tips of the left forefinger and thumb. Hold the hand about shoulder high and display the shell as in Fig. 1.

While displaying the shell as a half dollar with the left hand, shift the gimmicked coin in the right hand to finger palm position, holding it copper side against the fingers. Now raise the right hand, bring it over and hold it momentarily in front of the shell. Under cover of the right hand, drop the shell to the base of the left fingers, where it is held finger palmed (good side against the fingers), then take the gimmicked coin with the left forefinger and thumb from the right hand and hold it exactly as you did the shell. Next, draw the right hand to the right, revealing a copper instead of a silver coin, then show the right hand empty, Figs. 2, 3 and 4. The covering of the coin with the right hand and its subsequent removal should be done unhesitatingly—not too fast, not too slow. To the spectators it should appear that you merely passed your hand over the coin and it changed to copper.

Turn slightly to the right, take the fake coin between the tips of the right forefinger and thumb and display it copper side out.

Fig. 2

Fig. 3

Fig. 4

right forefinger and thumb from the left hand. Draw the left hand away, revealing the shell, and show the left hand empty. Apparently the copper coin turned back to silver.

Take the shell back in the left hand and hold it as before. The right hand, with the gimmicked coin finger palmed, is brought up and passed in front of the shell, but this time the right hand thumb palms the shell, Fig. 5, then the left forefinger takes the coin from the right finger palm, Fig. 6, and

Fig. 5

displays it as a copper coin while the right hand moves away to the right, Fig. 7. The coin has seemingly returned to copper.

Fig. 6

You are now holding the coin in the right hand exactly as you held the shell in the left. Bring up the left hand, and as you pass it in front of the coin you repeat the same series of moves you made a moment ago with the shell. That is, you drop the coin to the base of the right fingers, where it is held finger palmed (copper side against the fingers), then take the shell with the

While showing the copper side of the gimmicked coin in the left hand, drop the right hand to the side and shift the shell to finger palm position, where it is held good side against the fingers. Pass your right

Fig. 7

or classic palm position. Bring the right hand up and push the gimmicked coin from the left palm onto the fingers as you offer to repeat the trick without the use of the right hand. And to convince them that the right plays no part in the trick you will place it in your pocket. Put the right hand in the pocket. While it reposes there leave the shell in the main pocket and remove the regular half dollar from the match compartment and hold it classic palmed. Close the left hand, which action causes the gimmicked coin to turn over, copper side up.

Fig. 8

hand in front of the coin in the left hand as before, but this time add the shell to the front of the coin. Move the right hand away, but do not show it empty yet. Lower the left hand, show both sides of the shell covered coin (the shell covers the copper side of it making it appear to be silver) and the hand, then slowly turn the right hand palm outward and show it empty. Apparently the coin has returned to its original state—silver.

After showing clearly that your hands are empty except for the shell covered coin, rest coin and shell near the ends of the two middle fingers of the palm up right hand, opening of shell up. Turn the right hand over and inward, toss the coin onto the fingers of the left hand (which immediately closes) and retain the shell by pressure on its edges with the first and fourth fingers. (See Fig. 1, Mystery with a Half Shell!, page 266.) As the coin is thrown from the right hand to the left it lands copper side up on the fingers, but when the fingers close the coin turns silver side up onto the palm. Immediately open the left hand, showing the silver side of the coin. The spectators believe you were about to cause another change and are usually surprised when you show that nothing has happened. While showing the coin in the left hand, drop the right to the side and shift the shell to finger

A much less obvious method for causing the gimmicked coin to turn over in the left hand is as follows: Allow the coin to rest (silver side up) on the left hand at a position slightly left and inward from the exact center of the palm. (Fig. 8 shows the approximate position.) Partly close the fingers and bend the thumb inward (toward the palm) from the wrist joint. This raises the coin to a vertical position, Fig. 9. While completing the closing of the fingers, allow the coin to flop over, then return the thumb to its normal position. Now, if you should open your hand the coin would be lying copper side up near the base of the third and fourth fingers, but to get the coin as near to the center of the palm as possible, shake the fist up and down a time or two before you open it, which action causes

Fig. 9

coin to bounce back to the center of the palm.

Remove the right hand from the pocket (with the real half dollar classic palmed), snap the fingers over the left fist, then open it to show that the coin has seemingly changed back to copper.

To change the copper (gimmicked) coin back to silver, utilize the sleeving move called Devaluation (page 117), except you do not make the change from the back of the left hand, but from the palm. At the completion of this move you will be holding the real silver coin in the palm up left hand, while the gimmicked coin will be safely up the right sleeve. The coin can now be examined and your hands shown empty.

Although quite a few words have been necessary to describe the series of changes, they should take only about a minute to perform. Each change blends into the next one so quickly and smoothly it is impossible for the spectators to follow them. After the final change there is no clue to the mystery and the onlookers should be completely dazzled.

The Sympathetic Coins
MILTON KORT

Although this version of The Sympathetic Coins is similiar in effect to the standard one described on page 197, it differs slightly in two respects. First, only one piece of paper is required to cover the coins and, second, one of the four coins is copper. Because of these differences the trick is particularly puzzling to those who might know something about the standard method.

Requisites and Preparation: A pocket handkerchief, an expanded shell, two half dollars, one English penny, a gimmicked coin which shows copper on one side and silver on the other, and a piece of stiff paper (or thin cardboard) about four inches square.

Stack the coins and shell as follows: On top of the two half dollars place the English penny, then the gimmicked coin (copper side down), then the shell over the gimmicked coin. Have the coins in this order in one of your right pockets.

Working: Stand behind a table, show the piece of paper freely and place it aside. Show the handkerchief next and spread it on the table. Remove the stack of coins from the pocket with the right hand, spread them in a fan to show that you have three silver coins and one copper coin, Fig. 1.

Fig. 1

State that you should have four half dollars but you will attempt the feat with what you have.

Square the coins and hold them between the tips of the fingers and thumb of the palm down right hand, Fig. 2. The coins should still be in their original order: shell covered gimmicked coin (copper side down)

Fig. 2

is on top, then the English penny, then the two half dollars. Place the four coins on the center of the handkerchief and secretly lift off the shell, Fig. 3, and finger palm it

Fig. 3

(good side against the fingers) as the hand moves away. Pick up the square of paper with the left hand, and while you are showing it on both sides, drop the right hand to the side and allow the shell to turn over and lie hollow side against the fingers, then place the paper in the right hand over the shell, Fig. 4. Now with the left forefinger, slide the top (gimmicked) coin to the right inner corner of the handkerchief. Next, move the copper coin to the outer right corner and finally, the two regular half

Fig. 4

dollars to the inner and outer left corners, respectively, Fig. 5.

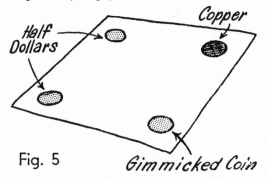

Half Dollars

Copper

Gimmicked Coin

Fig. 5

Take the paper and shell with the left hand, between the fingers underneath and thumb on top, place it over the coin at the outer left corner, releasing the shell at the same time. Be careful that the shell does not strike the coin as you do this, Fig. 6.

The most difficult part of the trick is now over, but the spectators think the trick hasn't begun. Pick up the real half dollar

Fig. 6

from the inner left corner of the handkerchief with your right hand, then lift the corner of the handkerchief with your left hand, *the fingers well underneath and thumb above.* Show the coin plainly, then place it underneath the handkerchief and push it forward toward the outer left corner. This is what you pretend to do. In reality, you place the coin between the tips of your left first and second fingers (Back Finger Clip) the moment the right hand is out of sight, then without hesitation, move the right hand forward to the outer left corner. Explain to the spectators that you are passing the coin through the handkerchief to join the other one underneath the paper.

Remove the right hand from beneath the handkerchief, show it empty, then lift the paper, showing two coins (real half dollar and shell). Without pausing, bring the paper back to the inner left corner, release that corner and take the paper from your right hand with your left. Properly done, it is impossible to get even the smallest flash of the coin between the left fingers because the paper is placed under the left thumb *before* the fingers are removed from beneath the corner of the handkerchief. The two coins are uncovered and the paper placed in the left hand in one continuous move.

The instant the left hand takes the paper from the right, that hand moves up and pushes the shell along side of the real half, which makes room for the second coin which will be added in just a moment. Now place the paper with its coin hidden underneath, back over the shell and real coin, making two real coins and a shell underneath the paper.

Repeat the above movements with the gimmicked coin from the inner right corner, then raise the paper and show three silver coins (two real halves and a shell). As the paper is returned, the fourth (gimmicked) coin is added, copper side up.

At this point the spectators are convinced that there are only three coins under the paper. Actually there are the two halves, the shell and the gimmicked coin, making four in all. Now take the real copper coin from the outer right corner of the handkerchief and repeat the previous moves for causing it to apparently pass underneath the paper. When you lift the paper the spectators will see three silver coins and a copper coin (actually two halves, shell and the gimmicked coin, copper side up).

At the completion of these moves you will be holding the paper in your left hand with the real copper coin clipped between the first and second fingers as in the previous moves. Take the paper and coin in the right hand, so the coin will lie on the fingers underneath the paper. This is done to free the left hand, which then touches and counts the four coins on the outer left corner of the handkerchief.

The copper coin, which is hidden underneath the paper, is in perfect position for the clean up move which follows. With the left hand, pick up the coins from the handkerchief and place them in an overlapping row on the paper in the following order: Gimmicked coin, shell, then the two halves. The English penny is still lying on the right fingers underneath the paper, Fig. 7.

Hold the palm up left hand under the left edge of the paper, then tilt the paper so the coins will slide off into that hand,

Fig. 7

Fig. 8

Fig. 8. As they slide off into the left hand the shell covers the copper side of the gimmicked coin, causing it to appear as silver, and the English penny, which was underneath the paper, becomes the bottom coin. Toss the paper aside, spread the coins in a fan and show them on both sides, which you can now safely do because the shell covers the copper coin and the coins are in the same order as they were on the paper. Apparently you have four regular coins, three silver and one copper.

The Modern Miser

Here is a practical, easy-to-do method for producing several coins. The effect is clean cut and there are several surprises in the routine to upset the theories of your viewers.

Effect: The magician reaches behind a spectator's lapel and extracts a half dollar. He tosses the coin into his left hand, plucks a second from the spectator's ear and drops it along side the first. He shows his hands unmistakably empty with the exception of the two coins, and immediately produces a third piece of silver from the spectator's lapel. He shows his right hand empty once more and pulls a fourth coin from the man's tie. To climax the routine a final coin is taken from his own trousers cuff.

Requisites and Preparation: An expanded shell, three regular half dollars, and a hook coin. In lieu of the expanded shell you can use the old style cut down coin and shell. In this case you would need only two regular half dollars and the hook coin. Regardless of which you use, have the shell covered coin and the hook coin in your right trousers pocket, one of the half dollars in the left trousers pocket, and one in the left trousers cuff.

A further preparation must be made before you begin. You must finger palm the shell covered coin and the hook coin in your right hand as follows: The shell covered coin lies against the fingers (opening of the shell away from fingers). On top of this is the hook coin, hook side out. After securing the coins from the right trousers pocket the left hand removes the coin from the left pocket, reaches under the right side of the coat and drops the coin into the top opening of the coat sleeve under the pretext of pulling back the shirt sleeve. Keep the right arm crooked at the elbow so the coin will not fall out. It only takes a moment to make this preparation and it is done at an opportune moment when attention is elsewhere.

Working: Begin the production by suddenly reaching behind a spectator's coat lapel. Produce the shell set and leave the hook coin fastened behind the lapel flap. Show the shell set as one coin and allow it to rest on the two middle fingers of the right hand near their tips. Turn the hand inward and over, toss the half dollar into the left hand and retain the shell by pressure on its opposite edges with the first and fourth fingers after the fashion described in Mystery with a Half Shell (page 265).

Without too much delay, reach out again with the right hand and produce the shell from the spectator's right ear, making a remark about it being a cash ear (cashier).

Show it as a genuine half dollar and drop it alongside the first coin in the left hand. Let it be seen that you have only the two coins. Very slowly exhibit your right hand empty, back and front, then produce the hook coin from the spectator's lapel. Lay this coin, hook side down, in the left hand with the other two.

Again show the right hand empty. Drop the hand to the side and retrieve the sleeved coin as you direct attention to the three coins in your left hand. Back palm the coin, then slowly move the hand out, palm upward (so the spectators can see your empty palm), and extract that coin from beneath the man's tie, using the method described in Producing a Coin from a Spectator's Clothing (page 19). Drop this coin into the left hand with the other three, show the right hand empty and take the final coin from your own trousers cuff. Place it with the others, making quite an array of money to have produced from apparently empty hands. Pocket the coins or retain a genuine one or two for your next trick and put the gimmicked coins away.

The Folding Half*

One trick that always creates a sensation and is remembered long after it is shown, is the Half Dollar in the Bottle. Practically every close-up performer has performed it at one time or another. Numerous magicians have featured it in their platform shows. Blackstone thought enough of it to use it in his elaborate theatre show a few years ago. Almost every magician has his own pet routine, so the standard version will not be dealt with here. Instead, I would like to present two of the best and most practical routines that I know of. Here they are:

---

* EDITOR'S NOTE: The folding coin was described in *More Magic* (1890), but its usefulness was not fully realized in that day.

The Half Dollar in the Bottle

RALPH DE SHONG, courtesy *The Bat*

Ralph says he prefers a Coca Cola bottle for this routine because they can usually be found almost anywhere. Their slight color and fluting help conceal the gimmicked half. You can carry your own bottle or borrow one. Be sure the bottle is clean.

The bottle is given to a spectator while you borrow a half dollar. When this is received, the spectator with the bottle is requested to bring it to you. You ask, "You have examined this bottle and find it to be an ordinary Coca Cola bottle? You see holes in the bottle, do you?"

If he answers "No," say, "Well, here is one," pointing to the neck of the bottle. If he answers "Yes," and points to the neck of the bottle, say, "No, that's an opening, I mean, did you find a *hole?*"

The borrowed half is held up as you ask, "Who gave me this half dollar?" As the spectator holds up his hand and replies, start to pocket same, but stop and add, "Oh, you only loaned it to me, didn't you?" This is an old gag, but it is still good.

Half is handed to spectator assistant as bottle is taken from him. He stands to *your* left. "Will you please examine this gentleman's half dollar? Do you find anything wrong with it? Are there any holes in the half?" As he examines the coin you continue, "What is the best test for a piece of silver money? That's right, the teller would drop it on the marble counter, wouldn't he? O.K., then you drop it on the floor and let's see how it rings."

While talking, your left hand moves in a casual manner to your left side coat pocket where you have the folding half. As your assistant drops the borrowed half to the floor, all eyes are on him and the coin. Bottle is in your right hand, the folding half taken from the pocket is inserted in the bottle neck, just barely in the top, as the good half hits the floor. This is perfect misdirection and gets over the one weak point in the trick—the insertion of the gimmicked coin in the bottle neck.

Pick up the borrowed half with your right hand as left hand holds bottle around the neck with bottle pointing horizontally to the right. Then say to your helper, "I want you to hold this bottle with your *left* hand, just as I do." Your left hand around the neck hides the folded half and his right hand replacing yours does the same. Your right hand, although holding the borrowed half, assists in the transfer of the bottle from your hands to his.

He is now holding bottle by the neck in his left hand, with the bottom of the bottle pointing toward you as you stand to his right. Hold borrowed half with left fingertips and thumb for audience to see. You apparently transfer the half to the right hand, but palm it in the left which is placed on the back of assistant's shoulder. Ask him to hold the bottle firmly as you expect to slap the bottle at the count of three. You then count to three, slapping bottle on the bottom with the right palm, opening the right hand quickly as it strikes the bottle. This slap causes the half to jump from the neck and appear unfolded inside the body of the bottle.

You now say to your assistant, "Will you kindly tell the audience what you see in the bottle? The spectator is often so dumbfounded that he cannot say a word, and that adds to the interest created. Remember, he has actually seen the half enter the bottom of the bottle! Allow him to look at it rather freely and do some rattling of the half as it is in the bottle. Now thank him and permit him to return to his seat as you continue to rattle the coin in the bottle. This little gag goes nicely here: "At this

stage of the experiment, I always match coins with the owner of the half dollar to see whether I get his half, or he gets my coke bottle—(look at him)—oh, you don't want to do that, eh? Well, we'll try to get it out for you then!"

During this by-play you have transferred the borrowed half from your left to your right palm, then let the bottom of the bottle rest on the half there. You advance to the owner of the half dollar, stopping along the path to show various spectators that the half is in the bottle. Hold the bottom of the bottle with your right hand and the top in the left, horizontally, and do a lot of rattling around of the gimmicked coin in the bottle. As you approach the owner of the half dollar, shoot the folded half out into your left hand with a quick jerk. Remember, the borrowed half is at the bottom of the bottle on your right palm. You will find that you can now rattle this good half against the bottom of the bottle, so that it sounds like it was in the bottle, by holding the bottle horizontally with both hands, cupping the right palm to give coin room to rattle around. This is one of the best parts of the trick. You ask the owner of the half to hold both hands cupped under the bottle and while rattling the half against the bottom of the bottle let it drop into his two hands. Next, set the bottle down on his outstretched hands on top of the half you have returned to him and say, "Sit there and try a while to get the half back in the bottle. If you succeed, you, too, will be a magician!"

Please note that both the entrance of the folding half into the bottle and the removal are covered by natural actions. Never let them suspect that the neck of the bottle has anything to do with the trick. The owner will invariably turn the bottle bottom up and examine it, for he (like the first spectator) will swear he *actually* saw the half drop out of the bottom of the bottle.

Folding coins tarnish because of the sulphur in the rubber. Use Wright's Silver Cream to polish. When you have reassembled the folding coin put some of this thick cream in the slot on top of the rubber. This hides the slot, is easy to do, and it will dry a near silver color.

Check rubber before each performance and renew often. Clean out the slot with a strong thread to remove broken particles of the rubber, etc.

Magic dealers can supply the proper size rubber bands for the folding half, but here is an idea of Rolland Hamblen's which I have found just as good as using the proper size band. Use any size that is handy. Begin by cutting the band, making one long piece. Wrap the band tightly around the pieces as you assemble them, letting about half an inch overlap the other end. Trim off two ends with a razor blade and finish off coin as described above. You will find, in most instances, a folding coin prepared in this manner can be used for a longer period of time before breakage of the rubber.

Second Method

STEWART JUDAH

Requisites and Preparation: A folding half dollar, a regular half dollar, a Coca Cola or pop bottle and a piece of fairly heavy paper approximately five inches square.

Have the two coins in the right trousers pocket. The paper already creased for The Coin Fold vanish (see page 61), and the bottle, are nearby.

Presentation: Reach into the right trousers pocket, come out with the folding half. Spin it in the air and catch it, toss it from hand to hand, and finally hold it daintily at the tips of the fingers. This shows with-

out saying so that you have but ONE coin.

Explain that under certain atmospheric conditions the coin actually becomes soft enough to bend. Now use the old bending watch move (*Modern Magic*) and seem to bend the coin. *Do not* bend the half at the folds, but hold it so the folds are across the coin—parallel with the floor.

After the bending demonstration, show the coin full face. Explain that you can bend it so small it will go into that bottle (point to the bottle). Actually fold the coin, but behind the fingers so the audience cannot see it. Pick up the bottle with the other hand and insert the folded coin, hit the bottle on the neck, and the coin opens out inside.

Exhibit the bottle so they can see that the coin is actually inside it. Pass the bottle from hand to hand, being sure the spectators see that your hands are otherwise empty.

Explain that if you can put the coin in the bottle, you can also remove it. Hold the bottle in your left hand, shake the coin out into your right hand, then exhibit it flat on the palm. Set the bottle down, toss up coin and spin it in the air, toss it from hand to hand, spin it again.

Say "Under certain conditions the coin will actually dematerialize completely." Wrap the coin in the coin fold paper, bang it on the table or on the bottle, holding the parcel in the right hand, and turn the hand around so the spectators can see the inside of the hand. (The coin is right at the edge of the paper, held in place by the right thumb, and would drop into the palm if grip were relaxed slightly.) Now turn the back of the hand to the audience and allow coin to slip from the folds of the paper into finger palm position. Tear the packet to pieces and toss pieces into the air so they flutter to the floor. Say "However, it doesn't go very far," and reach into right trousers pocket, leave the folding half and come out the the real half, explaining "It's still somewhat soft," and again go through the previous bending moves to demonstrate that it IS soft. "But as soon as the air chills it, the metal goes back to normal"—and with this, slap coin onto the table and hand it for examination.

The Magic Mint

Effect: A nickel, held between the forefinger and thumb of the right hand, is actually placed into the left hand after the spectators have satisfied themselves that the hands are otherwise empty. Following a couple of mystic passes, the left hand is slowly opened and, in addition to the nickel, there is also a half dollar. The half is placed in the pocket, while the nickel is retained. The nickel is taken in the left hand and allowed to become warm, then slapped into the right hand where it is seen to have expanded to a half dollar. The five cent piece is gone.

The two parts of the routine can be used as an entity or as separate items. The author has employed it for years to fool magicians.

Requirements: A genuine half dollar, a folding half and a nickel. Although magicians are quite familiar with the folding half, no one has ever suspected its use in this trick, so subtly is it utilized.

Preparation: Place the real half dollar in the right sleeve, allowing it to slip up to about the elbow. Bend the folding half and hold it concealed, partly behind the nickel and partly under the right thumb. The nickel is held between the right thumb and forefinger, Fig. 1.

Working: Let the hands be seen otherwise empty. Show the front and back of your left hand and place the nickel in its palm, still retaining hold with the right thumb and forefinger, Fig. 2.

Fig. 1

Slowly close the left fingers over the coin, removing the right thumb first and then the forefinger, letting it be clearly seen that you take nothing away from the left hand.

Fig. 2

Remark about everybody being interested in money and ways to make it. Tell spectator you will show him how to make his money increase tenfold. Slowly open your left hand, allowing the half to unfold as this is done. The nickel will be on top of the half dollar. Bounce the hand up and down a little, letting the coins jingle together. Say "You see my money has multiplied and I still have my original investment. This is the profit (point to the half), so I'll put it in the bank." While saying this, show the folding half and drop it in your pocket, permitting it to be seen that it really goes into the pocket and that nothing is removed in the process.

Toss the nickel back and forth between

the hands, making sure the spectator sees that this is the only coin you have at this point. The real half is still up the right sleeve. Hold the five cent piece horizontally by its edges between the right forefinger and thumb. Turn the left hand palm downward, and as you bring the hands together to deposit the nickel in the left hand, "squirt" it into the left sleeve. (See The "Pumpkin Seed" Vanish, page 101.) Close the left hand as if it held the nickel. Show the right hand empty and drop it to your side, allowing the half dollar to slip from the sleeve into the hand. Say, "By holding the nickel a moment, the heat from my hand warms the coin and softens it; softens it so much that if I should slap it into my hand like this, it will flatten out to the size of a half dollar." Suiting the action to the words, apparently slap the nickel into the right hand, where it is seen to have changed to a half and there is, of course, nothing else in the hands.

After a few minutes have elapsed and, when the spectator is not watching too closely, lower the left arm, allowing the sleeved coin to drop into the left hand. Take the half dollar in the left hand and place it in the pocket along with the nickel.

The effect is both startling and mysterious. It is a beautiful thing to behold. Master this and you will have one of the most effective tricks possible with coins.

Biting a Piece from a Coin

Gene Gordon

The magician shows a half dollar and apparently bites a piece from it. He removes the piece from his mouth and tosses it toward the mutilated coin, which is seen to instantly restore itself.

Requisites and Preparation: One folding half and either one of the outside pieces from another folding half. The folding

coin is in the right trousers pocket and the extra piece of coin is carried hidden in the mouth between the teeth and cheek (on either side of the jaw) until ready. You will experience no discomfort with the piece in this position and it offers no hindrance to the speech.

The effect can be presented as an individual feat or incorporated into almost any routine where a folding half is utilized.

Working: Remove the folding half from the pocket. Show it, letting it be seen that your hands are otherwise empty, then hold it vertically (folds running across it and flat surface toward spectators) between the left fingers in front, and thumb at the rear, Fig. 1.

Fig. 1

Bring the coin up to your mouth, then under the pretext of biting a piece from it, bend the top section down behind the coin and hold it in place with the tip of the thumb, Fig. 2. The rugged edge of

Fig. 2

the coin gives the illusion of teeth marks. To enhance the illusion the piece is exposed between the teeth, Fig. 3.

Fig. 3

Remove the piece of coin from your mouth with your right hand, then as you make a motion of tossing it toward the mutilated coin, thumb palm it and release the folded down section of the folding coin with the left thumb. The coin seems to mend itself instantly and visibly. Show it on both sides, then take it with your right hand and place it AND the extra piece in the pocket.

If you dislike carrying the extra piece of coin in your mouth, simply have it concealed in your right hand and just pretend to remove it from your mouth. Finish as described.

A little acting (or mugging, as it is known in the profession) will add greatly to the effect.

SECOND VERSION

TOM HOLLINGSWORTH

This is more of a gag than a trick, but when it is presented under the proper circumstances it is good for quite a chuckle.

Here is the effect: The performer shows a penny, bites a piece from it, then spits out a broken tooth.

Requisites and Preparation: A penny, from which has been cut a small, rough, crescent-shaped piece, Fig. 1, and an imitation tooth (sold in novelty shops as Yank-a-tooth). Have the tooth in your mouth or hidden in your right hand as you prefer.

Working: Show the penny between the tips of your left forefinger and thumb, hiding the missing portion with the fingers.

Fig. 1

Bring the coin up to your mouth and as you pretend to bite a piece from it, revolve the coin and display it with the cut out portion visible. Utter a cry of pain as you contort your face and bring the tooth to your lips, or if you have the tooth in your hand just pretend to remove it.

The coin cannot be restored, so just place it and the tooth in your pocket and continue with the next effect.

With either version the excuse for biting the coin is to test it to see if it is genuine.

Coin Through a Card
(The Folding Quarter)
DAVE COLEMAN

Almost everyone is familiar with the old stunt where a nickel is pushed through a dime-sized hole in a card. It has been used for many years as an advertising giveaway. Dave Coleman learned as a boy that to accomplish the feat all you had to do was bend the card across the hole, bring the ends together slightly and the coin would slip through.

A few years ago he received an advertising card from his friend and brother magician, Paul Le Paul. This card differed from the standard ones in that instead of a round hole it bore a triangular shaped one, and the wording said a quarter could be pushed through it, but it didn't say HOW. Thinking perhaps this could be done magically, Dave began to speculate on a possible solution. What he finally came up with fooled Le Paul, who had only intended it as a gag in the first place.

Effect: A borrowed quarter is placed in the center of a handkerchief and its four corners passed through a smaller, triangular shaped hole in a piece of cardboard. While a spectator holds the four corners of the cloth the performer causes the card to pass over the coin without folding or tearing it. The quarter and the card can then be examined. There is no clue to the mystery and it cannot be done except by the method explained below.

Requisites and Preparation: A folding quarter, a silk handkerchief (about 18 inches square) and a heavy card with a triangular shaped hole through which a quarter cannot normally pass, Fig. 1.

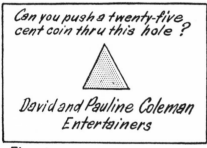

Fig. 1

Have the quarter in the right trousers pocket, the silk in the breast coat pocket and the card in any other pocket.

The card could be an advertising card or simply any card with a hole in it. If you should use such a card for advertising it would be wise always to carry a folding quarter, otherwise it might be rather embarrassing if a person should hand you your own card with a request that you demonstrate the trick for him.

Working: Remove the card, hand it to a spectator and ask him to see if he can push a quarter through the hole without bending or tearing the card. While he is thus engaged, obtain the folding quarter from your pocket and hold it finger palmed in your right hand. Offer to show him how to do it. Withdraw the silk from your pocket, show it, and spread it on the table. Take the quarter from him with your right hand and toss it onto the center of the handkerchief. This is what you pretend to do. In reality you execute The Bobo Switch (page 10) as you retain his quarter and throw the folding coin instead. With the aid of the two hands, gather the corners together and push them through the hole in the card, then slide the card down next to the coin, Fig. 2.

Call attention to the condition of things —the coin cannot escape because it is se-

Fig. 2

curely locked in by the card. Have a spectator hold the bunched together corners in one hand so the center of the handkerchief will hang down. Grasp the folding coin with both hands, then under cover of the card, fold the coin and slide the card off the center of the silk as the quarter returns to its original form. Take the handkerchief from the spectator, show the form of the coin again, then grip the handkerchief (and coin) by its center between the fingers and thumb of the palm down right hand allowing the corners to hang down. Pretend to shake the coin out, actually retain it in the handkerchief and drop the real quarter from the hand, Fig. 3. The illusion is that the coin drops from the silk. Place the handkerchief (with the coin in its center) back in the pocket, as it attracts no suspicion. Attention is then directed to the coin and card, which you hand to the owner of the coin for him to attest again to the fact that the coin cannot be passed through the hole.

It must be magic!

Fig. 3

Chapter XIII

STAGE COIN MAGIC

A Comedy Coin Routine · Coin in the Banana · Coin in Ball of Wool and Nest of Boxes · Flight Three

Although coins are more suited for use in close-up tricks they have been used for many years in stage tricks. During the vaudeville era quite a number of magicians made reputations for themselves by being specialists. For instance, there was Gus Fowler with his clock act, Arthur Lloyd with his "any card called for" act, Ade Duval with his silk act, and still earlier, Howard Thurston with his card act and T. Nelson Downs with his coin act.

Coins are still used by almost every type of performer—be his show big or small. I have seen Virgil and Willard the Wizard use coins to excellent effect in their big shows. Lyceum magicians from Eugene Laurant and Ed Reno down to Loring Campbell and myself have all used coins in their acts at one time or another.

Following are a few of the old favorites. They have stood the test of time and are as good today as they were when first shown. None of the tricks is new in effect, but each has a novel twist or a bit of something which adds to its entertainment value.

The first is by an old-time showman, Dave Coleman, who taught it to me several years ago. I have used it in my own show ever since, so I know its worth.

A Comedy Coin Routine

DAVE COLEMAN

Every top flight magician I know uses comedy in some degree in his show. Even though you may be a serious type performer a laugh now and then helps make your show more enjoyable. In this world of today we need to forget our troubles—we need a few laughs. This trick is designed with that in mind.

The trick is fine for presentation before almost any group, providing there are a few children present.

Effect: The performer asks for two boys to assist him in a trick. One boy stands on his left, the other on his right. He then shows some coins, which he has the boy on the left count onto a tray. There are six. The count is confirmed by the boy on the right, then the coins are placed in the hands of the boy on the left for safekeeping. With the aid of a magic wand, which the performer says is magnetized, he produces four coins from different parts of the body of the boy on the right. Each coin is produced on the tip of his wand, then tossed toward the boy on the left, who is then supposed to hold ten coins. But when he counts them onto the tray there are only nine. The tenth is found in the boy's pocket.

Requirements: A coin producing wand. The old-style wand as used by T. Nelson Downs is shown in Figs. 1 and 2. A coin, which was cut into three pieces and fastened to springs, fitted into one of the ends. It was caused to emerge and appear as a genuine coin on the tip of the wand by pushing a button near the other end. By reversing the operation the coin would

Fig. 1

Fig. 2

of sizes, shapes, and finishes, but try to obtain one which looks like what it is suppose to be—a plate or tray—not a piece of gaily colored magical apparatus. In the bottom of the tray is a slide, which must hold at least three coins for this routine, Fig. 4. When tray is tipped into the hand

Fig. 4

enter the wand and the ends would close making the wand appear free from trickery, even at close range.

The suspicious ends have been eliminated on the later versions. The newest model, invented by Don Boss, is constructed to take a regular folding coin, which fastens to a clip at the end of the wand, Fig. 3. Wand operates the same as the others.

A multiplying coin tray. Although one can be purchased from a magic dealer you can make one yourself if you are handy with tools. Coin trays come in a variety

the coins in the slot fall out along with those on top.

A pair of comedy glasses, which are constructed as follows: Purchase from the dime store a pair of child's spectacles (or sun glasses) and two brightly colored drinking cups with the bottoms of such size to fit the eye pieces of the spectacles. Knock the lenses from the spectacles, cut the bottoms from

Fig. 5

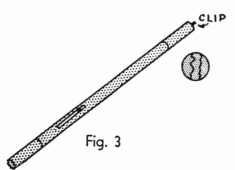

CLIP

Fig. 3

the cups, then with Duco cement, glue a cup to each eye piece of the spectacles. The finished product should look like Fig. 5.

You will also require ten half dollars. Never use palming coins, except at a distance. If the spectators realized that you were not using real money they would lose interest in the trick. In this case, with boys assisting in the trick and viewing the coins from close range, it is important that real money be used.

Preparation: Have three coins hidden in the slide of the tray, six visible on top, and one in your right trousers pocket. The tray, wand, and glasses are on your table.

Working: Say, "For my next trick I need two honest boys." As the hands go up, look them over, adding, "This trick has to do with money so I must have honest boys." Finally indicate a couple and ask them to come up on the stage. As they come forward, rush them up a bit by saying, "Hurry, hurry! Take your time, but hurry up!"

While waiting for the boys, casually place your right hand in your trousers pocket, finger palm the coin, and remove the hand. When the boys arrive on stage stand one on your left, the other on your right. Step to the left side of the boy on your left, place your left hand against his chest and as you push him back a few steps secretly load the coin from the right hand into his right hip pocket, saying, "Don't stand too close to the footlights, you might pop your corns." (This is a funny line even if there are no footlights.) As you suddenly push him backward he is caught off balance. During this brief action the deed is done. Of course, it is best that the boy not be wearing a coat. However, you will find after a little experience that a coat will offer no hindrance in loading his pocket. You will simply raise the tail of his coat a bit and drop the coin in his pocket in the action of moving him back. Repeat the action with the boy on your right. Ask the boys their names and shake hands with them. (If you have any comedy business with the boys this is a good spot for it.) Suppose the boy on your left is Harry and the other one's name is George. Say to them, "The reason I picked you two particular boys is because we are going to use money in this

trick and I want boys I can trust." To the small fry down in front: "Don't you think they have honest faces?" The kids will chorus a loud "No!" Continue: "Well, you will have to admit that they do have faces."

Pick up the tray with your right hand, show the coins to the two boys, then have the boy on your left hold out his hands. Tilt the tray so the six visible coins will slide off into his hands. (Be careful to tilt the tray from the right end, otherwise the three from the slide will fall out into his hands with the others. It might be wise to have some identifying mark on one end of the tray so there can be no accidents.) Ask the boy to count the coins onto the tray one at a time. "Count them so everybody can hear, especially those (point to the rear of the audience) back there in the cheap seats." After Harry has counted the coins walk over to George and tell him you want to check up on Harry. Dump the six coins into his hands and as he begins the count stop him and tell him to count a little louder. Everytime he counts a coin onto the tray, say, "Louder! Speak up—they can't hear you. Would you mind talking a little louder, please," etc., so that by the time he gets to six he is yelling at the top of his voice. Ask him again how many there are. He will yell, "Six!" "Well, you don't have to yell." This counting business is very funny if handled right. It gets funnier and funnier up to the point where he yells six and you tell him he doesn't have to yell.

Go back to the boy on your left and tell him that when you dump the coins into his hands you want him to close them quickly over the coins so you can't get any out. Dump all the coins into his hands, including the three from the slide. "Hold your hands up high—about even with your head. This (point to his head) is your head."

Place the tray on the table, pick up the coin wand, walk over to the boy on your

Fig. 6

right and say, "When you came up here a moment ago I heard a clicking sound on your shoes. Do you have cleats on your shoes?" Whatever is his reply, show him the magic wand and say, "This magic wand is magnetized. It is very sensitive to all metals. Hold up your foot." As he does so, touch his toe with the wand producing a coin on it tip. Hold it up and exclaim, "Look! He has half dollars for cleats! I'll take it off." Place the tip of the wand in the palm of the left hand, Fig. 6, wrap fingers around coin, Fig. 7, then pretend to remove it as you withdraw wand and touch its tip to fist, Fig. 8. "And I'll toss it over there with the ones Harry is holding." Go through the motions of tossing coin toward boy on left as you open, then

show the left hand empty. Ask Harry if he felt it. If he says, "Yes," say, "Oh, you're feeling pretty good, eh?" If he replies "No," state, "He's not feeling so good!"

Ask George how many coins Harry should now have. "Seven," he will say. "That's right. Now hold up your other foot." Produce a coin from the tip of his shoe with the wand, pretend to take it off and hand it to him, saying, "Here, you hold it." As he holds out his hand, whisper to him to pretend that he has it. "Got it?" "Yes," he replies. "Okay, throw it over to Harry." (I have been doing this trick for several years and not once have I had a boy fail to cooperate on this score.) After

Fig. 8

he goes through the motions of throwing the coin across to Harry ask him how many that makes Harry have. He will reply, "Eight." "That's right. Now hold up both feet." The expression on his face as he realizes what you said gives you another laugh. Occasionally a boy will lie down on the floor and put both feet into the air, which is even funnier.

Take him by the left ear and say to the audience, "Look at that ear! Did you ever see an ear like that?" Touch his ear with the wand and apparently produce another coin. Show it on the tip of the wand, look at his ear again and explain to the audience, "That must be a cash ear (cashier)."

Fig. 7

Pretend to remove coin and toss it toward Harry as before. Ask George how many coins Harry has now. "Nine," he will say. "That's right," you reply. "Did you see it go?" Whatever George answers say, "What you need is glasses." With the left hand, pick up the comedy glasses, holding them so they appear as two drinking glasses. "I don't mean this kind (quickly slip glasses on George), I mean this kind." Since the glasses act as "blinders" he can only see straight ahead. His actions in turning from side to side to see what is going on around him will prove very amusing.

"I need one more coin. Do you have any more hanging around anyplace, George?" Begin touching him on different parts of his body as if hunting for another coin, then apparently see one in his hair. Produce it on the wand and exclaim, "Looks like the barber forgot his tip when he cut your hair." Repeat the business of removing the coin from the tip of the wand and throwing it over to Harry, then ask George how many coins Harry has now. "Ten," he will answer. "That's right," you reply. "Let's count them and see." Remove the comedy glasses from George and lay them aside with the wand. Pick up the tray, give it to George as you tell him to take it over to Harry, then tell Harry to open his hands and count the coins one at a time onto the tray.

Appear expectant while Harry counts the first six coins onto the tray, then confident as he continues the count up to nine. When he stops counting on nine say, "Go ahead, count the other coin." He will say that there are no more. Step between the boys, take the tray, look at George and say, "There should be ten coins, shouldn't there, George?" He will agree. Count the coins yourself and upon finding only nine ask Harry what he did with the other coin. He will explain that that is all he had. Of course, you know he has it in his hip pocket

but you have to be subtle in having him produce it. Point to his shirt pocket and ask him what he has in it, then have him feel his trousers pockets. If he doesn't feel his hip pockets ask him what they contain. When he feels the coin in his hip pocket and sheepishly removes it and drops it onto the tray you have your climax. The audience will greet this act with applause. Give Harry a scornful look, then smile so he will know it was all a joke.

Thank the boys. Give each one a piece of bubble gum, or a souvenir and have them return to their seats.

From experience, I can say that this is an entertaining routine which is good for a lot of comedy. The number of laughs you get will depend on your ability as an entertainer. Jokes as a rule do not sound funny in print, but if these are delivered correctly and with a fair amount of acting, everybody will have a good time.

Coin in the Banana

Here is a dandy comedy trick that is suitable for children's shows or for performances where children are present.

Effect: The magician asks for the loan of a half dollar, which he has marked for future identification, then has it brought to the stage by a boy from the audience. He gives the boy a banana to hold while he takes the marked coin. As he causes coin to vanish he states that it will appear in the banana, but when he turns to the boy he sees that the boy has eaten the fruit. Thinking that perhaps the boy swallowed the coin along with the banana the magician has the boy open his mouth. Pretending to see it in his throat, the magician thrusts the end of his wand in the boy's mouth and comes out with the missing piece of silver on its tip. The coin is removed from the wand and returned to its owner, who identifies it as his own.

Requisites and Preparation: A coin producing wand (as described in the previous trick) and a banana, which are on your table.

Working: Ask a gentleman for the loan of a half dollar and request that he mark it for future identification. While this is being done, choose a boy, then have him bring the coin up on the stage. This procedure not only saves time but prevents you having to leave the stage.

Have the boy stand on your left, then shake hands with him and ask him his name. Let us suppose it is Billy. "Billy, do you like bananas?" He will naturally reply that he does, so take the banana from the table, partially peel it and give it to him to hold in the hand not holding the borrowed coin. Say to him, "Now, I want you to hold the banana while I do a trick with the half dollar." As you take the coin from him whisper to him to eat the banana, which he gladly does as you move away.

Pay no attention to him eating the banana but proceed to vanish the coin as follows. Hold the coin in your left hand and execute The French Drop, (page 37) as you pretend to take it in your right hand. (After this sleight you will have the coin finger palmed in your left hand and your right hand closed.) Pick up the wand with your left hand (which helps to conceal the finger palmed coin), wave it over your right hand, then as you open and show it empty say, "I will cause the coin to vanish from my hand, fly through the air, and appear in the ban. . . ." Up to this point you have been turned slightly to the right, but as you pronounce these last words, turn and stop suddenly as you see the boy cramming the last bit of banana into his mouth. The spectators will be paying little attention to you—they will be watching and laughing at the boy who is apparently putting you

on a spot by eating the banana. When you notice the boy finishing off the fruit just stand there without changing the expression on your face, which, if properly acted out, will build the laugh.

"Billy, I didn't mean for you to eat the banana. I was going to cause the half dollar to appear in the banana, and you have eaten it. You must have chewed up the coin with the banana and swallowed it. Did you feel anything rough go down your throat?" Regardless of his answer continue, "Maybe you didn't swallow it. Maybe it's stuck in your throat. Open your mouth." Peer in and say, "Wider." Pretend to see it as you exclaim, "There it is! I can see it! Just a minute, I'll get it with my magnetized wand." Transfer the wand to your right hand (which you have been holding in your left) and tell the boy to open wider and say "ah." As he does so place the tip of the wand in his mouth, then say "A-h-h-h," yourself, as you remove the tip of the wand from his mouth and exhibit coin on the end of the wand.

Pretend to remove it with your left hand but allow the gimmicked coin to slip into the wand and exhibit the borrowed one, which you have had in your left hand all the time. Give the coin to the boy as you thank him for his assistance and have him return it to its owner, who identifies it as his own.

Coin in Ball of Wool and Nest of Boxes

This version of an old classic carries a fine pedigree because for years it was a program item of Dana Walden, a lyceum magician who was popular in the early twenties.

I am grateful to my good friend, Rolland Hamblen, for furnishing the routine.

Effect: The magician borrows a half dol-

Fig. 1

lar and has it marked in such a way that the owner will positively be able to identify it when he again sees it. Holding the coin in plain view, he requests a boy to step up and help him. He gives the boy a wine glass of water to hold in one hand, then after covering the coin with the handerchief he has the boy hold it in his other hand directly over the glass. Apparently by accident the boy drops the coin, which falls into the glass. Upon uncovering the glass he finds it empty, except for the water. To rectify matters the performer turns to his table for his wand but when he turns back

to the boy he finds that the water has disappeared also. More confusion. First, the magician says, he will get back the water. With the aid of an awl, which he uses to make a hole in the boy's elbow, and a funnel he proceeds to pump the water out of the boy and the glass is again filled. However, that still leaves the half dollar to be found.

Attention is next directed to a mahogany box, which has been hanging in full view all during the performance. Taking down the box, it is unlocked and opened, disclosing a second box which just fills the first. This box, when removed and opened, is seen to contain a large ball of wool, which when unwound, discloses a small ribbon-wrapped parcel. Inside the ribbon is a tiny metal box, which is encircled with rubber bands. When these are removed and the box opened there is a second, smaller box inside. This box is unlocked and opened. In it is the missing half dollar, which the gentleman identifies as his own.

Requirements: A special set of two boxes. The set I use was constructed by Owen Brothers. The largest box is about five and a half inches square and is ordinary, Fig. 1. The inner box, about four and a half inches square, appears ordinary but has a slot in the bottom, in which fits a metal slide. This slide is for the passage of the coin into the ball of wool and the

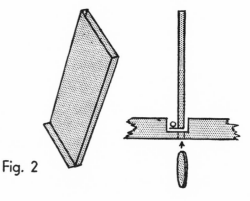

Fig. 2

inner nest of boxes. The slide is removable and is held in place with a long pin, which fits through the bottom part of the box, Fig. 2. The boxes are fitted with locks and handles.

Two small, nickel plated boxes. The lid of the smallest locks automatically when it is closed, and the box is just large enough to hold a half dollar. This box fits into a

Fig. 3

slightly larger box which does not lock. Boxes are shown in Fig. 3. My boxes were made by Carl Brema. In lieu of these boxes any small box, such as an aspirin box, may be used.

About 25 or 30 yards of heavy bright colored wool yarn.

Several yards of three-quarter inch ribbon.

A number of rubber bands.

A glass bowl large enough to hold the ball of wool.

A dissolving coin glass and glass disc, Fig. 4. This is simply a small glass which has a bottom about the size of a half dollar. It can be purchased at almost any magic shop.

A pocket handkerchief.

A regular magic wand.

A trick funnel. This is the familiar

Fig. 4

Fig. 5

double funnel which holds a quantity of water in its secret compartment, Fig. 5.

A magic awl—also a dealer item, Fig. 6.

Preparation: Nest the two metal boxes, insert the coin slide under their lids, then

Fig. 6

wrap the outer one with rubber bands, Fig. 7. When the boxes are later pulled off the slide the rubber bands will force the lids shut and lock the inner one.

After tying one end of the ribbon to the

Fig. 7

key to the nickel plated boxes, wrap it around them in such a manner that they will be completely covered with only the slide protruding. Place a few rubber bands around the ribbon to hold it in place. Fig. 8 shows how the package should look.

Fig. 8

Wind the yarn around the package, leaving the slide sticking out from the ball, **Fig. 9.**

Place the ball in the smallest wooden box so that the end of the slide will fit in

Fig. 9

the slot in the bottom. Insert the pin, locking the slide in. Lock the box, deposit it in the larger box, lock it and hang it on the goose-neck stand as shown in Fig. 1.

Have the bowl, dissolving coin glass (three-quarters full of water), funnel (its compartment filled with water), and the wand on your table. In your right trousers pocket place the glass disc and the key to the wooden boxes. And have your pocket handkerchief in your left coat pocket.

Working: Begin by requesting the loan of a half dollar from some gentleman in the audience. Have him scratch on it his initials or some mark he can identify. While he is doing this casually place your hand in your right trousers pocket and finger palm the glass disc. Walk down, take the half dollar from him with your right hand and hold it plainly in view as you return to the stage. Have a boy come up to help **you.** Stand him on your left and give him

the glass of water to hold in his left hand.

With your left hand, remove your handkerchief from your coat pocket and throw it over the marked half dollar, which you still hold in your right hand. Grip the glass disc through the handkerchief with your left hand as the right finger palms the coin. Immediately hand the boy the handkerchief with the glass disc (which he thinks is the half dollar) and have him hold it in his right hand directly above the glass of water. As you do this whisper to him to drop the coin, which he does. Reprimand him for dropping the coin as you take the handkerchief from him, show it, then lay it on the table. Tell him to remove the coin from the glass and you will start over. Casually place your right hand in trousers pocket and leave the half dollar there. He will reply that there is no coin in the glass. (The glass disc in the bottom of the glass is invisible.) Whisper to him to drink the water when you turn your back. Tell the spectators that in order to get the coin back you will need your wand. Turn to your table for your wand and as you do so the boy drinks the water much to the merriment of the spectators. Turn back to the boy and as you do so notice that the water is gone. By this time the spectators are wondering how you will get out of your predicament and you appear quite puzzled yourself.

Tell the boy that you need the water for another trick. "There is only one thing I can do in a case like this. . . . I'll have to get the water back." The boy's reaction to this remark will amuse the audience. Pick up the magic awl and say, "All I have to do is make a small hole here for the water to come out." Pretend to push the awl into his right elbow a couple of times. Then place it back on the table, pick up the glass and have him hold it in his left hand underneath his right elbow. Take up the funnel, show it empty, then hold it underneath his elbow with your left hand as you grip him by the wrist and pump his arm back and forth. Allow the water to flow from the funnel into the glass, filling it again, Fig. 10. This bit of business is always good for laughs. It seems so ridiculous to see water being pumped out of the boy they just can't keep from laughing. After

Fig. 10

this operation, place the glass and funnel back on the table.

Say to the boy, "Well, we have the water back but what are we going to do about the gentleman's half dollar?" Ask him if he can reimburse the man for the half he lost. Then after having a bit of fun with the boy along these lines, direct his attention to the hanging boxes and say, "Perhaps the coin went in that box. Let's see." Have the boy remove the box and place it on the table. While he is doing this place your right hand in your trousers pocket, finger palm the marked half dollar and remove the key. Hand the key to the boy and have him open the box, then ask him what he sees inside. "Another box," he will answer. Have him remove it, unlock it and look inside, then take the box from him with your left hand and place it on your right, directly over the coin. To show the audience what the box contains, tip it forward and as you do so insert the coin in the slot in the bottom of the box, the action being covered completely by the box. "A ball of wool," you

say. "Let's take it out." Turn the box upside down apparently to let the ball fall out into your hand, but actually to permit the coin to slide down into the inner set of metal boxes. (Actually the fingers have to pull the ball out.) While still holding the box upside down, grip the ball and pull it out. Close the lid of the box, place it on the table, drop the ball of wool in the glass bowl and hand it to the boy to hold as you take the end of the wool and start pulling. Stand some distance from the boy as you wind the wool into another ball.

As you keep pulling and winding your ball gets bigger while the one in the glass bowl gets smaller and smaller until finally the wool is exhausted and only the ribbon-wrapped package remains. Have the boy show the package, then remove the rubber bands and hand the end of the ribbon to you. Quickly pull this away, leaving the metal boxes in the bowl. Have the boy show the boxes to the audience as you stand some distance away and briefly explain what it is. Now direct him to remove the rubber bands, open the box and take out the other one. The key to the box is attached to the end of the ribbon, which you still hold in your hands. Hand him the key end of the ribbon, have him unlock the box and remove the half dollar. Tell the spectators that if everything went as it should, that must be the borrowed coin. Thank the boy for his assistance and have him return the half dollar to its owner, who identifies it. Thank him for the loan of the coin and bow to acknowledge the applause you will receive.

The trick is an act in itself.

Flight Three

GLENN HARRISON

This trick is not only fine for the parlor —it makes an excellent program item as well.

Effect: The magician requests two members of his audience to assist him in the experiment. One of the volunteer assistants is given three marked coins to hold while the other counts ten more coins into a small pail. The coins are then emptied into his hands with the request that he hold them tightly. The performer takes the three marked coins and causes them to vanish one at a time. When the second helper counts his coins he has thirteen—among them the three marked coins!

Requisites and Preparation: A small sand pail of the dime store variety (or a more expensive copper one), sixteen half dollars, and a roll of half inch adhesive tape. Six of the coins are prepared as follows: Cut twelve half inch squares of tape and fasten a square to each side of the six coins. Number three of them, on one side only, and place them in your right trousers pocket. Number the other three in the same manner then add a few markings (to represent initials, etc.) to the squares of tape on the reverse side of the coins. The reason for this will be explained later. Have these three coins in your left trousers pocket and the pail containing the ten coins nearby.

Begin the trick by removing the three coins from your right trousers pocket. Pass them to three different spectators with the request that each mark his coin on the blank square, and also remember its number.

While talking and directing the proceedings, casually place your left hand in your left trousers pocket, finger palm the three coins, and remove the hand. (Right here I might say that articles may be successfully stolen by just going into your pocket after them, *IF* you do it casually and non-chalantly and when there is no crucial attention on yourself. The main trouble with most amateurs is that they look and act so guilty that the spectators become suspicious.) After the three coins have been secretly removed from the left pocket, pick up the pail by the handle with the left hand. This gives that hand something to do while your right hand receives the three marked coins back from the spectators. Ask a spectator on your right to hold the pail for a few moments. Then dump the three marked coins into your left hand and give them to a spectator on your right to hold. This is what you pretend to do. In reality you retain the three marked coins finger palmed as you apparently dump them into your left hand. For a full description of this sleight see Vanish for Several Coins (a), page 45. Although the sleight is mainly used to vanish several coins, it can be used as an exchange just as well. In this instance the left hand is not carried away closed, because you have three other coins in that hand with pieces of adhesive tape stuck to them. Merely perform the sleight, retaining the three marked coins in your right hand, then immediately show the other three in your left hand. They appear to be the same identical coins. The illusion is perfect.

Give the three coins in your left hand to a spectator on your left to hold. If possible choose someone who was not too close to the three spectators who marked the coins. This is so there will be no danger of them recognizing their marks. As you hand the three coins to the spectator the others will get a flash of the tapes on the coins and naturally assume them to be the ones marked by the three spectators. Although this is a small point it is an important one that will be remembered later.

Turn your attention now to the spectator on your right holding the pail, and ask him if he has counted the coins in the pail. Upon receiving a negative answer, take the pail from him with your right hand, grasping it by the rim with the fingers inside and the thumb outside. This places the finger palmed coins inside the pail, held in position and covered by the fingers. Have him hold his hands cupped together, slowly and openly pour the ten coins into his hands, then have him count them back into the pail one at a time. Hold the pail in such a manner he cannot see inside of it while he counts. As the coins are dropped into the pail they make quite a clatter, so anytime after the first coin is dropped release your three coins one at a time to coincide with his coins falling into the pail. This, of course, accomplishes the work of the old multiplying money tray. When he has counted all ten coins into the pail, with obviously empty hands, pour the coins (now 13) into his cupped hands, cautioning him to hold them tightly so that "I will not be able to see or touch them." The only weakness in the entire routine occurs at this point. There is some danger of the spectator noticing the three marked coins falling into his hands, but this can be covered by paying attention to the following detail: Do not pour the coins slowly into his hands but simply invert the pail over his hands and for a moment or two leave it over his hands as you look him directly in the eye and stress the importance of his holding the coins tightly. If your personality and power of suggestion are what they should be, he will do as you say and close his hands tightly and there will be no cause for suspicion.

Announce that you intend passing the three marked (?) coins held by your assistant on the left, into the hands of your assistant on the right. Have your helper on the left give you one of the three coins he is holding. Vanish it using either The Bobo Complete Vanish, or the Complete Thumb Palm Vanish, Chapter IV. After vanishing the coin explain that perhaps your moves were a bit too fast for them to follow, so offer to do it slower as you take the next coin and vanish it using the Sucker Vanish, (page 50). Take the third coin from him in your right hand and act as if you are about to cause it to fade away also, then suddenly change your mind. Say that you will permit your helper to vanish this last coin. Show the coin in your right hand, then pretend to place it in your left but retain it palmed in your right. Go through the motions of placing the non-existent coin in his hand and have him close his hand. Ask him if he can feel it. (If you are not too close to the other spectators whisper to him to say "Yes.") Most people will cooperate and say "Yes." If he says "No" (which seldom happens), make some remark about him not feeling so good. Have him throw the coin (?) toward the spectator on your right who is holding the other coins. Direct all your attention to him as he makes the throwing motion, then turn to the other spectator and inquire if he felt the coin arrive in his hands. As you do this dispose of the palmed coin in your right coat pocket (or sleeve it and dispose of it later). Have the spectator open his hands and count the coins. He will, of course, have 13. Have him remove the three marked coins from the rest (he will be able to identify them quickly by the squares of tape on them) then carry them to the spectators who marked them and have them identify their marks. They are the same coins!

Chapter XIV

THE MISER'S DREAM

Versions of Robert-Houdin, T. Nelson Downs, et al. · Glenn Harrison Version · M. S. Whitford Version · A Miser's Dream Routine · Perpetual Coins

One of the most illustrious of the conjuring tricks with coins—found in the programs of all the great magicians of the past, and carried to the heights in the world of variety entertainment by T. Nelson Downs, "King of Koins," during the golden age of vaudeville. Like so many of the classic feats of magic, the origin of this effect is lost in the obscurity of the past. No magical historian seems to know definitely who introduced it, nor when. Robert-Houdin included it in his *séances fantastiques* in the forties of the last century, and described it for the first time in print in his *Secrets de la Prestidigitation et de la Magie* in 1868, but did not claim its invention, nor did he shed any light on its origin.

It must have made its appearance about the time the modern silk hat began to appear upon the heads of Europe's gentlemen of fashion; that was about 1840. About 1792 men had begun to wear beaver hats, which resembled the modern top hat except for ornamentation with strings and tassels. The trick could have slipped into the repertoire of some conjurer around the beginning of the nineteenth century, for about that time the hat began to endear itself to the hearts of the conjuring fraternity as a storehouse for small livestock, omelettes, and quantities of other strange goods. Since we can find no record of a conjuring feat in which coins collected from the air were deposited in a three-cornered hat, we shall say it *was* the top hat—and the silk topper at that—that inspired the nameless inventor who devised the feat.

Titled "The Shower of Money" in Robert-Houdin's book, the trick appears in its basic form: "When you first come forward on the stage, you have in the right hand a five-franc piece, palmed after the Italian method (*vis.*, thumb palmed). On your other side, you have beforehand placed in the left *pochette* seven five-franc pieces.

" 'Will some one of you gentlemen oblige me with a hat?' When the hat is handed to you, take it in the right hand, and while, in the act of turning round, the left hand is masked by your body, take from the *pochette* the seven five-franc pieces, which should be so placed as to be readily got hold of. You then take the hat in the same hand, in such manner as to let the coins lie flat against the inner lining. (The illustration depicts the hat held in the left hand, the fingers clipping the coins against the sweatband in the familiar manner. The first coin was pinched from the flame of a candle.) 'Look, gentlemen; to begin with, don't you see that five-franc piece just going to burn itself in the flame of that candle? Let us secure it!'

"While speaking as above, you have moved the hand close to the candle, and at the final moment you have brought the coin to the tips of the fingers.

" 'Here it is, you see! dear me! it is quite hot, I will put it here in the hat.'

"At the moment that you put the right hand into the hat, as though to place therein the coin, you palm this by the Italian method, as before, but at the same time you let fall from the left hand one of the seven coins which you are holding against the inside of the hat. If these two movements are simultaneous, the illusion is perfect, and the spectators must perforce believe that it is really the coin in the right hand which has just fallen into the hat."

The other coins are caught, one from a lady's handkerchief, one under the collar of a gentleman's coat, one in a child's hair, one under a fan, one in a shawl, one floating in air, etc., and each time the pretence is made of dropping the coin into the hat, but each time the coin is palmed and one let fall from the left hand's stock. The last coin (the palmed one) is caught and let fall openly into the hat.

Houdin advocated vanishing the eight coins by means of the *tourniquet*, but went on to explain that this production of coins served as the introduction to a stage trick which he called "Shower of Gold." "A gold vase, covered with a silk handkerchief, is instantaneously filled with golden coins; and lastly, the hat which has been used for the reception of the five-franc pieces is found crammed with an enormous quantity of bank notes. These notes, as may be well imagined, are of the 'Bank of Elegance' description, bearing, instead of the words 'five hundred francs,' 'five hundred times,' or the like, in the same kind of print. At a little distance they cannot be distinguished from the genuine article."

Compars Herrmann, the original Herrmann, introduced the trick to the United States in 1861, and according to Henry Hatton and Adrian Plate (authors of *Magician's Tricks—How They Are Done*)

has never been surpassed in the performance of it. Herrmann acted out the trick in a very melodramatic manner, these gentlemen tell us, and this greatly heightened its effect. When Herrmann went into the audience to borrow a hat, he had one coin, a silver dollar, palmed in his right hand, and as an excuse for keeping the hand closed, he carried his wand. In his left hand he had twenty-five or thirty-five coins, and that hand grasped the lapel of his coat. The moment he received the hat, he passed it to his left hand and thrust that hand into it so the fingers pressed the coins against its side, while the thumb, resting on the outside, clasped the brim. Turning the hat crown upwards and still clinging to his wand the performer boldly extended his arms and requested one of the audience to feel them, to convince everyone he had nothing concealed there. This examination completed, Herrmann turned toward the stage, and as if to prepare for work, tossed his wand ahead of him, at the same time dropping into his sleeve the coin palmed in the right hand. When he faced his audience he showed his empty right hand, back and front, without saying a word. Suddenly, he clutched at the air and then eagerly peered into his hand. Nothing there. He repeated this action once or twice, to no avail, and then, as if in despair, pressed his hand to his brow and dropped it to his side. That dramatic gesture enabled him to get possession of the sleeved coin, which he palmed. He again grasped at the air, caught a coin, and triumphantly showed it to the audience. He tossed the coin fairly into the hat—but took it out again almost instantly, kissed it fondly, and apparently threw it back. This time he palmed it, and dropped a coin from the left hand's stock instead. The right hand was always withdrawn from the hat with its back to the audience, and the palmed coin never seen. The now-familiar variations followed—a coin was pushed through the side of the hat; coins were shaken out of a lady's handkerchief, or from a man's beard, etc. But the little melodrama of the miser—his despair, his triumph, his glee over his increasing wealth—must have been most effective in 1861. Today, such a bit might be greeted like a performance of Uncle Tom's Cabin!

The most complete description of the trick in all of conjuring literature is that given by T. Nelson Downs in his book *Modern Coin Manipulation*. Downs' reputation rests upon the act which he called "The Miser's Dream," and we can do no better than to set it down here just as he put it into his book.

T. Nelson Downs' Original Version

(From *Modern Coin Manipulation*, Chapter II)

By T. Nelson Downs, 1900.*

The above original conception of the author's has, he believes, been more extensively imitated and counterfeited than any other known Magical Act. In this chapter it is proposed first to give an outline of same, and then to explain all the different "sleights" necessary for its accomplishment, which the author desires to emphatically state were all, without exception, invented by himself some sixteen years ago. He mentions this fact for the information of those who may be in doubt as to the origin of the back palm.

The stage is devoid of any kind of furniture, with the exception of an ordinary property side table, which is totally unprepared. The performer enters and asks

for the loan of a hat. Upon obtaining the necessary article it is placed crown downwards on the table. Professor now turns up his sleeves to the elbows, and his hands are shown to be quite empty back and front with the fingers WIDE APART. The hat is now taken (without the slightest suspicious movement) in the left hand. The right hand next makes a grab in the air, and there are two coins, which he places in the hat. This is repeated till about 20 coins have been caught, but during the whole time the back and front and fingers of right hand are shown to be absolutely empty, and not once do they approach the body. By way of variation, a coin is sometimes passed through the side of the hat, being unmistakably heard to fall within; or a half dollar is thrown in the air, completely vanishing, and the hat held out (a second or two afterwards) to catch the coin, which is also heard to fall into the same. A coin is placed between tips of first and fourth fingers of right hand, and pushed against bottom of hat, whereupon it instantly vanishes into the interior, making itself heard as it mingles with the other coins. The right hand now catches a dozen or 20 coins at once, dropping them all into the hat. This is continued until an enormous number of half dollars is collected. These are turned out on to the table. One is now taken in the left hand and passed completely through one and then both knees, then passed from hand to hand. Now the audience is asked to name any number, which we will say is 15, whereupon the performer proceeds to catch one at a time the half dollars on the tip of his wand, immediately passing each one invisibly into right hand, where it makes its appearance between the first finger and thumb—this being continued until the whole 15 are produced. Six coins are now vanished and both hands shown empty, when the former are produced in a fan from the back of the left hand. In conclusion, after several other sleights hereinafter described, the performer gathers up all the coins on the table —somewhere about 40—makes the pass with this huge pile, when lo! they have vanished, but are immediately reproduced in a shower from the bottom of the vest.

As the above depends chiefly on what is termed the "Continuous Front and Back Hand Palm," it is proposed to describe this in minute detail first. The object is to con-

Fig. 2

Fig. I

ceal a coin in the hand, yet at any moment showing back and front quite empty, extending the fingers and thumb as well, but immediately producing the coin when desired at the finger tips.

If the reader desires to excel in this particular sleight, he should first of all select a coin which best suits his fingers. The author always uses a half dollar as being best adapted to the size of his hands. The smaller the coin used the more difficult to successfully carry out the trick. It is therefore, advisable, perhaps, to start with a larger coin, say a dollar, and follow this up gradually with smaller coins, until you find one which exactly suits the width of your fingers.

To commence the trick the coin is placed on the front of the hand, being gripped between the tips of the first and fourth fingers, Fig. 1. You now draw down the two middle fingers until the points rest

behind the coin at its lower end. If you now exert with these two fingers a slight pressure on the lower part of the coin it revolves between the first and fourth fingers, Fig. 2, and, upon the performer now extending carefully the two middle fingers, these stretch out in front of the coin (see Fig. 3, which represents a back view) which is now held in the same position as at first, except that it is at the back instead of the front of the hand, the coin being quite

Fig. 3

invisible and appearing to have vanished. To cover this movement, which, of course, should be executed with lightning-like rapidity, the performer makes a short movement with the hand as if about to throw the coin away. The slight movement facilitates the deception to a great extent. Now, to make the coin reappear, the above movements are simply reversed. This novel movement should be acquired by both hands, which should perform it with equal free-

Fig. 4

Fig. 6

dom and ease. With considerable practice this can be accomplished with more than one coin. Fig. 4 shows the author's hand with six coins back palmed. [**Editor's Note:** There is some doubt about Downs or any other performer ever doing this. Legend has it that Downs himself was able to back palm three coins.]

The above is the original form in which the trick was invented by the author 16 years ago, but since then he has naturally made vast improvements in same, and the following is the correct manner in which he performed the "Continuous Front and Back Hand Palm" at the Palace Theatre, London, in 1899, for six consecutive months. . . .

When the coin has been reversed to the back of the hand, as in Fig. 3, the little finger moves away from the coin, which is left gripped between the first and second fingers. The third and fourth fingers are now spread wide apart, Fig. 5, to show there is nothing between them. The third

finger moves up at the back of the hand behind the coin, which it pulls between it and second finger, where it remains gripped as in Fig. 6, enabling the performer to show the back of the hand, and demonstrate that there is nothing between first and second or third and fourth fingers. Now, the thumb pushes the coin through from the front of the hand to the back, still

Fig. 7

gripped between second and third fingers, enabling the front of the hand to be shown, with the first and fourth fingers extended as in Fig. 7. The little finger next comes up behind the hand and grips the coin in exactly the same way as the third finger did previously, enabling the first, second, and third fingers to be shown empty, Fig. 8. The second finger now grasps the coin from the back, so that it is now held as before in Fig. 7, between two middle fingers, again allowing performer to show there is nothing between first and second or third and fourth fingers. The coin is then picked

Fig. 5

Fig. 8

Fig. 10

Fig. 11

Fig. 9

in an absolutely correct manner, a considerable amount of practice is necessary. However, to produce many brilliant effects it is only essential that the performer should be acquainted with one or two of the moves, but if the reader ever desires to become a strictly first-class Coin Manipulator he should practice, practice, and keep on practicing until all the above sleights become second nature to him, and he can defy even expert conjurers to tell where the coin is.

All the above should be done with both hands as mentioned before, thereby enabling the performer to exhibit some combinations that appear nothing short of supernatural.

[Editor's Note: Magical authorities differ on the value of this set of finger gymnastics designed by Downs to prove that the hand is empty. Some stamp it as bad magic—a needless effort which contributes nothing to the Miser's Dream and achieves but one result—that of isolating the coin so even the most ignorant spectator can tell exactly where it is, and follow its

up with the first finger and gripped between that and the second finger, as already seen in Fig. 5. Next, the fingers are bent round towards the palm, and with the assistance of the second and third fingers the coin is transferred to the palm of the hand, Fig. 9, thereby allowing the performer to show the back of the hand with all the fingers and thumb extended, Fig. 10. It is now picked up with the two middle fingers, and replaced between first and second fingers, being exactly the reverse of the previous move, enabling the front of the hand to be now shown. By next placing the third finger up behind the coin, the same can be placed at back of thumb, Fig. 11, where it lies gripped in the fleshy part, so that the performer can now show front of hand empty, but with the fingers extended. The hand is now closed, the coin being allowed to drop in, and then opened, whereupon the coin is produced. The author uses all the above passes in his entertainment, and, of course, to work the Back and Front Palm shuttlings back and forth between the fingers with the greatest of ease. It has been stated that Downs never used the moves illustrated in Figures 5 to 11. I am unable to find any record of his using them other than his book. However, I have vivid recollections of Downs' amazing skill. I have seen him execute a series of sleights with coins that was little short of miraculous, doing things one would not believe possible, and doing them so effortlessly—with even less effort than the average magical enthusiast expends to palm a single coin! Therefore I'm almost willing to believe that Downs could execute this series of "hide the coin" moves and make them look like a smoothly executed set of movements, in which the hand was shown both sides, and the fingers opened and closed and wriggled freely to prove their innocence. Downs was a great artist—too consummate an artist to overdo any sleight—if he used this, or any part of it, you may rest assured he would use it where it fit in best, and to achieve a certain effect. Like all great artists, Downs strove for simplicity; his best effects were achieved by the simplest means possible, and he DID simplify his methods as the years went along.]

Having described the principal secret of this Act, the author will proceed to explain the Act itself and then the various additions. Before going on the stage, the performer places 20 half dollars in his right-hand waistcoat pocket, and 15 in his right-hand trousers pocket. A hat is borrowed, and, while taking the same in his left hand, the coins from the waistcoat are palmed in his right, and placed like a flash of lightning under the bent-over side of the rim on the outside of the hat, Fig. 12, which is placed with the same hand crown downwards on the table. Now, if the coins have been placed neatly and properly on the rim when the hat is turned over,

Fig. 12

they will remain where you put them, but this is the most delicate part of the trick, as unless you are exceedingly careful some, or all, will fall as the hat is put on the table, and, in the words of a popular song, "There would be no show that night." With practice, however, this can be accomplished.

[Editor's Note: Downs made sure that no accident would mar his performance by using his own "topper," which was handed up to him by one of the musicians. This hat was just right for gripping the load of coins, which he transferred to the brim as the hat was passed from hand to hand, and he could set the hat on the table crown downwards without the slightest fear of the coins falling. This "prop" topper had a brass plate riveted to the inside of the crown, to amplify the sound of the coins dropping. And he actually used a Kellar coin dropper and palming coins in a later version of the trick!]

The performer now casually turns up his sleeves, and remarks, "With the permission of the ladies I will remove my cuffs, or rather turn them up to the elbows." The hat is now taken up with the left hand, the fingers of which get hold of the coins under cover of the rim. The hat is next passed into the right hand to show the left empty, and the artiste will find with practice it is quite easy to pass the coins with the hat from hand to hand. The hat is now taken by the edge nearest the audience, and, with right hand, turned over so that the fingers of the left hand containing the 20 coins are brought into the inside of hat, Fig. 13, in position for the money-

Fig. 13

catching. The right hand is now shown empty, and makes a grab in the air at an imaginary coin, immediately placing it (apparently) in the hat, where it is heard to fall, but, in reality, it is a coin dropped from the left hand. This is repeated, and, as the hand goes to the hat to make a pretense of dropping in a coin, two coins are quickly palmed in the right hand. You look in the air for more coins, and one of those palmed is now produced at the finger tips (the mode of which is described under "Production of Any Number of Coins At The Finger Tips," page 316) and visibly dropped into the hat. You now produce the second one, but, instead of placing this in the hat, one is dropped from the left hand at the same moment that the right hand approaches the top of the hat, thereby inducing the audience to believe that the visible coin was really placed in the hat. This is repeated as often as desired, and, by means of the "Continuous Front and Back Hand Palm," before described, the right hand can at any moment be shown apparently empty. [**Editor's Note:** Downs used this sleight very sparingly.]

Additional effects are produced accord-

ing to the fancy of the performer. The apparent passing of a coin through the bottom of the hat never fails to bring forth plenty of applause. This is accomplished by holding the coin in the manner depicted in Fig. 14. The back palm is now made, Fig. 15, one coin being at the same time dropped from the left hand into the hat, creating the necessary "jingle," and the illusion is perfect. A similar effect can be produced by holding the coin between the tips of the

Fig. 14

first three fingers and thumb and pretending to push it through the side of the hat. What really happens is that the coin is pushed by the hat down between the fingers

Fig. 15

(the back of the hand facing the audience) which hide it, one, of course, being dropped by the left hand to create the necessary deception. It is well to pay particular attention to these little moves, as they invariably create more *furore* than the bigger and more difficult sleights.

A coin is now apparently thrown in the air, and caught in the hat a few seconds later. The coin is, of course, palmed in the act of throwing up the hand, and the hat is held out in the left hand as if waiting for the coin, which, at the right moment, is dropped from the left hand.

[Editor's Note: Those who witnessed Downs' performance of the Miser's Dream will remember the ability he had of dramatizing everything he did. In catching the coins, he was deliberate at the start, and gradually increased the tempo as he neared the climax. And he varied the procedure as much as possible to keep one wondering where this endless supply of wealth was coming from. Coins were produced from the elbow, the trousers cuff, the knee, the tip of the shoe, even from a horn held up by one of the musicians in the orchestra pit, and coins were sometimes caught with the palm of the hand to the audience.

For the "additional effects" such as passing a coin through the bottom of the hat, Downs had a manner of setting the stage for the effect so that you knew something special was going to happen. By some trick of manner he placed you in an expectant mood—"set" you for something. And when the "something" happened, you were pleased, for you knew you had seen something special. It was his ability as an actor that enabled him to "put over" these episodes. His was "the grand manner"—no Shakespearean actor knew more of the tricks of the stage than did Downs. Unforgettable are his manner of carrying himself, his dramatic gestures, his postures suggestive of ballet or fencing, and his grand demeanor. His patter sparkled with sly wit, and he delivered it with a timing and inflection that caught and held your attention. But the many little tricks he employed to put over his so-called "additional effects" cannot be described adequately in print. For example, when a coin was apparently thrown into the air and caught in the hat a second later, he put a bit of business to it that made it most amusing. He would wait briefly for the coin to drop into the hat. It did not. He would look at the audience, puzzled at this failure, and turn his head in the opposite direction, still scanning the horizon for the coin. At this point he would release the coin from the left fingers, and it would land in the hat with a loud clink that caused him to turn his head and look at the hat in surprise. Then he would steal a sly look at the audience. As Downs did it, this bit was a sure laugh— but only a master of timing and a finished actor could make it such an effective bit. It was the succession of such effective bits that made the act.

He knew and used all the artifices ever invented to make the coin catching procedure more effective. To make the coins land with a greater clatter, he would lift the hat sharply as the left fingers released a coin, thereby increasing the impact with which the coin struck its fellows in the hat. And coins were stolen by shaking the hat so they could be clipped under the left fingers. In this manner a few extra coins could be "caught" after the left hand's stock had been exhausted. In some of his presentations he has been known to switch the hats—on the trip back to the stage from the audience, where great quantities of coins had been seemingly produced from the spectators. He would switch for a hat filled to overflowing with coins, and since you saw such a great quantity, you must of necessity believe he had produced such a tremendous number! But this was "magic for magicians" and it is doubtful whether he ever used such a routine for the public.

The trip into the audience, in which he invariably found a few coins "in their whiskers," was a succession of laughs. He would dip his hand into the hat and shower the coins from his fingers, brazenly stealing loads which he shook from their sleeves, neckties, handkerchiefs—even from a spectator's nose—"the gentleman who always blows himself about this time!" His patter sallies such as "Tomorrow night, East Lynne," or "Next season we'll carry two giraffes (pronounced Jy-raffes)," sound inane in print, but they always brought laughs. His skill was great, and his touch was sure—he was an incomparable artist—always.]

When the first load of coins is exhausted, the performer makes a bold move. He pretends to hear someone make a remark that he gets the coins from his pockets—"Which pocket?" he replies: "The left one?" and places his hand into the pocket so as to suit the action to the word—"No, the right one?"—now placing his right hand into the pocket, which forthwith palms the 15 coins previously placed there. "No, ladies and gentlemen, if I were to place my hands in my pockets you would all see me. Please, see that my hands do not approach the body." Meanwhile, he has got the palmed 15 coins on to the rim of the hat as explained at the commencement of this description. The hat is then placed, if desired, on the table, crown downward, and the hands shown perfectly empty. The same process is now repeated.

If the above movements are executed with a certain amount of *sang froid*, and without appearing to be in a hurry to place the hands in your pockets, not one in a thousand would guess that you were "load-ing"—it being such a barefaced proceeding the audience would never dream that you would be so bold as to deceive them in this decidedly simple yet effective manner.

Now, when this last lot of coins becomes exhausted, another ruse is resorted to by the performer. His right hand dives into the hat and rattles the coins to show they are real ones, at the same time letting them pour in a shower from the hand into the hat. He repeats this once or twice, and then palms, say, a dozen, which, of course, enables him to go on catching them singly (producing them at finger tips as previously described)* or to make a grab in the air and produce the 12 in a fan, Fig. 16, with the remark that "When I desire more than one I make this move." The

Fig. 16

above can be repeated, if desired, but it will usually be found that 30 to 40 coins will take some time to "catch," provided the performer is not unduly quick about it. This must be avoided, and the artiste must go about his business in an easy manner, without any jumps or jerks so common with unfinished performers. To practice before a looking-glass is all very well, but before your friends is better, as they are thereby enabled to give you hints as to mistakes, etc., which it is impossible for you to see yourself in a glass.

Next comes the

---

* EDITOR'S NOTE: The Downs Palm could be used here, and the coins dropped into the hat as caught. See page 3.

PRODUCTION OF ANY NUMBER OF COINS AT FINGER TIPS

Before the hat is replaced on the table the audience is asked to name any number, which we will suppose is 15. The performer, who has in the meantime been "jingling" the coins in the hat, quickly palms the desired number, and replaces the hat on the table (to palm the correct number instantaneously requires considerable practice, but the author is enabled through constant exercise to tell exactly how many he picks up by the feel and weight). Both hands are now shown empty by means of the "New Change-over Palm." The magic wand is taken in the left hand, and the coins caught on its extreme end one by one, each being then invisibly passed from the wand to the right finger tips. The wand used is, of course, the old "Half Dollar" Wand, but the one the author has been in the habit of using was improved by him to the extent that it works noiselessly, this being brought about by a series of minute pieces of rubber operating in the "Coin" end of the wand, which prevent the edges of the opening "clicking" together when the half dollar is caused to appear or vanish. [**Editor's Note:** Downs later abandoned the coin wand, and simply produced the required number of coins in a fan at his finger tips, in the manner to be described here.]

The coins are palmed in the right hand. To produce them one by one at the finger tips, the two middle fingers are bent down towards the coins as in Fig. 17. The third finger pushes up the bottom one (that nearest the wrist), same being immediately gripped between that finger and the second which instantaneously places the coin between the tips of the first finger and thumb, the second one being placed behind this, and so on till the whole 15 have been "produced." The left hand, of course, makes a motion of catching a coin on the wand

Fig. 17

each time and shows the coin, which is withdrawn into the wand in the act of throwing it towards the right hand.

The coins are now counted one at a time from the right hand into the hat. If, by any chance, you should have made a mistake in the number asked for, it is easy when counting them at the conclusion to "miscount" one or two. [**Editor's Note:** In Downs' hands, each coin added to the fan in the right hand appeared with a very audible click. If he had palmed too few coins, there was an occasional click unaccompanied by a coin, the procedure being analogous to the false count with cards. When the coins were counted aloud into the hat, the left hand held in reserve a few extras clipped against the hat as in Fig.13, and the right hand made the gesture of dropping a coin when actually the coin was released from the left hand's stock. Chicanery, Downs called it, but he was prepared for any emergency. When the methods of an acknowledged master are analyzed, is it any wonder that the proverb, "Genius is the infinite capacity for taking pains" is universally accepted?]

TO PASS A COIN THROUGH THE KNEES

To bring about the above effect a half dollar is palmed in the right hand, and another taken between the second and third

Fig. 18

through your knee. This can be repeated once or twice. The performer then pretends to overhear a remark, "Pass it through both knees," and replies "Through both knees? Oh, certainly; however, it's more painful," and he repeats the trick, apparently passing the coin through both knees, making, of course, not the slightest difference in the *modus operandi*.

THE ELUSIVE PASS

The performer takes, we will say, six coins between the foremost sections of the middle and third fingers of the right hand, spreading out at the same time the other fingers, presenting to the public the back of his hand. The left hand now approaches the right as if to take away the coins Fig.

Fig. 19

finger tips (the latter of course visible to the audience). Left hand is now shown empty, and the visible coin placed on the left fingers in readiness for the back palm, the left hand being placed horizontally against the right knee. The right hand now points at the coin in the left hand in a casual sort of way (in reality to show nothing between the fingers or at the back of the hand), then shows the front of the hand (in the meantime, of course, reversing the coin to the back of the hand), and places it in a similar position on the opposite side of the knee to the left. Fig. 18 will show the correct position. The coin is now back-palmed by the left hand—at the moment of doing which the coin back-palmed in the right hand is brovght to the front, the same having apparently passed completely

19, and, in fact, really takes them away the first time. Then, apparently overhearing a remark to the effect that they are not in the left hand, he opens it and shows the coins. Same are again taken between the tips of the second and third fingers of the right hand, and the left hand makes the motion of taking the coins, while, under cover of the fingers of the left hand, the two fingers of the right hand containing the coins are bent round the thumb of the left hand, and the coins left palmed in the right hand, the two fingers immediately returning to their original position, the left hand moving away as if it contained them, Fig.

Fig. 20

20. The above movements are made very clear in the accompanying drawings, though they may appear almost impossible of execution. In the first place, the different moves should be made very slowly with, say, 2 coins; but the reader will understand that in the actual execution of this feat before an audience everything is done so quickly that it is quite impossible for a spectator to tell whether the coins are really taken in the left hand or not. . . .

Now, upon the left hand being opened and shown empty, the right hand can also be shown empty by means of the following

NEW CHANGE-OVER PALM

When the left hand is opened, the right hand, which contains the coins palmed, is brought face to face with the left one, and

Fig. 21

the coins transferred to the palm of the left hand, which is immediately turned round (under cover of the right) to show (apparently) that there is nothing at the back, and then the right hand can be shown empty back and front, Fig. 21. The left hand is next turned round under cover of the right hand, and the coins repalmed in right, Fig. 22. This is an exceedingly difficult sleight, and requires a considerable amount of delicacy in manipulating. It is very desirable to have the coins all of the same size and thickness, otherwise one or

Fig. 22

more may slide out from the rest in the act of transference.

The coins can then be produced as fancy indicates by catching them one at a time, or in a fan from the back of the left hand; but a suitable mode of production will readily suggest itself to a performer who has thoroughly mastered the above two passes. The author can safely state that when once proficient in both of the above the performer can do practically just as he likes with half a dozen coins, and he therefore considers it one of the most useful passes in existence.

DOWNS' NEW "CLICK" PASS

As the trick about to be described relies almost entirely on the above-named new and original "pass," the author has thought it only fair to give it the above title. Once acquired it becomes a most useful and one of the most puzzling and deceptive sleights extant.

The mode of performing it is as follows: Ten coins are placed unmistakably in the left hand. All are satisfied that the coins

Fig. 23

Fig. 25

are really in the left hand, they being heard to fall therein. The right hand now picks up an ordinary glass tumbler and holds the hands wide apart. The coins are commanded to pass *one at a time* from the closed left hand into the glass held in the right, which they proceed to do, the beautiful part of the experiment being that each coin is distinctly seen and heard to fall into the tumbler. After about, say, eight coins have passed, the performer pretends to hear someone say that there are no coins in the left hand. He immediately opens the left

hand and shows the two remaining coins. The hand is closed, and the two that are left pass singly into the glass held in the right, in the same manner as their predecessors.

To produce the above illusion it is necessary to study carefully the accompanying drawings, which explain fully the "click" pass before referred to. The coins are first placed in the right hand, as in Fig. 23, and the hand is then quickly turned over, the coins being apparently transferred to the left hand, but in reality the third and fourth fingers of the right hand arrest their fall, Fig. 24 (thereby creating a sound or "click" as if the coins had fallen into left hand), and forthwith palm them in the right hand. If the foregoing be tried once or twice it will be seen what a perfect illusion it produces. Now with the right hand (containing the palmed coins) pick up the tumbler as in Fig. 25. By slightly relaxing the muscles of the palm of the right hand, the coins are released one at a time and fall into the glass, Fig. 26. A considerable amount of practice and delicacy of manipulation is essential to ensure the coins dropping singly. The additional effect of being able to show two coins in the left hand, after eight have passed into the tumbler, is brought about by finger-palming in the left hand two dummy coins pivoted together which admits of their

Fig. 24

being spread apart to look like two coins. These are shown, and in the act of again closing the left hand, they are reverse palmed, the fact of their being riveted together enabling this to be accomplished with ease.

The author can confidently recommend

Fig. 26

the above trick as being one of the best with which he is acquainted. . . .

DOWNS' NEW FAN PASS

This is another favorite pass invented by the author. The coins are held as in Fig. 27. The right fingers now allow the coins to slide down one after another with a jingle into the palm of the left hand which forthwith closes up on the same, but just as it does so the two middle fingers of the right hand grip the coins and immediately palm them in the right hand. If this is carried out neatly, and under cover of the movement of the left hand, the

Fig. 27

spectators will be absolutely convinced that the coins still remain in the left hand.

The foregoing is a very useful method of causing the disappearance of a number of coins after having produced them in a "fan."

THE DOWNS' EUREKA PASS

This is described on page 205 of this book. Downs said of it:

The author has the extreme pleasure, in the following description of the pass to which he has given the above title, in taking the reader into his confidence and explaining to him fully what the writer conscientiously believes to be his most novel, puzzling and prettiest feat:

The pass is used for the vanishing of any number of coins, up to 20, one at a time.

THE "TURNOVER" WITH FORTY COINS

This feat the author considers to be one of the best in his whole act, for the simple reason that no one has yet even attempted to duplicate it publicly. Others have tried it and have got as far as making the coins turn *one way*, but there they stop, it being next to impossible for them to make them return without the use of the other hand.

Fig. 28

The coins are spread from the very tips of the fingers of the right hand to the wrist, Fig. 28. Now, by slightly contracting the palm the whole row turns completely over

Fig. 29

in pretty fashion. Fig. 29 shows the coins in the act of turning. Fig. 30 shows them turned completely over. Now by a delicate jerk with the tips of the two middle fingers the coins are made to assume their original position. The author is able to turn the coins over quite slowly and also do the reverse movement in the same manner.

Fig. 30

This makes the trick look more effective, but it is exceedingly difficult of accomplishment, though, of course, it can be done with sufficient practice. The author fears that at first sight some of the sleights mentioned in this book may appear impossible of successful execution, and he therefore begs to say that he has described nothing but what he has accomplished himself, each of the experiments herein contained being quite practical.

TO PALM AND MAKE THE PASS WITH FORTY COINS

[Editor's Note: Here a paradoxical situation arises. The move as described is not possible to execute with thirty to forty coins. However, we shall give it in the author's own words, for what it may be worth.]

Now to describe the correct method as employed by the author. The pile of thirty to forty coins (they were dumped out of the hat onto the table after having been "caught") is taken between the fingers in exactly the same manner as described in "The Elusive Pass." The right hand now makes a motion of passing the coins into the left, but in reality the two fingers holding the coins bend round and palm them in the right hand, in the position shown in Fig. 20, the left hand closing at the same time and the right hand keeping in an upright position pointing at the left. The left hand is now shown empty. The right hand can be brought down to hang in a natural position by slightly bending the third finger round on to the top of the coins which keeps them from falling, and the same can be produced in any manner the performer desires.

The author's favorite method is to produce them in a shower from under the vest. This is accomplished in the following manner: As the right hand (containing the coins) lifts up the edge of the vest with the first finger and thumb, the third finger, which it will be remembered is supporting the coins, pushes them under the vest. The stomach is now expanded and the hand can almost be withdrawn, and by gradually drawing in the abdomen the coins escape a few at a time and fall into the right hand which is waiting to receive them.

[Editor's Note: The vanish Downs actually used was quite similar to the Vanish for Several Coins, page 45. After the "Turnover" the coins are lying on the palm of the hand as in Fig. 30. The hand simply tilts and simulates the action of pouring the coins into the left hand, held immediately below as if actually receiving coins. The coins in the right hand slide down and are held in a stack on the curled second and third right fingers, and as they slide down and come to rest in a stack they make a sound like the actual pouring of coins from one hand into the other, which helps to create the necessary illusion. The back of the hand pouring the coins is to the audience during the action, and the cupped left hand conceals the fact that it receives nothing. Performed with no lost motion, this vanish is most deceptive.]

There you have it—the most complete exposition of The Miser's Dream in all of magical literature, by the greatest master of the feat in the history of magic. It would command attention today, and get top billing, for Downs' "Miser's Dream" was more than a trick. It was a piece of characterization—just as much as Cardini's act is today.

Over the years, the top hat as a receptacle for the coins has given way to a variety of more modern containers—a champagne bucket (often gimmicked to conceal and deliver loads of coins), a child's toy sand pail, a cocktail shaker, a glass tumbler with the side slotted just above the bottom, so the same coins can be caught over and over again by changing the glass from hand to hand, a champagne glass, etc. I have seen Downs himself use a straight-sided metal pail or can. And tons of coin catchers and weird contrivances have been sold to amateur magicians to eliminate the sleight of hand in catching the coins. A few of the coin droppers, such as the Kellar coin dropper, have much merit, and as we mentioned elsewhere, Downs used a Kellar dropper in a later version of the trick.

Owen Clark made a thumb tip in which a folding coin was concealed, and used it in his version of the trick, the coins as he caught them being tossed into a glass bowl. (See The Stanley Collins Section, Chapter XV.) The celebrated Felicien Trewey is said to have presented a pantomime version of the feat with no coins at all, the sound effects being produced off stage to enhance the illusion. Al Flosso convulses his audiences with his version of this celebrated trick.

The Miser's Dream deserves to be revived as a program item. It is far more stageworthy than Cup and Ball routines, and it displays the abilities of the performer just as much. Of the modern versions of the trick, we present several having great audience appeal in the pages that follow.

The Miser's Dream

GLENN HARRISON

One of the main reasons The Miser's Dream is so seldom seen today is because most of the routines in print are outdated, too difficult for the average performer, or are not suitable for modern presentation.

This routine by Glenn Harrison is pure entertainment. The only sleight of any consequence in the entire routine is the simple thumb palm. Not only is the routine thoroughly practical in every respect, it is easily adaptable to either straight or comedy presentation. If you like to make your audience laugh, this is for you. The routine has a novel beginning and an ending that is guaranteed to leave the most blasé audience weak from laughter.

The number of coins the performer uses will depend on several factors—the speed at which he works, the length of time he wishes to consume, and his ability. It is better to use a small number of coins and have confidence in your handling of them than to use a greater number and not be sure of yourself. You might start with a small number and progress to a larger number. It is better to use a smaller number of coins which are easier to handle, and concentrate on each production, than to produce a great number in rapid succession without rhyme or reason. I remember seeing a magician who produced countless numbers of lighted cigarettes from the air so rapidly the spectators hardly realized what was taking place. On the other hand I have seen magicians produce only a half dozen cigarettes in such a manner that the appearance of each cigarette was an event.

For some reason or other it is more effective to seemingly pluck coins from different objects around the stage and different parts of your body than to get them from the air. Of course, the very essence of the mystery depends on the performer's ability to convince the spectators that there are coins all about him just waiting to be picked. Make each production a real event. If you pretend to see a coin on the flame of a candle, pluck it off like a flower. There is no mystery in simply having a coin appear at the fingertips as you reach into the air. Make each production as magical as possible. Act out your part, imagine yourself a real magician and that you actually have the ability to produce money from the air.

To make an event out of apparently extracting a coin from the air do it this way: Turn your gaze upward as if looking for something, then pretend to see it. Follow its flight as it moves slowly about. Suddenly reach out and as you pretend to catch it, quickly bring the coin into view at your fingertips. Look at your treasure, then at the audience as if to say, "Look what I've found —a silver dollar!" Show it, drop it into the pail, then repeat the process. Produce the next one from your elbow or knee. Vary the production. Pluck each coin from a different place and I think you will find that the production of a coin from yours or a spectator's clothing is much more amusing than if the coin was taken from the air. Imagine that the coins are actually there—all you have to do is pluck them.

Requirements: 20 to 24 silver dollars or palming coins, a white silk handkerchief,

a small metal pail, a flash bill, a coin holder to hold six or eight coins, and a box of matches or cigarette lighter.

If you plan to use real silver dollars, select some well worn ones from the 1922 or 1923 issues. The 1921 vintage is too rough and thick. For a night club audience a copper or chromed champagne bucket or ice bucket is a must, but for mixed audiences where children are present a child's sand pail is ideal.

Preparation: Have one silver dollar and the flash bill in your wallet, which is in your inside coat pocket. Silk is in your left breast coat pocket. Put six or eight coins in the coin holder and fasten it under the lower left edge of your coat. Place about eight coins in your left trousers pocket and one in the right trousers pocket. Rest the pail on its side on your table and arrange

Fig. 1

the remaining coins inside it in an overlapping row, Fig. 1. Wedge a small article on either side of the pail to prevent it from rolling and dislodging the coins.

The first part of the routine works very well with soft music but is also very effective with patter.

Routine: Begin by removing your wallet. With your right hand, extract the flash bill with the silver dollar hidden behind it and covered by your fingers. Show the bill, then take a match, or your lighter, and set fire to it. The bill will burn rapidly toward your fingers, and just as it is almost consumed toss it and the coin into the air about eighteen inches. The coin will go higher than the burning bill but a flare will follow part way and expire, leaving nothing but the silver dollar, which drops into your hand. On first trial you may drop the coin because you will be distracted by the burning bill and fumble the coin as it descends. But just ignore the burning bill and keep your eye on the coin and you will have no trouble catching it. Apparently the bill is transformed by fire to a silver dollar.

Pick up the pail with your left hand in the following manner: Extend the fingers well inside and bring the coins together in a stack as you lift the pail away from the table. Turn to the left and as you pretend

Fig. 2

to toss the coin into the pail, thumb palm it and release one with the left fingers, which falls with a clink to the bottom of the pail, Fig. 2. The timing on this action is very important. If the left hand releases a coin too soon or too late the illusion is lost. A fraction of a second off in timing will mar the effect. The coin should strike the bottom of the bucket the exact instant that one would had it actually been dropped from the right hand. There is nothing difficult about this procedure—the right hand with its coin enters the mouth of the

bucket and thumb palms the coin. At the same time the left hand releases one coin. Practice this over and over until you can do it perfectly every time. While the right hand is engaged in producing the next coin the left hand readies a second coin for quick release. Simply slide a coin downward from the stack so it is barely held by the fingertips, then it can be released instantly, without fumbling, Fig. 3.

Fig. 3

Continue picking coins from nowhere, varying the operation as much as possible until only two coins remain under the left fingers and one is thumb palmed in the right. For a bit of comedy, reach for a coin and failing to get it, rub your fingers together. Look with disappointment at your hand, then turn to the audience and say, "I guess that wasn't a coin." Immediately look out and say, "Oh, there it is." Reach out and produce it. Pretend to drop it into the pail but thumb palm it and drop one from the left hand. Now you have one coin in each hand.

Produce another coin and show it in your right hand. Go through the motions of tossing it high into the air—really thumb palm it and follow its invisible flight with your eyes. Then as it falls, thrust out the bucket to catch it. The moment your eyes reach the bucket release the coin from the left hand, permitting it to fall. If properly acted out this bit of pantomime is very effective. Now only one coin remains thumb palmed in your right hand. Seemingly pluck the last piece of silver from the air and drop it openly into the bucket. Now pour all the coins into your right hand, place the bucket aside and remove the silk from your breast pocket. Spread it over your palm up left hand, then dump the coins audibly onto the silk and close the left fingers over them. Open the hand and dump them back into the right hand and exhibit them in an overlapping row. Apparently repeat the action of pouring the coins into your left hand but execute the Vanish for Several Coins (a), (page 45), retaining them in your right hand and closing the left hand and turning it over. The sound created by this sleight produces the illusion that the coins did actually arrive in the left hand. The right hand drops innocently to the side and the left hand throws the silk, apparently full of coins, into the air. Seemingly the coins disappear in midair and the silk floats to the floor. If you are working with an orchestra have the drummer hit the bass drum the instant the handkerchief reaches the floor. For some reason this is funny to an audience.

With your right side toward the spectators, stoop, and as you pick up the silk with your right hand, steal the load of coins from the holder with your left hand. Now you have a number of coins in your right hand, hidden by the silk. Turn to the right and apparently shake the coins from the silk into the bucket. This is a strong finish but you are prepared for an encore. Toss the silk into the air, catch it with your right hand, and as you step to the other side of the table transfer the silk to your left hand, over the load of coins. Again hold the silk over the bucket, give it a little shake and more coins stream out.

This concludes the first part of the routine and you can stop here. But if you wish to continue you can do so with excellent effect by proceeding with

PHASE TWO

Ask for the assistance of two men. As they come forward casually place your hands in your trousers pockets and finger palm the eight coins in your left hand and the single coin in your right hand. Remove your hands from your pockets, pick up the bucket with your left hand and hold the load inside of it as previously described. Do this in a casual, off-hand manner as the men come forward and the action will never be noticed.

Stand one man on your left, the other on your right. Reach out and pretend to pluck a coin from the clothing of the man on your left and apparently toss it into the pail. Actually you thumb palm it and drop one from the left hand instead. Produce one or two more from his clothing, then take the end of his tie with your right hand and shake a coin from it (the one you had thumb palmed) into the bucket. Tell him he can do the same thing. Instruct him to reach into the air after a coin, with his left hand. He gets nothing, so tell him to try again but throw the coin into the bucket. After he makes a grab into the air have him hold his fist over the bucket and open it. As he opens his hand allow a coin to drop into the pail from your left hand. The illusion is that he caught a coin and dropped it into the pail.

Now turn to the man on your right and ask him to blow into the bucket. Meanwhile you have transferred the bucket to your right hand and the left still retains the load of coins. Place your left hand to his

Fig. 4

nose and stream the coins into the bucket, Fig. 4. This is good for a laugh but the business that follows is even funnier. Immediately whisper to him to remove his handkerchief and pretend to blow his nose. While the spectators are laughing turn to the spectator on the left and as you begin conversing with him steal a load of coins from the bucket. Don't worry about anyone seeing you do this. They will be laughing and watching the man on your right and paying little attention to you. Look around in surprise as he blows his nose into the handkerchief. You will know when he does this as there will be a burst of laughter from the audience. Take the handkerchief from him with the hand that contains the coins and as you exclaim, "You are cheating me!" stream the coins from the handkerchief into the bucket.

Quickly thank the men and dismiss them.

EXTRA

Here is a brilliant bit of business that will fit well into the first part of the routine, especially if you are working before a smaller audience. The single coin in your right hand has a daub of wax at its center. When you are down to one coin in your left hand, instead of throwing the right hand coin

into the bucket, stick it flat against the bottom of the bucket—the wax will make it adhere. At the same time release the coin from the left hand. Apparently the coin has penetrated the bottom of the bucket! Now place the bucket over the top of a tall, clear glass tumbler, the coin being directly over the mouth of the glass. Remove a coin from the bucket, hold it about 12 inches above the bucket and drop it. When it strikes the bottom of the bucket it will jar loose the waxed-on coin underneath, causing it to drop into the glass. It makes a very pretty visible penetration, heightened by sound effects!

The Miser's Dream

M. S. WHITFORD'S VERSION

Here is another modern version of this old classic that should appeal to many. The routine is unique in that the performer produces fourteen dollar size coins without the benefit of gimmicks or body loads. Nothing is used but the coins, a transparent glass to drop the coins in as they are produced, and the two hands. And best of all it is just as effective when performed at close range as at a distance.

Requisites and Preparation: A glass of the high ball type with a recessed bottom large enough to hold seven dollar size palming coins. These glasses are obtainable in grocery stores, and come packed with pickles or relish, put out by the Glazier-Crandle Pickle Company and the American Lady Company. It should not be too difficult to find a glass suitable for the trick in a dime or department store.

Also required are fourteen thin type palming coins, which must be made smooth by polishing their flat surfaces on an emery stone or emery cloth. Most palming coins available today are so roughly embossed they are difficult to handle in a stack and slide apart noiselessly. If the palming coins you have are of this variety simply grind down their rough surfaces with a rough emery stone then smooth them with a finer stone or a fine grade emery cloth. The milled edges should not be disturbed—the sharper they are the better. There are quite a number of tricks in this book that can be made easier to perform by the use of smooth coins, so it is advisable to prepare

Fig. 1

a few and have them on hand. Downs prepared his coins in this manner.

Have the glass on the table, mouth down, with seven of the coins stacked in the recessed bottom, Fig. 1. The coins cannot be seen (except from above) because of the

Fig. 2

Fig. 3

scientific principle known as refraction of light. The remaining seven coins are in your right trousers or coat pocket.

Working: Secretly secure the seven coins from your pocket and hold them together in the Downs palm position (see The Downs Palm, page 3). Pick up the glass with the left third and fourth fingers on top of coins and reverse glass, fingers holding coins securely in recessed bottom, Fig. 2. This is the same way you would hold a glass to drink from it. Turn slightly to the right and permit your right palm (fingers apart) to be seen empty as you reach out and produce the first coin, Fig. 3. (For methods, see The Downs Palm, page 3, and Four Coins to a Glass, page 160.) Drop the coin into the glass, then shake the glass, rattling the coin inside. Do this after each coin is produced so the spectators can actually hear as well as see the coins in the glass.

Face the spectators, then with the back of the right hand toward them, pluck the next coin from the end of your tie. Keep the back of your right hand toward the spectators as you get the third coin from behind your left knee. Produce the next one from the elbow of the bent left arm, then swing back to the right and catch the fifth from the air in the same manner as you did the first.

Face the spectators again and apparently pull one out of your hair. Hold your nose with your right forefinger and thumb and as you pretend to blow the last coin from your nose, release the coin from the hand and catch it in the glass.

Apparently the trick is over but actually you are only half through. Next comes the procedure of getting the seven coins from the bottom of the glass to the right hand and into the Downs palm position. This is accomplished as follows: Bring the glass over the right hand (which is held in a loose fist and back outward), apparently set the glass on top of the fist, with the right thumb and first finger in the same position as they were in when they held the first stack of seven coins. At this point, the left third and fourth fingers lower the coins from the bottom of the glass into the right thumb (Downs palm) palm position. Immediately on releasing the coins from the left fingers, the left fingers slide to the top of the glass, pick it up and shake the coins already in it. Set the glass back on the right fist and return the left third and fourth fingers to the same bottom hold as before. This is misdirection and does not affect the trick. Now your right hand is loaded with seven more coins ready to be produced as at the beginning.

Produce these coins one at a time, varying the procedure as much as possible.

Now slowly pour the fourteen coins from the glass into your right hand and place the glass on the table. Slowly pour the coins from your right to your left hand. Arrange them in the left palm in an overlapping row, starting near the wrist and spreading them almost to the base of the fingers. Bring the left hand over to the right and apparently pour the coins back into the palm up right hand, but execute the Vanish for Several Coins (a), page 45, retaining the coins in the left hand as the right closes

and pretends to hold the coins. The sound produced by this sleight creates the illusion that the coins were actually dumped into the right hand.

Keep the right hand closed as though holding the coins as you reach over and pick up the glass by its rim with the left thumb and first finger, back of hand pointing toward audience. Pretend to throw the coins from the extended and raised right hand into the right sleeve. Shake the right arm as though the coins were going down the sleeve, across the back and down the left sleeve into the glass, which is held about hip high. With the left hand, release most of the coins slowly and let them fall into the glass, keeping the glass in motion, causing the coins to rattle. Retain two or three coins in the left hand and pretend some of the coins stuck in the left sleeve. Grasp the left sleeve at the elbow with the right hand and shake it, at the same time releasing the remainder of the palmed coins from the left hand which fall into the glass apparently out of the sleeve.

Patter suggestions: "I had a friend and his name was Bill. He never worked and never will. He always had a glass in his hand (pick up glass) and he always had money (at this point produce first coin). He wore those beautiful hand-painted ties (produce coin from tie), tailor made suits (produce coin from knee). He hung around swanky joints (produce coin from elbow of bent left arm). He travelled a lot (move right arm through air and produce coin at fingertips with arm extended). He kept his hair well trimmed (produce coin from hair). He always blew himself when in a crowd (blow one from nose into glass).

(At this point execute the move of transferring coins from bottom of glass into right Downs palm.) "I asked Bill how he could have money and not work. Since we were old friends and had attended school together, he agreed to tell me. The secret was—*magic*, my boy! You just wish for money, reach out and there it is. So I said, 'Why not try it?' I wished there was a coin right out there (with eyes pointing to a spot in front of you), so I reached out and there it was (reach out and produce coin, act surprised, and drop coin into glass). Maybe there is something to magic, let's try it again." (Continue to produce the remaining coins. After producing the last set of seven coins, reach out in the air, pretend to get a coin, and drop it into glass—no noise. Put your forefinger to your mouth and say, "Hush money.")

At this point you pour the fourteen coins from glass into right hand, and then into left hand. You apparently throw them back into right hand, but retain them in left hand. "This is the way magicians use their sleeves to do magic—up the right sleeve, across the shoulder, down the left sleeve into the glass." Go through motions as described previously.

A Miser's Dream Routine

Jack Makepeace

This version combines several standard sleights and tricks in an interesting and novel routine, which can be varied according to the performer's ability.

Requisites: Five thin palming coins, a wine glass, and a small dish with a rim high enough to conceal the five coins when they are placed therein. The dish is on the table.

As you begin you have the five coins concealed in the Downs palm position of your right hand and you are holding the wine glass by its stem with your left hand. With your left side toward the spectators, reach out with your right hand which is held palm outward) and produce the first coin from

the air. Drop it into the glass, then pluck a second one from a different spot. (For a description of these moves see The Downs Palm, page 3, or Arthur Buckley's method in Four Coins to a Glass, page 160.) Vary the production. Get a coin or two from the air, two or three from different parts of the clothing, and the last one from the air.

Empty the coins into your right hand and place the glass on the table. Now perform the Roll Down Production of Four Coins (page 204), or any other flourish, then drop the coins one at a time into the left hand. The left hand stacks the coins in the palm in preparation for the next move.

With the fingers and thumb of the palm down right hand, grasp the top four coins by their edges, lift them up and away from the left hand, which retains the bottom coin palmed and turns palm inward. Right hand deposits its four coins in the dish as the left hand grasps the glass by its rim between the fingers and thumb in such a manner that when the coin is released from the palm it will drop directly into the glass. Take one of the coins from the dish with the right hand and show it. Hold the hands some distance apart and as you make a motion of throwing the coin toward the glass, classic palm it. Pretend to follow its flight to the left hand and the instant your eyes reach the glass, release the coin from the left palm, permitting it to fall into the glass. Rattle the coin in the glass, then transfer the glass to the right hand, which holds it exactly as it was held by the left hand. With the left hand, take a second coin from the dish. Then as you go through the motion of throwing it toward the glass, palm it and release the coin from the right palm, which falls into the glass on top of the first one. Continue this action, alternating hands, until you have four coins in the glass, one hidden in your left palm, and none in the dish. Apparently the dish still contains one coin. Pretend to remove it with the left hand and toss it toward the glass. Release the coin from the left palm so it falls into the glass on top of the others and show the right hand empty.

Pour the coins from the glass into the right hand and place the glass on the table. Pretend to dump the coins into your left hand but retain them in your right hand as you execute the Vanish for Several Coins (a), (page 45). Keep the left hand closed as if it actually held the coins and pick up the glass by its rim with the fingers and thumb of the palm down right hand. Make a throwing motion toward the glass with the left hand as the right hand streams the coins into the glass. Apparently you have thrown all five of the coins invisibly into the glass.

Jack Makepeace sometimes elaborates on the routine by first producing a glass of wine from underneath a handkerchief. After drinking the wine he produces the coins as described and drops them into the glass. To climax the routine he vanishes the coins and glass with the aid of a handkerchief.

It is not within the scope of this book to give the details of the wine glass production as it is quite familiar to most magicians and is sold by magic dealers. The vanish is standard, too. It is the method wherein the glass is covered by a handkerchief (the familiar double variety containing a ring the size of the rim of the glass) and the glass disposed of in a well or servante. The handkerchief is lifted away, apparently with the glass underneath, and tossed into the air. As the handkerchief) descends it is caught by two corners and shown on both sides. The glass and coins have disappeared!

This routine will fit nicely in manipulative acts—and can be presented either in pantomime or with patter. One effect blends into another smoothly and logically.

Perpetual Coins

HARRY BERNARD, *courtesy*
The Linking Ring

After showing both hands unmistakably empty, the performer reaches behind his right knee and produces a coin. He takes it with his left hand and drops it in his pocket. Suddenly a second coin makes its appearance at the fingertips of the right hand. This one is placed in the pocket but another one appears. The effect is similar to the old familiar continuous cigar production and is continued *ad infinitum*.

Requisites and Preparation: Two matching half dollars and a small cookie or cracker.

Have the cookie in the left pocket and a coin in each sleeve. Keep the elbows bent so the coins will not fall out prematurely.

Working: Stand facing the spectators and show both hands empty on both sides. Lower the right hand to the side, catch the coin on the cupped fingers as it falls from the sleeve and produce it from behind the right knee. While this is going on, lower the left hand, catch the coin from that sleeve and hold it concealed in the hand by its opposite edges between the tips of the first and fourth fingers, which is the front finger hold (see The Front Finger Hold, page 5.)

Bring the right hand up in front of your chest, holding it palm inward (fingers extended) as you display the just-produced coin between the tips of the thumb and forefinger. Keeping the left hand palm inward, bring it up to the right hand and take the coin from that hand between the tips of the left forefinger and thumb. In this action the hidden coin is secretly transferred from the left to the right hand. The actual mechanics are as follows: You are still facing the spectators and both hands are backs outward as the left hand approaches the right hand to take the coin. Move the left hand to the right until the left fingers overlap the backs of the right fingers to the second knuckles and press the hidden coin flat against the backs of the two right middle fingers. Retain the coin in this position by right first and fourth fingers, which press together against opposite edges (see The Back Palm, page 5).

Take the visible coin between the tips of the left forefinger and thumb. Under cover of this and the action of swinging the body to the left, transfer the stolen coin in the right hand from back palm position to front finger hold by a simple reversal of the regular back palming movement. The coin is still held by the right first and fourth fingers, but now it is on the palm side of the hand. Show the coin just taken by the left hand at the left fingertips and apparently put it in the coat pocket. When the left hand is in the pocket, grip the coin in the front finger hold and remove the hand, holding it palm inward as you swing

to the right and produce a second coin with the right hand.

An easy and pretty method for causing the coin to suddenly appear at the fingertips follows: Keeping the back of the hand toward the spectators, make a little grab in the air. As this is done release pressure on the lower edge of the coin with the little finger and clip its top edge between the first and second fingers. With the aid of the thumb, suddenly lever up the coin, causing it to make a visible appearance at the fingertips.

Show the right hand on both sides, then as you take the coin with the left hand secretly transfer the other coin from the left to the right hand as before. Produce this coin as described. Catch six or eight coins in the same manner, but don't overdo it. As the left hand enters the pocket the last time it leaves the coin and brings out the cookie hidden in the hand. When removing the last coin, the cookie is transferred to the right hand, then produced and eaten.

Chapter XV

THE STANLEY COLLINS SECTION

T. Nelson Downs · William J. Hilliar · L'Homme Masqué · Allan Shaw · Owen Clark · Charles Morritt · The Purse Trick · Three Coin Monte · The Jumping Sixpence · The Esscee Half Crown and Wafers Trick · Two Heads and a Tail · The Esscee Front and Back Manipulation

The Editor of this volume, my friend John Braun has suggested that I shall add to it, impressions of a few of the coin manipulators whose acts I have witnessed during the past half-century. I shall make no other attempt at chronological order than to start with that outstanding personality whose name is synonymous with coin manipulation, the famous KING OF KOINS.

T. Nelson Downs

In company with my friend Louis Nikola, I witnessed the performance of T. Nelson Downs during the first week of his engagement at the Palace Theatre, London in 1899. I shall never forget his stately entrance from the Prompt side of stage, every leisured step he made being accompanied by a bow and a smile. As done by Downs, this made a dignified and arresting entrance, one which I am certain only he could have made without appearing ridiculous.

Downs was unquestionably a wonderful handler of coins and every inch a showman. Unfortunately I took no notes of his act at the time and now at this late hour can recall very little more of the actual details of the performance than the famous Miser's Dream and sleights with the coins. Some very neat front and back palming with seven cards concluded an act that proved entirely to the taste of the fashionable and very conservative patrons of the Palace Theatre of half a century ago.

I have often been asked by young conjurers if Downs really did all the seemingly impossible sleights that are illustrated in his book *Modern Coin Manipulation*. I can answer definitely that on the stage at any rate, he did *not* do all those weird and wonderful moves; he had too keen a sense of stage values to indulge in tomfooleries. He did, however, do the turn-over of a spread of coins on the hand, a feat which I personally found no difficulty in performing almost at the first attempt.

William J. Hilliar

The great friend of Downs when he was in London was William J. Hilliar who at that time was living in Brixton, London, S.W. There he and I would foregather on Sunday afternoons to work out and practice coin sleights together.

Hilliar was a dextrous handler of coins, with a delicacy of touch that particularly appealed to me. His own version of the Miser's Dream left nothing to be desired.

L'Homme Masqué

On the occasion when I saw this superb artist at the St. James's Hall in London some fifty years ago, he gave one of the most entrancing presentations of the classic money-catching trick that I have ever seen. Judged by modern standards, relatively few coins were produced, probably not more than a dozen, but all made their appearance without the back and front repetitions that all too frequently turn an artistic trick into a mere exhibition of finger-flinging. I ought to add that L'Homme Masqué did none of the passing of coins through crown and similar absurdities; he was an *artist*.

Since the money-catching trick was not always included in his programme, I count myself very fortunate on being present when it was performed by L'Homme Masqué.

Allan Shaw

We have had scores of jugglers, many of them with almost breath-taking feats of incredible difficulty; but there was only one *artist* in juggling, the incomparable Paul Cinquevalli. As with juggling, so it is with coin manipulation. Of the comparative few conjurers who have achieved distinction in this very exacting branch of manipulation, one only of those whose performances I have personally witnessed can be classed as an artist: Allan Shaw. He combined every ideal; an engaging personality; an unerring sense of the theatre; an original and truly amazing coin technique and above all, the grace and fine taste of the born artist.

Shaw would have none of the cramped fingers or the jerky, unnatural back-and-front ugliness that spoils so much of the work of the poetry of motion. His opening trick with a hard felt hat and one coin, if baldly written up as a magazine article, might seem almost banal. In Shaw's hands

it was a gem. A coin, apparently thrown into space, was heard to fall into the hat. Almost immediately the coin was taken out from under the crown just as if it had forced its way through the felt. That was the effect he created, not once but several times in succession. The coin was simply palmed in the right hand and the sound of a coin falling inside the hat was produced by a snap of the forefinger on the sweat-band.

Shaw's work to be fully appreciated, had to be seen at close quarters. I had the privilege on several occasions of witnessing some of the most beautiful artistry with coins that I am ever likely to see again.

It gives me the greatest pleasure to write these few words in appreciation of a great artist.

Owen Clark

Alfred Owen Clark, to give him his full name, would have been the last man in the World to suggest that his metier was sleight of hand. Essentially an inventor of highly original mechanical tricks, he had little or no time for manipulation *qua* manipulation. Judge then of my surprise when one morning in Caledonian Market, London, where he and I often met, both on the look out for bargains in antiques, he was full of enthusiastic excitement over an entirely new approach to the coin catching trick which is such a favourite of mine. His invention was to have none of the usual flourishing movement of hand and fingers and no handling of the receptacle which was to receive the coins. His hand was to have fingers wide apart and to be shown slowly back and front before each coin made its appearance. Furthermore, each coin as it was produced was to be dropped into a clear glass bowl. It really sounded too good to be true.

Shortly after this talk, I had a note from Owen notifying me that I might see this new coin miracle at St. George's Hall. Accordingly I went and saw it performed exactly as he had described the effect to me. The broadside production of the coin between finger and thumb of right hand was made just as it was promised that it should be made; there was not a semblance of flourish and the dropping of coins in the glass salad bowl was certainly a perfect synchronization. But alas! to echo the words of the late lamented Bernard Shaw, it was "Too true to be good."

On my appearance in his dressing room, Owen hailed me with "Well! what about your Miser's Dream now?" "Owen," I said, "I congratulate you most heartily on being able to do the trick at all. How ever you managed to handle a coin with your poor thumb handicapped with that great poultice on it, is a mystery to me." Owen's face was a study. I think now that I was rather brutal, for Clark had an idea there that might be made a practical trick if developed by some mechanical genius. I do know that Clark never really forgave me for my sarcasm at his expense.

The "poultice" to which I referred was a sort of false thumb* carrying a folding coin which was made to spring open between thumb and forefinger. But unfortunately, it literally shrieked its presence.

The glass bowl, ornamented with the metal-plated rim familiar to many salad bowls, was mounted on a tripod. A thin wire stretched across the mouth of the bowl, when struck with the hand, released one of the coins hidden in the thick rim. This part of the business was above reproach.

A more apt title for this article would be The Gentle Art of Making Enemies.

* EDITOR'S NOTE: In Will Goldston's *Secrets of Famous Illusionists* (1933), Clark's "false thumb carrying a folding coin" is described, titled "The Superfine Coin Fake."

Charles Morritt

Although Morritt made no specialty of coin manipulation, he included at one time in his repertoire two very effective tricks. From a very soft Panama hat he would produce not a few coins, but several hundreds. The loads, under cover of effective misdirection, were stolen from behind the left lapel of his Dress Coat. This concealment of small and soft articles behind lapel was a dodge very much favoured by Morritt.

Another engaging trick that he featured for some time was based on the old Fairground and Race-course swindle, the Purse Trick. Having obtained the assistance of two male members of his audience, he seated them one on each side of him and handed to each a small purse. To the man on his left he addressed himself somewhat as follows: "I want you, Sir, to imagine that you have two half-crown seats in the Stalls of a theatre. Here are two half-crowns to represent your preferment." (This is a silver coin about the size of our half dollar.) Into a purse apparently went two half-crowns and the closed purse was handed to the care of Mr. Left. The man on the right was told to imagine that he had two seats in the Gallery of the theatre, these to be represented by two pennies. Mr. Right then took charge of a purse containing presumably the two pennies. (The large copper English pennies.)

The two men were told they must now wish to change places in the theatre. On opening their respective purses, the surprised helpers found that their coins had somehow or other changed places.

Morritt was a master of the purse trick, the actual performance of which seems little known among conjurers. The moves are not easy to describe in words, but if our good artist can supplement my explanations with a sketch showing the hold of the coins at the commencement of the trick,

I think I can make the thing intelligible to a handler of coins. At the outset, the grip of the coins to be substituted must be clearly understood, for it is upon this little known grip and attendant subtlety that the deception is so good. Two pennies are gripped between the index and third fingers *at their roots* as shown in Fig. 1. This hold,

Fig. 1

demanding no thumb restriction and permitting the fingers to be outstretched with perfect freedom, is a particularly useful one that has been overlooked or neglected by conjurers. It is mainly upon this hold of coins that the Race-course Purse Trick depends.

The two pennies are then concealed by overlapping the two half-crowns *in line with the fingers* and NOT across them, Fig. 2. Thus, two half-crowns can be openly

Fig. 2

exhibited on the extended right hand of the conjurer which otherwise appears to contain nothing. But this is not all. The two half-crowns are carelessly tossed on to the open flat left hand and then back to their original penny-covering position in the right hand. On this return to the right hand, care must be taken that the pennies are entirely covered, a simple matter, as experiment will prove.

Now unless the exchange is made absolutely convincing the trick will fail. It is a move easier to demonstrate than to explain in writing. As a purse is picked up and shown to be empty with the left hand, the right turns over to permit all four coins to be gripped and shown between thumb and first and second fingers. The silver coins by this act are in view of the audience. All four are dropped unmistakably into the purse; but as if to assure the audience that there is "no deception," the two half-crowns are taken out and shown again. Now comes the two moves that must be neatly and convincingly made. Held between thumb and forefinger of the right hand the two half-crowns actually go inside the purse; but the hold on them is not released. Smoothly and naturally they are withdrawn and passed behind the purse as the left hand closes it. The purse with the concealed half-crowns under it is *tossed* across to the left hand and similarly tossed back to the right hand. Mr. Left then receives his purse from the left hand of the conjurer whose right hand now holds and grips the two half-crowns in the roots of the first and third fingers as already explained.

All is now ready for the second exchange. Two pennies taken from the left trouser pocket and laid over the gripped half-crowns serve to make possible a repetition of the series of moves I have already described. The conjurer is, of course, left with a duplicate set of pennies at the end, to be disposed of at a convenient moment.

I have outlined the trick just as Morritt performed it and very effective it was in his hands. Morritt, who was blessed with a very large, fleshy hand, could hold four or five coins in this Purse Grip with ease and certainty.

I should add that the purses should be of the single snap variety and about 3¼″ wide by about 2¾″ deep.

Three Coin Monte

In his Magical Monthly for July 1913, Servais LeRoy tells of a trick with three pennies that was done in a tramcar in Madrid by an "ingenious gentleman of ragged appearance." LeRoy describes the effect in these words:

". . . displayed the pennies on his open hand, one near the tips of the fingers, one near the base of his fingers, and one in the centre of palm. He showed them back and front, and then moistened a small piece of paper, and stuck this to one coin. He then moved coins, altering their positions, sliding one over the other. During this movement he slips the paper from one coin to the other, very neatly when actually doing it, and rather clumsily as a blind. Then we had to wager as to where the paper was—under which coin."

If that WAS the exact effect of the trick that LeRoy witnessed, it has not the cleañ and open procedure of the trick as I saw it performed by a sharper in a shop in Shafterbury Avenue, London when I was in my late teens. Let me describe the trick as I saw it. After showing three mint new pennies back and front, my nimble friend moistened a paper wafer and stuck it on the head side of one of the coins. All three laid, tail side up, in a row on the counter, the

one with the wafer being between the two others. So that it could be lifted clear without any fumbling, each coin slightly overlapped the near edge of the counter. Starting with the one at his left, each coin was lifted and turned to show that the water was where I supposed it to be, viz. between the two others. After making a very straightforward and simple transposition of the three coins, he asked me to guess which one was labelled. Needless to say I was always wrong.

Now let me explain the simple sleight. Simple, indeed, it is in theory, but it needs delicate and smooth handling. The important thing is to understand and get the correct hold of the coins. The edge of coin which projects over the edge of counter or table is pressed slightly down with the thumb *which must be held in line with the edge of table* so that the opposite edge can be taken by the index finger. Thus lifted, the plane of the coin will be almost in line with the forefinger, Fig. 3.

The wafer, which should be no more than five-eighths of an inch in diameter, must be of soft, porous paper and wetted on both sides. A piece cut from a cheap newspaper serves the purpose admirably.

Let us now imagine that our three pennies are in a row on table, the one carrying

Fig. 3

the wafer being between the other two. Pick up No. 1 and turn hand palm up to display the under side of the coin, Fig. 4, and replace the coin on table. Pick up No. 2 in the same manner and show that it is the one with the wafer. Now as the hand

Fig. 4

turns knuckles up to replace this coin, the middle finger-tip sweeps across the under surface and carries the wafer away, a steal which is quite undetectible if correctly handled. Instantly this middle finger, carrying the wafer on its tip, is curled back into the palm in which position the stolen wafer is well out of sight. When next the hand turns palm up to show the under side of No. 3 coin, it will be found that with the second, third and fourth fingers curled back toward the palm, the wafer on the middle finger tip is completely hidden. In the act of replacing this last coin, the middle finger presses the wafer on to the under side, the greater movement of the turning hand covering the lesser movement of the middle finger.

Any transposition of the coins may now be indulged in, always provided that the moves are straightforward and in no way misleading.

When I first saw this trick, it was performed with all coins showing the tail side uppermost. A variation could, of course, be made by having the coin with the wafer showing a head, as opposed to the two others showing the tail sides; but this would be very bad conjuring.

The Jumping Sixpence

I first saw this curious little feat performed many years ago by a sailor, but did not find out the exact way to do it until some years later. A small coin, a sixpence or a farthing (about the size of our dime), laid on the wrist is made to turn completely over or even to be propelled several inches in the air by merely giving a turn of the hand to the left.

There is no hard and fast rule for achieving this little trick; the best way must be found out by personal experiment. All that I can do is to indicate the general procedure.

Lay the small coin on the wrist just below that part which is known to Palmists as The Bracelets. Now with fingers outstretched, bend the end joint of thumb and bring the tip of the forefinger on to the thumb nail. The tendency at this stage will be for the free fingers to bend inwards; they must be kept rigidly outstretched. Now by turning the hand sharply to the left, a peculiar snap of the wrist tendons, quite audible with strongly developed wrists, gives the necessary impulse to the coin. The best plan for determining the exact placing of the coin is to press with left thumb on the right wrist and feel for the necessary click of the tendons.

Another method to bring about the desired click of the tendons is to bring the middle finger hard on the ball of the thumb and then make the always necessary turn of the hand to the left.

Although this little feat is by no means a novelty, I do not remember ever having seen an explanation of it in print.

An original method of propelling quite a large coin high in the air, is one that can create a deal of amusement. A much larger coin, a penny or a half-crown piece is laid on the middle joint of the second finger. Without the slightest movement of the hand itself, the finger bent on its middle joint kicks the coin with a spin some two feet or more in the air. The feat looks so simple that an onlooker will always want to try to imitate it. All that happens in his hand is that the coin slithers on to the floor without being raised an inch above the finger; and unless he is in possession of the simple secret he will never succeed in emulating the trick.

The secret depends on the knack of being able to bend the end joint of a finger without bending the middle one, a control that is very easily acquired. If then the end joint is flexed and kept flexed as the middle joint is bent, the coin on knuckle will be impelled upwards with considerable force. In performance, of course, the fact that the end joint is flexed must not be known to an onlooker; it must appear that the finger, extended perfectly straight, merely bends at its middle joint. This means that the bending of the two joints must be simultaneous action.

I have described the feat as performed on the middle finger. If end joint control is made easier on any other finger, it can, of course, serve the purpose of the feat equally well.

The Esscee Half-Crown and Wafers Trick

If this little informal conceit is handled as it should be handled, there is not a false or unnatural move in it. In addition to a half-crown and a penny, preferably a smooth, well-worn one, two gummed wafers about the size of a farthing, and a pen or a pencil must be readily accessible.

Both sides of the half-crown taken from

left trouser pocket are made identifiable by means of the two individually marked stickers. This half-crown changes into a penny. After both hands have been shown unmistakably empty except for the exposed penny, the left returns to trouser pocket and brings out the original marked half-crown.

There is a particular reason why the half-crown shall be taken from left trouser pocket. When it is brought into view, it has behind it a penny which, being smaller than the silver coin, is perfectly concealed. The two coins, as one only, are held between the thumb and forefinger as if in readiness for the French Drop, but with hand turned to display the face of the half-crown instead of its edge.

So soon as the stickers are marked one is picked up and stuck on the face of the half-crown. It should be made clear without necessarily drawing attention to the fact, that the right hand, before it picks up the second wafer, contains nothing. Now comes a really very pretty move. To turn the half-crown over, the ball of the right thumb presses on the lower edge of the half-crown and the index and second finger go behind so that they completely cover the penny, Fig. 5. The penny can thus be slid off to

Fig. 5

Fig. 6

be concealed behind the first and second fingers as seen in Fig. 6. As the right hand moves away to obtain the second gummed wafer, the penny is passed to the orthodox finger grip at the roots of the second and third fingers. The thumb and index fingers being free, pick up the second wafer and stick it on the reverse side of the half-crown still held in the left fingers.

The half-crown has now to be exchanged for the penny, the preparation for which is made by shifting the penny from the roots of the second and third fingers to the roots of the first and second fingers. The right thumb, then passing under the half-crown, clips the coin in the familiar thumb grip to allow the penny to take its place between the thumb and forefinger of the left hand. Smoothly done this has a very pretty effect.

From the thumb grip, the half-crown is transferred to the finger palm position as the left hand with its penny passes to the right hand. The penny, then balanced on the edge of the right forefinger, is spun high into the air by being kicked up with the thumb in the way a coin is usually spun for tossing purposes. As all eyes, including the conjurer's, follow the upward flight of the coin, the half-crown is quietly and unobtrusively dropped into the LEFT sleeve. Both hands can now be shown freely. Displaying the penny in the right hand, the

conjurer says: "I am not going to insult your intelligence by asking you to believe that our half-crown has by some metamorphic process been turned into a penny. No, my friends; I merely exchanged the one for the other; and had you watched me as closely as you ought to have done, you would have seen my left hand steal the silver coin back into my trouser pocket. Here it is, you see."

During this harangue, the left hand, dropped to the side, receives the half-crown from the sleeve; and the thing is done.

Two Heads and a Tail

Although strictly speaking this little trick is more for the sharper than for the conjurer, it has a surprise as well as a catch. I contributed it to one of the English conjuring magazines (I forget which one) many years ago, but as I have never seen or heard of it being done by conjurers, I must conclude that it has been either overlooked or forgotten.

It is based on the well-known principle of arranging that the under one of two pennies held between the thumb and forefinger of the right hand shall turn over as it is dropped on to the palm of the other hand.

The two pennies and a farthing which are needed for the trick are stacked in this order: Penny, tail side up; on that a farthing head side up, and finally on top, the other penny, head side up. With the coins thus stacked and held between the thumb and forefinger, the right hand should be about a foot above the palm of the waiting left hand. If now the thumb *only* releases its hold on the undermost penny, instead of falling flat, the coin will make a complete turn, taking with it the hidden farthing. To all appearances, a penny alone is dropped, head side up, on the palm of the left hand;

but unknown to the onlookers, a farthing is concealed under the penny. The second penny is then fairly dropped, head side up, but permitted to overlap the first, so that the head side of both coins is evident. After sliding the overlapping penny flush on the other, the conjurer enquires of his audience: "Now can you tell me whether the bottom coin is head or tail up?" The response is, of course, that it is head side up. Lifting the two pennies together as one, the conjurer reveals the farthing showing its tail side up. (American performers can use two half dollars and a dime, or nickel.)

N.B. Do not make the mistake of referring to the bottom coin as the "penny"; always use the word "coin."

The Esscee Front and Back Manipulation

As usually performed, the turning of the hand from back to front to induce the onlookers to believe that the said hand contains nothing, serves only to convey the impression that although a coin is actually in the hand, the conjurer is clever enough to prevent its presence being seen. That, at its very best, is bad technique.

In these unfortunate days, when mere finger-flinging is regarded as ideal conjuring, the fact that all unnatural moves are bad, seems never to enter into the minds of the misguided. Finger-flinging has about as much relation to magic as a Jazz Band has to Music.

Here is my own method for showing both sides of the hand without making any perceptible finger movement or unnatural turn of the hand. Start by passing the coin to the back of the hand by the familiar Downs move, but immediately the coin is behind the fingers, release the little finger grip. The index finger will thus be slightly out of line with the other three fingers, all of

Fig. 7

which are perfectly free, Fig. 7. Now as the hand slowly turns on the axis of an imaginary line drawn as an extension of the space between the second and third fingers, the third finger is passed over the face of the coin until the edges of the nails of the index and third fingers touch each

Fig. 8

other, Fig. 8. The third finger then slides the coin between the second and third fingers, between which it projects on the front side at right angles when the back of the hand is exhibited. From this position, the coin can be gracefully produced between the thumb and index finger.

That is the mere action of the sleight, but to perform it deceptively, the movement of the third finger must be out of the range of sight of the onlookers; it should not be made until the hand is palm down. The entire action must be done without bending any one of the fingers and with no movement of the hand except the action of turning it over.

Chapter XVI

ROUTINES

The successful magician is fundamentally an entertainer. To be a good entertainer you must please your audience. One of the best ways I know to please an audience is to present your tricks in a smooth-flowing routine.

People like to be mystified and entertained. They like to believe in fairy tales and fancy. Blend a few good tricks together in a logical routine, clothe them in patter and the results will repay you a thousand-fold!

Following are several tried and tested routines which may be of some help. At least they will give you a foundation upon which to build your own routines.

No. 1

WITH A SINGLE COIN

I. Begin the routine by showing a coin in your right hand. Exhibit the left hand empty and close it in a loose fist with the fingers underneath. Rest the lower edge of the coin on the back of the left hand and pretend to push it through the hand, utilizing the moves described in Through the Hand (b), (page 67).

II. Remove your handkerchief, throw it over the coin, then cause the coin to apparently penetrate the cloth by performing Through a Handkerchief (a) or (b), (page 68). The first version (a) is the old standby where the coin is covered with the handkerchief and a small pinch of cloth secured at the base and rear of the coin with the left thumb. In the action of showing the coin

again it is brought outside the handkerchief, then worked through the fabric.

In the second method (b) the handkerchief is spread over the palm up left hand. Right hand pretends to deposit coin on handkerchief above left palm, but retains it thumb palmed and drops it in left hand under cover of lifting rear edge of handkerchief and showing left hand empty.

III. Climax the routine by vanishing the coin, employing Method One, With a Handkerchief (page 53). Hold the coin chest high in the left hand. As right hand spreads handkerchief over coin with an inward movement, clip coin between right forefinger and thumb, carry it back and drop it in left breast coat pocket.

No. 2

WITH A SINGLE COIN

I. Secretly obtain and back palm a half dollar. Produce it from a spectator's tie as described in Producing a Coin from a Spectator's Clothing (page 19).

II. Using a method from Chapter III, vanish, then produce the coin from behind your right knee.

III. Now place the coin on your left leg and hold it in position with tip of right thumb. Turn the coin over, forming a fold of cloth over it, steal it out with right hand, slap leg with left hand, then produce it from behind leg with right hand as you perform Through the Leg (b), (page 63).

IV. After causing the coin to apparently penetrate your leg, flip it into the air a couple of times with right hand. Then as you bend down to place it back on left leg toss it into left hand. Rub leg with right fingers, show coin gone, then produce it with left hand from behind leg by performing Rubbed Through the Leg (page 64).

V. Place coin outside right trousers pocket and form a fold of cloth over it. Steal it out and cause it to apparently penetrate the pocket after the fashion of Through the Leg (third effect, above). Reach in pocket, partially remove coin, drop it back and pretend to place it in left hand. Toss non-existent coin into air as you do the Pocket Vanish (page 52).

No. 3

WITH A SINGLE COIN

I. Have a coin and a handkerchief in left coat pocket. Reach in with left hand, palm coin, bring out handkerchief and as you show it on both sides transfer coin to right hand. Spread handkerchief over right hand. Grip coin through fabric with left hand, then shake it from folds into right hand by doing The Switchover (page 85).

An alternate way of producing the coin is to employ the moves from The Switchover to show the handkerchief empty. Then spread it over left hand and close hand into a fist. Load coin into fist from right hand, have spectator pull one corner of handkerchief while you pull opposite corner. This causes coin to rise mysteriously from left fist. See The Appearing Half (page 87) for complete description of moves.

II. Cause coin to penetrate handkerchief by doing either version of Through a Handkerchief (page 68), or see second trick, Routine No. 1, for outline of moves.

III. Wrap the coin in handkerchief, then push the four corners through a borrowed ring. Have corners held by two spectators

and cause the ring to pass over the coin as you execute the non-mechanical version of Coin Through a Ring (page 172).

IV. Vanish coin by employing Method Two of With a Handkerchief (page 55). In this effect the handkerchief is spread on the table and the coin back palmed in right hand as it is placed underneath. When the handkerchief is jerked away coin is dropped in right coat pocket.

If a table is not handy simply hold coin in left hand and cover it with handkerchief. As you quickly remove right hand to caution spectators to "Watch," toss coin in left coat pocket after the fashion described in the third method of With a Handkerchief (page 56).

No. 4

Requisites and Preparation: A double faced coin, two English pennies, a half dollar, and a pocket handkerchief.

Have handkerchief and one English penny in left coat pocket, the remaining English penny in the right coat pocket and the regular half and the double faced coin together in the small match compartment of the same pocket.

I. Reach in right coat pocket, finger palm regular English penny, bring out double faced coin (silver side showing) and half dollar and place them on palm up left hand as two silver coins. Cause them to change to two copper, back to two silver and finally to one copper and one silver by opening and closing hand. This is Presto Chango (page 245). At the finish of this trick double faced coin will be concealed in the left hand and regular copper and silver coins visible in right hand. Toss them onto table for examination.

II. Reach in left coat pocket, leave gimmicked coin, bring out handkerchief and do your favorite version of Silver or Copper

Extraction (page 174). In this mystery, copper and silver coins are wrapped in handkerchief. Spectator chooses one. This coin is magically extracted from the handkerchief, leaving the other inside.

Have a spectator remove remaining coin from handkerchief and while he is thus engaged, steal the regular copper coin from your left coat pocket, keeping it concealed in hand in preparation for next trick.

III. Take the half dollar with right hand and as you wrap it in handkerchief and give it to a spectator to hold, leave copper coin inside with half dollar. Vanish copper coin and cause it to apparently penetrate the cloth and audibly join the silver coin as you perform Copper Penetration (page 178).

No. 5

Requisites and Preparation: Two copper coins, a silver coin, and a pocket handkerchief.

Have handkerchief and one copper coin in left coat pocket, remaining copper and silver in right trousers pocket.

I. Remove the two coins from right pocket, show and place them on table. Take copper coin in left hand and silver coin in right hand; cause them to transpose themselves twice by doing the first two moves of the Fourth Method of Copper and Silver Transposition (page 132). After this trick place the coins back on the table.

II. Apparently cause the coins to transpose a third time by doing the first version of Copper and Silver Transposition (page 129). Here are the bare bones of the trick: Pick up silver coin with right hand, pretend to place it in left hand but retain it palmed in right. Take up copper coin with right hand and thumb palm it. Open right hand and drop silver coin on table. As you make pass around left fist with right hand, load in thumb palmed copper coin as de-

scribed in the trick, then open left hand showing transposition. Place both coins on table.

III. Pretend to place both coins in left hand but palm them in right as you do The Click Pass (b), (page 14), apparently causing the two coins to travel from left to right hand.

IV. Do Coins in the Teeth (page 146) next. This is another transposition effect in which the coins are placed between the teeth a few times before placing them apparently in the left hand. Coins again travel from left to right hand.

V. Remove handkerchief from left coat pocket; do Silver or Copper Extraction and Copper Penetration which are the last two tricks of Routine No. 4.

No. 6

Requisites and Preparation: Three English pennies, a half dollar, a nickel, a small pellet of wax, and a pocket handkerchief.

Have handkerchief and one English penny in left coat pocket, a second English penny up your right sleeve, and the remaining English penny (with the pellet of wax stuck on it) and the half dollar stacked together and hidden behind the nickel, which is held between the tips of right forefinger and thumb in preparation for doing Much from Little (page 80).

I. Show left hand empty on both sides and call attention to nickel in right hand. Cause it to change into an English penny and a half dollar by doing Much from Little. While showing the two coins in left hand, drop right to side, catching sleeved penny as it falls from sleeve. Execute the Utility Switch (page 11) as you retain the copper coin with waxed-on nickel in left hand and show regular copper and silver in right hand. Toss them onto table for examination.

II. Go to left coat pocket, leave penny and nickel, bring out handkerchief. Finish the routine by performing the last two tricks from Routine No. 4.

No. 7

Requisites and Preparation: Two English pennies, a half dollar, and a pocket handkerchief.

The handkerchief and one English penny are in your left coat pocket; other English penny and half dollar are on the table.

I. Open with the third version of Copper and Silver Transposition (page 131). In this effect you pick up the half dollar with the right hand, pretend to deposit it in the left hand but retain it palmed in the right instead. Left hand is closed. Take up the English penny with the right hand and back palm it as you close your fingers. Drop the back palmed penny onto the palm of the left hand as both hands are opened and the transposition shown.

II. Finish by performing the last two tricks from Routine No. 4.

No. 8

I. Cause a half dollar to change to an English penny in a spectator's hand by employing the first version of The Ghost of a Coin (page 188). To perform this trick have an English penny concealed in finger palm position of your palm down right hand as you show a half dollar at the fingertips of the same hand. Toss the half dollar into your left hand, place in a spectator's hand and close his fingers over it. This is what you pretend to do. Actually you execute a switch and toss the English penny and place it, instead of the half dollar, in the spectator's hand. When he is commanded to open his hand a moment later he will be surprised that he holds a copper coin. The

silver coin remains hidden in your right hand.

II. Take the copper coin from him with your right hand and openly place it in your right trouser pocket. Leave the silver coin, thumb palm the copper coin as you remove your hand. Form a fold in the cloth outside pocket (secretly inserting coin), then cause it to apparently penetrate pocket by doing Through the Pocket (a), (page 65).

III. Place coin on the left leg and hold it in position with right thumb. Form a fold of cloth over coin and steal it out with right hand, slap leg with left hand, then produce it from behind leg with right hand as you perform Through the Leg (b), (page 63).

IV. Vanish the coin, using The Bobo Complete Coin Vanish (page 49). In this method you thumb palm the coin as you pretend to place it in your left hand, then under cover of making a few passes over that hand the coin is dropped in the upper left breast coat pocket.

No. 9

Requisites and Preparation: A half dollar with a fitted shell, a quarter, and a glass disc the size of a half dollar.

Have glass disc in right trousers pocket, the quarter and shell covered half in right coat pocket.

I. Place right hand in coat pocket, palm quarter and bring out shell covered half and show as one coin. Do How to Make Money (page 266). In this trick you retain the shell in right hand as you toss half into left. Produce shell (as half dollar) from behind left elbow and place it along side real half in left hand. Slip quarter into shell as you take it in right hand. Pass shell and half over each other and cause the half to suddenly change to a quarter as the half nests in the shell. Show shell covered half and quarter in right hand. Toss half and quarter into left hand and retain shell in right hand. Show real half and quarter in left hand.

After remarking that the quarter is a profit on the original investment, pick it up with right hand and place it in right trousers pocket along with shell. Finger palm glass disc and remove hand from pocket.

II. Now do The Ghost of a Coin (see first trick, Routine No. 8, for description). This makes a good stopping point, but if you wish to continue you can do so as follows: After the spectator has opened his hand and found the glass disc, pick it up with your right hand and switch it for the half dollar as you pretend to toss it into your left hand. Snap right fingers over left hand, then open it, showing that glass disc has apparently turned back to silver.

III. Pick up coin from left hand with right hand and openly place it in right trousers pocket. Leave glass disc in pocket and cause coin to apparently penetrate pocket by performing Through the Pocket (see second trick, Routine No. 8, for description).

IV. Next, perform Through the Leg (see third trick, Routine No. 8, for description).

V. Follow with Rubbed Through the Leg (see fourth trick, Routine No. 2, for description).

VI. Vanish the coin, employing Kneezy Vanish (page 50). To recall this vanish to your mind here is a brief description of it: Show coin in right hand. Pretend to place it in left hand but retain it palmed in right. Slap left knee with left hand. Produce coin from behind right knee with right hand. Repeat same gesture but actually place coin in left hand. Slap left fist against left leg and while pretending to produce coin from behind right knee, drop coin in left coat pocket. Pretend to transfer nonexistent coin from right to left hand, then toss "it" into air.

No. 10

Requisites and Preparation: Three quarters, a half dollar with fitted shell, and a clip underneath lower right edge of coat.

Place one quarter in clip and have other two in right trousers pocket. Shell covered half is visible in right hand.

I. Display shell covered half as one coin and cause it to multiply to two, change back to one, then double itself again by doing Mystery with a Half Shell (page 265). At the completion of this trick show the half and shell in the left hand as two coins. Put shell in right trousers pocket, finger palm a quarter and bring out second quarter visible at the fingertips.

II. Toss half dollar from left hand and visible quarter from right hand onto table, then cause them to change places, pass from one hand to the other and finally change to three quarters as you do Quarter and Half Dollar Transposition (page 139).

No. 11

I. Have six half dollars in right trousers pocket. Reach in with right hand, classic palm five coins and bring out the sixth visible at the fingertips. Magically produce the five coins, employing the routine called One to Six (page 93).

II. Place the six coins on the table in two parallel and vertical rows of three coins each. Do Three and Three (page 153) as you cause the three coins in left row to travel one at a time from left to right hand.

III. Put four coins away, then pick up remaining two (a coin in each hand), cross wrists and cause left hand coin to join coin in right hand by executing The Inseparable Pair (page 144).

IV. Vanish the two coins, using two of your favorite methods from Chapter IV.

No. 12

Requisites and Preparation: Four half dollars and a pocket handkerchief.

Have the handkerchief and two halves in left coat pocket—the other two coins in the right trousers pocket.

I. Place left hand in left coat pocket, palm the two coins and bring out handkerchief. Unfold and show it on both sides, then throw it over palm up left hand and two concealed coins. These are the opening moves of Double Penetration (page 71). Continue by removing the two halves from right trousers pocket. Show them and pretend to place them on handkerchief over left palm but palm them in the right instead. Close left hand and jingle two coins in hand under handkerchief. Bring trick to climax by causing them to apparently penetrate the cloth, then toss them on the table. Two coins are concealed in right hand. To get rid of them place handkerchief in pocket, leaving the coins there as you do so.

II. Pretend to place both coins in left hand but palm them in the right as you do The Click Pass (b), (page 14), apparently causing the two coins to travel from left to right hand.

III. Again cause the two coins to come together in the right hand by doing The Inseparable Pair (see third trick, Routine No. 11, for description).

IV. Repeat the transposition effect, only this time in a different manner as you do Coins in the Teeth (see fourth trick, Routine No. 5, for description).

V. A fitting climax would be to vanish the two coins completely by employing two different methods from Chapter IV, or put one of them away (or vanish it) and carry on with one of the single coin routines, which are Routines 1, 2, and 3.

No. 13

Requisites and Preparation: Four half dollars, a pocket handkerchief, and two pieces of paper about four inches square.

Have the two squares of paper on the table, the handkerchief in a handy pocket, and the four coins in your right trousers pocket.

I. Before announcing a trick secretly obtain and palm the four half dollars. Produce them one at a time by performing The Touch of Midas (page 90). In this production a coin appears in your left hand every time the wrist is touched by a spectator.

II. Remove handkerchief from pocket, spread it on table, place a coin on each corner and cover the outer two coins with the squares of paper. Cause all to come together and join the coin underneath the outer left square of paper by doing the first version of The Sympathetic Coins (page 197).

III. Put three coins away, borrow a man's ring and do Coin Through a Ring (see third trick, Routine No. 3, for description). Return ring.

IV. Vanish the coin, employing Method Two, With a Handkerchief (page 55). To perform this vanish spread the handkerchief on table, place coin underneath and back palm it. As you jerk handkerchief off table to show coin gone, drop coin in right coat pocket.

No. 14

MILTON KORT

Requisites and Preparation: A leather dice cup, five half dollars, and a silver dollar.

Have the dice cup, with one half dollar in it, on the table, the silver dollar in the left trousers pocket, and the remaining four half dollars palmed in your right hand.

I. Open with The Touch of Midas (page 90) or One to Four (page 92). If the latter is used you would have the four half dollars in your left trousers pocket; finger palm three of them as you bring the fourth out visibly, and begin the production as described in the trick. After you have produced the four coins drop them in the dice cup, making five there because of the one which was there from the beginning.

II. Show the hands empty, then do The Traveling Centavos (page 164). In this effect the coins are caused to pass one at a time from the right hand into the cup held in the left hand. At the completion of the trick there will again be five half dollars in the cup.

III. Empty the five coins into the right hand, palm one and toss the remainder onto the table. Pick up one coin with the left hand, slowly and deliberately drop it in the left trousers pocket. Apparently cause the coin to penetrate the pocket as you do Through the Pocket (b), (page 65). You have left four coins.

IV. Pick up one coin with your right hand, pretend to push it into the left fist but retain it in the right hand as you do The Tunnel Vanish (page 24). After this vanish there will be three coins on the table with a fourth concealed in your right hand, which is just the arrangement you want to perform the next trick.

V. Do The Gadabout Coins (page 182) up to the point where the left hand deposits a coin in the pocket, finger palm the silver dollar and remove the hand the instant the right hand opens to show its three coins. Hold the left hand palm up with the fingers curled slightly to hide the dollar. Now pretend to place two coins in your left hand

as in the regular version of the trick, palming them instead. Drop the third coin in the right trousers pocket, ditching the other two at the same time. Command the two half dollars that you ostensibly placed in your left hand a moment ago to change to a dollar, then open the hand and drop the big coin onto the table.

Variations: Instead of showing a silver dollar in your left hand at the finish you can show almost any article that can be hidden in the hand. For instance, you could cause the two silver coins to change to two Chinese coins, to a thimble, a ball, or a rabbit's foot. Simply have the article in your left trousers pocket and palm it out as described in the above routine.

Several startling and unusual transition effects can be accomplished utilizing this idea. Suppose you wish to progress from coins to thimbles. Have one thimble in your left trousers pocket and three in your right trousers pocket. Steal the single thimble as you did the silver dollar and get the three in the right pocket on the second, third, and fourth fingers of the right hand as that hand enters the pocket the last time. Show the single thimble in your left hand as you remove the right hand with the last three fingers curled in to hide the three thimbles. Keep the back of the right hand toward the spectators, place the single thimble from the left hand to the right forefinger and do a couple of sleights with it. Finally vanish it, and as you reach behind your knee or elbow to produce it, extend the other fingers and bring the hand out with a thimble neatly capped on each of the four fingers.

Very startling!

Entertaining coin routines should consist of effects that blend logically and smoothly, one into the other, making for a continuity that builds to a definite climax. And don't forget the importance of surprise!

No. 15

TOO MANY COINS

Milton Kort

Requisites and Preparation: Six half dollars and an English penny, which are in your right coat pocket.

I. Seat yourself at a table, remove the seven coins retaining one half dollar palmed in your right hand and toss the others onto the table. Arrange them in two parallel and vertical rows about six inches apart, with the copper coin occupying the inner position of the left row. Do The Flying Eagles (page 152), but do not sleeve or completely vanish the last coin. Keep it hidden in your right palm.

Say "Everytime I do this trick someone says, 'No wonder you fooled us, you use too many coins.'" Suiting the action to the words, pick up a half dollar and put it in your right coat pocket, still keeping the extra one hidden in the right hand.

II. Now do the improved version of Winged Silver (page 151). At the completion of this feat you will have four half dollars and the English penny visible in your left hand and the extra half dollar hidden in your right hand. Drop the five coins from your left hand onto the table and repeat the remark about using too many coins. Tell them that you will get rid of one and do it again. Pick up the copper coin with the right hand, put it in the small compartment of the right coat pocket, dropping the palmed coin at the same time in the pocket proper. This is done so you can quickly obtain the copper coin later. Now there are four half dollars on the table.

III. Cause the four coins to apparently penetrate the table by performing The Magical Filtration of Four Half Dollars (page 193). Repeat the objection about using too many coins, then drop one of them in

your right coat pocket. Now there are only three left.

IV. These three coins are caused to pass from your left to your right hand one at a time as follows: Execute The Click Pass (a), (page 14) as you apparently drop two of the coins in your left hand, retaining one palmed in the right. Toss the third coin into the left hand, then after going through the motions of causing one to pass from the left to the right hand, open both hands and dump two from the left and one from the right hand onto the table.

Pretend to place the two coins back in your left hand, but execute The Click Pass again as you retain one palmed in the right. Take up the third piece of silver and allow it to rest on the cupped fingers of the palm down right hand. Repeat the tossing motion with the left hand, allowing the palmed coin in the right to drop onto the one on the fingers. Open both hands, drop one coin from the left and two from the right.

Take the single coin with the right hand and palm it as you pretend to place it in the left. Pick up the remaining two coins with the right hand and allow them to rest on the cupped fingers of the palm down hand. As you again pretend to toss a coin from the left hand to the right, clink the coins together in the right hand, then open the left and show it empty. Drop the three coins from the right hand. Repeat the talk about using too many coins, then dispose of one in your right coat pocket. Two half dollars remain on the table.

V. Do The Inseparable Pair (page 144) next. After this, explain to the spectators that to make it easier for them to tell the coins apart you will substitute one for the copper coin. Which you do.

VI. Cause the copper and silver coins to change places by performing the first version of Copper and Silver Transposition (page 129). State that perhaps you are still using too many coins. Put one in the pocket and leave one on the table.

VII. Vanish the last coin, using The Bobo Complete Coin Vanish (page 49).

No. 16

ROLLAND HAMBLEN

Requisites and Preparation: For this routine you will require, besides an expanded shell and five half dollars, a George Boston Combination Coin Box, and a Lippincott Coin Box. This last item, obtainable through the dealers, is so constructed that a coin can be secretly loaded into it while it is securely locked. In lieu of this you can use the silver boxes from your old Coin in the Ball of Wool trick, or any other nest of boxes small enough to go into the pocket. I prefer the Lippincott box, because it can be loaded in a flash.

Have the Lippincott box, prepared for loading, in your right trousers pocket; fill the Combination Box with four halves, put it and the shell in the right coat pocket; the remaining half dollar goes in the left coat pocket.

I. Reach in your right coat pocket, remove the Combination Box, open it and dump the four coins onto the table. After having the box examined, return it to your right coat pocket and palm the shell. Pick up the four halves from the table and toss them one at a time into your left hand. As you take them back in your right hand, secretly add the shell to the top one, then perform The Peregrinating Halves (page 273). At the completion of this trick the four halves will again be on the table and the shell concealed in your right hand.

II. Reach in your right coat pocket, leave the shell, bring out the Combination Box and place it on the table. Show the box again, then as you drop the four coins one

at a time into it with your right hand, secretly obtain and hold finger palmed, the half dollar from the left coat pocket.

Pick up the box with your right hand and deposit it squarely over the finger palmed coin in the left hand. Now as the right hand adds the lid to the box the secret turn over is made and the lid is put on the bottom. Remove the lid again and place it on the table. The single coin in the recessed bottom convinces the spectators that the coins are still in the box. Pick up the box with the right hand and place it on the back of the left as that hand retains the four coins finger palmed and turns over for the purpose.

Have a spectator place the lid on the box himself, then tap the lid with his forefinger. As he does so, release the coins from the hand allowing them to clatter to the table.

Do not remove the lid from the box at this point, but take the box between the fingers and thumb of the palm down right hand and pick up the four coins from the table with your left hand. Now allow the bottom section of the box to right itself as you drop it onto the coins in your left hand. The extra half is not noticed among the other four coins because the box still covers it. The get-away for the extra half is easy, for all that is necessary is to slide the box off the hand with the coin hidden in the recessed bottom, then place it back in your coat pocket. The instant the hand enters the pocket allow the coin to drop into the finger palm position, then remove the hand.

III. Have a spectator choose one of the four coins from the table and mark it with a knife so he can identify it later. Take the marked coin with your palm down right hand, execute The Bobo Switch (page 10) as you toss the duplicate into your left hand, and retain the marked one in your right. Keep the duplicate coin in plain view in your left hand while you go to your right trousers pocket, load the marked coin in the Lippincott box, remove it and place it on the table. Perform a few flourishes with the duplicate coin, then vanish it. Have the spectator remove the coin from box and identify his mark.

The vanish of the duplicate coin may or may not be a complete vanish; use the one you prefer. If it is not a complete vanish dispose of the coin as you drop the others in your pocket after the spectator has identified his mark.

Remember, these routines are offered to show what can be done by combining several tricks. With a little thought in regard to the proper placement of coins in the pockets it is possible to link together two, or even three routines.

A perfect example of what can be accomplished along these lines is this next and final routine.

No. 17

SPECIOUS SPECIE

J. G. THOMPSON, JR.

Jim has pointed out to me that, in magic, originality is measured largely by how well versed the reader is. Therefore, to be a trifle different from those inventors who preface their writings by stating that their creativeness extends only to such and such variation, twist or improvement, he asked me to enter in the record that *nothing* in the following routine is original. However, as you read the material he has prepared, keep in mind that the bigger liar you can make him, the happier he will be.

Required will be: (a) Liberty Head Half and U. S. penny; (b) a quarter; (c) a double faced coin (showing a half dollar on one side and an English penny on the other); (d) a matching English penny; (e) an old-

style shell or a stretched half; (f) a fitted half for the shell or a regular half, if the stretched shell is to be used; (g) a pencil; (h) a pocket handkerchief.

Placement of the articles will be: (a) and (b) in the lower right vest pocket; (c) in the left trousers pocket; (d) in the right trousers pocket; (e) in the left coat pocket; (f) in the right coat pocket; (g) in the upper left vest pocket; (h) in the outer breast coat pocket;

Working: Before anyone is conscious of what you are about to do, thrust both hands into your trousers pockets and finger palm the two coins. With the right hand, reach under your coat to your left armpit, pull up the shirt sleeve slightly and, after crooking your left arm at the elbow, drop the palmed coin into the sleeve. Duplicate the procedure with your left hand, allowing the coin to fall into the right sleeve and bring out (a) and (b) from your vest pocket.

(To eliminate the get-ready just described, utilize sleeve pockets—see page 112.) Then you would have (c) in the right one and (d) in the left one. With this set up, there is no danger of a premature appearance of a coin.

PART I

State that you are going to engage in a little gambling game in which the odds are all in favor of the spectator. With the quarter inside the shell, display the half and old penny, sliding them over and under each other. The last time the penny goes under, slip it between the quarter and shell and press it into position. Ask the spectator to extend his left hand, place the coins therein, close his hand around them and tell him to hold both hands behind his back, transfer one of the coins to the other hand, then extend both fists, backs up, in front of him. While he is doing this, drop your right hand to your side and finger palm the double faced coin, which falls onto your fingers, with the silver side toward the fingers.

Promote an even bet that you can choose the hand holding the silver coin. In making your choice, select the one in which you originally put the coins since it is more likely to be in that hand.

Whether right or wrong, have him open the hand containing the half. With your right fingers, turn it over as you pick it up, so that he will remember that he saw both sides, and apparently throw it into your left hand, which should immediately close. Actually you execute The Bobo Switch (page 10) as you retain the Liberty half and throw the other one instead. If the spectator sees anything, it will be a flash of silver just before your left hand closes.

Hold your left fist beside his, back up, reach inside your coat and get the pencil from the upper left vest pocket, ditching the half there at the same time.

Use the pencil as a pointer and promote another bet as to the resting place of the copper coin. After he chooses his hand, have him open it to disclose the quarter. In opening your hand, drop the fingers slightly so the coin rests thereon and turn the hand counterclockwise to a palm up position so the copper side will show. As you open your hand, put the pencil in your right coat pocket and finger palm the half dollar.

Have the spectator extend his free hand, place the gimmicked coin, copper side up, on his fingers and fold the latter into a fist, so that, when he next opens them, the silver side of the coin will be visible.

Take the quarter from the spectator with your right fingers and apparently toss it into the left hand, but execute The Bobo Switch instead and throw the half dollar. Immediately go to your right coat pocket, leaving the quarter and retrieving the pencil, which should then be waved grace-fully over your left fist.

As you open the left hand to show that the quarter has grown to a half, replace the pencil in your upper left vest pocket and bounce the half several times on your left palm so that both sides show, finally grasping it between your left thumb and forefinger.

Remove the handkerchief from your breast pocket with the right hand; as you gently shake it open, drop your left hand to your side and allow the English penny to fall into finger palm position, meanwhile spreading the handkerchief by means of a bouncing movement over the back of your right hand. Hold up the left hand with the half still at your fingertips and drape the handerchief over it. As this is done, drop the half in your right sleeve, at the same time levering up the penny with your left thumb into position formerly occupied by the half. (See Switching, page 112.)

Have the spectator grasp the coin through the handkerchief with his free hand and ask if he can guess where the copper coin is. While this is going on, drop your right arm and finger palm the genuine half as it falls from your sleeve.

As soon as he opens his hand and sees the silver coin where he thinks the copper should be, pick up the gimmicked coin between your right thumb and forefinger. When he removes the coin from under the handkerchief, perform the One-Hand Switch (page 12), bringing the real half in view and finger palming the gimmicked coin.

Toss the genuine half into his hand, take the handkerchief from him and stuff both hanky and gimmicked coin into your breast pocket, thus leaving him with two unprepared coins to examine. Your hands are now empty.

This is a good place to stop, but, if you wish to continue with Part II of this routine, while the spectator is removing the copper coin from the handkerchief and you are executing the One-Hand Switch with your right hand, slip the left into your coat pocket and finger palm the shell, open side away from the fingers. Toss the genuine half to the spectator and, after a short examination, pick up both coins with your left fingers, dropping them on the shell so that the latter slips over the half. At the same time take the handkerchief and stuff it in your breast pocket. Then, remarking that you won't need the copper coin, pick it up with the right forefinger and thumb and deposit it in your trousers pocket, leaving the finger palmed coin there also. This leaves you with the shell and half in your left hand ready to move into Part II.

Due to the length of this article, little has been written regarding why certain things are done, but, if the routine is presented as described with a casual showing of empty hands, whenever possible, I can assure you that your audience will be completely bewildered by the numerous surprises.

PART II

While Part I is primarily for close-up presentation, Part II has been concocted as an entity which can be performed effectively for larger groups as well as just a few persons.

If you are following through from Part I, then you should drop back five paragraphs and continue on in the description after the first coin has been produced.

The shell and half should be placed in the small compartment inside the right coat pocket.

"To present a routine with coins, one must naturally have some before starting. I never worry too much about that, for there are usually a few sticking around."

Turn your left side toward the audience,

reach behind the left knee, at the same time stealing the shell and half from the pocket with your right hand, rub fingers of the left hand and show nothing there.

"If not here, always back here." Reach behind your right knee and produce the shell and half.

Exhibit what appears to be a single coin and lay it, opening of shell up, on the middle fingers of the right hand. Utilizing the basic move from Mystery with a Half Shell (page 265), retain the shell and toss the coin into your left hand.

"One coin doesn't go far these days, so let's see if there is another." Produce the shell from behind your right knee and lay it in the left hand overlapping the outer edge of the coin.

"I always feel sort of out of balance with two coins over here, or, as my family puts it—unbalanced. I'm going to move one to this hand." Cover the coins momentarily with the right hand, slipping the shell over the half and showing one coin in the left hand as the right hand moves away closed and empty.

"Ah, that's better—but not for long, for this one seems to have disappeared." Open the right hand and show it empty, displaying only one in the left.

"I'll try again." Place the half shell as one on the two middle fingers of your palm up right hand while you show your left empty. Execute the basic move from The Peregrinating Halves (page 273) as you retain the half finger palmed and place the shell in your left hand.

Up to this point you have been facing your audience. As the shell is taken in the left hand, swing to the left (a quarter turn) and close your fingers over the shell. Wave the left fist up and down, counting up to three. On "two," turn your right side toward the audience, reach behind your right knee and produce the half, at the same time dropping the shell into the left coat pocket and bringing forth your left fist as though it still contained the coin.

"Now everything is O.K. again . . . but, wait a minute! Now the other one is gone!" Open the left hand to show that this is so and display the single coin in your right hand. Flip it in the air.

"Since I seem destined to have only one coin, suppose I proceed with it. You know, the trouble with most persons is that when they see a magician place a coin in his hand, (execute The "Pumpkin Seed" Vanish, page 101, and 'squirt' the coin into your left sleeve while pretending to place it in the left hand), they begin to suspect that it is over here (show your right hand empty), while actually it is still where he put it." Point to your left fist. "That's why it comes as a complete surprise, when this hand is opened (left) and the coin is gone." Open the left hand and show it empty. "No, it's not here either." (Show the right one, dropping the left at the same time and catching the coin from your sleeve.) "I think it's up here." (Reach into the air with your right hand, apparently catch the coin and slap it on your left palm, exhibiting the coin which was there all the time.

For the next trick, utilize a patter line in which you describe what you saw another magician do one time, and do A Novel Vanish and Reproduction (page 121).

"There is scarcely a person who has not seen a magician place a coin in his left hand, squeeze it to nothingness and then produce it from his elbow." Using a method from Chapter III, vanish, then produce the coin from your left elbow.

"What actually happens is that the coin goes into the sleeve and penetrates the cloth at the elbow. I can see you don't believe that. Suppose I demonstrate a trifle differently. Here is a piece of cloth—a handkerchief. Imagine it to be the cloth at my elbow." At this point remove the handkerchief from your breast pocket and do Through a Handkerchief (a), (page 68).

"Perhaps you didn't quite catch that. I'll do it again." Pretend to repeat the same trick but perform With a Handkerchief (Number One, page 53), after which you show the handkerchief and both hands empty and say, "Since the coin seems to be irrevocably gone, there is very little else for me to do but to say thank you, and sit down."

Which you do.

Chapter XVII

LESSONS IN COIN MAGIC

Tools of the Trade

If you intend building a box or a house you will require some tools— a square, a hammer and a saw. If you want to be a master coin magician you must have some basic "tools." These "tools" are the basic sleights which you use to build your effects. The first four chapters contain all the "tools" you need to perform most all coin effects, but to make it easy for you, there are only four important *basic* sleights: The Classic Palm (page 1), The Thumb Palm (page 3), The Finger Palm (page 4) and The Bobo Switch (page 10). Of these there is only one that will require much practice and that is The Classic Palm. I consider it one of the most useful "tools" in the magician's entire arsenal of sleights. It is a great and wonderful secret that enables the performer to perform veritable miracles. Many laymen know that a magician can palm an object but they are never sure when this sleight is employed if the performer uses it well. Magicians know that other magicians are often mystified by

a trick that may depend upon the secret use of the classic palm.

In mastering the classic palm naturalness is the important thing. If the hand that conceals the coin is not held naturally, attention is directed to it and the trick fails. First, develop the ability to hold a coin in the palm. Do not concern yourself about how *unnatural* your hand might appear at this point—naturalness will come later. And you will probably discover that a coin with a sharp milled edge is easier to hold than a smooth-edged coin. Although the half dollar seems to be about right for most hands, you might find a quarter or even the silver dollar more comfortable. Practice holding a coin in the palm while performing other tasks such as driving your car, eating or reading. After a while you will discover that muscles will develop that will make the holding of the coin easier. Now you must learn to hold the hand naturally. Any self-consciousness must be overcome. When the classic palm is employed in a trick use that hand to gesture, to snap the fingers, to pull back the sleeves or to hold another visible object. It is a peculiar fact that an audience believes the hand can hold but one thing at a time. So if the hand with the palmed coin holds a visible object such as a wand, a pencil, a glass or even another visible coin, it is not suspected of any concealment.

Remember to grip the coin lightly. A firm grip causes the hand to appear cramped and unnatural. Actually the hold on the coin should be so slight that a tap from the other hand would dislodge it. So, first learn to hold the coin in the palm—hold it lightly as you perform some natural action with the hand and naturalness will come. When you have achieved this goal you can then devote all thought to the proper presentation of the trick at hand.

Technique

When you have mastered a few basic coin sleights you will need to know how to build them into entertaining mysteries. Here are a few suggestions. Let's consider technique on a coin vanish. After the move of pretending to place a coin in your left hand, you have it concealed in your right. First, master the mechanics of the sleight involved. Begin by actually placing the coin in the left hand. Stand before a mirror as you do this. When you pretend, does it look like you have placed the coin in your left hand? If it does, good! If it does not, then you need some more practice. Actually deposit a coin in your left hand, then try to simulate these exact moves but retain it in your right. Center your complete attention on your closed left hand as you say to yourself, "There it is." Believe it is there and the audience will believe it too. Do not open your hand quickly to show the coin gone. Take a moment—allow for the idea to sink in. After a pause, open your left hand and look surprised that the coin has

vanished. Turn your hand over and look for it on the other side. The coin is gone. Where is it? Look around—pretend to see it dangling on a spectator's ear. Reach over with your right hand, let the coin touch his ear as you pretend to pluck it off. Or produce it from his tie as explained on page 19.

Dr. E. M. Roberts has a baffling method for producing a coin from behind the left knee. Perform your favorite coin vanish, retaining the coin concealed in your right hand. Bend forward slightly and reach behind the left side of the leg with the left hand. With the first two fingers and thumb, grip a bit of cloth and pull the trousers to the left as if trying to extract a coin from the material. The left hand slips off the cloth with nothing. Now the right hand tries to extract it from that side of the leg in the same manner, but gets nothing. But it is in this action of reaching behind the leg that the coin is tossed behind the knee into the left hand, which catches it and holds it flat against the rear of the leg. The left hand tries again and this time gets the coin. The spectators see the left hand empty as it fails to find the coin. They also see the right hand empty as it comes away with nothing. So the production is a baffling one since both hands were apparently empty before the coin made its appearance.

Prior to the production of the coin from behind the knee, sleeve it in the right sleeve using the Delayed Action Method (page 100). Now both hands can be shown completely empty, and to convince the spectators further that the coin has actually vanished pull back your coat sleeves, unbutton your shirt sleeves and turn them back. The coin will be locked in the sleeve by the now tight fitting coat sleeve as it grips the forearm. Drop your arms to your side and show the hands all around. The coin cannot possibly be up the sleeve, the spectators reason, and they will wonder where it is. Relax a moment as you act as if the trick is over. Turn your sleeves back down. Suddenly remark, "Perhaps it is down here." Reach behind your left knee for it as described. Upon not finding it say, "No, not here; maybe it's here," you continue as you reach for it with your right hand (and toss it into the left hand) on the right side. "Oh, here it is!" you exclaim as you slide the coin into view with your left hand.

This vanish and subsequent reproduction of a coin is highly recommended. It is clean, convincing and completely baffling.

The point is—there is a lot more to a trick than the sleight. It's the manner, the presentation, the dressing—the technique!

This handling could be employed in almost any vanish. Suppose you have just performed the Sucker Vanish (page 51), after which the coin is in the right trousers pocket. Occasionally a person will reason that the vanished coin might be hidden in your pocket, and might even say so. Whether he does or not, thrust both hands into your trousers pockets, classic palm the coin in your right hand as both hands simultaneously turn the pockets wrong side out. Leave them out as you sleeve the coin in the right sleeve; pull your sleeves back as explained, finally producing the coin from behind your knee as explained.

This is a good technique!

Suppose you are adept with The Bobo Switch (page 10). Let's dress this up and build it into a real mystery. I will call it

Change in a Spectator's Hand

Effect: The performer shows a half dollar with his hands otherwise empty. He allows a spectator to hold it in his clenched fist. A moment later when the spectator opens his hand the half dollar has changed into a Chinese coin.

Requisites and Preparation: A half dol-

lar and a Chinese coin the size of a half dollar. The Chinese coin is preferred over another of like size because of the square hole in the middle which makes it easily found among other coins in the pocket. And it appears so completely different from coins people are familiar with.

Have the two coins together in your right trousers pocket.

Working: With the right hand, reach into your pocket, classic palm the Chinese coin and bring out the half dollar visible at the fingertips. Toss the half into your left hand, and as you direct attention to it, sleeve the Chinese coin in the right sleeve. Toss the silver coin back and forth a few times letting it be seen that your hands are otherwise empty. Do not call attention to the fact that there is just one coin. The spectators can see this. At the completion of the tossing have the half dollar in your open left hand. As you single out a spectator to assist, drop the right arm to the side, catch the Chinese coin on the cupped fingers as it falls from the sleeve, then finger palm it. Pick up the half from your left hand between the tips of the right first two fingers and thumb. Extend your left hand palm up toward the spectator and say, "Hold out your right hand in this manner." Just as he does so, switch the half for the Chinese coin as you aparently toss it into your left hand, employing the Bobo Switch (page 10); immediately close your left fingers over the Chinese coin and turn the left hand palm downward. At this point the Chinese coin should be held between the extended left fingers and thumb, just barely hidden by the fingers. It should appear that you are holding a coin in your left hand but that it isn't quite visible. In the meantime the right hand has palmed the half dollar.

Deposit the Chinese coin in the palm of spectator's hand, telling him to hold onto the half dollar tightly so you cannot get it away from him. With your right hand, help him close his fingers over the Chinese coin. And if you keep talking to him and cautioning him to hold the half dollar tightly so you cannot remove it, he will not see the Chinese coin nor will he suspect a switch. Don't make a big thing out of the switch —just do it with confidence and all will be well. He will believe he is holding a half dollar because that was all he had seen and, at this point in the effect, he can feel a coin in his hand and believes it to be the half.

Now, for complete safety, have him place his left hand on top of his right fist and grip it tightly. Illustrate with your own hands, and even though you have a coin palmed in your right hand this should not be difficult. It further strengthens the idea that your hands are empty. Step back a pace, and as you raise your hands in a gesture, cautioning him to hold tightly onto the coin, sleeve the half dollar in your right sleeve.

"Do you believe I can take the half dollar away from you from this distance and without touching you?" He will reply "No." "Well, I can't," you say, "but I can cause a transformation or change to take place." Ask him how much he is holding. He will reply, "A half dollar." Say, "All I have to do is snap my fingers." Snap your fingers dramatically, then tell him to open his hand. When he does he will discover the Chinese coin. He will turn it over to examine it and be completely baffled. He will often glance at your hands but he will see nothing. His facial expression makes the climax.

Because this effect is worked in a spectator's hands it becomes a small miracle and will be talked about long after others are forgotten.

Edward Marlo has developed the basic idea still further in his trick Copsil, pg. 364.

The Come and Go Coin

J. B. BOBO
Courtesy *The Gen*

Effect: A coin makes a mysterious appearance, rising from the folds of a handkerchief. It penetrates the cloth, then vanishes completely.

Method: A half dollar and a white handkerchief are in the right coat pocket. Reach into the pocket, conceal the coin in the hand and bring out the handkerchief. In unfolding it and showing it stretched out between your two hands, sleeve the coin in the right sleeve, employing the improved method for Delayed Action Sleeving on page 100. This is easy, as the hands are raised to shoulder height to unfold and show the handkerchief. As you slowly show the cloth on both sides allow the hands to be seen empty. Show the left hand empty while the right holds the handkerchief, then spead it over the palm up left hand so a corner lies on the left forearm. Ask a spectator to indicate the exact center with his forefinger. As he does this drop your right hand to your side and catch the half dollar as it falls from the sleeve. Or, you could steal the coin from a magnet, page 259. In either event, the coin obtained is finger palmed.

Say, "I will close my fingers over the exact center of the handkerchief, where you have indicated." And as you do so a fold or pocket will be formed in the cloth. With the right forefinger and thumb, pick up the corner from the left forearm and say, "I will hold this corner . . . and you hold this corner." Release your corner, quickly move your hand forward to the outer, diagonally opposite corner, pick it up in the same manner and direct spectator to hold it. It is in this movement that the coin is loaded from the right finger palm position into the pocket formed in the hanky held in the left hand. Here are the mechanics of the loading move: The left hand is palm up and the fingers closed to form a fold in the handkerchief. Right hand is palm down with a half dollar hidden in finger palm position. As the right hand travels from the inner corner on the left forearm to the diagonally opposite corner, it passes directly over the left fist. It is in this action that the coin is dropped into the left hand. The left fingers open about ½″ and the coin slips right into the fold, flat-wise, as the right fingers release it. There is absolutely no hesitation and the load is completely covered by the action of the right hand moving forward. You won't even be able to see it yourself if you do it properly! (For another description of this loading move see The Appearing Half, page 87.) All of this is done as you illustrate how you want the spectator to hold the other corner. After he picks up the proffered corner, your right arm returns to the inner corner and holds it. Say, "Don't pull on this corner, just hold it. I will do the pulling." Then as you pull inward on your corner the fold is pulled from the cloth and the coin rises into view, a pretty effect—and quite startling.

Now comes a pretty penetration. After the half dollar makes its appearance place it on the table or have the spectator hold it, then remove the handkerchief from your left hand. Show the left empty and again hold it palm upward as the hanky is draped over it as before.

Take the half dollar in your right hand holding it between the tips of the second finger and thumb of the palm up hand. Hold it directly over the center of the handkerchief and over the left palm. Close the left fingers over the coin but retain the right hand's grip. Immediately turn right hand palm downward and move it back to

the inner corner of the handkerchief on the left forearm, thumb palming the half in the action. The larger movement of the right hand traveling inward to the left forearm conceals the smaller movement of thumb palming the coin. Pick up the corner of the cloth from the left forearm between the tips of the extended first two fingers and carry it forward, exposing the empty left palm. Left fingers retain a small pinch on the fabric so that it won't be pulled away. Say, "Nothing in my hand;" then as you return the corner to its original position on the forearm the right hand drops the coin into the left where it is covered by the handkerchief. The left hand again assumes its original position with the fingers closed, apparently concealing the half dollar in the hanky. It should appear that you deposited a half dollar in the left hand, folded the cloth over it, showed the bare palm underneath and returned the handkerchief to its original position. This is a very deceptive move. The left hand is closed into a fist but the coin is underneath the fabric, not on top as the spectators believe.

Snap your right fingers over the left hand, then slowly open it to show that the coin is no longer there. At this point, if the fabric is not too heavy and if the portion over the left palm is taut, the coin can be seen through the material. The right hand slowly pulls the handkerchief from the left to reveal the coin in its palm. Apparently the coin penetrated the cloth! For another description of this penetration effect see Through a Handkerchief, page 70.

Tell the spectators you will explain the secret of the trick. Return the handkerchief to its original position on the palm up left hand with a corner again lying on the left forearm. Apparently you duplicate the same moves to make the coin penetrate the cloth, but this time it vanishes completely. Hold the coin between the tips of the second finger and thumb of the palm up right hand as you did before. Go through the motions of apparently depositing it in the fold of the handkerchief, but really carry it away, thumb palming it as you did previously while moving the hand back to pick up the corner on the forearm. Pick it up as before but this time do not carry the corner forward—instead, give it a couple of tugs inward. As you do so you will discover that the right hand with its thumb palmed coin comes in contact with the left chest at a spot directly above the breast pocket, and the coin goes "south." (A crumpled hanky in the pocket will help hold it open.) As you tug on the corner, say, "You can pull on this corner . . . or you can pull on this corner." Drop the inner corner, pick up the outer corner and add, "But never pull on *this* corner because if you do you will find that not only does the coin penetrate the handkerchief . . . it will vanish completely!" Slowly pull hanky away from the left hand. Show that hand empty, the hanky empty and let it fall to the table or floor. (This proves that the coin is not concealed in the folds of the cloth.) Return the handkerchief to your pocket.

The Goshman Pinch
ALBERT GOSHMAN

Here is a revolutionary sleight that should open new vistas for the coin magic of the future. Although it was evolved by Mr. Goshman and has been used by him and a few others for a number of years, it is new to the vast majority of coin workers. It is employed in the 3 tricks that follow and the reader will find many uses for it in others.

First, I would like to describe the move itself, then a trick which can also serve as an exercise, and finally the effects employing the sleight.

A coin is concealed underneath the palm up hand in a clip or pinch between the third and fourth fingers. It is completely unlike The Back Finger Clip (page 7);

Fig. 1

Fig. 2

the coin is pinched by its edge and lies closely to the back of the hand in an almost flat position, thus making it less likely to be detected. To grip the coin in this fashion slide it over the tips of the fingers as you would if you were going to back palm it, and grip it between the third and fourth fingers, the fourth finger slightly overlapping the underside of the third. This overlap is so slight that it does not appear unnatural. Fig. 1 shows the hand as it appears from above while gripping the coin underneath, and Fig. 2 shows how the coin is actually held. It will be noted that because of this slight overlap of the little finger underneath the third, the coin lies almost flat against the underside of the hand. Actually it should lie at an angle no greater than 45 degrees.

With a coin concealed in this position, a

Fig. 3

Fig. 4

second coin can be exhibited on the palm up hand and the hand will appear otherwise empty.

To use the pinch as a coin switch, begin with a coin concealed in the Goshman Pinch. Let's suppose this coin is an English penny. Lying visible on the palm up hand is a half dollar. Lower the tips of the fingers and permit the half dollar to slide off onto the table or palm up left hand. While attention is directed momentarily to the silver coin, drop the right hand to the side or out of the line of vision and turn it over. In turning it over, the copper coin is transferred from the back of the left hand to the palm as follows: Close the hand into a tight fist, then using the tip of the second finger, push the coin inward until its edge touches the palm, Fig. 3. The second fingertip is removed and the coin is revolved between the palm and the inside of the fourth finger, the axis being at points indicated in Fig. 4. The tip of the third finger aids in the revolving of the coin, then it presses it into the palm where it is held.

The transfer of the English penny from the Goshman Pinch to the palm can also be accomplished while the visible half dollar is retained in the hand, the transfer of the copper coin being made in the action of turning over the hand to show the other

side of the half. To accomplish this, have the silver coin lying visible on the fingers of the palm up hand. The thumb lowers on top of it and slides it forward to the tip of the forefinger, Fig. 5. Here it is gripped by its edge between the tips of the forefinger and thumb, then as the hand turns over to a palm down position the other fingers curl inward and the copper coin is transferred from the pinch to the palm as already described, Fig. 6. The transfer of the penny from the pinch to the palm is made while ostensibly showing the other side of the half dollar. And it should appear that you merely pushed the coin forward so you could turn it over and show

Fig. 5

Fig. 6

its other side. Thus the transfer of the hidden coin from the pinch to the palm is practically the same with or without the extra visible coin. The turning over of the hand which covers the secret transfer of the hidden coin from the pinch to the palm seems to be made to show the other side of the visible coin, or to deposit it in the left hand, or place it on the table. If a third coin is visible in the left hand, attention can be directed to it momentarily as the secret transfer is made. However, no misdirection is actually required if the sleight is under complete mastery. The transfer is made while the hand is executing a natural move.

Before describing any of the Goshman effects I would like to detail another trick which is not only a fine coin switch but an excellent exercise. When this is mastered the other tricks will come a bit easier. It is called

The Instantaneous Coin Change

Howard Schwartzman

Effect: The performer shows a half dollar lying on his palm up right hand. As he tosses it into his left hand it is seen to change instantly to an English penny. The palm up left tosses the copper coin back

into the right hand and as that hand returns it to the left it changes back visibly to a half dollar. This can be repeated *ad infinitum*. The effect is that the change takes place en route from the right to the left hand. Both hands are palms up at all times and only two ordinary coins are used.

Method: At the outset have the copper coin in the Goshman Pinch and the silver coin lying visible on the palm up right hand. The left hand is palm up, held higher than, and about a foot from, the right. As the right hand makes the tossing motion toward the left, the thumb is lowered on top of the silver coin and retains it while the pinched coin is released. As it flies upward into the waiting left hand the right immediately transfers the retained half dollar to the Goshman Pinch. The eye follows the flight of the coin in its journey upward into the left hand, which affords the necessary but brief misdirection for the transfer. The move is not covered but performed openly. It could be seen IF the eye was on the right hand at the specific moment of the transfer, but it is not. Because the eye follows movement it watches the flight of the coin into the left hand. The instant the coin is received in the left it is seen to have changed into a copper coin. When the eye returns to the right hand it is empty.

But the spectator is not given time for study. The copper coin just received in the left hand is returned to the right immediately by turning the left hand palm downward and tossing it back. The right hand apparently tosses the copper back upward into the left but retains it as described and throws the silver coin from the pinch. The left hand receives it, then it is seen to be a silver coin. This is repeated one or two more times, or as many more as possible without discovery.

In effect this is a coin switch. It can be

performed as described, or only once to affect a change as required for a specific trick. If used for a series of changes the pinched coin is finally brought to the palm as the hand turns over, takes the other coin from the left hand, then performs the Coin Flip (page 16) and places both coins in the pocket.

Impossible Marked Coins Transposition
ALBERT GOSHMAN

Here is the ultimate in modern close-up coin conjuring. This trick has been the exclusive property of Al Goshman, and with it he has baffled some of the country's most knowledgeable coin men. It is revealed here for the first time and I consider it one of the cleverest coin effects I have even seen.

Effect: Two marked coins are caused to change places two times in the cleanest manner possible.

Requisites: Mastery of the Goshman Back Pinch, a half dollar, two English pennies and a wick marking pen. This type of pen will put a large mark on a coin, so it can be seen easily.

Working: Begin with one of the English pennies palmed in the right hand, head side out. Show the other copper coin and the half dollar and have them marked with the pen on their head sides for identification. The marks convince the spectators that only these two coins are used in the effect. Place the marked coins on the table, marked sides up, the half dollar to the left of the copper coin.

With the palm down right hand, pick up the English penny between the tips of the first two fingers and thumb. Take up the half dollar in the left hand in the same manner. Call attention to the markings on the coins. Then in the action of turning

them over simultaneously and depositing them on the table, the marked English penny is back pinched and the other penny is placed on the table. Both coins slide off the palm up hands onto the table together and the hands appear empty. It should appear that you merely turned over the coins to show their tail sides. Now, as the right hand turns palm down and picks up the half dollar, the back pinched marked penny is transferred to the palm. The regular penny lies on the table, tail side up. And because it is tail side up the spectators assume it is the marked penny. The right hand tosses the half dollar onto the palm up left, marked side up. Call attention to the mark. With the right forefinger, point first to the silver coin lying on the open left hand, then to the copper on the table. Say, "Copper, silver." Up to this point nothing has taken place as far as the spectators are concerned.

Take up the half dollar from the left hand and toss it back. This is what you pretend to do. Actually you execute The Bobo Switch (page 10) and throw marked penny instead. The left hand immediately closes over the coin. Now take the regular penny from the table with your palm down right hand, then back pinch it as the hand turns over and tosses the half dollar onto the table. Immediately open your left hand to show the marked penny and leave it there. Call attention to the fact that the coins have changed places as you drop your right hand to your side and transfer the back pinched coin to the classic palm.

For the second transposition the moves are varied.

As you begin this phase of the routine you have the regular English penny concealed in your right palm; the marked penny is visible in your open left hand and the half dollar is on the table, markings showing.

Take the half dollar from the table with your right hand, and as you pretend to toss it into your left make The Bobo Switch and throw the regular penny instead. Close the left hand over the two coins and rattle them to show they are actually there. (If you find it easier to execute The Bobo Switch from finger palm position, have the penny there as you begin this second transposition.) With the finger and thumb of the palm down right hand, reach into the thumb side of the left fist, which opens slightly, and remove the regular penny, making sure it is tail side up, then place it on the table, tail side up. Apparently the left hand holds the half dollar but actually it holds the marked penny, while the half dollar is hidden in the right palm. Take the penny from the table, and back pinch it as you turn over and open your right hand to reveal the silver coin. Allow it to slide off the fingers onto the table. Open your left hand to reveal the marked penny and toss it onto the table. The back pinched coin is transferred to the classic palm and right hand is used freely to point to the copper coin in the left and the silver coin on the table. The coins have changed places a second time!

Mastering the moves for this trick will require time but the effect is worth it.

For another "impossible" coin transposition effect using gimmicked coins and the Goshman Pinch, see The Sun and Moon, Chapter XIX.

The Tenkai Pennies

The Japanese magician Ishida Tenkai, who once resided in this country, taught me this beautiful little trick quite some years ago. It is included here because it makes use of technique known only to a few of today's coins workers.

Effect: The performer shows two U.S.

pennies, one in the palm of each hand. The hands are closed, then opened again to show the pennies still in their respective places. With a minimum of movement the left hand's coin travels over to join the one in the right.

Method: Two U.S. pennies are used, plus a very pretty sleight. Begin by showing a penny lying in the palm of each hand. The hands are palm up and held below the eye level of the spectators, about 6″ to 8″ apart. Close the hands into fists, turn them backs up and work the fingers of each hand. The

Fig. 1

left makes only crumbling or rubbing motions but the right secretly slips its coin outside the hand with the aid of the thumb, where it is held between the third and fourth fingers in the Goshman Pinch, Fig. 1. It is held in this position so when the hand is opened a moment later it will be out of sight.

Turn your left hand palm up, open it to show the penny, and as you do, extend your right forefinger and use it to push the coin from the palm to a position near the left fingertip, Fig. 2. Say, "Remember, there is one penny here," close the left fingers, and apparently use the same move, this time with the left hand, to show the right hand's penny. Actually it is the left hand's penny

Fig. 2

Fig. 3

that is cleverly shown in the right hand instead, while a penny remains out of sight in the back pinch, Fig. 3. This maneuver is accomplished as follows: Immediately after showing the penny in the left hand and pushing it forward, place your left thumb on top of it, close the second, third and fourth fingers into a fist, turn hand palm down, and quickly deposit the penny on the palm of the right hand as that hand turns over and opens to receive it. The left forefinger follows through by pushing the penny forward onto the fingers of the right as you say, "And a penny here." The illusion is that you first showed a penny in your left hand and pushed it forward onto the fingers. You then closed that hand, opened your right to show a penny there, and pushed it forward in a similar manner onto the fingers. This technique is ingen-

ious and completely indetectable when performed correctly.

At this juncture the left hand is closed and held back up. The right is palm up with a penny lying visible on the fingers and one concealed underneath in the Goshman Pinch. Move the right hand further from the left as you give the spectators a view of the coin. As you close your right hand and turn it so it is back up, the back pinched penny is quickly pulled inside the fist with the aid of the thumb. Now there are two coins in the right but the spectators know of only one. All the moves have been executed in a deliberate, smooth and continuous manner up to this point, and the trick is over as far as you are concerned. Direct attention to the left hand, open it, and show it empty back and front. Call attention to the right hand and slowly open it to show two coins. Apparently the one in the left travelled invisibly to join its mate in the right hand.

A good trick to precede or follow this one would be Two Pennies on the Leg, page 143. The effects are similar but the methods differ.

Copsil

EDWARD MARLO
Courtesy *The Linking Ring*

Effect: A silver coin held by a spectator changes places visibly with a copper coin held by the magician.

Several elements in this routine make it a clear and startling transposition. The byplay with the silver coin tends to impress upon the spectator that he DOES hold silver, unmistakably; the copper coin isn't introduced until much later, so the audience is not confused by having to think of two objects at the same point in the routine. A few subtleties are introduced to throw the knowing ones off the track, and these

Fig. I

Fig. 2

Fig. 3

add to the entertainment. For the close-up version, the performer must be seated at a table, but the VISIBLE feature can be incorporated into any of the other silver and copper routines.

Requirements: A pencil clipped in the left inside coat pocket, with a copper coin under the clip as in Fig. 1. A duplicate of the copper coin is in the left coat pocket; a borrowed half dollar completes the list.

Routine: Place the half dollar on the palm of the right hand in the classic palming position. Do this deliberately, as if you were up to something.

2. The right hand approaches the left as if to place the silver into it. Actually you do let the half go into the left hand, but your whole attitude must be one of seeming to do the opposite. The position of the hands during this move is shown in Fig. 2.

3. The left hand, with the coin, now gives it to the spectator seated on your right. Meantime the right hand is curled suspiciously.

4. Addressing the spectator, say, "What I'm about to show you is hard to believe; therefore, would you be so kind as to examine the coin you hold so you will know it again. And please note the date." As these lines are delivered, the hands turn palm upwards in a sort of gesture to show, indirectly, both empty. (Gestures are pure personality traits, so it is left to the individual to use the one suitable to himself.)

5. While the spectator is noting the date, go into your inside coat pocket casually, to get the pencil clipped there; at the same time the right fingers draw away the copper coin as in Fig. 3, then classic palm it, the hand immediately bringing out the pencil.

6. "Just to make sure you will recognize the coin again, let us mark it with any initials you may prefer." During this, the performer has taken the coin with his left hand and placed it in front of himself near the edge of the table.

7. The coin is now pencil marked in the manner desired, the performer doing the actual initialing. This is important, for it affords the necessary cover for the palmed copper coin.

8. After marking the silver, the right hand places the pencil on the table to the left.

Fig. 4

Fig. 5

9. The right hand now picks up the coin and holds it at the fingertips, but concealed when viewed from the front, as in **Fig. 4**.

10. Now pretend to place the coin into the left hand as in **Fig. 5**; actually the right fingers merely hold it in the original position while the left fingers seemingly close around it.

11. The left hand now advances to the spectator to hand him the coin while the right moves back towards the edge of the table until it reaches the point shown in Fig. 6, which shows the relation of the hands to each other.

12. As soon as the spectator reaches towards your left hand the right fingertips snap the silver coin down on the table with a loud click as the left fingertips are brushed across spectator's palm.

13. The right hand moves out of the way to expose the coin in front of the performer as in **Fig. 7**. Note that it is near the table edge.

14. Look at the spectator as you say, "When I give you the coin make sure you grab it and hold it so it doesn't get away from you." As you tell him this, demonstrate by closing your right hand into a fist and then turn it palm up. Actually the right hand has the copper coin palmed, but this touch conveys the illusion of emptiness.

15. At this point look directly into the spectator's eyes and ask, "Do you understand?" As you say this, the right hand moves once more to pick up the tabled coin, but actually brushes it off into the lap. Right hand immediately lets the copper coin fall onto the fingertips and hand moves to the center of the table where the fingertips tap the copper coin against the table as if it were the silver coin just picked up, the fingertips effectively concealing the copper.

16. The right hand now places the coin into the spectator's hand, and as instructed, he closes it into his fist. A moment later both your hands are shown empty, so he must be convinced he holds the silver coin. Furthermore, the silver coin was the only coin in evidence during this by-play, so you

Fig. 6

Fig. 7

have formed a very clear picture in the minds of your watchers that the spectator is now holding the half dollar.

17. Say to him, "Would it be a good piece of magic if I managed to get the half dollar out of your hand without your knowing it?" Raise your hands with both palms facing the audience as you say, "As a matter of

Fig. 9

Fig. 8

fact I will do better than that." After this line drop the right hand into the lap while the left goes to the coat pocket to get the copper coin. You continue, "In my pocket I have an English copper penny to use for this unbelievable experiment."

18. While left hand is getting the copper coin out and onto the table, the right has picked up the lapped silver coin and classic palmed it. Right hand now comes up to pick up the tabled copper coin and place it in the left fingers as in Fig. 8, in readiness for the Visible Change.

19. The right next picks up the pencil and using it as a pointer between the copper coin and the spectator's clenched fist, performer says, "Not only will I get your half dollar away from you, but I will also give you this copper coin in exchange, and the operation will be painless. Hold tightly, now!"

20. The right hand puts the pencil down and makes a pass towards the spectator's hand. During this motion towards the spectator, the palmed silver coin is let slip to the right fingertips. The right hand then

goes over and across the copper coin held by the left; as right fingers cover the copper, the right thumb will automatically hit the copper coin and send it falling into the left finger palm, Fig. 9. The right fingers merely leave the silver in the fingers of the left hand as shown, and a Visible Change seems to have transpired. After the silver is in the left fingers, the right hand continues by making a throwing gesture towards the spectator's closed hand.

21. The right hand removes the visible silver coin from the left fingertips, spins it into the air, catches it and slaps it down onto the table as you say, "There is your marked half dollar."

22. Pick up the pencil with the right hand and tap the spectator's fist as you say, "If you will open your hand you will find the English penny." As all eyes are on the spectator opening his hand, the left takes the pencil and places it into the inside coat pocket, disposing of the palmed coin at the same time.

Copsil II
Stand-Up Version

Have copper coin under pencil clip as before, duplicate in left coat pocket, and borrow the half dollar. Proceed as before, up to the point where you give the spectator nothing; as there is no table now, you merely show the silver coin at the right fingertips. Now you must do a One Hand Switch. It must appear as if the right hand is actually giving the spectator the coin the left only pretended to give. Use the One Hand Switch on page 12; the spectator closes his hand over the copper coin, but thinks he receives the silver. The left hand now takes the copper coin from the left coat pocket and holds it in readiness for the Visible Change. Right hand has silver coin concealed. After the Visible Change the right hand spins the coin into the air, catches it on the palm, and maneuvers it into classic palm position. Hold out right palm, with silver coin on it, for spectator's examination. Then have him open his hand to show he has the copper coin. At this point you pretend to dump the silver coin from the right palm into the left, actually retaining it, and at the same time the right hand reaches for the copper coin on the spectator's hand. Pick it up and say, "I will take my English penny and here is your half." Here you take the copper coin and actually place it in your pocket. The left hand now gives the spectator what is supposed to be the silver, and again he closes his fingers over it, but he is again getting the copper while you retain the silver in your right hand as before. Caution him to hold tightly to his half, for you will attempt to get it out of his hand again. Make a grab towards his closed hand and at the same time let the palmed silver coin fall into finger palm position. Extend right fingers and with right thumb push out the silver coin as in Fig. 10. Let the coin fall from right fingers into open left palm. Say, "Of course you now have nothing in your hand." When he shows he has the copper coin act surprised, then say, "Sir, you must be a pickpocket!"

Right thumb pushes out coin from hand

Fig. 10

Thank him for his assistance and give him the half dollar while you take back your copper penny.

Alternative Stand-Up Ending

Proceed to the point after the first Visible Transposition. At that point you have the silver palmed in the right hand and the copper visible at the right fingertips, while the left is closed around the supposed silver. The left hand now crosses over to give the supposed silver to spectator on your right. It is natural for the right hand to move in toward the chest to permit the left hand to cross over, and it will be an easy matter for the right fingers to drop the copper coin into the breast coat pocket. The right fingers retain their pose of seeming to hold the copper coin. Now the stage is set for the final transposition. Recap the situation, then the right fingers push out the silver coin as in Fig. 10; toss the silver from open palm to open palm, showing only the silver coin in the hands, and when spectator opens his hand he finds the copper. This is a strong finish, for you close with just the two coins, the silver and the copper, after a series of almost incredible transpositions. This is an excellent introduction to the Expansion of Texture Expanded! on page 181.

Psychological Coins Through

SLYDINI

Courtesy *M-U-M,* and HARRY STANLEY, publisher *The Gen*

The now classic Coins Through the Table was introduced to the magical fraternity in 1914 by Han Ping Chien, a skilled Chinese magician, and even today the stratagem upon which it is based is called "the Han Ping Chien move." There are five versions of the feat in this book, counting this one, and each is the pet method of a skilled coin worker. Like the original, each demands perfection in coordinated movements, but the result is unexplainable illusion.

Slydini is probably the only magician since the wily Mr. Han to devise so many simple and effective methods for accomplishing the basic move, or so many clever variations for performing the trick. He can perform a routine of "coins through the table" effects, one after the other; each time he repeats the trick he tries earnestly (or so it seems) to make things easier for you to follow, but alas—whatever he does to help you "see" only increases your bewilderment. I believe Han Ping Chien himself would have been taken in by this version, in spite of his oriental wisdom, for the trickery is not sleight-of-hand, but timing and psychological misdirection, and who is proof against that? And this version, while in the tradition of the original, differs in that only six coins are used, and they do not pass down through the table top to congregate in the right hand.

Working: The coins can be half dollars or half crowns, but Slydini uses six silver dollars. The performer must be seated at a table, and the coins are spread in a line from left to right in front of him. A spectator is asked to sit at the side of the table on

the performer's right. When he is seated, the performer says to him, "Before I show you this, there is one request I'm going to make—when I ask you to give me your hand under the table, you must do so right away —okay?" When this has been clearly understood and agreed upon, the performer begins, "Here are six silver coins," and gestures toward them with his right hand.

They are picked up three in each hand, held by the edges between the thumb and first and second fingers; the palms are facing the spectators. Gesturing with each hand in succession the performer says, "Three—and three—do you think I could have done anything tricky so far?"

Fig. 1

As he asks this, he closes each hand around its coins, Fig. 1, shakes the hands so the coins jingle, then says, "Do you think I did anything tricky then? Well, never mind what you think—by the noise you know I'm still holding the coins. How many do I have in my right hand?" The right hand jingles its coins and the left drops to the table, then the patter continues.

"Come close and listen." The right hand is shaken close to the spectator's ear as he is asked, "How many here?" When he answers, the right hand is rested on the table

Fig. 2

Fig. 3

top as the left is lifted. This hand is closed very loosely and the spectator can actually see the edges of the coins at the thumb end of the fist, for the performer has now turned slightly to the left, Fig. 2. He asks, "How many here?" When the answer has been given, the performer says, "Once more—I want you to listen." The right hand is shaken, then the left, and the edges of the coins are seen through the end of the left fist exactly as before.

Pausing for a second the performer says: "Give me your hand under the table!" and immediately places his own *left* hand under; he does not touch or grasp the spectator's hand, but leaves the three coins on the front edge of the seat of his chair, between his two legs which he has separated sufficiently to allow placing them there. This is done in an instant and the hand is withdrawn immediately, still closed, so he can raise both closed hands as in Fig. 1 as he says to the spectator, "No, no—the other hand—wait a minute—which hand did you use?"

As he is saying this, he points and gestures first with his right hand, Fig. 3, then with the left. The reason for this is that by moving both hands for a second or two, the minds of the spectators are confused and

they will not remember which hand the performer put under the table—often they will not remember that one of his hands left their sight for an instant.

As soon as the spectator has placed his other hand under the table, the performer reaches under with his *right* hand, picks up the coins, then raises both closed hands again to the position shown in Fig. 2 and says, "Wait a minute—at what position is your hand under the table? Point with the other hand." The performer points as in Fig. 4 with both hands alternately, to spots on the table under which the spectator's hand could be.

The spectator will now understand and

Fig. 4

will point to a spot on the table top with his other hand. The performer points to the same spot with his left forefinger and says, "Here?" By this time the alternate movement of the performer's hands has "lost" the spectators—the whole business appears to them as if he is making sure the assistant understands clearly what he is to do. The thing seems decided when the performer says, "Here?" and follows with "Okay—give me your hand under the table now," and reaches under with *his* left hand. He touches the spectator's hand, and at the same instant slaps his right hand down on the table, palm open, and lifts it to reveal six coins. Then he shakes the spectator's hand under the table, and the climax is complete when he brings his left hand into view.

That there were three coins in each hand was well established. The hands never came close to each other, and the misdirection centering around the spectator's hand under the table left no clear track to follow. Yet somehow the coins in one hand joined those in the other, and the table top was no barrier.

If you wish to repeat Han Ping Chien's fine trick several times, start with the Coins Through the Table, page 190. When you have finished, say, "Did you see how that was done? No? Well, I'm going to let you in on a little secret. This is what confused you." Here you pick up the odd coin and pocket it, then say, "I'll give you another chance, and this time I'll make it easier for you. I'll use just the eight coins, all alike." Repeat the trick using the Third Version with just the eight coins—no odd coin. The effect is the same but the method differs enough to confuse. After the coins have passed this time, say, "Did you see how that time? No? Well, maybe I used too many coins. I'll do it once more, and to give you a better chance I'll use only six coins!" Now

you seem to be really trying to help them, but what chance do they have when you've changed your strategy completely?

This is a reputation making routine!

Stand-up Coins Across

C. L. SCHMITT

Courtesy *The Linking Ring*

The classic effect of causing a number of coins to travel from one hand to the other has appeared in print in numerous versions. This one, a stand-up version, merits inclusion here because of its fine points in handling and its unique sleeving move.

Effect: The performer very clearly counts out by dropping them one at a time, four half dollars from the right hand to the left, showing the left hand front and back before counting, then the right, after the counting. The coins are then dumped from the left hand into the right. Both hands are held fists closed about a foot apart and one coin jumps invisibly from the right hand to the left. The one coin is shown in the left hand, the three in the right. This is done three more times so that one at a time the coins jump from right fist to left; each time the hands are shown plainly and the coins are counted openly.

Working: Have one coin up your right sleeve as you gather four from the audience. Hold these in the right hand. Slowly show the left hand empty, front and back, then hold the coins up at the fingertips of the right hand, dropping them one at a time into the left, counting out loud slowly, one, two, three, four. As they are being displayed on the palm of the left hand, show the right on both sides and drop it to the side to secure the sleeved coin. Bring the arm up in a natural manner, opening the palm of the right hand (with the fifth coin in it) as you dump the four coins from left hand into right. Thumb palm one of the four retaining it in the left hand and making a fist.

Spread the four coins on your right hand with a forward jerky motion, just as you would when you spread a handful of change to find a nickel for the parking meter. This move is best described as jabbing your right hand foward at about chest level, stopping the forward motion of the hand and by the law of inertia causing the four to spread out evenly on the palm of the hand. Now here is the all important move, calling for practice, but it means everything to the effect. With practice you will learn that this spreading motion can space the coins so one lands on your upturned wrist under the edge of your coat sleeve. To do this, the hand must be held flat and level and the inertia movement must be just right to keep all the coins on the hand except the one which goes onto the wrist. It is best to practice with shirt sleeves rolled up, but later you can do it properly dressed. Now to continue: Close the hand into a fist over the three coins, the fourth resting on your wrist; slowly raise your fist to shoulder level but in front of your body, turning the arm slowly as you do this to bring the fingernail side facing the audience. As you do this, the "wristed" coin will slide very naturally down the sleeve, unperceived by the audience. Stand with your fists at about shoulder level, 18″ apart and 18″ in front of your body. Tell the audience you will make one coin jump between the two hands and if they will watch carefully half way between the two fists, they may see it go. With a slight shake of both hands you apparently do this, for you slowly open the left hand showing one coin. Place this one the table, hold left palm out level in front of you, slowly open raised right fist and slowly and deliberately drop one, two, three coins from right fist to left hand, then show the right

empty, very slowly. Drop the right hand, acquiring the sleeved coin; bring hand up to receive the three dumped from the left hand which again thumb palms one, then make the same sliding motion to put one on the right wrist, etc. This continues until the final coin and here is the clincher—the visible magic which jolts the reasoning of both layman and magician.

You have reached the point where three coins are on the table; the fourth is on the palm of the upturned left hand and the fifth (secretly, of course) in the right sleeve.

Drop the arm, secretly securing the sleeved coin. Bring the right hand up toward the left palm, holding the secret coin with your third and fourth fingers, extending the thumb and first finger as you would to pick up a coin. Pick up the coin on the left hand, and as you do so move forward slightly (to the left) with it held in right thumb and first finger; drop the secret coin into the palm of the left hand, close left into a fist and turn it over at chest height with knuckles up and finger nails down. (For a similar loading move see The Touch of Midas, page 90). The right hand continues its motion back to the right, holding the coin visible at the tips of the finger and thumb. Flip this in the air, catch it, make a tossing motion toward the left hand which opens, showing the coin has arrived, and now, while all eyes are on the left hand and coin, drop the right hand's coin in the right sleeve. This is very easy, for you are gripping this coin near the heel of the hand, held there by the right fingertips; your arm is up in the air, your sleeve is standing wide open. You simply drop the coin and your miracle is completed. You have invisibly transposed four coins one at a time from hand to hand. A brilliant effect to follow this fine routine would be Glenn Harrison's Miracle Coins to the Pocket, on page 168.

Penny and Nickel Transposition

HERBERT G. ZARROW
Courtesy M-U-M

This trick was inspired by The Tenkai Pennies.

Effect: Two coins of different denominations (they may be the same if desired) are shown, one in each hand and then magically made to appear in the same hand. This version employs a nickel and a penny.

Working: Show the penny on the palm of the left hand and a nickel on the right palm; both hands are held palms upward, fingers extending toward the spectators but with the hands slanting downward to the front, Fig. 1. The second, third and fourth fingers of the right hand bend inward, holding the nickel in the palm, while the forefinger and thumb are extended, Fig. 2. The right hand is revolved to the left, so the hand is palm downwards and the tip of the

PENNY

NICKEL

Fig. 1

Fig. 2

right index finger touches the first joint of the left second finger in a pointing action.

The right forefinger strokes along the left second finger until right finger's first joint rests on the penny. The penny is now pushed forward by the right forefinger until it reaches the first joint of the left second

PENNY

Fig. 3

finger—the bottom edge of the penny touches the first crease of the left second finger, Fig. 3. While the right forefinger remains on the penny, the left hand is turned to form a half closed fist, with the back of the hand up.

The right hand is given a quarter turn, clockwise, bringing the side of the forefinger to rest on the penny. The right second finger is extended to the underside of the penny, which is clipped between the right forefinger and the second finger. The exact positioning and clipping of the penny can be determined by experimentation for different hands, Figs. 4 and 5, page 374.

The right hand finishes with another quarter turn to a palm up position, with all fingers extended, displaying the nickel in the palm of the right hand. During this action, the left second, third and fourth fingers are closed into the palm and the left forefinger is extended, pointing to the

Fig. 4

Fig. 5

palm up, the thumb draws the penny into the hand by reaching behind the tip of the forefinger, releasing the grip of the forefinger and pulling the penny into the palm.

You have now shown a coin in the left hand and one in the right, with the same motions in each case, and the entire effect is a fast and continuously smooth one, depending primarily on timing. The patter is left to the performer.

A Trio of Vanishes
The Placement
Milton Kort

Turn your right side toward the spectators and show a coin held by its edges between the tips of the thumb and second finger of the palm up right hand. The left hand is open, ready to receive the coin. Turn the right hand over, palm downward, and move the coin directly over the palm of the left hand, Fig. 1. Then as those fingers begin to close over it, the right thumb rolls the coin to the tip of the third finger where it is revolved, then clipped edgewise between the second and third fingers as the left hand closes and the right moves away, dropping to the side. There should be no perceptible movement of the right fingers as the coin is rolled from the second to the

right second finger, the same position that was assumed earlier by the other hand. (The whole turning action of the hand and the clipping of the penny are performed with a slight swing of the hands from left to right.)

The nickel is now handled in the same manner as the penny was, the left forefinger stroking along the right second finger and pushing the nickel back to the tip of the right second finger. The left hand is now drawn to the left side of the body as the forefinger is drawn in to complete the fist. The right hand turns over, forming a fist, but be careful not to expose the clipped penny.

The left hand is now shown empty by turning it palm up. As the right turns

Fig. 1

third finger. The back of the right hand, as it is brought up to deposit the coin in the left, conceals the fact that the coin is retained. And it seems that the coin is actually seen in the left hand a moment *after* the right moves away. Only after the right hand moves out of the spectators' line of vision is the coin clipped and held between the two middle fingers. Now "crumble" the coin away in the left fingers, then open them to show its disappearance.

In the Well

MILTON KORT and DAVE HERTZBERG

The left hand is thumb up and held in a loose fist. Your right side is turned toward the spectators as you display a coin held horizontally by its edge between the tip of the thumb and second finger of the palm up right hand. With a wrist movement, the right hand turns palm down and deposits the coin into the top of the left fist, Fig. 2. The right hand does not release its grip on the coin but immediately withdraws it hidden by the back of the hand, which then drops to the side as the left closes completely, moves further from the body and makes crumbling motions. At the same

time, the right hand transfers the coin to classic palm. Open the left hand and show that the coin has vanished.

Under the Thumb

MILTON KORT and HUGH MACLEAN

Your right side is toward the spectators. The left hand, which is held open and vertical, is palm toward them. The coin is held vertically by its bottom edge between the tips of the thumb and second finger of the palm up right hand. Bring the right hand over to the left and press the top edge of the coin against the fold beneath the fleshy part of the left thumb, then lower the thumb over the coin as if to retain it, Fig. 3. At the precise moment the left thumb lowers over the upper portion of the coin, both hands turn over toward each other simultaneously, the left now closing completely but the right retaining the coin in its original grip. As the two hands turn over the back of the right comes up to conceal the coin from the spectators' view. The left hand moves away and the right drops to the side and adjusts its coin to thumb or classic palm. "Crumble" the coin with the left fingers, finally opening them to show it has disappeared.

The three vanishes will require a great

Fig. 2

Fig. 3

deal of practice to obtain naturalness, as they depend on "the permanence of retinal impressions" more than sleight-of-hand.

Following the pretended placement of the coin in the left hand in the last two methods it is a simple matter to thumb palm it from the grips used, then while making magical passes over the left hand with the right, the coin can be secretly dropped into the outer breast coat pocket in the same manner as in the Bobo Complete Coin Vanish (page 49).

And once the hands are separated, and before the left hand is shown empty, the coin secretly held in the right hand can be sleeved. The left hand would then be opened and both hands shown empty.

The Cartwheel Sleight

KIRK STILES

The title of this deceptive sleight refers to the "cartwheel" action involved rather than to an American silver dollar, for it is suitable for vanishing either a half dollar or a dollar. Holding the coin at your right fingertips, you appear to drop it into the left hand, from which it vanishes in due course.

The coin should rest on the tips of the two middle fingers of the left hand which is being held palm up to allow it to be seen after picking it up, or after it has been tossed into the hand. The right hand then comes over to the left and takes the coin between the thumb and middle fingertips as shown in Fig. 1, then moves away and turns palm up, or palm down, to show the coin once more, flat side to audience. Now, with the coin held parallel to the floor, the right hand returns to the left, which waits to receive it. As the coin moves over the left fingertips—the back of the right hand being toward the audience—the left thumb from above, and the left middle finger from be-

low, squeeze it at the center of the X mark in Fig. 1. The right thumb releases its grip, and as the right hand continues toward the center of the left palm, the right middle finger rolls the coin around counter-clockwise on the off-center hub formed by the left thumb and middle finger which continue to squeeze just tightly enough to offer moderately firm resistance. Continued pressure with the tip of the right middle finger will roll the coin exactly into the curve of the finger which gently closes around it. It appears as if you were droping the coin into your left hand; do NOTHING to disabuse the spectators of this notion.

The left thumb and finger separate and the coin is removed by the right hand which slips back; simultaneously the left hand closes slowly into a fist, seemingly adjusting itself to the bulk of the coin. In doing this, the left fist moves just a bit to the left, the eyes following it. Then the right hand, index finger still extended, points to the audience, the coin being concealed behind the middle finger which receives an assist from the third finger. This is only the most fleeting of gestures, as all attention must be directed immediately upon the left hand. Now the left fingers can crumble away the coin, or slap it through the leg, or toss it, supposedly, to the place where it is to appear.

This sleight can also be used for the vanish of two coins. Hold them 1/8" apart

Fig. 1

in the right finger grip. When the left thumb and finger squeeze them, the sound of the two coins dropping from the right fingers will be duplicated, but the coins actually go into right finger palm position. You can even make a "feint" pass—let the coins actually go into the left hand for the spectators to see, but in this case the left fingers must close over them in total silence, just as they will have to close when the coins are not there.

Now you see how the "cartwheel" gets into the title!

Progressive Production
BOB CARVER

When you need a few coins for a trick why not produce them magically? Here is a simple, easy method for the quick production of five half dollars.

Effect: The coin worker produces a coin from his left elbow, drops it into his left hand and immediately he has two. These are dumped into his right hand and three are shown. The three become four as they are tossed back to the left. And finally the four coins become five as they are returned to the right hand. No gimmicks; nothing but the two hands and the coins are required!

Working: If you can palm a coin and are familiar with the Utility Switch (page 11) you should have no difficulty in mastering this production quickly, as these are the basic moves required.

Begin with two coins concealed in classic palm position of your left hand. The other three are in the same position in the right hand, except that the topmost coin is jogged slightly forward, Fig. 1. The reason for this will become apparent later.

Raise both hands to about shoulder level, hold them palms inward to conceal the palmed coins and snap the fingers of both hands simultaneously as you say, "Watch!" Lower your right hand a few inches, release the jogged coin onto the cupped fingers and produce it from your left elbow. Say, "One," as you hold the left forefinger shoulder high and display the coin at the same level at the tips of your right fingers and thumb. This coin is now apparently deposited in the palm up left hand, which is held slightly cupped and about chest high to conceal its two coins. As the right hand swings over to deposit its visible coin in the left, it is brought down rather sharply, which causes the two in that hand to jingle. This audibly strengthens the idea that you did deposit a coin in the left hand while the right thumb palms its coin. Hold up two fingers of your right hand, lower your left to show two coins and say, "Two."

Pretend to dump these two from the left into the right hand which turns palm up to receive them. But in this action the two left hand coins are retained palmed as the thumb palmed coin in the right hand is released onto the two in that palm. Say, "Three," as the back outward left hand holds up three fingers and the right lowers to show its three coins. Bounce the coins around so they separate, but manage to keep one over the palm. Now pretend to dump

ONE COIN
JOGGED FORWARD

TWO COINS SQUARED
TOGETHER

Fig. 1

the three into the left hand, but one is retained palmed. The left hand immediately shows four coins, two just received from the right hand and two that were already there. Snap the fingers of your right hand over the left, then point to the coins and say, "Four."

After showing the four coins in your palm up left hand, dump all of them back into your right and say, "Five." Snap the left fingers over your right hand which shows the five coins.

The entire series of moves requires less than half a minute to execute. The appearance of the coins is enhanced by the counting and the jingling. They make their one-by-one appearance in such rapid succession that it is impossible to understand where they might be coming from.

Coins from Silk

JACK CHANIN

There are numerous versions of this trick, but this one ranks among the very best. Suitable for close up or stage, it is simple, direct and easy to perform, And it is a handy one to have on tap to produce coins to be used in other effects. Almost any size coins can be used. Mr. Chanin used coins up to 3″ in diameter!

Effect: The magician shows a silk handkerchief on both sides and drapes it over his left hand. Grasping the center with his right hand the handkerchief is reversed over that hand to reveal a coin. This is dropped into a dish on the table and the handkerchief is turned over the left hand to show a second coin. This is dropped into the dish and the moves are repeated to produce a total of four coins.

Requisites and Preparation: Four half dollars, an 18″ silk handkerchief and a small glass dish or bowl. For a stage presentation have the open handkerchief lying flat on a table. Near one inner corner are two coins in a stack, and near the other inner corner are the other two in a stack. The glass dish is nearby.

Working: Step behind the table, reach down with both hands simultaneously, finger palm the coins, two in each hand, then grasp the two opposite corners of the handkerchief and lift it from the table. With it held by the corners and stretched out between your hands show it on both sides. Release the left corner and hold that hand about chest high with the fingers pointing upward as the right drapes the hanky over it so the center lies directly over the left fingers. Now as the right hand moves over to the center of the hanky from above, the left thumb pushes up one of its coins from underneath. This is taken through the silk by the right fingers and thumb, and the handkerchief is reversed as it is thrown over that hand to reveal a coin, Fig. 1. Keep a light grip on the coin through the silk, and as you display it to the spectators move the hand back and forth so the coin will

Fig. 1

wobble and glitter in the light it reflects. Lower your right hand and allow the coin to drop into the dish.

Now you produce a second coin by reversing these moves as follows: Reach over with your palm down left hand, and as it takes the center of the handkerchief the right thumb pushes up a coin from that hand. The coin is gripped through the handkerchief as it is thrown back over the left hand. A second coin appears. Display it as you did the first, then lower your hand and drop it into the bowl. Repeat these moves to produce the next two coins. The production is performed at an even pace with the clattering of each produced coin into the bowl adding to the effect.

Produce only four coins. The effect is not improved by producing more.

If the trick is to be performed close-up a pocket handkerchief can be used, but a dark colored silk is preferred. In this case you would have two coins in your right pocket and two in your left. Palm these out at an opportune moment and perform the trick as described, dropping the produced coins onto the table or into an ash tray.

The Six Coins In Goblet

S. Leo Horowitz (Mohammed Bey)
Courtesy *The Sphinx*

This routine comes from a master of our craft. Not only is it a great platform trick, but a routine performed without apparatus, employing many basic and important sleights in coin conjuring.

Effect: The magician picks up a stemmed goblet and transfers it from hand to hand, showing both hands empty. Then he reaches in the air and produces one at a time, six coins; each as produced is tossed into the glass. He tips the coins out into his hand and spreads them upon the table.

One at a time he picks them up with his right hand and puts them into the left. He takes the glass with the right hand, and one at a time the coins are vanished from the left, dropping into the glass until three have arrived, when he shows that only three remain in the hand. The glass is put down and the three coins are laid on the table. The left hand now takes the glass; a coin disappears from the right and reappears in the glass. The glass is then transferred to the other hand, and a coin vanishes from the left hand and appears in the glass. Again the glass is transferred and a coin disappears to arrive with a clink, and the magician then pours the coins from the glass, showing the six original coins.

To the audience this seems to be one effect. To a magician it is a routine of coin sleights. Because of the way they are put together, each move looks open and natural. It does not seem to be a manipulative trick. Although some of the sleights are described on previous pages, it is suggested that the description be read with care and preferably with the equipment in the hand.

Requirements: Seven half dollars and a goblet.

Working: Using the trick as an opener permits the performer to have the extra coin which the audience knows nothing about, hidden in the left sleeve. However, it can be in a holder underneath the bottom left side of the coat.

Enter holding the glass in your right hand with the six coins edge palmed in the same hand; Fig. 1 shows the hand as seen by the audience. The left arm is bent at the elbow the same way as the right arm. After bowing to the audience, the left arm is extended and the fingers wiggled to call attention to the fact the hand is entirely empty. Then the glass is taken by the left hand as the body is turned so the left side is toward the audience, and the right hand

Fig. 1

shown empty. In making this transfer of the glass and turn of the body, the left thumb and first finger grasp the bowl of the glass, and the second and third fingers pick the six coins out of the palm of the right. Fig. 2 shows how the coins are held prior to the transfer of glass and coins from right to left hand. And remember — the coins are palmed EDGEWISE, rather than flat. (See The Edge Palm, page 2, and Down's method, pages 311 and 316.) This transfer is completely natural and covered by the turn of the body. When the right hand is shown, the body is again turned, the glass again transferred, and the coins set right back in the same edgewise palm position. Now reach into the air with the left hand as if attempting to catch something. Finding nothing, the glass is again transferred to the left hand, but this time the coins remain palmed in the right.

During this transfer, continue to stare in the air as if looking for something. Reach up with the right hand and pluck a coin from the air. This is done by pulling one from the bottom of the stack with the right third finger; when it is out far enough, catch it with the second finger and pull it

out far enough so it may be caught between the first finger and thumb. Tap the coin on the bowl of the glass, then drop it in. This same move is repeated five times. Never look at the glass or the coin, but keep searching in the air, trying to see the coins found there. All this time the left arm has remained bent so the sleeved coin does not make a premature appearance.

The coins are tipped out of the glass into the right hand, then the right first finger and thumb take the glass by the top edge and set it on the table. The coins are now laid out singly upon the table, but still the left arm is not straightened.

The coins are now picked up one at a time and each seemingly put into the left hand. There are six different moves and the final result is that the audience believes there are six coins in the hand; actually there are three in each hand. The first coin is picked up between the right forefinger and thumb, held long enough for the audience to see, then dropped upon the tips of the second and third fingers of the palm up right hand, and seemingly picked up by the left, which is back uppermost. Actually the left hand only simulates picking up the

Fig. 2

coin, and is turned palm uppermost and closed as if holding one. The coin is really palmed in the right hand. The second coin is picked up in the same manner, between the first finger and thumb of the right, and it, too is dropped on the tips of the second and third fingers, but as the hand is turned so its back is toward the audience, seemingly this second coin is dropped on top of the one they imagine to be in the left hand, and they hear it land. What happens is, the fingers of the left hand are slightly opened and the palmed coin dropped so it hits the one on the curled right fingers, then bounces into the left hand. Hitting the coin causes the click which makes the audience believe the second coin was dropped on the first in the left hand. (For another method for pretending to deposit two coins in the left hand see The Click Pass (a), page 14.) The coin on the tips of the right fingers is then palmed and the third coin picked up in precisely the same manner. This time, as the left hand is held open, the palmed coin drops on the one on the tips of the right fingers but is not permitted to bounce into the left. Both coins are pressed into the right palm. (Refer to The Click Pass (b), page 14 for illustration and another description of this sleight.) The audience at this moment believes there are three coins in the left hand; actually there is one, the other two being palmed in the right. The fourth coin is picked up and actually thrown into the left hand, in a manner duplicating the previous gestures. The two in the left are then jingled, the audience thinking they hear four. The fifth coin is picked up in the same identical manner, the two palmed coins are allowed to fall on it, and the three are then pressed into the right palm instead of the seeming "placing" of the coin in the left. The sixth and last coin is then actually thrown in the left hand, following the same moves previously

used. The left hand then jingles its coins.

The glass is then picked up with the right hand so the palm is over the mouth and the thumb and four fingers holding it. The left hand squeezes one coin so it extends out of the fist at the crotch of the thumb. The hand is waved toward the right, and at the same time the coin in the fist is allowed to drop back out of sight. At this moment one coin is released from the palm of the right and allowed to fall into the glass. These same motions are repeated twice. When three have reappeared the glass is set on the table. Now show that there are just three coins in the left hand by fanning them out at the fingertips. The fan of coins is then taken with the right fingertips and the left arm straightened so the sleeved coin can drop into the left hand, where it is palmed. Two of the three coins held in the right hand are dropped singly on the table as you count one, two, three, but you hold the third at your fingertips. The glass is then picked up with the left hand, the palm over the mouth, the thumb and four fingers holding it. The coin in the right hand is then dropped toward the glass (actually palmed) and the retrieved (sleeved) coin dropped from the left palm. The glass is then transferred to the right hand and the previous routine duplicated. Again the glass is transferred, this time back to the left hand, and the sixth and last coin is picked up by the right, thrown toward the glass, but actually back palmed. It is back palmed while the fingers are curled and with the back of the hand toward the audience. The fingers are then opened out as the wrist is twisted, turning the palm of the hand toward the audience. This convincingly shows the back and the palm of the hand to be completely empty.

There are now six coins in the glass held by the left hand, and one back palmed in the outstretched right. This hand is then brought toward the left and turned over, palm uppermost, at the same time bringing the coin from back palm position around to the finger palm. Simultaneously the left hand comes toward the right and turns the glass over so the coins are dumped into the right hand at exactly the same moment the extra coin is brought to finger palm position. The glass is turned mouth inward, then turned back mouth uppermost. Now the coins are counted one at a time as they are dropped back into the glass. The count is completely fair through the fifth coin. When the sixth is counted, drop the two coins as one into the glass, place the glass on the table, bow, and accept the applause of the audience.

Kort's Fourth

MILTON KORT

This trick, a version of The Sympathetic Coins, is by one of the nation's greatest close-up performers. Milton Kort deserves special praise for his generosity in contributing so many excellent tricks, sleights and ideas to this and the previous edition of *Modern Coin Magic*.

Effect: Four half dollars are placed on a spread out handkerchief, one at each corner. Two are covered with squares of cardboard. Two halves penetrate the handkerchief and join a third under one of the covers. Lifting the other cover, the fourth coin is seen to have changed to copper. And when the cover is raised from the other three, they too have become copper coins!

Requisites and Preparation: Four half dollars, four English pennies, a man's opaque handkerchief and two pieces of cardboard, each about 6″ square.

Have three of the copper coins in the left coat pocket and one in the right coat pocket. The four half dollars are in the right

trousers pocket and the cardboard can be on the table.

Working: Begin the effect by spreading the handkerchief on the table with the edges parallel to the table edges. Stand behind the table and explain that you will require four coins for the trick. Thrust both hands into their respective coat pockets and finger palm the coins as follows: The right finger palms its coin with the second and third fingers, while the left finger palms its coins with the third and fourth fingers. Then pretending the coins you need are not in the coat pockets, take your hands out, remove the four half dollars from the right trousers pocket, and place them in a row along the edge of the handkerchief nearest you.

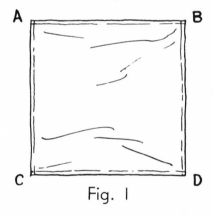

Fig. 1

Pick up a square of cardboard in each hand and show them back and front, keeping the coins in the hands concealed. Drop one at corner A of the handkerchief and the other at corner B, Fig. 1. With the right hand, pick up a half dollar as the left raises the cardboard at corner A of the handkerchief. Drop the coin on this corner of the cloth and cover it with the cardboard. Lift the cover at corner B with the left hand while the right takes up a half dollar and apparently tosses it on the handkerchief under the cardboard. Actually the copper coin from the hand is dropped and the half dollar finger palmed. The square of cardboard conceals this switch, making it completely indetectable. Move the two remaining visible half dollars to corners C and D. As far as the spectators are concerned the trick has not begun.

With the left hand, pick up the cover at corner A and transfer it to the right hand, covering the finger palmed half. Show both sides of the cardboard, then as it is returned to corner A the half dollar goes along underneath.

Pick up the half at C with the right hand while the left raises corner C, fingers underneath, thumb on top. The right hand with its coin goes under hanky and moves up to corner A, pretending to push the coin up through the cloth there. As the right hand with the half is withdrawn it passes underneath corner C held by the left hand, which clips and retains the coin so the right comes out empty.

With the right hand, take up the cover from corner A, displaying two half dollars there. Without any hesitation the cardboard is transferred to the left hand, which releases its grip on corner C of the handkerchief and holds its half dollar underneath. Point to the two halves at corner A with the right hand.

The right hand now takes the cover and its hidden coin from the left and shows both sides, keeping the coin concealed with the fingers. The left immediately picks up the two half dollars at corner A, turns them over and drops them back. The right hand follows without any hesitation and replaces the cardboard over them, loading the third coin.

Take up the visible coin at corner D with your right hand, raise that corner of the cloth with the left and carry the coin underneath. Pretend to push it up through corner A, then bring the hand out with the coin finger palmed. Lift the cardboard

from corner A with the right hand to show three coins. The left hand picks up the three halves, shows them and holds them together between the thumb and first two fingers, then as the right drops the cardboard over them, they are retained and the three copper coins dropped instead. The left hand is holding the three half dollars as described, with the tip of the little finger resting on the table and just as the right moves the cardboard over, apparently to cover them, the coppers are dropped while the three silver coins slide into finger palm position. Apparently you have shown the three silver coins and covered them again with the cardboard.

State that you will attempt to cause the last half dollar to pass from underneath its cover to join the other three silver coins. Snap your fingers, then pick up the cover from corner B with the right hand and transfer it to the left, covering the three half dollars hidden there. Instead of a half dollar at corner B there is a copper coin! Now remove the cover from corner A with the right hand to reveal three copper coins there, a really surprising climax.

Now you have three half dollars hidden in your left hand and one in your right. Retain the cardboard covers in your hands until the spectators have looked over the copper coins, then toss the squares onto the table, pick up two coppers with the right hand and two with the left and place them and the concealed half dollars in the pockets.

Motile

Dr. Jacob Daley
Courtesy *The Phoenix*

In this method for performing The Sympathetic Coins, the first covering motion is the cornerstone. Performed in a brisk manner this is as indetectable as a trick can be.

Requirements: Four half dollars, two playing cards, a cloth covered performing surface, or the rug on the floor.

Working: "I have discovered a rather odd property of cards and coins." You are covering each of the four coins as you speak. "Two coins, when properly covered, will develop this odd property which I want to demonstrate. What the secret of this property is, I do not know. Seemingly a kind of static electrical charge is developed when certain coins are covered in a specific sequence by cardboard,—in this instance, playing cards. I can't tell in advance which coins match up, therefore I simultaneously touch the coins with my fingers and cover them with the cards."

Hold the cards at their sides, in the middle with the tips of the fingers and thumbs of the right and left hands. Think of the coins being labelled as in Fig. 1, A, B, C, D. Cover B and C with cards. The backs of three fingers rest on the coins as the cards are brought down momentarily covering them; remark: "Um-m-m—I feel no electrical tingle from these . . ." As you say this, move the right hand and its card to the right a few inches, exposing coin B. Transfer the cards from the right hand to the left hand, and from left to right, freezing the left hand. The right hand covers

Fig. 2

coin D in like manner; the left hand moves to the left exposing coin C. You say, "No, these don't seem to match either. No tingle." The left hand covers C again, and you then bring the card in the left hand to the right hand, transferring cards. Freeze the right hand in its position.

Now, here is the crux of the whole trick! The left hand, holding the card as in Fig. 2 and pressing down on coin C with the backs of the fingers as shown, slides coin C up to A under cover of the card. The right hand has come down over the area where the coin was, dropping its card and freezing into immobility.

The left hand has brought its stolen coin up to coin A, then moves to the left carrying the stolen coin C along with it and shows coin A.

You say, "Aha—a tingle! These match!"

Slide the hidden coin, under cover of the card, to the right, dropping the card over coin A, and automatically over the stolen coin. You will be amazed at how delightfully simple this sliding action is. There is no strain in your fingers, nothing to reveal that the steal has taken place! Master this simple move, or please don't do the trick!

Pick up coin B with the right hand. Vanish it by any simple vanish you do well. It must vanish by seeming to place it in the

A   B

Fig. 1

C   D

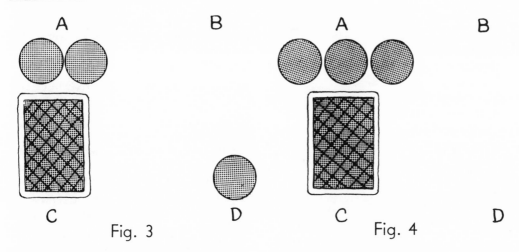

A   B   A   B

C   D   C   D

Fig. 3   Fig. 4

left hand but retain it in the right.

Hold the left fist over card at A, crumple the coin to nothingness, and with the left fingers pick up the card at A revealing that the coin has joined its mate. Transfer the card from the left hand to the right covering the finger palmed coin hidden there. The left fingers reach up to the coins at A and adjust them so they are next to each other horizontally, Fig. 3.

Take the card from the right hand with the left fingers and cover the two coins. A coin still lies completely unsuspected on your right fingers. No loading takes place here.

Pick up coin D with the right fingertips and thumb and drop it into the left hand; now and *only* now, just as you are about to close the left fingers about the visible coin, pause, and reach down with the right fingertips, pick up the card at A and show that there are still only two coins there. When you replace the card you place the palmed coin down with its mates. This delay makes the difference between a cute trick and a masterly one!

The right fingers now pick up the coin from the left hand and you proceed to vanish it, again using a vanish that ends with the coin retained in the right. Crumple

the left fingers showing coin has disappeared; pick up the card at A with the left fingers and transfer it to the right fingertips covering the retained coin which you have finger palmed.

Use the card to adjust the three coins in a horizontal line, as in Fig. 4. Transfer the card and coin at the fingertips to the left hand, and replace the card over the three adding the extra coin below the line of the three. The three coins will project beyond the cover afforded by the card; this doesn't matter, for the one you are concerned with hiding, is concealed. See Fig. 5.

The card at C, which has lain dormant throughout the whole routine is bent upward lightly by the tips of the left fingers, then the right fingers go underneath and pretend to take out the non-existent coin.

Hold the right hand as though it contained a coin, pretend to place it in the left palm and close left fingers into a fist. Hold the hand over the card at A and "crumple" vanish the 'coin'; the right hand simultaneously picks up the card at C; you use it as a wand, running the edge of the card over your fingers as you 'vanish' this coin. This rather effective click precedes showing the left hand empty.

Use this card as a lever to flick the other

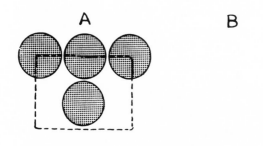

A   B

C   D

Fig. 5

card out of the way, thus revealing all four coins together, Fig. 5.

Dr. Daley asked, "If you like this effect and decide to do it, please, please practice it at least 50 or 100 times; as simple as the sequence is, when you do it, it must be without conscious thought or apparent effort."

The Waiter's Tip

SILENT MORA THE MAGICIAN

This little trick caused a waiter's eyes to pop, as well as much merriment among the passengers in the dining car of a train. The occasion, a group of magicians going from Chicago to attend the 1946 I.B.M. Convention in St. Louis, Missouri. Mora tells it in these words:

"The diner was comfortably cool on this hot summer day, and in such surroundings every magician present wanted to entertain the others by doing his 'pet specials.' I must admit we all did our bit, and while the magicians were entertaining each other, many other diners were very interested onlookers.

"Finally, as the train was nearing St. Louis, we all departed for our seats in the other cars, but before we left the diner I called our waiter to our table and while he was watching, I slipped a silver dollar under my napkin for him.

"He hurriedly put his hand down on the napkin, saying, 'Here's ONE buck that ain't going to disappear,' and lifting the napkin he found—NOTHING! His tip had vanished, and the other waiters were laughing at the surprised look on his face. That silver dollar had really vanished, and the waiter, amazed, threw the napkin on the table. I picked it up by the center and draped it over my right hand, then called, 'George, will you please catch hold of the center of the napkin,' which he did, and he, turning it so the folds fell over his hand, found the vanished TIP staring him in the face."

Method: The corner of the folded napkin should be pointed toward where the waiter is standing. With finger and thumb of the left hand, catch the very tip of the corner and lift it up half way. Right hand, holding the coin at tips of thumb and first finger, places it on the lower part of the fold, then left fingers let the lifted corner drop over it.

That is what the waiter sees, but he does not notice that when you have made the placement, the right hand turns back upwards, and with no further movement of the thumb and fingers, the hand is withdrawn from the fold and drops to the side, the coin still unmoved from its first position between your thumb and first finger. You can palm it now, and you are ready for the moment when the waiter throws the napkin on the table. Pick it up with the left hand and drape it over the right. When the hand is covered, the palmed coin is brought to the fingertips, and when the waiter catches the napkin in the center he feels the coin inside, and he will gleefully reveal it to the folks watching.

Don't do any fancy work with your

hands. The movements are all simple and natural, and anything extra would spoil the effect. The optical illusion known as the persistence of vision is working for you, just as it is in T. J. Crawford's Illusive Coin Pass and Dai Vernon's Coin Vanish, pages 29-32, and there is nothing in the entire realm of coin magic more deceptive. Mora sometimes uses the move to (apparently) put a coin in a coin purse, snapping the purse shut with the left hand, and here, too, it is a perfect illusion.

'Silver Lining'

MILBOURNE CHRISTOPHER
Courtesy *The New Phoenix*

For attention-getting effectiveness, this "quickie" coin production will be hard to beat. Milbourne Christopher often uses it as an "ice-breaker," and credits it with getting him many publicity stories. Since it can be used as an effect by itself, or as an introduction to a coin routine, you will find it useful to know. Once you learn it, you will never be without a trick to do so long as you have a half dollar in your pocket, for you can borrow the dollar bill!

Effect: A dollar bill is shown front and back, at the very tips of the fingers, then rolled into a cylinder. A half dollar appears magically from the rolled bill.

Method: The trick depends upon the easily learned sleight used to conceal the coin as both sides of the bill are shown. This sleight is a variation of one used to conceal a coin when showing both sides of a card—see Glenn Harrison's Coins and Cards, Chapter IX. Dino Mazza's illustrations show every step of the move.

The dollar bill is held in the right hand as in Fig. 1, the half dollar concealed behind it, clipped by the thumb and first and second fingers as shown by the dotted lines. When the hand turns around to show the back of the bill as in Fig. 3, the thumb slides the bill down as the fingers draw the half dollar upward as in Fig. 2. The coin is now concealed by the fingers, and since the bill is held at the very fingertips, the full surface of both sides is seen. The bill is again turned so its face is toward the spec-

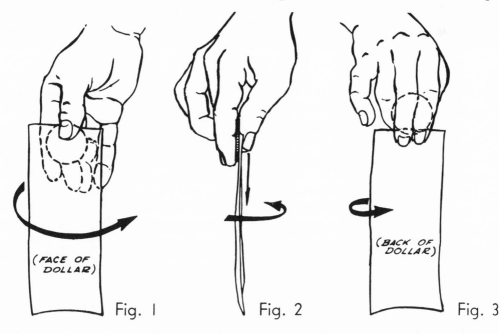

(FACE OF DOLLAR)   Fig. 1

Fig. 2

(BACK OF DOLLAR)   Fig. 3

Fig. 4   Fig. 5   Fig. 6

tators as in Fig. 1, by reversing the moves just described. Now the forefinger is brought around as indicated in Fig. 4, clipping the coin against the middle finger, and the thumb is removed as in Fig. 5. The left fingers now grasp the lower end of the bill, Fig. 6, and roll it upward toward the body, Fig. 7, forming a cylinder which

is held in place by the thumb on the outside and the middle finger inside, Fig. 8, the coin being held in place by these same fingers. Now if you were to tilt the cylinder toward the table and release the pressure of the fingers, the half dollar would slide out and drop with a resounding clink.

When the bill is displayed as in Fig. 1, you say, "Have you ever noticed the words at the top of a dollar bill, 'SILVER CERTIFICATE'?" and you point to the words. As you show the bill on both sides and roll

Fig. 7

Fig. 8

it into a cylinder, say, "That is exactly what a dollar bill is—a certificate of silver." As you reach the position shown in Fig. 8, the cylinder is pressed flat; the half dollar is still inside, but the flattened cylinder is now held with the fingers and thumb on the outside. "You can even hear the silver in the certificate," you say as you rap the packet sharply on the table. "And here is the silver!" So saying, allow the half dollar to drop out onto the table.

You can have the half dollar with the bill in your billfold if you use your own bill; or, have the coin sleeved in the right sleeve and borrow the bill. Your hands would be seen empty; you would receive the offered bill in your left hand and pass it to the right, which just the moment before had dropped to the side and obtained the sleeved coin. [U. S. Currency changes in recent years have taken silver certificates out of circulation and silver half dollars may soon vanish. But 'Silver Lining' remains a real gem!]

Dollar Flight

Glenn Harrison

Here is another "coin passe" effect employing silver dollars and a completely different handling.

Effect: Two silver dollars are seen lying on the table several inches apart. One is held in each hand. The right hand opens, palm up, and tosses its coin to the table, then turns palm down and covers it. The left hand slaps its coin to the table a few inches to the left. Both hands now lie flat, a coin under each. Now the left hand is raised. No coin is seen. Right hand is then lifted to show both coins.

Working: Show two silver dollars on the table, one to the right, one to the left. With your right hand, pick up the coin on the left and pretend to place it in your left hand, but retain it palmed in your right. The left hand closes into a fist over the table. Now take up the coin on your right with your right hand, hold it for a second, then as you turn your hand palm up, back palm the coin and toss the other onto the table. The effect is that you picked up the right hand coin, held it in your closed hand a second then tossed it back onto the table to show all fair. The apparently empty right hand and the "clang" of the coin striking the table adds to the illusion that all is fair. Say, "I will place my right hand over the coin on the table." As you say this the closed left hand, which has been finger-side up, turns palm down and pretends to lay its non-existent coin on the table. At this precise moment the right hand has completed its turn to a palm down position and releases its palmed coin, which falls to the table beside the one already there. The left hand is brought palm down and flat on the table at the instant the right hand releases its palmed coin, and the sound of this coin striking the table completes the illusion of a coin actually being under the left hand.

Both hands now lie palm down, flat on the table a few inches apart. Apparently there is a dollar under each hand, but both are underneath the right. Slowly lift your left hand from the table, turn it palm up and show it empty. The coin is gone! Lift your right hand to show both under that hand.

Stand-Up Coin Opener

Royal H. Brin, Jr.

Effect: Two half dollars are placed in the left hand, the right being shown empty. They magically fly apart so there is one in each hand. The one in the right is placed in the pocket, but immediately rejoins the other in the left hand.

Method: There are really three half dollars. One is concealed in the left sleeve, one held openly in the right hand, and one in the left. As attention is called to the coins, the right hand is held out, palm up, its coin resting about an inch from the finger-tips. The left hand is raised chest high, and its coin is held between thumb and first finger.

The right hand is now turned over and closed into a fist; if this movement is timed correctly the coin will be tossed almost automatically into the right sleeve, but to the spectators it is apparently held in the closed fist.

The closed fist is immediately raised and moved to the left, to meet the approaching left hand. The left hand pushes its coin into the right fist, as you say, "Let's put the two halves together."

Continue, "Now the left hand is empty . . . ," and show that it is, then drop it to the side as you go on, ". . . and there are two half dollars in the right." Turn your gaze to the right hand, moving it to focus attention on it. Meanwhile the coin in the left sleeve has dropped into the left hand, where the last three fingers curl around it. Raise the left hand again and point toward the right fist, as you continue, ". . . or a total value of one dollar, right?"

Look at the audience a moment for confirmation, and whatever their response, say, "No, that's wrong. There's one half dollar in each hand." Open both hands to show that to be the case.

Take the coins between the thumb and forefinger of each hand, respectively, and display them for a second or two, letting the audience see the hands otherwise empty. Then drop both hands to your sides as though the trick were all over, saying, "You weren't watching very closely." Meanwhile the coin in the right sleeve slides down into the cupped middle, ring, and little fingers

of the right hand, ready for the finish.

Raise both hands chest-high again, a half dollar held openly between thumb and forefinger of each hand, and another concealed by the closed last three fingers of the right hand, as you say, 'This time let's put one half into the pocket." Put the left hand into left coat pocket, leave the coin behind, and bring out the left hand, showing it empty. "Now we have one hand empty," looking at the open left hand, "one half in the pocket," as you gesture toward the pocket with the left hand, "and one coin in the right hand," as you gesture toward the right hand with the left.

"But it takes just a tap on the pocket," tap the outside of the pocket with the left hand and at the same time let the visible half drop from the right thumb and finger into the hand, clinking against the concealed half, ". . . and the coins are back together again!" Open the right hand and show the two halves are there indeed.

You have obtained a double magical effect, safely disposed of the extra coin, and are all ready to continue with any other coin moves.

Frank Ducrot's Coin Fold

STEWART JUDAH

The standard coin fold, a very useful method of vanishing a coin by wrapping it in a small piece of paper, is explained on pages 60 and 61. A number of ingenious dodges have been devised to take it out of "The Boy's Book of Magic" class and put it into the conjurer's bag of tricks, but the orthodox method can still be deceptive in the hands of a man who knows his business.

The famous Frank Ducrot, who edited the magic magazine *MAHATMA* back at the turn of the century, made a few little changes both in the method of folding and

Fig. 1

Fig. 2

Fig. 3

in the handling that I believe you'll like. Frank explained it to me over 30 years ago. I was with him on several occasions when he used it in his public shows to vanish the coin in The Coin and Nest of Silver Boxes, and it's still good today. I know, for I use it!

Frank used a piece of paper 6″ wide by 6½″ long, and the folds had been made beforehand, Fig. 1; after he had borrowed the coin and had it marked, making the little packet, or "coin fold" as we say, was but the work of a moment. The paper lay on his left hand, his left thumb in the top middle square. The coin was placed on the center square, the thumb clipping it against the paper supported by the fingers. The top was folded down, Fig. 2, the bottom folded up, and the sides folded in, first one, then the other. He held the paper so the audience could see him fold it around the coin. When folded, Fig. 3, the packet could be turned in any direction and the coin could not drop out. He tapped it against the table, even tossed it onto the table where it landed with a "clunk." Then, pretending to overhear some remark about it, he would look up

innocently, pick up the packet, and holding it at his fingertips, slowly unfold the sides, then the bottom, and there was the coin, safely between the folds.

He took it out, held it up, and said, "Oh no—it's still here," and apparently slipped it under the top fold as they had seen it before; he turned the bottom fold over it, then the two sides, and tapped it on the table again in the fairest possible manner. But this time deception had entered the picture and the coin was in position to "go south" so the packet could be burned, or torn to the bits which fluttered to the floor like a miniature snow shower.

The second time, the top fold was down as before, but he did not slip the coin back *under* this fold. The action and gesture were the same, but this time he held the paper so the audience could not SEE what took place. When he seemed to be slipping the coin under the top fold, he was sliding it *over* the fold where it was held by the thumb until he could bring the bottom fold over it, then fold down the two sides and tap the packet on the table again. The coin was now in the usual one-end-open fold and could be slid out into his fingers at his leisure.

Even the small boys who knew things were taken in, so convincingly did he "fox" them when he put the coin back in the packet.

Handkerchief Coin Vanish

EDDIE JOSEPH
Courtesy Abbott's Magic Mfg. Co.

This is one of the simplest vanishes for one or more coins in the whole conjuring arsenal, for all you need is a plain, fancy or borrowed handkerchief. It has "gone the rounds," even to appearing in print in various forms and credited to various people, and we include the originator's version here because we believe it to be as useful as the Coin Fold.

Method: A handkerchief is spread on the table and the coin (or several small coins) placed in the center as in **Fig. 1.** Fold corner C up on top of A, as in Fig. 2.

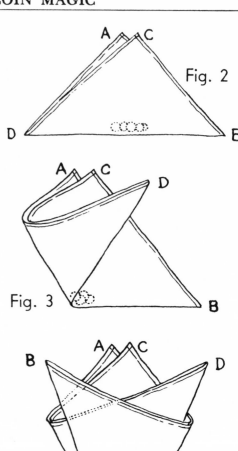

Fig. 2

Fig. 3

Fig. 4

COINS

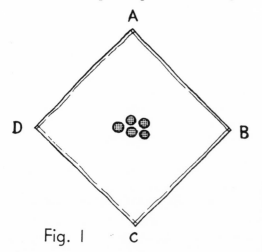

Fig. 1

Fold corner D over to the right, about in line with AC, as in **Fig. 3.** Corner B is then folded to the left as in **Fig. 4.** Now, everything depends upon the way you pick up the corners to keep the coins in the little bag that will form. Gather B into the left thumb crotch and take A between the left thumb and index finger; gather D into the right thumb crotch and grip C between the right thumb and index finger as in Fig. 5. Jounce the coins on the table a couple of times then pull the hands apart, letting

Fig. 5

Fig. 6   *COINS IN TROUGH*

will find that after the hanky has been displayed as in Fig. 6, you can bring the corners A and C together in the left hand, and the coins will stay in the trough at the center. Grasp the center in the right fingers, holding the coins in the folds like the egg in the Egg Bag; you can now let go with the left fingers and slap the ends of the hanky across the left palm, creating the illusion of nothing there.

As simple as this is, you will have to work with it until you can handle it convincingly. Then it will look like magic when you do it!

Al Leech's Coin Trick

Beautiful as it is to behold in the hands of an Al Goshman or Dai Vernon, the coin effect known as Spellbound has always seemed, to me at least, to lack a suitable conclusion. In the usual routine, a half dollar changes to an English penny and back again in a series of really bewildering transformations. In conclusion, the performer either pockets the coin or hands it to a spectator, in a manner designed to convey the impression that only one coin is used.

Somehow, I've always felt that this sort of ending is "bad theater," and that if at all possible a surprise twist should be introduced. The following bit of business was devised in an effort to create such a surprise ending.

I shall not go into the entire Spellbound routine, which has been published by Louis Tannen in *Stars of Magic,* but instead will describe a shorter and very simple version, which incidentally is quite easy to do.

Props and Preparation: A half dollar, an English penny, and a brightly colored button about the same size as the coins. The button is in the right hand trouser pocket.

Method: Display the silver coin in the

go of B and D by loosening the thumb crotch grip of each hand, but holding onto corners A and C. The hanky will now be stretched horizontally, Fig. 6, and the coin (or coins) will lie at the center in a little trough or channel which forms in the diagonal fold toward you, if you've done everything as you should. A couple of trials will give you the idea. After you get "the hang of it," you can gather all four corners into the left hand (keeping them separated and labelled in your mind), then jounce the coins on the table. To vanish them, the right hand comes up, takes corner C as explained, the left taking A; the corners B and D are released, the hanky stretched out as in Fig. 6 and the coins are gone.

If a single coin is used, it will run down the trough into your hand when the hanky is tilted, and can then be palmed.

When several small coins are used, you

left hand, which is palm up. It is gripped at its opposite edges by tips of the thumb and second finger. The English penny is concealed in the right hand, in the finger palm.

The right hand now approaches the left, to stroke the half dollar as in Fig. 1. In doing so, the right thumb goes behind the half. The left thumb and second finger now relax their grip, allowing the half to fall into the finger palm position at the base of the two left middle fingers. The right hand now moves away to the right in a stroking motion, at the same time depositing the English penny between the left thumb and second finger, in the precise position originally occupied by the half dollar.

Grasping it between the thumbs and forefingers of both hands, the penny may now be shown on both sides, but be careful not to flash the half dollar concealed in the left finger palm.

Next, place the penny in the right hand, in position for the change, and repeat the effect, stroking the coin with the left hand. At the conclusion, the penny is hidden in the right finger palm, and the half dollar is displayed between the right thumb and forefinger.

Take the coin for a moment in the left hand, and gesture with it, to show the hand otherwise empty. The coin should be held near the rim, with the left thumb on top and the second finger underneath.

Now, pretend to transfer it to the right hand, actually retaining it in the left. The move I use for this is quite natural and easy to do. The right hand, concealing the penny in the finger palm, is held waist high, fingers pointing to the left, in a relaxed position. The left hand now moves over to the right pretending to place the half dollar in the right palm. As the edge strikes the right palm, the coin is auto-

ENGLISH PENNY
FINGER-PALMED

Fig. 1

matically pushed back between the left thumb and second finger, concealing it from view. The right hand closes as if containing the coin, and pretends to place it in the right trouser pocket.

Above all, don't make a "move" out of the pretended transfer. It should be done casually, exactly as if you were placing a coin in your pocket, which in itself is a natural and everyday occurrence. As you pocket the coin, make a remark to this effect: "Actually I don't need this half dollar, because I always carry a spare behind my ear." As you say this, the left hand, containing the concealed half dollar, goes to the right ear, and squeezes the earlobe between the thumb and forefinger. Pretend to extract a half dollar from behind the ear and display the coin. While this is taking place, the right hand has plenty of time to get rid of the penny in the trouser pocket, and secure the button in the finger palm.

As the half dollar is displayed in the left hand, the right emerges from the pocket and takes the coin for a moment. Next, the coin is placed in the left hand in position for the final change. The right hand strokes the coin, Fig. 1, leaving in its place the button. The left hand now displays the button, with the half dollar remaining concealed in the left finger palm.

Finally, the left hand disposes of both button and half dolar in the left trouser or coat pocket.

The Great Purse Game
Al Baker's Version
Courtesy of Louis Tannen

For many years the nimble-fingered gentry plied their trade of Three Card Monte and The Shells and the Elusive Pea at the country fairs throughout America, and many a rural visitor returned to his home sadder but wiser after trying to beat "the other man's game."

In England and Australia the unwary victim was separated from his hard earned money by means of the Great Purse Game, an entirely different but extremely clever swindle. Although in recent years Card Monte and the Shell Game have become widely known among the magical fraternity, the purse secret has not been widely circulated. Stanley Collins describes Charles Morritt's masterful presentation in this book on page 334, but Morritt's handling depended upon a sleight he called the Purse Grip, mastery of which may be impossible for some because of the size of individual hands. Therefore it is with particular pleasure that we present Al Baker's version of this clever close-up effect.

In working, the operator had a number of small purses lying on a tray. Picking one up he would unmistakably drop two silver half dollars into it, snap it shut, and toss it from hand to hand several times in a casual manner. It was then dropped in full view on a tray with the other purses and after slightly mixing, they were offered for sale at fifty cents each. It was comparatively easy for the unsuspecting victim to

keep his eye on the prize purse and after a hurried purchase he would open it to find not silver, but two copper coins.

This trick, like all good tricks, will require some practice but if the interested performer will follow the instructions carefully he will find that the moves are natural and blend together to form a perfect illusion.

Requisites and Preparation: Two copper coins, preferably English pennies, two half dollars and a small snap-open type coin purse made of soft leather. The half dollars should be in the purse before beginning the trick, and the two copper coins are held in finger palm position in the right hand as in Fig. 1, which also holds the purse as shown.

Method: Right hand with copper coins finger palmed picks up loaded purse as shown in Fig. 1, then hand is straightened out flat and palm up allowing the purse to cover the two coppers now lying on the fingers, Fig. 2.

Fig. 1

Fig. 2

Fig. 3

Fig. 4

Fig. 5

Fig. 6

The purse is then tossed through the air from hand to hand as hands are held three or four inches apart as in Fig. 3. It will be found that the coins will travel along underneath and in close contact with the purse without any danger of being seen, and purse will fall on fingers as in Fig. 2. After three or four tosses, the fingers of the right hand are curled around the copper coins and return to the position shown in Fig. 1. From this position, the right hand passes the purse to a spectator with the request that he open it. He finds two half dollars, which are taken by the performer with the thumb and index finger of the right hand, and spectator is asked to examine the purse. While this is being done, the performer straightens his hand out flat allowing the silver coins to cover the two coppers as in Fig. 4.

Taking the open purse from the spectator, the two silver coins are openly dropped into it, but unknown to the audience the two copper coins are allowed to drop with them. The purse is then snapped shut with the left fingers, and again tossed at a slight distance from one hand to the other. At the same time the magician remarks, "Who'll give me fifty cents for the purse?" Receiving no ready reply, he opens it and says, "Perhaps you think the coins are counterfeit," and at the same time reaches in and removes the two silver coins and holds them up for inspection. Then placing one of the coins momentarily between his lips, he holds the remaining half on his right hand with edge protruding as in Fig. 5, and the coin is apparently tossed into the purse. In reality it is tipped over, or dropped, into the slightly open fingers of the left hand as the right is turned completely over, the index finger being allowed to actually enter the purse, the palm of the right hand now facing the audience, Fig. 6.

This is repeated with the second coin, purse is snapped shut with left fingers and again is tossed from hand to hand, but this time the silver coins are under the purse. After several tosses, the fingers of the right hand are curled around coins and hand resumes the position shown in Fig. 1. The purse is then offered to a spectator who on opening it finds not silver but two copper coins.

When tossing the purse from hand to hand, do it with a careless manner and you will find that the coins will travel underneath without the least suspicion of anything being concealed.

When apparently tossing the coin into the purse as in Fig. 5, let me stress again that

it must protrude *over* the finger exactly as shown, for the reason that the flash of silver creates the perfect illusion.

In Al Goshman's hands the Great Purse Game is a convincing illusion—one of his prized program items.

The Passe Coins

` John Brearley

Some years ago, John Brearley included a version of The Purse Game in his book *ConJUNIORing*, and reminisced:

"Morritt raised this humble close-quarter trick to the dignity of a stage illusion, and when one considers that the sole apparatus consists of two purses of the snap variety and six coins, it has something to recommend it. Furthermore, there is ample opportunity for movement which makes it ideal for stage presentation."

Effect: Two assisting spectators are seated at card tables on either side of the stage. In the absence of tables, the assistants can hold trays. Each is given a purse to examine. One is given two English pennies and the other two half crowns. The performer puts the coins in their respective purses, which are then left in the custody of the two spectators. The coins change places.

Method: First of all, the examination of the purses is stressed. The coins are placed on the two tables. The conjurer goes from one table to the other after each operation, which imparts a lively tempo to the trick. He has two half crowns finger palmed in the right hand, and these can be stolen after the purses and coins are in the hands of the assisting spectators. Approaching the "penny" table, he drops the two pennies in the purse, then closes it. The purse is then opened and the pennies dropped out on the table. The two coins are again picked up with the right hand, between the index finger and thumb, the second, third and fourth fingers being slightly curled. The finger palmed half crowns are dropped into the purse which is immediately shut with a snap. At the same time the fingers of the right hand straighten out and hide the pennies. Emphasis is given to the fact that the coins are really in the purse by shaking it near the spectator's ear, for the jangling of the coins is heard, and it is during this operation that the pennies in the right hand are shifted to the finger palm position.

Now comes a ruse which "lifts the trick into the miracle class." The purse is put on top of the finger palmed pennies, and against all conjuring ethics, the performer says, "No palming," and deliberately throws the purse, together with the hidden pennies, from hand to hand exactly as ex-

plained in the Al Baker version. The noise made by the hidden pennies is assumed to be the coins within the purse.

Finally the purse is taken in the left hand and given to the assistant, with a request to feel the coins through the leather. The pennies remain finger palmed in the right hand.

The above moves are repeated with the other assistant, and it only remains to work up excitement for the denouément.

"Due to the modesty of the apparatus used," says Brearley, "it is a useful 'extra' to include in one's bag against the emergency which sometimes arises through having to 'cut' an item in one's planned program owing to its unsuitability." The trick is interesting to youngsters as well as adults, and this stage version can be presented as a straight coin transposition effect rather than with the Purse Game plot and patter.

Chapter XVIII

SELECTED COIN TRICKS

The tricks in this chapter have been selected from the repertoires of expert coin workers. They require a mastery of the techniques explained in previous chapters, and their entertainment potential is "built in." But it is not enough merely to stand before an audience and "do" them. You have to win audience approval for them by ENTERTAINING with them, too! And to entertain with them, you will have to employ all the arts of the theatre, and these, unfortunately, are best learned through experience. We can give you step-by-step directions so you can duplicate the tricks, but only by your own ability can you transform this cold print into something that will delight an audience!

Passing the Buck

THOMAS JAMES OSBORNE
Courtesy Mrs. Thomas Osborne
and Louis Tannen

The author considers this routine one of the finest ever developed for close-up presentation. It has movement, surprise after surprise, mystery and eye appeal. And it can be performed in pantomime.

Effect: From four cards, four coins are magically produced. Then the cards are placed in a row on the table. The coins vanish one by one, appear under the cards and jump around in a manner that is impossible to follow. Finally a coin is placed underneath each of the cards but they magically accumulate at one end.

Requisites and Presentation: A deck of poker size playing cards with the following five cards on top: 4 of Diamonds, 3 of Clubs, 5 of Hearts, 8 of Hearts and the Ace of Diamonds. Poker size cards are suggested because they are wider than bridge size and therefore aid in concealing the coins.

Five well-worn and smooth half dollars. For quieter handling the older coins create less noise than the newer ones.

Working: As you begin the trick have the five coins finger palmed in your right hand and the deck, back up, in dealing position in your left. Stand behind a cloth-covered table facing the audience. Holding both hands chest high, the left thumb pushes the top card over so the right can take it between the thumb and extended fore-

Fig. 1

Fig. 2

Fig. 3

Fig. 4

Fig. 5

finger, Fig. 1, face of card toward the spectators. Due to the peculiar hold you have on the 4D you are able to push the top coin off the stack onto the back of the card. The right thumb is taken away from the back of the card for a moment while the card is held between the forefinger and the curled-in second finger. The thumb pushes the coin to the back of the card as shown in Fig. 2. As this move is made the left thumb riffles the deck to cover any noise that might be made by the coin.

The hands are lowered to several inches above the table, and in transit the right hand turns over the card and hidden coin so both can be held by the left thumb and second and third fingers, Fig. 3. As soon as this is done, the right hand moves away. The left hand now deposits the card and

the hidden coin on the table, Fig. 4, being careful that the coin does not make a noise. These moves are repeated exactly to get the next three cards on the table, with a coin under each.

Finally the fifth card (AD) is taken by the right hand and the last coin is pushed against the back of this card. Now lower your right hand, keeping the face of this card to the spectators, while your left drops the deck in the pocket. The left hand takes hold of the card and the hidden coin, so the right hand can be shown empty, Fig. 5. The right hand retakes the card, the coin hidden underneath, as the left is shown empty, Fig. 6. Now turn the card over with

Fig. 6

Fig. 7

Fig. 9

Fig. 8

Fig. 10

the fingers hiding the coin, Fig. 7. Then bend the fingers inward, sliding the coin almost off the card so a fuller view of the back can be seen. (See Stewart Judah's handling of the pennies in his Turnover Sleight, Chapter XVIII, Penny Prestidigitation.) Straighten the fingers, turn the card face up and take it with the left hand between the fingers on the face and thumb underneath, Fig. 8. Snap the back of the card with the right second finger. Hold the right hand palm up; the left, holding the card and coin as just described, drags the outer end of the card inward and over the right hand a few times, paint brush fashion, finally leaving the coin exposed as in Fig. 9. Drop the coin onto the table and place the card out of the way.

The first and most difficult part of the trick is now completed. From now on be sure to use the correct cards and have these in the positions shown, to learn the routine. Fig. 10 shows the state of affairs at this juncture, face up cards in a row on the table, a coin hidden under each one. One coin

is exposed and lying on the table between you and the 8H.

Say, "This trick is known as 'passing the buck'. Watch this coin as it passes invisibly from my hand to the eight of Hearts." Pretend to place the coin in your left hand but retain it in your right. Then as the left crumbles away the non-existent coin, allow the one hidden in the right hand to drop into finger palm position for the next move. Open your left hand and show the coin vanished. With the palm down left hand lift the outer end of the 8H with the tips of the fingers and thumb and turn it inward and over onto the coin hidden in the right fingers. The thumb immediately drops on top of the card to hold it there while the left hand points to the coin just exposed on the table, then draws the coin inward a few inches. Now the right hand places the card with its hidden coin on the table, face down, Fig. 11.

Take up the visible coin with your right hand and pretend to place it in your left, this time performing a different vanish but again retaining it finally in right finger palm position. Take up the 5H with your

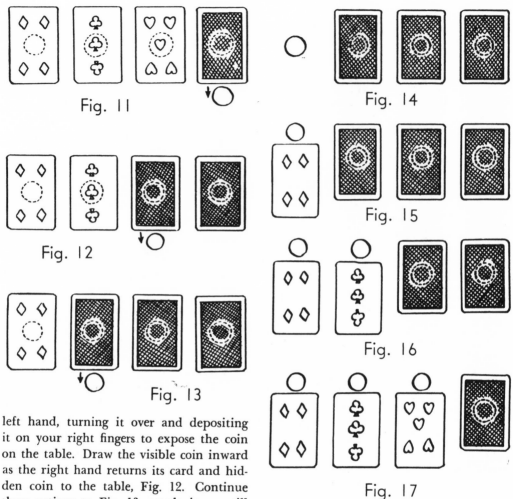

Fig. 11

Fig. 12

Fig. 13

Fig. 14

Fig. 15

Fig. 16

Fig. 17

left hand, turning it over and depositing it on your right fingers to expose the coin on the table. Draw the visible coin inward as the right hand returns its card and hidden coin to the table, Fig. 12. Continue these actions to Fig. 13, employing a still different method to vanish the coin. Vanish the next coin and find it under the 4D. At this point, three cards are face down on the table, a coin hidden under each, and visible at the left end of the row is a half dollar, Fig. 14. The 4D is face down in your right hand covering a coin.

Employ the "paint brush" move to produce this coin, Figs. 5 to 9. Keep the coin in your hand while you place the 4D face up on the table, as in Fig. 15. Pass the coin to the 3C, leaving the two exposed coins on the table, while the 3C hides the coin in the hand.

Again using the "paint brush" move, produce the hidden coin from the 3C, and keep the coin in your hand, laying the 3C on the table as in Fig. 16.

Pass the coin to the 5H. Lift up that card and show the three coins on the table. Produce the hidden coin from the 5H in the same manner as before, show the coin in your hand and lay the 5H on the table as in Fig. 17.

Pass the coin in the hand to the 8H, lift that card and show four coins on the table, keeping the 8H in your right hand hiding the extra coin. Return the 8H and hidden

Fig. 18

Fig. 19

Fig. 20

Fig. 21

Fig. 22

Fig. 23

Fig. 24

coin to the table, leaving everything as in Fig. 18. Show both hands empty.

Say, "I will now push a coin under each card, after which the coins will all come together under one card." So saying, lift up the outer end of the 8H with the left hand, being careful not to expose the hidden coin there, Fig. 19. Take the coin as in Fig. 21, push it under the half-lifted 8H and leave it there.

Repeat the foregoing move with the coin in front of the 5H, leaving the coin under the card, Fig. 20.

"And I'll place a coin under the three of Clubs." Pick up the coin in front of the 3C, and as you pretend to slip it under the forward end of the card, palm it, fingers only going underneath. The coin is picked up as in Fig. 21 and after the pretended deposit it is in the palm, Fig. 22. Repeat the move with the 4D and its coin, hiding

the coin on the drawback as in Fig. 23. The right hand is palm downward; in its palm is one half dollar while a second lies on the curled-inward fingers. The cards are all face up on the table with a hidden coin under the 5H, two under the 8H, Fig. 24.

You now order the coin to pass from underneath the 4D to the 8H. Make a magical pass or snap your fingers, then lift the 4D to show the coin is no longer there. The 4D is lifted by its outer end with the palm down left hand and turned back onto the right fingers as in previous moves. Fig. 25 shows how the right hand holds the card with the coin hidden underneath. And, though it cannot be seen, a coin is also in the classic palm. The left hand now lifts the 8H to show that the coin has arrived, Fig. 25.

With the right hand place the 4D over the two exposed coins, adding the hidden

Fig. 25

Fig. 26

Fig. 27

coin which is under it. Then drop the 8H face down on top of the 4D, as in Fig. 26.

Now order the coin under the 3C to join the others. Lift up the 3C to show the coin has gone and at the same time let the classic palmed coin in the right hand, drop onto the curled fingers where it is covered with the 3C. With your left hand, lift the two cards (4D and 8H) and show the three coins. Place the 3C down over the coins, adding the hidden one, then drop the other two cards on top as in Fig. 27.

Pretend that the coin under the 5H has passed. Lift the card but the coin is still there. Drop the 5H face down on top of

the other three cards, then vanish this last coin, keeping it hidden in the hand and showing all four coins together under the four cards.

Bobo Variation

Instead of employing the cards noted in the foregoing description, the author favors the four Aces. These would be on top of the deck so the Ace of Spades would go at the right end instead of the 8H. Then you could tell your audience that you were going to show them a Four Ace trick and before they realize it they are seeing a coin trick. This is especially good for magicians because of the unusual way the cards are dealt off in the beginning. The handling would be the same but you would have the four Aces face up on the table with a coin hidden under each (exactly as in the original version), the fifth coin in classic palm of the right hand.

Say, "You have all heard that there is money in cards." With the right hand, deal two cards from the deck, face up, onto the table, then place the deck aside. As the left hand picks up both cards together the coin in the right hand is dropped onto the fingers, the two cards then taken in that hand over the coin. Now perform the Coin Production from Two Cards (page 88), as you say, "Yes, there is money in cards." The coin appears from between the two, which are then dropped on top of the deck and the trick finished as in the original version.

When you vanish the coins, and this is done a number of times, make sure you vary your methods. Chapter III describes more than you would need. Use a different method for each vanish, and, if you wish, at the end you can vanish the last coin completely by employing a method from Chapter IV.

Practice the routine so every move is like clockwork and you will have a beautiful mystery that your audience will enjoy seeing and you will enjoy performing.

The Mexican Gadabout Coins
MILTON KORT

Here are two routines based on The Gadabout Coins described on page 182. If you can perform that one well, these can be quickly mastered.

Effect: The performer takes from his pocket a small Mexican coin purse and hands it to a spectator with the request that he remove its contents. Upon finding three Mexican pesos he is directed to place them on the table. The purse is placed aside in full view. The operator then places two of the coins in his left hand and one in his pocket. Opening his left hand he shows that the coin has returned, for there are now three. This is repeated two more times, each time the pocketed coin joining its mates in the left hand. Finally, when the left hand is opened it contains not the three coins but a beautiful Mexican ring. The purse is opened and in it are the missing coins.

Requirements: Two leather Mexican coin purses, each large enough to hold three pesos.

Seven silver Mexican pesos.

A Mexican finger ring. Any ring will do.

A pocket handkerchief.

Preparation: Put three of the coins in one purse and three in the other. Have the purses in the right coat pocket, the ring in the left coat pocket, the handkerchief and the single peso in the right hip pocket.

Working: With the right hand, reach into the coat pocket; conceal one purse in the hand and bring out the other visible at the fingertips. Place the visible purse on the table and ask a spectator to open it and dump its contents onto the table. He finds three Mexican pesos. Take the empty purse from him with your right hand, execute The Bobo Switch, page 10, and place the loaded purse on the table in full view. Immediately reach into your right hip pocket, leave the empty purse, palm the coin and bring out the handkerchief which you use to wipe your hands. Return hanky to pocket. As far as the spectators are concerned nothing has happened to this point, but this is the situation: On the table lies a supposedly empty purse, but actually it contains three coins; three coins are visible on the table, while the fourth is hidden in your right hand.

Work The Gadabout Coins as described in the original version up to a point near the end where the left hand deposits a single coin in the pocket and leaves it there. Here the similarity ends. When the left hand is removed from the pocket it has the ring concealed in finger palm position. The right hand immediately takes one of the coins from the table and pretends to place it in the left, which is held palm up in a slightly cupped position (to conceal the ring later). The right hand actually retains the coin classic palmed and the left hand closes as if holding it. Pick up the second peso with the right hand and repeat the previously described maneuver of apparently placing it in the left hand, but this time execute The Click Pass (b), (page 14), retaining coin palmed in the right hand with the first. Close the left hand which supposedly holds two coins—actually it holds only the ring as both coins are in the right hand. Remove the last coin from the table with your right hand, execute The Coin Flip (page 16) for effect, then place it and the two concealed coins in the right coat pocket. Wave the right hand over the left, then open the left to show that instead of the two coins it now holds a ring. Ask the spectators if they would like to know what happened to the coins. Upon receiving an affirmative answer direct attention to the purse that has been lying on the table all during the trick. Ask that the purse be opened—when this is done the missing pesos are found inside.

Second Version

In this version the Mexican ring is not required—just the seven pesos and the two purses.

Preparation: Load each of the purses with three coins as before and place one in the left coat pocket. The other and the single coin are together in the right coat pocket.

Working: Remove the purse from the right coat pocket and direct a spectator to empty the three coins onto the table. Return the empty purse to your right coat pocket and remove the hand with the coin classic palmed. Do The Gadabout Coins exactly as described in the previous version, up to the point where the left hand places a single coin in the left coat pocket. Leave the coin in the pocket but bring out the purse hidden in finger palm position. Continue the routine exactly as described in the previous version so that when the left hand is opened at the finish it will contain, not the two coins as expected, but the purse. A spectator opens the purse and discovers the coins.

This, like the foregoing, is a double-barreled mystery.

Nuts To You

JERRY McDERMOTT

This trick has been one of my favorites since Jerry showed it to me some 12 years ago. For simplicity and surprising climax it is hard to beat.

The performer removes 25 cents—two dimes and a nickel—from his pocket and places the coins on the table. He deposits a nickel and one dime in his left hand and the remaining dime in his pocket. When he opens his hand the pocketed dime is seen to have returned, for he now holds three coins—two dimes and a nickel. He performs this two more times. Finally he deposits two dimes in his pocket and the nickel in his hand and asks, "What does the hand hold now?" "A nickel," will be the reply. "No," says the performer, "and if you don't believe me, NUTS to you!" When he opens his hand that is exactly what he does have—a nut. The hands are otherwise empty.

Requisites and Preparation: Three dimes, one nickel, and a nut are required. These five items are in a handy right pocket.

Working: The handling is simple and basic. If the reader is familiar with the Utility Switch (page 11) and The Bobo Switch (page 10), the working will be automatic.

With the right hand, reach into your right pocket, finger palm one of the dimes, bring out the other two and the nickel visible at the fingertips, and place them on the table. If a table is not available any flat surface will do, even a spectator's open hand. And the dime need not be finger palmed—it can lie on the curled fingers of the palm down hand. But if the angles are bad it would be safer to keep the dime hidden in finger palm position, at the base of the third finger.

Call attention to the coins. "25 cents," you say. With the right first two fingers and thumb, pick up the nickel and drop it into the upturned and slightly cupped left hand. Take up a dime next and drop it AND the concealed dime into the left hand, which immediately closes. "15 cents," you say, for apparently the hand holds a nickel and a dime; actually it holds a nickel and two dimes. Pick up the remaining coin and carry it to your pocket. Do not leave it there, but finger palm it and remove the hand from the pocket. As this is done, ask, "How much in my hand?" The answer will be, "15 cents." "No," you say, "I have 25 cents." Open your left hand, show the 25 cents and place the three coins back on the table.

"Permit me to do that again. Here are the three coins." Point to them with your palm down right hand (which has a dime finger palmed) and show your left hand empty. Take up the nickel with your right fingers and drop it into your cupped left hand. Do the same with a dime. Open your left hand, pick up the two coins together between the thumb and first finger of your right hand, and as you display them show your left empty front and back. Then hold it cupped and palm up again as the right hand drops the visible coins and the concealed dime therein. Say, "Once more, 15 cents in the hand and a dime in the pocket." Saying this, pick up the remaining dime and place it in your pocket. Do not leave it there—finger palm it as before as the hand is brought out. Again ask how much is in your left hand. "15 cents," will be the reply. "No," you say, "I'm afraid you are not paying close attention. It's 25 cents!" Open your left hand, show the two dimes and the nickel and return them to the table.

The right hand, with its hidden coin, takes up the nickel and places it in the left. As you deposit a dime alongside it say "15 cents." Open the left hand and show the two coins to the spectators on your left. Pretend to toss the coins into your right hand but retain the dime while the right shows the nickel just received and the dime that was already there. As you show the two coins to the spectators on your right,

repeat, "15 cents." (For another description of this move see Utility Switch, page 11.) Dump these two coins into the cupped left hand, then take up the last dime with your right, place it in your pocket and leave it there. Again ask how much the hand holds and again the reply will be, "15 cents." Open your left hand, show 25 cents and place the coins on the table. Three times you have ostensibly placed 15 cents in your left hand and a dime in your pocket, and each time the dime has returned to make 25 cents.

Now you perform the trick a bit differently. Place a dime in your pocket, leave it there and bring out your hand with the nut concealed in finger palm position. Pick up the nickel and as you pretend to toss it into your left hand execute the Bobo Switch (page 10) and throw the nut instead. The left hand closes over it. As you take up the remaining dime and place it in your pocket, ask the spectators what you hold now. Regardless of the answer, open your hand to show the nut and say "Nuts to you!" The appearance of the nut comes as a complete surprise and makes for a humorous ending.

You can use a walnut, pecan or peanut, or a metal nut for a bolt. If you wish, you could use the metal nut from the Brema Magic Nut Trick then follow with the nut from the string.

A wood screw can be used instead of the nut. In this case the punch line would be "You are screwy!" Or, if they are folks you don't know, use the line, "No, there's something screwy here!" as you roll the screw out onto the table.

Rip-o

JACK CHANIN

Even though this trick has been on the magical market for a number of years very few magicians seem to be familiar with it.

It has become a stand-by in my repertoire since it is always well received by all types of audiences.

Effect: The magician borrows a half dollar and a handkerchief. He puts the coin underneath and twists it in the cloth so its form can be seen. Pretending to hear remarks that the form is not actually the coin, he rips away the center of the handkerchief to expose the half. He enlarges the hole and the coin drops through to the table, then mends the handkerchief magically and returns it undamaged to its owner.

Requisites and Preparation: A small square of cloth is required, in which a duplicate coin is wrapped. The best material is cut from an old pocket handkerchief, which because of its age will rip easily. The cloth should be about 3½" square. Place a half dollar in the center, gather the corners together and wrap a rubber band several

CUT OFF HERE

Fig. 1

times around the cloth at the base of the coin. When the excess is cut away the finished product looks like Fig. 1. For the sake of explanation I'll call this package Rip-o.

You will also require a knife that can be opened with one hand. The one I use carries the name "Christy" and came from a cigar store. Have the knife in your right coat pocket and Rip-o in your left coat pocket.

Working: First ask for the loan of a

white pocket handkerchief, then a half dollar. While these are forthcoming, casually place your left hand in your coat pocket and finger palm Rip-o, flat side against fingers and remove hand. The right hand receives the borrowed handkerchief, then transfers it to the left where it is held by one edge to help conceal Rip-o. Take the coin from the spectator and hold it vertically between the tips of the extended fingers and thumb of the palm inward right hand. The coin is held about chest high as the left hand drapes the handkerchief over it. Permit the form of the coin to be seen through the center of the cloth. The left hand, with the concealed Rip-o, is palm inward and pointing to the right. Now the left hand twists the coin in the center of the handkerchief so its form can be seen. That is what appears to happen, but actually this action is only simulated. As the left hand moves over to the right the coin under the handkerchief is allowed to drop down to a finger palm position. This is done as the left hand pretends to grip the coin through the cloth and twist it. In this action the right fingers and thumb take the protruding portion of Rip-o as the left hand immediately begins a twisting motion. At the beginning of this motion Rip-o is not visible to the spectators but is brought gradually into view during the final, simulated twists. When the left hand moves away it appears that the spectator's coin is twisted into the center of the handkerchief held by the right. The illusion is perfect, Fig. 2.

With the forefinger and thumb of the palm down left hand, grip the handkerchief (and the tail end of Rip-o) directly underneath the coin as your right hand drops away with its finger palmed coin. Keep the flat surface of the coin toward spectators as your right goes to your pocket, leaves the finger palmed coin and brings out the knife. Pretend to hear someone say that the form

Fig. 2

ner of the cloth, lift it up and carry it back to the left forearm. Return the corner to its original position; as you repeat this action the right thumb and forefinger steal away the torn portion of cloth, and the thumb pulls it behind the fingers out of sight. The right hand returns its corner to its original position and releases its grip as the left fingers make rubbing motions from beneath on the center of the fabric. Finally flatten out your left hand to show the handkerchief restored. Pick up the knife from the table with your right hand and place it and the torn piece of cloth in your right coat pocket. Show the handkerchief undamaged and return it and the coin to their owners.

Actually the coin that is returned is not the one you borrowed. It is the one from Rip-o. But if you want to perform the trick with a marked coin do it this way: Proceed as described up to where it is time to return the coin. Ask, "Who gave me this coin? You did! Oh, thank you." Place the coin in your coat pocket, switch it for the marked one, then as an afterthought remove it and return it to the spectator.

under the handkerchief is not the coin. "Sure it is," you say. "Listen. You can hear it." Tap the coin in the cloth with the knife. "Doesn't that sound like a coin? No? Well, I'll show you." As quickly as possible extend the blade of the knife and thrust it through the cloth to reveal a portion of the coin. The ripping of the cloth must be done quickly and with no warning, for maximum effect. The spectators will usually gasp at this point because it looks exactly as if you have cut the borrowed handkerchief. Thrust the blade of the knife back into the cloth and tear a larger hole so the coin will tumble out onto the table. The right hand then closes the knife and puts it on the table.

"See," you say, "it is a coin! Some people think I'm trying to fool them." This is the high point of the trick. The spectators have seen you cut the coin from the handkerchief and wonder what you are going to do about it. And they will laugh at the spectator because they believe you have ruined his handkerchief. So now you proceed to repair it magically. This is how you do it: With the first and second fingers of the palm up right hand, grip the outer cor-

Vanishing Coins and Purse

Glenn Harrison

Effect: A small coin purse is tossed to a spectator who opens it and finds a Chinese coin. The coin is removed and returned to the performer who places it in his trousers pocket. While the purse is being examined the performer removes his handkerchief, drapes it over his left hand, and places the purse in the fingers of that hand on top of the handkerchief. Several coins in small change are borrowed from the spectators, who drop them into the open purse. Performer snaps purse shut and places it underneath the handkerchief, then a spectator is permitted to hold it through the cloth. At command, the coins disappear. The spectator shakes the purse and hears nothing. He then removes the handkerchief to discover that he holds only the metal frame of the purse, the leather section and the coins having disappeared.

Requisites and Preparation: Secure two small coin purses with metal frames and snap tops. Cut away the leather portion of one, but do not destroy this as its use will be explained later. Have the skeleton frame in your left trousers pocket.

Two matching Chinese coins with square holes. To one of these tie a length of black elastic. The other end is tied to a safety pin fastened to the inside of the coat near the right shoulder. The coin should hang about 4″ above the bottom of the coat and near the right trousers pocket.

The other coin is in the regular purse in your right coat pocket. And have a handkerchief in your right hip pocket.

Working: Remove the regular purse from your pocket, toss it out and have the Chinese coin removed. Patter about its mysterious qualities, then retrieve it and place it in your right trousers pocket. While the purse is being examined your right hand goes for your handkerchief while the left secures the skeleton frame and holds it hidden in the hand. Both hands come out of the pockets at the same time and the handkerchief is draped over the left. Take the purse back with its snap open and place it in the fingers of the left hand, over the handkerchief. Ask for the loan of some small change and permit the spectators to drop the coins in the purse themselves. While they are doing this, your right hand, which has been resting on your hip under your coat, secretly secures the coin on the end of the elastic. After collecting several coins remark that you will also need your Chinese coin. Your right hand then goes into your trousers pocket—where you had

openly placed the other Chinese coin when it was removed from the purse, and comes out with the one on the elastic. Turn slightly to your left and deposit the Chinese coin in the purse. The left fingers then grasp the coin through the handkerchief and purse; this frees the right hand which snaps the purse shut. Shake purse so the coins jingle, being careful not to expose the elastic. The right hand then carries the purse underneath the handkerchief and lets go, the elastic drawing purse and contents underneath the coat. A slight turn to face the audience should accompany this move. Immediately the skeleton frame in left hand is brought up from underneath as the right grasps it from above, and both hands guide the frame (only) into the hands of a spectator who is cautioned to hold it very carefully.

Now command the coins to leave the purse. To prove they have gone, have the spectator shake it violently. Since nothing can be heard, he and the spectators will be puzzled. Then invite him to remove the purse from beneath the handkerchief and open it. The surprise comes when he discovers he holds nothing but the skeleton frame. And the spectators will be highly amused when you direct him to open the purse and feel inside for the missing coins.

Permit the owners of the vanished coins to believe their money is gone forever as you perform another trick, after which a handful of change is removed from one of your pockets and the proper coins returned to the lenders.

Follow-up Effect

A fine feat to follow the foregoing is this one which makes use of the discarded leather portion of the coin purse and The 21¢ Trick (see the Homing Coins, page 239, for description).

If this finish is used you would begin by borrowing two nickels, a dime and a penny from the spectators. In the right trousers pocket you have the leather portion of the purse containing the gimmicked coins for the 21¢ Trick. At the outset, when the Chinese coin is taken back from the spectator, you slip it into this leather portion of the purse as you pocket it. With this set-up you would perform the trick as described, and explain that the leather portion of the purse and its contents traveled to your pocket. Remove it, take out the Chinese coin first and put it back in your pocket as it is not used, then remove the four gimmicked coins as the ones you borrowed. Hold the leather portion of the purse mouth toward yourself and return the gimmicked coins to it, coin by coin, nesting them as you do so. Now remove the nested set as a nickel and put it in your pocket. Then pretend to throw away each of the remaining coins and show the purse empty.

Still the borrowed coins have not been returned. You can return them as previously explained or seize an opportune moment by reaching back underneath the coat for the vanished purse. Open it enough to release the Chinese coin on the elastic, then carry it to the trousers pocket and dump the change into the hand. Bring out the coins and return them to their owners. This is quite easy and it appears that you merely went into your pocket for the change.

Chinese Money Trick

SILENT MORA

Courtesy *The Sphinx*

This trick comes from the hands of an old master of magic, Louis J. McCord, professionally known as Silent Mora. Because it has stood the test of time and because it will be "new" to the present generation of coin workers, we are proud to include it.

Fig. I

You will require the three unusual coins shown in the illustrations. The round coin is Chinese and slightly larger than the U.S. half dollar. The oval is a 17th century Japanese coin, I believe. The third, because of its shape, is called "man-money." Genuine coins such as these will not be easy to find, but imitations can sometimes be had. If the necessary coins cannot be located in the coin shops, coins resembling these can be made from brass. You will be repaid for your trouble in locating these coins with a trick that will be new to present day audiences.

Preparation: Have the oval coin in your left coat pocket, the "man-money" in your right coat pocket and the round coin concealed in your right sleeve or hand.

Working: Begin by producing the round coin from a spectator's lapel. Place it in the trousers fold and vanish it (see Pocket Vanish, page 52.) Reproduce it and pretend to bend it a few times, employing the old bending move familiar to all magicians. Hand the coin to a spectator with a request that he try it. While all eyes are on him, steal the oval coin from your left pocket and hold it finger palmed. Take back the round coin, bend it again, then say, "Never grip the coin by its ends or you might get it out of shape." Bring your hands together. The round coin is at your fingertips, the oval concealed in your left hand. Under cover of pretending to stretch it, conceal the round coin in your right hand and bring the oval coin into view. Pass it out for inspection. Meanwhile get rid of the round coin in your right coat pocket and steal the "man-money" coin. Turn your body away for an instant to hide this action. Take back the oval coin. Your right hand holds the "man-coin" secretly between the top joints of the two middle fingers and the base of the thumb. Say, "The most difficult part of the trick is to get the coin back in shape again. If you pull on the sides too much, it will get completely out of shape." Bring the "man-money" into view, still pulling on it. The appearance of this unusual coin provides ample misdirection for dropping the oval coin in the pocket or sleeving it.

The trick Quick Change by C. Thomas Magrum in Chapter XVIII uses the coin transformation idea, but with coins more readily obtainable.

Pouring Pennies Through a Table

MIKE ROGERS

Here is a genuine eye-popper, mystifying and funny, that takes less than a minute to perform.

Effect: A glass of pennies is "poured" through the table.

Requirements: A bottomless glass, a real glass and about 40 pennies. The glasses used should be slightly taller than regular tumblers, and can be clear plastic.

Working: You are seated at a table with your audience in front of you. In your lap is the bottomless glass. On the table is the real glass containing the pennies. With your right hand, shake the glass, then pour the pennies on the table. The shaking is necessary to establish the sound effect that is later all-important in the illusion created.

Sit back in your chair, resting both hands in your lap. The right hand is still holding

the real glass, the left is on the bottomless glass. Look at the pennies. Sit forward, and bring the fake glass to the top of the table with your left hand; leave the ordinary glass in your lap, and with the right brush the coins around on the table. While the right hand is thus engaged, return the left to the lap, leaving the fake glass on the table. This exchange of glasses is unnoticed and natural since the trick is with coins and not a glass.

Attempt to pick up the coins with your right hand but be clumsy; without comment decide to scoop them into the glass on the table. Pick up the fake glass with your right hand and place it in your left, which carries it to the edge of the table, holding it with its top visible above the edge and the bottom below, this being the position to receive the pennies a moment later as they are scooped in. The right hand drops to the lap, picks up the real glass and slips its mouth loosely over the bottom of the fake glass, the left gripping both together as the right returns to the top of the table and begins scooping in coins. They fall right through the fake glass into the real one held below it, Fig. 1. Pause a time or two during the scooping, letting the top of the bottomless glass be seen. When all the coins are in, the right hand comes back, grasps the fake glass by its top and brings it above the table as the left hand carries the genuine glass underneath. Now shake both hands simultaneously, Fig. 2. This is very illusive. The effect is that you are shaking a glass of pennies above the table. The movement is there, but the sound comes from the other glass. The spectators will not notice that the glass they see is empty. After shaking the non-existent coins a few times, pour them right through the table. At least, this is what you appear to do, and the timing must be just right. As the right hand turns its glass over above the table, the left also turns over its glass, emptying the pennies in the lap. The sound fits the action. Together they create the illusion that you did actually pour the coins through the table. Yet this seems so utterly incredible it appears funny. The real glass is left in your lap and the left hand quickly grabs as many coins as it can, then brings them up and tosses them onto the table. There is no harm done if some of the pennies are left in the lap.

Fig. 1

BOTTOM OF FAKE GLASS IS NESTED IN REAL GLASS

Fig. 2

There is no need to switch glasses again unless you want to. If you do, take advantage of the surprise created by the climax to sit back in your chair and drop the right hand holding the fake glass to your lap. Brush the coins around on the table with your left hand while the right leaves its glass in the lap and brings up the real one. The coins can now be scooped into the real glass and placed aside.

The Seven Penny Trick

TERRY LYNN

From *Principles and Deceptions*
Courtesy Mrs. Arthur Buckley

Effect: The performer takes seven pennies from the table one by one with his right hand and counts them into his left hand. Now a spectator is requested to extend his right hand palm up, and the pennies are counted one by one into his hand. Turning his hand over after he closes it, performer asks him how many coins he has. On hearing him state "Seven," one coin is caused to leave his hand and appear in performer's, which is held underneath. He counts his coins back into the performer's hand and he has but six. The trick is repeated with six, then five coins.

Working: After counting the coins from the table into your left hand, they are counted into the spectator's hand as follows: Take them one by one between the tips of your right first two fingers and thumb and deposit them one by one in the palm of the spectator's right hand until five are in. The sixth is only touched to the others in his hand without releasing it. It remains hidden behind your fingers as that hand drops to the side. Now turn your left hand over above his and dump the last penny onto the others, then request him to close his hand quickly over them. Ask him how many he has and he will reply, "Seven."

Raise your right hand and pretend to extract a penny from underneath his hand, then have him open the hand and count the coins. He will have only six.

Counting the coins into his hand one by one makes the operation seem very fair, and the sound of the sixth touching the others convinces him that it went in his hand. The illusion is perfect, and dumping in the last coin is the "clincher."

Repeat the trick with six pennies, then with five, each time using Milt Kort's line "Perhaps I used too many coins. This time I'll do it with six," etc. And each time you perform it caution him to close his hand quickly so the coins can't escape. You can tell him you simply pull one penny through a hole in the back of his hand. The trick becomes more perplexing with the second or third performance.

The Runaway Coin

John Giordmaine

Effect: A small coin purse is removed from the pocket and handed to a spectator with the request that he open it and empty its contents on the table. The performer returns the purse to his pocket and holds out his hand so the spectator can count the coins into it. He counts 10 pennies. Performer then counts the pennies back into the spectator's hand and has him hold them tight. Stepping back a bit, he commands a coin to leave the spectator's hand. The spectator opens his hand and counts only nine coins. Reaching into his pocket, the performer removes the purse, then hands it to the spectator who opens it and finds the missing penny.

Requirements: Ten matching pennies and a small, snap top change purse.

Working: Perform the trick as outlined in "Effect," employing the stratagem used in The Seven Penny Trick to retain the ninth coin. After the spectator counts the pennies and finds one missing, reach into your right pocket, drop the coin in the purse (which has purposely been left open), snap it shut quietly and bring it out. Hand it to the spectator who opens it and finds the errant coin.

Penny Prestidigitation

John Braun

"I'm sure you've heard of the famous *Threepenny Opera*," says the performer as he sits down at the Close-Up table. "I want you to see my seven penny act." With that introduction he begins a routine using seven U.S. pennies, and all but one of the tricks is in this book.

Requisites and Preparation: Seven copper plated steel pennies. These were issued during World War 2, and are still available, but you will have to have the plating done. While only three are actually necessary, it is simpler to have them all the same to avoid confusion.

A bent penny. This need not be steel, but it should match the others.

A Chinese brass coin about the size of our quarter, with hole in center.

Two playing cards. You can use blank face cards with your name, address and telephone number printed on them, for giveaways.

A pocket handkerchief.

Penny Ante (Tannen catalogue item No. 406). This trick, which is the ancestor of Stewart Judah's Coins and Matchbooks routine, Chapter XIX, also uses matchbooks gimmicked with magnets. It sells for $1.00.

The bent penny is in a right pocket and the matchbooks in a left pocket. Have the other items on the table and you are ready.

The Routine: Begin by spreading the handkerchief on the table and performing The Sympathetic Coins, page 197, using four pennies and the two playing cards. However, a subtlety is introduced which will be explained later, and there's a little difference in the way the pennies are handled, as it is easier to do the trick with pennies than larger coins.

2. Next perform the Seven Penny Trick in this chapter. Do it at least twice, three times if you have a good audience. Each time perform it with one less coin, using Milt Kort's line, "Perhaps I'm using too many coins. We'll put one away and do it with six," etc.

3. Now comes the Bent Penny trick. Do it exactly as described on page 186. You will have to steal the bent penny from your pocket to perform the trick, but this is a simple matter. Use a second spectator and have him squeeze the penny, but he squeezes too hard, bending the coin. Leave the bent penny on the table and secretly pocket the one hidden in your hand.

4. Remove the two matchbooks from your pocket and do Penny Ante. Pocket the matchbooks after completing the trick.

5. Finally, the big finish. Use the six pennies and the Chinese coin and do Coins Through Table, Fourth Version, by Stewart Judah, (page 192).

Now the Sympathetic Coins variations. The routine follows the original Yank Hoe method, but uses pennies instead of half dollars, and playing cards instead of squares of paper. The penny at the right front corner is stolen when covered by the card, exactly as explained, and held clipped against the underside of the card, completely covered by the tips of the first and second fingers. On a soft surface this steal is very easy. Now comes the Judah addition, a Turnover Sleight. After the penny is stolen and the vacant place covered with the other card, you casually show both sides of the card in the right hand before covering the coin in the upper left corner of the handkerchief.

Fig. 1

Fig. 2

Fig. 1 shows how the card is held. The tip of the thumb is on the back, first two fingers underneath; now the hand is turned back up so the face of the card can be shown, but the coin, under the fingers, has been drawn back until the fingertips have an almost negligible hold on the card. The coin is completely concealed between the thumb and first and second fingertips, Fig. 2. The fingers always seem to be at the very edge of the card, which can be shown "clear" before it is placed over the coin in the upper left corner. This sleight is easy with a penny; the coin is shuttled back and forth as the hand is turned over to show both sides of the card, and the concealment is complete.

The right fingers now pick up the coin from the left inner corner, as left fingers lift that corner, fingers well underneath the handkerchief and thumb above. Show the coin, then place it underneath the hanky and push it forward toward the left front corner, pretending to pass it upward through the cloth. That's what you SEEM to do. The right fingers actually leave the coin on the tips of the left two fingers and move without hesitation toward the left upper corner. Now, with a slight upward movement of the right fingers, one of the coins under the card will be thrown on the other with an audible "clink." Apparently the coin has passed through the fabric.

Remove the right hand from beneath the handkerchief, show it empty, then lift the left outer card so they see the two pennies. Without pausing, bring the card back over the left fingers; the left thumb lifts to receive it, and the hand comes away with the card at the left fingertips, the coin again clipped underneath, completely concealed between the thumb and first two fingers in readiness to show both sides via the Turnover Sleight and again be placed over the two pennies in upper left corner. But this time the left fingers execute the sleight. This action is repeated for the coin at the right inner corner and finally the (nonexistent) coin still covered in upper right hand corner is passed in the same manner, but just pretending this time. With pennies, there is scope for considerable "abandon" in the handling of the cards and coins, as you will find after a few trials.

There are other good tricks with pennies in this book, both with apparatus and without, so you can vary the routine to suit your desires.

Dollar to Dollar
JACK CHANIN

Effect: The performer shows an American silver dollar, his hands otherwise empty. As he rubs the coin with his fingertips it is seen to transform itself into a dollar bill. But for the bill, again his hands are empty.

Requisites and Preparation: Fold a dollar bill in half across its narrow width, then again the same way. Now fold it into thirds so you have a package as long as the width of the bill and about ½" wide. Fold this into thirds the long way, tucking one end under a corner to prevent it from unfolding. When you finish you will have a package approximately ½" wide by ⅞" long, small enough to be concealed behind a silver dollar. Fig. 1 shows how to fold the bill.

You will also require a silver dollar. The folded bill and silver dollar are together in your right trousers pocket.

Working: Reach in your pocket, finger palm the bill and bring out the coin visible at the fingertips. Toss the coin into your left hand and sleeve the bill in your right sleeve. Just let it tumble off your curled fingers into your sleeve as you raise that arm in a natural gesture. (See Delayed Action Sleeving, page 100.) Show the coin, flip it into the air and toss it from hand to hand. And as you do this let it be plainly seen that you have nothing concealed in your hands.

Finally take the silver dollar in your left hand where it is held between the tips of the first two fingers and thumb. Drop your right arm to your side and catch the folded bill on the curled fingers as it drops from the sleeve, then grip it between the extended first two fingers and thumb as that hand comes up and takes the coin from the left hand. As the coin is received by the right hand an edge slips between the bill and the fingers, Fig. 2. Now, holding your hands in front of your chest, you first show the left hand empty, then the right, as follows: After displaying the left hand take the silver dollar and the folded bill together and hold them between the tips of the extended first two fingers and thumb. As the

Fig. 1

END IS
TUCKED IN
TO PREVENT
UNFOLDING

Fig. 2

Fig. 3

the bill and begin to bring it into view; the coin slips behind the left end of the bill where it is held by the left thumb. The silver dollar has transformed itself into a paper dollar! The open bill is stretched between your two hands, being held by the extreme ends with the coin concealed behind the left end. Pop or snap the bill a couple of times, then show your right hand empty. Then as you pop the bill again a couple of times, the coin is transferred from behind the left thumb to behind the right thumb at that end of the bill. Now you take the bill in your left hand as the right steals away the coin and finger palms it. While displaying the bill in your left hand the right sleeves the coin and you let it be seen you have nothing else in your hands. Pocket the bill and retrieve the sleeved coin later. Or, if you wish, retrieve the coin while the left hand shows the bill; pass it to the right hand and place it and the coin together in your right pocket.

Stewart Judah's Half Dollar Vanish

This title might be a bit misleading, for any coin could be vanished in the manner I am about to describe. In fact, I am going to do it as a feature trick using a large brass or silver foreign coin to give it an "exotic" flavor.

Effect: The coin is displayed and placed on the palm of the left hand, which is then closed into a fist and held back up, about waist high. Performer taps the closed hand with a small stick or wand, then pushes it into the hand until the end on the thumb side is completely inside. He gestures with his right hand, then pulls the wand through from the little finger side, taps the closed fist, and shows the left hand empty. The wand is tossed to the table, and the coin is found in the pocket or elsewhere.

transfer of the coin is made from the right to the left hand, the right thumb pushes the bill completely behind the coin where it remains out of sight as the left hand takes both together. The left thumb holds the bill concealed behind the coin now and the right hand is shown all around. The coin and bill are taken again in the right hand and held as shown in Fig. 3. With the coin thus daintily displayed the left hand is once more shown empty.

Now bring the fingers of both hands together and under this cover quickly unfold

Method: While any coin can be used, a half dollar size coin makes the best showing. The wand should be 9″ long. It can be made from a teak chopstick by cutting off all but 9″ of the large end, or it can be made from a dowel stick ¼″ to 5/16″ diameter.

The gimmick is a small piece of "re-usable adhesive." I use Plasti-Tak, made by Brooks Manufacturing Co., Cincinnati, Ohio 45231. Magician's wax won't do. Roll a piece into a ball about 5/16″ diameter. It is a white substance, easy to work, and does not leave sticky blotches on the hands or objects it touches. Flatten the little ball to about the size of a dime and stick it on one side of the half dollar. (A smaller piece would be used for a smaller coin, and vice versa.) You can have the coin in your pocket, or on your table, adhesive side down, for this adhesive only works when it is pressed on.

The coin can be displayed carelessly, so long as the waxed side is not shown, but it need not be handled gingerly. The spectators don't know what's coming! Place it on your left palm, wax side to palm; close the hand, and turn it back of hand up. Do NOT close the fingers tightly on the coin, but allow it to lie in a tunnel formed by the loosely closed fingers, waxed side up, Fig. 1. Take up the stick or wand in the right hand, toss it in the air, catch it, and push it into the left fist over the top of the

Fig. 2

Fig. 3

Fig. 1

coin and not touching it until it is completely inside and about flush with the side nearest your left thumb, Fig. 2. Now close the left fingers tightly, pressing the stick against the adhesive. Over half of the stick protrudes from the little finger side of the fist. The empty right hand comes over, takes hold of the stick by gripping it between the thumb and forefinger at A, Fig. 3; left fingers allow it to be removed, and the coin goes out with it, stuck to the end in contact with it, and beautifully screened by right hand. The stick is lifted straight up; left fingers relax and allow the coin to go out, then close tightly. Right hand now taps left fist with stick, and the fingers open showing coin gone. Stick is rolled out of the adhesive by right fingers and tossed to the table, making a clatter; right hand goes to pocket, plunges in, peels or "rolls" off the adhesive leaving it in pocket, and comes out with the coin, which is also tossed onto the table. Or, have a duplicate appear elsewhere. This vanish can be used in close-up work, or in a "stand-up" act, and is useful in any trick where coin is switched and will be vanished to appear elsewehere.

Thumb Tax

Howard Schwarzman

On page 90 there's a trick called The Touch of Midas. Here is a humorous version of the same effect with a simpler and different handling.

Effect: With a spectator assisting, the performer produces four half dollars and a penny, one at a time.

Requisites and Preparation: Four half dollars and one penny. Concealed in the left finger palm is a penny covered by a half dollar. In the right hand are hidden three half dollars, two together in classic palm position and one in finger palm position.

Working: Approach a spectator and say, "Excuse me, but I think you have something on your sleeve." With your right hand, pretend to pluck the finger palmed coin from his sleeve as you bring that coin into view at your fingertips. Show the coin briefly and simulate placing it in your left hand, actually retaining it in right finger palm position as the left turns over to expose its half dollar. Be careful that the half dollar does not slide from its original position to expose the penny. A slight curl-

ing of the third finger will keep the half in place. Ask the spectator to hold out his right hand. Go through the motions of taking the exposed half dollar from the palm up left, but retain it finger palmed as that hand turns over, and the right hand brings into view again its finger palmed half. It should appear that the right hand lifted the half dollar from the left as that hand turned over. Deposit the coin on the back of the left hand, then bring that hand near and slightly above the thumb side of the spectator's hand; tilt your hand slightly clockwise so the coin will slide off the back of your hand onto the palm of his. While the spectator is concerned with catching the coin, your right hand has dropped to your side and a half dollar is released from the palm onto the curled fingers as illustrated and described on page 90. The palm down left hand now tugs on the spectator's thumb, then turns palm up to reveal the original finger palmed half dollar (with the penny still concealed underneath). Apparently you have "milked" the coin from his thumb. Repeat the foregoing moves as the right hand pretends to pick up the coin from the left. Retain it finger palmed as that hand turns back up and the right hand brings its coin into view. Place it on the back of the left hand as before and again allow it to slip off into the spectator's hand, which now holds two half dollars. Grasp his thumb again and give it a tug, then turn over the hand to reveal the same half dollar once more. Repeat the previous moves to produce the third coin and put it into the spectator's hand. He now holds three half dollars. Concealed in finger palm position of your palm down left hand is the half dollar still covering the penny.

Milk his thumb once more, then turn the left hand palm up and show the half dollar. The right actually removes the half this time but the penny is retained finger palmed as the left turns back up and the half dollar is deposited on its back. Tilt the hand so the half will slide off onto the other three in the spectator's hand. Give the tip of his thumb a tiny pinch, then turn the left hand over to reveal the penny. As you drop it into his hand say, "Tax."

Wanderful

HOWARD SCHWARZMAN

This routine employs the basic moves from Thumb Tax for a platform or stage presentation.

On the table is an Old Fashioned cocktail glass and a magic wand. The penny is not used. The four half dollars are concealed in the two hands exactly as in Thumb Tax.

Begin by picking up the wand with the right hand. Grasp it loosely at the center with the left, then as that hand slides to the end, the finger palmed coin is brought into view, apparently from the tip of the wand. Flip the coin into the air and catch it in finger palm position in the left hand as the right returns the wand to the table. Pretend to take the coin from the left hand with the right but retain it concealed as the right brings its finger palmed coin into view. This is the basic move that is employed four times to produce the four coins. Place this coin between the tips of the forefinger and thumb of the palm up left hand, the flat side of the coin toward the audience and the fingers curled just enough to conceal the finger palmed coin. Take up the wand with the right hand, holding it near one end. Push its opposite end under the left thumb and behind the visible coin, then as you lower your hands over the table use the tip of the wand to flip the coin from the fingertips into the glass.

Produce the next three coins in exactly

the same manner. The fourth coin, however, is not flipped into the glass but tossed into the air and caught with the right hand, which pretends to return it to the left but retains it classic palmed. The closed left hand, pretending to hold the coin, is raised to about chest level as the right takes up the wand again. Insert its tip into the bottom of the left fist and hold it there as the right hand is removed. The left hand supports the wand while the right forefinger points to the left fist. All the right fingers are closed except the forefinger, which curls around the center of the wand, pressing it against the thumb and across the backs of the fingers. Holding the wand in this manner with the right hand, the left is opened to show the coin vanished. The right hand presses the tip of the wand to the palm of the left, which then closes over it. Remove the right from the center of the wand and stroke the lower end downward in a "milking" movement over the glass. On the second or third stroke release the coin into the glass, apparently "milked" from the end of the wand. Lay the wand on the table and show the four coins in the glass.

This production can be used alone, or to introduce a platform trick requiring four coins. It is actually Phase 1 of the next routine, which is called

A Wanderful Production

HOWARD SCHWARTZMAN

Effect: With the aid of his wand, the magician produces four coins one at a time, dropping them into a glass on his table. Then, forming a handkerchief into a bag, the coins are dropped in and caused to disappear. After showing the handkerchief on both sides, he drapes it over his left hand. Grasping the center of the cloth with his right hand, he reverses hanky over that hand to reveal one of the missing coins.

This one is dropped into the glass, and the other three are produced in succession, in similar fashion. Following the fourth coin, he reverses the hanky again, this time producing a shower of coins—enough to fill the glass!

Requisites and Preparation: 24 to 48 palming coins or half dollars, the exact number depending on the thickness of the coins and the ability of the performer.

A man's handkerchief. The regular white pocket variety works fine, but a paisley pattern, or printed silk handkerchief such as is sold for the breast pocket is preferred.

An Old Fashioned cocktail glass, a wand, and a box with a lid, about 6″ x 12″ x 4″ high. This box conceals the stack of coins,

REAR OF TABLE

Fig. 1

holds the props for the routine, and elevates the glass during the production and vanish of the first four coins. These props are arranged as in Fig. 1: the glass and handkerchief on top of the box, and concealed behind it, the stack of coins, which can be prepared as for An Extra Load for the Miser's Dream (in this chapter). The wand lies beside the box.

Working: Perform Wanderful just as described. When you finish, lay down the wand, spill the coins into your hand, drop them into the glass one at a time, and take your bow. That concludes PHASE 1 and you are ready for

PHASE 2

Showing the handkerchief, fold it into a bag for the Handkerchief Coin Vanish (Chapter XVII). Hold it at the corners in the left hand, keeping the corners "labelled" in your mind; with your right hand take two of the coins from the glass and drop them one at a time between corners A and C, so they will be inside the bag. Take the remaining two (this should be a 1, 2, 3, 4 action) and seem to drop them in the same as the first two, but this time drop them between corners AC and DB (refer to the illustrations in Handkerchief Coin Vanish) where they will be outside the true "bag" portion, but held inside the double folds. Take the corners with the right hand and jounce the coins on the slightly cupped left fingers, to jingle them. This jolting action will dislodge the two in the "outer folds" so they will slip out into the left hand where they are finger palmed. Now grasp corners A and C and separate the hands for the Handkerchief Coin Vanish. When the hanky is stretched between the hands, the coins have apparently vanished. Actually two are finger palmed in the left hand and you will have to finger palm the two in the trough in the hanky; this is how you do it: Bring corners A and C together in the left hand and insert the right, palm down, into the "U" now formed, pressing the fingers over the coins. The left hand moves outward and down and the right, finger palming the two coins, turns palm up. The hanky is now draped over the right hand concealing the coins. The left hand grasps one of the corners projecting at the right fingertips and tosses the hanky into the air, while the right hand picks up the wand, catches the hanky on the tip as it descends, and twirls it on the wand, proving conclusively the coins have vanished. Take the hanky off the wand, place the wand on the table, and you are ready for

Now you have two coins concealed in each hand, in finger palm position. Jack Chanin's Coins From Silk (Chapter XVII) is used to reproduce them. You are standing behind the table. Begin the routine just as described. The first coin is stolen from the left hand, but is dropped into the glass with the right, which holds it through the cloth with the fingers. The left hand makes a stroking motion over the corners of the hanky as the coin is revealed, gathering the corners of the hanky as coin is dropped. This action brings the hand directly over the stack of coins. As the second coin is dropped in the glass with the left fingers, the right hand is over the stack. When the third coin is dropped in, the left hand in this stroking action is again over the stack and steals it. At this point you have the stack concealed in the left hand and the hanky draped over the last single coin in the right hand. Grasp the coin through the cloth with the left fingertips, reverse the hanky over the left hand, reveal the single coin and drop it into the glass with the left fingers. The silk now covers the left hand and the stack. With the right hand, grasp all the coins through the hanky, reverse hanky over cupped right hand, then let the coins pour out of the hanky and shower into the glass. This final production is startling and unexpected, and the steal blends so well with the "reversing action" in draping the hanky over each hand alternately, that there is no clue as to where the coins came from. Using the set-up for An Extra Load for The Miser's Dream will facilitate matters and the load of coins will be more "maneuverable."

Truly, the "money-catching" plot has both universal appeal *and* variety!

Rising Coin Through Handkerchief
RICHARD N. OSLUND

Effect: A half dollar, covered with a handkerchief, penetrates and rises through it.

Working: Stand facing your audience as you show a half dollar and a man's handkerchief. Hold the coin vertically and about shoulder height between the tips of the fingers and thumb of the palm up left hand. The handkerchief in the right hand is held by one edge, between the extended first two fingers and the curled-in third and fourth fingers—the thumb remaining free. Raise the handkerchief and draw it back over the coin from the front, the right hand moving inward toward the left forearm, and cover the coin. The right, still retaining its grip on one edge of the handkerchief, reverses its motion and uncovers the coin to show it still there. Now, as you repeat the foregoing moves exactly, apparently to cover the coin again, steal it away from the left hand by taking it between the thumb and forefinger of the right as it moves inward without hesitation to the left forearm. The right hand releases its grip on the edge of the handkerchief, moves forward in its original path, deposits the coin in the left fingers behind a fold of cloth, continues on forward a few inches and stops. As the hand is brought to a halt, point the forefinger upward and say "Watch." Drop the right hand to the side so the handkerchief-covered left hand will receive all the attention. Push the coin up into view from behind the handkerchief. Apparently it penetrates, rising through the cloth. Hold this position for a moment, then take the coin in the right hand as the left shows the handkerchief undamaged.

The moves used in this effect are very similar to those employed in a complete coin vanish, With a Handkerchief, NUMBER ONE (page 53). Instead of the right hand dropping the coin in the breast coat pocket as in that trick, it is brought forward and deposited in the folds of the handkerchief for the penetration effect.

A Funny Finish for a Coin Routine
J. B. Bobo

Although this is not magic, it is 100% entertainment. If you are a working magician you will value this routine as much or more than the trick you use it with. It makes an excellent climax for A Comedy Coin Routine (page 294), as it brings the trick to a humorous and entertaining finish.

After terminating A Comedy Coin Routine the magician offers to divide the 10 coins between the two boys and himself. He asks the boys how they like the idea, and naturally they agree that it is a good one.

Explain that since you also assisted in the presentation of the trick, you too should receive a share of the money. The boys agree to this. "There are 10 coins," you say, "and we can't divide three into 10 and come out even. So that everything will be fair this is how we will do it. Here is the tray and the 10 coins. My assistant will help us divide them." She takes the tray in one hand and holds the coins in the other. Direct her as follows: "Put one coin on the tray for the boys." She does this. "Now give me one." She hands you a coin. "Put another on the tray for the boys." When she has complied, ask, "How many is that for the boys?" "Two," she replies. "Okay, give me two." She gives you two coins. "Now put another coin on the tray for the boys." When she has done this ask, "How many does that make for the boys?" She will answer, "Three." "Well, give me three." Your assistant hands you three coins. By this time it becomes obvious that the boys are not receiving their just share. Their reaction to this lopsided division creates a funny situation that is enjoyed by the audience and the boys alike.

Continue by directing your assistant to put another coin on the tray for the boys. After this is done ask, "How many is this for the boys now?" "Four," will be the answer. "All right, give me four." She dumps all four coins from the tray into your hands. The boys get nothing. The surprised look on their faces makes your climax.

Do not under any circumstances try to create the impression that you are cheating the boys. The audience would not take kindly to this. But properly presented it will bring a good laugh from the audience, and so the boys won't go away empty-handed give them *something. This is important!* Give them a souvenir of the show, a small toy, a balloon or a piece of candy, but be sure to reward them, and thank them for helping as you usher them off.

The Camera Coin
Paul Morris

Effect: In this novel trick the performer shows two cards blank on both sides, and a half dollar. He claims the coin contains the world's smallest camera, and he would like to use it to make a picture of a spectator. The date on the coin is checked, then it is placed between the cards—because the camera operates best in the dark—and they are held up ready to make the picture. "Click." The performer says the picture has been made, and hands the cards to the spectator to separate and see the results. The spectator finds not his own picture but head and tail views of the coin, one on each card. The coin has vanished, The date on the photograph is checked and it is the date on the coin.

The cards are now placed face to face and from them the performer shakes silver confetti, explaining that the pictures of the coin are disintegrating. When he separates the cards they are blank on both sides.

Requisites and Preparation: Two blank playing cards prepared as follows: Photograph the head and tail sides of a coin, full size; cut out the two pictures and paste one on each card.

A half dollar with a date the same as the one in the photograph.

A confetti dropper. This is made like a giant, hollow clothes pin, and holds about a tablespoon of confetti. Soldered to it are two small safety pins so it can be fastened

Fig. 2

Fig. 3

Fig. 1

underneath the bottom edge of the coat, Fig. 1.

Silver confetti. Make this from silver-colored paper.

Load the dropper with "silver" confetti and pin it underneath the bottom left edge of your coat. When you want a handful of confetti cup your fingers underneath the dropper, and as the heel of the hand presses inward the jaws open, delivering the confetti into the hand. Have the special cards and the half dollar in a convenient pocket.

Working: Remove the half dollar, hand it to a spectator to look over and tell him it contains the world's smallest camera. And add that with his permission, you would

like to use it to make his picture. While he is looking the coin over, ask that he remember the date on it. Now bring out the two special cards, explaining that the camera works best in the dark, and that they will be used as a darkroom. You now show the cards blank on both sides. To do this, hold one in each hand, picture side down. Fig. 2 shows how the right hand holds its card. The left holds its card in the same manner and simultaneously duplicates the moves made by the right.

Grip the left side of the card with the fingers and begin to turn the hand over. When the card reaches the position shown in Fig. 3 press the tip of the thumb against the middle of the photograph and continue to turn the hand over until it reaches the position shown in Fig. 4. To all appearances the cards have been turned over; actually only the hands have turned, and the cards remain picture side downward. To return the cards to their original positions,

Fig. 4

simply reverse the moves. The sleight is a deceptive one as a few trials will show, and can be employed in other tricks using business cards, small slates, etc. With this move you can apparently show one or two cards blank on both sides. Carl Herrmann is said to have used the sleight in the middle of the last century, and Dai Vernon describes a version of it in *Hugard's Magic Monthly*, June, 1949.

After showing the cards apparently blank on both sides, place them together, and under cover of squaring them, turn the bottom one over. Now the pictures of the coins are together between the cards. While holding them together and squared, show them on both sides and explain that you will use them as a dark room for making the picture. Take the coin from the spectator and slip it between the cards. Press them together to hold the coin in place, and hold them out at arm's length between the fingers and thumb of the right hand. Then while moving the spectator around for a better angle, allow the coin to slip out into finger palm position. Finally exclaim, "Hold it! Click! I've got it! Here, take a look." Hand him the cards and request that he separate them so he can see his likeness. As he does this sleeve the coin or drop it in your pocket. He opens the cards and finds, not *his* picture but a picture of the coin—tail side on one card, head side on the other—and the half dollar has vanished. Pretend that nothing like that had ever happened with the trick before. Explain that because the camera was an experimental model it

must have backfired and made a picture of itself. Ask him to check the date on the coin in the picture to see if it is the same as was on the coin. It is!

Direct him to place the cards together with the pictures inside. While he is doing this, drop your left hand to your side, steal the load of confetti and hold it in the curled second, third and fourth fingers. Turn slightly away as you make the steal. Take the cards from him with your right hand, bring up your left and transfer them to that hand, holding them vertically, the

Fig. 5

CONFETTI HELD
IN LEFT FINGERS
BEHIND CARDS

long sides between thumb and forefinger, with the other fingers curled behind, Fig. 5. Now shake the cards slightly and allow the confetti to fall, apparently from between the cards, to the floor. While it flutters down say, "Oh, I forgot to tell you—the picture the camera makes is not permanent. It is now disintegrating." Explain that the confetti is the silver from the coin crumbling away. Bring your left hand to your right, reverse the bottom card so it will be picture side down, and hold a card in each hand for the turnover move. "Here are the two cards," you say. Show them apparently blank on both sides, as you did earlier. "No more picture." Place the cards in your pocket.

Suggestion: You might have a pair of extra blank cards in your pocket which you could show in case someone wanted to look them over.

George Kaplan suggests that a glass disc the size of a half dollar be placed in with the confetti. Then, after the confetti falls from your hand you could release the disc, letting it fall to the floor. In this event the half dollar would be called a ghost camera —the disc would be the ghost of the coin, the confetti the silver from the coin.

Jerry Andrus recommends placing two half dollar size metal discs in with the confetti. They would be what's left of the photos with the silver removed.

Coin to Confetti

Here is another use for the confetti dropper. Have it loaded with silver confetti. Show a half dollar in your right hand and steal the confetti in your left. Bring up the left and pretend to push the coin through the back of the hand, using the method described and illustrated on page 183. Squeeze your left hand, apparently crumbling the coin to silver dust. As the confetti flutters from your left hand, sleeve the coin in the right sleeve. This is a pretty and startling vanish of a coin.

An Extra Load for the Miser's Dream

Described by JOHN MULHOLLAND

Some 40 years ago, T. Nelson Downs told me the secret of a method he used at various times to get a 40-coin load during a performance of the Miser's Dream. Its practicality was so obvious that I made the equipment and have used it often. Its major advantages are that the load is not from the body, getting it is invisible, and the gimmick can be disposed of easily.

Requirements and Preparation: 36 to 40 coins, according to their thickness and the size of the magician's hand, have minute holes drilled through their centers. The drilling should be done on a lathe so the holes will be in the exact centers. The coins Tommy used were drilled by a jeweler and the holes were so small as to be invisible except under the closest inspection. The coins I use are nickel plated British pennies and have holes the size of a fine human hair.

The drilled coins are strung on what Tommy called florist's wire, a very fine, strong wire used by florists in binding flowers to make bouquets. A florist friend helped me to get a quantity of this wire and I do not know of any other source. After the coins are strung, the ends of the wire are drawn together and twisted so tightly the coins are immovable. The extended ends of the wires are made into a loop big enough to go over the thumb easily and twisted until secure, then the left-over ends are cut off. This load of coins is put on a servante back of a chair, or behind something on the table. In either instance the wire loop extends into the air where it is invisible because it is so fine. This wire cannot be seen at a distance of two feet.

Working: When the magician is down to his last palmed coin he plucks that coin from a chair back, or an object on the table, and in so doing, sticks his thumb through the wire loop. The load of coins will be picked up and hang concealed at the palm, leaving the fingers free. When performer wishes to produce these coins all he has to do is to squeeze the stack and the wire will break, releasing the coins. At the end of the production the wire is dropped to the stage where it is invisible.

Climax to the Coin Pail

NEIL FOSTER

The smart looking "Champagne Bucket" type of pail is often used nowadays as the

Fig. 1

two arms of the gimmick, bringing the coins into the hand. The left hand passes the pail to the right hand, which repeats this operation of gripping it so the fingers enclose the load and steal it into the hand, then the pail is placed on the table.

With a load of coins in each hand, start pushing coins up one at a time with the thumbs and dropping them into the pail. The coins are dropped from each hand alternately, clunk, clunk, clunk, and the tempo speeds faster and faster. Then with half the load left in each hand, make catching gestures with each hand and with open palms allow 'handfuls' of coins to cascade into the pail. Worked smartly to this climax and building the tempo to a crescendo, this is an automatic applause-getter.

The Miser's Dream with Paper Bag

Courtesy *Genii*

HARRY LOUINE, King of Koins

Harry Louine (his real name is L. N. Miller) devised this routine for The Miser's Dream while logging 5000 hours with the U.S.O. during World War II; it enabled him to perform this celebrated feat under all sorts of handicaps, eliminated carrying a top hat as well as certain other equipment. Mr. Miller was born in Marshalltown, Iowa, where he got his inspiration to become a magician from the famous T. Nelson Downs, and toured vaudeville for many years. Downs himself conferred upon Mr. Miller the right to use the billing "King of Koins."

The Miser's Dream is always well received when properly presented. The idea that a magician can seemingly pluck money from the air fascinates all types of audiences, and the trick has been featured on the programs of many famous magicians of the past and present. There is something whimsical

receptacle into which the magician drops the coins he catches from the air. The ring and knob on each side disguise droppers that provide as many as 24 coins, and the coins drop with a resounding clatter. Here's a tried and tested climax for your coin pail Miser's Dream.

Attached to the inside of the bucket are the 2 holder gimmicks shown in Fig. 1. These are made to hold dollar size coins.

After the performer has exhausted the 24 coins in the knob droppers, he steals the dollar loads in setting the pail on the table. The left hand grips the pail with the fingers enclosing the load on the left side and the middle finger draws upward between the about using a paper bag in which to collect the coins extracted from the air, and the resounding "klunk" when a coin is dropped into the bag is just as telling in its effect upon the spectators as if it were dropped into a tin bucket. Mr. Miller's description is a sort of "Bare Bones of the Trick," but it will serve to explain the construction of the bag and give the coin worker a skeleton upon which to build. The Miser's Dream has been dealt with in considerable detail in Chapter XIV.

In this version, the paper bag used instead of the hat usually employed, is gimmicked by pasting a small upside down pocket inside the mouth, in which the first load is concealed. Also pasted inside, but right side up, is a smaller bag of the candy store variety.

The bag is flat when it is picked up from the table. It is snapped open in the best grocery store manner, the hand covering the small pocket, and shown empty by permitting the audience to look inside. It can be turned upside down and the initial coin load will not fall out, but as it is turned right side up, the load slips out of the pocket into performer's hand, and the routine begins.

A few coins are produced from the air and dropped into the bag. The bag is dropped to the floor, the coins serving as ballast to keep it upright. More loads are stolen as needed and produced, the coins being dropped into the bag. When the supply is almost exhausted pick up the bag and hold it with the hand in which the coins are concealed, just as the hat or pail would be held. Now pretend to gather more coins from the air. But you just pretend to drop them into the bag. The same coin is produced over and over again, in the conventional manner, while the other hand releases coins one at a time and they fall into the bag until the supply is ex-

hausted. Take a handful of coins from the bag and pour them back, stealing a few as you do this. Produce these from the air; pass one through the bag; toss one into the air where it disappears, hold out the bag and it drops in, etc. All the standard moves can be employed.

Finally dump the coins from the bag onto a tray or plate and use them for sleights and a few tricks. (See Down's routine in Chapter XIV.) You are limited only by your own ability, and the length of the routine you wish to present.

For a climax the coins are apparently dropped into the bag, but actually they go into the smaller bag inside. The bag is then blown up and burst and—the coins have vanished!

A Surprising Routine
ROLLAND HAMBLEN

Once associated with Floyd Thayer, the late Rolland Hamblen was a valued and true friend who taught me many fine things in magic. Here he combined tricks and apparatus to make an entertaining routine.

Effect: A borrowed and marked half dollar is held tightly in a spectator's hand while the performer waves a lighted match around it, claiming the heat will soften the coin enough to permit him to remove the silver. By rubbing the back of the spectator's fist he apparently extracts a nugget of silver. The spectator opens his hand and finds the coin he holds is now devoid of metal of any kind and completely transparent, yet the milling and design can still be seen.

Stating that the transparent coin is worth about a nickel, the performer reaches behind his knee and produces the remaining part of the half dollar in the form of 45 pennies! These he dumps into the spectator's hands and asks him if he would trade all of that for the contents of a small box which he then removes from his pocket. The spectator agrees to make the trade so he is handed the box and a key. He opens the box and finds inside his own marked half dollar.

Requisites and Preparation: You will require, besides the packet of matches, a glass disc the size and thickness of a half dollar, or a plastic coin; a wad of tin foil about the size of a large pea; a Lippincott Coin Box, marketed by Harold Martin and obtainable from most dealers; and an Ireland penny dropper as used in Ireland's Fifty Cent Routine (Ireland catalog No. 77).

Have the Ireland dropper loaded with 45 pennies and hanging on the right hip pocket. The Lippincott box, prepared for loading, is in the right coat pocket. The key for the box is in any handy pocket. In the pocket with the Lippincott box is a packet of matches and the wad of foil. The plastic coin is finger palmed in your right hand.

1. Borrow a half dollar and have it marked with a pen knife for future identification. Perform Silver Extraction exactly as described on page 187, leaving the marked coin in the right coat pocket while you bring out the wad of foil hidden in your hand, and the packet of matches visible at your fingertips. Do not load the coin in the Lippincott box at this time. The match is waved around the spectator's hand and the foil is extracted. He then opens his hand to discover the plastic coin.

2. Tell him the plastic coin and the nugget are worth about five cents. Reach back with your right hand, quickly obtain the 45 pennies from the dropper and produce them from behind your right knee. "Here is the rest of the 50 cents," you say as you dump the coins into his hands.

3. While the spectator is recovering from his surprise, reach into your right coat pocket, load the marked coin in the Lippincott

box, bring it out and place it on the table in front of him. Tell him the box contains something of equal value, and rather than be burdened with the weight of the pennies, it would be much better to trade them for the contents of the box. After he agrees to make the exchange, remove the key from your pocket and hand it to him with the request that he examine the box first, then open it. Inside he finds a half dollar and on it his mark!

The Penton Coin Switch
CHARLES PENTON

Many tricks require that the magician borrow a coin and switch it for a duplicate. The following method accomplishes this so naturally there need be no fear of detection.

Ask for the loan of a coin. Have it marked and held up so everyone can see it. Now you take the coin, hold it up and pass it to someone else to hold, or drop it in a glass. It is during the action of taking the coin from the spectator and holding it up for all to see that the switch is made. Here are the mechanics: Hold the duplicate in

Fig. 1

your right hand with the first two fingers in a sort of unorthodox finger palm. The coin lies over the middle joints of these two fingers, which curl in slightly, holding it as in Fig. 1.

To accomplish the switch the spectator must be holding his coin properly. It

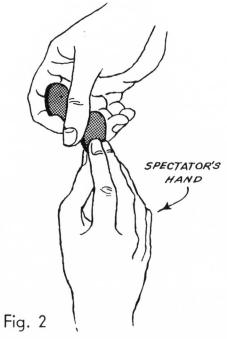

SPECTATOR'S
HAND

Fig. 2

should be held vertically, near the tips of his fingers. After he has marked it ask him to hold it up. This will put it in correct position for your taking it and making the switch. With your coin gripped as described, the right hand takes the spectator's coin from above between the ball of the thumb and the side of the third finger between its two outer joints, Fig. 2, (the performer's view). The spectator still holds his coin, which is about to be taken away in the performer's right hand. The duplicate is still gripped by the slightly curled first two fingers. As the right hand carries away the spectator's coin gripped as shown and described, it immediately turns palm up, and in so doing the marked coin is pushed into the finger palm by the thumb, which then slides the duplicate to the tip of the forefinger. This coin is now held up by the tip of the right forefinger and thumb, so it can be seen clearly by all.

Several basic methods for switching coins will be found in Chapter II of this book.

A Lippincott Coin Box Routine
J. B. BOBO

Here is a routine employing The Penton Coin Switch and the Lippincott Coin Box, a small wooden box, so constructed that a coin can be secretly loaded into it while it is securely locked.

Have the Lippincott box, prepared for loading, in your right coat pocket. Hidden in your right hand is a half dollar with a few marks on it. Ask for the loan of a half dollar. Have it marked, then execute The Penton Switch as you take it from the spectator and give it to a second person to hold. If he should look at it he will see your markings which he will take for those put on by the lender. As the second spectator holds the coin high, reach into your right coat pocket, load the marked coin in the Lippincott Box, bring it out and hand it to the first spectator to hold. Now take the duplicate coin from the spectator—everyone thinks this is the borrowed one—and vanish it completely employing a method from Chapter IV. Tell the audience the coin went into the box. Have the box examined, then opened. The spectator removes the coin and identifies his mark. Apparently the borrowed half dollar disappeared and reappeared inside a locked box.

The trick is a good one.

The Dam Coin Trick

This is the name associated with one of the most baffling coin tricks invented in recent years. It originated in Germany, was brought to this country by Dick DuBois and marketed by Gene Gordon. It is now becoming fairly common, since the secret is sold by every dealer and many novelty shops. It employs a principle new to magic and the effect on an audience is startling.

Effect: A drinking glass is shown with

its top covered by a square of rubber held in place with a rubber band. On top of the rubber is a quarter and partly underneath the quarter is a dime. The dime is removed. The forefinger presses lightly on top of the quarter and it magically penetrates the rubber and falls into the glass. Everything can be examined.

Requisites and Preparation: A piece of thin rubber measuring approximately 5″ square. This material is called dental dam and can be purchased in at least two thicknesses, at a dental supply store, or the dealers can supply it.

You will also need a drinking glass, a rubber band, a fairly new quarter and a dime.

When the glass is brought forth with the rubber stretched over the top, the quarter and dime appear to be on top. The dime *is* on top of the rubber but the quarter is actually underneath, held in place by a pocket formed in the rubber. Due to the transparency of the rubber when stretched, the quarter appears to be lying on top.

To prepare: Balance the quarter on the right second finger tip while gripping the square of rubber with the two hands, thumbs on top, fingers underneath. Stretch it both ways until you think it is about to break, then push the quarter up tightly against the center. Hold it pressed tightly to the center of the rubber as you release tension, and as you do so the rubber will contract and grip the edges of the coin, holding it there. A small ledge of rubber is formed pocket-fashion around the edge of the quarter. A few trials may be necessary at first to get the coin placed in the rubber properly, but once the knack is acquired it becomes easy and takes only half a minute to prepare. Another method, which may be easier for some, is to place the quarter on the top of a small bottle, the mouth of which must be smaller than the coin.

Stretch the rubber dam two ways between the hands and lower it over the coin, then press down a little more so the rubber will grip the coin when the hands are relaxed.

With the rubber and quarter thus prepared, place the piece over the mouth of a drinking glass and hold it in place with a rubber band. You can now slip the edge of a dime underneath the quarter, which adds to the illusion that the quarter is really on top of the rubber.

Working: Bring forth the glass prepared as above and call attention to the two coins. Ask a spectator to choose a coin. Using the magician's choice, the dime is removed and placed aside. With the forefinger, tap the quarter sharply and it will apparently penetrate the rubber and fall into the glass. You may now permit the spectators to examine everything.

There needs to be no fear of detection when performing the feat. Close, visual inspection by the spectators will not reveal that the quarter is covered by the transparent rubber.

The rubber prepared as explained can be carried in the pocket for a short length of time and the trick presented apparently impromptu. Bring it out in the left hand, rubber held folded loosely over the quarter. A quarter is removed from the right pocket and apparently slipped under the fold of the rubber, but the coin is retained concealed in the right hand as the fold falls away to reveal the quarter. Reach into your right pocket, leave the concealed coin and remove a rubber band. Now stretch the rubber over a glass and present the trick as previously described.

Jay Marshall suggests pushing the quarter through the rubber sideways instead of flatways. To do this simply grip the edge through the rubber, lift coin up a bit, turn it to a vertical position and push it through. Greater care in preparation and handling is necessary for this push-through version.

After preparing the rubber with a quarter you will find that a dime can be slipped right in next to the quarter and held in place with it. A slight push from the top will dislodge the dime and a harder push will loosen the quarter. Place the rubber over the glass with the quarter and dime underneath. Another dime lies visible on top with the quarter. Remove the dime, pretend to place it in your left hand, but retain it in your right. Tap quarter lightly with your left forefinger, dislodging the dime hidden underneath, which drops into the glass. Apparently the dime passed through invisibly. Now say you will make the quarter penetrate visibly. Tap the quarter and it goes through. A spectator can be permitted to perform this task with perfect safety. This almost knocks 'em out of their seats!

In a similiar fashion the familiar Dime and Penny set can be used for a slightly different version. Place a regular dime in the pocket underneath the quarter in the rubber. From above only the quarter is visible, and it seems to be lying on top of the rubber. Cover the top of the glass with a square of cardboard and place the gimmicked dime and penny on top of this, the penny on top of and slightly overlapping the dime. By pressing lightly on the penny as you slip it completely over the dime, the dime apparently penetrates the cardboard and the rubber. Then the penny is taken away and shown on both sides, and finally the cardboard. Now the quarter is caused to penetrate as in the regular method.

Howard Strickler had an impromptu version using a dime and a glass pill bottle. The bottle measures approximately 1⅛″ diameter and 3″ tall. The plastic cap has a hole slightly smaller than a dime drilled through it. Bottle and cap are shown in Fig. 1. A dime is "loaded" in a 2½″ square

Fig. 1

of dental dam and placed in the left coat pocket. The bottle and cap are in your right coat pocket. Have a dime with some small change in a trousers pocket.

Take the change from your pocket, remove the dime and put back the other coins With your left hand, remove the prepared rubber square from the pocket with the thumb covering the dime. Pretend to place the dime on the rubber, but retain it in your right hand as the left thumb moves away to reveal the dime in the dam. Apparently you placed the dime on the rubber in your left hand. Reach into your right pocket, leave the hidden dime and bring out the bottle. Have someone look it over and remove the cap. Take back the bottle and place the rubber over its mouth so the dime lies right over this opening. Take the cap and slip it on the bottle. The dime can now be seen through the hole in the cap, and the capped bottle can be shown freely. Hold the bottle in the right hand and bring it down sharply against the palm of the left, which action dislodges the dime from the rubber and it falls into the bottle. Rattle the dime in the bottle, then pass it to a spectator to examine and disassemble.

The Miller Routine
For The Miser's Dream

CHARLES EARL MILLER
Courtesy of *Genii*

The money-catching trick, or "Miser's Dream" is one of the finest effects in all of magic. Dai Vernon says it is the only trick that appeals to all audiences, and in his opinion is the greatest single effect in magic. The trick is not easy to do. It requires timing, skill and plenty of "address." Just to walk out with a handful of palming coins and drop them into a hat or tin can doesn't require much except nerve, and I am sorry to say I have seen too many perform this classic feat in this way. The true student will follow the routine as outlined here and appreciate the finer points that make the trick an excellent bit of fantasy.

A soft hat is preferable as the receptacle in which to drop the coins, but the writer often uses a paper sack—a hardware size eight bag, as a regular grocery bag is not strong enough and the bottom will tear. Or, a small champagne or ice bucket will do very nicely. The whole idea here is that the receptacle should be as inconspicuous as possible, and all attention should be on the catching of the coins. For that reason my champagne bucket is not shiny or silvered, and I use it to bring on a few items I use—a piece of rope, a couple of packs of cards, a piece of paper and a box of matches. I remove the items and go into the coin catching routine. The trick can be used at the beginning or whenever you please; I find it the best opener one can have.

Requirements: Twenty to thirty coins. The exact number is not critical; on occasions I have used as few as twelve. Twenty-five works out very nicely. I like silver dollars, but now and then I use halves.

STACK OF COINS

Fig. 1

Not palming coins, for at the finish the coins are displayed. Besides, palming coins don't sound like real money. Have the coins you are going to use in the left trousers pocket, and one coin of the same value in your right trousers pocket with some small change.

I assume that the student is familiar with the sleights used, as they are all explained in the other "Miser's Dream" Routines in this book. One thing I wish to emphasize is that the receptacle is held at an angle as shown in Fig. 1. This is important. For one thing it is less tiring, but the main reason is for the sound. The coins fall farther in dropping from palmed position. Make sure that the hand holding the palmed coins against the brim of the hat (or side of the receptacle) doesn't move. This is a fault one sees most often in performances of this trick. Now we're ready to go—

"Ladies and gentlemen, here's how a magician really makes a living. Deep down in everyone's heart is a desire to make money and make it fast. I'll show you how to make money without working for it. For this purpose I use a champagne bucket.

Most people would use this to collect champagne in—I use it to collect money in." (If you use a hat, the lines here would be, "For this purpose I use a hat. Most people use a hat to collect heads in—I use it to collect money in." Or, "For this purpose I use this paper sack. Most people use a sack to put groceries in. I use it to collect money in.")

"I also use a pair of hands, a great deal of nerve and lots of hope."

Take a penny from your right trousers pocket, at the same time palming the half, or dollar. At the same time your left hand goes into left trousers pocket and steals the stack of coins there. To do this, first display the hat and place it on the table, then with both hands go into your pockets. Toss the penny into the hat; immediately pick up the hat with the right hand and cover the stack palmed in the left. An alternate way is to hold the hat in the right hand. Dive into the left trousers pocket, get the stack and immediately pass the hat to the left hand. Actually you simply lay it over the left hand. Make no attempt to do any sleights. The left hand is held palm upward and the coins are along the fingers, spread out so the brim can be taken in a moment. Now go into the right trousers pocket and remove the penny only. Either put the penny on the table or simply hold it while you adjust the hat into the position for catching. That is, the left hand will now grasp the hat by the brim, ready to release the concealed coins one at a time, as explained on page 324.

Throw the penny into the hat. When you reach in to remove it, release one of the coins from the left hand, catch it and conceal it in the right as you pick up the penny. Show penny and toss it back into the hat. This leaves you with the first coin for production. Say:

"A penny isn't worth very much. I'm after the big money (turn the hat upside down and let the penny fall out). You know, the air is full of particles of silver and all you have to do is gather them together—like this (produce palmed coin at fingertips)—real money, spends and everything." (Apparently throw coin into hat; really retain it in right hand and allow the bottom coin of the stack in left hand to fall. Time this perfectly, for upon this illusion depends the success of the whole trick). "I'll try it again (produce a coin and repeat the move same as before). Isn't it wonderful? All you have to do is reach for it— I wish I had Howard Hughes' reach (coin from air). This must be the kind of thing a miser dreams about (coin from air). I could keep this up for a week but it's such a nuisance carrying it about (produce coin from trouser leg). Money isn't everything but it is nice to have if you've mislaid your credit card (coin from elbow). This looks like one of those rare ones—maybe I should save it (place in pocket, but palm it out again). It's so easy—makes me feel like a millionaire—you think I want to be a millionaire? Not I! I just want to live like one. (Produce another apparently from the air, toss it away, palming it so it appears to have vanished on the upward toss. Lean a little to the left and extend the hat, dropping a coin from the left hand as you pretend to catch one in the hat). It must be hush money. You can hardly hear it go! (Produce the palmed coin apparently from your left cuff). This is known as getting it on the cuff. (Now pretend to take the coin off the bottom of the hat. During these productions keep shaking the hat so the coins make a lot of noise). Money doesn't go very far these days, and it sure gets there in a hurry. (This remark is made between productions. Then take a coin out of the hat and look at it). By the way, I wonder if this is all tax free and deductable? (Throw the coin back; this leaves you with one still palmed. Downs palm this—see Chapter 1, Page 3—and make a turn to the right. Hand seems empty, yet you can produce a coin). Look! (Catch the coin and do the coin roll—see Chapter IX, Page 201—and let coin drop off the fingers into the hat). They say money talks, but it also walks. Now watch! (Scoop up a handful of coins from the hat, pour them back but retain several in your right hand). About five dollar's worth; not bad at that for a few moment's work. You know, I don't have to do this for a living—I happen to have married money.

"By the way, I see some coins floating around right among you, so I'll go into the audience just to see how the other half of the world lives. (Go into the audience and produce the first coin from the air—very close to a person). I have enough to last me for the rest of my life—provided I die tomorrow! (Now start producing the coins from the clothing of the members of the audience; from coat lapels, the cuffs, neckties, the handkerchiefs, etc.). You simply look for them and collect them. Some people don't believe I really catch these from the air. Neither do I. (As you do this you can use the following optional patter lines:) Money, money. It's only money—and I wouldn't do this if it weren't for the money . . . It is much easier than passing around a tin cup (use the word HAT if you are catching coins in a pail or bag). I did this trick for the income tax collector. I asked him if he would like me to teach him how to do it. 'No,' he said, 'You just make them and I'll collect them.' They say the richest man in the world is the one with the most money. I taught this trick to a Scotchman once. He died, poor fellow, from sheer exhaustion. But money isn't everything. You can't buy poverty with it. You know, a man worth ten million dollars is just as happy as a man with twelve million!"

Have a member of the audience reach into the air and pretend to catch a coin. Hold the hat underneath his hand and ask him to drop coin in. As he does so, allow one of the coins to fall from the stack. It appears as though he dropped a coin in the hat. Now have a coin palmed in the right hand. Ask a spectator on your right to reach into the air with his left hand and catch an imaginary coin. Then grasp the heel of his hand with your right hand. Ask him to open his hand, which is held about a foot above the hat. Just as he opens, let the palmed coin slide out of your supporting right hand. It appears as though he drops the coin. (Practice this well, for it is one of the prettiest moves in the routine). "Thank you. You are quite a magician yourself."

Now ask another spectator to stand up. Select one not too close to you, and have him reach into the air. He pretends to catch a coin. Instruct him to put it into his pocket as you say, "You may keep that one for yourself."

As you return to the center of the stage or room, take the opportunity of again grabbing a handful of coins in the right hand. Scoop them out of the hat and let some fall back but retain a few concealed in the fingers. Grasp the hat with the right hand and steal some in the same way with your left hand. Take the hat with your left hand and start producing the coins one at a time, rather rapidly, saying, "Well, I haven't done so badly after all, but you know you can save a lot of time by catching a lot together—like this—instead of one at a time. Especially if you are greedy—like I am." (You catch the coins as you are talking. Now quickly take the hat into the right hand, make a big grab and catch the coins palmed in the left hand in a bunch. Allow these to fall all together into the hat. This makes a definite climax.

COIN REPALMED

Fig. 2

Bow to your applause).

"You know, ladies and gentlemen, I'm sure this will prove to you the truth in the old saying—Rich or poor—it makes no difference as long as you have money. I have been rich and I have been poor, and believe me, being rich is much better."

SOME ADDITIONAL TIPS

When producing a coin from the air, make it appear as though you were actually picking it from a spot in the air. The coin is made to appear at the exact spot, and the way to create this illusion is to get it to the fingertips in just a fraction of a second on the way there. The hand reaches forward. You make the coin appear at the fingertips but the hand continues in a forward direction about two inches, then starts backward. The timing is very critical, but when properly done the coin appears to be actually plucked from the air. A good way to

practice is to suspend a few coins by threads from some high spot. Now move about and "catch" them as if you were actually picking them out of the air. Practice to make your pretended catches look like the real thing.

As each coin is produced it should be wiggled to make it catch the light and "scintillate." At times it is well to spin the coin in the air and catch it in the right hand just before pretending to drop it in the hat. Most of the time, this simulated dropping is badly done. It LOOKS like the magician is palming the coin and dropping another in its place from the hand holding the brim of the hat. The fault lies in the fact that the coin is badly retained or repalmed in the right hand, and the dropping occurs out of time. The actual dropping should be under cover of the right hand when it covers the left completely as in Fig. 2; then the audience sees no telltale movement of the left fingers in pushing the lower coin off the stack. And one thing more—use the thumb crotch palm sparingly.

In loading the stack of coins with the left hand stealing them from the pocket, please note that the hat is placed right over the hand. The left hand pushes out the crease in the crown, and the right now goes to the trousers pocket and secures the penny. It is clipped between the first and second fingers so it will not be out of sight when right hand adjusts hat into proper position.

In this routine, performer produces about eight coins before going into the audience to "take up a collection." More than eight becomes too repetitious. Robert-Houdin caught only eight, and this is still a good routine. T. Nelson Downs caught a bowlful, but when you are great you can take liberties!

Chapter XIX

TRICK COIN MISCELLANY

If you have studied and practiced the things taught you, you should, by now, have a fine collection of coin sleights to your credit. The mastery of sleight-of-hand and the mastery of coin magic go hand in hand. Skill is all important in the performance of most coin tricks but there are many that can be made better, more baffling and easier to perform through the use of gimmicked coins. Sometimes an effect can be improved upon with the subtle use of a tricked coin. A purist might feel that sleight-of-hand is the only way. This is wrong! The old adage, "All is fair in love and war" is just as true when applied to coin magic. What difference does it make HOW the trick was accomplished just so it did what it was supposed to do—mystify! The effect is the thing! If the effect can be made better with a shell or folding coin, by all means use it.

The performer might bring forth a deck of cards for a trick. If the cards belong to the magician they are usually suspected of being tricked. Not so with the coins! Coins are taken for what they appear to be—coins. They are not suspected of being tricked unless the performer through careless handling invites suspicion.

Virtual miracles can be performed with tricked coins. How else could one perform that wonderful effect, The Cap and Pence? How could a real, ungimmicked coin be put in a bottle? And is there a cleaner method for performing the "coins across" effect than the one called The Peregrinating Halves? The Silver and Two Copper Transposition and Half Crown and English Penny Mystery (The Sun and Moon) are modern miracles—real jet-age magic! The shell coins, the folding coins and the nesting coins are marvelous aids that can help to create effects baffling in the extreme.

The tricks explained in this chapter are good magic, for they are prized effects from the repertoires of the world's great close-up entertainers and performers. Use them!

Trick Coins

Besides the gimmicked coins described in Chapter XI there are numerous others, some of which have been perfected since the publication of the first edition of this book in 1952. I am indebted to Conrad Haden for supplying much of the information and description of the following coins and their uses.

The New Folding Half

The coin works the same as the one described on page 286 except with this one no rubber band is visible around the edge. The band is concealed by a three-part shell that covers one side and the edge of the coin. It is cemented in place and can be removed to replace a broken rubber band. The New Folding Half is a perfect replica of the genuine article and is preferred by many to the older variety.

Regular folding coins are available in nickel, quarter and half dollar sizes.

Spinning Nickels

The edges of the nickels are filed off to 83 degrees, one sloping toward the head side, the other toward the tail side. When these are spun on a smooth, clean surface they will always fall head or tail respectively. One would think they would fall toward the lower side but they actually fall toward the higher side.

Magnetic Coins

The most popular of these are made up in the quarter and the half dollar size. They are gimmicked by adding a piece of steel so they will adhere to a magnet.

These coins are useful in performing many tricks, including the one described on page 258. Other methods for handling magnetic coins are described in The New Quarter and Half Dollar Transposition, and The Come and Go Coin. Such a coin can be used in almost any trick where it is necessary to vanish a coin completely. Have a felt-covered magnet fastened underneath the right edge of your coat. Pretend to deposit the coin in your left hand but retain it hidden in your right. Either before or after showing the left hand empty, the right secretly slips the coin onto the magnet. A coin can be obtained from the magnet in the same manner. Its uses are many and varied, as a few trials will show.

Regular Shell Coins

These are cut-down coins with matching shells. They are available in nickel, quarter and half dollar sizes, as well as the English penny.

Expanded Shells

An expanded shell is made to fit over any regular, matching coin of like denomination. They can be had in three denominations—quarter, half dollar and dollar. See the chapter on The Shell and Folding Half (page 265) for tricks employing shell coins.

Squirting Coins

The Squirting Nickel, described on page 264, is also made in the half dollar size and is examinable.

Stack of Halves

This is made like the Stack of Quarters. See pages 253 and 255 for tricks using this gimmick.

The Chinese Quarter

One side of this coin is a quarter, the other a Chinese coin. It is made like the Double Faced Coin described on page 243, and many of the effects usually performed with that coin can be adapted for this one. Although the quarter size is the most popular, it also comes in the half dollar and dollar size. The half dollar and dollar sizes are rarities because of the extreme scarcity of the proper size Chinese coins used in making them. Recently, however, these sizes are being made up with manufactured brass coins which resemble Chinese coins, called The Chinatown Quarter, etc. Stewart Judah's Chinatown Dollar Routine uses a coin of this type. (See page 459.)

The area within the hole in the Chinese side is usually painted white or flesh color. A small square of white adhesive tape is preferred rather than the white paint because it will more closely resemble a white surface such as a pocket handkerchief or table cloth. The same holds true when the hole is painted flesh color and the coin is displayed on the palm of the hand. Very convincing!

The fact that one side is a Chinese coin with a hole makes for greater contrast and this gimmicked coin is preferred in some instances to the Double Faced Coin.

Dime to English Penny

Conrad Haden

Although regular coins are employed in Much From Little (page 80), the trick can also be performed with gimmicked coins. With the gimmicked coins a dime changes to an English penny. One side of the penny is recessed to take the dime, and one side of the dime matches a portion of the penny. When the dime is pressed home the penny can be shown on both sides.

The outfit is also made with a nickel instead of a dime.

This list does not cover ALL the gimmicked coins available—only the better known ones. There are stretched and elongated coins, double faced coins with matching shells and novelty coins of several kinds. Imagine most any combination, and chances are it is available!

The New Quarter and Half Dollar Transposition

Here is a new and superior handling for The Quarter and Half Dollar Transposition described on page 139. In this version a magnet is used as a holdout for the extra coin instead of a clip. The reader will discover many uses for this clever device for secretly obtaining or disposing of a coin. Naturally a silver coin will not adhere to a magnet so it must be gimmicked with a piece of steel to give it the proper quality. The handling is simple. Anytime a coin is needed the performer simply turns the fingers of his right hand under the lower edge of his coat to the magnet fastened there and slips off the money. Reversing the process gets rid of the coin. Either action is practically invisible since the coin lies right at the fingertips, but out of sight under the coat. This handy utility device will aid in the performance of numerous effects.

The magnet is like the one described on page 258 but in this instance it is placed in a flat felt bag slightly longer than the magnet. To this "tab" end is fastened a safety pin so it can be pinned underneath the lower right side of the coat with its lower end no more than an inch from the bottom. Locate the proper spot by allowing the right hand to hang naturally and relaxed at your side. You can have one pinned at each side if your routine requires.

Requirements: A gimmicked half dollar, a gimmicked quarter and two regular quarters.

Preparation: Have the gimmicked quarter attached to the magnet under the coat, the two regular quarters and the tricked half dollar in the right coat pocket.

Working: Reach into your right coat pocket, finger palm one of the quarters and bring out the other two, visible at the fingertips. Place both coins on the table, the half dollar a few inches to the left of the quarter. Continue as in the original version to the climax where the two quarters are shown in the left hand. Show these to the spectators to the left, then as you show them to the spectators on the right turn your body slightly and get rid of the concealed half dollar in the right hand by sticking it to the magnet as described.

This is a clean and easy method for getting rid of the half dollar. And since the coin is always ready on the magnet, it can be stolen secretly and employed in any trick you wish.

The Come and Go Coin, Chapter XVII, requires that a coin be secretly stolen, and will follow this trick very nicely.

The Sun and Moon

ALBERT GOSHMAN

Like the Impossible Marked Coins Transposition, this is another miracle coin effect by a master of the craft. Properly performed it is impossible to fathom.

Effect: The performer shows clearly and convincingly that he has just two coins, one copper, one silver. These are caused to transpose themselves twice in his hands in an amazing manner.

Requisites: Two coins are required. One is a regular English penny, the other is a gimmicked English half crown. It is in two parts and is constructed like the familiar Dime and Penny; that is, one part shows an English penny on one side and a half crown on the other. The other section is a shell that shows the head side of a half crown. The parts fit together loosely and when nested appear as one coin, a half crown.

Working: At the outset it is necessary that you convince the spectators your hands hold just two coins. Performing The Coin Roll (page 201) with the two coins and both hands creates immediate interest and convinces the onlookers that your hands are otherwise empty. And by doing this no one would suspect that one coin is gimmicked.

Now hold the English penny in your left hand and the half crown in your right. Grip the coins flatwise near their edges between the tips of the fingers and thumb and show them and your hands on all sides. Call attention to the half crown in your right hand as you say, "Silver." Turn attention to the English penny in your left hand and say, "Copper." While the left hand displays the copper coin, the right steals the shell off its coin and palms it. To do this, simply press the half crown into your palm, retain the shell and allow the two-faced coin to drop onto your curled fingers, copper side up. The right hand now deposits the two-faced coin, silver side up, in the left hand in finger palming position at the base of the two middle fingers. Say, "Copper and silver," as you point to the coins with your right hand. Take the copper coin from the left between the fingers and thumb of the palm down right hand. As the right moves away close the left, causing the two-faced coin to turn over, copper side up. Then as you say, "Watch the copper become silver," execute the Goshman Pinch on the copper coin held by the right hand. Turn your hand palm up, then slide the visible silver coin forward with the thumb to a position near the tip of the forefinger. It should appear that you merely closed your hand over the copper, then opened it to show it changed to silver. Turn your attention to your left hand and say, "And the silver becomes copper." Open that hand to show the copper side of the two-faced coin. The instant attention is drawn to the left hand, turn the right hand palm down and transfer the back pinched penny to the palm. The shell is held between the tips of the forefinger and thumb as this action takes place. At the completion of the transfer you should be holding the shell visible and opening downward, at the tips of the forefinger and thumb of your palm down right hand, and the penny concealed in your palm. The two-faced coin lies visible, copper side up, in your palm up left hand. The two coins have changed places.

The trick is now repeated with different moves.

As you begin this second transposition both hands are palm down. The left holds the two-faced coin, copper side out, flatwise and visible between the tips of the fingers and thumb. The right hand, with its palmed penny, holds the shell in the same manner. As the coins are thus held announce that you will repeat the trick.

Bring both hands up to a position in front of the chest and transpose the two visible coins by sliding the two-faced coin across the front of the shell into the right hand while the left takes the shell. Then as you say, "This is an English trick," the right hand deposits the two-faced coin in the eye, copper side out, where it is worn like a monocle. This frees the right hand which now takes the shell from the left and executes The Bobo Switch (page 10), tossing the regular English penny from the right palm to the left hand, which immediately closes. At the completion of this switch you will be holding the penny in your closed left hand, the two-faced coin in your eye, copper side out, and the shell finger palmed in your right hand.

With the first finger and thumb of your right hand, remove the two-faced coin from your eye and deposit it, copper side out, between the tips of your left forefinger and thumb, the other fingers remaining closed. While calling attention to the visible penny (two-faced coin) held in your left hand, drop your right to your side and take a new grip on the concealed shell. Adjust it to a front finger palm position (see Fig. 2, page 5). Remove the two-faced coin from your left hand with your right, gripping it between the extended fingers and thumb so it overlaps slightly the hidden shell. Open your left hand and hold the English penny in practically the same manner, that is, hidden behind the fingers, in finger palm position. Both hands assume the same positions at about chest height. Visible at the tips of the right fingers is the two-faced coin, copper side toward spectators. Hidden behind the left fingers and held in position by the thumb, is the regular English penny, Fig. 1, (performer's view).

Gesture first with your right hand, then with your left as you say, "Watch the copper become silver and the silver become copper." Slowly draw the double faced coin

Fig. 1

down behind the fingers so it slips noiselessly into the shell. (Great care will be necessary to prevent the coins from "talking.") And as it sinks down behind the fingers you continue, "The sun sinks in the west and rises in the east." Turn your attention to the left hand as it slowly pushes up into view its copper coin. Look back at your right hand as it pushes up the half crown. "The sun goes down and the moon comes up." And that is the effect—the copper sinks from view and rises as a silver coin. The silver, supposedly held by the left hand, becomes copper. This climax is both startling and pretty, so make the most of it. Slowly lower your two hands so the spectators can see that they hold nothing else.

The trick is completely incomprehensible!

The Silver and Two Copper Transposition
CONRAD HADEN

Here is one of the cleanest and most ingenious coin mysteries of the present age. It seems impossible in effect, yet is quite easy to perform.

Effect: The performer shows three coins in his left hand, two copper and one silver. He closes his hand over them, then removes the silver coin with his right hand and holds it in his otherwise empty hand some distance from his left. Without a suspicious move of any kind the hands are opened. The right hand that a moment ago held the half dollar now holds the two copper coins, while the left holds the half dollar. Two coins have changed places with one coin!

The three coins are again shown in the left hand. The fingers close over them and the right hand removes the silver as before. This time the half dollar is deposited in the coat pocket. A moment later the left hand is opened to show the silver coin back in

that hand and a spectator removes the two coppers from performer's pocket. The pocket is now empty and the three coins can be examined, as they are genuine.

Requirements: A regular half dollar. A regular English penny. An early American cent. This coin is about the size of a quarter.

A gimmicked coin that is in two parts. When the parts are nested they appear as a half dollar on one side and an English penny on the other. When they are separated they appear as two coins, an English penny and the early American cent.

Preparation: Place the two ungimmicked copper coins in the right coat pocket. "Unnest" the gimmicked set and place it, together with the half dollar, in the small change compartment of the same pocket. Crumple a handkerchief and place it in the breast coat pocket to hold pocket open slightly so the gimmicked set can be dropped in secretly, later.

Working: Remove the three coins from the change compartment and arrange them in an overlapping row on your palm up left hand as follows: The American cent goes near the base of the two middle fingers, the English penny overlaps the forward edge of the cent and the half dollar overlaps the forward edge of the penny. After displaying them in your left hand, close the hand and turn it over. This will cause the two copper coins to nest as one. Show your right hand empty and with fingers wide apart reach into the left fist with the forefinger and thumb (thumb on the bottom) and remove the nested set, silver side up. Close the fingers and slide the coin down out of sight into your hand. With the hand closed and turned over the copper side of the coin will be upward.

Remind the spectators of the position of the coins. Since they saw you remove the half dollar from your left hand with your right, they naturally assume that the left hand must contain the two coppers. "Two copper coins in my left hand and the silver coin in my right. Is that correct?" you ask, then say, "No, it's the other way around." Separate the nested coins in your right hand by lifting off an edge with the tip of the thumb and sliding them noiselessly apart. "Here are the two copper coins," you say as you open your right hand and show the cent and English penny. Open your left hand and say, "And here is the half dollar!" Two copper coins have mysteriously changed places with one silver coin!

Offer to repeat the trick. Arrange the three coins in your palm up left hand as before. Repeat the moves already described, to the point where the right hand removes and shows the gimmicked set as a half dollar. "This time I will put the half dollar in my pocket." Suiting your actions to your words, place it in your right coat pocket, but do not leave it there. Thumb palm it as you remove your hand and ask, "What is in my left hand?" When a spectator replies, "Two copper coins," say, "No, it's the half dollar." Open your left hand and show the half dollar. "The copper coins should be in my pocket. Would you remove them, sir?" To make the task easier, turn your right side toward him and raise your right elbow. As this is done your right hand comes up naturally to your breast coat pocket and the gimmicked set is dropped in. With the pocket held open slightly by the handkerchief, and the coin in thumb palm position, this task can be accomplished quickly and imperceptibly. The spectator removes the copper coins from your pocket and finds it otherwise empty. All three coins are tossed onto the table where they may be examined if the spectators so wish.

If you wish to have the coins examined in the beginning you can start the trick with all the coins in the right coat pocket—

the nested, gimmicked set in the small compartment, copper side out, and the three regular coins in the pocket proper. Remove the three genuine coins from your pocket and place them on the table for the spectators to look over. Do not invite examination as this would draw suspicion to the coins. They are genuine and the spectators can see this if they look them over.

Take up the coins and place them in a row on your palm up left hand as you announce a trick. Close your left hand and turn it over. With your right forefinger and thumb, reach into your left fist, remove the two copper coins and drop them into your right coat pocket. "What is in my left hand?" you ask. "A half dollar," will be the reply. "That's right," you say as you open your hand to show the coin. "I just wanted to see if you were paying close attention." Reach into your pocket, separate the gimmicked set and bring it out as two copper coins. Although no magic has taken place you have switched the regular copper coins for the gimmicked set. Now begin the trick in the manner originally described.

Alternate Version

Use an expanded half dollar shell (see page 265) instead of the genuine coin and repeat the moves as described. You will find that when the left hand closes over the three coins all will nest together and appear as a regular half dollar. The right hand removes the entire set and shows it on both sides as a half dollar. Place this in your pocket. Open your left hand and show it empty. Both copper coins have vanished!

In Chapter XII of this book, SHELL AND FOLDING HALF, there are eleven good tricks using this most ingenious gimmick, the shell coin, and there are at least thirteen more in this Chapter. Guard its secret carefully!

A Quarter and A Half

MOHAMMED BEY (S. LEO HOROWITZ)
and
JOHN MULHOLLAND

QUARTER   HALF DOLLAR

Fig. I

"I devised this routine many years ago," says Mohammed Bey, "and people still find it more interesting than many more elaborate and difficult coin effects."

Effect: The performer shows his hands empty except for two coins, one a quarter, the other a half dollar. He calls attention to the fact that one of the coins is small and the other large, and that their value is noted on one side only, then shows those sides. Turning the coins head sides up, he points out that now the only way to tell the difference between the two is by the difference in their size. Then he states that he can confuse the minds of the spectators by sliding one coin under the other several times so they will be unable to distinguish which coin is the half or which is the quarter. But in the process both have become half dollars, so now it IS impossible to tell which is the quarter. They are shown very slowly and again slide one under the other, and again the performer has one half dollar and one quarter.

Requisites and Preparation: The larger coin has a shell. The small coin is quite unprepared. At the beginning of the routine have both coins together, the smaller one on top of the shell covered half in a right hand pocket.

Working: Take the coins from the pocket with the right hand. Show the left empty and call attention to that fact. Then call attention to the two coins and transfer them to the left hand where they are taken between the first finger and thumb. Attention is now called to the empty right hand, as you say, "Except for these two coins, my hands are quite empty." As you say this, take hold of the edge of the larger coin

between the right first finger and thumb and draw it away from the quarter. Now there is a coin in each hand, Fig. 1. This is the point where you talk about confusing the minds of the spectators. Slide the small coin under the larger, and by this method transfer each to the opposite hand. Then, as if continuing the mixing, put the small coin on top of the larger so both are held by the first fingers and thumb of the left hand. The instant the left has the two, the right hand makes a quarter turn and takes hold of the large coin by its edges, between the first finger towards the audience and thumb towards the body. The second finger comes up against the bottom of the large coin. The moment the right hand has hold of the large coin, the left thumb pulls the small one away.

Seemingly, start again sliding the small coin under the other. Actually, as soon as the smaller coin is about half way under the larger, lift the shell off with the first finger and thumb of the right hand and push it between the first finger and thumb of the left. The actual large coin is balanced upon the second finger of the right hand. The shell, in being pushed between the finger and thumb of the left, goes over the small coin, and shell and coin are held together in the left fingers. The large coin is actually between the shell and the small coin when it is gripped, so it does not have a chance to fall off the right second finger. The instant the left hand has a grip on the shell, the large coin is pulled back by the first finger and thumb of the right hand taking hold of both edges. At this point in the effect there is one large coin in each hand.

Here the first finger of the right hand slides onto the top surface of the coin so the edge can be gripped between the first and second fingers. The thumb then goes under the coin and raises it so it is turned over. When the coin is reversed it is slid back under the shell and hidden small coin, the two are lined up exactly, gripped with the right thumb on top and first and second fingers underneath, and when firmly grasped, the left fingers are released. The right hand now makes a half turn so the position of the two coins is reversed. As soon as this has been done, the left fingers (back of hand up) take hold of them, and by twisting the wrist turn them back to their original position. When that turn is completed they are again taken by the right hand, and the left draws out the under coin (the real half) and turns it face up. The effect is that both sides of the two coins have been shown.

Now, apparently you are holding two half dollars—the actual large coin in the left hand and the small coin covered by the shell in the right. Bring the two together, slide the shell from the top of the small coin to its original position covering the large one, and again show that you hold one small coin and one large one in two otherwise empty hands.

A variation of Mohammed Bey's trick, titled How To Make Money, appears on page 266 of this book.

John Mulholland has taken Bey's routine a step further by using a shell on the small coin, too. After he finishes making both coins large and returns them to their original sizes, he makes both of them small, and he will tell you in his own words just how he does it:

Mulholland's Quarter and Half Routine

Shortly after Mohammed Bey showed me his wonderful effect I found that its greatest audience appeal came from the premise that the eyes of the spectators were misled rather than that the coins were changed in size. This led me to what my friend Leo was kind enough to say was an addition to his trick.

It should be noted here that at the time Leo invented his trick, the designs of the half dollar and of the quarter were the same. This permitted saying, "Here are a half dollar and a quarter. The metal and design are identical—the size is the only difference. Watch closely because I am going to confuse your eyes." Today's coins, because they are of different designs, require a patter change. But there is no more difficulty in doing the trick with a shell over the quarter than with an "honest" quarter.

When the climax of Leo's trick has been reached the magician is holding a large coin and a small one. Both are placed on his outstretched left hand, the quarter on the fingers, the half on the palm. Pointing with the first finger of the right hand, he says, "Let me help you. This is the little coin— it is the quarter. This is the big coin—it is the half dollar. Watch as I confuse your eyes again. And remember—except for these two coins, I have nothing in my hands to distract your attention."

The right hand, held vertically (palm inward and fingers pointing to the left) then picks up the quarter by gripping opposite edges between the tip of the thumb and first finger with the tip of the second finger underneath, and moves to the half dollar

Fig. 1

so the tip of the second finger can touch it and press it to the palm, Fig. 1. With both hands working in unison the shell is picked off the quarter (right thumb and forefinger raise it upward) and the left is turned so its back is toward the audience. In turning, the left is held so as to mask both quarter and shell. The left hand closes until the half is transferred from the palm to the fingers; then it is opened and held palm up, and goes under the fingers of the right hand which holds the two quarters. At this point the half dollar is hidden by the right hand; the fingers of both hands are flat and together and bent at the knuckles at right angles to the palms.

The right hand pushes the quarter shell toward the left thumb as the fingers of the left hand press the shell-covered half into the back palm position of the right hand. The hands are then separated, the left thumb pulling the quarter shell onto the left fingers as the hands move apart. Each hand is seen to hold a quarter, the shell in the left, the real coin in the right. The performer holds his hands still and says, "Remember, one of these coins is a half dollar and one is a quarter, but isn't it difficult to be certain which is which?"

The hands are brought together again and the left thumb presses down on the edge of the shell in order to raise the opposite edge slightly so it will go easily over the real quarter. The right thumb pulls the shell so as to aid in nesting the quarter inside, and simultaneously the tips of the left fingers retrieve the back palmed half. The hands are then moved apart, the right holding the shell-covered quarter and the left, the shell-covered half. These moves seem to be the same act of sliding one coin over the other used throughout the routine. Now the hands are held out so everyone can see the quarter in the right hand and the half in the left.

Note: In moving the half from the palm of the hand to the fingers, before the audience is permitted to see the two quarters, the coin has been turned over so the shell is underneath. This position insures that both will stay together when back palmed.

To conclude the trick, I hold one coin on the palm of each hand. Each is face down, which brings the shells to the palm, and each is in position to be classic palmed. The hands are turned over and the coins permitted to drop on the table so they may be examined, although it is quite unnecessary to suggest such action. And in turning over the hands, the shells remain in the palms so only the coins drop.

I found, after I had been doing this routine for some time, that throughout all the moves the illusion was just as perfect to the performer as to the spectators. This led to performing the trick while standing behind a spectator, and, with arms around him, performing the trick so he had a back view. When the trick is done in this way the spectator is apt to move his head back and forth and block the performer's view of his actions; therefore it should NOT be attempted in this manner until it can be done without looking at the coins. When I do this trick I ask one spectator if he has ever been back stage to watch a magician, and then offer him that opportunity.

J. B. Bobo likes the version where the trick is done in front of the eyes of a pretty girl as she sits on my lap. The trick is no more difficult to do in this way—except for the mental hazard!

A Surprise Routine with the $1.35 Trick
CONRAD HADEN

This is the standard effect with the $1.35 Trick but with a surprise ending.

Effect: The performer shows four coins totaling $1.35—a dime, a quarter and two half dollars, which are deposited one at a time in his left hand. He removes a half dollar, and places it in his pocket and asks what amount remains in his hand. When the reply is "Eighty-five cents," the performer says, "That's right, but in Chinese money!" He opens his hand and drops onto the table a Chinese coin, which may be examined as it is genuine.

Requirements: The $1.35 Trick. This consists of a dime, a quarter and two half dollars which when nested appear to be a regular half dollar.

Working: Show the four gimmicked coins in a row on the table, good sides up. Hidden in finger palm position of your left hand is a Chinese coin, and the hand is held palm up in a cupped position to conceal the coin. With the right hand, take the coins from the table one at a time and deposit them in the left, nesting them as you do so. The cut-down half goes in first, then the quarter and dime. Finally the last, the shell half dollar, is placed in with the others so it fits over all. Close your hand on the coins, then with the forefinger of your right (fingers wide apart) reach in and remove the nested set as one coin. Show it on both sides and place it in your pocket. Ask the spectators what amount remains in your left hand. They will reply, "Eighty-five cents." "That is correct," you say, "But it is in Chinese money." Open your hand,

show the Chinese coin and drop it on the table. Your hands are empty and the coin can be examined. The finish is both surprising and humorous.

Another trick using this gimmicked set of coins is described on page 241.

Stoppard's Peregrinating Coins
JAMES T. STOPPARD

On pages 273-276 of this book there's a trick called The Peregrinating Halves. The following routine was evolved from it into an excellent trick suitable for close-up or platform.

Effect: After showing a small change purse, the performer removes the leather part, opens the remaining metal frame and extracts four half dollars which he places in a row on an easel. He now takes the coins from the stand and holds them in his left hand, billiard ball fashion. He removes the coins from his left hand and holds them in his closed right. Taking up a glass with his left hand, he holds it some distance away as the right makes a throwing motion toward it, where one coin is seen and heard to arrive. The right hand opens to show three coins. These are caused to pass into the glass one at a time in the same manner. The coins are taken from the glass and again displayed on the easel. He now returns them one at a time to the bottomless purse, and all he has left is the skeleton frame and his empty hands.

Requisites and Preparation: An easel that will display and vanish four coins (dealer item).

A skeleton purse. Buy a medium sized coin purse with a snap top. Remove and discard the leather portion. Cut a piece of brown or black cardboard the shape of discarded portion of the purse and slip it into the jaws of the frame so the finished product resembles a real purse.

Four half dollars. Silver dollars show up best from the stage.

An expanded half dollar shell that will fit any ordinary half dollar.

A glass tumbler.

The glass and easel are on the table. The prepared purse and the four coins, with the shell covering one of them, are together in your left trousers pocket.

Working: With the sleeves rolled back, reach into your left trousers pocket, classic palm the four coins (shell covering top one) and bring out the purse visible at your fingertips. "This is my moronic money purse in which I keep all my worldy wealth," you say as you hold up the purse. "Not in *this* part." Pull off the bag-shaped cardboard and throw it away. *"But in this part."* Wiggle your right forefinger through the empty frame as you hold it in your palm up and slightly cupped left hand. With your right forefinger and thumb, reach into the opening of the frame, remove the shell-covered coin from your left palm and bring it into view, apparently extracting it from the purse. Place the coin on the easel. Remove the next two coins from the purse in the same manner and put them on the easel. When you reach in for the last one pretend to find nothing. As the right forefinger and thumb enter the purse, the two middle fingers of that hand clip the coin from the left palm, then curl in so it can be edge palmed as right hand comes away without a coin. Shake the purse and show it and the left hand empty. "I could have sworn there was another one in there," you say as you look in the purse. Still holding the frame in your cupped left hand, reach in again with your right forefinger and thumb for the last coin. As you feel for it, the right two middle fingers carry the palmed coin behind the left fingers where the right thumb and forefinger take it and bring it into view, apparently from the purse, as you

say, "Oh, it was way down in the bottom." Put the last coin on the easel alongside the others, close the skeleton frame and drop it onto the table.

With your right hand, take the shell-covered coin from the stand and place it shell side up and edgewise between the tips of the thumb and forefinger of your left hand. Place the next coin between the first and second fingers and so on until all four are held billiard-ball fashion, Fig. 1.

Fig. 1

Turn your left hand palm out so the flat surfaces of the coins face the audience, and so they can see you have nothing but the coins in your hand. After showing your left hand, stand facing the spectators and hold that hand palm up and about chest height. Beginning with the coin held between the third and fourth fingers, the right hand removes three of them one at a time and holds them in a fan at the tips of the fingers. Here are the exact mechanics: Take the first, inside coin, between the tips of your right forefinger and thumb. Move the hand to the right, and as you raise it slightly and look at it, count, "One." Move the right hand back and take the next coin in front of the first, holding it with the tip of the second finger. Carry these two away as you did the first and count, "Two." The

SHELL

Fig. 2

Fig. 3

third coin is taken in the same way, and as the right hand displays them count, "Three." As the right hand moves away from the left with its fan of three coins, bring the left fingers together and release the coin from its shell, which drops down behind them into finger palm position. The coin falls from its shell into the hand *after* the right hand has moved away and at the exact instant that you count "Three." All eyes, including your own, will be on your right hand and the coin falling from its shell will not be seen as it drops behind the fingers to the finger palm. The right hand now moves back and takes the shell in front of, and overlapping the three coins, and they are displayed fan-wise as you count "Four," Fig. 2. There must be no change in tempo in removing the coins from the left hand and displaying them in the right. At this point you are still facing the audience, the right hand holds the fan of coins, the left is palm inward and pointing to the right.

As the left hand now turns palm down and reaches for the glass on the table, the coin it conceals is shifted to classic palm position. The left hand grips the glass by the rim from above between the tips of the

fingers and thumb, Fig. 3. The right turns palm down and draws the coins into the hand as it closes. This causes the shell to slip over one coin. Hold the hands about two feet apart and make a tossing motion with the right toward the left, and at the same time release the coin from the left palm, so it falls into the glass. One coin has apparently passed from your closed right hand into the glass. Rattle the coin in the glass, then return it to the table. Now open your right hand and show the three coins in a fan (shell covers one). While holding the fan show the front and back of the hand so the spectators can see that you have only three coins. Return them to the left hand where they are held as before, and again the shell-covered coin is between the thumb and forefinger. Show the front and back of the left hand and say, "Three."

Duplicate your previous moves to cause two more coins to travel from the right hand into the glass. Finally you will be left with the shell-covered coin. Hold it in your left hand between the tips of the thumb and forefinger as before. Now, while showing your right hand completely empty, release the coin from the shell and catch it in the finger palm, then take the shell between the tips of the first two fingers of your right hand. The left hand has shifted its coin to the classic palm and holds the glass ready to receive the last. As the right hand makes a tossing motion it thumb palms the shell and the left hand drops its palmed coin into the glass, completing the illusion. Four coins have passed invisibly from your right hand into the glass.

Turn slightly to your left, hold the glass high and rattle the coins. While doing this drop your right hand to your side and shift the shell, opening up, to finger palm position. The hands are now brought together and the coins poured from the glass into the right hand, one going into the shell. The right hand counts three half dollars back into the glass. Count the last, shell-covered coin "Four," but do not drop it into the glass. It is placed on the easel. Then the other three are taken from the glass and placed on the easel along side the first. Four coins are seen by the spectators on the easel as the glass is placed aside.

Now you are going to return the coins to the skeleton purse. This is how you do it: Take up the skeleton frame and hold it again in your palm up, and cupped left hand. With the right hand, take one coin from the stand, pretend to deposit it in the purse but thumb palm it. Pretend to take up the next coin but allow it to slip into the easel and bring the thumb palmed coin into view. Make believe you put the coin in the purse, but again thumb palm it. Treat the next coin in the same manner. The shell-covered coin remains on the easel. It is also allowed to slip secretly into the stand as the thumb palmed coin is brought up. Say, "Some people think I am hiding the coins in my hand." Place the coin on the stand while you show the right hand empty with a flourish and ignore any request from the spectators to show your left hand. Finally pretend to take up this last coin but

let it slip into the easel and go through the motions of placing this non-existent coin in the purse. Snap the frame shut and toss it from hand to hand, casually showing your hands empty and saying, "So now I know where my money is when I want it."

Walt Rollins' Coins Through Table

Effect: Four coins of different sizes and denominations—a quarter, a half dollar, an English penny and a silver dollar—pass through the table one at a time into a clear glass cup underneath.

Requisites: A quarter, a half dollar, a silver dollar, an English penny and a double faced coin, copper on one side and silver on the other. The English penny and half dollar must match the copper and silver faces of the double faced coin. Have the English penny on your right knee, for this must be performed seated at a table. The other coins are in the right coat pocket, and the clear glass coffee cup is on the table.

Working: Display the four coins on the table and while commenting on their denominations and difference in size, pick them up in the right hand and toss them into the left, holding back the quarter in the right finger palm. Pick up the cup in the right hand, holding it by the handle, which appears normal and fair. Carry the cup under the table and position it between the knees. Now announce that you intend to pass the coins one at a time through the table top into the cup, and finish by saying, "The quarter will be the first to go." Slap the left palm down on the table, and let the quarter drop from the right fingers into the cup at the same instant. Lift the left hand to show the half dollar, double faced coin with copper side up, and the dollar. Bring up the cup and empty the quarter onto the table.

Pick up the three coins (half dollar, copper penny and dollar) in the right hand, toss them into the left but hold back the half in right finger palm; then with the right hand pick up the quarter, drop it into the cup and carry it under the table to the between-the-knees position. Say, "The half dollar is next." With the back of the left hand to the audience, push up the double faced coin so the silver side shows to the spectators, then slap the left palm down onto the table, at the same time dropping the finger palmed half into the cup with the right. Lift the left hand showing the copper side of the double faced coin and the silver dollar on the table. Empty the half dollar and quarter out of the cup, a little to one side.

Now the copper coin and the dollar are picked up in the left hand, while the right drops the half and quarter into the cup and carries it under the table. Say, "The dollar is the toughest." The left hand is closed into a fist and rests thumb up, but the dollar has been allowed to slip down until its edge rests on the table. Thump the fist on the table as the cup is jiggled underneath so the clink of the coins will simulate the arrival of the dollar; then the cup is brought up in the right hand and the quarter and half are tossed towards the left hand. Simultaneously the left hand moves away leaving the dollar, then puts down the double faced coin, copper side up, about 6" away. This is the well known Han Ping Chien sleight using a cup in the right hand. The hands move simultaneously—the right tosses the coins out of the cup towards the loosely held left fist, which moves away leaving the dollar with the half and quarter, but making no tell-tale movement of the fingers as it does; the fingers open well away to put down the copper coin. This is very deceptive, but the timing must be just right.

The copper side of the double coin now shows as the penny, the only coin left. The right hand takes the half, the quarter and the dollar and tosses them into the cup, but holds back the half. The left fingers take up the copper coin and close over it. Start to put the cup beneath the table, hesitate, then give matters a final check before proceeding. The left hand puts down the double coin, copper side showing, then takes it up again and secretly turns it so it will drop out of the fist silver side up. Now the coins in the cup are tossed toward the left hand, and the hand moves away, fist still closed but leaving the double coin on the table, silver side up to mingle with the coins spilled out of the cup. This is Han Ping Chien strategy again. The patter line is, "The English penny is in the left hand, and the quarter, half dollar and dollar are in the cup." They've just seen the left hand pick up the copper penny; they see three silver coins seemingly spill out of the cup, and they see the right fingers put them back into the cup. If the timing is right, the illusion will be perfect, and while there is no coin in the left hand now, the spectators will believe the copper is there. Go beneath the table with the cup; pick up the real penny from the knee; slap the left hand palm down on the table and allow the copper coin to drop from the right fingers into the cup, then raise the left hand showing nothing there. Slip the double coin out of the cup and leave it in your lap, then bring up the cup and toss the coins onto the table. There are exactly four honest coins there now, so examination can proceed.

The difference in the size of the coins always makes an impression on the spectator, for he follows a recognizably different coin each time, and each time he is fooled. Dai Vernon, Edward Marlo, Al Goshman and U. F. "Gen" Grant have all commented most favorably on this deceptive routine.

The Coins and the Matchbooks

Stewart Judah's Routine

The performer shows two matchbooks and places one on his palm up left hand. Three quarters are on the table, and one is covered with the other match packet. The quarter beneath the matchbook on the table is caused to pass beneath the book in the left hand. The coin in the hand is again covered with the book and the second quarter travels down the performer's sleeve to join its mate. The two coins are shown freely in the left hand and again covered with the matchbook. The last coin leaves its position beneath the book on the table and is discovered underneath the matchbook in the left hand.

Requirements: Four gimmicked quarters, each having a wafer of steel inside, to adhere to a magnet.

Two matchbooks, each gimmicked with a small magnet. Remove eight matches from the center of a matchbook; place a small magnet in this vacancy and hold it in with a piece of masking tape or cement. Prepare the second match packet in the same manner, Fig. 1.

Preparation: Place one quarter between the two matchbooks and have these in a

Fig. 1

handy pocket. The three remaining quarters are placed in another pocket. The spectators are never aware of the fact that four coins are employed in the mystery.

Working: Remove the quarters and the matchbooks and place them on the table, the coins in a stack, the matchbooks together. Grasp the opposite sides of the two books at their striking ends between the tips of the right thumb and second finger and lift them together from the table. Turn the hand palm up and show the bottom of one book, then turn the hand palm down again. With the left thumb and second finger, grip the top book by its opposite end while the right hand moves away with its packet and turns over to show the bottom. Both packets are then placed on the table, a few inches apart. Apparently you have shown the matchbooks on all sides but a quarter remains hidden under one of them.

Pick up the three quarters and apparently toss them onto the table in a haphazard manner. Actually, the coins are pushed into a wide V formation, about 6" or 8" apart. With the right hand, pick up the matchbook with the concealed coin and deposit it on the palm up left hand. Cover the coin to the left on the table with the other book. Go through the motions of pretending to remove an invisible coin from beneath the packet on the table, and toss it toward the left hand. With the right fingers grip the cover on the left hand, press down slightly, and slide it off to the right to reveal the quarter in the left palm. Immediately deposit this matchbook alongside and directly below the one on the table so they are side by side and about ¼" apart. Do this in an offhand manner, quickly and directly. Toss the coin from the left to the right hand and back and forth a few times, finishing with it in the left.

Pick up the matchbook covering the quarter and place it (with its concealed coin) squarely on top of the quarter in the left hand. The fact that you did not take the original packet from the table will not be noticed if you work the effect smartly. Now the situation is this: The match packet lying on the palm up left hand actually covers two quarters while the one on the table covers nothing. Place this book over the center quarter on the table.

Take up the visible quarter from the table (on the right) and say, "This one will travel down my sleeve to join the other." Pretend to deposit the coin in the top opening of the left coat sleeve but drop it in the shirt pocket instead. Show your right hand empty as you remove it from beneath the coat, and shake the sleeve slightly. Show that the coin has arrived in the left by sliding the packet away with the right. Two coins are now displayed in the left hand as the right deposits its matchbook alongside and below the coin on the table, as was done earlier. Toss the coins from hand to hand, finishing with both in the left hand.

With the aid of the first and second fingers and thumb (first finger going between the two packets), lift both together, move them forward, and cover the spot supposedly occupied by the quarter with the cover held between the thumb and forefinger; then place the other packet (with its hidden quarter) on the left palm with the other two coins. Go through the motions of causing the last quarter to jump from its position under the packet on the table to join the other two in the left hand. Lift the packet from the table and show the coin gone. Slide the packet off the left hand and show three coins together. Toss them from hand to hand as before, then onto the table. The trick is over and the coins and matchbooks are pocketed.

When the routine is performed smoothly and with no hesitation between moves the effect is startling and mysterious.

The Stack of Nickels and Die

J. B. BOBO

This coin effect is a "reformed" version of a swindle that has been used by gamblers to defraud, but it makes an excellent trick for the coin worker. It was shown to me by a magician shortly after the publication of the first edition of this book, and I wish I knew his name so I could give him credit! I have used it hundreds of times for laymen and magicians and found it to be a real baffler.

Effect: The operator brings forth a roll of nickels, a small die and a small, conical brass cup with a hole in the top. He permits the die and cup to be examined, and while this is being done unrolls the nickels and stacks them on the table. The stack is shortened by removing a few, then the die is placed on top of the nickels with the six-side up. He then places the brass cup over the nickels hiding the die from view, but calls attention to the fact that it can be seen through the small hole in the top. The problem is to turn the die over while thus covered, so the opposite side, the Ace-side, will be on top; performer proposes to do this without touching the cup with his hands or removing it from the top of the stack. And he will accomplish this feat by manipulating the die with a toothpick, through the small hole in the top of the cup. At this point he discovers he has no toothpick. As he turns away for a moment to obtain one, an onlooker (?) lifts the cup, steals the die, then replaces the cup.

Having obtained the toothpick, the operator turns again to the spectators and explains once again that he will attempt to turn over the die underneath the cup with the aid of the toothpick. Just as he begins to insert the pick into the hole he notices a look of doubt on the faces of the spectators. "Surely you don't doubt that I can do it," he protests, and usually someone will state that he does not believe it can be done. "Would you bet that I cannot do it?" asks the performer. Someone will accept and bet that the feat cannot be accomplished. How could it be? There is no die there to turn over! After the bets are made the performer inserts the tip of the toothpick in the hole of the cup and apparently turns over the die, because he immediately lifts the cup and there is the die on top of the stack of coins and it is Ace-side up! The operator collects his winnings and permits everything to be examined.

Requirements: Two small dice approximately 5/16″ square.

Two conical brass cups each approximately 1″ high and 1″ in diameter. Each has a small hole in the top. One cup is of such a size that it will fit snugly over the fake stack of nickels (described below) and lift them away. The other is slightly larger so it *will not* pick up the gimmicked stack when the die is on top. The spectators know of but one cup.

A fake stack of six nickels with a square hole through five of them, for concealing a duplicate die. See Fig. 1.

A roll of nickels from the bank. Remove six from the roll and add the fake (containing the die, six-side showing) to one end and reroll the coins in the wrapper.

A toothpick.

Besides the apparatus just described you will need a "shill," an assistant who will "do the dirty work" for you—that of stealing away the die while your back is turned. This person should seat himself close to the table so he can perform his task quickly when the time comes. Tell him beforehand to take his time and act as if he were trying to ruin your trick. Even a poor actor can convince an audience that what he is doing is unfair, but he must also indicate that the spectators act as if nothing has happened.

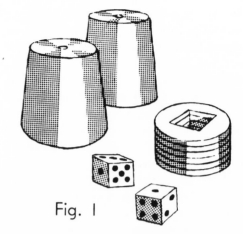

Fig. 1

Preparation: Have the largest of the two brass cups in your right coat pocket. The roll of nickels prepared as explained is in a handy pocket together with the small cup and the other die.

Have the toothpick in the kitchen or another room if performing in your own home. Otherwise have it some distance behind you in your bag or among your other apparatus.

Working: Remove the roll of nickels, the die and the small cup from your pocket and place them on the table. Permit the die and cup to be examined. Remove the wrapper from the coins, being careful that the fake stack is not exposed. As long as the fake stack is kept together with the other coins, everything appears to be okay. Stand the nickels on the table, then remark that perhaps the stack is too tall. Lift off about half the stack, place six or eight from the bottom aside, and return the remaining group to the original stack. The fake stack is still on top. Deposit the die on top of the nickels, six-side up, then cover with the cup. Say, "The die is on top of the nickels with the six on top. I'll show you." Lift the cup, call attention to the six showing on top, show the cup empty and place it back over the die.

Now announce that you will attempt to

turn the die completely upside down so the Ace will be on top, and that you will do this without removing or touching the cup with your hands. "To accomplish this I shall use a toothpick." Feel in your pockets for a toothpick. Upon not finding one say, "Excuse me, I believe I have one back here." Turn away to obtain the pick. Leave the room if necessary. Do not hurry. Give your assistant time to steal away the die and replace the cup.

Return with the toothpick and continue with the trick as if nothing has happened. "I will now attempt to turn over the die with the toothpick. To do this I have to work through this tiny hole on top of the cup." Stop short of actually inserting the tip of the pick in the hole and pretend to observe a look of doubt on the faces of the spectators. Say, "I have a feeling you don't think I can do this." Ask if anyone doubts your ability to accomplish this feat. When you get a reaction ask if he would like to make a wager. Whether anyone does or don't won't make any difference. Merely state, "Well, I bet that I can." Someone will reply, "I'll bet you can't." Make small bets if you wish, then insert the tip of the toothpick in the cup and pretend to turn over the die. "There," you say, "I've done it!" Immediately press down on the cup to lock in the fake, then lift it away exposing the die with its Ace-side up! Without any hesitation place your right hand in your coat pocket, leave the loaded cup and bring out the empty one. Do not fear detection. The spectators are stunned when they see a die where they were sure there was none. And the Ace is on top as you promised! Casually place the empty cup on the table. Say nothing about examination but everything is now free from trickery and can be examined if the spectators wish. About the most anyone will do is give the cup a casual examination. It will now be obvious why two cups are employed instead of one. It is much simpler to make the exchange. And the larger cup will not pick up any of the nickels while the die is on top of the stack, in case someone should try.

The spectators will realize that they have witnessed a clever swindle, but they will be at a loss to explain it.

Retrieve the stolen die from your helper later.

I know of few coin tricks that have a greater impact on an audience than this one.

The Stack of Quarters
J. B. Bobo

One of the oldest and most effective close-up coin tricks, "The Cap and Pence" or "Stack of Quarters," as it is generally called in this country, was described in *Hocus Pocus Junior*, in 1634. It has been in the repertoires of many famous magicians even to this day. Numerous variations have appeared in magical literature but there still remains one weak point—the exchange of the real coins for the fake stack. Perhaps this is the reason so many have passed it by for tricks easier to perform. The switch in the following version is not only easy and natural but completely deceptive.

Effect: The magician shows six quarters and a small leather cone. He stacks the coins and places them on the back of a spectator's outstretched hand, then covers them with the cone. At command the quarters penetrate the spectator's hand and fall to the table. A moment later when the cone is lifted six pennies are seen occupying the spot originally held by the quarters. Everything can be examined and the performer's hands are empty.

Requirements: A fake stack of six quarters hollowed out to conceal six pennies. Six pennies. Six quarters, which you may provide or borrow. It's best to have them.

A small, flat rubber band.

A leather cone to fit loosely over the stack of quarters. This can be made from a thin piece of leather from an old wallet.

A conical wooden form, over which the leather cone must fit. The form and leather cone are shown in Fig. 1, page 253.

Preparation: In the right coat pocket have the nested cones, and fake stack of quarters loaded with the six pennies with the rubber band around to hold them in place. Six loose quarters are in the left coat pocket.

Working: Thrust both hands into your coat pockets. With the right thumb, slide the rubber band off the fake stack and finger palm it with its opening toward the fingers; then remove the right hand holding the nested cones between the first two fingers and thumb. Simultaneously remove the left hand from its pocket with the quarters lying in a short, overlapping row at the base of the two middle fingers. If you wish to borrow any or all of the quarters do this first, then hold them as described while the right hand removes the nested cones and gimmick from the right pocket.

Announce a trick with a leather cone and six quarters. Deposit the nested cones on the table in front of a spectator, then with the aid of both hands quickly square the quarters and hold them in a stack by their edges between the forefinger and thumb of the palm down right hand. Drop them singly in a horizontal row on the table. Call attention to the fact that the leather cone fits over the wooden form, and state that since the form plays no part in the mystery you will place it aside. With the right forefinger and thumb, lift off the leather cone, place it back on the table and move the form to one side.

Actually the wooden form need not be introduced into the trick at all but it seems

a good idea to employ it since the spectators sometimes think it plays some unknown part in the mystery.

Point to the leather cone with your right forefinger as you direct someone to look inside to see if it is empty. While the spectator is thus engaged, slide the coins off the table one at a time into your left hand with the tip of your right forefinger. The two hands are then brought together as if to take the coins in the right hand, but the fake is brought into view instead, as follows: After the last coin from the table is caught in the left hand they are shaken to square them so they lie at the base of the two middle fingers in a finger palm position. As the right hand moves toward the left apparently to take the coins, the right fingers bring the fake stack to the fingertips where it is held with the opening down and toward the thumb. It is deposited momentarily on top of the coins in the left hand; then the left retains the six loose coins finger palmed as the right hand brings the fake stack into view. This action of apparently taking the coins from the left hand, but retaining them and bringing into view the fake stack, is all one continuous move and is not observed, since attention is on the leather cone. Even if someone should be watching your hands there is nothing to detect since the action is a natural one, duplicating exactly the action of taking the coins from left hand with the right.

After the spectator has examined the cone and confirms that it is empty, direct him to hold out his right hand, palm downward. Under the pretext of steadying his hand grasp it from the little finger side in such a manner that your thumb will lie on the back of his hand and your fingers underneath, curled just enough that he cannot detect the finger palmed quarters. A view of this action is shown in Fig. 2, page 256. Deposit the fake stack of coins on the back of his hand, and if the nested pennies should rattle a bit the illusion of separate coins will be enhanced. Even up the stack with right fingers (the construction of the gimmick permits this), then pick up the leather cone with the right hand, show it empty and slowly lower it over the coins. Lift the cone again for a "last look" at the coins and place it back. Pause a moment here to set the stage for the climax. Suddenly snap your right fingers, releasing the finger palmed coins from your left hand and allowing them to clatter to the table. A split second later, grasp the cone at its base with your right forefinger and thumb, lift it AND the fake together to expose the six pennies on the back of the spectator's hand. Apparently the quarters penetrated the spectator's hand, leaving in their place the pennies.

Loosen your grip on the cone, allowing the gimmick to drop into your cupped hand; toss the cone on top of the quarters, and with one continuous movement bring your hand back to your right coat pocket and drop the fake therein. The clatter of the quarters striking the table and the appearance of the pennies serve as ample misdirection for getting rid of the gimmick. Now everything can be examined.

Instead of permitting the coins to fall to the table they can be caught in a small dish or an ash tray which can be held by the spectator with his left hand. This confines them and prevents their rolling off the table as they sometimes do. Using a receptacle to catch them allows the feat to be performed while standing or when a table is not available.

Other methods for performing this excellent trick can be found on pages 253 and 255 of this book.

In *Hocus Pocus Junior,* the stack of coins or "counters" passes through the table, leaving a small die instead of pennies.

Magnetic Stack of Quarters
MILTON KORT

Effect: Five borrowed quarters are placed in the magician's left palm, the hand then closed and turned over. The empty right hand is placed palm down on the back of the left and a quick up and down motion of the hands is made. Lifting the right hand, the coins are seen lying on the back of the left, apparently having penetrated upward through that hand. The trick is repeated.

Now the stack of quarters is placed on the back of a spectator's hand and covered with a leather cone. On command the coins penetrate his hand and fall to the table. They are returned and the cone shown empty.

Requisites and Preparations: A gimmicked stack of five quarters, made as follows: Three are hollowed out and contain a magnet. They are then soldered together in a slightly uneven stack. Each of the other two quarters has a piece of steel embedded, to make them adhere to the stack of three containing the magnet. With the single quarters at the top and bottom of the stack the five can be handled as a unit.

A leather cone to cover the stack, like the one described on page 253.

The stack of quarters, with the loose ones at top and bottom, is in the right sleeve, and the leather cone is the left coat pocket.

Working: Remove the leather cone from your pocket and place it on the table or hand it to a spectator to hold. Borrow five quarters, or supply your own. Hold them in a stack in your palm up left hand, close the hand into a loose fist and turn it over. Move the palm down right hand over the back of the left. Both hands moving together now make a quick up and down motion, causing the coins to apparently penetrate upward through the back of the left hand. Here are the exact mechanics for accomplishing this effect: As the hands are quickly raised and lowered together, the left revolves slightly to the left, which action causes the coins to fly upward out of the thumb end of the left fist. Centrifugal force holds the coins to the palm of the cupped right hand, which deposits them on the back of the left hand as that hand returns to its original position and both hands are lowered and brought to a halt. This up and down motion of the two hands should not exceed 8″. The right hand is lifted to show the five coins in a stack on the back of the left. Most coin workers are familiar with this Bob Hummer move which is usually performed with one coin.

State that you will repeat the trick. Ask a spectator to remove the coins from the back of your left hand and place them on your palm as that hand turns over to receive them. While he is doing this, drop your right hand and receive the "magnet" stack on the curled fingers as it drops from the sleeve, then hold it finger palmed. Maneuver the coins in the left hand to finger palm position, close the hand and turn it over. As the left hand turns over, the palm down right hand is brought on top of the left with its fake stack of quarters. The two hands make their previous up and down movements but no coins are transferred this time. The left hand retains its stack of ordinary coins and the right is lifted to disclose the gimmicked stack on the back of the left hand. Actually you have done nothing but it appears that the coins have again traveled upward through the back of the left hand. As the right hand is lifted to disclose the fake stack the top coin is knocked off, apparently accidentally. Pick up the balance of the stack and place it on top of this coin so the two single coins will be together at the bottom. With the palm down right hand, lift the fake stack from the back of the left which remains immo-

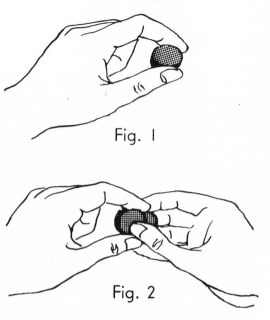

Fig. 1

Fig. 2

bile. Then the right turns palm up and places the stack between the tips of the left forefinger and thumb, Fig. 1. The loose coins are now at the top of the stack and the left second, third and fourth fingers curl inward concealing the finger palmed stack of ordinary coins.

The gimmicked coins are now counted, apparently one at a time, in this manner: The palm up right hand is brought up to the left hand holding the visible coins. The top coin is pulled off the stack with the right thumb, which presses down on it from the top, and the first and second fingers which take it from below. Move the right hand with its coin about 4″ from the left as the coin is taken and you count "One." The counted coin now lies on the pad of the second finger and the edges are gripped between the first and third fingers, the thumb resting lightly on top. The right hand moves up to take the next coin, the first coin goes underneath the stack and the thumb goes on top. Slide the top coin off onto the first, Fig. 2, and show and count two coins. Again the right hand approaches the left, apparently to take another coin, but since the remaining three are a unit a switch is made. The two coins are placed underneath the fake stack and retained by the left forefinger and thumb as the right takes the fake stack and you count "Three." Now the right hand holds the soldered stack; the left holds the two single coins, and all are held in exactly the same grip as before. The right hand carries its stack of three to the bottom of the two coins in the left hand. The right thumb slides the top coin off onto the stack as the hands separate and you count "Four." Repeat this move to take the last coin on top of those in the right hand and count "Five." You have now apparently counted and shown five separate coins. These are held in the right hand with the top two single coins slightly fanned and the illusion is complete.

Ask a spectator to hold out his right hand, back up, above the table. Bring up the fake stack and as you deposit it on the back of his hand allow the top coin to slip off, apparently accidentally. Pick up the remainder of the stack and place it on top of this coin, so the soldered stack is now between two single coins. Grasp his wrist lightly as if to steady it, with your palm down left hand, which still holds the five regular coins. With your right hand, pick up the cone and place it over the fake stack on the back of his hand. Count, "One, two, three!" On the count of three, tap the top of the cone with the tip of the right forefinger, and at the same instant release the single coins from the left hand, allowing them to fall to the table. With the right forefinger and thumb, grip the leather cone at the base and lift it and the fake stack from the back of his hand. Tilt the top of the cone forward, permitting the fake stack to drop into the hand, then toss the cone onto the table. The surprise created

by the apparent penetration of the coins through the spectator's hand and their subsequent dropping to the table affords ample opportunity to sleeve or pocket the gimmicked stack.

Return the quarters to their owners.

Chinatown Dollar Routine
STEWART JUDAH

This table routine with a dollar size brass Chinese coin and a silver dollar moves rapidly from one surprise to another, holding the interest of the spectators because of the "guessing" angle, and brings into play such varied subtlety that an explanation by the onlookers is next to impossible.

Effect: A brass, dollar size Chinese coin and a silver dollar are placed on a folded handkerchief. The top portion of the hanky is folded over the coins; performer removes and places the silver dollar under the table, explaining, "That would leave the brass coin," and shows this is true. Replacing the dollar, he covers the coins again, this time removing the brass coin and placing it under the table. "That should leave the dollar," he says, "but if I snap the brass coin like this (he snaps it under the table top) it jumps up, leaving ME the dollar." The brass coin is now on the hanky and he brings the silver from beneath the table.

With the right hand he now folds the hanky around the brass coin while left holds the silver dollar under the table, where he snaps it—and comes out with the brass coin. The empty right hand picks up an end of the folded hanky and the silver dollar slides out on the table.

Now the performer proposes a little guessing game, offering 100 to 1 the spectators will guess wrong. He covers the coins, saying, "I will remove one coin," which he holds concealed but taps it on the table, then allows a spectator to feel the hanky to make sure there's a coin in the folds. He continues, "I have cast a spell so you cannot guess which coin remains. I'll wager my dollar you cannot guess correctly." His right hand with concealed coin goes under the table and the spectator makes his guess. Regardless which coin he names, when the hanky is turned back he sees he is wrong—the performer bringing the named coin from beneath the table.

For the final surprise the performer takes a coin in each hand, showing them fairly. The right hand with the brass coin goes under the table and the left is brought down flat on the hanky. The spectator is asked if he can now name the coin under the left hand, and whatever he names, he fails again, for there is no coin there—it has penetrated the table top and is now clinking against the other in the right hand, which brings out and drops both on the hanky—a brass Chinese coin, a silver dollar.

Requirements: A Chinatown dollar, which is a trick coin showing a silver dollar on one side, on the other a dollar size brass Chinese coin with a square hole in it. The area within the hole is white to match the hanky when the coin lies on it brass side up. An "honest" brass coin to match the

FOLD DOWN (SEE ARROW)
TO COVER THE COINS

"HINGE" FOLD

Fig. 1

Chinatown dollar, and a white handkerchief, are also needed.

The handkerchief should be folded in quarters and the creases ironed. With the closed fold at the top and the open edges at the right hand side and bottom, fold it toward you and crease it again with the iron. Now when the folded hanky is lying on the table with the closed fold toward you, the crease can be grasped without fumbling and the hanky opened or closed like a book, when covering or uncovering the coins. This is important.

Working: Start with the hanky opened to quarter size and the two coins lying in the lower right square as you sit at the table, Fig. 1. The Chinatown dollar is to your right, silver side up. The silver side of this coin passes for a silver dollar throughout the routine. The brass coin is to your left. Now you are ready for

PHASE 1

With coins in position, take hanky with right fingers at top center and "hinge" it towards you, covering the coins. Remove the silver dollar, placing it momentarily on right side of folded hanky. Then with the right hand carry it under the table as you say, "If I take away the silver, that would leave the brass coin." With left hand, uncover the coin, showing that you speak the truth. Put the silver coin back and cover the coins as before. This time the right hand removes the Chinatown dollar, brass side up, and places it on the folded hanky, then carries it under the table while you say, "If I take away this one, that should leave the dollar; but if I snap the brass coin under the table, it jumps up—(uncover with left hand and show brass coin in hanky)—leaving ME the dollar," and right hand brings from under the table the gimmicked coin, silver side up, and places it alongside

the brass coin, Fig. 1, in position for

PHASE 2

Pick up the brass coin with left hand and place it on top of the silver. Now pick up the stacked coins with left first and second fingers and thumb so brass side of gimmicked coin is next to and covered by fingertips. Turn left hand palm down (Fig. 2), pull back the "honest" brass coin with the left thumb as if doing the Downs Change with playing cards, and place the gimmicked coin, brass side up, on the hanky. The edge of the coin toward you must be just above the "hinge" crease of hanky, as in Fig. 3. Left hand, its coin concealed by the fingers, rests well away, back of hand up. Right hand, with thumb on top and fingers underneath, grasps hanky and folds down the top third over coin, then makes another fold with fingers under and thumb on top, this time turning over the coin and bringing the silver side up inside hanky, which now looks like a flat tube (Fig. 4). The spectators think you have the silver coin in your left fingers. Carry the hand under the table, snap the coin against the under surface, bring it out, slap it down on the table and move the hand away, revealing the brass coin. Pick up right hand end of the hanky with the obviously empty right hand and let the silver dollar slide out into view on the table. Immediately fold the hanky as at the start; place the two coins in the lower right hand square, the brass coin to the center, and the gimmicked coin silver side up and about 1″ in from the right edge. Now you are ready for

PHASE 3

This is the 100 to 1 Challenge. With right hand, thumb on top and fingers underneath, fold hanky over the two coins.

Fig. 2

"HONEST" BRASS COIN

BRASS SIDE UP

SILVER SIDE DOWN

Fig. 3

Fig. 4

Say, "I shall remove one coin," and suiting the action to the word, remove the brass coin in right fingers, but don't allow it to be seen. Keep back of right hand up, and fingers cupped over coin to conceal it; tap the coin on table so they know you've taken one away. Now, with left fingers covering the center of the gimmicked coin in the folded hanky, have a spectator feel hanky so he knows there's a coin there. Don't let him touch the center, or the "jig is up" for your challenge. Say, "I want you to name the coin in the handkerchief. But let me warn you—I have cast a spell so you cannot guess which one it is. I'll wager my dollar against your nickel you can't guess which coin is in the handkerchief." The right hand, with its coin finger palmed, goes under the table. Left hand takes a position at the edge of the hanky as if about to uncover the coin—fingers are on top, but thumb is inside and secretly UNDER the edge of the coin nearest you. The spectator makes his guess. If he should say, "The brass coin," simply unfold the hanky and show him he's wrong, at the same time slapping the brass coin on the hanky with the right hand as you say, "No, that's the dollar—I removed the brass coin."

If he names the silver dollar, a bit of maneuvering and perfect timing are necessary. First, you turn over the gimmicked coin as you uncover it, so the brass side will be up when it comes into view. This is easy, for your thumb is under the coin in readiness to turn it over if necessary. When the brass coin is in view, say, "I'm afraid you guessed wrong," and give them an instant to see it's the brass. Then reach out with the right hand, which has the real brass coin concealed in thumb palm position; pick up the gimmicked coin, execute the Bobo Switch (page 10) and put down the real brass coin in upper left square of the hanky as you say, "This is the brass coin. I removed the silver dollar." As you are saying "silver dollar," slap the gimmicked coin silver side up, below and to the right of the brass coin. The Switch, which should be timed with the line "This is the brass coin," should look as though you merely picked up the coin, moved it a little and slapped it down again.

Practice to make the entire action fit the three patter lines. When the brass coin is in full view after being uncovered, the right

hand reaches for it; as you say, "This is the brass coin," you have picked up the gimmicked coin, switched it for the REAL brass coin and slapped it down again. As you say "I removed the silver dollar," the action of slapping down the silver coin must be completed—all this in one smooth, natural sequence. The psychological process that makes this sequence of moves go unchallenged is the fact that they SAW the brass coin lying on the hanky while you said, "I'm afraid you guessed wrong." Do this with confidence and don't worry—it "whizzes by" every time!

After a brief pause, you are ready for

PHASE 4

Pick up both coins with the right hand; drop the gimmicked coin silver side up into the left, the brass coin remaining in the right. Exhibit the coins lying on the fingers, one in each hand. Close both hands, but get the brass coin in the right hand in the thumb palm position. Both hands are backs up. Slap down the dollar from the left hand as if doing the Han Ping Chien coin trick, but immediately pick it up so silver side goes against left palm when fingers are closed. Now apparently slap down the brass coin with the right hand in the same way; actually you do the Han Ping Chien move, allowing the coin to fall out of the LEFT hand, brass side up. Left fist remains closed, apparently still holding the silver dollar, but now away to the left a little from the brass coin on the table. The right hand with real brass coin thumb palmed rests back upward, fingers relaxed, to the right. Fingers of this hand now pick up the brass coin and carry it under the table. The left hand is placed flat on the hanky as if covering a coin, and once again you ask the spectator whether he can tell you which coin is under your hand. Whatever he answers, show him there's nothing under the hand, at same time letting the coins clink and bringing out the right hand so you can drop both on the table, but make sure the silver side of the gimmicked coin is up.

Now you are back where you started. You can pocket the coins, switch for a real dollar, and replace them on the table when you put the hanky away, but it is not necessary. Most people have seen silver dollars. The Chinese coin might get looked at, but the spectator now has several unexplainable things to occupy his thoughts, so I don't bother with switching and passing for examination.

To brush up on the Han Ping Chien move, see pages 190-193. Doing the move with the two coins finishes off the routine very nicely, for your "spell" has obviously made it impossible for the spectator to win at your little guessing game, and such matters are very perplexing.

The Witch-Doctor's Coin

HORACE GOLDIN
Courtesy *The Sphinx*

When John Mulholland baffled me with this trick some years ago, then told me it was explained in *The Sphinx,* I could hardly wait to look it up and learn how it was done. Since then it has become one of my favorite coin mysteries.

The trick evolved from the old, familiar ring on the string trick. The famous Horace Goldin was interested in improving the trick and brought it to its present state of perfection. He preferred a Chinese coin over the ring and thought it better showmanship to put the coin on the string than to take it off. And he wanted to eliminate the handkerchief which was used in the old version with the ring. He felt that both the coin and string should bear examination

since the trick was suitable only for small groups. He tried out a coin with a shell but discovered the shell was too light. Then he had another outfit made with the shell as thick and heavy as possible, and that seemed to be the solution. The ideal coin seemed to be the German three mark piece. Two such coins were actually required—one for the shell, the other for the coin, which was cut down slightly so the shell would fit loosely over it. Because these particular coins have no milling on their edges they were ideally suited for the trick. A 3/16" hole is drilled through the center of each. With or without the shell the coin appears the same.

Briefly, the story Goldin told with the trick concerned a witch-doctor and his fancy get-up. He would tell of the jewelery, the ornaments and coins the man wore strung around his neck. One of the coins he wore was a Kaiser Wilhelm II drei mark piece of old Germany, and it seemed he could do strange things with this coin, etc.

Effect: There are two routines, one requiring two assistants, and one performed unassisted. In both instances a coin with a hole in it is caused to pass magically onto a shoelace.

Routine No. 1: Begin by telling about the witch-doctor, his fancy jewelery and coins, and his powers with them. Remove the shell covered coin and shoelace (which is round, black and about 27" long) from your pocket and place the lace on the table. Show the coin and tell the spectators what it is. It cannot be examined at this point and there is no need for inspection as nothing has happened yet.

Hold the coin with shell side up, and push the shoelace up through the hole until the coin is at the middle. Then the two ends are brought together and held in one hand. The weight of the coin as it hangs in the loop is enough to hold the shell tightly in place. The coin should swing back and forth, however, so no one gets a good chance to look at it because the shell just might be visible.

While swinging the coin ask two gentlemen to assist; instruct one to stand to your right and the other to your left. As soon as the men are in position take hold of the coin with your left hand. The right continues to hold the ends of the lace. Hand one end of the string to the man on your left and instruct him to take a very firm grip on it, suggesting that he wind the end around one finger. (There is a very important point to note at this part of the trick. The shell must be on the side of the coin towards the right. In other words, it cannot be on the side of the coin near the gentleman on your left who is holding the lace.) When the man has a firm grip on the shoelace, which you have handed him with your left hand, both hands are brought together. The left hand, palm down, takes hold of the lace and the coin as the right slides the shell along the string. The left hand seems merely to be holding the lace though actually it is masking the coin on the lace. The shell is slid slowly along the string, care being taken to hold the face of the shell towards the audience. It will be found that with proper care neither the audience nor the two volunteers have a chance to glimpse the hollow bottom of the shell. When the shell is almost at the end of the string, the left hand slides along, merely, so it seems, to hold the string as the coin (shell) is taken off. As soon as the coin (shell) has been removed, give that end of the lace to the helper on your right. The instant he has a firm grip on it run your left hand along it, back to the volunteer on your left and caution him not to release his grip for an instant. Now run your left hand back to the center, pressing down upon it, and ask the men not to pull the lace taut but to allow just a little

slack. Asking each man to hold his end with a firm grip almost invariably makes them pull a little. Actually you have your hand on the lace to hide the real coin, but by your manner and instructions you seem to be explaining how you want the string held.

The left hand remains motionless on the lace and the coin while the right holds up the shell, and everyone is asked to watch the witch-doctor's coin. In showing the coin, it is held by the thumb pressing it against the second and third fingers. The back of the shell is entirely on the second and third fingers, and the thumb goes on top just far enough to hold it. The hand is held palm toward the audience as their attention is called to the "coin." Then with a sweep the right hand is brought down and under the left, turning palm up in the movement. The instant the hand is palm up the thumb releases its grip and the hand is straightened out. The left hand is also partially straightened so only the ends of the fingers are curled (to mask the coin) and the lace under the second joints. These details are given in full because of the fact that when the hands are brought together in this manner the coin will be right up against the left sleeve. The next two moves run together into one which will completely mask what actually is done: The right hand slides the shell into the left sleeve as the left hand is raised, Fig. 1. Because of the weight of the shell it will slide up the sleeve as the left arm is raised. That is the way the shell is caused to disappear and the shell is, of course, thought to be the real coin by the spectators. The instant the shell has been tipped (it is *not* thrown) into the sleeve, the left hand, as it is raised, releases its grip on the coin on the shoelace and moves toward the left. Simultaneously, the right hand moves toward the right. Both hands catch hold of the string, the left hand

Fig. 1

with the thumb and the right with the tips of the fingers. The left hand is still back up and the right is still palm up. Seemingly both hands are merely lifting the center of the lace upon which hangs the coin. The coin seems to have been thrust on the string and this climax is very effective. The magician then lets go of the shoelace, steps back and asks that both the string and the coin be examined.

Routine No. 2: The foregoing version of the trick was Goldin's favorite. And since I prefer this one, I have taken a few small liberties with it to suit my own handling. This version requires no assistants.

Begin as you would in the previous version by removing the lace and the shell-covered coin from your pocket. Show the coin and explain what it is. Show the hole in the coin and explain that you use a foreign coin because Uncle Sam frowns on the mutilation of his currency. Thread the shoelace through, then hold both ends together in your left hand and swing the coin back and forth like a pendulum, but with the shell side toward the audience. With the right forefinger and thumb, grasp the coin flatwise near its right edge; release the ends of the lace held by the left hand from above, so these fall down and hang below

the coin. Show your left hand empty front and back, then slip the fingers of the now palm inward hand between those portions of the lace hanging down on either side of the coin, and grasp it by its edges between the thumb on top and the forefinger on the bottom. Show your right hand empty front and back, and while attention is directed to it briefly, the left thumb relaxes its pressure from the top of the shell, permitting the coin to tumble out onto the curled fingers, Fig. 2. Don't worry about this move being detected. It will not be seen because the eyes of the spectators are simply not on that

← SHELL

Fig. 2

hand at the moment the move is made. When the eyes do return to the left hand they again see the shell and everything appears as it was. The action appears perfectly normal. Apparently you have simply shown your left hand empty, then taken the coin in that hand so you could show the right empty. Now take the shell flatwise between the tips of your right first finger and thumb, slide the shell forward off the lace and snap it down audibly onto the table. Because it is thick and heavy it sounds like a genuine coin when snapped down. Grasp the lace on the palm side of the left hand with your right and pull it down until only about 3″ of the end protrudes from the top of the left hand. For a brief moment the lace is stretched out between the palm up left hand (with fingers curled to hide coin) at one end and the palm down right hand holding the other. The coin, with the lace running through it, lies hidden in finger palm position of the left as both hands are brought together and the ends of the lace tied in a hard knot. And since the fingers of the left hand must be together and slightly curled to conceal the coin, hold the right in the same manner as you tie the ends of the string together. Now move the knot down so it lies midway between the top of the left hand and the bottom of the loop, Fig. 3.

Pick up the shell from the table with your right hand and show it; then as you pretend to deposit it in the left hand behind the curled fingers, thumb palm it and bring the tips of the two middle fingers to the surface of the coin in the left hand. Retain this position a moment as you turn slightly to your left and open your left fingers completely to give a view of the situation to the spectators. It should appear that you simply placed the coin (shell) in your left hand on top of the lace held there. Now as you take away your right hand the coin apparently

Fig. 3

penetrates the lace visibly as it drops to the bottom of the loop. A split second later, the right hand sleeves the shell, then moves over so the thumb can slip through the loop. The left hand changes its grip on the lace so its thumb also goes through the loop, and the coin is displayed on the lace which now hangs from the thumbs of the two palm outward hands. Hold this position for a few seconds for the climax to reach its full impact. This is a startling and pretty finish to a baffling mystery!

Get rid of the sleeved shell as you return the lace and coin to the pocket.

Coin on the Stick

J. B. BOBO

This routine makes use of a coin similar to the one used in The Witch-Doctor's Coin trick except this one must be smaller and made of copper. It stems from a Washer on a Stick routine that was taught me by Rolland Hamblen.

Effect: With a minimum of moves, and in the fairest possible manner, a coin with a hole in it is caused to pass onto a stick held by a spectator.

Requirements: A copper coin with matching and loose-fitting shell, each with a 3/16″ hole drilled through their centers.

A stick cut from a small diameter dowel about 9″ or 10″ long, with rounded ends. The stick should slip freely through the hole in the coin and the ends are rounded to permit quick insertion through at the proper time.

Working: As you begin the trick both hands are palms up; the coin is held shell up, flatwise and parallel to the floor between the tips of the left forefinger and thumb. The right hand grips the stick at the middle between the forefinger and thumb. The stick thus held is brought to a vertical position as the left hand turns palm down and slips on the coin, shell side down, from above until it contacts the right forefinger and thumb. This is done to show how the coin fits onto the stick, Fig. 1. Show your left hand empty, then turn it clockwise, thumb downward and palm outward, and grip the sitck immediately above the coin by the curled-in third and fourth fingers, with the forefinger and thumb taking the coin by opposite edges. The right hand now releases its grip on the stick while the left, holding the stick and coin as just described, turns counter-clockwise, turning the stick end for end in the process. At this point the stick, which is gripped below the coin, is almost in a vertical position. The curled-in third and fourth fingers still hold it near its lower end; the coin, which is shell side up, is held at the middle of the stick between the left forefinger and thumb while the second finger is curled loosely around the stick, supporting the coin from underneath.

Show your right hand empty, front and back, and while doing so permit the coin to slip out of the shell onto the top side of the third finger, the second finger moving out of the way to release the coin from the

Fig. I

SHELL

COIN HELD BY EDGE BETWEEN TWO MIDDLE FINGERS

THIRD AND FOURTH FINGERS CURL AROUND STICK

Fig. 2

shell. Here the coin is gripped by its edge between the second and third fingers, Fig. 2. The left hand is palm inward and the fact that the coin is now separated from the shell is unknown. All they can see is the shell which is taken to be the coin. Now slip the coin (shell) off the top end of the stick and place it on the table. The left hand now turns palm downward bringing the stick to a horizontal position.

Ask a spectator to hold the ends of the stick for you, and as you direct him how to hold it, the right hand slips the stick to the right out of the left hand, which still holds the coin gripped by its edges between the two curled-in middle fingers. The stick is taken between the tips of the two outstretched forefingers, Fig. 3, then returned to the left hand by the right, where it is

Fig. 3

again held by its center to permit the spectator to hold the two ends. But in doing this the right hand slips the stick back through the partially closed left and through the coin, a quick, easy and natural action. Practice this move so the return of the stick to the left hand through the coin will appear to be a natural maneuver. With the stick held as just described the spectator is invited to take it by the ends. The left hand retains a light grip on the middle of the stick as the right picks up the coin (shell) from the table and carries it underneath the left hand where it is pressed into the left palm. Caution the spectator to hold the ends of the stick tightly, then direct him to take a firmer grip with his fingers and thumbs, to insure against a possible accident at the crucial part of the trick.

Now straighten the left fingers and draw them back over the edge of the coin, causing it to spin on the stick. The effect created is that you placed a coin in your left hand and immediately passed it onto the stick. Take a step backward so the spectators will receive the full impact of this pretty and effective climax. While the stick and coin are examined drop the shell in your pocket.

A Copper and Silver Release
Stewart Judah

Effect: A small silver coin about the size of a dime, and a copper coin about like a U.S. penny, each having a hole drilled through the center, are threaded on a piece of string and the ends held by a spectator. The performer spreads a handkerchief over the coins and asks the spectator to name his favorite coin. Then he reaches under the hanky, drops the silver coin on the table or floor, leaving the copper still on the string when the hanky is removed.

Required: A nesting set of coins made like the familar Penny and Dime set; that is, a copper shell coin into which nests a two-faced coin—silver on one side and copper on the other. However, when squeezed between the fingers, the nested set fits together tightly and appears to be a complete copper coin. Un-nested, it passes for a copper coin and a silver coin. This set has a .047″ diameter hole drilled through the exact center.

You will also need a matching silver coin with a .047″ hole drilled in the center. Have this in a right hand pocket.

Working: Exhibit the "un-nested" set as a copper and a silver coin, then have the spectator hold the piece of string, which is about 15″ long, by the two ends. Take the end in his right hand from him and thread on the copper shell so the honest side faces him. Thread on the double faced coin with the silver side towards him, and leave them in the center of the string about 2″ apart, the string loosely stretched between his hands. Caution him not to let go the ends, but maneuver the string so he cannot see the gimmicked sides of the coins. Now shake out the folded handkerchief, draping it over the coins, again cautioning him to hold tightly. Ask him to name his favorite coin—copper or silver. Let's say he names silver. You have had ample time to obtain the silver coin with the hole in it from your pocket; carry it concealed under the hanky, squeeze the nested set together, drop the silver and whip off the covering. The copper coin is still threaded on the string, and now it will pass all but microscopic examination. The silver coin is off, and except for the hole, it is an honest coin.

If he names the copper coin, the procedure is the same. Since you haven't told him WHAT you intend to do, he is left to assume that you intended to leave the selected coin on the string.

The tightly nested set can be "un-nested" by shaking it in a drinking glass.

The Magic Coin Block Routine
STEWART JUDAH

Stewart Judah has a wonderful way of blending tricks together into smooth, entertaining routines. He can take a simple effect and make a miracle of it. This close-up routine is built around two well known pocket tricks, both so old now they come under the "old chestnut" classification—the Magic Coin Block, and the very old penny, block and ring trick explained in every "Boy's Own Book." (At least such was the case when I was a boy!) Look what happens after they've passed through Mr. Judah's hands!

Effect: On the table the audience sees a small green card with a penny at one end, at the other a small, bright metal ring; on the ring sits a small red plastic block, and on top of the block, another metal ring. Performer lifts off the top ring, dropping it on the table; then he overturns the block in the middle of the card. This is merely to show the apparatus, for he immediately

stacks the block and top ring on the lower ring as before, announcing that he wishes to show the spectators an optical illusion with the penny. He sets the block and ring assembly over the penny, traces an imaginary circle around it with his finger, then gravely removes the top ring, dropping it on the table; the block is lifted off and overturned on the card, but the penny in the lower ring is gone! To bring it back, he sets the block over the now vacant ring, replaces the other ring on top and lifts away the assembly—and there's the penny!

Flushed with success he repeats the trick. Again he covers the penny with the assembly, and again top ring and block are removed; the penny is gone. But alas—the knowing ones seem to suspect something, so performer lifts the remaining ring revealing the penny hidden by the disc of paper pasted to the ring. To make the penny disappear he simply covers it with the ring, and it stays "gone" until the ring is lifted off.

"The other day," he explains, "when I was doing this trick, a man challenged me to do it with the other ring." As he says this he puts away the gimmicked ring, so there's nothing but the plain ring, block and penny left on the green card. Again he sets the block on the ring and the assembly over the penny. When he lifts the block and tosses it to the table, the penny is gone. He removes the penny from his pocket and everything can be examined.

Now he says, "I'll do it again—with two coins this time, and you may choose the coin I am to use. Here's a penny and a dime. Which shall I use?" Let's say the spectator chooses the penny. The performer sets the block over the ring, the assembly over the penny. Now he picks up the dime and drops it in his pocket, explaining that the dime will change places with the penny on the table. The block is lifted, turned over on the table, and there in the ring is the dime! The wonderful man removes the penny from his pocket and everything can be examined.

Requirements: The trick called "The Magical Coin Block" is carried by all magic dealers. Buy two of these, for you'll need two of the shell coppers supplied. Get two bright plated key or harness rings 1½″ in diameter, and some green, stiff paper cards, size 3″ x 5″, and about file card weight. Glue a circle cut from one of the cards over one of the rings, and trim it carefully so no ragged edges show when this ring is set over the penny. The paper on the ring matches the card and conceals the penny when set over it, creating the "optical illusion" that the penny has disappeared. Have a dime, and one of the shell pennies loaded with a real dime, in the change pocket of your right coat pocket, and a real penny to match the shell in your right trousers pocket. On the table have the green card. At the right hand end is one of the penny shells, honest side up; at the other end is the gimmicked ring, on it the block, felt side down, and the plain ring on top of all.

Routine: Display the props and patter about the optical illusion. Place the block assembly directly over the shell penny. The finger describes the imaginary circle, then the top ring is removed and dropped on the table away from the card, so table top can be seen through it. The block is then removed and tossed on the table, or set down on the card and turned over. The penny is gone, due to the ring with the "false bottom" over it. Offer to bring back the penny. Set block over the ring on card, then pick up the ring from the table and place it on top of all. When you lift off the whole assembly the penny has miraculously returned. At least YOU say it has.

Repeat the disappearance of the penny. When you have taken off the top ring and

overturned the block, pretend to hear suspicious remarks about the disappearance, and explain the illusion. Pick up the ring, revealing the penny—it was there all the time—show the matching paper disc pasted over the ring, and set ring over the coin so they "see how it's done."

All this is "praising Caesar before you stab him," for they will have NO explanation for what follows. Say, "The other day when I did this, a man challenged me to do it with this ring (here you hold up the plain ring) and that posed something of a problem. I guess he thought I was a magician! Well, there I was. The least I could do was to try it." Put away the gimmicked ring, and handle the block and ring so they see there's nothing wrong with them. You can even pick up the penny and move it a little.

Set the block over the ring, then place the assembly over the penny. Draw the mystic circle. Lift off the block with the right index finger and thumb, and as you do, the middle finger sweeps across the bottom of the block "stealing" the clinging shell penny into the right palm; block is tossed to the table, and all this is accomplished in one smooth, simple movement. The penny is gone; the right hand goes to the trousers pocket, comes out with the penny which is tossed to the table (shell penny is left in pocket) and all is clear—everything can be examined. After they've looked, take back the penny and drop it into the right coat pocket.

Offer to do the trick again, this time with two coins. Remove the dime and the shell penny loaded with a matching dime, from the change compartment in right hand coat pocket, and place them on the card as a penny and a dime. Have spectator designate the coin you are to use. Say he names the penny. Exactly as before, set the block over the ring and the assembly over the penny. Now pick up the dime and drop it in your right trousers pocket. Explain, "The dime is in the pocket, and the penny you chose is under the block. I shall cause the dime in my pocket to change places with the penny! Watch!" Snap your fingers over the block, lift it off, steal the shell penny and toss block onto the table. There, in the ring, is the dime; if there are any "grabbers" they can grab, for you are way ahead of them. Your hand goes to the right coat pocket, leaves the shell and brings out the penny as you say, "The penny has traveled to my pocket," and you toss it to the table.

If spectator chooses the dime, pick up the dime and put it in your pocket as you say, "You want me to use the dime? Just as you wish! I'll cause the dime to change places with the penny on the table." Cover the penny with block and ring as before, then say, "Watch!" and snap your fingers. Remove block, steal away shell, toss block to table, remove penny from your pocket (leaving shell) and slap the penny down on the table. Again all is clear!

The Flash Silver and Copper
GERALD BRUNING (BRUNO)

Effect: A copper and a silver coin are displayed and wrapped in a small square of paper. A spectator feels the parcel to make sure the two coins are still there, then it is placed in an ash tray. A lit cigarette is touched to the parcel; there is a flash of fire; the silver coin is still in the ash tray, but the copper penny has disappeared. When the spectator lifts the ash tray, there is the copper on the table. This can be used as the finale of your copper and silver routine, or by itself, for it is very effective.

Requisites and Preparation: You will need a half dollar size nested "set" made like the familiar Dime and Penny. The silver coin is a shell that fits snugly over a double faced coin, one face of which is an English penny, the other, silver to mate with the silver shell, so the nested set will be a complete silver coin. Due to the fact that the two-faced insert fits snugly, the coin can be handled freely as a silver coin. An English half crown and copper penny make a nice set, but there are other combinations.

In your wallet have several sheets of flash paper about 6" square. And you need an honest copper coin matching the one in your "coin set." Have the set "un-nested", with the matching copper coin in your right coat pocket.

Working: During your close-up performance, slip the extra copper penny under the ash tray. This can be done easily as you move the tray, slipping the finger palmed copper under it as you "clear a space" just before starting this feat. (Read **The Free and Unlimited Coinage of Silver**, page 213, for similar operations).

Take the silver shell and double faced coin out of your pocket and exhibit them side by side on the table as a silver and a copper coin. From your wallet remove the piece of flash paper, place it on the table, and set the copper penny in the center with the silver shell overlapping about an inch. Fold the paper over the coins forming a little flat parcel, but leave the coins overlapping. Have someone feel the top of the parcel to assure himself the coins are still there. When you pick up the packet to put it in the ash tray, slide the shell over the penny with your thumb and squeeze gently as you put it down, to lock the set. Borrow a lit cigarette or lighter and touch the package. After the flash, only the silver coin remains, and you show it on both sides. Ask one of the spectators to lift up the ash tray. Under it he finds the copper penny, and you give the silver coin another squeeze before dropping it on the table. Turn over both coins, pocket them and go on to the next trick. Everything looks honest!

The coin set can be "un-nested" by shaking it in a drinking glass.

Quick Change

C. THOMAS MAGRUM

Effect: In this series of eye-popping changes a silver dollar transforms itself into a half dollar, which quickly becomes a copper coin, then vanishes leaving the hands completely empty. The dollar is reproduced but it is bent. The performer slaps it onto his hand to straighten it, then passes it for inspection.

Requisites: Two American silver dollars, one of which is bent. A double faced coin that shows a half dollar on one side and an English penny on the other.

Preparation: The bent dollar is up your left sleeve; the double faced coin is finger palmed in your right hand, copper side out, and the regular dollar is visible at your fingertips.

The experienced coin worker will have no difficulty in getting the coins into these positions, but here is a suggestion. Have the three coins together in your left inside coat pocket. Reach in with your right hand, remove the bent dollar from your pocket and drop it into the top opening of your left sleeve; the left arm bent at the elbow prevents the coin going farther. Now finger palm the double faced coin and bring the regular dollar out, visible at your fingertips. A quick glance inside your hand will tell you if the double faced coin is copper side out. If it is not, take the dollar momentarily in your left hand to show it as the right drops to the side and turns over the double coin. Take the dollar back in the right hand. Or, the entire arrangement can be made openly at an opportune moment while attention is elsewhere.

Stuff a crumpled handkerchief in your left breast coat pocket to hold it open for the vanish of the coin, and be sure that the shirt sleeves are pulled back tightly against the forearm to facilitate the sleeving moves.

Working: With the bent dollar in your left sleeve, the double faced coin finger palmed in your right hand, copper side out, and the regular dollar held visible at the fingertips of the same hand, call attention to the dollar and toss it into your left hand a couple of times. On the third toss execute The Bobo Switch (page 10), retaining the dollar and tossing the double faced coin so it lands in the left hand *silver* side up. Immediately close your left into a fist and snap the right fingers over it. Open the hand and show the double faced coin as a half dollar. Show it a moment, then close your fingers over it again, permitting it to turn copper side up. The hand slowly opens—the coin has now become an English penny! It is a simple matter to turn the coin over as the hand closes over it. Have it lying at the base of the two middle fingers and it will turn over automatically as the hand forms into a fist. Or, use the method illustrated in Figs. 8 and 9, pages 281 and 282. While all eyes are on the left hand, sleeve the dollar in the right sleeve.

At this point you have the bent dollar in your left sleeve, the regular dollar in your right sleeve and the double faced coin lying copper side up in your open left hand.

Vanish the double faced coin by means of The Bobo Complete Vanish (page 49), the crumpled handkerchief in your breast coat pocket facilitating this. After the vanish show both hands completely empty. Apparently the trick is over. Relax, drop your left arm to your side and retrieve the bent dollar as it falls out onto the cupped fingers. Now bring your left hand up closed, make a little "squeeze" as you turn attention to the hand, then open it to show the bent dollar.

Feign surprise that the coin is bent. Toss it from hand to hand so the spectators can see your hands otherwise empty. Now as the left hand takes the coin and shows it, the right drops to the side and secures the regular dollar from that sleeve onto the cupped fingers, where it is transferred to the classic palm. Bring the right hand up with its concealed dollar and take the bent coin from the left hand with the fingers and thumb of the right. Toss it into the left hand a few times. Finally make The Bobo Switch, retaining the bent coin in your right hand and throwing the good one. Quickly close the left hand over it and sleeve the bent coin in your right sleeve. Slap the left hand coin onto the palm up right hand as you bring your hands together sharply, then lift the left to show that you have apparently flattened out the coin. Show your hands empty and permit the dollar to be examined. While attention is on it, retrieve the bent coin from your sleeve and pocket it.

The patter can be about inflation, deflation, foreign exchange, the poor shape our currency is in, and the bright prospect of prosperity.

Knickel Head

CHARLES SMITH
Courtesy *The New Phoenix*

The occasion often arises for using something of a humorous nature—a little trick, gag, or bit of business that amuses as well as entertains. Sometimes such items are more welcome and fit in better than baffling magic. The trick I am about to describe is designed strictly for laughs.

Effect: The performer shows a nickel, then presses it to his forehead and it stays there. He removes it, and as he drops it into a spectator's hand he says, "The trick is easy with this coin. Would you like to try it?" The spectator gasps as he discovers

that the coin resembles a huge thumbtack, for affixed to it is a good sized nail! The performer's hands are empty.

Requisites and Preparation: Solder a short, stubby nail, such as a roofing nail, to one side of a nickel. Have this prepared coin and a regular nickel in your right trousers pocket and you are ready to perform.

Working: Thrust your right hand into your pocket, finger palm the gimmicked coin and bring out the good one visible at the fingertips. Call attention to the nickel but do not show both sides of it. Press it flat against your forehead and it will stay there. If you have difficulty making it stick, tilt head back slightly. Exhibit the coin on the forehead long enough for everyone to see it, then remove it with your right hand. Ask a spectator if he would like to try it. As he extends his hand, drop the gimmicked coin and retain the regular one. Immediately sleeve the coin in the right sleeve so when the spectator's eyes turn to your hands they are seen to be empty. You need not hurry to get rid of the coin because the spectator will be so taken aback by the coin that appears to be a huge thumbtack, it will be a few moments before he thinks to look at your hands and then it will be too late. Do not call attention to the fact your hands are empty—the spectators can see that for themselves.

The fun comes when they speculate on how you could perform such a feat. The inference is that you caused the coin to adhere by pushing the nail into your skull. Although they will *know* this was not what you did, they will look at your forehead just to make sure. It's good for a laugh.

The Big Nickel

JOHN GIORDMAINE

Novelty stores and magic dealers sell a large coin resembling a jumbo nickel, approximately 3″ in diameter. Although the coin is usually sold as a paper weight or for a souvenir, it has been used by magicians for numerous effects. John Giordmaine, the famous Canadian magician, has a delightful routine with the coin that he has made famous in his country as well as in the U.S.A. Here it is.

Effect: In the trick, which is simple, direct and surprising, a borrowed nickel changes into a huge coin.

Working: Ask for the loan of a nickel while searching through your own pockets for one. This gives you an opportunity for getting the big coin out of your left coat pocket and into your left sleeve. Once in the sleeve the arm is held bent at the elbow so the coin will not fall out. Or you can have the big nickel in your left inside coat pocket where it can be removed under cover of the coat and dropped into the upper inside opening of the sleeve.

As you begin the trick the coin is hidden in your left sleeve. Ask for the loan of a nickel. Receive it in your right hand, then place it in your left and close the fingers over it. Open your hand, show the nickel and take it back in your right. Return the nickel to your left hand, close your fingers over it and ask a spectator to hold out his hand, palm up. Turn your closed left hand back up and hold it about six inches above and directly over his. Open your left hand, dropping the nickel into his hand. Pretend to be surprised that nothing happened. Take the nickel from him with your right hand, then as you duplicate your previous moves pretend to put the coin back into your left, but retain it hidden in your right. Close the left hand and as you begin to move it back over his hand stop suddenly and ask, "Have you seen this trick before?" At this precise moment drop your left hand to your side and catch the big nickel from your sleeve on your cupped fingers, which

immediately close over it as the hand is raised and returned to its original position above the spectator's hand. The spectator will reply that he has not seen the trick before. Now quickly open your left hand, allowing the big nickel to drop onto his hand for a big surprise. Apparently the small coin grew to a bigger one! Under cover of his amazement drop the nickel in your right hand into your pocket.

For an extra surprise after the big finish of the trick you can use this idea suggested by the late W. W. Larsen. Have a crumpled $5 bill in your right coat pocket, then as you secretly pocket the nickel palm out the bill and hold the hand suspiciously. This will be noticed by the audience and someone will want you to open your hand. Reluctantly open your hand and show the bill.

An Alternate Effect

In this effect you begin with the big nickel hidden in your left sleeve as before. Ask for the loan of a nickel, then change your mind. "Instead," you explain, "I'll draw an imaginary circle on the back of my left hand about the size of a nickel." Close your left hand, then using the right forefinger, draw a circle on the back of the hand. "This magic circle on the back of my hand will make an impression on the inside similar to a nickel—sort of a ghost coin." Turn your left hand palm up and open it. The spectator sees nothing. "Can you see the impression?" you ask. "You can't?" you exclaim with considerable surprise, at the same time dropping your arm to your side and securing the big nickel as it falls from the sleeve. Bring your hand up again, closed. "In that case," you continue, "I'll draw a bigger circle and try to get a bigger impression." This time draw a circle about the size of the big nickel on the back of the left hand, then turn your hand over and open it to disclose the big coin. As the spectators gasp a bit, remark, "Makes quite an impression, doesn't it?"

Incidentally, it will!

The Photo Coins

ROLLAND HAMBLEN

The following routine was developed over a period of years, for table work in cocktail lounges. Not only is it an excellent version of an old trick, but it has proved most effective as an advertising medium.

Effect: Two copper coins are shown, one in each of the two palm up hands which are held just above the table. One coin is head side up, the other is tail side up. The performer quickly turns his hands palm down on the table and asks the spectators to tell him which hand covers the head-side-up coin and which covers the one tail-side-up. The trick is repeated, but when he lifts his hands this time both coins are seen under one hand.

Now a small piece of photographic paper is autographed by a spectator and sandwiched between the coins. These are left in full view on the table. A card is selected and waved over the coin sandwich. The coins are separated and on the tiny paper is a replica of the selected card.

Requirements: Two matching English pennies.

An English penny with a shell.

An identification card case.

A quantity of tiny photographs of playing cards of a size to fit under the shell covering the English penny. These are made by photographing a number of black playing cards so the image of each on the finished print will be approximately ½" wide by about ⅞" long.

A number of small blank playing cards. These are actually small pieces of blank photographic paper cut the same size as the small card photos.

A supply of "frame" cards, about the size of a business card, each with a cut-out a trifle larger than the card photos. These cards can carry your advertisement. The frame card has a strip of scotch tape stuck on the back and across the window for the purpose of affixing the small card photograph at the conclusion of the trick, as a "give-away" or advertising card. These cut-out cards, with scotch tape stuck on, are protected by placing two back to back between a piece of folded plastic. This arrangement prevents the cards from sticking to each other and they can be peeled easily from the plastic.

A short pencil.

A deck of playing cards.

Figure 1 shows the open identification case. On one side, underneath the plastic are two of the advertising "frame" cards. A second card is carried for a second performance if working at a different table later. In the compartment on the other side is the shell-covered English penny with the tiny playing card, face down, underneath the shell. And four tiny blank cards are seen

Fig. I

Compliments

Your Name Magician

COIN

BACK OF CARD SHOW-ING SCOTCH TAPE ACROSS WINDOW

protruding from underneath a strip of leather on the same side of the case.

Preparation: The two regular English pennies are in either the right or left trousers pocket. The pencil is in the left coat pocket, and the identification case, with a rubber band around it, is in the right coat pocket.

Working: Remove the two English pennies from your pocket and explain that you are going to present an old gambling game called "heads and tails," and that you will do all the work. Place the pennies on the table about 9″ apart, one head up, the other tail up. Now pick up the coins and hold one head side up in the left palm and the other tail side up in the right palm, the back of each hand touching the table. Moving both hands in unison, they are turned over quickly, palm down, on the table, each hand covering a coin. Ask which hand covers the head up coin and which covers the tail up coin. Regardless of the answer, lift both hands and show that what was head is now tail and what was tail it now head side up.

Apparently you repeat the trick but this time when you lift your hands from the table both coins are seen under one hand. This is accomplished by propelling the coin from the right to the left hand a split second before the left completes its turnover. This is an old move, familiar to most magicians. It can be mastered in a short time if it should be unknown. Sometimes the same move is used to cause two small coins to change places. After you ask the spectators this second time which hand covers which coin, lift the right first to show nothing under it, then the left to show both together. This little trick, as simple as it is, is completely mystifying if performed adroitly. The best time to make the toss-over is on the second turnover as this is when trickery is least expected.

Take up the two coins, pretend to place both in your left hand but retain one in your right. This hand then goes to the right coat pocket as you explain that you will next require some photographic paper. Leave the coin in the pocket and bring out the identification case. Open it so the spectators can see the four strips of photo paper protruding from their pockets. Now the case is partially closed to shield the following action: The two middle fingers of the right hand enter the leather pocket and bring out the shell-covered coin as the thumb slides a piece of photo paper on top of it. The coin and paper are placed carefully on the table in front of you. This shell-covered coin is taken by the spectators to be one of the two regular coins they saw a moment ago placed in the left hand. Now remove the paper from the coin, show it all around, then replace it on top of the coin and shell. Next, place the penny from the left hand on top, making a sandwich. The situation now is that the photographic paper is sandwiched between the shell-covered penny on the bottom and the regular penny on top. Between the shell and its coin is the tiny photograph of a card.

Introduce the deck of cards and force a card corresponding to the photo beneath the shell. While the card is being shown around, lift off the regular coin and the shell below, explaining that you would like someone to mark the blank (?) paper for future identification. The paper he marks is not the blank piece but the one with the photo of the card on it, blank side up. This is how: Have the selected card placed face down on the table. Place the regular coin, shell and blank piece of paper sandwiched between, in the left hand while the right goes to the pocket in search of a pencil. Not finding one there, the left fingers push the regular penny into the right hand, retaining the shell with the blank paper on top; then left hand goes to the left coat pocket for the pencil. The shell and paper are left in the pocket; the pencil is brought out and handed to a spectator as you request that he mark the supposedly blank piece of paper. The tip of the right forefinger holds the paper to the coin, ostensibly to keep it from slipping, but actually to safeguard against having the paper prematurely examined. Cover the initialed paper with the other penny. As far as you are concerned now, the trick is over, for between two regular coins is a marked piece of photo paper which the spectators believe to be blank but which carries the photo of the card on its under side. Nearby is the selected card, face down.

Ask a spectator to pick up the selected card and hold it over the coins a moment. Caution him not to hold it too long as it might overexpose the picture. Now have the selected card turned face up on the table and explain that if conditions were right there should be a photograph of the card on the piece of paper between the two coins. Have the top coin removed and the initials on the paper verified, then turned over to reveal the photograph of the selected card.

Leave the two coins on the table for examination as you remove one of the frame cards from your identification case. Stick the tiny photograph of the card on the scotch tape over the window in the card, and give it to the spectator whose initials it bears, as a lasting momento of a trick they will remember.

The Bowling Coin Wand
J. A. BOWLING
Manufacturing rights reserved.

The finest and most practical wand for producing a coin is this one, which was designed by J. A. Bowling for use in our show. Since very few were made it has been an exclusive item for a number of years. The great advantage of this wand over others is the simple, rugged construction which makes it ideal for professional use.

Its parts consist of a 14" long piece of 5/8" diameter metal tubing, a 12" length of doweling and a special folding coin. The coin is in 3 pieces. Two outer sections are hinged to the center piece. Small springs are attached so the coin will spring open when it makes its appearance from the wand. The center section is fastened to the end of the dowel so the outer sections will fold backward to form a triangle. With the coin thus folded it will slide easily into the wand.

There is a slot near the end which is held by the hand. A small round head screw in the dowel protrudes through the slot, which permits the right thumb to slide the dowel backward and forward. Pushing the screw forward causes the coin to spring into view at the outer end of the wand. The left hand apparently removes the coin from the wand, but it is actually drawn back in and out of sight. The tip of the wand is placed directly over the left palm. The hand is closed over the tip, folding the coin backward while the right thumb operates the slide, drawing the coin inside. This construction does not permit the coin to be shown on both sides, but that is unimportant. The wand is painted black, with white tips to resemble the traditional magician's wand. A carrying case will protect it from damage while traveling.

This wand is an invaluable aid in performing A Comedy Coin Routine (page 294), or any other routine that requires the use of a coin wand. The Coin in the Banana, page 298, details an excellent use. To use the wand merely to produce a number of coins from the air is not good magic. Such use would invite suspicion. But used as an accessory, it can add much!

Nail Through Half Dollar

PAUL MORRIS
Courtesy *Hugard's Magic Monthly*

This effect was evolved from a lighted cigarette through a half dollar trick by William Meyers in *The Linking Ring*. Mr. Morris liked the cigarette effect but since he did not smoke, developed a similar routine using a huge nail. Howard Schwarzman, Al Goshman, Del Cartier and Charlie Kalish contributed ideas and suggestions. Several methods of handling will be described.

Effect: A huge nail is pushed through a borrowed half dollar.

Requisites and Preparation: A 50d or 60d (5½″ to 6″) nail.

A half dollar with a hole to permit one of these nails to be pushed through.

A colored pocket handkerchief.

Have the handkerchief in the outside breast coat pocket, the nail in the left coat pocket and the gimmicked half dollar in the right sleeve. The gimmicked coin may be in your right palm and sleeved later, if you prefer. If you choose to use your own half dollar, have it in the left trousers pocket.

Working: Remove the nail, regular half dollar and handkerchief from your pockets and toss all three items onto the table. Invite the spectators to look them over. While they are doing this you may sleeve the half dollar so the hands can be shown empty without calling direct attention to this fact.

Have a spectator spread the handkerchief over your outstretched left palm. As he does this, drop your right arm to your side and retrieve the sleeved gimmicked coin in your right hand, then finger palm it. With your right hand, pick up the regular half dollar from the table and hold it vertically about chest height as the left hand throws the handkerchief over it. Under cover of the cloth a switch is made. Instead of tak-

Fig. 1

ing the regular coin which is at the fingertips of the right hand, the left takes the finger palmed coin through the handkerchief. The right hand allows the regular coin to slip down to finger palm position as it comes out and grips the gimmicked coin through the cloth, Fig. 1. The spectators are unaware of the finger palmed coin in the right hand, as it holds the handkerchief. While holding the gimmicked coin in this manner—and you will note that the right thumb and forefinger are directly over the hole in the coin—a spectator is permitted to feel it through the fabric. With your left hand, pick up the nail, carry it underneath the handkerchief and push it through the coin. Then turn your right hand palm up, and with the aid of the left throw the handkerchief back, revealing the coin with the nail through it, Fig. 2. Slide the nail back and forth through the coin with the left hand. The regular coin in the right hand is hidden by the handkerchief.

Turn the right hand over, palm down, so the handkerchief will fall down over the gimmicked coin. Grip the nail through the cloth with the left hand, pull it out and let it drop to the table. Take the gimmicked coin through the handkerchief from the outside with the left hand as the right re-

Fig. 2

leases its grip and goes underneath. There it takes the gimmicked coin from the left between the thumb and forefinger, deposits the good coin in the left fingers and throws the handkerchief back on the left forearm to reveal the coin undamaged. The right hand now has the gimmicked coin finger palmed. The left lowers and drops the regular coin onto the table. Taking the handkerchief by the corners of one side, hold it stretched between the hands. The palms are toward the spectators, but the curled-in fingers of the right hand hide the coin and the hands appear empty. Place the handkerchief and the coin in the pocket.

Howard Schwarzman uses a playing card instead of a handkerchief to hide the coin as the nail is pushed through. At the outset the nail would be on the table and the gimmicked coin finger palmed in the right hand. A regular half dollar would be visible at the tips of the fingers of the same hand. Now while showing a playing card in the left hand the right performs a one hand switch as follows: slide the regular half dollar down to thumb palm position, where it is held a moment as the thumb pushes up the gimmicked coin to the fingertips, and the thumb palmed coin turns over into finger palm position. Keep the hole in

the coin hidden as the left hand folds the card over it once. The right hand holds the card as the left pushes the nail through it and the coin. You may permit the spectators to peek down into the folded card to see the coin on the nail. Pull the nail out with the left hand, and drop it to the table as the left releases its regular coin onto the table. The gimmicked coin then is allowed to slip out into the right fingers where it is hidden or covered by the card.

Switching a regular coin for the one with a hole in it should pose no particular problem. The more natural the switch the better. Two methods have already been described. Here are two more:

Have the regular coin, nail and handkerchief lying on the table. Hidden in your right hand is the gimmicked coin. Pick up the regular coin with your right hand, and as you pretend to toss it into your left perform The Bobo Switch (page 10), throwing the gimmicked coin and retaining the regular one. The left hand holds the gimmicked coin visible but with the thumb covering the hole, as the right hand takes up the handkerchief and throws it over the left. Continue as described.

This is the second switch. The handkerchief, nail and regular coin are on the table, while the gimmicked coin is hidden in your right sleeve. Allow the hands to be seen empty without calling attention to the fact. As the spectators look over the three articles, drop your right arm, retrieve the sleeved coin and hold it classic palmed. Now two actions take place almost simultaneously. First, the palm down right hand picks up the coin from the table. Immediately following this action the left takes up the handkerchief, and as it shakes it open the right puts the regular coin in the Goshman Pinch (see Chapter XVII), turns palm up and slides the gimmicked coin forward onto the fingertips with the thumb covering the hole. The spectators get a brief view of the coin and the empty right palm before the handkerchief is thrown over it. Now the left hand takes the gimmicked coin through the cloth while the right transfers the regular coin from the pinch to the classic palm. From here the effect is continued as described.

But remember—the sleights are only a means to an end. It is the effect that counts. The easiest and most natural way for you is the best way.

And let's don't overlook the mechanical coin for accomplishing a similar effect. The coin is gimmicked with a small, round trap-door which swings open to permit a pencil to be pushed through. It closes when the pencil is withdrawn. This coin, which looks ordinary, can only be shown on one side but the effect, nevertheless, is excellent.

In the effect, a regular coin is switched for this gimmicked one, a pencil pushed through it, the pencil withdrawn, the coin switched back for the regular one and returned to its owner.

Zella's Space Coins
U. F. "GEN" GRANT
Courtesy *The New Phoenix*

This clever routine uses the Chinatown Quarter (described under "Chinese Quarter" in TRICK COINS, this chapter) and a playing card or business card, either yours or borrowed. It almost works automatically!

Requisites: A Chinatown Quarter set, which consists of a Chinese coin with a hole in the center, a special coin showing the Chinese coin on one face and a quarter on the other, and a matching "honest" quarter. Have the regular quarter in the right trousers pocket, and the Chinese coin set, with the business card or playing card, in the right coat pocket. If a playing card is used, it should be a deuce.

Method: Remove the playing card from your pocket and hold it in the left hand with the back up. Take out the ungimmicked Chinese coin and place it on the back of the playing card. The back of the card will show through the hole in the coin, and since this routine is performed literally "right under the spectator's nose," this is a strong point. Next, remove the gimmicked coin, quarter side showing, and place it on the back of the playing card, just behind the Chinese coin. Now the right hand grasps both the card and the coins, the fingers going on top of the coins and the thumb underneath the card. Holding the coins against the card, the right hand turns palm up so the coins are now underneath the card.

"Now we will place the Chinese coin on top." With these words, your left fingers slide the gimmicked coin from under the card; the Chinese side will be showing, and you keep your left thumb over the hole until the coin is placed in the center of the now face up card. Thanks to the white spot in the hole of the gimmicked coin, the spectator apparently sees through the hole as before. Holding the coins in place with the right fingers, snap the card with the left fingers, then turn it over. The Chinese coin *was* on top, and should now be underneath, but the spectator sees that it is still on top, now on the BACK of the card. Slide the coin from beneath the card—it is seen to be the quarter.

Place the coins on the back of the card as at the start. Holding both against the card, turn it over as before. Slide the gimmicked coin from underneath, covering the hole with the thumb as before, and place it on top of the card.

"This time I will place the Chinese coin in my pocket." Remove it from the top of the card (covering the hole) and place it in the right trouser pocket. Snap the card and then turn it over. The Chinese coin is seen back on the card. Remove the honest quarter from the pocket and place it on the card. Now both coins can be examined, and performer is "left clean at the finish," as the ads stress.

You can present this routine with a Copper and Silver set, but the strong point in the routine, the hole in the Chinese coin, is lost. But the routine makes an excellent introduction to the next trick, which is called

The Phantom Coins

U. F. "GEN" GRANT

Courtesy *The New Phoenix*

The performer, pretending to be concerned over the spectator's inability to tell which coin is where, offers to repeat the trick, this time with large coins to make it easier to follow, and he places a half dollar and an English penny on the table, asking the spectator to look them over. Now he puts them slowly and fairly into the spectator's hand, and asks him to cup his other hand over them and shake them up. Facing the spectator, performer asks him to extend his arms and open his hands just a trifle so he (performer) can remove one of the coins. He removes the half dollar and lets the spectator get a good look at it in the process, puts the half in his pocket, has spectator close his hands, then asks him which coin he now holds in his hands. He will say, "The copper penny." Ask him if he will bet it's the copper penny; then, regardless of his answer, have him open his hands and sure enough he will have the copper penny.

"Let's try that again," says the performer, as he brings the half dollar from his pocket. "The larger coins do help," he says as he places the half with the penny as before and has the spectator cover the coins and shake them up again. Again performer re-

moves a coin from the spectator's hands, this time the copper penny, and places it in his pocket. Again spectator is asked which coin he holds, and this time he will say "The half dollar." This time you tell him you think he is mistaken, then ask him if he would be willing to bet it's the half dollar. Again have him open his hands and —again he finds he has the copper coin, and you bring the half dollar from your pocket.

Requisites: An English penny, a half dollar, and a Double Faced Coin (page 243) showing an English penny on one side and a half dollar on the other. Have the special coin in the little change pocket at the top of the right side coat pocket. The regular half and the English penny are in the pocket proper.

Method: Remove the two regular coins and place them side by side on the table. Have the spectator look them over, then you place them in his extended left hand, which he holds out palm up. Have him cup his right hand over them, concealing them as he shakes them up to mix them. Now have him hold his hands out toward you (stand facing him) and open them just enough so you can remove one of the coins. Remove the half dollar, and let him get a good look at it as you place it in your pocket. As soon as you remove the coin, he is asked to close his hands, then to tell you which coin he holds. He will usually say "The copper," but your follow-up question, "Would you wager you have the copper?" will disturb him; regardless of his answer, say, "You are exactly right—look—you DID have the copper coin. You're improving. Let's try that once more."

This time you reach into your pocket and bring out the gimmicked coin, silver side showing, and place it silver side up in his hands so he holds both coins again. Ask him to cover them as before and shake them up. Have him extend his hands toward you, and open them just enough so you can reach in and remove one coin. Remove the gimmicked coin, copper side showing, and let him see it; close his hands with your left hand as your right pockets the copper coin.

Again ask him which coin he holds, and when he says, with more confidence than previously, "The half dollar," tell him you think he must be mistaken, and it's a good thing he didn't wager this time, for he has the copper coin—and YOU have the half dollar. As you say this, remove the honest silver coin from your pocket and again, both coins can be examined.

The strong point here is that the coins are examined at the start and at the finish. The gimmicked coin is slipped in and out with the greatest of ease, and there's something very disarming about doing the trick right in the spectator's hands, so slowly and fairly that he sees every move you make.

SECOND METHOD

This is the original method that appeared in *The New Phoenix*. After the copper and silver coins have been looked over, you drop the English penny into the spectator's breast coat pocket and place the half dollar in your right coat pocket. Make certain that both your hands are seen to be empty after you place the coin in the spectator's pocket.

Ask him which coin he has. He will, of course, say the English penny. Ask him to remove it from his pocket to make certain. At the same time, you reach into your right coat pocket and remove the copper-silver coin, half dollar side showing.

Again take both coins, showing them as an English penny and a half dollar, your hands otherwise empty. Drop the coins into the spectator's outside breast pocket. Now you remove the copper-silver coin, showing it as the English penny, and place it into your right coat pocket. Once again ask him

which coin he has in his pocket. He will reply that he has the half dollar. As you tell him you think he is mistaken, reach into your pocket and bring out the real half. Then ask him to check and see if he doesn't have the penny!

This routine is based on Grant's Slow Motion Bill Switch, and with coins is even more effective than with bills. Pages 243 to 253 of this book explain other routines using the double faced coin, probably one of the oldest faked coins in the history of conjuring. Guyot (1706-1786) explains the method for making the copper-silver coin in his book *Nouvelles Recreations!*

The Queen Bows

U. F. "Gen" Grant

The plot of a coin or coins passing into a glass covered by a pack of cards or a tray has found much favor with conjuring headliners over the years. Roterberg explains three versions in *New Era Card Tricks* (1897) and the celebrated Nate Leipzig often used a sleight-of-hand version which is explained in *Dai Vernon's Tribute to Nate Leipzig* (Lewis Ganson, 1962). Magicdom's top idea man "Gen" Grant offers a version here that has much to recommend it.

Effect: A coin is shown and marked by a spectator, then folded into a little square of paper. A playing card, the Queen of Hearts, is clipped to a penny matchbox, then the packet containing the coin is slid under the clip. The card, coin packet and matchbox assembly is stood on a small tray, and the tray set over a drinking glass. Now a spectator is asked to stand at the rear of the card and blow on it, as this will make the Queen bow. He blows—the Queen-matchbox-packet assembly topples over, and the coin is seen and heard to drop into the glass, still covered by the tray.

Requisites: A Canadian nickel, or a coin

gimmicked with a piece of steel so it will adhere to a magnet. A small Alnico magnet. A Queen of Hearts. A small non-magnetic tray (aluminum, brass or opaque plastic). A drinking glass. A small square of paper—see page 61, The Coin Fold. A wick-type marking pen.

Preparation: Tape or cement the magnet inside one end of the drawer of the matchbox. Slip a trumpet-type paper clip over the middle of one end of the face side of the cover of the matchbox, and put the cover on the box so the paper clip is at the magnet end of the box. Have the box in your coat pocket, and the coin you are going to use in the change compartment of that pocket. The marking pen can be in your pocket, or on your table with the card, the glass, the tray and the square of paper for the coin.

Method: Bring out the coin and the marking pen and have a spectator mark it. Bring out the matchbox, and slip the Queen into the paper clip. Stand the box on end on the tray, so the box acts as a stand to support the card. Take back the coin, wrap it in the Coin Fold (there are two methods in this book) and in tapping the packet against the glass, steal the coin. Slip the coin packet into the paper clip in front of the Queen so she can take charge of it. Set the tray over the hand concealing the coin so the coin will adhere to the bottom of the tray (the magnet end of the matchbox is right over the coin). Then place the tray over the mouth of the drinking glass. Due to the principle of magnetism involved, this operation can be performed with the utmost freedom; all you have to watch is that the matchbox is well centered over the coin. Actually the tray is now held at the tips of the fingers and set over the glass in the fairest possible manner.

When the Queen bows, you say, the coin will disappear. But the Queen is a royal personage and has to be forced to bow—so you have a spectator stand behind the glass so he can blow on her back which tickles her and makes her bow. He blows—the assembly topples over and the coin drops with a musical clink into the glass. Lift off the tray, have the coin identified; tear up the coin fold packet, and slip the matchbox into your pocket. You can leave another matchbox on the table, with a paper clip on it, if you like. And if you use the Frank Ducrot Coin Fold explained in Chapter XVII, you can leave the little packet, too. And the card! But make sure you get your coin back, for it may "cost you" to replace it.

Hanktration

ED. MARLO AND TAKESHI NEMOTO

Here is an unusual climax you can easily incorporate into Milton Kort's Coins Through the Table routine on page 276 of this book, for you will be working with the necessary "props."

Effect: After you have passed the last coin through the table into the spectator's hand, offer to give him a chance to see how the coins penetrate. This time everything will be "above board." The four coins are stacked on a small handkerchief which is stretched over the mouth of the glass and held in place drumhead fashion by a rubber band. The coins are spread on the drumhead so everyone sees just four. They are stacked again; performer removes the top coin, pushes it sharply downward on the drumhead, and it drops with a clatter into the glass. There are only three coins left in the stack, the performer's hands are empty, and spectator can remove the rubber band and examine everything, for the gimmick is now well out of the way.

Requisites: Four half dollars, an expanded shell, a wide mouthed glass (a double Old Fashioned glass is just right) a strong rubber band and a small square of silk. This is not magician's "silk," but a hanky made by cutting a man's silk pocket handkerchief into quarters and hemming the cut edges.

Method: Since this is designed to follow Kort's fine routine, after the last coin has passed through the table into the spectator's hand offer to give everyone a better view of the process. And this time everything will be completely "above board"—none of that "under the table stuff."

Load the shell on one of the coins and place it on the left hand in finger palm position, then stack the other three on it while you count "One, two, three, four." With the right hand lift off the shell and the three coins above it, leaving one coin behind in the left hand which turns palm down, then picks up the small square of silk while the right hand spreads the four coins on the table (three coins and shell) in an overlapping row.

Spread the hanky over the palm up left hand, taking care the finger palmed coin is not seen. With the right hand, stack the coins on the shell and set the stack on the hanky, over the concealed coin. Press the stack downward with the left thumb, which will jam the shell over the hanky tightly enough so you can now take hold by the sides with your two hands and concealed coin will not fall out. Lift the stacked coins on the hanky over the mouth of the glass, spread hanky drumhead fashion and hold it over the mouth of the glass with the left fingers while the right hand encircles glass with the rubber band. Then spread the coins to show there are just four, as in Fig. 1. Actually only three coins are spread—the shell and coin set is not touched. Stack the coins again and show your hands empty.

Now pick up the top coin of the stack with the right thumb and fingers and show

Fig. 1

it as you say, "I'll cause this coin to penetrate the handkerchief and drop into the glass, so watch closely and you'll see just how it's done." With the left thumb and fingers, grip the glass to steady it and keep the drumhead stretched. Bring the coin in the right hand in front of the three stacked coins holding it at an angle of 45 degrees, the lower edge resting on the handkerchief and just touching the front edge of the shell. The right thumb is against the back edge of shell and stack as in Fig. 2. The right fingers must be stretched out straight as shown.

Push the coin sharply downward with the tips of the right fingers, Fig. 3. You are actually pushing it under the stack and against the right thumb. The pushed coin will dislodge the "jammed" coin under the hanky and go into the shell, causing the dislodged coin to fall with a clatter into the glass. The whole thing is over in a fraction of a second, and the closest watcher will not see what actually took place.

After you have the "just right" grade of silk for the hanky, you will have to practice until you get the "feel" of the operation. You will find that you can right matters immediately if the "pushed" coin is not perfectly covered by the shell, for your straightened fingers are over the stack for

Fig. 2

PUSH

AUDIENCE

Fig. 3

SIDE VIEW

off into your hand and dump them on the table (palming off the shell), then push the covered glass toward a spectator and have him examine it to his heart's content, as you remark, "Well, that makes everything clear, I hope!"

Made In Japan
By Ron Bauer

This is a presentation for the Chinatown Quarter (or Half, or Dollar). The only props needed are the Chinese coin, the fake coin, and a five inch square of linen (as opaque as possible). This piece of linen need not be hemmed; however, you might print at one edge, or attach a small sticker which reads, "Made in Japan." Have the folded piece of linen and the Chinese coin in the right coat pocket. The Chinatown Quarter (or coin) can be brought out with a handful of change (Chinese side down), removed and placed on table. Replace rest of change in pocket.

Presentation runs along the lines of ". . . it's amazing the number of items that are made in Japan these days. And the quality! You have to watch a lot closer than you used to . . . for instance, this is the latest . . . I think they've gone a bit far, don't you?" Pick up coin and apparently examine it closely. "You know, it's a good thing I brought along the tester or some of you might think I'm not being entirely truthful . . . after all, this is one of the better ones." Right hand removes the square of cloth from the coat pocket, secretly finger palming the Chinese coin with it. Spread out the cloth square on the palm up left fingers. "As you can see, it's quite simple in construction. Oh, yes —be sure to get the Japanese make—it's a lot cheaper . . . anyway, this is how it works . . ."

an instant, and you have a better view of the situation than those in front. Keeping the fingers straight, as shown, seems to be the secret.

When you see all is clear, tip the coins

Pick up the fake coin by its edges with

the right fingers and place it on the cloth over the left fingers. Now close the left hand, pause, and open hand to show the change as in the standard method. Pause to let the effect sink in. "Now you can see there is a slight flaw in its construction. Here, take a closer look . . ." As you say this, reach over with right hand to pick up the coin. Actually your right index and middle fingers cover it and your thumb slips under its edge. You then clip it between thumb and forefinger. If done properly, the coin will actually be completely concealed as you pick it up. The right hand then moves toward a spectator and apparently drops it into his hand. Actually you release the Chinese coin only, retaining the fake in the clipped position. (This is the easiest switch imaginable, and it works!)

As a "clean up," try the following: The left thumb presses the linen square against the left palm as the left hand is revolved into a palm down position. At the same time, the right hand starts revolving palm up. Both hands are moving simultaneously and toward one another until you've covered the palmed coin in the right hand with the linen. The right thumb then comes around to grip the linen square against the right fingers, at the same time pressing the fake coin against the fingers through the cloth. At this point, left hand has released the linen and then regripped another edge so it may be snapped between the two hands. Now the linen can be taken by the right hand and pocketed. And naturally you ditch the fake coin at the same time.

Blasted

Courtesy LOUIS TANNEN

This is one of the most popular "dealer" coin tricks of recent times. The basic trick is as near to being "self-working" as we can

expect to get, yet it looks impossible; and by introducing a little skill, the performer can be "left clean at the finish," which is, to say the least, a very desirable state to be in.

Effect: A small metal tray, a British half crown and a copper penny are shown. The silver coin is placed on the tray and a champagne glass inverted over it. The copper coin is pushed against the foot of the glass, and with a sharp click seems to penetrate the glass, for it is seen resting on the tray under the glass with the silver coin. Now both coins are placed unmistakably on the left palm. Both hands are closed—spectator names either copper or silver—the hands are opened and there is a coin in each hand. And it is easy to leave both coins, the tray and the glass on the table as you go on to the next trick.

Requirements: You receive a decorated metal tray about 3½ inches diameter, the champagne glass, and a gimmicked coin. This is a British silver half crown piece, gimmicked like the familiar Dime and Penny set. The silver coin is bored out to become a shell, and there's an insert with a silver face on one side and a copper penny face on the other. The insert nests perfectly in the silver shell, and when shown carelessly will pass for a perfect silver coin. A copper penny to match the copper face of the insert comes with the trick, but you will also need a matching half crown if you want to leave the outfit for inspection.

The Secret: Look at the inside surface of the tray. You will notice that it presents a "crowned" appearance—that is, the center is higher than the surface around the rim. Hold it between the two hands, fingers underneath and thumbs on top. Press down on the center with the thumbs. Due to the metal used and the way it is stamped, the center of the tray can be pushed down, and as it "snaps" down it will make a sharp clicking sound. It will stay down until pressure is applied, when it will "snap" up again. This "snapping" action of the metal is the motive power that accomplishes the trick. With the copper insert nested inside the silver shell so it looks "honest," place the silver coin, slightly off center and shell side up, on the tray. Cover the coin with the inverted glass. Place your right hand on the foot of the glass, press down and the apparatus will do the rest. A second coin, copper, will appear alongside the silver. When you press down on the glass, the center of the tray snaps back into its normal position, and the reaction causes the silver shell to fly up, uncover the copper insert, and settle down again alongside or partly over the copper; the glass prevents the shell from turning over. It happens in a split second, too fast for the eye to follow. After a few trials you will find the right "off center" position for the coin.

Presentation: Have the glass and tray on the table, with the center of the tray pushed down and ready "to operate." The gimmicked silver coin and the copper penny are in a right hand pocket, and the matching half crown is in a convenient place.

Bring out the gimmicked half crown and copper penny and place them on the table before you, the silver coin to the right. Call attention to the two coins and ask a spectator to name one of them. If he names the silver, pick up that coin and place it shell side up and off center on the tray. Then take the penny and drop it into the glass. If he names the copper, pick it up first and drop it into the glass. Then place the silver coin in position on the tray. This gives the impression that the coin named is the one used, but in either case the silver coin goes on the tray. Now remove the copper coin from the glass, invert the glass and place it lightly on the tray, covering the

coin. DO NOT put any pressure on the glass at this point!

Pick up the copper coin, holding it at the tips of the right fingers. Rest it lightly on the foot of the glass, fingers in front of coin, thumb at back. Let the coin be seen resting on the glass, then slide all four fingers downward, covering the coin from view. As the fingers slide down over the coin, withdraw the thumb completely so coin will snap down flat on the foot of the glass with a clicking sound. The pressure of the fingers will cause the tray to revert with a snap to its normal position, and so bring about the appearance of the copper coin alongside the silver, under the glass.

The appearance of the copper coin under the glass is so surprising that you have all the time needed to carry away the concealed penny as the fingers are removed from the foot of the glass. As the right hand moves away with the concealed coin, the left approaches the glass, lifts it by the foot, turns it mouth upward and passes it to the right hand which takes it by the stem between the index finger and thumb, a perfectly natural position which helps to conceal the finger palmed penny. The left hand lifts the tray from the table and displays the two coins while the right returns the glass to the table. The left hand returns the tray to the table and now you do the clean-up move.

The right hand, with the "honest" copper penny finger palmed, picks up the fake coin, copper side showing, and places it on the open palm of the left hand. Right hand returns to the tray, picks up the silver shell, and places it part way over the copper fake. The left thumb is now brought over the coins so its rests lightly on them as the left hand remains palm up.

Ask spectator to call out either silver or copper. Start to turn the left hand palm downwards, and as you do so, the left thumb pushes the shell over the fake coin as both hands close. Move the closed hands forward, backs of hands uppermost and about 24 inches apart. Squeeze the left hand as if squeezing the coins away, then open both hands to show a silver coin in the left and the copper in the right. Toss the copper coin onto the palm up left hand, then pick up both coins, holding them fanned out at the tips of the right fingers; show them both sides, and replace in the right hand pocket. Leave the gimmicked coin behind, get hold of the "honest" silver half crown, bring out the silver and copper coins again, drop them on the tray, and push tray, glass and coins to one side. The effect is complete and the gimmicked coin is gone, leaving you "clean."

These instructions cover the actual handling of the apparatus and the routine for making the coin apparently pass through the glass onto the tray, which is astounding enough. But the coins cannot be looked at until the trick is over, and it would seem good magical strategy to use British half crowns and pennies in a previous trick or routine, to familiarize the audience with these coins and thus "lull them into a false sense of security" about their being just silver and copper coins. People DO like to look at strange coins! An excellent trick to lead up to this one would be Señor Mardo's version of The Flying Eagles on page 153. Here four copper coins and four silver are used, and they are all just innocent coins even though they are the unfamiliar British pennies and half crowns. Or, The Coins Through the Table, page 190, using British copper pennies and the half crown as the odd coin. Or the Stewart Judah version, page 192. By the time you've finished the routine, everyone is satisfied that the coins are honest, and they've satisfied their curiosity about them. Now when you bring out the tray, the glass, a silver half crown and a large copper penny, you are in the clear. And by the time you've progressed to this point in this book, you should know this and a great deal more without having it pointed out to you!

Blasted, Jr.
Courtesy LOUIS TANNEN

This excellent "dealer's item" works on the same principle as Blasted, except that no glass is used, and the coins are a U.S. penny and a nickel. The gimmicked coin is a "Nickel and Penny set" precision made like the familiar Dime and Penny. A small brass tray is supplied, and a clear plastic cover instead of the champagne glass. To complete the list of properties you must have a penny that matches the insert, and a nickel that matches the shell. You can perform the trick without any sleight-of-hand at all, and with the easiest of sleights you can leave the coins, tray and cover for inspection after performing. Since the instructions for Blasted apply for Blasted, Jr., there is no need to repeat them.

Pennies and nickels are such common coins that the gimmicked coin in this case should excite no curiosity. But if you want a penny and nickel routine to "condition" your spectators for this "miracle" use Stewart Judah's Coins Through the Table on page 192—it is described using pennies and a nickel.

There are a number of excellent tricks in this book that require only small coins —pennies, nickels and dimes. When gimmicked coins are required, they are inexpensive in the small denominations. A very entertaining coin routine can be devised using such small coins and the necessary gimmicks. If you wish to try your hand at routining, you'll find excellent material in the book to choose from.

Chapter XX

LATEST COIN BOX MAGIC

Al-'N-Nate • The Mulholland Box and 4 tricks therewith • Kort's Paul Fox Coin Cups Routine (2 versions) • The O-Korto Box Routine (2 versions) • Stiles' Okito Box Routine • Okito Change for a Half (2 versions) • Gag Penetration With an Okito Box • Okito Box Glittering Finale • Judah's "Mystic Coins" Routine • A Stopper With the Okito Coin Box • Okito Box Coin Vanish

The coin box of Professor Hoffmann's day, called The Vanishing Halfpenny Box in *Modern Magic* (1876) was ". . . a little round box, made of boxwood, about an inch deep, and of such diameter that its internal measurement exactly admits a halfpenny . . . The top and bottom of the box are lined with some bright colored paper, and it is used with a halfpenny, one side of which is covered with similar paper. If this halfpenny be placed in the box with the papered side upwards, it is taken to be the bottom of the box, which appears empty . . ." There was a lid to put on, and the camouflaged coin could either seem to be in the box, or gone after being put in, by shaking the box up and down, or laterally. It had no room to move laterally, so shaking it thus would not give away its presence. Later models would vanish any halfpenny, for a matching disc dropped from the lid to cover the coin.

These principles are still in use today, but Theo Bamberg (Okito) advanced coin box magic by great leaps and bounds when in 1909 he invented the Okito coin box and some of the subtleties possible therewith, which are covered in Chapter X. There have been other significant developments since this book first appeared in 1952,

and we present here the latest magic with this most popular of the coin worker's apparatus pieces, the Coin Box.

Al-'N-Nate

J. B. BOBO

Courtesy *Louis Tannen*

This trick gets its name from Al Baker and Nate Leipzig who first popularized it. The Al-'N-Nate Coin Box used in this routine is a utility item, in that numerous other routines can be performed with it.

Effect: The performer shows four half dollars and an English penny and stacks them in a metal cup that has a hole in the bottom. After placing the filled cup on the center of an outstretched handkerchief, the corners are gathered up, forming a bag. Then holding this bag a few inches above the table, the magician commands the coins to leave the cup and pass through the cloth and the table. He then reaches underneath the table and produces the five coins. The handkerchief is lowered to the table and spread out. The box is seen to be empty because the fabric can be seen clearly through the hole in the bottom. Everything can be examined, the spectators finding no clue to the mystery.

Requisites and Preparation: A special Al-'N-Nate coin box. This is similar to the Bert Kalmar box described on page 232, but with several improvements. The Al-'N-Nate Box is not only superior in design and construction; its weight makes it easier to handle and affect the secret turnover. Like the Kalmar box, this one also has a hole through its recessed bottom. But unlike the Kalmar box, this one will not accept a regular coin in the recess.

Fig. 1 shows a cross sectional view of the Al-'N-Nate box, which is usually turned from solid brass for proper weight and balance. The box accepts five half dollar size coins, but its recessed bottom takes a special coin. In this case the special coin is an English penny which has been turned down to a smaller diameter. Its tail side, which is ground smooth, has glued to it a circle of white cloth to match a man's handkerchief. For clarity, this special coin will be called the disc. With the disc in the recessed bottom of the cup, which lies mouth up on a handkerchief, it appears empty. What appears to be the handkerchief through the hole is actually the disc. The illusion is that the cup is empty.

You will also require four half dollars and an English penny.

Working: As you begin the trick the four halves and the English penny are in the box and the disc is finger palmed, cloth side outward, in the right hand. Dump the coins onto the table with the left hand, then place the cup in your palm inward right between the forefinger and thumb, Fig. 2. With the left hand, pick up the first two silver coins, one at a time, and drop them in the cup. As the left hand reaches for the third silver coin the right hand lowers the cup onto the finger palmed disc, which slips into the recessed bottom. The right hand is now open and palm up as the left drops the third half dollar into the cup, then the

Fig. 1

Fig. 2

FINGER PALMED DISC
CLOTH SIDE OUTWARD

fourth. The copper coin is placed in last, head side up, to match the disc in the recessed bottom.

Ask for the loan of a gentleman's handkerchief, and as you gesture toward the lender, turn the box over. It still appears the same but now it is mouth downward, and the coin seen is actually the copper side of the disc. Ask the spectator to spread the handkerchief on the table. Pretending that he is not doing it right, take the box from your right hand, leaving the five coins finger palmed, and place it on the table. Both hands now busy themselves smoothing the handkerchief.

If you are seated at a table you can grasp the handkerchief corners nearest you and draw them over the edge of the table, depositing the stack of coins on the leg in the action; then the smoothing of the handkerchief is continued. The coins remain on the leg for the time being.

In either event, the cup is now picked up and placed on the handkerchief a bit off center. Gather the corners and hold them in your left hand. The hand is raised a bit so the cup is suspended in the handkerchief "bag" a few inches above the table. As the corners are gathered up and the handkerchief lifted, the box turns over. While pretending to blow in the handkerchief, steal a glimpse of the box to see if it has turned over properly, and that the disc is still in the recess. If not, a slight movement of the handkerchief should put everything in order. Command the coins to leave the cup and penetrate the handkerchief and the table. Reach under the table with your right hand (pick up the coins on the leg, if seated), bring up the five coins and drop them on the table. Lower the handkerchief so the cup will rest on the table. Open the handkerchief so the spectators can see the apparently empty cup, the cloth on the disc appearing as the handkerchief through the hole. The half dollars and English penny have apparently penetrated the handkerchief and table.

The trick is over, but a final finishing touch is added. Press down gently on the cup so the disc will stay in its place in the recessed bottom, and draw it along the handkerchief to a spot an inch or so from the inner edge. Drop all the coins in the cup, one at a time. With the palm down right hand, slide the cup inward and off the cloth to the edge of the table and pick it up between the thumb underneath and the fingers on top. As the hand is turned palm up, the cup is turned over onto the base of the middle fingers. As the left hand lifts the cup away the disc remains behind, finger palmed, and the coins are dumped onto the table. The right hand then reaches across the handkerchief to its farthest corner, picks it up, and as the left points to the table say, "See, there is no hole in the table." Return the handkerchief to its owner. All may now be examined; the coins are ordinary and it will be found that none will fit in the re-

cessed bottom, increasing frustration.

The foregoing routine is only one of many possible with the Al-'N-Nate coin box, which can also be made up in quarter and dollar sizes.

The Mulholland Box

Described by JOHN MULHOLLAND

Through a cross-breeding of the Okito box and the Al-'N-Nate trick I produced a box with which several startling tricks can be done. These are particularly strong when combined with other coin magic to form a routine, for with this box one coin, or six, can be made to disappear and reappear. Also, a single coin placed in the box by a spectator can be pushed through the box and the hand of the magician. And while it is possible to show the tricks with this box while standing, most magicians will find them particularly suitable for close-up table magic.

I begin by taking the box from my pocket, filled with six coins and with the cover in place. Three of the coins are half dollars and three are copper coins of half dollar size. For the coppers I use Chinese coins having square holes, but British pennies are excellent. As both box and coins are unprepared, everything may be examined. However, rather than put suspicion in the minds of the spectators by asking to have the several items examined, it is better to have the dates on the coins noted, and let them feel the weight of the box.

Requisites and Preparation: A round metal box with a separate cover is the only prop known to the audience. Both box and cover are made of one piece of metal (preferably brass), turned on a lathe. The sides of the box are 1/32″ thick and the bottom 1/16″. The opening is just large enough for a half dollar to drop in easily and yet not rattle when inside. When six half dollars are in the box the sides are just high enough for the top coin to extend 1/32" above the top edge. The sides and top of the cover have the same thicknesses as the sides and bottom of the box, and the sides of the cover go exactly halfway down the sides of the box. A ⅜" hole is drilled through the center of both the box and cover.

Also needed is a half dollar cut down, except at the center, to form a disc 1/32" thick. The center of the coin is left full thickness and just under ⅜" in diameter. This fake when finished is a thin disc showing the head side of the half, with an extending plug at the center of such a size as to fit easily, but not loosely, into the hole at the bottom. When the disc is in place on the bottom, and the box filled with coins, it will have the same appearance when right side up as upside down.

Note: When I introduce the box of coins, all are unprepared. Any gimmicked coins needed for other effects are carried separately and substituted as needed. Because of the coin on the string and other tricks with Chinese copper coins having center holes, my box holds three half dollars and three copper coins exactly the size of a half. One side of these pseudo coins carries my name in Chinese characters and on the other are the characters for New York and America. Rather than bother going into the counterfeiting business it is suggested that British pennies and U.S. half dollars be used. And it should please you to know that all the various tricks that can be done with the regular Okito box can be done with this one.

To Cause Six Coins to Disappear Inside A Closed Box

Working: The cover, the box and the six coins are shown to the audience, in that order. After the cover has been looked at it is placed at the edge of the table to the right of the magician. After the audience is satisfied with the innocence of the box, it is held opening up between the first and second fingers and thumb of the right hand. A spectator is instructed to place all the coins on the table, and to make certain each is head side up. He is then asked to drop them in the box, one at a time, being careful that every coin is head side up when it goes in. Assuming three silver and three copper coins are used, he is told first to put in a copper coin, then a silver.

As these instructions are being carried out, the magician takes the disc-fake from his pocket, or lap, with his left hand, and holds it finger palmed with the face toward the fingers.

After the spectator has put one copper coin and one silver into the box, the performer asks, "You know the half dollar is in the box because you can still see it, but you can no longer see the copper coin; are you absolutely certain it is still in the box?"

No matter what he replies, the performer says, "Because of the hole in the bottom you can still see the copper coin." So saying he places his first finger on top of the half dollar, and by turning his hand, brings the box bottom side up. After the copper coin has been shown, the spectator is told that the next coin to go in must be a copper coin, heads up, and the remaining coins must go in with silver and copper alternating, and always heads up. During these instructions the magician has turned the box right side up, brought his hands together, and placed it on top of the disc so the plug goes into the hole in the bottom. The spectators are so interested in making certain the instructions are followed that no attention will be paid to this action, and the box is held on the outstretched fingers of the left hand while the remaining coins are put in, one at a time. Now they *know* all is fair!

When the box has been filled, performer reminds the spectators what has been done, ending by saying, "And of course, you realize that no matter how tightly I press, it is impossible to squeeze six solid coins through the little hole in the bottom." As he makes this statement he closes his hand, and very obviously presses hard. The box has been on the fingers while being filled. In closing his hand the magician simultaneously turns it over, palm down. After giving it a hard squeeze, he turns his hand palm up and opens his fingers. These actions will have changed the position of the box from the fingers to the palm, and at the same time turned it over so the disc-fake is uppermost. Now the right hand picks up the box and sets it on the table. In picking it up it is first slid along the left hand into the finger palm position where the coins are left when the box is taken away. Because the left hand is turned as the box is removed no one sees or knows about the palmed coins. They are pocketed or placed on the lap as the performer, with his right hand, picks up the cover and puts it on the box.

Now the spectators are reminded that the covered box contains six coins which one of their number put into it. Performer picks it up as he talks, saying they will recall that a copper coin was the first one put in, and he points to the bottom but takes care not to raise the box high enough so the open bottom can be seen. Now he rests the box on the tips of the fingers of the palm up left hand, removes the cover, and states he is certain everyone will recall that the silver coin was the last one put in.

In lifting the cover he raises it just high enough to be free of the box, and holding it parallel to the floor, moves his hand toward the audience. The cover is gripped by the first and second fingers on opposite sides and the hand so held that the top can always be seen. Once the spectators have had a chance to see the silver coin the cover is replaced, and the way it is put back seems to be exactly the reverse of the way in which it was removed. Actually the box is turned over as the cover is replaced, and this is done by a subtle move Okito showed me about 45 years ago. As the hand moves toward the box the side of the thumb hits the top edge and pushes it over. Because of the way the cover is held the second, third and little fingers completely hide the turnover from the audience. After trying this a few times you will find that turning over the box in this way becomes automatic.

At this point the cover is on an empty box and the disc-fake at the bottom is in finger palm position. The box is lifted by the right hand and the disc left behind and finger palmed. As the box is raised the left hand turns over and takes hold of it, gripping it with the thumb covering the hole at the bottom and the first finger over the hole in the cover. Thus held, the finger palmed disc cannot be seen even though the palm of the hand is facing the audience.

Now the performer sets the box on the table and withdraws his left hand. With his right he removes the cover, or asks one of the spectators to take it off, to disclose that the coins have disappeared.

To Return The Six Coins to the Box

Working: The six coins are taken from their hiding place and finger palmed in a stack in the left hand. With his right, the performer turns the box bottom up and strikes the table several times with the top edge, remarking about it being made of one solid piece of metal. Then he transfers it, still bottom side up, to the left hand where it is held over the stack between the thumb and the tips of the fingers holding the coins.

Stating that the cover, too, is made of one piece of solid metal, he strikes it on the table several times, and as it hits the table, he pushes the box down over the stack with his left thumb. The noise made by striking the cover on the table will drown any click this action may make. The cover is turned over and slid, upside down, into place under the box. The instant it is in place the closed box is taken by the right hand, turned over, and placed on the table. The cover is removed so everyone can see the box filled with coins, then it is picked up and slowly turned so the coins can spill out upon the table.

Coin Penetrating Box and Hand

Effect: A half dollar is dropped into the box and the cover put on. The covered box is placed upon the back of the left hand and the thumb and fingers of the hand extended. A cigarette is dropped into the hole in the cover. The magician takes hold of the top tip of the cigarette and pushes down. The cigarette is seen to go so far into the box as to penetrate not only the bottom but through the hand and push the coin through. Then it is pulled free and dropped on the table. The box is opened to show that it no longer holds a coin.

Working: As with the standard Okito box routine, this effect begins by putting a coin into the box and making the secret turnover as the cover is put in place. The box is then placed on the palm of the left hand where it remains while the magician borrows a cigarette. He takes the proffered cigarette with the right hand and places it on the table. The box is then picked up from the left palm, and when the left hand has been turned over, is placed on the back of that hand. During these moves the coin is held palmed in the left hand. The borrowed cigarette is picked up and dropped

into the hole in the top of the box where it is left standing. Actually it goes through the hole in the bottom as well. The tips of the right fingers then take hold of the very end of the cigarette and press down. For an instant this is what actually is done; then, loosening their grip, the fingers slide down the exposed length of the cigarette and the illusion of pushing it through the box and the hand is perfect. The instant the fingers touch the top of the box the palmed coin is released and permitted to drop onto the table, then the cigarette is withdrawn and dropped.

The first finger and thumb of the right hand takes the closed box from the back of the left. Then the first finger and thumb of the left take hold of the box itself, and the right fingers the cover. In the correct position both hands must be backs up, and the fingers of the right hand above those of the left. The hands are then pulled apart and simultaneously turned palms to the audience. The cover will be removed from the box, and the inside of the cover and the box will be facing the spectators, cover in the right hand, box in the left. After very little practice, showing the box to be empty in this manner can be done quite slowly without anyone realizing what actually took place.

This manner of taking the cover off the inverted box, as well as having a hole through both cover and box, I thought of when I was but a boy. In 1918 Okito's praise of both ideas has, through the years, been a source of pride.

Another Coin Penetration

This effect can also be done with an Okito box. After a coin is put in and the cover put in place, the box is rested on a business card the magician holds. With the index finger of the free hands he rubs the

Fig. I

underside of the card. After several rubs the finger is brought out from under the card with the coin balanced on it. Both the card and the empty box are then shown to be free of trickery. Instead of a business card, a playing card can be used effectively.

Working: After the coin is put in, the box is reversed when the cover is put on. Then it is placed on the tips of the fingers of the left hand so the left thumb rests on the "near" top edge. As the right hand brings the edge of the card to the bottom edge of the box, the left thumb presses on, and tilts the box just enough so the card can be slid between it and the coin. The right hand holds, and very lightly crimps, the card with the thumb on top and the fingers underneath, so the card will better hold the weight of the box. Once the coin is under the card it is held by the tip of the middle finger, Fig. 1. After the first finger of the left hand has rubbed the underside of the card several times, it goes under the coin, and as the coin is released by the right second finger, brings it out balanced on the tip.

The trick is particularly impressive when a borrowed business card is used.

Paul Fox Coin Cups Routine

MILTON KORT

Effect: A brass cup is given for examination along with seven coins. The coins are dropped in the cup and it in turn is placed on the back of the left hand. The right hand covers the cup for a moment, presses down and the coins apparently penetrate cup and hand and fall to the table. The right hand is lifted and the cup shown empty. The performer states that he will, contrary to all rules of magic, repeat the trick. Once again the cup is filled with coins and placed on the back of the left hand. And once again it is covered with the right. But this time when the right presses down it is the cup that penetrates while the coins remain on the back of the hand.

Two methods will be described: the first must be performed while seated at the table; the second is designed to be performed while standing.

Requisites and Preparation: A set of Paul Fox Coin Boxes and eight quarters. (See page 233 for a description, and other uses for these cups.) One of the quarters is stuck with magician's wax in the recessed bottom of the gimmicked box and the other seven are in the regular box. All are together in the right coat pocket.

Working: While seated at a table, bring both boxes from your pocket, leave the gimmicked box in your lap and place the regular one on the table. Empty the coins onto the table and pass the box for examination. While this is being done get the prepared cup in finger palm position in your right hand. While the spectators look over the coins, pick up the ordinary cup and switch it for the gimmicked cup as you apparently toss it into your left hand. (The Bobo Switch, page 10, works fine for this.) Ask the spectators to note the number of the quarters as the left hand places the prepared cup on the table. The right hand moves to the edge of the table and drops the ordinary cup in the lap. Place the coins in the cup one at a time, making sure that the last one to go in matches the one in the recess of the prepared cup. Now the cup is picked up with the right hand and placed in the left, but as it travels from the table to the left hand it is turned over, as follows: As the right hand picks up the cup from the table the thumb presses inward and downward on the top inner edge. The fingertips, which rest against the outer side, slip underneath the box as it tips back, and it is removed from the table held flatwise with the thumb against the inner single coin and the fingers against the loose coin. As the right hand moves toward the left, the box completes its revolution and is deposited mouth downward at the base of the two middle fingers of the palm up left hand. The move is a simple one that excites no suspicion, for it appears that you simply picked up the box from the table and deposited it in your left hand. Explain that either side of the hand can be used for the trick; lift the cup up and away, leaving the stack of coins finger palmed in your left hand as you turn that hand over and place the cup on a spot at the base of the third finger knuckle. The cup is empty but appears full owing to the single coin visible in the recessed bottom.

The palm down right hand moves over the left hand and cup, then with a backward and forward rubbing motion the cup is secretly reversed, mouth side up. The best way to accomplish this is to place the heel of the right hand over it and turn it inward and over, then slide it back to its original position on the left hand. The right hand then presses down and at the same moment the left releases its coins which clatter to the table. The right hand is lifted and the cup is seen to be empty. Apparently the coins penetrated the cup and the hand!

Return the cup to the table with the right hand as the left drops to the lap casually and finger palms the unprepared cup.

Again pick up the coins with your right hand and drop them into the prepared cup. State that you will repeat the trick. The left hand with its hidden regular cup is brought to the top of the table while the right picks up the prepared cup from the table, reverses it secretly as before, and deposits it mouth downward on the back of the left hand. Place the palm down right hand over the cup on the back of the left, and repeat the rubbing motions, finally pressing down and palming the cup as the left hand releases its palmed cup, which falls to the table empty. The right hand is raised and the stack of coins is seen on the back of the left hand. This time the trick worked in reverse. Instead of the coins penetrating the cup and the left hand, it was the cup which passed through, leaving the stack of coins, a surprising ending indeed! Immediately move your right hand to the edge of the table and drop palmed cup in the lap. The cups and coins may now be examined.

In *the Stand-up Version* the effect is identical but the handling is slightly changed.

Begin the trick with the prepared cup finger palmed in your right hand and the regular cup loaded with the coins, visible in your left. Dump the coins onto the table; have the cup looked over, then the coins. While the coins are being examined, pick up the cup with your right hand and switch it for the gimmicked cup as you pretend to toss it into your left hand. The right hand drops the unprepared cup in the left sleeve while pretending to adjust the sleeve or the wrist watch.

Now cause the coins to penetrate the left hand and the cup, as in the first version, then return the cup to the table. Announce that you will repeat the trick. While the right hand deposits the coins in the box the left drops to the side, retrieves the unprepared box as it drops from the sleeve, and finger palms it. The trick is now continued as in the first method. At the finish the regular cup will be on the table, the coins on the back of the left hand and the gimmicked cup concealed in the right. With the right hand, pick up the quarters from the back of the left hand, turn that hand palm up and drop the coins into it. Jingle the coins a moment, then square them with your right hand, pick them up and place them, with the hidden coin box, in your pocket. The other box is shown unprepared and placed in the pocket.

The O-Korto Box Routine

MILTON KORT, WALTER WILSON
AND RON BAUER

Effect: Four coins are dropped in an Okito box and the lid placed on. The box is deposited on the back of the left hand, the coins leave the box, penetrate the hand and drop to the table. The performer places the box back on the table, turns his head away, and directs a spectator to place one coin in, remembering which side is up and place the lid on. But the spectator has difficulty in getting a coin in the box. The box is now either too small or the coin too big. The performer turns facing the spectators and has no trouble whatsoever putting the coins in.

He now places the coin-filled box on the back of his left hand and presses down from the top with his right. This causes the coins to penetrate the hand and fall to the table. The right hand is lifted and the box is empty. The coins are returned to the box, it is again placed on the back of the left hand and covered with the right. But this time the box penetrates the hand, leaving the coins on the back of the hand. Coins and cup may be examined.

Requisites and Preparation: A set of O-Korto Coin Boxes. The set consists of four pieces—one lid and three bottoms. The lid will fit all three bottoms. The bottoms look exactly alike but differ somewhat. One box bottom is like the Okito coin box (page 217). The second looks the same but its inside diameter is slightly smaller and will not permit the insertion of a half dollar. The third bottom looks like the other two but is recessed deep enough to take a coin, like The George Boston Coin Box (page 230). This box and the Okito box will each hold four half dollars.

Five half dollars, one of which is stuck in the recessed bottom of the Boston-style box with a small dab of magician's wax. The other four halves are in the regular Okito box with lid placed on. This is on the table while the "Boston" box and the small box are hidden in your lap as you sit at a table.

Working: Begin the routine by performing Coins Through Box and the Hand (page 221) with the four coins, or any trick with the box and the coins. Finish with the box, lid and coins on the table. Steal the small box from your lap with your right hand, then take the bottom of the Okito box from the table and as you pretend to toss it into your left hand, switch and throw the small box instead. With the right hand, pick up the lid, place it on the box and return both to the table. Tell the spectator you will turn your head away while he places one of the coins in the box, remembering whether it is head or tail up, then puts the lid back on. Add that you will attempt to "divine" the side that is up. As you turn your head, drop your right hand to your lap, leave the regular box on your left knee and finger palm the "Boston" box. The spectator will be very disconcerted by the fact that none of the coins can be placed in the box. Face him again to see what the trouble is. Bring up your right hand, pick up the bottom of his box and apparently toss it into your left, again making a switch and throwing the "Boston" box. Place this box on the table. Now pick up the coins one at a time with your right hand and drop them into the box. This dumbfounds him because he now sees you dropping coins into a box that a moment ago would not accept a single coin! Keep the back of your hand toward the spectators during these actions so you won't expose the bottom still concealed there. While showing the box and coins with your left hand, the right moves to the edge of the table and drops the small box into the lap.

With the right hand, take up the "Boston" cup and reverse it as was explained in the foregoing trick, then place it mouth downward on the palm up left hand. Display it there for a moment; then as the right hand lifts it away, the coins remain in left finger palm position as that hand turns over so the box can be placed on the back. Although the box appears filled with coins because of the single visible coin in the recessed bottom, it is empty. From now on the moves follow those in the Paul Fox Coin Cups Routine just explained. Briefly, the right hand covers the box, secretly turning it over. As it presses down, the left hand releases its coins onto the table and the right is raised to disclose an empty box on the back of the hand. Apparently the coins have penetrated the box and the hand. Place the box on the table.

Offer to repeat the trick as the left hand drops to the lap and finger palms the regular Okito box bottom from the left knee. Once again the coins are placed in the "Boston" box on the table. The right hand picks it up, reverses it and deposits it on the back of the left hand which has now been brought up to the top of the table to receive it. Cover the box with your palm down right hand and press down. Immediately

the left hand releases its palmed box which falls to the table. As the right hand is lifted it carries away the box palmed, disclosing the four coins in a stack on the back of the left hand. Instead of the coins passing through the hand as before, the box penetrated and left behind the coins.

Remark that you should not have repeated the trick, and dispose of the Boston box by dropping it in your lap.

O-Korto Box Routine No. 2

[Milton Kort wishes to share credit for the following routine with Ron Bauer, Walter Wilson, and Ed Marlo. And special thanks are due Conrad Haden for the beautiful job of producing the boxes. The points of difference and the added refinements of this routine will be at once apparent to the student, but some may prefer the first version, some this. So we've included both!]

Requisites and Preparation: The O-Korto Boxes, consiting of C, the cover (we abbreviate to save space); A, the ordinary box; S, the box with the inside machined smaller than the diameter of the halves; and F, the George Boston type box with a half dollar built into the underside. Also needed are four matching half dollars (they must be the same style as in F) i.e., Liberty, Franklin or Kennedy. The four halves are in F, covered with C and held in left hand. A is in left sleeve, or on your lap if you are seated. S is palmed in right hand.

Working: 1. Right hand removes C from F and place it to one side. Left hand dumps halves on table. F remains in left hand.

2. Right hand places halves into F one at a time.

3. As right hand reaches for C, left hand "relaxes" at wrist and fingers close slightly. This action will reverse box so

the bottom recessed coin is uppermost. C is now placed on F. (Alternate method: After coins are dumped on table, box is set down. C is retained in right hand which rests on table. LEFT hand places coins into F one at a time. Left fingers go on top of F and slide it a few inches across table toward you. As this is being done, the left thumb slips under it. Now the right hand moves with C toward F. At the same time, the left hand turns palm up. Now you may place C on F, but be sure to give the spectators a flash of the recessed coin.)

4. Right fingers lift F off of left fingers and place it on back of left hand. Naturally, the four halves are retained in left finger palm as in standard method for Okito box.

5. Tap box with right fingers, and coins apparently penetrate box and hand.

6. Right hand picks up F and drops it into palm up left hand, retaining C. The standard Okito box "Drop Move" is done, showing F to be empty. (See the paragraph above Fig. 13 on page 220.)

7. F and C are placed on table to the right and slightly forward.

8. Right hand pushes coins toward spectator, and you tell spectator to pick up any two and drop them into the box. Right hand picks up F and tosses it into left hand, actually switching for S. The right hand immediately picks up one of the halves in a gesture toward the box. (This movement is only to aid in covering the switch.)

9. Left hand offers S to spectator as right drops its half onto table. Tell spectator that as long as he's going to try the trick, he should start with two. He soon finds he can't even get one into the box!

10. Wait for effect to register, and then say, ". . . well, if you don't want to try, I'll do it again . . ." Take S from spectator

with right hand and switch for F as you toss it back to left. Right hand immediately goes for the coins and begins placing them into the box. (NOTE: Be careful not to expose coin on bottom of F when you catch it in left hand.)

11. "This time I'll do it without the lid so you can follow closer . . ." Right hand picks up C and places it in right coat pocket, leaving S at the same time.

12. During Step 11, you secretly reverse F by the "relaxing action" explained in Step 3.

13. F is again placed on back of left hand, secretly leaving the coins finger palmed in left.

14. Right palm apparently presses on F and coins again "penetrate" hand. Under cover of pressing on F, the heel of the right hand secretly reverses it.

15. Right hand is raised to show F is empty and then places it on table slightly away from you.

16. "I shouldn't repeat that, but in case you missed it, I'll try it again . . ."

17. Right hand slowly places halves into F one at a time. (NOTE: First half is placed into the box tails up, and the others heads up.) During this action, secretly get A into palm position in left hand.

18. Right hand places thumb on upper edge of F nearest performer. The first and second fingers are placed on the side of F farthest from performer. The right thumb pushes back and downward, causing the box to pivot on its edge and allowing the first and second fingers to slip under it. F is now being held by thumb on coins in box and fingers covering recessed coin. F is then placed on back of left hand with recessed coin showing. (This turnover is very deceptive.)

19. Right hand is shown empty and then placed palm down on F. Press. Nothing happens. Press again, and at the same time

release A from left palm. As A hits the table, right hand grasps F and lifts up to show coins on back of hand.

20. "Well, it didn't exactly work out the way I expected . . ." Right hand goes to pocket, leaves F, and brings out C. The audience may now examine the props. (NOTE: When leaving F in pocket, watch out for "talking" of one box against another.)

There you have it—a "sense-confounding" problem with a little brass box and a few coins—and you can take your choice of two excellent routines.

Fig. I

Fig. 2

A Coin Box Routine

KIRK STILES

Effect: An Okito coin box, a half dollar and an English penny are examined by a spectator. The magician drops the copper coin in the box, places the lid on and holds it in his hand. A tap from the forefinger causes the coin to apparently penetrate the box and fall to the table.

The performer now holds the half in his closed left hand and places the copper coin in the box. The box is held in the right hand some distance from the left but the two coins change places.

Using different moves, the penny is again placed in the box and the half dollar held in the other hand. But once more the two coins transpose themselves.

Requisites and Preparation: An Okito box, two half dollars and an English penny.

Have the half dollar and the English penny in the box, and it on the table. The other half dollar is hidden in your lap as you sit at the table.

Working: After the spectator is satisfied that the two coins and the box are innocent, it is taken in the right hand as in Fig. 1, resting on the two extended middle fingers

while the thumb and forefinger hold the top from opposite sides. The top is lifted and held vertically just clear of the box. In this position the forefinger is a bit lower but does not touch the bottom of the box.

Invite the spectator to drop in the English penny, or do it yourself. The left hand is palm up and the forearm is resting on the table. The right hand now approaches the left in a slight upward and downward arc, replacing the lid in transit and a split second before it is received in finger palm position of the left hand. Release your grip on the box with the right hand and ask, "Do you happen to remember if the coin showed head or tail?" Few spectators will ever know, but if one should, you may verify his opinion for the others. Take the box back in the right hand, lift the lid as in Fig. 2, showing the coin inside. Replace the box in the left hand using the same arcing motion as before. This time, however, the right forefinger catches the box from below and tips it inward and over onto the two middle fingers of the left hand as the lid is placed on, apparently as before. But now the bottom of the box is upside down with the penny resting underneath on the left fingers. This movement which tips the box over can be made to appear exactly like the genuine action of placing the top on. The move represents considerable thought and is completely undetectable if the proper amount of practice is given to its mastery.

Now the right hand slides the box off the left fingers and holds it by its sides between the thumb and forefinger with the second finger curled underneath supporting the English penny silently from below, Fig. 3.

Fig. 4

Fig. 3

Carry the box above the table and say, "This is a funny box. If I tap the top with my finger like that, the coin falls right through." Tap the top of the box once with the tip of the left forefinger and release the coin so it falls to the table, apparently through the bottom. Now hold the left hand underneath the box. As the right releases the bottom of the box it is allowed to trip over the tip of the second forefinger so it revolves and lands right side up in the left hand. The top is tossed opening up alongside it, then both parts are placed on the table. A more detailed description of this turnover move, together with an illustration, will be found on page 220.

Push the English penny aside and pick up the half dollar with the right hand. Toss it into the left, close the fingers over it, then turn the hand over so the fingernails are facing the table. Lower the fingers a trifle

with the coin resting on them. Hold the coin gently against the heel of the hand and have the third finger 'walk' it to the position shown in Fig. 4. In this position the coin protrudes at a slight angle from the hand.

While this is being done the right hand places the lid on the box. Touch the top of the closed box with the tip of your right forefinger and say, "The coin is not here." Show the right hand empty and say, "It is not here." Close the second, third and fourth fingers of the right hand, keeping the forefinger extended, tap the back of the left and add, "It is not in here." Now, using the moves shown and described on page 79, turn the left hand over and steal away the coin between the tips of the right thumb and second finger. The spectators see no visible finger movement of either hand as the right takes the coin and the left continues turning and raises about 3" from the still pointing right forefinger. After a very brief pause, the left hand reaches out, opens and slaps the top of the coin box. The cover, being slightly loose, makes a metallic click as if a coin might possibly have fallen through into the box. The left hand is now turned palm up and shown empty. And during this brief action the right has remained completely immobile.

With thumb and two middle fingers of the left hand, the box is picked up from the table and carried to the right hand where it is accepted by the thumb and fore-finger, the thumb and second finger still retaining their grip on the half dollar. With the left hand, lift the top and turn it over, the inside facing upward. The key move now is to pretend to pour the coin from the bottom of the box into the top. As the left hand removes the top, the right tilts the lower part slightly away from the spectators lest they see it to be empty. The pouring is a continuation of the tilting movement. At the precise instant for maximum sound effect, let the coin drop from the pinch into the top of the box. Continue the rotation of the bottom just as you would if you really were spilling out the coin. For prac-tice purposes actually spill the coin out into the lid, then duplicate these movements with the coin coming from the pinch. Show the half dollar actually in the lid, then empty it onto the table and place the two parts of the box down beside it.

Lower your right hand below the table to make an adjustment of your chair posi-tion, and finger palm the half dollar from your lap. Bring up the hand, pick up the half dollar from the table and toss it into your left hand where it lies in finger palm position. Next, take up the English penny with your right hand and toss it into your left so it slightly overlaps the inner edge of the half dollar. Now pretend to toss both coins into your right hand, but execute the Utility Switch (page 11) as you throw only the copper and retain the silver coin. The right hand immediately shows two coins, the English penny which was just received and the finger palmed half dollar, then drops its coins onto the table.

Take up the English penny with the right hand and place it between the second joint of the forefinger and thumb of the palm inward left, which still conceals the dupli-cate half dollar, Fig. 5. Now pick up the

bottom of the box with the right hand and hold it directly under and touching the left little finger. The left thumb now permits the English penny to slip down into the hand, but be careful that it does not clink against the finger palmed half. The mo-ment the copper disappears from the spec-tator's view, the finger palmed silver coin is allowed to drop into the waiting box be-low. The sound created by the half drop-ping into the box is taken to be that made by the English penny, but that coin remains hidden in left finger palm position. Now the right hand raises the box and deposits it between the tips of the left forefinger and

Fig. 5

thumb. Without hesitation, the right hand picks up the lid and places it on the box. You then take the box from the left hand, shake it to rattle the coin inside, and say, "The English penny," and set the box on the table.

The left hand, with its finger palmed English penny, points to the half on the table as you say, "And the half dollar." Bring the left hand, palm down, over the half and pretend to draw it off the table, but drop it into the lap as the left hand closes over its concealed English penny. Raise the left fist and say, "The half dol-lar." Touch the box on the table with the tip of the right forefinger and add, "The

English penny." Gesture again with the left fist and repeat, "The half dollar." Pick up the box from the table with the right hand and give it a shake as you reiterate, "The English penny. You saw the English penny drop through the bottom of the box." Shake the box again. Move the left hand again and say, "You saw the half dollar go through the top of the box. Now for the most difficult feat of all. To make them change places!"

The right hand taps the box three times on the back of the closed left hand. Move the hands about a foot apart and say, "And now the English penny is back in my hand." Open it. "And the half dollar is back in the box!" Put the box on the table and remove the lid. Simultaneously drop the English penny from your left hand onto the table as the right dumps the half dollar out of the box.

Okito Change for a Half

MILTON KORT AND CASS DMUCHOWSKI

Effect: A half dollar, when placed in an Okito box, changes to a quarter, two dimes and a nickel—change for a half.

Working: A quarter, two dimes and a nickel are finger palmed at the base of the third finger of your right hand as you show an Okito box and a half dollar. Drop the 50 cent piece into the box and as you place on the lid execute a secret turnover of the bottom, placing the lid on the reversed bottom. (See pages 218 and 219 for methods.) Hold the box in the palm up left hand at the base of the two middle fingers with the thumb pressing on top, and rattle it. Now the right hand takes the box and rattles it again. But as it takes it the half dollar is left behind in the left finger palm and the open bottom of the box is brought down over the coins hidden in the right hand. Although this move is not difficult,

care must be exercised to prevent the spectators getting a flash of the half and the smaller coins. A slight turning of the body from left to right will aid in concealing the coins as the transfer is made. Rattle the coins in the bottom of the box slightly.

Ask a spectator if he would like to see the half dollar change. He will reply that he would. Both hands move together, each performing two different but simultaneous moves. As the palm down left hand removes the lid from the box and places it on the table, opening up, the right thumb is lowered onto the upside down bottom; that hand turns palm down and deposits the box bottom on the table, mouth up. It should appear that you merely removed the lid from the box and placed it and the bottom on the table. Call attention to the coins inside, then dump them out to show CHANGE FOR A HALF.

Second Version

MILTON KORT

This effect is exactly the same as the previous one, only the handling is different.

You begin the same way; that is, hidden in finger palm position of the right hand are a quarter, two dimes and a nickel. Show the Okito box empty and drop the half dollar in it. This time the lid is placed on fairly, with no secret turnover. Ask a spectator if he would like to see the half dollar change. Upon receiving a positive reply, the box is opened and the change is dumped onto the table. That is exactly what appears to happen. After placing the 50 cent piece in the box the closed box is held near the tips of the fingers and thumb of the palm up right hand, the fingers of which point slightly to the left. The box rests near the tips of the fingers and the thumb presses down on the lid from the top. Now the palm down left hand lifts the lid from the box; the right thumb presses down on the half dollar in the box, retaining it and the box pressed against the fingers as that hand turns inward and over, releasing its finger palmed coins onto the table. The illusion is that the coins fell from the box. The left hand, still holding the lid, brings it opening downward on top of the reversed bottom held in the right hand, and that hand places the entire box in the left at the base of the two middle fingers. Any sound made by the half dollar rattling in the box is covered by the lid being placed on. The move of returning the lid to the box and taking it in your left hand is made quickly, and immediately following the dumping of the coins onto the table. At this point the box lies at the base of the two middle fingers of the palm up left hand with the half dollar in the reversed bottom resting on the fingers. The right hand lifts the box away from the left, leaving the half dollar finger palmed in that hand, which turns inward to conceal it. The palm down right hand holds the box between the fingers and thumb a few inches above the table, and the two parts are dropped openings up onto the table, using the method described on page 220. The half dollar has changed to a quarter, two dimes and a nickel, and the box is empty. Dispose of the finger palmed half dollar at your convenience.

Gag Penetration with an Okito Box

MILTON KORT and RON BAUER

Effect: In this humorous effect a half dollar is placed in an Okito box. It is rattled and placed on the back of the palm down left hand. The right hand taps the box, and as the coin apparently penetrates the box and the hand it changes to a silver dollar.

Working: Hidden in your left coat sleeve

is a silver dollar. Show a half dollar and the empty Okito box with the hands otherwise empty. Drop the half dollar in the box; make the secret turnover as the lid is put on, and toss the box to the left hand with the coin going along in the reversed bottom. Place the right thumb on the lid to hold it in place and rattle the box. While doing this, drop your left arm to your side, retrieve the sleeved silver dollar and hold it classic palmed. That hand is now brought up and held palm down at about waist level as the right hand places the box, minus the half dollar, on the back of the left hand. The right hand, with its finger palmed half dollar, turns inward and the forefinger taps the top of the box. The left hand immediately releases its dollar which clanks to the table. The box is lifted from the hand and shown empty, using any familiar turnover move. The half dollar apparently penetrated the box and the hand but in doing so changed to a silver dollar.

Say, "I'll do that again if you will put it back in the box!"

The feat is especially good for magicians and adds a humorous touch to a routine with the Okito coin box.

Okito Box Glittering Finale

GERALD BRUNING (BRUNO)

This idea from the clever mind of Bruno makes possible a very good finale for an Okito box routine, for you show the spectators in slow motion how the coin penetrates the box.

Effect: You place a half dollar into the box, put on the lid and point out that there is a hole in the bottom of the box. They are to concentrate on that hole, and as you shake the box a stream of glittering silver particles pours through because, you say, "The coin disintegrates into small particles and escapes through the hole!" When the interior of the box is shown, the coin is no longer there.

Requisites and Preparation: The coin box used must have a $1/8''$ hole drilled in the exact center of the bottom. (An Okito box with a hole drilled in both the lid and the box is not unusual, for S. Leo Horowitz has devised some excellent routines with such a box.)

In addition, you will need a gimmick or receptacle for the glitter. This is a cylindrical box made from $1\frac{3}{16}''$ diameter clear plastic tubing. A disc of thin, clear plastic is cemented over each end of the gimmick; the end that will be the bottom should have a $\frac{3}{16}''$ diameter hole in the exact center. The overall height of this gimmick is $1/4''$. See Fig. 1. Fill this with glitter and cement a small disk of silver or aluminum foil over the hole. Place the loaded gimmick in your right coat pock-

Fig. 1

et with the foil covered end towards your body.

Routine: Near the end of your regular Okito box routine, when opportunity permits palm the glitter gimmick in your right hand, foil side away from the palm. Your left hand picks up the empty Okito box and places it bottom up over the concealed gimmick. The foil side is now against the inside of the bottom of the box. The left hand now takes the box from the right, still bottom up, between the index finger and thumb, middle finger supporting the gim-

mick. The right hand picks up a half dollar from the table, places it in the lid of the box, then picks up the lid so it rests on the middle fingertips of the palm up hand, the coin visible, lying in the lid. The left hand now sets the upside-down box and the concealed gimmick into the lid, so the coin is inside the box. Now the right hand shakes the box so the coin can be heard rattling, then transfers it to the left palm, bottom of box still up. Right hand now takes a pencil or pen and inserts it into the hole, calling attention to it and asking the spectators to concentrate on it, for, you explain, "The coin will disintegrate and make its escape through this hole, in slow motion so no one will miss it." While you seem to be using the pencil as a pointer, you have actually used it to poke a hole through the foil over the hole in the gimmick. Now take the box from the left hand with the right thumb under the lid, and index and middle fingertips on bottom, index finger over the hole, and turn hand palm up. When you command the coin to disintegrate, remove the index finger from the hole, shake the box gently, and allow the glitter to stream out into an ash tray, or handkerchief spread out on the table. When the gimmick is empty, set the box on the tips of the palm up left fingers, but in doing so execute the Okito box turnover so box rests bottom up on left hand with the lid over its bottom. After the right hand points to the little heap of glitter, and stirs it with the index finger, the box is taken away from the left hand, leaving behind the half dollar and gimmick. While the right hand drops the box, then the lid on the table (both will turn opening up in falling), the left turns back upward concealing the palmed gimmick and coin. Box and lid now lie empty on the table. When you gather up the handkerchief or move the ash tray out of the way, "go south" with the palmed "evidence" in left hand so all will be clear.

The handling of the coin box is dealt with at length in Chapter X, pages 217-230.

Stewart Judah's "Mystic Coins" Routine

The dealer's ad read:

"A clever new pocket trick performed with precision apparatus that does the trick for you.

"Four palming coins are covered with a chrome cap. Everything is then placed on top of the hand. At a tap, one coin penetrates the hand, dropping on the table. Only three coins are now left under the cap, which is laid on the table. Vanish a coin and it reappears under the cap. Various combinations can be worked out with this interesting equipment. You receive the chrome cap, coins and instructions. $2.00."

Five palming coins come with the outfit. One of these is gimmicked—it has one plain side to match the plated inside of the cap, and it will wedge in so cap can be shown empty. I cemented a disc of black construction paper inside the cap, and covered the plain surface of the gimmicked coin in the same way. These surfaces could be enamelled red or green, and that would be fine, too, but I was not equipped to do it.

Working and Routine: With the cap mouth up, put in three of the palming coins, then the gimmicked coin, black side up; place the last real coin on top. When ready to perform, place the "cap" of coins in your left hand, coins resting on palm. Slide the cap off the coin next to the palm so it remains in palming position; lift cap off the stack, set it on the table, and spread the coins in an overlapping row on the back of the hand, gimmicked coin on top

of all with coin side uppermost. Pick up the cap, slide it over the row of coins scooping them up and squaring the stack so they are all underneath. Explain that you will drive one coin through the hand. Slap the cover sharply with the right hand, allow palmed coin in left to drop to the table; lift off the cap, showing it empty, and set it down on the table forcibly enough to dislodge the wedged coin. Now count the three coins onto the table, arranging them in a row to the rear of the coin that penetrated.

Pick up the three coins one at a time with the right hand, at the tips of the thumb and fingers, counting "One," the second under the first counting "Two," and the third under the two, counting "Three." Holding left fingers curled and palm of hand up, apparently drop or toss them into that hand. In reality you push off the upper two only, retaining the third with the tip of the right thumb against the first joints of the fingers, exactly as explained in Al Baker's Magical Filtration of Four Half Dollars, page 195. You say, "Three coins in the left hand—and one in the right," and here you pick up the coin remaining on the table with the fingers of the palm down right hand. Now a transposition takes place —one coin leaves the left hand and passes over to join the one in the right. Lay out the coins in two vertical rows—two on the left, and another row a little to the right from the right hand. Your hands are empty.

Now line up the coins in a horizontal row; this doesn't mean anything, but it looks good. Take away the coin at the right end of the row. Say, "We'll cause this coin to vanish and pass under the cap." The cap has been sitting there in full view, and you haven't been near it. Use any sleight-of-hand coin vanish to apparently transfer the coin to the left hand, where you "crumble" it away; lift the cap with empty hand, and they see the coin. Right hand reaches out, picks up the gimmicked coin and places it in the pocket as you say, "This time we'll use just three coins," leaving palmed coin also.

Line the three into a horizontal row. You are now ready for the "grabbers," for the cap is innocent and the gimmick is gone. Pick up one coin in the left hand, two in the right. Left hand slaps down its coin, letting it be seen there is but one, then picks it up as you say, "One coin in the left hand." Right hand apparently slaps down its two coins, and spectators see two on the table; right hand rests back up with fingers relaxed, and left hand is closed as if holding a coin. However, you've tricked them again, for you used the Han Ping Chien move, and the condition right now is: The left hand has dropped its coin, but seems to hold one in the closed fingers; the right hand has dropped one coin, and holds one concealed in thumb palm. The right fingers pick up the two coins on the table. All three are now in the closed right hand, but you say, "And two coins in the right." Now you can make the coin in the left (?) fly invisibly into the right hand, or cause it to pass through the table into the hand. The Han Ping Chien move is explained on pages 190-193.

Can't you visualize how good this would look made up with foreign copper or silver coins, or Chinese coins with the square hole?

A Stopper with the Okito Coin Box
JOHN J. LIND

Effect: The performer exhibits an empty Okito coin box in his palm up left hand. A spectator drops a half dollar into the box, the lid is placed on, and a playing card slipped underneath so box can be carried away on the card. The empty left hand is formed into a fist held thumb side up, and card and box are set on the fist. The box is lifted from the card, the coin rattled inside, then returned to the card. A tap from the right forefinger causes the coin to penetrate the box and card and drop to the table; box is then placed mouth up and empty on the table, with the lid beside it.

With the aid of the card, the performer lifts the lid from the table and slowly slides it onto the box. A moment before the lid completely covers the box it is seen to be empty by a spectator. The performer causes the half dollar to vanish, and a spectator finds it inside the box.

Requirements: An Okito coin box as pictured in Fig. 1, page 217, two matching half dollars and a playing card or business card.

Working: Have the playing card and one of the half dollars on the table. The box lies opening up on the palm of your left hand. The lid is held in the right hand mouth down, with the duplicate half dollar concealed under it, the lid being gripped with the index finger and thumb, the second finger curled underneath supporting the coin. Extend your left hand and direct a spectator to drop the half on the table into the box. Now the right hand covers the box with the lid. Actually the box is secretly inverted so lid is placed on the bottom with the duplicate coin in between. This is a Stewart Judah move, accomplished as follows: At the start of the covering operation, the right hand holding the lid is over the left wrist. As the hand moves toward the tips of the left fingers, the right little finger contacts the forward edge of the box and turns it over so the lid is placed on the now upside down box, the action being completely covered by the back of the right hand. As the right hand moves away from the left, the covered box lies at the base of the left fingers. Without hesitation the left thumb pushes it forward to a position near the tips of the fingers. At this point in your left hand (from palm up) you have a half dollar, the inverted box, another half dollar and finally the lid.

Pick up the card with the right fingers and slip it underneath the box (and coin) in left hand, picking all up on the card. Gesture with the left hand letting it be seen empty, then allow the box and coin to slide off the card and back onto the palm up left hand. Show both sides of card—your right hand is plainly empty. Again slide the card under the box, but this time between the box and the coin, then lift all away between the right first two fingers underneath and thumb on top of lid. At this point the coin lies on the extended first two fingers of the palm up right hand; on top is the card, the inverted box, the duplicate coin and the lid. Show the left hand empty and form it into a loose fist. The right hand now rests the card and box on top of the fist, and as this is done the hidden coin is allowed to sink into fist. Now comes a subtlety all magicians will appreciate. The right hand picks up the box from the card and shakes it back and forth, causing the coin under the lid to rattle. It sounds like a coin rattling in the box, and you can give the illusion an "assist" if you raise the lid just a little during this "rattling" bit. Place the box back on the card and announce that you will cause the half dollar to penetrate the box and card. As the right forefinger taps the top of the box once, the left fist relaxes and the coin drops with a clatter onto the table.

Take the card from the left fist with the fingers, carrying away the box. Tip the card to allow the covered box to slide off onto the left hand, which has turned palm up to receive it. Drop the card onto the table. The left thumb now pushes the box

forward to the tips of the fingers where it is gripped by its sides between fingers and thumb, which now point upward. Grasp the lid by its sides between the fingers and thumb of the palm down right hand and quickly move both hands together, first upward, then downward, separating them and depositing the box opening up, with the lid opening downward beside it and still covering the duplicate coin. With a little practice you will "get the hang" of this move, for the coin will stay in the lid, held there by centrifugal force, like the ball stays in the cup in the familiar Cup and Ball move. You "smack" down the box and lid, both hands operating together, and at the finish of this maneuver the box lies right side up on the table, and beside it, the lid, open side down, still covering the duplicate coin. In practicing, tilt the covered box slightly so the coin will rest on the inside of the lip of the lid when the hands separate, and you will find it an easy matter to smack box and lid on the table without betraying the presence of the concealed coin.

Take the card in the right hand and slip it underneath the lid and concealed half. Bring it toward the box, and with left hand assisting, slide the lid and coin off the card onto the right edge of the box so the far right edge of lid will rest on the table. The lid now rests at a 45 degree angle, propped over the edge of the box. (This works best on a cloth covered table or a close-up pad,) At this point the box can be seen empty, and attention is called to this fact. With your right forefinger, continue sliding the lid (with concealed coin underneath) onto the box until it is almost covered. Just before the lid falls "home," allow a last view of the box, then push lid on completely. The concealed coin drops in unison with the lid, and the "clink" will be accepted as the noise made by the lid settling into place, again deceiving the ear. Vanish the visible half dollar, then in your best dramatic manner push the box toward a spectator and request that he open it. Inside he will find the vanished coin (?) and during the moment of surprise you will have "gone south" with the evidence so all will be clear.

(Carlos H. Colombi is credited with this "cover load" Okito coin box stratagem. You will find it useful in coin box routines.)

Okito Box Coin Vanish

Oran Bailey Dent uses an Okito Box as a vanisher for the coins that arrive one at a time in such tricks as Frame Fantastique, or audibly, in Copenetro. The box is shown, four half dollars dropped in, and the turnover move made as the lid is put on. The coins now rest on the palm but the box can be shaken before it is taken by the other hand and placed in view on the table. When the apparatus in which the coins are to appear is picked up, the stolen coins are left behind.

After displaying the apparatus, a spectator is invited to assist. Pick up the coin box, say something about the coins, then remove the cover and glance inside as if looking at the coins you are talking about. Replace the cover, making the turnover

move again so cover is now on properly, and hand box to the spectator. Ask him to hand you the coins one at a time.

When he removes the cover and finds the coins missing, he will react—probably by laughing—and the audience will wonder what happened. So you explain, "Oh, I forgot to tell you. The box has the same effect on coins as current prices. It makes them invisible. See?" Tip the box forward so audience can see inside, then say to assistant, "Will you please hand me the invisible coins, one at a time?" Usually he will play along with you and go through the motions of handing you a coin. Take it from him, seriously, at your fingertips, and pretend to toss it through the air into the piece of apparatus. You can make the second coin pass "the hard way" by "banking it" off the wall; you can accidentally drop one, have spectator pick it up, and then pass it; and you can toss one of them from behind your back with your left hand —very difficult that way. All this is pure make-believe, but it is as entertaining as the passing of the cards from one packet to the other in the classic Cards Across trick. And, as with the Miser's Dream, in some cases the coins can be heard to arrive. When the apparatus is uncovered, there they are, so they must have arrived invisibly!

BEST WISHES WITH YOUR NEW COIN ACT!

BIBLIOGRAPHY

(No attempt has been made to include ALL references to material on coin conjuring.)

Art of Magic, The—T. Nelson Downs (1909)

Best in Magic, The—Elliott (1948)

Bull's-Eye Coin Tricks—L. L. Ireland and Ed. Marlo (1942)

Classic Secrets of Magic, The—Elliott (1953)

Coin Magic—Jean Hugard (1935)

Coin Tricks—Tom Osborne (1945)

Coining Magic—Ed. Marlo (1957)

Convincing Coin Magic—Farelli (1946)

Cylinder and Coins, John Ramsey's—Farelli (1948)

Dai Vernon Book of Magic—Dai Vernon (1957)

Dai Vernon's Tribute to Nate Leipzig—Vernon and Ganson (1962)

Dime and Penny, The—Lloyd E. Jones (1945)

Fine Art of Magic, The—G. Kaplan—(1948)

Greater Magic—Hilliard and Hugard—(1938)

Handle With Gloves—Jack Chanin—(1941)

It's Easier Than You Think—Buckingham—(1952)

Magic As A Hobby—Elliott—(1948)

Magic of the Hands, The—Victor—(1937)

Magic of Slydini, The—Slydini—(1960)

Magical Ways and Means—Al Baker—(1941-1946)

Magician's Tricks—Hatton and Plate—(1910)

Magic Without Apparatus—Gaultier (1914-1945)

Malini and His Magic—Dai Vernon (1961)

Modern Coin Manipulation—T. Nelson Downs—(1900)

Modern Conjurer, The—C. Lang Neil—(1903)

Modern Magic—Hoffman (Angelo Lewis)—(1876)

Modern Magic Manual—Jean Hugard—(1939)

Money Magic—Will Blyth—(1926)

More Magic—Hoffmann (Angelo Lewis)—(1889)

Okito Coin Box Routines—Mohammed Bey (S. Leo Horowitz)—(1963)

Okito on Magic—Theo Bamberg—(1952)

Principles and Deceptions—Buckley—(1948)

Professional Magic Made Easy—Elliott—(1959)

Quality Magic—Okito (Theo Bamberg)—(1921)

Routined Manipulation—PART 1—Ganson—(1950)

Routined Manipulation—PART 2—Ganson—(1951)

Routined Manipulation Finale—Ganson—(1954)

Secrets of Conjuring and Magic—Robert-Houdin—(1878)

Sleight of Hand—E. Sachs—(1877, 1946)

Stars of Magic, SERIES 1, 2, 8, 9, 10 and 11 (Louis Tannen, Publisher)

Tarbell Course in Magic, The—Vols. 1, 2 and 3—Dr. Harlan Tarbell—(1941-1942-1943)

World's Best Book of Magic—W. Gibson—(1927)

* * *

Magical Journals—The files of The Sphinx, The Jinx, The Linking Ring, The New TOPS, The New Jinx, The Phoenix, The Gen, The Magic Wand, The Magazine of Magic, Genii the Conjurer's Magazine, Hugard's Magic Monthly, Hade-E-Gram, Pentagram, The Magician, and Stanyon's Magic, plus Lloyd Jones's The Bat.

INDEX